Bringing
the Gospel of Luke
to Life

OPENING THE SCRIPTURES

Bringing
the Gospel of Luke
to Life

Insight and Inspiration

GEORGE MARTIN

Our Sunday Visitor Publishing Division
Our Sunday Visitor, Inc.
Huntington, Indiana 46750

Our Sunday Visitor Publishing Division
Our Sunday Visitor, Inc.
200 Noll Plaza
Huntington, IN 46750

bookpermissions@osv.com
1-800-348-2440

ISBN 978-1-59276-034-3 (Inventory T1180)
LCCN: 2011937805

Cover design by Rebecca Heaston; interior design by Sherri L. Hoffman
Cover image by The Crosiers

Royalties from the sale of this book go to the Catholic Near East Welfare Association to assist the Church in the Holy Land.

PRINTED IN THE UNITED STATES OF AMERICA

To my children:
Ann, Therese, Maureen, Paul, and John

CONTENTS

PREFACE

The two disciples who walked with the risen Jesus on the road to Emmaus exclaimed afterward, "Were not our hearts burning [within us] while he spoke to us on the way and opened the scriptures to us?" (Luke 24:32).

We too would like the Scriptures opened to us so that we could understand their meaning, their significance, their message. No book can duplicate what Jesus did for the two disciples on the road to Emmaus or replace the guidance of the Holy Spirit. But a book can explore what meaning the words of Scripture had for their first readers and what message an inspired author conveys by his words. The aim of this book is to bring the Gospel of Luke to life for its readers. The Gospel comes to life for us in two stages. First, its words come to life for us when, as twenty-first-century Christians, we gain insight into their original first-century meaning and context. Then, as followers of the risen Jesus, we can be inspired to apply that gospel message to our lives today.

While this book has some features of a commentary, it is not a scholarly commentary. Many issues and questions that are of legitimate interest to scholars are passed over. The focus of this book is on what Luke's words meant when he wrote them, with an eye toward their meaning for readers today. This book is intended for men and women who want to read and understand Luke's Gospel as Scripture, as God's word conveyed in human words.

Reading a Gospel as Scripture is like having a good conversation. Conversing requires listening. Good listening means paying close attention to what the other person is saying; it can also mean noting what is implied and what may be left unsaid. This book will closely examine the text of Luke's Gospel, sometimes commenting on the meaning of the words the author uses, sometimes drawing out an implication, occasionally noting what is left unsaid.

A good conversation presumes the two parties share some common background. For example, a conversation about American politics requires that those conversing have a shared knowledge of the American system of government and political parties. Similarly, understanding the Gospel of Luke requires some knowledge of Jewish life and thinking in Palestine in the first third of the first century. What Jesus did and said must be understood in light of the context in which he lived. This book tries to fill in some of that background, as far as we can reconstruct it today, to help make sense of the teachings and actions of Jesus.

Another factor that makes good conversations possible is knowing the person we are talking with. Often our conversations revolve around interests and concerns that arise from our experiences and personal situations. What was Luke's situation, and what were his concerns? This book adopts the commonly held view that Luke's Gospel was written about A.D. 85, possibly in Greece, and was addressed to a Church that was largely made up of Gentile converts. Luke is concerned in his two-volume work of his Gospel and Acts to show how God's plan of salvation that began with Israel is fulfilled in Jesus and in salvation being extended to Gentiles as well as to Jews. How could a crucified Jew be God's agent for the salvation of Gentiles? Luke addresses this by compiling "a narrative of the events that have been fulfilled among us" (1:1). He shows how Jesus' crucifixion was not the tragic failure of his mission but the working out of God's will as made known in Scripture. The salvation being extended to Gentiles is not a departure from God's plan but the fulfillment of what God began with Israel. Luke writes so that his readers "may realize the certainty of the teachings you have received" (1:4). Luke wants to make sense of the events involving Jesus so that his readers can be confident of the gospel message.

A short essay at the end of this book addresses the writing of Luke's Gospel. Rather than saying more in this preface about the Gospel of Luke, we will let its character and purpose unfold as it is read.

This book focuses on the Gospel that is "According to Luke," the title it bears in the oldest manuscripts. It does not try to compare or synthesize what Luke wrote with the other Gospels. It is difficult to carry on four conversations at once; it is easier to pay attention to one person at a time. After paying close attention to the Gospel according to Luke, you can later compare what Luke wrote with what Matthew, Mark, and John wrote. For each passage of Luke, this book indicates where similar material may be found in the other Gospels.

This book deals with the text of Luke's Gospel as it has come down to us in the Bible. It does not go into matters like the sources Luke may have drawn on, nor does it raise questions like "Did this really happen exactly as Luke presents it?" While such considerations can have validity, it is the

Gospel of Luke as we have it that is inspired Scripture for us. This book presents what I hope is a responsible interpretation of the Gospel of Luke, laying out the meaning I find in Luke's words. I make no claim that my interpretation is the only possible reading of Luke: there are riches of meaning in a Gospel that no single exposition can capture.

Interspersed throughout my exposition of Luke's Gospel are questions "for reflection." They indicate ways that a reader might ponder and apply the text. Using these reflection questions is optional; much more important are the questions that Luke's Gospel itself poses for you. If reading a Gospel as Scripture is like having a conversation, then listening to the words of Scripture is only half of the conversation; the other half is our response. This book cannot supply your side of the conversation; you must do that yourself. This book can lay out Luke's side of the conversation as I understand it and raise issues for you to reflect on and respond to. The most important issues, invitations, questions, and challenges will be those that the Gospel itself puts to you.

Luke's original audience did not usually read his Gospel but listened to it being read aloud at a gathering of Christians, perhaps for the Eucharist. We too listen to the Gospel of Luke being read aloud in the context of worship. In the Catholic liturgy, after a passage from Luke is read the reader proclaims, "The Gospel of the Lord." The reader does not say, "The Gospel of Luke." Even though we are listening to words written by Luke, our real conversation partner is the Lord Jesus. We listen to Jesus teaching even if it is Luke who gives expression to Jesus' words. It is Jesus who invites our response, even if it is Luke who conveys Jesus' invitation.

One response to reading a Gospel is prayer. There is a long tradition in the Church of "sacred reading" (*lectio divina* in Latin). This type of reading involves paying careful attention to a passage of Scripture, verse by verse and word by word, and pausing for reflection and prayer. My fondest hope is that this book will prove useful as an aid to sacred reading. I suggest that those who wish to use this volume for prayerful reading return to the words of Scripture after having read the exposition, offer a brief prayer asking for the guidance of the Holy Spirit, and enter into conversation with the one who speaks to them through the Gospel of Luke.

ACKNOWLEDGMENTS

I drew on the knowledge and insights of many biblical scholars in writing this exposition of Luke's Gospel. Footnotes acknowledging my debts to them would have complicated a book intended to be as simple as possible, but my debts are real nonetheless. Some of the commentaries and studies I consulted are listed in the bibliography at the end of this book. My indebtedness to these scholars does not, of course, imply their endorsement of my interpretation of Luke.

I am also indebted to many individuals for their help and encouragement. Among them I must single out Mary Martin and Susan Manney, who read the manuscript and made many suggestions. I am grateful to Our Sunday Visitor for publishing this work, and to its acquisitions editor, Bert Ghezzi, for their help and enthusiasm. Kevin Perrotta edited the manuscript for content and frequently rescued me from my ignorance; I and my readers are indebted to him.

Above all, I am grateful to my wife, Mary, for gracefully accepting that my idea of a Florida retirement has been to spend my time studying and writing about Scripture.

NOTES ON THE FORMAT AND TEXT

Each section contains the text of the Gospel of Luke (printed in boldfaced type) accompanied by a verse-by-verse exposition.

Everything else, printed in smaller or different type, is auxiliary material and consists of

- *Orientations* to certain passages in Luke's Gospel, when such introductions might be helpful
- After the text of each passage of Luke, *Gospel parallels* indicating where similar material may be found in the other Gospels, along with Old Testament (*OT*) and New Testament (*NT*) references to material that bears on the passage from Luke
- *Old Testament quotations*, when reading them in conjunction with a passage of Luke might throw light on the passage
- Questions for the reader's *reflection*
- *Background* information pertaining to the world of Jesus
- *Comments* that explore implications of Luke's Gospel

An index og *background* material and *comments* may be found at the end of this book.

Scripture citations that do not include the name of a biblical book are to the Gospel of Luke. For example, the citation 9:20 would refer to chapter 9, verse 20, of Luke's Gospel.

Scripture citations follow the chapter and verse numbering used by the New American Bible. Other translations sometimes employ slightly different numbering (for example, in Malachi and some of the psalms).

The New American Bible requires preservation of certain of its conventions, including its paragraph breaks and square brackets around words not found in all ancient manuscripts. When poetry is set here as prose, the New American Bible requires that slashes be used to indicate line breaks.

The Catholic Church and most Orthodox Churches accept as canonical Scripture the books of Baruch, Judith, 1 and 2 Maccabees, Sirach (Ecclesiasticus), Tobit, and Wisdom (Wisdom of Solomon), along with some additional material in the books of Daniel and Esther. Protestant Churches do not accept these writings as part of the biblical canon, but some Protestant Bibles include them in a section labeled Apocryphal Works.

ABBREVIATIONS USED FOR BOOKS OF THE BIBLE

Acts...................Acts
Amos..................Amos
Baruch................Baruch
1 Chron.............1 Chronicles
2 Chron.............2 Chronicles
Col...................Colossians
1 Cor...............1 Corinthians
2 Cor...............2 Corinthians
Dan...................Daniel
Deut..................Deuteronomy
Eccl.................Ecclesiastes
Eph...................Ephesians
Esther................Esther
Exod..................Exodus
Ezek..................Ezekiel
Ezra..................Ezra
Gal...................Galatians
Gen...................Genesis
Hab...................Habakkuk
Hag...................Haggai
Heb...................Hebrews
Hosea.................Hosea
Isaiah................Isaiah
James.................James
Jer...................Jeremiah
Job...................Job
Joel..................Joel
John..................John
1 John...............1 John
2 John...............2 John
3 John...............3 John
Jonah.................Jonah
Joshua................Joshua
Jude..................Jude
Judg..................Judges
Judith................Judith
1 Kings..............1 Kings

2 Kings...............2 Kings
Lam...................Lamentations
Lev...................Leviticus
Luke..................Luke
1 Macc...............1 Maccabees
2 Macc...............2 Maccabees
Mal...................Malachi
Mark..................Mark
Matt..................Matthew
Micah.................Micah
Nahum.................Nahum
Neh...................Nehemiah
Num...................Numbers
Obad..................Obadiah
1 Pet................1 Peter
2 Pet................2 Peter
Phlm..................Philemon
Phil..................Philippians
Prov..................Proverbs
Psalm(s)..............Psalms
Rev...................Revelation
Rom...................Romans
Ruth..................Ruth
1 Sam................1 Samuel
2 Sam................2 Samuel
Sirach................Sirach
Song..................Song of Songs
1 Thess..............1 Thessalonians
2 Thess..............2 Thessalonians
1 Tim................1 Timothy
2 Tim................2 Timothy
Titus.................Titus
Tobit.................Tobit
Wisd..................Wisdom
Zech..................Zechariah
Zeph..................Zephaniah

Bringing the Gospel of Luke to Life

Insight and Inspiration

CHAPTER 1

ORIENTATION: *Luke begins with a carefully crafted one-sentence preface that presents the nature and purpose of the work he is writing—the Gospel of Luke and the Acts of the Apostles.*

Preface

¹ Since many have undertaken to compile a narrative of the events that have been fulfilled among us, ² just as those who were eyewitnesses from the beginning and ministers of the word have handed them down to us, ³ I too have decided, after investigating everything accurately anew, to write it down in an orderly sequence for you, most excellent Theophilus, ⁴ so that you may realize the certainty of the teachings you have received.

OT: 2 Macc 2:19–32
NT: Acts 1:21–22; 6:2–4; 10:36–42

1   Luke notes that **many have undertaken to compile a narrative of the events that have been fulfilled among us**. By **events** he has in mind the events of Jesus—his deeds and teachings, his crucifixion and resurrection. Since he refers to them as having been fulfilled **among us**, Luke also has in mind the events of Jesus being extended to the people of his day through the preaching and life of the Church. Luke does not write that these events occurred but that they **have been fulfilled**, implying fulfilled by God. Luke will recount in his Gospel and Acts how God accomplished his purposes through Jesus and the early Church, fulfilling what he began with Israel, fulfilling the Scriptures. The profound significance of **fulfilled** will be particularly evident in the final chapter of Luke's Gospel. Writers before Luke have **undertaken to compile a narrative** of the events of Jesus. A **narrative** is an ordered account, a coherent presentation.

Luke does not name the **many** who have compiled narratives about Jesus. Luke has Mark in mind as one of them; he will draw on Mark's Gospel as a source for his own. Another source available to Luke is a collection of Jesus' teachings, a collection that Matthew also used as a source for his own Gospel. Luke had other sources, too, for there is material in his Gospel not found in the other three Gospels.

3

Since earlier writers have produced narratives of the events of Jesus, Luke will do the same (verse 3). Luke does not disparage their work but uses them as a precedent. Luke will have his own aims as he writes (verses 3–4), making his narrative distinctive.

2 Previous writers compiled narratives of the events of Jesus, **just as those who were eyewitnesses from the beginning and ministers of the word have handed them down to us**. The Gospels are based on the accounts of **those who were eyewitnesses from the beginning**, those who, in the words of Peter, "accompanied us the whole time the Lord Jesus came and went among us, beginning from the baptism of John until the day on which he was taken up from us" (Acts 1:21–22; see also Acts 10:37–41). These eyewitnesses became **ministers** (servants, helpers) **of the word** (Acts 6:4; 10:42), bringing "the word of the gospel" to others (Acts 15:7). During the half-century between Jesus' resurrection and Luke's writing, the message of Jesus has been **handed** on by the original ministers of the word and their successors (see 1 Cor 11:2, 23; 15:3). What was handed on was used by Luke's predecessors as the basis of their accounts, and it will be the basis of Luke's narrative as well.

3 Since others have recorded the events of Jesus (verse 1), Luke writes that **I too have decided, after investigating everything accurately anew, to write it down in an orderly sequence**. Every word Luke uses to describe his endeavor is full of meaning. Luke has spent time **investigating**, studying, interviewing; his narrative will be based on research. He has investigated **everything**, making a thorough study of the events of Jesus and the spread of the gospel message. He has investigated **accurately** and carefully in order to ascertain the truth. He has investigated everything **anew**, taking a fresh look. The Greek word translated **anew** can also mean from the beginning. Luke's narrative will begin with the conceptions of John the Baptist and Jesus (1:5–38). Because Luke has made a careful and thorough investigation, his account will be trustworthy.

Luke will produce a coherent narrative: he will **write it down in an orderly sequence**. The notion of an **orderly sequence** does not necessarily mean in chronological order; it means a systematic presentation that shows the connection between events. Luke will organize his material to highlight its significance.

Luke used his abilities to do research and write in the service of the gospel message; Luke himself was a "minister of the word."

For reflection: How can I use my abilities in the service of the Gospel?

Luke's orderly account, based on careful research, is **for you, most excellent Theophilus**. The name **Theophilus** means beloved of God and was a common name among Gentiles and Greek-speaking Jews. Luke calls Theophilus **most excellent**, a form of address used for governors (Acts 23:26; 24:3; 26:25) and nobility. We know nothing about Theophilus save that he was a person of high status and probably a convert (see verse 4). Although Luke is dedicating his work to Theophilus, he almost certainly has a broader readership in mind as well. Some scholars suggest that Theophilus may have been Luke's patron, supporting him while he did his research and writing.

Patrons: See page 216

4 Luke tells Theophilus that he is writing his carefully researched narrative **so that you may realize the certainty of the teachings you have received**. Theophilus has already **received** instruction and is acquainted with **teachings** about Jesus, presumably indicating that he is a convert. Luke wants him to **realize the certainty** of what he has been taught. In the Greek of Luke's long sentence (verses 1–4), the word **certainty** is the final word, giving it emphasis. Luke writes to assure Theophilus of the **certainty** and reliability of the gospel message.

BACKGROUND: GREEK LANGUAGE AND CULTURE Alexander the Great (ruled 336–323 B.C.) of Macedonia (northern Greece) conquered the eastern Mediterranean world. Thereafter the Greek language became the common international language and the everyday language of many of the lands he conquered. Many Jews living outside Palestine adopted Greek as their language; Jews living in Egypt translated the Hebrew Scriptures into Greek in the third and second centuries B.C. The New Testament was written in Greek as the most commonly understood language. Even Paul's letter to Rome was written in Greek, not Latin. The early Church, being overwhelmingly Greek-speaking, used the Greek translation of the Old Testament as its Scripture. Greek culture, including philosophy, architectural styles, and enjoyment of the theater, had Jewish adherents in some of the larger cities of Palestine, including Jerusalem, but does not seem to have penetrated the small villages and rural areas of Galilee. *Related topic: What languages did Jesus speak? (page 117).*

Theophilus might need reassurance. Christians were a scorned minority: "this sect is denounced everywhere" (Acts 28:22). Skeptics could ask troubling questions. If Jesus is the Messiah, why was he crucified? Why do Jews reject him? Why has the Church become largely Gentile? Luke will write an ordered account of what God accomplished through Jesus to show the continuity in God's plans despite unexpected turns.

Luke's writings can give reassurance not only to Theophilus but to everyone who is beloved by God, helping us see more clearly how God's plans unfolded in Jesus and in those who became his followers.

For reflection: Where am I in need of reassurance about my beliefs? What questions trouble me?

The elegance of Luke's opening sentence (verses 1–4) would have been noted by educated Greek readers of his day. It was expected that serious books would have a preface stating their nature and the author's aims. (2 Maccabees, also written in Greek, has such a preface, considerably wordier than Luke's—2 Macc 2:19–32.) Although Luke will employ simpler styles in the remainder of his work, the sophisticated Greek of his preface would have assured readers of his competence.

ORIENTATION: *Luke shifts from the elegant Greek of verses 1–4 to the style and idiom of books like Genesis, Judges, and Samuel in his account of events surrounding the birth of Jesus. His Old Testament tone invites readers to understand what God is doing now as a continuation and fulfillment of what God did in the past.*

Zechariah and Elizabeth
⁵ In the days of Herod, King of Judea, there was a priest named Zechariah of the priestly division of Abijah; his wife was from the daughters of Aaron, and her name was Elizabeth. ⁶ Both were righteous in the eyes of God, observing all the commandments and ordinances of the Lord blamelessly. ⁷ But they had no child, because Elizabeth was barren and both were advanced in years.
OT: Deut 6:25; 1 Chron 24:1–19

6

5   The Old Testament uses the reigns of kings as a way of indicating when someone lived or something happened (Judith 1:1; Jer 1:2; Dan 1:1; Zeph 1:1), and Luke does the same: **In the days of Herod, King of Judea, there was a priest named Zechariah**. The reign of **Herod** the Great lasted from 37 to 4 B.C. Luke calls him **King of Judea**. Luke sometimes— as here—uses **Judea** as an alternative name for Palestine (6:17; 7:17; 23:5) and sometimes as the name of a region within Palestine (1:65; 2:4; 3:1; 5:17; 21:21). **There was a priest named Zechariah** who lived during Herod's reign. Israelite priesthood was hereditary; every male descendant of Aaron was eligible to serve as a **priest** (Exod 28:1; 29:8–9; Num 18:1). This priest was **named Zechariah**, a common name in the Old Testament. He was **of the priestly division of Abijah**. There were twenty-four divisions, or groupings, of priests (1 Chron 24:1–19); **Abijah** was the ancestral head of one of these divisions (1 Chron 24:10). **His wife was from the daughters of Aaron**: she too was a descendant of Aaron. **Her name was Elizabeth**—Elisheba in Hebrew, the name of Aaron's wife (Exod 6:23).

Judea: See page 40

Priests and Levites: See page 302

BACKGROUND: HEROD THE GREAT Two individuals are called Herod in the Gospels: Herod the Great, who ruled when Jesus was born, and his son Herod Antipas, who ruled Galilee during Jesus' public ministry. Herod the Great's father was an Idumean, a people of Edomite ancestry, who had been forcibly converted to Judaism in 129 B.C. Herod the Great's mother was an Arabian princess, making Herod and his sons half-Jewish at best in the eyes of many. Herod the Great's father was an administrator employed by Rome to oversee Judea. After his father was poisoned by Jewish opponents, Rome made Herod king of Judea, Samaria, Galilee, and some territories to the east and south. Herod the Great was ambitious, shrewd, and ruthless in eliminating any who stood in his way. He undertook projects in a manner that bordered on megalomania, dotting his kingdom with palaces, massively redoing the Temple complex in Jerusalem, and building temples to the Roman emperor in other cities. He had ten wives and many children, some of whom he murdered on suspicion that they were plotting against him. Herod the Great ruled from 37 to 4 B.C. At his death, Rome divided up his kingdom among three of his sons. Archelaus was made ruler of Judea, Samaria, and Idumea, but governed so incompetently that Rome removed him in A.D. 6 and appointed Roman governors to rule his territory. Philip was given rule over a territory that lay north and east of the Sea of Galilee and included Bethsaida and Caesarea Philippi. He ruled well until his death in A.D. 33 or 34. A third son, Herod Antipas, was made ruler of Galilee and of a region east of the Jordan River. *Related topic: Herod Antipas (page 99).*

---

6 Zechariah and Elizabeth not only have priestly heritage; more importantly, **both were righteous in the eyes of God, observing all the commandments and ordinances of the Lord blamelessly.** Luke literally writes that they were walking in all the commandments and ordinances, an Old Testament idiom for following God's ways (see Deut 26:17; 30:16). Moses told the Israelites, "Our justice before the LORD, our God, is to consist in carefully observing all these commandments he has enjoined on us" (Deut 6:25). Elizabeth and Zechariah fulfill Moses' words. They are just and **righteous in the eyes of God** because they keep **all** of God's commandments, and keep them **blamelessly**. They are model Israelites, living up to what God asks of them.

Lord: See page 137

For reflection: Do I keep all of God's commandments? How blamelessly do I observe them?

7 **But they had no child, because Elizabeth was barren**—had not borne a child. Nor was she likely to do so now, for **both were advanced in years.** Children were seen as a blessing from God (Gen 1:28; Deut 28:4, 11; Psalms 127:3–5; 128:1–4) and childlessness a tragedy, even a disgrace (1:25; see Gen 30:22–23; 1 Sam 1:1–6). Childlessness could be a punishment from God (Lev 20:20–21)—but why would God deny children to a blamelessly upright couple like Elizabeth and Zechariah? Perhaps God has something special in mind for them, as he had for another couple who were childless and well advanced in years: Abraham and Sarah (Gen 16:1; 17:17; 18:11).

For reflection: What has been my biggest disappointment or tragedy? How do I understand it in light of God's care for me?

The Announcement of the Birth of John

8 Once when he was serving as priest in his division's turn before God, 9 according to the practice of the priestly service, he was chosen by lot to enter the sanctuary of the Lord to burn incense. 10 Then, when the whole assembly of the people was praying outside at the hour of the incense offering, 11 the angel of the Lord

appeared to him, standing at the right of the altar of incense. [12] Zechariah was troubled by what he saw, and fear came upon him. [13] But the angel said to him, "Do not be afraid, Zechariah, because your prayer has been heard. Your wife Elizabeth will bear you a son, and you shall name him John. [14] And you will have joy and gladness, and many will rejoice at his birth, [15] for he will be great in the sight of [the] Lord. He will drink neither wine nor strong drink. He will be filled with the holy Spirit even from his mother's womb, [16] and he will turn many of the children of Israel to the Lord their God. [17] He will go before him in the spirit and power of Elijah to turn the hearts of fathers toward children and the disobedient to the understanding of the righteous, to prepare a people fit for the Lord." [18] Then Zechariah said to the angel, "How shall I know this? For I am an old man, and my wife is advanced in years." [19] And the angel said to him in reply, "I am Gabriel, who stand before God. I was sent to speak to you and to announce to you this good news. [20] But now you will be speechless and unable to talk until the day these things take place, because you did not believe my words, which will be fulfilled at their proper time."

OT: Gen 17:15–22; 18:9–15; 1 Chron 24:5

8 **Once when he**—Zechariah—**was serving as priest in his division's turn before God**: each division, made up of around three hundred priests, served for a week in the Temple twice a year. Service in the Temple was service **before God** because the Temple was the place of God's special presence (1 Kings 8:10–13).

9 **according to the practice of the priestly service, he was chosen by lot to enter the sanctuary of the Lord to burn incense.** Priests were assigned different duties by **lot** (1 Chron 24:5). We might consider this a way to assign duties randomly and impartially, but in the biblical world casting lots was a way of putting a decision in the hands of God (Lev 16:7–8; Joshua 18:6; Acts 1:23–26). Zechariah was chosen to enter **the sanctuary of the Lord**. The **sanctuary**, or Temple proper, had three rooms or sections lined up in a row. The innermost room was the Holy of Holies (1 Kings 6:16), the place of God's special presence; in Solomon's Temple it contained the Ark of the Covenant (1 Kings 8:6). Only the

high priest could enter the Holy of Holies, and only once a year, on the Day of Atonement (Lev 16:11-16). In front of it was the Holy Place (1 Kings 8:8), a room with an altar for burning incense, lampstands, a table for the showbread, and auxiliary items (Exod 30:1–6; 1 Kings 7:48–50). The third room or section served as a vestibule leading to the Holy Place. Twice a day, morning and afternoon, a priest chosen by lot entered the Holy Place **to burn incense** on the altar. A later Jewish writing indicates that a priest was generally allowed to do so only once in his lifetime.

Temple: See page 519

Today is Zechariah's day of a lifetime: **he was chosen by lot—selected by God—to enter the sanctuary of the Lord to burn incense**. This is the closest he will ever be to God's special presence in the Holy of Holies; this is the highest act of worship he will ever carry out as a priest.

10 **Then, when the whole assembly of the people was praying outside at the hour of the incense offering**: Jews came to the Temple for "the three o'clock hour of prayer" (Acts 3:1), during which the afternoon incense offering was made. While Zechariah is inside making the incense offering, a **whole assembly of the people** is gathered in the outside courts **praying**. While priests have special roles, the whole people of God is to be a worshiping people.

For reflection: When are my times of prayer?

11 We can imagine that Zechariah was already excited to be in the Holy Place offering incense. And then an **angel of the Lord appeared to him, standing at the right of the altar of incense**! Luke tells where the angel stood but not what the angel looked like.

Lord: See page 137

12 **Zechariah was troubled by what he saw, and fear came upon him.** The Greek word translated **troubled** can also mean agitated or terrified. Zechariah is startled by the angel's appearance and overcome with **fear**. This is a normal human reaction to encounters with the divine or divine messengers (Isaiah 6:5; Dan 8:15–17; 10:5–9).

13 **But the angel said to him, "Do not be afraid, Zechariah."** The angel tries to calm Zechariah, telling him **do not be afraid**. Similarly, when Daniel became faint at the appearance of an angel, the angel told Daniel to fear not (Dan 10:12, 19). Zechariah is to have no fear **because your prayer has been heard**—heard by God. Zechariah would have recited a prayer for God's people as he made the incense offering, but is that the **prayer** that the angel has in mind? It might appear that the angel is referring to a different prayer, for God's answer to Zechariah's prayer is that **your wife Elizabeth will bear you a son**. Elizabeth and Zechariah had undoubtedly prayed to have children—but were they still praying for children now that they were advanced in years (verse 7)? Or was God answering a prayer they had prayed in the past before giving up hope? We can only speculate at this point in Luke's account.

For reflection: Have I ever had prayer answered after I had given up hope and stopped praying?

BACKGROUND: ANGELS The Hebrew and Greek words translated as "angel" also mean "messenger," and angels appear in early Old Testament writings as messengers of God. These messengers are not always clearly distinguished from manifestations of God himself (Gen 16:7–13; Exod 3:2–6). Some Scripture passages speak of members of God's heavenly court, sometimes calling them "the sons of God," meaning "heavenly beings" (Job 1:6), or calling them the "host," or army, "of heaven" (1 Kings 22:19–22), an expression that can also refer to stars (Deut 4:19). Cherubim are heavenly beings, too (Ezek 10:18–20; see also Gen 3:24), as are seraphim (Isaiah 6:2). Thus the Old Testament speaks of a variety of heavenly beings without relating them to one another, without calling all of them angels, and without defining their nature. Individual angels are not named until late Old Testament writings; Raphael (Tobit 5:4; 12:15), Gabriel (Dan 8:15–16; 9:21), and Michael (Dan 10:13) are the only three angels named in the Old Testament. Michael, the prince or guardian angel of God's people (Dan 12:1), contends with other heavenly beings who are the guardians of other nations (Dan 10:13, 20–21). Speculations about angels multiplied late in the Old Testament era and are reflected in Jewish writings that did not become part of Scripture. The perplexing account in Genesis of "the sons of heaven" (literally, "sons of God"; see Job 1:6) who had intercourse with women (Gen 6:1–4) developed into a story of the fall of some angels who led humans into sin. The chief of the fallen angels was given various names, including "Satan." At the time of Jesus, angels were generally thought of as human in form (2 Macc 3:26; Dan 8:15–16) but with heavenly rather than earthly bodies, not needing to eat or drink (Tobit 12:19). *Related topics: Nonbiblical writings (page 342), Satan (page 108).*

The angel tells Zechariah that Elizabeth will bear a son **and you shall name him John**. The name **John** in Hebrew means "Yahweh has been gracious" (Yahweh is the personal name of God in the Old Testament, which the New American Bible renders as LORD—Exod 3:15). God is indeed being gracious to Elizabeth and Zechariah, giving them a son. It was normal for a father to **name** a newborn son, but being given his name by a divine messenger recalls a similar instruction to Abraham when he and Sarah had Isaac in their old age (Gen 17:19). God's involvement in naming a child indicates that God is about something special (see also Gen 16:11; Isaiah 7:14; Hosea 1:4, 6, 9). In accord with his name, John will play a role in God's gracious plans for his people.

God's name: See page 546

For reflection: How have I most clearly experienced God's graciousness?

14 **And you will have joy and gladness.** The son Elizabeth will bear will bring **joy** and **gladness** to his parents—and not only to them: **many will rejoice at his birth**. We might interpret the **many** as relatives and friends of Elizabeth and Zechariah who will **rejoice** with them over the birth of a child at long last. But as the angel goes on to explain why **many will rejoice at his birth**, it becomes clear that **many** means a large number of God's people and not simply those who know Zechariah and Elizabeth.

15 Many will rejoice over John **for he will be great in the sight of [the] Lord**. There is greatness, and then there is being **great in the sight of [the] Lord** God. Someone who is considered great by others may or may not be considered great by God; someone who is a nobody in the eyes of the world can be great in the sight of God. The angel goes on to tell why John will be great in God's estimation. First, **he will drink neither wine nor strong drink**. The word translated **strong drink** does not mean distilled spirits but simply an alcoholic beverage other than wine, chiefly barley beer or ale. John will abstain from alcohol. Those who dedicated themselves to God by taking a nazirite vow drank no alcoholic beverages (Num 6:1–4), but neither were priests to imbibe while serving in the Temple (Lev 10:8–9) or Samson's mother during her pregnancy (Judges 13:3–4, 7, 14). As in all these cases, John's abstinence will indicate that he is dedicated to God's service.

Secondly, John will be great because **he will be filled with the holy Spirit even from his mother's womb**. Samson was "consecrated to God from the womb" (Judges 13:5), as was Jeremiah (Jer 1:4–5); John will be likewise dedicated to God while in **his mother's womb**. Even before he is born, John **will be filled with the holy Spirit**. The Old Testament precedents for being **filled with** or inspired by **the holy Spirit** suggest that John will be a prophet, someone who speaks for God (Num 11:25–26; 2 Sam 23:2; Isaiah 61:1–2; Ezek 11:5; Joel 3:1). God selected John, even before he was born, to play a special role and will fill John with the Spirit so that he will be equipped to carry out this role.

The Spirit: See page 100

For reflection: When did God select me for his service? How have I been equipped to carry out my service?

16 John will be great in the sight of God because he will be filled with the Spirit so that **he will turn many of the children of Israel to the Lord their God**. The expression **children of Israel**, literally, "sons of Israel," is an Old Testament idiom for the Israelites, the people of God. The Old Testament characteristically speaks of repentance as turning to or returning to God: "Return, O children of Israel, to him whom you have utterly deserted" (Isaiah 31:6). John will **turn many** to God. Here **many** may imply not all; John will meet rejection as well as acceptance. Being filled with and empowered by the Holy Spirit does not guarantee unmitigated success.

17 The angel expands on John's turning the hearts of many to God. **He will go before him in the spirit and power of Elijah**. In context, the **him** before whom John will go is the Lord God (verse 16). **Elijah** was the great wonder-working prophet of the Old Testament (1 Kings 17—2 Kings 2). He was taken up into heaven (2 Kings 2:11) and was expected to return to prepare people for a "day of the LORD" when God would judge his people (Mal 3:23–24; Sirach 48:4, 10). The angel does not say that John is Elijah come back to earth but that John will carry out his mission with the **spirit** and **power** of Elijah—the Holy Spirit (verse 15), the power of God at work through him. The angel says that John will **turn the hearts of fathers toward children**, echoing the prophet Malachi's description of

13

what Elijah will do in preparation for the "day of the Lord" (Mal 3:24; see also Sirach 48:10). John, carrying out what was expected of Elijah, will mend human relationships in preparation for God's judgment. Turning to God (verse 16) includes making right our relationships with one another.

The day of the Lord: See page 91

> Lo, I will send you
>   Elijah, the prophet,
> Before the day of the LORD comes,
>   the great and terrible day,
> To turn the hearts of the fathers to their children,
>   and the hearts of the children to their fathers.
>
> Mal 3:23–24

John will also mend relationships with God. That seems to be the sense of turning the hearts of **the disobedient to the understanding of the righteous**. Here **understanding** means way of thinking; **the righteous** are those who are right with God. Those who are disobedient will begin to think rightly as a necessary step for setting themselves right with God. John's work, in summary, will be **to prepare a people fit for the Lord**, ready to stand before him.

We can now understand some of the angel's previous words a little better. John will be the answer not only to the prayers of Zechariah and Elizabeth to have a son but also to Zechariah's priestly prayer on behalf of the people of Israel (verse 13). Many will rejoice over God's sending of John (verse 14) to turn hearts to God.

While the angel has spoken of John going before **him**, meaning God, and preparing a people fit for the **Lord** God, there is a second level of meaning in the angel's words. Jesus will be called Lord as God is called Lord; John will go before Jesus, who will baptize with the Holy Spirit (see 3:15–17).

For reflection: What can I do to touch hearts and help prepare people to be with God?

18 While the angel has said quite a bit about John and what he will do (verses 15–17), Zechariah's mind is on the promise of his birth (verse

13). **Then Zechariah said to the angel, "How shall I know this?"** Another translation would be, "By what shall I know this?" Zechariah asks for a sign to confirm that Elizabeth will bear a son. Zechariah tells the angel why he asks for a sign: **for I am an old man, and my wife is advanced in years**, well past childbearing. There are Old Testament precedents for asking for a sign (Abraham—Gen 15:7–8; Gideon—Judges 6:17, 36–37; Hezekiah—2 Kings 20:8). God even invited King Ahaz to ask for a sign (Isaiah 7:10–11). But shouldn't an angel's delivering a message be a sufficient guarantee of its divine origin and truth? What sign does Zechariah need in addition to an angel appearing to him in the Holy Place?

19 **And the angel said to him in reply, "I am Gabriel, who stand before God."** The angel speaking to Zechariah is not just any old angel. He is **Gabriel**, who revealed God's hidden designs to Daniel (Dan 8–12; Gabriel is identified by name at Dan 8:16 and 9:21). He is one of seven angels **who stand before God** and are specially available to serve him (see Tobit 12:15; Rev 8:2). Zechariah should appreciate that God has sent one of his first-class messengers! Gabriel continues, **I was sent to speak to you and to announce to you this good news**, the good news that Elizabeth would bear a son who would turn the people of Israel to God. **Good news** has come into English as the word "gospel." Gabriel has told Zechariah the gospel truth, as it were, but Zechariah would not accept it.

Gospel, good news: See page 59

20 Having asked for a sign, Zechariah is given a sign that leaves him speechless: **but now you will be speechless and unable to talk until the day these things take place, because you did not believe my words**. Zechariah asked, "How shall I know this" (verse 18), because he **did not believe** Gabriel's **words**. Zechariah did not understand how he and Elizabeth could have a child in their old age, and he limited what he thought God could do to what he could understand. Nevertheless, the things that Gabriel said would happen **will be fulfilled at their proper time**—in God's timing. God's word is always fulfilled. Zechariah will be **unable to talk until the day these things take place**. It is not apparent what **day** Gabriel is referring to, since he has not only spoken of Elizabeth bearing a son who is to be named John (verse 13) but of John

carrying out a ministry as an adult (verses 15–17). Zechariah must have been left wondering how long his speechlessness would last and what would have to be fulfilled for him to talk again.

For reflection: Do I limit what God can do to what I can understand?

Luke's readers who are familiar with Genesis might note parallels between two couples: Abraham and Sarah, and Zechariah and Elizabeth. Both couples were childless in their old age, received a divine message that they would have a son, were told what to name him, and expressed skepticism (see Gen 17:15–17; 18:10-12). Abraham and Sarah marked a new beginning in God's plans. Zechariah and Elizabeth also stand at the beginning of God doing something new, but in continuity with what he began with Abraham and Sarah.

Elizabeth Conceives

²¹ Meanwhile the people were waiting for Zechariah and were amazed that he stayed so long in the sanctuary. ²² But when he came out, he was unable to speak to them, and they realized that he had seen a vision in the sanctuary. He was gesturing to them but remained mute. ²³ Then, when his days of ministry were completed, he went home. ²⁴ After this time his wife Elizabeth conceived, and she went into seclusion for five months, saying, ²⁵ "So has the Lord done for me at a time when he has seen fit to take away my disgrace before others."

21 **Meanwhile the people were waiting for Zechariah and were amazed that he stayed so long in the sanctuary.** A "whole assembly" of people were praying outside while Zechariah was inside the **sanctuary** making the incense offering (1:10). The rhythms of Temple ritual were sufficiently fixed that people noted Zechariah's delay and were **amazed** by it.

22 **But when he came out, he was unable to speak to them.** A later Jewish writing indicates that, upon coming out of the Temple after offering incense, priests would pronounce a blessing on those assembled (see Num 6:22–27). Zechariah could not do so, for **he was unable to speak,**

as Gabriel had decreed (1:20). The people **realized that he had seen a vision in the sanctuary**. They do not necessarily know that an angel appeared to him, but it is apparent that Zechariah had some kind of encounter with the divine that left him in shock and unable to speak. **He was gesturing to them but remained mute.** The word translated as **mute** can also mean deaf; it will emerge that Zechariah is deaf as well as speechless (see 1:62). Zechariah tries to convey what happened to him by **gesturing**—but how does one express Gabriel's words in gestures? Luke's account leaves Gabriel's message known only to Zechariah and the reader.

23 **Then, when his days of ministry were completed, he went home.** Even though he cannot speak, Zechariah continues to carry out his priestly **ministry** in the Temple until the week of service for his division of priests is **completed** (see 1:8). Then **he went home.** We will later learn that he and Elizabeth lived in a town in the hill country of Judah (1:39–40)—an area adjacent to and south of Jerusalem.

For reflection: Do I try to continue to serve God despite physical impediments or other limitations?

24 **After this time his wife Elizabeth conceived.** Being "advanced in years" (1:7) does not mean that Zechariah and Elizabeth have stopped having intercourse. **Elizabeth conceived**, just as the angel Gabriel said she would (1:13); God's plans are unfolding. **She went into seclusion for five months.** The point of her going into **seclusion**—literally, hiding herself—would seem to be to prevent others from learning that she is pregnant. Elizabeth explains her going into seclusion by **saying,**

25 **"So has the Lord done for me at a time when he has seen fit to take away my disgrace before others."** Elizabeth recognizes that her pregnancy is a gift from God: **so has the Lord done for me**. She had not become pregnant during her normal childbearing years but has done so **at a time when** God **has seen fit**. In the culture in which she lived, her childlessness was a **disgrace before others** (see Gen 30:22–23; 1 Sam 1:1–6). God has now taken away her **disgrace**.

Elizabeth considers her pregnancy a gracious gift from God. But why is this a motive for her to hide herself? How can her **disgrace before**

others be removed if no one learns that she is pregnant? We would expect her to announce her pregnancy to everyone to testify to God's graciousness and to remove the stigma of barrenness. But Elizabeth instead keeps her pregnancy a secret, leaving us wondering.

With Elizabeth in seclusion and Zechariah speechless, they are the only ones who know that Elizabeth is pregnant. God will incorporate this into his plans.

The Announcement of the Birth of Jesus

²⁶ In the sixth month, the angel Gabriel was sent from God to a town of Galilee called Nazareth, ²⁷ to a virgin betrothed to a man named Joseph, of the house of David, and the virgin's name was Mary. ²⁸ And coming to her, he said, "Hail, favored one! The Lord is with you." ²⁹ But she was greatly troubled at what was said and pondered what sort of greeting this might be. ³⁰ Then the angel said to her, "Do not be afraid, Mary, for you have found favor with God. ³¹ Behold, you will conceive in your womb and bear a son, and you shall name him Jesus. ³² He will be great and will be called Son of the Most High, and the Lord God will give him the throne of David his father, ³³ and he will rule over the house of Jacob forever, and of his kingdom there will be no end." ³⁴ But Mary said to the angel, "How can this be, since I have no relations with a man?" ³⁵ And the angel said to her in reply, "The holy Spirit will come upon you, and the power of the Most High will overshadow you. Therefore the child to be born will be called holy, the Son of God. ³⁶ And behold, Elizabeth, your relative, has also conceived a son in her old age, and this is the sixth month for her who was called barren; ³⁷ for nothing will be impossible for God." ³⁸ Mary said, "Behold, I am the handmaid of the Lord. May it be done to me according to your word." Then the angel departed from her.

OT: 2 Sam 7:11–16; Psalm 2:7; 89:2–5, 27–38
NT: Matt 1:19–20, 24

26 **In the sixth month** of Elizabeth's pregnancy (1:24) **the angel Gabriel was sent from God to a town of Galilee called Nazareth**. Gabriel, one of seven angels who stand in God's presence (1:19; see Tobit 12:15;

Rev 8:2), was previously sent to Zechariah in the Holy Place of the Temple (1:11–20). Now Gabriel is sent to **Nazareth**. Although Luke calls it a **town**—literally, a city—Nazareth was a nondescript farming village of several hundred people that is not mentioned in the Old Testament. Its obscurity may be the reason why Luke tells his readers that Nazareth is in **Galilee**, a region in the northern part of Palestine. Gabriel's two missions take him to two decidedly different places. The Temple is the unique center of Jewish worship; Nazareth is just one of many small farming villages. Why would God send an important messenger like Gabriel to a place like **Nazareth**?

Angel: See page 11
Galilee: See page 114

27 Gabriel is sent by God **to a virgin betrothed to a man named Joseph**. Jewish marriage involved two stages. Usually between the ages of twelve and thirteen, a young woman was **betrothed** by her father to a young man. Betrothal was more than engagement: a betrothed couple was considered married and were spoken of as husband and wife, even though the bride continued to live in her father's house and the couple refrained from sexual relations. A year or so after betrothal the husband would bring his wife to live in his house, and they would begin to have sexual relations. Gabriel is sent **to a virgin betrothed to a man named Joseph**: they are in the first stage of marriage, and she is still a **virgin**. Joseph is **of the house of David**, meaning that he is a descendant of David. **The virgin's name was Mary**: Luke again specifies that she is a **virgin**. Jews who valued their heritage often named their children after

---

BACKGROUND: NAZARETH was an insignificant farming village located on a hillside overlooking the Jezreel Valley in southern Galilee. The remains of ancient Nazareth lie beneath the modern town of Nazareth and have been only partially excavated. Archaeologists tell us that the village was a few acres in size at the time of Jesus and had several hundred inhabitants. Remains from the first century suggest that houses in Nazareth were rather insubstantial, with fieldstone walls and thatched roofs. No luxury items of any kind have been found on the site. Nazareth is not mentioned in the Old Testament; its unimportance is reflected in Nathanael's question "Can anything good come from Nazareth?" (John 1:46). There was nothing to distinguish Nazareth from other small farming villages in Galilee during the years Jesus called it home.

Old Testament figures, just as Christians today might give saints' names to their children. **Joseph** is the name of one of the twelve sons of Jacob (Gen 30:24); **Mary** is a form of the name Miriam, the sister of Aaron (Exod 15:20). If their names are any indication, Joseph and Mary come from families that honor Jewish tradition.

Marriage practices: See page 540

Gabriel is not only sent to small, insignificant Nazareth; he is sent to a young woman who is insignificant in the culture of the time. She has none of Zechariah's status as a priest making a once-in-a-lifetime incense offering in the Holy Place; she is a village girl entering marriage with another villager.

28 **And coming to her, he said, "Hail, favored one! The Lord is with you."** Luke provides no setting for Gabriel's appearance to Mary, but the Greek word translated **coming** means entering, and it may convey that Mary was indoors when Gabriel came to her. Luke expresses Gabriel's greeting as **Hail**, the usual Greek greeting, equivalent to the English hello; it literally means rejoice. Gabriel's message to Mary should bring her joy. **Favored** means favored by God; God has chosen Mary to be the privileged recipient of his graciousness. That is why Gabriel is sent to this young woman in an insignificant village. **The Lord is with you** assures Mary of God's presence to her, and it has the connotation that God will assist her in carrying out some mission (see Gen 26:24; 28:15; Exod 3:12; Judges 6:12, 16; Jer 1:8). But what would God want a young village woman to do for him?

Lord: See page 137

For reflection: How have I experienced God's favor? How has God been with me and assisted me as I serve him?

29 Although Gabriel's greeting invites Mary to rejoice, that is not her initial reaction. **But she was greatly troubled at what was said and pondered what sort of greeting this might be.** Mary is perplexed, even **greatly troubled,** by Gabriel's words, for they convey that she is someone special to God and imply that God has something for her to do. That is apparently not how Mary thinks of herself. She does not say anything

but **pondered** the implications of an angel **greeting** her as God's favored one and assuring her of God's presence and assistance. She might have to think differently of herself in light of Gabriel's words.

For reflection: How have I reacted when I have experienced God's special favor or call? How did it change the way I think of myself?

30 Gabriel addresses Mary's consternation. **Then the angel said to her, "Do not be afraid, Mary, for you have found favor with God."** Gabriel's sudden appearance can frighten a person, as was the case with Zechariah and Daniel (1:11–12; Dan 10:5–11). Gabriel tells Mary, as he told those to whom he earlier appeared, **do not be afraid** (1:13; Dan 10:12). She is to have no fear because she has **found favor with God**; she is God's "favored one" (verse 28). To find favor with God echoes an Old Testament expression for being esteemed by God and pleasing to him. God told Moses, "You have found favor with me and you are my intimate friend" (Exod 33:17; see also Exod 33:12–13). The expression is used in modern Hebrew for really liking someone; God really likes Mary.

31 Gabriel goes on to explain how God's favor will be borne out in Mary's life. **Behold, you will conceive in your womb and bear a son, and you shall name him Jesus.** Gabriel's words could be taken as simply a prediction of what will happen and what Mary is to do when it happens: Mary is betrothed to Joseph and in the normal course of events she will move into his house and they will begin to have sexual relations. She will become pregnant and deliver a son; she is to name him Jesus. **Jesus** is an Aramaic form of the name Joshua, the name of Moses' right-hand man (Exod 24:13; 33:11). Jesus was a popular name among Jews in the first century, and there would be nothing out of the ordinary in Mary's son being given this name. Yet there is more to Gabriel's words than first meets the ear. They follow an Old Testament pattern of God or God's messenger telling of the conception and birth, and often naming, of a child (Gen 16:11; 17:19; Judges 13:3; Isaiah 7:14), a pattern Gabriel followed in announcing the birth of John to Elizabeth and Zechariah (1:13). God does not send birth announcements without a reason. The fact that Gabriel tells Mary of the conception and birth of Jesus indicates that Jesus, like John, will be someone special and carry out an important role in God's plans.

32 Gabriel explains how Jesus will be special and what role he will play: **he will be great and will be called Son of the Most High**. The Psalms extol God as great (Psalms 48:2; 86:10; 135:5; 145:3), and Jesus will also be **great.** Gabriel told Zechariah that his son John would be great in the sight of God (1:15) but Jesus will be **great** in a far more exalted way: Jesus **will be called Son of the Most High**. In the biblical view, what one is **called** expresses what one is. **The Most High** is a title for God (Gen 14:18–22; 2 Sam 22:14; Dan 4:21). Jesus will be called and will be Son of God.

What would Mary have understood by her son being called Son of God? In the Old Testament, a variety of individuals were referred to as sons of God, including kings, righteous Israelites, and angels (2 Sam 7:14; Job 1:6; 2:1; Psalm 2:7; 89:7; Wisd 2:18; 5:5; Sirach 4:10). Being a son of God indicated that one enjoyed some kind of special relationship with God but did not specify what that relationship was.

Son of God: See page 25

Gabriel gives a reason why Jesus can be called Son of God: **the Lord God will give him the throne of David his father.** To have **the throne of David** means to rule Israel (1 Kings 1:48; 2:24). God promised David that his descendants would occupy his throne forever (2 Sam 7:11–16; Psalm 89:2–5, 27–38). God said of the king who would rule after David, "I will be a father to him, and he shall be a son to me" (2 Sam 7:14), providing the basis for later kings being thought of as sons of God (see Psalm 2:7). Jesus will be a kingly Son of God who will be given the throne **of David his father.** Joseph is "of the house of David" (verse 27), as would be his children.

> And when your time comes and you rest with your ancestors, I will raise up your heir after you, sprung from your loins, and I will make his kingdom firm . . . And I will make his royal throne firm forever. I will be a father to him, and he shall be a son to me . . . Your house and your kingdom shall endure forever before me; your throne shall stand firm forever.
>
> 2 Sam 7:12–14, 16

Presumably Mary is continuing to ponder what the angel is telling her (see verse 29), and she has been given a lot to ponder. She will bear a son who will be great, who will be called Son of God, who will rule over God's people. They have been ruled by Rome for over a half-century; does this mean that her son Jesus will win Jewish freedom and reestablish the dynasty of David?

33 Before Mary can take in the full implications of Gabriel's words, he makes an even more sweeping pronouncement: **and he will rule over the house of Jacob forever, and of his kingdom there will be no end**. The **house of Jacob** is an expression for Israel, the people of God (Isaiah 2:5; 8:17; 48:1). Jesus will not be like David's descendants, who sat on his throne one after another; Jesus will rule **forever**. Jesus' kingdom will not come to an end as David's kingdom did with the Babylonian conquest of 586 B.C.; **there will be no end** to Jesus' **kingdom**. It is now evident that Gabriel is speaking about the Messiah whom many Jews expected: a descendant of David empowered by God to usher in a new age.

Messiah, Christ: See page 257

34 Yet Mary is puzzled by Gabriel's words. **But Mary said to the angel, "How can this be, since I have no relations with a man?"** She does not ask how her son could rule over the house of Israel forever but how she could have a son at all. Mary's puzzlement is in turn puzzling. She is betrothed to Joseph and would be expected to bear children after they began to live together. Yet Mary asks **How can this be?** She gives the reason for her asking how can this happen: **since I have no relations with a man**. The sense seems to be, "I do not have a husband with whom I am having sexual relations."

Mary's words have been interpreted in a number of ways. Saints Gregory of Nyssa (lived about 330-395), Ambrose (lived about 339-397) and Augustine (lived 354-430) proposed that Mary was vowed to maintain her virginity. While this interpretation made sense in light of Christian esteem for virginity, it makes less sense in terms of the Jewish view of marriage. The primary purpose of marriage was to beget children—fulfilling God's command to "be fertile and multiply" (Gen 1:27), continuing the father's family name and providing support for parents in their old age. For a wife to be childless was a disgrace (see 1:25). Few Jews chose lives of virginity; those who did so did not get married. In a first-century Jewish context, Mary and Joseph's getting married meant they planned to have sexual relations and children. This is not to say, however, that their plans weren't changed by Gabriel's message and its fulfillment: from early centuries the Church has proclaimed Mary to be ever virgin.

Another way that Mary's words might be interpreted: she may have understood Gabriel's words as a statement of what was to happen immediately rather than after she and Joseph began to live together. She would then be asking how she could conceive now, since she was not having sexual relations with a man.

For reflection: How do I understand Mary's words to Gabriel?

35 Whatever the proper interpretation of Mary's words might be, Gabriel answers her "How can this be?" question. **And the angel said to her in reply, "The holy Spirit will come upon you, and the power of the Most High will overshadow you."** Gabriel employs the Hebrew poetic practice of using two expressions to speak of the same thing: **the holy Spirit** and **the power of the Most High**. The Holy Spirit is the creative power of God—the "mighty wind," or Spirit, of God that swept over the waters at creation (Gen 1:2; the same Hebrew word means wind, breath, or spirit). Psalm 104 proclaims, "When you send forth your breath, they are created / and you renew the face of the earth" (Psalm 104:30; see also Judith 16:14). The breath that God breathes into humans gives them life (Gen 2:7). The Holy Spirit, the power of God, will **come upon** Mary and **overshadow** her, enveloping her in God's creative and life-giving power. Her son will be conceived not through human agency but by God.

The Spirit: See page 100

Therefore the child to be born will be called holy, the Son of God. Gabriel's **therefore** is explanatory: because Jesus will be conceived through the Holy Spirit, **therefore** he will be **holy**, set apart for God's service. Because Jesus will be conceived through the Holy Spirit, **therefore** he will be called and will be **the Son of God**.

Gabriel earlier said that Jesus "will be called Son of the Most High," connecting his sonship with his being the Messiah who will rule forever (verses 32–33). Now Gabriel speaks of Jesus being **the Son of God** in a far more profound sense: he will be begotten by God. God will proclaim him to be his beloved Son (3:22; see also 9:35); Jesus will speak to and of God as his Father as no one had ever done (2:49; 10:21–22; 22:29, 42; 23:34, 46; 24:49). The son whom Mary will bear will be uniquely **the Son of God**.

For reflection: What does it mean to me that Jesus is the Son of God?

Mary pondered Gabriel's first words to her (verse 29) and now he has presented her with the virtually imponderable: she is to be the mother of the Son of God.

36 Unlike Zechariah (1:18), Mary has not asked for a sign to confirm that Gabriel's words are true. Gabriel nevertheless gives her a reassuring sign, perhaps because he has communicated a far more profound message to Mary than he delivered to Zechariah: **behold, Elizabeth, your relative, has also conceived a son in her old age, and this is the sixth month for her who was called barren**. Gabriel refers to **Elizabeth** as Mary's **relative**. She is often thought of as Mary's cousin, but Luke does not use the Greek word for cousin; he uses a word that means **relative** and covers a variety of relationships. Elizabeth who is in **her old age** and was

---

BACKGROUND: SON OF GOD The title "son [or 'sons'] of God" carries a variety of meanings in the Old Testament. It is applied to angels and members of the heavenly court (Job 1:6; 2:1). It is used to refer to the people of God (Exod 4:22; Deut 14:1). A king in the line of David could be referred to as a son of God (2 Sam 7:14; Psalm 2:7), as could a devout Israelite (Wisd 2:18). It is not, however, a title explicitly associated with the Messiah: no prophecy refers to the Messiah as the Son of God. When the title "Son of God" is applied to Jesus in the Gospels or in Paul's letters, it carries a far greater meaning than in the Old Testament, since it refers to Jesus' unique relationship with God as his Father. This is particularly developed in the Gospel of John. Paul focuses on what Jesus is able to do to bring us salvation because he is the Son of God (Rom 5:10; 8:3, 32; Gal 4:4–5; Col 1:13). In later centuries, the Church reflected on what Jesus' sonship meant in terms of his divinity. The Council of Nicaea in 325 proclaimed that the "Lord Jesus Christ, the Son of God" is "true God from true God, begotten not made, consubstantial with the Father"—"one in Being with the Father" in another translation of the Nicene Creed. The Council of Chalcedon, held in 451, proclaimed that Jesus Christ is one person with two natures, a divine nature and a human nature, so he is both fully divine and fully human.

---

considered **barren** has **conceived a son** and is in the sixth month of her pregnancy. Mary would not have known this, for Elizabeth has been in seclusion and Zechariah speechless (1:20, 24). God's giving of a son to Elizabeth in her barrenness is a sign that God can give a son to Mary in her virginity.

37 God can give sons to the barren Elizabeth and to the virgin Mary, **for nothing will be impossible for God**. When Sarah laughed at the idea of having a son in her old age, God told Abraham, "Is anything too marvelous for the LORD to do?" (Gen 18:14). If we accept that God is God, then we must accept that he can do all things (see Job 42:2; Jer 32:27; Zech 8:6).

> For reflection: When or how do I place limits on what God can do? On what God can do for me?

38 Gabriel has told Mary what will happen but has not asked whether she consented to it. Mary does not wait to be asked: **Mary said, "Behold, I am the handmaid of the Lord. May it be done to me according to your word."** The Greek word translated **handmaid** is literally slave. When used to characterize one's relationship with God, it connotes absolute submission to God, complete availability to do God's will, wholehearted compliance with whatever God asks. This is Mary's response: she proclaims that she is God's **handmaid**, his slave, ready to do all he asks. She puts aside whatever plans and expectations and hopes she had for her life so that God's will may be carried out. She tells Gabriel, **may it be done to me according to your word**: let it happen to me as you have said. Mary responds to God with acceptance, submission, and faith, believing Gabriel's words. **Then the angel departed from her**, having carried out his mission. Mary is left to ponder what God is doing through her and to marvel at it.

Servant, slave: See page 454

> For reflection: How willingly do I embrace all that God asks of me? All that he might ask of me? How can I make Mary my model?

Catholics believe that Mary, like John (1:15), was called from the womb to play a role in God's plan of salvation—called, however, from the moment of her conception. By virtue of the redemption won by her son, she was preserved from the sin of Adam (see Rom 5:12) which came to be called original sin. Yet Luke's account does not read as if Mary was aware of her privileged place in God's plans before Gabriel appeared to her. We can better appreciate the greatness of Mary if we accept that she grew in her understanding of herself and her role rather than assume that she knew from the beginning how everything would unfold.

Mary Visits Elizabeth

39 During those days Mary set out and traveled to the hill country in haste to a town of Judah, 40 where she entered the house of Zechariah and greeted Elizabeth. 41 When Elizabeth heard Mary's greeting, the infant leaped in her womb, and Elizabeth, filled with the holy Spirit, 42 cried out in a loud voice and said, "Most blessed are you among women, and blessed is the fruit of your womb. 43 And how does this happen to me, that the mother of my Lord should come to me? 44 For at the moment the sound of your greeting reached my ears, the infant in my womb leaped for joy. 45 Blessed are you who believed that what was spoken to you by the Lord would be fulfilled."

OT: Judges 5:24; Judith 13:18
NT: Luke 8:21; 11:27–28

39 **During those days**, after Gabriel had appeared to her, **Mary set out and traveled to the hill country in haste to a town of Judah**. Gabriel told Mary that her relative Elizabeth was pregnant (1:36), and Mary goes to see her. She travels to the **hill country** of the territory that had long ago been allotted to the tribe of **Judah**, a region adjacent to and south of Jerusalem. Luke does not name the **town** that is her destination; by the sixth century it came to be identified with En Kerem, five miles west of Jerusalem. From Nazareth Mary **traveled** at least eighty-five miles, a journey of five or more days on foot. It would have been highly unusual for a young woman to travel unaccompanied, but Luke does not go into Mary's travel arrangements. He notes that she travels **in haste** but does

27

not explain why she is in a hurry. Gabriel told Mary that Elizabeth was pregnant despite her old age, and he used her pregnancy as a sign that God could accomplish the impossible (1:36–37); we might speculate that Mary was eager to see this sign for herself. We might also speculate that she was eager to be with Elizabeth because of what they had in common: they were unexpectedly becoming mothers through the favor of God; their sons would play major roles in God's unfolding plans.

40 On reaching her destination Mary **entered the house of Zechariah and greeted Elizabeth**. Although **Zechariah** served in the Temple in Jerusalem (1:8–23), he, like most ordinary priests, lived outside Jerusalem (see Neh 11:3). Mary **greeted** Elizabeth: in the biblical world, a greeting was usually more than a quick "hello" (this is presumed in Acts 18:22; 21:7). Luke does not recount the words Mary used to greet Elizabeth, but if Elizabeth's greeting to Mary is an indication (verses 42–45), Mary's greeting might have expressed her joy that Elizabeth had been shown favor by God and become pregnant.

41 **When Elizabeth heard Mary's greeting, the infant leaped in her womb.** Elizabeth is six months pregnant (1:36) and by now familiar with her infant's stirring and kicking in her womb. But **Elizabeth, filled with the holy Spirit**, is inspired to understand the significance of her infant's leaping the moment she heard Mary's greeting. She realizes that her infant leaped in joy in response to Mary and the child she is carrying (verse 44). Elizabeth, inspired by the Holy Spirit, grasps that Mary is an extraordinary woman carrying someone extraordinary in her womb.

The Spirit: See page 100

42 Elizabeth's inspired insight cannot be contained; she **cried out in a loud voice and said, "Most blessed are you among women, and blessed is the fruit of your womb."** Elizabeth's words echo Old Testament praise for Israelite heroines. The prophetess Deborah proclaimed Jael to be "blessed among women" for slaying an enemy general (Judges 5:24–27). Judith was praised as blessed "above all the women on earth" for slaying another enemy general (Judith 13:18). Mary is **blessed**, however, not for causing death but because she is bringing forth life—extraordinary life. Mary is **blessed**—blessed by God; she is the **most blessed among**

women. Elizabeth is inspired to recognize what Gabriel proclaimed: Mary is God's "favored one" (1:28).

> *Then Uzziah said to her: "Blessed are you, daughter, by the Most High God, above all the women on earth."*
> Judith 13:18

A beatitude—declaring someone blessed or fortunate—usually tells why or how a person is blessed. Elizabeth tells Mary, **blessed is the fruit of your womb**. Again, **blessed** implies blessed by God. **Fruit of your womb** is a biblical idiom for offspring (see Gen 30:2; Deut 7:13; 28:11). Mary's child is **blessed**, and Mary is blessed because of her child. In the culture in which Mary lived, a woman's greatness came from the children she bore (see 11:27). Elizabeth, inspired by the Holy Spirit, perceives the greatness of the child whom Mary is carrying and Mary's resulting greatness.

Beatitudes: See page 169

43 **And how does this happen to me**—why have I had the privilege—**that the mother of my Lord should come to me?** The Greek word translated **Lord** has a range of meaning. It can be a respectful form of address for someone with authority; the New American Bible sometimes translates the word as sir (13:8; 14:22; 19:16) or master (12:37, 43). The word is also used as a title for God; Mary told Gabriel, "I am the handmaid of the Lord" (1:38). What is the meaning when Elizabeth refers to the child in Mary's womb as **my Lord**? She certainly has profound respect for Mary's child and acknowledges that he will be her lord or master. But since she is "filled with the holy Spirit" (verse 41), her words are prophetic: Jesus will be called Lord as God is called Lord (see 2:11; John 20:28; Phil 2:11). Elizabeth asks in awe, how does it happen that the mother of **my Lord** should come to me?

Lord: See page 137

44 Elizabeth tells Mary how she knows that Mary is the mother of her Lord: **For at the moment the sound of your greeting reached my ears, the infant in my womb leaped for joy.** The Holy Spirit prompts both Elizabeth and her child. "Filled with the holy Spirit even from his

mother's womb" (1:15), Elizabeth's infant, John, **leaped for joy** at the presence of Jesus in the womb of Mary. John is to go before the Lord, preparing a people for him (1:17). His leaping in joy at his first encounter with Jesus foreshadows the fact that it is Jesus, as well as God, whose way he will prepare. Elizabeth, likewise "filled with the holy Spirit" (verse 41), perceives the significance of her infant's leaping: they are in the presence of one whom Elizabeth must acknowledge as her Lord (verse 43), carried in the womb of Mary.

For reflection: When have I experienced the greatest joy over the presence of Jesus?

45 Mary is blessed because of the one she bears, and blessed for another reason as well. Elizabeth proclaims, **Blessed are you who believed that what was spoken to you by the Lord would be fulfilled.** Mary **believed** what was spoken to her **by the Lord** through the angel Gabriel. She is blessed because of her faith that what God said **would be fulfilled**—that she would conceive through the Holy Spirit and bear a son who would be called Son of God and rule over God's people forever (1:31–33). That is a lot for a young woman to believe! But Mary believed and submitted herself to God's word: "May it be done to me according to your word" (1:38). With inspired insight, Elizabeth proclaims Mary **blessed** because she **believed** the word of God that **was spoken** to her. Mary is a model for hearing the word of God and acting on it (see 8:21; 11:28).

For reflection: How eager am I to hear and embrace the word of God? How is Mary a model for me?

The scene of Mary and Elizabeth greeting each other invites our meditation. On one level it is a touching encounter between a young woman and an older relative, both unexpectedly pregnant. We might imagine their feelings, their concern for each other, their love. But they are not simply pregnant; they are pregnant through the design of God, and Mary's son will be the Son of God and Lord. Luke's account invites us to join Elizabeth in being guided by the Holy Spirit as we ponder the profound significance of Mary's pregnancy for her and for us.

For reflection: What insight or lesson do I take away from Elizabeth's encounter with Mary?

ORIENTATION: *Elizabeth told Mary that she was most blessed among women (1:42). Mary responds by praising God for what he has done for and through her. Mary's hymn echoes psalms and other Old Testament prayers of praise.*

Mary Praises God

⁴⁶ **And Mary said:**
    "My soul proclaims the greatness of the Lord;
⁴⁷   **my spirit rejoices in God my savior.**
⁴⁸ **For he has looked upon his handmaid's lowliness;**
    behold, from now on will all ages call me blessed.
⁴⁹ **The Mighty One has done great things for me,**
    and holy is his name.
⁵⁰ **His mercy is from age to age**
    to those who fear him.
⁵¹ **He has shown might with his arm,**
    dispersed the arrogant of mind and heart.
⁵² **He has thrown down the rulers from their thrones**
    but lifted up the lowly.
⁵³ **The hungry he has filled with good things;**
    the rich he has sent away empty.
⁵⁴ **He has helped Israel his servant,**
    remembering his mercy,
⁵⁵ **according to his promise to our fathers,**
    to Abraham and to his descendants forever."
⁵⁶ **Mary remained with her about three months and then returned to her home.**

OT: 1 Sam 2:1–10; Psalm 34; 136
NT: Luke 6:21, 25

46 **And Mary said** in response to Elizabeth's praise of her, **My soul proclaims the greatness of the Lord.** Mary does not deny that she is blessed by God, but directs attention to the **Lord** God, who blesses her. **My soul** is a poetic expression for oneself (see Psalm 34:3)—one's whole

self, not just a component. The Greek word translated **proclaims the greatness of** means to magnify, exalt, extol, glorify. Mary's prayer fulfills the invitation of Psalm 34 to "magnify the LORD."

Lord: See page 137

> My soul will glory in the LORD
> that the poor may hear and be glad.
> Magnify the LORD with me;
> let us exalt his name together.
>
> Psalm 34:3–4

47 my spirit rejoices in God my savior. The expression **my spirit** means oneself and is equivalent to "my soul" (verse 46; see Isaiah 26:9). Mary **rejoices** and delights in **God**, who is her **savior**. A **savior** rescues from distress; God is praised in the Old Testament for being the savior of his people (Exod 15:2; 2 Sam 22:3; Judith 9:11; Psalm 18:47; 118:14). Mary will go on to say how God has been her **savior**.

The first two sentences in Mary's prayer say roughly the same thing in different words, using a parallelism that is a common in the psalms (see Psalm 34:4). Mary's prayer echoes the prayer of Hannah as she left her son Samuel to serve in God's temple (1 Sam 2:1–10). Mary's prayer manifests that she is thoroughly steeped in the prayers of Scripture, and they supply the phrases and structure of her outburst of praise.

> My heart exults in the LORD.
>
> 1 Sam 2:1

For reflection: How have the psalms and other biblical prayers influenced the way I pray?

48 Mary states her reason for glorifying and praising God: **For he has looked upon his handmaid's lowliness.** In response to God's message to her spoken through Gabriel, Mary proclaimed herself to be the **handmaid**—female slave—of the Lord (1:38). She claims no status for herself, no standing independent of what God has in mind for her; she makes herself completely available to God for whatever he will do with her. She is a lowly village girl in the eyes of the world, and she embraces being lowly before God as well. Because of her **lowliness** God has **looked upon** her. The sense of **looked upon** is "singled out with affection." Mary does not need to spell out the results of God's looking upon her kindly; it is already in the forefront of her mind and Elizabeth's mind. Mary has conceived and is carrying a child whom Elizabeth acknowledges as her Lord (1:43). Mary knows that her child will be great and be called the Son of God; he will rule over God's people forever (1:32–33). God has filled Mary's **lowliness** with the greatest motherhood a woman will ever have. There is a correlation between lowliness before God and the greatness of what God is able to do: the emptier we are, the more God can fill us.

> *For reflection: What has God been able to accomplish through my lowliness and emptiness?*

Elizabeth is the first to proclaim Mary blessed because of what God is doing through her and because of her response to God (1:42, 45), but she will not be the last. Mary realizes that **from now on will all ages call me blessed**. Every future generation will look upon Mary as someone specially favored (1:28, 30) and **blessed** by God. The words **from now on** signal a turning point. The conception of Jesus inaugurates a new stage in human and divine history; God has taken a decisive step that will affect **all ages** to come.

49 Mary rephrases her reason for praising God, and the reason as well why all coming generations will call her blessed: **The Mighty One has done great things for me.** The Old Testament refers to God as **the Mighty One**, highlighting his power (2 Sam 23:1; Psalm 132:2, 5; Isaiah 1:24; 49:26; 60:16). The "power of the Most High" has overshadowed Mary (1:35); **the Mighty One** has done the **great** thing of conceiving Jesus in her womb. **Holy is his name**: in the biblical worldview, one's **name** is not an arbitrary label but an expression of one's identity. To say God's **name** is **holy** is equivalent to saying that God is **holy**. God is preeminently **holy** (Lev 11:44–45; Psalm 99:3, 5, 9). God glorifies his name through deeds that manifest his holiness (see Psalm 111:9; Isaiah 29:23; Ezek 36:23). What God is doing through Mary reveals the might and holiness of God.

> *Let them praise your great and awesome name:*
> *holy is God!*
>
> Psalm 99:3

50 Mary in her praise proclaims a third attribute of God: **His mercy is from age to age.** In the Greek translation of the Old Testament, **mercy** translates a Hebrew word that has connotations of faithful loving-kindness and mercy; the word is used to characterize God's covenant relationship with his people. God is faithful to his people and lovingly cares for them with kindness and mercy: that is what Mary expresses when she speaks of God's **mercy.** God's mercy endures **from age to age,** literally, to generations and generations. Generations come and go; "God's love"— his faithful loving-kindness and mercy—"endures forever" (Psalm 136:1). God is merciful **to those who fear him.** To **fear** God is to revere him as God and to serve and obey him (see Deut 10:12–13). Psalm 103 proclaims, "The LORD's kindness is forever, / toward the faithful from age to age" (Psalm 103:17). Another translation would be, "The LORD's mercy is from eternity to eternity toward those who fear him." Mary's prayer continues to echo the Scriptures.

> *Praise the LORD, who is so good;*
> *God's love endures forever.*
>
> Psalm 136:1

For reflection: When have I been most aware of God showing mercy on me?

51 **He has shown might with his arm.** The Old Testament speaks of God's **arm** as a figurative way of referring to his power (see Exod 6:6; Deut 4:34; Psalm 17:7; 98:1; Isaiah 40:10). Mary proclaims that God **has shown might,** literally, "done a mighty deed." God, the Mighty One, has done something great for Mary (verse 49), conceiving Jesus within her. He has **dispersed the arrogant of mind and heart.** To be proud and **arrogant** is the opposite of fearing God (verse 50). The Old Testament speaks of God scattering or dispersing his enemies to convey his victory over them: "Your strong arm scattered your foes" (Psalm 89:11; see Num 10:35; Psalm 68:2). The image is of enemy soldiers fleeing in all directions

before an advancing army. When has God **dispersed the arrogant of mind and heart**? Mary could be referring to what God had done in the past. Yet the context of Mary's prayer is what God is doing through her by the conception of Jesus. In this context, Mary seems to speak of the arrogant being scattered through Jesus.

52 **He has thrown down the rulers from their thrones.** If Jesus is to rule over the house of Jacob (1:33), then other rulers must be displaced. God's people are presently ruled by Herod the Great, governing on behalf of Rome. Mary speaks as if **rulers** such as Herod have already been **thrown down** by God. Gabriel told her that God would give her son Jesus the throne of David and that he would rule forever (1:32–33), and Mary believed God's word spoken through Gabriel (1:45). She has such great conviction about what is going to happen that she speaks of it as if it has already happened. God has taken the decisive step, conceiving Jesus within her. The outcome is certain: the arrogant will be dispersed and rulers will be thrown down. Mary praises God not only for conceiving Jesus but also for the assured consequences of his coming.

God has thrown down those in high places **but lifted up the lowly**. The word **lowly** can mean the poor and powerless, those with no social standing. It can also mean those who are humble and without pretensions. Those who lack social status may find it easier to be humble than those with money and power. Mary is lowly in both senses: she has neither social standing nor pretensions about herself. God looked with kindness upon Mary in her lowliness (verse 48) and through her son **lifted up the lowly**. Mary continues to speak about what will happen as if it has already happened. She also continues to echo Scripture in her praise (Sirach 10:14; see also 1 Sam 2:8; Psalm 147:6).

> The thrones of the arrogant God overturns
> and establishes the lowly in their stead.
>
> Sirach 10:14

53 Jesus' coming brings reversals of fortune. The proud and powerful are thrown down by God and the lowly lifted up; **the hungry he has filled with good things,** but **the rich he has sent away empty**. God has a special concern for those in need—for Israelites groaning in slavery in

Egypt (Exod 3:7–10), for widows, orphans, and aliens (Deut 10:17–18; 24:17–22; 26:12–13), for the hungry and oppressed (Psalm 107:9; 146:7; Isaiah 58:6–7). Mary proclaims that in conceiving Jesus within her God is acting to care for the **hungry**, filling them **with good things**. Mary may not know the details of how the hungry will be filled, but her words express her conviction that they will be filled because Jesus will be God's instrument of mercy.

> He satisfied the thirsty,
> > filled the hungry with good things.
>
> Psalm 107:9

For reflection: What good things has God given me?

The rich, however, **he has sent away empty**. It was presumed at the time that there was a limited supply of goods and wealth; if some were **rich,** others of necessity were poor. Those with a surplus must be emptied for the hungry to be filled.

At this point we might preview what Jesus will say decades later: "Blessed are you who are now hungry, / for you will be satisfied. . . . But woe to you who are filled now, / for you will be hungry" (6:21, 25). Did Mary have an inspired premonition of what her son would teach? Or did Jesus imbibe his mother's views as he grew up (see 2:51–52)?

54 **He has helped Israel his servant**. God calls the people of **Israel** his **servant** (Isaiah 41:8; 44:1; 45:4). The Greek word for **helped** suggests an image of taking hold to support. In conceiving Jesus in Mary, God has come to the aid of his servant people Israel, grasping them, supporting them. God has done so **remembering his mercy**: God's **mercy**, his faithful love that endures from age to age (verse 50), is why he conceived a son in Mary. She praises God once for his might and holiness (verse 49) but twice for his **mercy** (verses 50, 54), highlighting it.

> The LORD has made his victory known. . . .
> Has remembered his faithful love
> > toward the house of Israel
>
> Psalm 98:2–3

55 God acted **according to his promise to our fathers, / to Abraham and to his descendants forever**. God told **Abraham**, "I will bless you abundantly and make your descendants as countless as the stars of the sky and the sands of the seashore" (Gen 22:17); all the people on earth would find blessing in Abraham (Gen 12:3). God made more promises to the **descendants** of Abraham, those whom Jews looked back upon as **our fathers**. Now these promises find fulfillment through the son conceived in Mary, the instrument of God's merciful help.

Mary's prayer ends with the word **forever**: God's mercy (verse 54) outlasts the ages.

For reflection: How can Mary's prayer serve as a model for my prayers?

56 Luke skips ahead to conclude his account of Mary visiting Elizabeth: **Mary remained with her about three months and then returned to her home.** We might presume that Mary would stay to help out during and after the delivery of Elizabeth's baby, but Luke will not mention Mary being present when John is born (1:57–80). Adding **about three months** to the sixth month of Elizabeth's pregnancy (1:36) doesn't establish that Mary stayed until John was born, for pregnancies were sometimes thought of as lasting ten lunar months (Wisd 7:1–2) rather than nine months (2 Macc 7:27), and we don't know which duration Luke had in mind. Mary returned to **her** home: although betrothed to Joseph (1:27), she had not gone to live with him yet.

The Birth and Naming of John

[57] **When the time arrived for Elizabeth to have her child she gave birth to a son.** [58] **Her neighbors and relatives heard that the Lord had shown his great mercy toward her, and they rejoiced with her.** [59] **When they came on the eighth day to circumcise the child, they were going to call him Zechariah after his father,** [60] **but his mother said in reply, "No. He will be called John."** [61] **But they answered her, "There is no one among your relatives who has this name."** [62] **So they made signs, asking his father what he wished him to be called.** [63] **He asked for a tablet and wrote, "John is his name," and all were amazed.** [64] **Immediately his mouth was opened, his tongue freed, and he spoke blessing God.** [65] **Then fear came upon all their**

neighbors, and all these matters were discussed throughout the hill country of Judea. ⁶⁶ All who heard these things took them to heart, saying, "What, then, will this child be?" For surely the hand of the Lord was with him.

OT: Gen 17:9–14; Lev 12:3
NT: Luke 1:5–25

57 **When the time arrived for Elizabeth to have her child she gave birth to a son.** The Greek word translated **arrived** is literally "was fulfilled": the angel Gabriel told Zechariah that his words would "be fulfilled at their proper time" (1:20), and that **time** has come. **Elizabeth**, who had been barren and is advanced in years (1:7), **gave birth to a son**, as Gabriel had said she would (1:13). "Nothing will be impossible for God" (1:37); what God promises, God fulfills.

58 **Her neighbors and relatives heard that the Lord had shown his great mercy toward her.** Elizabeth had gone into seclusion for the first five months of her pregnancy (1:24) but presumably resumed normal life afterward. Her **neighbors** and **relatives** hear that she has given birth to a son: news spreads quickly in villages. They perceive that her bearing a son means that **the Lord had shown his great mercy toward her**. Elizabeth was past normal childbearing years; for her to have a son is due to the **great mercy** of God, taking away the disgrace of barrenness (1:25). Her neighbors and relatives **rejoiced with her**. Gabriel told Zechariah that the birth of their son would bring them "joy and gladness, and many will rejoice at his birth" (1:14). God's word spoken through Gabriel continues to be fulfilled.

For reflection: What is the greatest mercy God has shown me?

59 **When they came on the eighth day to circumcise the child**: circumcision of Jewish males incorporated them into God's covenant with his people (Gen 17:9–14); it was "the mark of the covenant" (Gen 17:11). Circumcision was done **on the eighth day** after birth (Gen 17:12; Lev 12:3). Elizabeth and Zechariah observe all of God's commandments (1:6); their son is circumcised on the proper day. Neighbors and relatives (verse 58) **came** to celebrate the circumcision. **They were going to call him**

Zechariah after his father: neighbors and relatives expected that the child would be named after his father.

Naming a son does not seem to have been deferred until circumcision during Old Testament times (see Gen 21:2–4; 25:25–26; 29:32–35); we do not know what was the customary Jewish practice at the time of Zechariah and Elizabeth. The normal Greek practice was to name children seven to ten days after birth, and so Luke's first readers would have taken naming on the eighth day as unexceptional.

60 **but his mother said in reply, "No. He will be called John."** Gabriel had told Zechariah that their son was to be named **John** (1:13), and Zechariah had presumably communicated this to Elizabeth. Zechariah cannot speak (1:20), so Elizabeth speaks for them. The Hebrew name that comes into English as **John** means "God has shown favor" (using God's personal name—Yahweh); it was not an unusual name in priestly families (1 Macc 2:1–2). Luke does not explain the meaning of John's name, but it is highly appropriate: God had shown favor to Elizabeth and Zechariah and would show favor to his people through their son (see 1:16–17).

God's name: See page 546

61 **But they answered her, "There is no one among your relatives who has this name."** If a son was not named after his father, it was customary to name him after one of his other **relatives**. But no one in the families of Elizabeth and Zechariah is named John. Breaking with customary practice in naming John is a sign that he is someone out of the ordinary. His significance will not lie in his family heritage but in who he is and what he will do (see 1:15–17).

62 **So they made signs, asking his father what he wished him to be called.** The relatives and neighbors who gathered for the circumcision are not willing to accept Elizabeth's choice of an uncustomary name. Did they think she hadn't consulted with Zechariah and had picked a name without his consent? Their making **signs** to communicate with Zechariah indicates that he is deaf as well as mute: the two conditions often went together in the ancient world.

63 **He asked for a tablet**—a small wooden board covered with wax, written on with a stylus; the wax could be smoothed for reuse. Zechariah **wrote, "John is his name."** Gabriel told Zechariah that they were to name their son **John** (1:13) and that **is** his name, assigned before he was conceived. **All were amazed** that Elizabeth and Zechariah violate custom in naming their son.

64 **Immediately his mouth was opened** and **his tongue freed.** Gabriel told Zechariah that he would be "speechless and unable to talk until the day these things take place" (1:20), and that day turns out to be the day of John's naming. Zechariah insists that their son be named John (verse 63), and **immediately** he is able to speak again. His first words after months of silence are praise and thanksgiving: **he spoke blessing God**. His last words before being struck mute expressed skepticism that God would do what Gabriel said he would (1:18). But what Gabriel said would happen has happened: Zechariah's speechlessness, Elizabeth's bearing a son, many rejoicing over his birth, naming him John, Zechariah's speech being restored (1:13–14, 20). As a consequence, Zechariah has moved from questioning God to **blessing God**. Zechariah can believe that John will grow up to fulfill Gabriel's words about what he will be and do (1:15–17).

For reflection: How has God dealt with my skepticism or doubts? Why can I believe that God will fulfill his promises to me?

65 **Then fear came upon all their neighbors, and all these matters were discussed throughout the hill country of Judea.** A feeling of awe or **fear** is a normal reaction to a manifestation of divine presence or power (see 1:12). **All these matters** would include Elizabeth's giving

---

BACKGROUND: JUDEA This was the region of Palestine around and to the south of Jerusalem. It was originally the territory of the tribe of Judah, which gave it its name. Israelites from this region who had been in exile in Babylon returned to Judea after 538 B.C. Thereafter they began to be called Judeans, which passed through Greek and Latin and came into English as the word "Jews." Luke sometimes uses Judea as an alternative name for Palestine (Luke 4:44; 7:17; 23:5) as well as the name of the region within Palestine (Luke 1:65; 2:4; 3:1; 5:17; 21:21).

birth to a son in her old age after lifelong barrenness, the child being given an uncustomary name, Zechariah's months of muteness and his sudden healing. God had to be behind these events, and this filled the **neighbors** of Elizabeth and Zechariah with fearful awe: God was doing something next door to them. Naturally they talked about it, and word spread **throughout the hill country of Judea**, the region in which Zechariah and Elizabeth lived (1:39–40).

66 **All who heard these things took them to heart.** News of the unusual spreads, but these were not simply unusual events: they were indications that God was about something special in the birth of John. The events surrounding his birth were **things** to take seriously and ponder, and **all who heard** about them **took them to heart.** Many Jews longed for God to act powerfully to restore Jewish independence from foreign domination and overcome injustice and evil, fulfilling promises made through the prophets. Could John's birth mark the beginning of God's acting decisively on behalf of his people? **What, then, will this child be?** What will this child become? What role will he play in what God is doing? Luke's account gives the reader a sense of anticipation.

Jewish expectations at the time of Jesus: See page 69

Luke concludes his account of the birth and naming of John with his own comment: **For surely the hand of the Lord was with him.** The Old Testament uses the expression **the hand of the Lord** to convey the power of God (Joshua 4:24; see Exod 7:4; 13:3; 15:6); the hand of the Lord being **with** or upon someone means that he is empowered and guided by God (1 Kings 18:46; 1 Chron 28:19; Ezra 7:28; Ezek 1:3; 3:14, 22). **Surely** someone born to a previously barren women in fulfillment of an angel's words has been sent by God to carry out a special work, and surely God will empower and guide him to accomplish his mission. By adding this final comment, Luke invites his readers to join those pondering what this child will be and to share their sense of anticipation.

For reflection: What element in Luke's account of the birth and naming of John has the greatest significance for me?

41

ORIENTATION: *His voice restored, Zechariah blesses God (1:64), praising him for what he will accomplish through Jesus and John. Like Mary's prayer of praise (1:46–55), Zechariah's prayer has many echoes of psalms and other Scriptures.*

Zechariah's Prophetic Prayer of Praise

⁶⁷ Then Zechariah his father, filled with the holy Spirit, prophesied, saying:

⁶⁸ **"Blessed be the Lord, the God of Israel,**
> **for he has visited and brought redemption to his people.**
⁶⁹ **He has raised up a horn for our salvation**
> **within the house of David his servant,**
⁷⁰ **even as he promised through the mouth of his holy prophets from of old:**
⁷¹ **salvation from our enemies and from the hand of all who hate us,**
⁷² **to show mercy to our fathers**
> **and to be mindful of his holy covenant**
⁷³ **and of the oath he swore to Abraham our father,**
> **and to grant us that, ⁷⁴ rescued from the hand of enemies,**
> **without fear we might worship him ⁷⁵ in holiness and righteousness**
> **before him all our days.**
⁷⁶ **And you, child, will be called prophet of the Most High,**
> **for you will go before the Lord to prepare his ways,**
⁷⁷ **to give his people knowledge of salvation**
> **through the forgiveness of their sins,**
⁷⁸ **because of the tender mercy of our God**
> **by which the daybreak from on high will visit us**
⁷⁹ **to shine on those who sit in darkness and death's shadow,**
> **to guide our feet into the path of peace."**

⁸⁰ The child grew and became strong in spirit, and he was in the desert until the day of his manifestation to Israel.

> OT: Gen 12:1–3; 15:1–21; 17:1–14; 22:16–18; 2 Sam 7:11–16
> NT: Luke 1:13–17, 30–35, 64

67 **Then Zechariah his father, filled with the holy Spirit, prophesied.**
Luke's **then** may refer to the moment when Zechariah's speech was
restored and "he spoke blessing God" (1:64). His wife, Elizabeth, had been
"filled with the holy Spirit" when she heard Mary's greeting (1:41), and now
Zechariah is also **filled with the holy Spirit**. He **prophesied**: the Spirit
inspires men and women to prophesy (Num 11:26; 2 Sam 23:2; Ezek 11:5).
Zechariah's voice is restored so that he can provide God's perspective on
the events that are taking place. Zechariah does not prophesy in a "Thus
says the Lord" format. Rather, Zechariah blesses God, praising him for
what he has done and will do. Zechariah's prayer of praise is inspired just
as a psalm praising God for his deeds is inspired (for example, Psalm 105).

The Spirit: See page 100

68 **Blessed be the Lord, the God of Israel.** The opening words of
Zechariah's prayer were already used in the book of Psalms to mark the
end of three collections of psalms (Psalms 41:14; 72:18; 106:48). To proclaim a man or woman blessed is to recognize their good fortune, but the
word **blessed** has a different sense when used in prayer to God. **Blessed
be the Lord** means "may the Lord be praised" and is an implicit invitation to others to praise the Lord. The **Lord** is **the God of Israel**: God
could be praised as the creator of the universe (Psalm 104:1) or as king
over all the earth (Psalm 47), but Zechariah's praise focuses on God as
the God of Israel. God is about something new, but it is a continuation
and fulfillment of what he has done for his people **Israel** in the past.

Lord: See page 137

> Blessed be the LORD, the God of Israel,
>   from all eternity and forever.
> Amen. Amen.

Psalm 41:14

Zechariah explains why the Lord God is to be praised: **for he has
visited and brought redemption to his people**. God's visitation, his
personal intervention, can be to punish (Amos 3:14–15) or, as is the case
here, to help (Ruth 1:6; Jer 29:10; Zeph 2:7). Zechariah proclaims that God
has visited his **people** and **brought redemption** to them. **Redemption**
means release from bondage, as when a captive is ransomed or a slave is

43

freed. God's great act of redemption for his people was his freeing the Israelites from slavery in Egypt, an act that Deuteronomy refers to as his ransoming of them (Deut 7:8; 9:26; 13:6; 15:15). Zechariah will go on to indicate what God's new act of redemption will involve. His listeners might think that Zechariah is speaking about his son John—that John's birth is the result of God visiting his people and that John will be God's instrument of redemption. But what Zechariah says next indicates that he does not have John in mind but Mary's yet-to-be-born son. Zechariah, "filled with the Spirit" (verse 67), is prophesying about Jesus. God has **visited** his people in the conception of Jesus; God has come on the scene in Jesus. God has **brought redemption to his people**: Zechariah, like Mary (1:51–55), speaks about what will happen as if it has already been accomplished. God is freeing his people through Jesus; the outcome is certain, even if Jesus has not yet been born.

69 Zechariah continues to praise God for what he is doing. **He has raised up a horn for our salvation**. A **horn** evokes images of a bull or wild ox holding its head high or tossing its horns in a display of its power; it is a biblical idiom for strength (see 1 Sam 2:10; Psalm 89:18). By extension, a **horn** could stand for a powerful person and is used as a symbol for a mighty descendant of David, an anointed one, or messiah (Psalm 132:17). That is its significance here: God has raised up a horn **within the house of David his servant**. David, though king, considered himself to be God's **servant** (2 Sam 7:18–21). To be of **the house of David** means to be a descendant of David and hence of the tribe of Judah, David's tribe (see Sirach 45:25). Since Zechariah is a priest, he and his son John are of the tribe of Levi. Zechariah is not prophesying about John but about Jesus, who will be given "the throne of David his father" (1:32).

Messiah, Christ: See page 257

> There I will make a horn sprout for David's line;
> I will set a lamp for my anointed.
>
> Psalm 132:17

God is raising up Jesus within the house of David **for our salvation**. While we think of **salvation** as being given eternal life, the word originally had the broader meaning of any rescue from danger and distress or deliverance from death. Zechariah will go on to indicate what form the salvation brought by Jesus will take. Zechariah praises God for raising up a horn for **our** salvation, literally, a horn of salvation for us. Zechariah is not speaking about what God did for previous generations but about what God is doing now, for **our salvation**.

For reflection: What has God done for my salvation? What is God doing right now?

70 God is sending Jesus to bring salvation **even as he promised through the mouth of his holy prophets from of old**. Jesus is the fulfillment of God's promises, made **through the mouth of his holy prophets**. God **promised** salvation for his people and is carrying out his promise by sending Jesus. Zechariah speaks broadly of **prophets from of old**. One of these prophets would be Nathan, who prophesied to David that God would establish a house—dynasty—for him and that his descendants would rule from his throne forever (2 Sam 7:11–16). Other prophets laid the groundwork for the expectation that one of David's descendants would be the Messiah (see Isaiah 9:5–6; 11:1–5; Jer 23:5; Ezek 34:23–24; 37:24). These prophecies often portrayed a future in which evil would be overcome and God's people would enjoy peace and a renewed relationship with God (see Isaiah 9:1–4; 11:6–9; Jer 23:6; Ezek 34:25–31; 37:23, 25–28). Gabriel told Mary that her son would be given the throne of David and that he would rule forever (1:32–33); this will fulfill what God promised through prophets.

71 God is sending Jesus to bring the salvation promised through prophets (verses 69–70), specifically, **salvation from our enemies and from the hand of all who hate us**. As noted earlier (see verse 69), the word **salvation** means rescue from distress or deliverance from death. **Hand** is a biblical idiom for power. The act of **salvation** that God is carrying out for his people through Jesus includes rescue from their enemies and from the power of all who hate them. This continues what God has been doing since he freed the Israelites from slavery in Egypt so that they could be his people. The book of Judges is a series of stories about

God rescuing his people from their enemies. Zechariah's prophecy need not refer to any specific **enemies**; rather, Zechariah may be echoing traditional expressions to convey that God is rescuing his people from what oppresses them. The psalms use similar language to celebrate God's deliverance of his people (Psalms 18:18; 106:10).

> He rescued them from hostile hands,
> freed them from the power of the enemy.
>
> Psalm 106:10

72 God is acting **to show mercy to our fathers and to be mindful of his holy covenant**. For Jews, **our fathers** are, above all, their founding fathers, Abraham, Isaac, and Jacob. Taken by itself, the first clause is cryptic: how does God's raising up a horn of salvation in the house of David **show mercy to our fathers**? It is best to consider the second clause first and then return to the mercy shown the fathers. The **holy covenant** is God's covenant with Abraham, as the next verse makes clear. God promised Abraham that he would be the father of a great nation that would be a blessing for all peoples (Gen 12:1–3; 22:17–18); God made this promise part his covenant, or agreement, with Abraham, also promising to give his descendants a land of their own (Gen 15:18–21). For his part, Abraham was to live blamelessly in God's presence and be circumcised (Gen 17:1, 10). God is acting **mindful** of his covenant with Abraham—remembering what he promised and fulfilling his promises. The conception of Jesus marks a new stage in God's relationship with his people, a covenant relationship that began with Abraham.

To show mercy to our fathers can perhaps be best understood as having roughly the same sense as God being mindful of his covenant: God has shown the **mercy** promised to the **fathers** as part of his covenant with them. **Mercy** translates a Hebrew word that has connotations of faithful loving-kindness and that is used in the Old Testament to characterize God's covenant relationship with his people (see 1:50). God entered into a covenant with Abraham out of mercy and is now mercifully fulfilling his covenant promises.

For reflection: How have I experienced God's mercy and love?

73 God is acting mindful of his covenant **and of the oath he swore to Abraham our father**. God **swore to Abraham** that he would give him numerous descendants who would be a blessing for all peoples (Gen 22:16–18; see also Gen 26:3). The letter to the Hebrews interprets God's oath as an additional guarantee of the promises he made to Abraham as part of his covenant with him (Heb 6:13–18). God is fulfilling his sworn promises by sending Jesus.

> *I swear by myself, declares the* Lord, *that . . . I will bless you abundantly and make your descendants as countless as the stars of the sky and the sands of the seashore; . . . and in your descendants all the nations of the earth shall find blessing.*
>
> Gen 22:16–18

How is Jesus the fulfillment of God's covenant promises to Abraham? Zechariah prophetically proclaims that God is acting through Jesus **to grant us that,**

74 **rescued from the hand of enemies, without fear we might worship him**. God is raising up Jesus to bring "salvation from our enemies and from the hand of all who hate us" (verse 71) so that, **rescued from the hand of enemies**, God's people can live **without fear**. Freed from external oppression and interior anxieties, God's people are able to **worship him** without constraint or distraction. The word translated **worship** means to carry out religious service and covers not only acts of worship but all that is done in service of God. Paul uses the same word when he writes, "God is my witness, whom I *serve* with my spirit in proclaiming the gospel of his Son" (Rom 1:9; emphasis added). God's purpose in giving Abraham descendants as countless as the stars of the sky and the sands of the seashore (Gen 22:17) is to create a people who will worship and serve him. After the Israelites occupied the land that God was giving them, Joshua reminded them of what God had done: he had called Abraham, he had freed the Israelites from slavery in Egypt, he had given them a land (Joshua 24:1–13). Joshua then exhorted the Israelites, "Now, therefore, fear the Lord and serve him completely and sincerely" (Joshua

24:14). Jesus will bring what God began in Abraham to fulfillment; Jesus will **rescue** God's people from all that prevents them from serving him completely and sincerely.

For reflection: What prevents me from serving God completely? Where do I stand in need of Jesus' rescue?

75 God's people will worship him **in holiness and righteousness**. The Greek word used here for **holiness** has the connotation of being devoted to God. **Righteousness** involves obeying God's commandments (as Zechariah and Elizabeth do—1:6), carrying out our obligations to him and treating others justly. Rescued from enemies, God's people will worship in holiness and righteousness **before him all** their **days**. They will live in God's presence their whole lifetime. Worship is not an occasional act but a way of life. Jesus will enable God's people to live in the manner for which they were created, responding to God's loving mercy (verse 72) with service and worship.

76 Zechariah, continuing to speak prophetically, turns his attention to his eight-day-old son. **And you, child, will be called prophet of the Most High.** Everyone who heard about the extraordinary circumstances of John's birth and naming was wondering, "What, then, will this child be?" (1:66). Zechariah answers their question. John will be acknowledged to be a **prophet of the Most High** God. A **prophet** speaks on behalf of God under the inspiration of the Holy Spirit (2 Sam 23:2; Isaiah 61:1–2; Ezek 11:5), and John has been filled with the Holy Spirit even while in Elizabeth's womb (1:15). Zechariah tells his infant son that he will be recognized as a prophet because **you will go before the Lord to prepare his ways**. Gabriel told Zechariah that John would "go before him," meaning before God, and would "prepare a people fit for the Lord" (1:16–17). Zechariah's words also echo a prophecy of Malachi: "Lo, I am sending my messenger / to prepare the way before me" (Mal 3:1). John will be the **prophet** or messenger of the Most High God, preparing the way for God.

Luke's readers can find a second level of meaning in Zechariah's words. Elizabeth, filled with the Holy Spirit, acknowledged the infant in Mary's womb to be "my Lord" (1:41, 43). Jesus will be called Lord as God is called Lord; John will go before Jesus to prepare the way for him (see 3:2–6, 15–17).

Lord: See page 137

77 How will John prepare the way for God, and for Jesus? He will **give his people knowledge of salvation through the forgiveness of their sins**. John's mission is to **his people**, meaning God's people. As often in the Old Testament, **knowledge** means experience; John will not give lectures about salvation but will help God's people experience it. While **salvation** can mean any rescue from danger or death, here it refers to what God's people receive **through the forgiveness of their sins**. John's mission will be to help rescue God's people from their sins and from the consequences of their sins. That is the greatest rescue a man or woman can receive.

78 Sins will be forgiven and salvation experienced **because of the tender mercy of our God**. Jews prayed for God to forgive their sins out of his **mercy** for them: "Have mercy on me, God, in your goodness; / in your abundant compassion blot out my offense" (Psalm 51:3). The word translated **tender** is elsewhere translated "affection" (Phil 1:8), "compassion" (Phil 2:1; 1 John 3:17), or "heartfelt" (Col 3:12). The Greek word literally refers to one's inner parts (see Acts 1:18: "all his insides spilled out"). Used figuratively the word conveys being profoundly moved; we use the expression "gut reaction." The **tender** mercy of God is his profound, heartfelt compassion for us, forgiving our sins and granting salvation.

For reflection: Do I accept that God is profoundly moved by compassion for me?

Zechariah proclaims that **by** the tender mercy of our God **the daybreak from on high will visit us**. The Greek word translated **daybreak** means rising or springing up. Translating it as **daybreak** applies it to the rising of the sun, which is the sense required by the following verse. The word is also used for the springing up of plants, and it is sometimes used for a shoot: "I will raise up a righteous shoot to David; / As king he shall reign and govern wisely" (Jer 23:5). Some of Luke's first readers may have understood the **daybreak** to be a shoot or descendant of David who would rule from his throne—a messiah. **From on high** means from heaven, the dwelling place of God (see Psalm 144:7); **from on high** is equivalent to "from God." Zechariah earlier proclaimed that God "has visited" his people (verse 68), referring to the conception of Jesus. Zechariah now says that a daybreak sent by God **will visit** us, referring to what Jesus will accomplish in the future.

79 Jesus will be sent by God as a daybreak, or rising sun, **to shine on those who sit in darkness and death's shadow**. Zechariah's words evoke a prophecy of Isaiah that speaks of a great light shining on those who have been in darkness and gloom; the great light is a poetic allusion to the birth of a newborn prince who will rule from David's throne (Isaiah 9:1, 5–6). Jesus, of the house of David (verse 69), will be a daybreak shining light on those **who sit in darkness**. Being **in darkness** is an image for being oppressed, physically or spiritually (see Psalm 107:10; Isaiah 9:1; 42:7; 59:9; Micah 7:8). Jesus will be a rising sun that will vanquish **death's shadow**: no matter what lesser light casts a shadow, the shadow disappears in direct sunlight. Zechariah's imagery of a sunrise dispelling darkness and shadows means that Jesus will triumph over the forces of evil, even over **death**. Jesus will **guide our feet into the path of peace**. Just as a light guides those who walk in darkness, so Jesus will **guide** God's people, leading them **into the path of peace**. The word translated as **path** is sometimes translated as "way"; Luke will use it to refer to the way of discipleship, to being a follower of Jesus (Acts 9:2; 18:25–26; 19:9, 23; 22:4; 24:14, 22). **Peace** is not simply the absence of strife but a condition of harmony, wholeness, fullness. Jesus will be a light guiding **our feet**— guiding us—into following the way of life that brings total well-being.

> The people who walked in darkness
> have seen a great light;
> Upon those who dwelt in the land of gloom
> a light has shone.
>
> Isaiah 9:1

Zechariah's prophetic prayer ends on the note of **peace**. Zechariah has praised God for what he has done through the conception of Jesus and what he will accomplish through John and Jesus. His prophecy is filled with Old Testament phrases and images but does not go into the specifics of how Jesus will accomplish his mission. Zechariah is certain that God is visiting his people in Jesus and will do great things for them, but he has not been given the details of what will happen.

For reflection: Do I have a confident sense that God will work things out for me without my knowing how he will do so?

80 Luke concludes his account of the birth and naming of John by summarizing what happens in the coming decades, thereby setting the scene for the beginning of John's ministry. **The child grew and became strong in spirit**. The word **spirit** can refer to the human spirit, the self ("my spirit rejoices in God my savior"—1:47). John grew up and matured, becoming a **strong** person. **Spirit** can also refer to the Holy Spirit. Although John was "filled with the holy Spirit" from his mother's womb (1:15), he nonetheless **grew** in the Spirit. Life in the Spirit is not static but a process of growth. **He was in the desert until the day of his manifestation to Israel.** The **desert** is the rocky and barren eastern portion of Judea as it slopes down to the Jordan River and the Dead Sea. John's **manifestation to Israel**, his first public appearance, will take place near the Jordan River (see 3:2–4).

Luke does not say what John did during his years in the Judean wilderness before he began his ministry. Some have speculated that he spent time with the Essenes at their settlement near the Dead Sea. While there are some similarities between John's ministry and Essene beliefs and practices, there are also marked differences. John had his own distinctive ministry, whatever influences he might have been exposed to.

Essenes: See page 395

CHAPTER 2

The Birth of Jesus

¹ In those days a decree went out from Caesar Augustus that the whole world should be enrolled. ² This was the first enrollment, when Quirinius was governor of Syria. ³ So all went to be enrolled, each to his own town. ⁴ And Joseph too went up from Galilee from the town of Nazareth to Judea, to the city of David that is called Bethlehem, because he was of the house and family of David, ⁵ to be enrolled with Mary, his betrothed, who was with child. ⁶ While they were there, the time came for her to have her child, ⁷ and she gave birth to her firstborn son. She wrapped him in swaddling clothes and laid him in a manger, because there was no room for them in the inn.

NT: Luke 1:26–38; Acts 5:37

1   **In those days a decree went out from Caesar Augustus**. Luke is recounting the birth of Jesus, so **in those days** is roughly six months after the birth of John and fifteen months after Gabriel appeared to Zechariah (see 1:36). **Caesar Augustus** ruled the Roman empire from

---

BACKGROUND: ROMAN EMPIRE At the time of Jesus, the Roman Empire included all the lands bordering the Mediterranean Sea and extended through western Europe as far as Britain. The Roman general Pompey had intervened in a Jewish civil war in 63 B.C., conquering Jerusalem and pushing aside the ruling Jewish Hasmonean dynasty, thus bringing Palestine under Roman domination. This was a time of transition within the Roman government, as power became consolidated in an emperor and conquered lands gradually came under direct Roman rule. In this transitional period, Rome sometimes ruled through client kings, such as Herod the Great and his sons. The Roman government was content to have the Herods rule on its behalf as long as they did so competently, were loyal to Rome, and paid taxes. Other regions were ruled as Roman provinces by governors sent from Rome. Judea became a Roman province in A.D. 6 after Rome deposed Herod's son Archelaus for incompetence. During Jesus' public ministry, Pontius Pilate was the Roman governor of Judea and some adjacent areas. In A.D. 66, many Jews in Palestine rebelled against Roman rule, with disastrous consequences. Rome put down the revolt, destroying Jerusalem in A.D. 70. *Related topics: Herod the Great (page 7), Herod Antipas (page 99), Pontius Pilate (page 617).*

---

27 B.C. to A.D. 14. He brought peace after an extended period of strife and civil war, and was so revered that some hailed him as "savior of the whole world" and a god. He decreed **that the whole world should be enrolled**—that a census be taken as a basis for taxation. Augustus did not rule the **whole world,** but Romans considered the Roman empire to be the whole civilized world. Mention of **the whole world** provides a universal setting for Jesus' birth; Jesus will bring salvation to the whole world.

2 **This was the first enrollment, when Quirinius was governor of Syria.** A Roman named Publius Sulpicius **Quirinius** was appointed **governor of** the province of **Syria** in A.D. 6. After Herod's death, Archelaus, one of his sons, ruled Judea until he was deposed by Rome in A.D. 6. **Quirinius** was charged with bringing Judea under Roman rule through a governor. One of his assignments was to take a census as a basis for taxes being collected. This led to a Jewish uprising. Taxes had been collected by Herod the Great and his sons, but some Jews found paying taxes directly to Roman overlords offensive. Not many joined their rebellion, and it was squelched (see Acts 5:37).

Luke seems to date the census and the birth of Jesus to the time when Quirinius was governor of Syria, and this creates a difficulty. Gabriel appeared to Zechariah "in the days of Herod" (1:5)—Herod the Great, who died in 4 B.C. Jesus is born not much more than fifteen months later, well before Quirinius became governor. Some maintain that Luke's account is confused. Perhaps, rather, he compressed a complex situation into two verses. Taking censuses was common Roman practice, and several were taken in provinces during the reign of Augustus. Herod the Great would have taken censuses in his realm as a basis for taxation. The Greek word translated **first** in **the first enrollment** can mean before, which is its sense in John 15:18. Some scholars suggest that verse 2 be translated, "This enrollment happened before Quirinius was governor of Syria." In this interpretation, the **enrollment** could be one taken during Herod's reign. Luke might mention Quirinius because he was associated with a notorious census, remembered because it led to a revolt. Interpreting verses 1 and 2 in this way makes sense of what would otherwise be an inconsistency in dating. Luke later indicates that he does not know the exact year of Jesus' birth (3:23).

3 **So all went to be enrolled, each to his own town.** Censuses were usually not taken door-to-door but at registration centers. One's **own town** might mean the nearest place of registration or the place of one's origin. **All** comply with the order **to be enrolled**. This too might indicate that the census was not that of A.D. 6, when some refused to comply (as Luke well knew—Acts 5:37).

4 **And Joseph too went up from Galilee from the town of Nazareth**: Joseph, like Mary, lives in **Nazareth** (see 1:26–27). He travels **to Judea, to the city of David that is called Bethlehem, because he was of the house and family of David**. This is the second time Luke has pointed out that Joseph is of **the house of David** (see 1:27); any children of his will also be descendants of David. The **city of David** referred to here is **Bethlehem**, the village of David's family (1 Sam 16:1–13); in other contexts the oldest section of Jerusalem is called the city of David (2 Sam 5:7; 1 Kings 2:10; Neh 3:15). The shortest route from **Nazareth** to **Bethlehem** meant a trip of about eighty-five miles, a journey of four or more days on foot.

Galilee: See page 114
Nazareth: See page 19
Judea: See page 40

5 Joseph traveled from Nazareth to Bethlehem **to be enrolled with Mary, his betrothed**. Unlike what rebels will do in A.D. 6, Joseph complies with the census; Jesus is born into a law-abiding family. It is not clear why Joseph had to go to Bethlehem as the ancestral home of his family to **be enrolled**; one speculation is that he may have owned land there

---

BACKGROUND: BETHLEHEM lies about five miles south of Jerusalem. Its name means "house of bread," perhaps because grain crops were grown in adjacent fields (see Ruth 1:22–2:23). King David's family lived in Bethlehem (1 Sam 16:1–13), giving it its chief claim to fame in the Old Testament. It was otherwise not an impressive village. The prophet Micah called it "too small to be among the clans of Judah," but nonetheless prophesied that "from you shall come forth for me / one who is to be ruler in Israel" (Micah 5:1). Micah's prophecy was the basis for an expectation that the Messiah would not only be a descendant of David but would also come from Bethlehem (Matt 2:4–6; John 7:42), but this expectation of a Bethlehem origin was not shared by all at the time of Jesus (see John 7:27). Bethlehem was likely still a rather modest village at the time of Jesus' birth.

and the enrollment was for a property tax. Nor is it completely clear why **Mary** went with him; the head of a family could usually enroll his entire family. Perhaps Joseph and Mary wanted to be together when their child was born. Luke refers to Mary as Joseph's **betrothed**: a betrothed wife usually continued to live in her father's house. Now, however, Joseph and Mary have apparently begun to live together: Mary is to be enrolled with Joseph, not with her father's household. Continuing to refer to her as **betrothed** (see 1:27) may signify that while Joseph and Mary are living together, they have not had sexual intercourse. Although Mary **was with child**, she made the trip to Bethlehem. We need not imagine Mary and Joseph considered this an extraordinary hardship; in a peasant society, pregnancy is more likely considered routine rather than a delicate condition.

Marriage practices: See page 540

6 **While they were there**: Luke does not tell us how long Joseph and Mary stayed in Bethlehem. We might imagine that it was a quick visit to register for the census, but it could equally well have been for an extended stay with relatives since they had to travel there anyway for the census. Consequently speculations about the risks of Mary traveling while on the verge of giving birth have no basis in Luke's account. While they are in Bethlehem, **the time came for her to have her child**. Luke literally writes that the days were fulfilled for her to give birth: the birth of Jesus fulfills Gabriel's announcement that Mary would conceive and bear a son (1:31).

7 **and she gave birth to her firstborn son.** The word **firstborn** indicates that Mary had no children prior to Jesus; it does not imply that she had children after him. This is evident from a grave inscription for a Jewish woman who died in 5 B.C.: "In the pains of giving birth to a firstborn child, fate brought me to the end of my life." This woman died giving birth; her firstborn was her only child. That Jesus is Mary's **firstborn** means that he has privileges of a firstborn son (Deut 21:15-17) and must be consecrated to God (Exod 13:2; Num 18:15-16). **She wrapped him in swaddling clothes**—strips of cloth wrapped around the limbs of an infant to ensure they would grow straight. **Swaddling** an infant was standard practice; even Solomon, born in the palace of David, was swaddled (Wisd 7:4).

Mary **laid him in a manger**. The word **manger** is used for a stall for animals and for a trough for feeding them. Since Jesus was **laid** in a **manger**, the meaning here is a feeding trough, used as a makeshift cradle. Mary made use of a manger **because there was no room for them in the inn**. While we usually think of an **inn** as a commercial lodging for travelers, the Greek word Luke uses is not so specific and only means a place where one might stay. It is translated as "guest room" at 22:11, referring to the "large upper room" where Jesus ate his last supper with his disciples (22:12). When Luke clearly refers to commercial lodgings, he uses a different, more specific Greek word for inn (10:34). It is unlikely that there were commercial lodgings in Bethlehem; the village was small and did not lie on a trade route. Travelers normally received hospitality from relatives or friends (see 11:5–6) or even from strangers. As a descendant of David, Joseph would have had relatives in Bethlehem, and he and Mary would have stayed with them while in town.

When it came time for Mary to give birth, **there was no room** for her to do so where they were staying. Another translation would be there was no *place*: where they were lodging was not a place to give birth. Ordinary people often lived in one-room houses which afforded little privacy. Houses in Bethlehem, as in other villages in the limestone hills

---

BACKGROUND: THE CAVE OF JESUS' BIRTH Ancient tradition locates the birth of Jesus in a cave. The earliest testimony comes from Justin Martyr, who was born in Neapolis (today's Nablus), thirty miles from Bethlehem. Around the year 150 he wrote: "When the child was born in Bethlehem, since Joseph could not find a lodging in that village, he took up his quarters in a certain cave near the village; and while they were there Mary brought forth the Christ and placed him in a manger" (*Dialogue with Trypho*, 78). Justin Martyr's testimony is significant because of its early date and because he was a native of Palestine, familiar with local traditions. The *Protevangelium of James*, a second-century apocryphal gospel, also places the birth of Jesus in a cave. So does Origen, an Egyptian Scripture scholar who moved to Palestine around A.D. 235. Origen wrote, "In conformity with the narrative in the Gospel regarding his birth, there is shown in Bethlehem the cave where he was born, and the manger in the cave where he was wrapped in swaddling clothes. And this sight is greatly talked of in surrounding places, even among the enemies of the faith, it being said that in this cave was born that Jesus who is worshiped by Christians" (*Against Celsus*, 1.51).

---

of Judea, were sometimes built in front of or over natural or man-made caves used as animal shelters. Outside the Gospels, the most ancient references to Jesus' birth have him being born in a cave. That is a likely setting for Jesus' birth: because the room where they were staying was not a suitable place for giving birth, Mary and Joseph made use of a nearby cave normally used to shelter animals. There was a **manger** on hand for feeding animals, and this became Jesus' first cradle. In the fourth century, Helena, the mother of Constantine, had a church built in Bethlehem; a cave beneath the church is revered as the place of Jesus' birth to this day. The icons of the eastern Churches depict a cave as the birthplace of Jesus.

Hospitality: See page 314

Houses: See page 186

If Jesus was born in a cave and laid in an animal feeding trough, then we should neither exaggerate nor minimize the circumstances of his birth. Caves in Palestine are not dank, dreadful accommodations; they have been used to shelter humans as well as animals even into modern times. Nonetheless, birth in a cave with a feeding trough for a cradle is hardly a mark of exalted social status. Jesus, who will lift up the lowly (1:52), was born into this world as one of its lowly ones.

For reflection: What significance do I find in the circumstances of Jesus' birth? What is their most important lesson for me?

A Proclamation of Who Jesus Is

⁸ Now there were shepherds in that region living in the fields and keeping the night watch over their flock. ⁹ The angel of the Lord appeared to them and the glory of the Lord shone around them, and they were struck with great fear. ¹⁰ The angel said to them, "Do not be afraid; for behold, I proclaim to you good news of great joy that will be for all the people. ¹¹ For today in the city of David a savior has been born for you who is Messiah and Lord. ¹² And this will be a sign for you: you will find an infant wrapped in swaddling clothes and lying in a manger." ¹³ And suddenly there was a multitude of the heavenly host with the angel, praising God and saying:

14 **"Glory to God in the highest
and on earth peace to those on whom his favor rests."**
OT: Isaiah 40:9; 52:7; 61:1–2
NT: Luke 2:1–8

8 **Now there were shepherds in that region** around Bethlehem. Some later Jewish writings consider **shepherds** to be inherently dishonest, but there is no evidence that this was the view in the first century. Caring for sheep and goats was an ordinary if low-status occupation, along with farm work and fishing. These shepherds were **living in the fields and keeping the night watch over their flock.** Literally, "they were living out of doors and watching the watches of the night over their flock." It was necessary to guard sheep and goats against thieves and wild animals, keeping watch through the night if the flock remained in open country. These shepherds remained **in the fields** with their flock, taking turns staying awake. Nighttime was customarily divided into three or four watches (see 12:38; Matt 14:25).

9 **The angel of the Lord appeared to them and the glory of the Lord shone around them.** Although they were surely not expecting it, an **angel of the Lord appeared to them**. Luke does not name the angel but it will, like Gabriel (1:11–20, 26–38), bear a message from God. The **glory of the Lord** is the splendor of God's presence, often manifest in God's dwelling tent or temple (Exod 40:34–35; Num 17:10; 2 Chron 7:1–3; Ezek 43:4–5; 44:4). God's **glory** is like a brilliant light that **shone** around the shepherds, vanquishing the darkness of the night. **They were struck with great fear,** a normal reaction to an encounter with the divine (see 1:12).

Angels: See page 11

The "daybreak from on high" that will "shine on those who sit in darkness" (1:78–79) is first manifested by God's glory shining on shepherds keeping night watch. Why shepherds? A prosaic answer might be, because no one else was awake at the time. A better answer is that shepherds represented the lowly whom God would lift up through Jesus (1:52), and it is fitting that the lowly be the first to hear about his birth.

10 **The angel said to them, "Do not be afraid,"** just as Gabriel told Zechariah and Mary not to be afraid (1:13, 30). The angel tells the shep-

herds that they are to have no fear, **for behold, I proclaim to you good news of great joy**. The **good news** that the angel brings the shepherds should replace their "great fear" (verse 9) with **great joy.** For Jews, proclamations of **good news** could bring to mind prophecies that announced good news (Isaiah 40:9; 52:7; 61:1–2). One prophecy speaks of a messenger "who brings glad tidings, / Announcing peace, bearing good news, / announcing salvation" (Isaiah 52:7). Now an angelic messenger has come bearing **good news** for the shepherds—and not only for them: it is good news **that will be for all the people.** The primary meaning of **the people** is God's people; the good news is about how God is visiting and redeeming his people (1:68). Yet **all the people** also foreshadows all the people of the earth, "the whole world" (2:1). Luke's two-volume work—his Gospel and Acts—shows that what God began with the Israelite people is extended through Jesus "to the ends of the earth" (Acts 1:8).

> How beautiful upon the mountains
>> are the feet of him who brings glad tidings,
> Announcing peace, bearing good news,
>> announcing salvation, and saying to Zion,
> "Your God is King!"
>
> Isaiah 52:7

For reflection: Do I hear the gospel as good news for me? Does it bring me great joy?

BACKGROUND: GOSPEL, GOOD NEWS The English word "gospel" comes from the Anglo-Saxon word godspell, which means "good news." "Good news" is in turn a literal translation of the Greek word euangelion used by Matthew and Mark (Matt 4:23; 9:35; Mark 1:1, 14–15). Luke uses the related verb euangelizo, which means to proclaim good news. These Greek words give us such English words as "evangelist" and "evangelization." New Testament authors did not invent the word euangelion; it is found in ancient Greek literature as a term for a message of victory or another message that brought joy. The Greek translation of Isaiah uses forms of this word: "Go up onto a high mountain, / Zion, herald of glad tidings; / cry out at the top of your voice, / Jerusalem, herald of good news!" (Isaiah 40:9). Paul, whose letters predate the written Gospels, was the first New Testament author to use the word euangelion as an expression for the message of Christ: "Our gospel did not come to you in word alone, but also in power and in the holy Spirit" (1 Thess 1:5).

Mention of the proclamation of **good news** could have triggered another association for some of Luke's first readers. A Roman proclamation hailed Caesar Augustus as a "savior" who brought peace; it maintained that his birth was "good news" for the world. Now an angel proclaims that someone else's birth is good news, someone who is a savior (verse 11). In his two-volume work Luke will not challenge Roman authority head on, but he will subvert any claim that it is the ultimate authority.

11 The angel proclaims what the good news is: **For today in the city of David a savior has been born for you**. Referring to Bethlehem as **the city of David** is a subtle reminder that Jesus is a descendant of David (see 1:27, 32, 69; 2:4). The shepherds would have understood a **savior** to be someone who rescues from harm and distress (Judges 3:9, 15; Neh 9:27). God acts as a savior for his people (Exod 15:2; 2 Sam 22:3; Judith 9:11; Psalm 18:47; 25:5; 118:14); Mary rejoiced "in God my savior" (1:47). Zechariah spoke of a "horn for our salvation" being raised up in the house of David (1:69): God will save his people through Jesus. While the angel proclaims that **a savior has been born,** he does not explain what kind of salvation he brings. The rest of Luke's Gospel will flesh this out.

The angel tells the shepherds that the good news is about what happened **today . . . for you**; today is a day of salvation for the shepherds. Similarly, today is a day of salvation for Luke's readers if they embrace the savior whom his Gospel proclaims.

The angel goes on to tell the shepherds that a savior has been born **who is Messiah**. Different Jews had different expectations of who the **Messiah** would be and what he would accomplish. One common expectation was that he would be a descendant of David who would restore Jewish independence and usher in a golden age. Luke's Gospel has already made it clear that Jesus is the Messiah (1:31–33; 68–69); it will be left to Jesus to teach what kind of Messiah he is (see 9:20–22).

Messiah, Christ: See page 257

The child born in Bethlehem is not only savior and Messiah; he is also **Lord**. The word translated **Lord** means someone with authority; it can be a title or designation for God (1:6, 9, 11, 15, 16, 17, etc.). The angel announces that Jesus is **Lord** but does not explain the nature of Jesus' lordship and authority. Clearly, though, Jesus is Lord in some profound sense: otherwise why would an angel announce it? Luke's readers likely know that Jesus is called Lord as God is called Lord (see Phil 2:11).

Lord: See page 137

For reflection: What do I have in mind when I acknowledge Jesus as my Lord?

12 The angel adds, **and this will be a sign for you** that a child has been born in Bethlehem who is savior, Messiah, and Lord. **You will find an infant wrapped in swaddling clothes and lying in a manger.** The word for **infant** has the connotation of newly born. Since Bethlehem is a small village, there are probably not too many newborn infants in it. The infant will be wrapped in **swaddling clothes**, which is normal practice and of itself not much of a sign. The shepherds will find him **lying in a manger.** While using an animal feeding trough as a makeshift cradle was not usual, it was probably not unheard of; other poor or displaced families may have done the same. What then is the **sign** that the angel is providing the shepherds? In one sense it is the conjunction of the specifics supplied by the angel: they will **find** only one swaddled, newborn infant lying in a feeding trough in Bethlehem that night.

In another sense the **sign** provided by the angel indicates something about this child. Although he is a savior sent by God (see 1:68–69), the Messiah whose rule will last forever (1:32–33), and Lord, yet he is **lying in a manger** because his mother had no proper place to give birth and no regular cradle (2:7). We would not expect one who is savior, Messiah, and Lord to enter the world in such a lowly manner. The humble circumstances of his birth are a sign foreshadowing the paradox of his life: he is a Lord who serves those under him (22:27); he is a Messiah who suffers and dies (9:20–22); he is a savior who saves others (19:10) by not saving himself (23:35–39).

For reflection: What is the significance for me of Jesus' lying in a manger?

13 **And suddenly there was a multitude of the heavenly host with the angel.** The word **host** means army. The Old Testament refers to stars as the host of heaven (Isaiah 34:4; 45:12; Jer 19:13; Zeph 1:5) and uses the

same expression for angels (1 Kings 22:19–21), which is its meaning here. A **multitude** of other angels **suddenly** appears and joins the **angel** who is speaking to the shepherds. The birth of Jesus is an event of cosmic significance. The heavenly multitude is **praising God** for what he is accomplishing by the birth of Jesus, **saying:**

14 **Glory to God in the highest and on earth peace to those on whom his favor rests.** Some scholars suggest that the sense is brought out by adding words that are implied: There is **glory to God in the highest** and there is **on earth peace to those on whom his favor rests**. While God's glory can be his splendor (verse 9), here **glory** seems to refer to the honor and praise given him. The **highest** means the highest heaven, God's dwelling (see 1:78; 19:38; 24:49; Psalm 148:1). God is glorified in heaven because of the birth of Jesus. And **on earth** the birth of Jesus brings **peace to those on whom** God's **favor rests**. As in Zechariah's prayer (1:79), **peace** is not simply the absence of violence but a condition of harmony, wholeness, well-being. God sends peace **to those on whom his favor rests**. God's **favor** is his free choice, his good pleasure. God chose the Israelites to be his people, making a "covenant of peace" with them (Isaiah 54:10). "Mindful of his holy covenant" (1:72), God has sent Jesus so that his people, rescued from enemies and freed from fear, might be holy and righteous (1:74-75). That is the **peace** God is sending to those whom he has chosen. No limit is placed on God's choice: his chosen include his people Israel (1:68), but God may also show his favor to others—potentially to all the people of the earth. World peace does not come from an emperor; peace in its fullest sense is God's gift through an infant lying in a manger.

For reflection: How have I experienced God's favor and peace?

Responses to the Birth of Jesus
¹⁵ **When the angels went away from them to heaven, the shepherds said to one another, "Let us go, then, to Bethlehem to see this thing that has taken place, which the Lord has made known to us."** ¹⁶ **So they went in haste and found Mary and Joseph, and the infant lying in the manger.** ¹⁷ **When they saw this, they made known the**

message that had been told them about this child. ¹⁸ All who heard it were amazed by what had been told them by the shepherds. ¹⁹ And Mary kept all these things, reflecting on them in her heart. ²⁰ Then the shepherds returned, glorifying and praising God for all they had heard and seen, just as it had been told to them.

NT: Luke 2:8–14

15 **When the angels** who had appeared to the shepherds (2:13–14) **went away from them to heaven, the shepherds said to one another, "Let us go, then, to Bethlehem to see this thing that has taken place."** The **thing that has taken place** is the birth in **Bethlehem** of a savior, Messiah, and Lord, whom the shepherds will find lying in a manger (2:11–12). The shepherds say that this is something **which the Lord has made known to us**: it was revealed to them by an angel surrounded by the glory of God (2:9). They decide to **go** and **see** for themselves what **has taken place**, even if this means leaving their flock unguarded (see 2:8).

Angel: See page 11
Bethlehem: See page 54
Lord: See page 137

16 **So they went in haste**, in eager response to the angel's message, just as Mary went in haste to Elizabeth in response to the angel Gabriel's words (1:36–40). The shepherds **found Mary and Joseph, and the infant lying in the manger.** The Greek word for **found** has connotations of finding something after searching for it. The angel told the shepherds "you will find an infant … lying in a manger" (2:12); his words were an invitation to seek out the infant and a promise that they would find him. They responded to the invitation, and the promise was fulfilled. Luke speaks of **Mary and Joseph** although normal cultural practice would have been to mention the husband before the wife (see 1:5); putting **Mary** first may reflect her special blessedness (see 1:42–45, 48–49).

For reflection: How quickly have I responded to God's invitations and instructions?

17 **When they saw this**—an infant lying in a manger—**they made known the message that had been told them about this child.** The

63

shepherds told Mary and Joseph what the angel had told them: the infant born in Bethlehem that day is a savior and Messiah and Lord, whom they would find swaddled and lying in a manger (2:11–12).

18 Mary and Joseph were not the only ones the shepherds told about an angel's announcing the good news of the birth of a savior, Messiah, and Lord: **All who heard it were amazed by what had been told them by the shepherds.** Those whom they told—presumably people in Bethlehem and the vicinity—were **amazed**, astonished by what they heard. But that seems to have been the extent of their reaction. Luke gives no indication that any of those told about the birth of Jesus sought him out. Their response is like someone being told, "God is offering you eternal life" and saying "Wow!" but doing nothing to take up God's offer.

19 **And Mary kept all these things, reflecting on them in her heart.** All of **these things** certainly include the shepherds' report of the angel's announcement that her son is savior, Messiah, and Lord. But Mary would have in mind as well all that led up to the birth of her child: Gabriel's startling promise that she would bear a son through the overshadowing of the Holy Spirit, a son who would rule over a kingdom that would last forever (1:26–38), and Elizabeth's surprising pregnancy and her proclaiming Mary blessed by God (1:39–45). Mary has had nine months to ponder what God is doing through her; the shepherds' report is one more thing to ponder. Mary is apparently included in the "all" who where "amazed" by the shepherds' words (verse 18), but her response is more than astonishment. Mary **kept all these things**: the Greek word **kept** has connotations of preserving something, being concerned about it, treasuring it. Mary treasured the events that had unfolded, **reflecting on them in her heart**. The Greek word for **reflecting on** means putting things together, pondering them. In the biblical view, the **heart** is the seat of thinking and feeling and willing. Mary takes to heart the amazing things that are happening and tries to fathom their meaning. **Mary** is a model of treasuring all that God says and does, meditating on his word, pondering his plans for our lives.

For reflection: How often do I meditate on Scripture? On what God is doing for and through me?

20 **Then the shepherds returned** to their flock (2:8), **glorifying and praising God.** Angels praised God over the birth of Jesus, "saying: 'Glory to God in the highest'" (2:13–14). The angels have returned to heaven (verse 15); shepherds carry on their praise, glorifying God **for all they had heard and seen**. They had **heard** the good news an angel proclaimed about the birth of a child in Bethlehem (2:10–12); they had **seen** the child lying in a manger **just as it had been told to them**.

Like Mary's pondering in her heart, the responses of the shepherds are also an example for us. They believed what an angel told them and went in haste to find Jesus. They told others about the birth of a savior, Messiah, and Lord; some scholars see them as the first evangelists in Luke's two-volume work. They praised and glorified God for all they had been privileged to hear and see.

For reflection: What is the specific lesson for me in the responses of the shepherds?

Obedience to God's Law

²¹ **When eight days were completed for his circumcision, he was named Jesus, the name given him by the angel before he was conceived in the womb.**

²² **When the days were completed for their purification according to the law of Moses, they took him up to Jerusalem to present him to the Lord,** ²³ **just as it is written in the law of the Lord, "Every male that opens the womb shall be consecrated to the Lord,"** ²⁴ **and to offer the sacrifice of "a pair of turtledoves or two young pigeons," in accordance with the dictate in the law of the Lord.**

OT: Gen 17:10–12; Exod 13:2, 11–15; Lev 12:1–8; Num 18:15–17;
1 Sam 1:11, 22–28; Neh 10:37
NT: Luke 1:31, 35; 2:7; Gal 4:4

21 **When eight days were completed for his circumcision**: circumcision, carried out **eight days** after birth, was "the mark of the covenant," a sign that a man was a member of the people of God (Gen 17:10–12; Lev 12:3). Joseph and Mary follow God's law and have Jesus circumcised. **He was named Jesus**: like John (1:59), Jesus is given his name at circumcision.

The name **Jesus** comes from the Greek form of an Aramaic form of the name Joshua, which was popularly understood to mean "Yahweh," that is, the LORD, "saves," but Luke does not go into the meaning of Hebrew or Aramaic words for his Greek-speaking readers. The significance Luke sees in Jesus' name is that it was **the name given him by the angel before he was conceived in the womb** (see 1:31). Mary and Joseph obey both God's general laws and God's specific instructions to them delivered by Gabriel.

22 Luke does not recount anything further about Jesus' circumcision but jumps ahead about a month, to **when the days were completed for their purification according to the law of Moses**. After giving birth to a son, a mother was ritually unclean for seven days and continued to avoid contact with anything sacred for the next thirty-three days (Lev 12:2, 4). At the end of this period she would make sacrificial offerings in the Temple and be ritually clean again (Lev 12:6–8). There were no corresponding restrictions or procedures regarding new fathers, since it was giving birth that made one ritually unclean. Nonetheless, Luke speaks of **their purification**, which might be taken to mean that he thought Joseph as well as Mary needed to be purified. Perhaps, though, he is speaking of Mary's purification as a family affair, something they both had to be concerned about. Luke was familiar with the passage in the law that deals with purification after childbirth (see verse 24) and would have known that it did not apply to fathers.

Clean and unclean: See page 140

Thirty-three days after Jesus' circumcision, when Mary and Joseph went to the Temple to make the purification offerings, **they took** Jesus **up to Jerusalem to present him to the Lord**. The family is staying in Bethlehem (see 2:39), roughly five miles from **Jerusalem**. Their visit to the Temple in Jerusalem has two purposes: to make the sacrificial offerings that completed Mary's purification and to **present** Jesus **to the Lord** God, whose dwelling on earth was the Temple.

23 Luke explains what lies behind their presenting Jesus to the Lord: Mary and Joseph do so **just as it is written in the law of the Lord, "Every male that opens the womb shall be consecrated to the Lord."** The

sense of **opens the womb** is "the first to open the womb," that is, the firstborn (see Exod 13:2, 12); Jesus is Mary's firstborn (2:7). To be **consecrated to the Lord** meant to belong to him. The book of Nehemiah speaks of the firstborn of children (literally, sons) and animals being brought to the Temple (Neh 10:37). Firstborn animals were offered as sacrifices to God; firstborn sons were redeemed (Exod 13:15; Num 18:15–17) for five shekels (Num 18:16)—ransomed, as it were, from God, to whom they belonged.

> *Consecrate to me every firstborn that opens the womb among the Israelites, both of man and beast, for it belongs to me.*
>
> Exod 13:2

While Luke goes on to describe the offering presented in the Temple as part of Mary's purification (verse 24), he says nothing about Joseph and Mary paying five shekels (about twenty days' wages for an ordinary laborer) to redeem Jesus. This leaves the impression that Jesus remains **consecrated to the Lord**, permanently belonging to him. An Old Testament precedent might be Samuel, who had been given to God by his mother, Hannah, before he was conceived (1 Sam 1:11). After he was weaned she left him in God's Temple in the care of the priest Eli (1 Sam 1:22–28). Jesus will not remain in the Temple as did Samuel, but he will nevertheless be entirely **consecrated to the Lord**.

The Greek word Luke uses for **consecrated** is the word for holy; Gabriel told Mary that Jesus "will be called holy" (1:35). His holiness is his consecration to God: Jesus belongs to God and is dedicated to his service.

For reflection: What is my idea of holiness? How am I striving to be holy?

24 Mary and Joseph bring Jesus to the Temple to present him to God **and to offer the sacrifice of "a pair of turtledoves or two young pigeons," in accordance with the dictate in the law of the Lord**. Such **sacrifice** is offered forty days after the birth of a son to complete the purification of the mother (Lev 12:2, 4, 6–8). The **law of the Lord** called for offering a yearling lamb and a pigeon or turtledove (Lev 12:6) but made allowance for those who were too poor to afford a lamb; their sacrificial

offering could be **a pair of turtledoves or two young pigeons** (Lev 12:8). Joseph and Mary qualify for the less expensive offering, indicating that they are poor—what we would think of as the working poor. Jesus, who will lift up the lowly (1:52), is born among the lowly.

> *If, however, she cannot afford a lamb, she may take two turtledoves or two pigeons.*
>
> Lev 12:8

The poor and the rich: See page 198

Luke noted that Zechariah and Elizabeth observed "all the commandments and ordinances of the Lord blamelessly" (1:6). He portrays Joseph and Mary doing the same. Luke has mentioned "the law of Moses" or "the law of the Lord" three times in three verses to explain why Mary and Joseph did what they did. Paul will write that Jesus was "born under the law" (Gal 4:4). Jesus represents a new stage in God's dealings with his people but is firmly rooted in what God has done and required in the past.

For reflection: What example do Joseph and Mary set for me?

Simeon's Encounter with Jesus

²⁵ **Now there was a man in Jerusalem whose name was Simeon. This man was righteous and devout, awaiting the consolation of Israel, and the holy Spirit was upon him.** ²⁶ **It had been revealed to him by the holy Spirit that he should not see death before he had seen the Messiah of the Lord.** ²⁷ **He came in the Spirit into the temple; and when the parents brought in the child Jesus to perform the custom of the law in regard to him,** ²⁸ **he took him into his arms and blessed God, saying:**

²⁹ **"Now, Master, you may let your servant go**
    in peace, according to your word,
³⁰ **for my eyes have seen your salvation,**
³¹   **which you prepared in sight of all the peoples,**
³² **a light for revelation to the Gentiles,**
    and glory for your people Israel."

³³ The child's father and mother were amazed at what was said about him; ³⁴ and Simeon blessed them and said to Mary his mother, "Behold, this child is destined for the fall and rise of many in Israel, and to be a sign that will be contradicted ³⁵ (and you your‑self a sword will pierce) so that the thoughts of many hearts may be revealed."

OT: Isaiah 42:6; 46:13; 49:6; 52:9–10; 66:13
NT: Luke 2:22–24

25 **Now there was a man in Jerusalem whose name was Simeon**, named after one of Jacob's twelve sons (Gen 29:33). **This man was righteous and devout**. Being **righteous** means obeying God's laws (see 1:6); to be **devout** means to revere God and carefully carry out religious duties. Simeon did what God required of him and he hoped for what God promised: he was **awaiting the consolation of Israel**. Many Jews at the time of Jesus had hopes that God would act to restore his people, freeing them from evil and foreign rule, fulfilling promises made through the

---

BACKGROUND: JEWISH EXPECTATIONS AT THE TIME OF JESUS Jews in Palestine were ruled by Rome or by Rome's client kings, and their taxes were burdensome. The high priest served at the pleasure of Roman authority—one reason why many devout Jews, who revered the Temple, had low regard for those who controlled it. The situation Jews found themselves in fell far short of what God had promised his people through prophecy: rule by a descendant of David, an era of peace and prosperity, God mani‑festly dwelling in his Temple in Jerusalem, Jews returning from other lands to dwell in the land God promised to their ancestors, Gentiles either turning to the God of Israel or being subject to the rule of Israel, and God's Spirit being poured out. Any Jew who took these prophecies seriously had to be struck by the disparity between how things were and how prophecies promised they would be. Expectations were fanned by various nonbiblical writings in the two centuries before Jesus which spoke of God acting soon to set things right. Different Jewish groups envisioned different scenarios for what God would do. Some expected God to act directly; some expected God to act through one or more messiahs. Some foresaw the conversion of Gentiles to allegiance to the God of Israel; others foresaw their destruction. Some thought the end of the present age was near and that God's final triumph over evil was not far off. While there was no agree‑ment over how God would bring an end to the unsatisfactory situation in which God's people found themselves, many shared the expectation that God would do something about it. *Related topics: The age to come (page 487), Kingdom of God (page 381), Messiah, Christ (page 257), Nonbiblical writings (page 342).*

---

prophets. Simeon expresses these hopes as God's **consolation of Israel**, echoing prophecies of Isaiah that speak of God's consolation, or comfort, for his people (Isaiah 40:1; 49:13; 51:3, 12; 52:9; 57:18; 66:13). **Consolation** has a note of intimacy, of God comforting his people "as a mother comforts her son" (Isaiah 66:13). **And the holy Spirit was upon him**: the Holy Spirit who filled Elizabeth and Zechariah and John (1:15, 41, 67) and overshadowed Mary to conceive Jesus (1:35) rests upon Simeon. The following verses tell how the Holy Spirit inspires and guides Simeon.

Jerusalem: See page 516
The Spirit: See page 100

As a mother comforts her son,
so will I comfort you;
in Jerusalem you shall find your comfort.
Isaiah 66:13

For reflection: How have I experienced God's consolations?

26 **It had been revealed to him by the holy Spirit that he should not see death before he had seen the Messiah of the Lord.** The **Spirit** inspired prophets to speak for God (Isaiah 61:1–2; Ezek 11:5; Joel 3:1); the Spirit reveals what God wants made known (see 1 Cor 2:9–10; Eph 3:4–5). The Holy Spirit in a personal message for Simeon **revealed to him** that he would **not see death** before he **had seen the Messiah of the Lord**. To **see death** is an idiom for experiencing death, for dying (Psalm 89:49; see John 8:51; Heb 11:5). Simeon waited for the "consolation of Israel" (verse 25) that God would accomplish through his **Messiah,** and the Holy Spirit had **revealed** to him that he would not **see** death until he had **seen** the Messiah. Luke does not tell his readers Simeon's age or how long ago this promise was made to him; Simeon's words in verse 29 might imply that he was elderly and had been waiting for the Messiah for quite some time.

Messiah, Christ: See page 257

27 **He came in the Spirit into the temple**, led by the Spirit to be at the right place at the right time. **Temple** courtyards encompassed more than thirty-five acres and were often bustling with people. The **Spirit** guided

Simeon to recognize the one whom he was awaiting **when the parents brought in the child Jesus to perform the custom of the law in regard to him.** Mary and Joseph brought Jesus to the Temple to present him to the Lord in accordance with **the custom of the law** (2:22–23; see Exod 13:2; Neh 10:37). They did not go to the Temple to meet Simeon; their encounter was arranged by **the Spirit.**

Temple: See page 519

For reflection: How have I experienced the promptings of the Spirit?

Luke mentions the law of God three times in three verses (2:22–24) and mentions the Spirit three times in the next three verses (verses 25–27), with the last verse also mentioning the law. These repetitions are Luke's signals that law and Spirit converge in Jesus. The law is the terms of God's covenant with his people; Jesus comes in fulfillment of the covenant (see 1:54–55, 68–73). The Holy Spirit is the creative and life-giving power of God (Gen 2:7; Judith 16:14); God is doing something new and life-giving through Jesus (see 4:14–21).

28 Enlightened by the Holy Spirit to recognize who the infant Jesus is, Simeon **took him into his arms.** Simeon not only sees the Messiah but is able to hold and embrace him. Simeon **blessed God,** praising and thanking him for sending the Messiah and for allowing him to live long enough to see him.

29 Simeon blessed God, saying **Now, Master, you may let your servant go / in peace according to your word.** The word **now** is emphatic: **now** is the consolation of Israel (verse 25), **now** Simeon can die. The Greek word translated **Master** is not the word usually translated Lord but has much the same meaning; the Greek translation of the Hebrew Scriptures sometimes uses **Master** to refer to God. Simeon calls himself God's **servant,** literally, his slave; Mary used the feminine form of this word when she called herself the "handmaid" of the Lord (1:38). Simeon respectfully addresses God as a **servant** addresses his **Master.** To be **let . . . go** means to set free, to be released from a duty, or to be sent away; here it has the connotations of being dismissed from service and departing from this life. Simeon has lived to see the Messiah, as it had

been promised **according to your word** (see verse 26); now he can die **in peace.** Peace is God's gift on those he favors (2:14); Simeon has been given the favor of seeing the Messiah. Even though Simeon will not live to see Jesus carry out his mission, he can die with the satisfaction of having seen and held him. It is as if Simeon had been set as a watchman to await the Messiah; now that the Messiah has come his duty is over and he can be dismissed from this service.

Servant, slave: See page 454

For reflection: What is the chief service God has assigned me?

30 Simeon explains why he can die in peace, which is also his reason for praising God: **for my eyes have seen your salvation**. Simeon has **seen** the infant Jesus, and he has been enlightened by the Spirit to realize that Jesus is God's **salvation**. The word **salvation** means rescue; in the Old Testament it is used for God's rescue of his people and his victory over their enemies. Moses told the Israelites, "Stand your ground, and you will see the victory the LORD will win for you today" (Exod 14:13; "victory" could also be translated "salvation"). Jesus is God's agent sent on a rescue mission; through him God's people will be "rescued from the hand of . . . enemies" (1:74). Simeon does not explain how this will happen; he simply thanks God for having **seen your salvation**—for having seen Jesus.

For reflection: Where am I most in need of Jesus' rescue?

31 **which you prepared in sight of all the peoples**: God's salvation has been made ready to be seen by everyone. The following verse indicates that **all the peoples** includes Gentiles as well as Jews. Isaiah prophesied that God would comfort his people by restoring Jerusalem and that this would be displayed "in the sight of all the nations" (Isaiah 52:9–10).

> *Break out together in song,*
> *O ruins of Jerusalem!*
> *For the LORD comforts his people,*
> *he redeems Jerusalem.*
> *The LORD has bared his holy arm*

in the sight of all the nations;
All the ends of the earth will behold
the salvation of our God.

Isaiah 52:9–10

32 The salvation God is granting through Jesus is **a light for revelation to the Gentiles.** This is the first clear statement in Luke's Gospel that **Gentiles** are included in God's salvation—good news for Luke's Gentile readers. Gentiles have hitherto not been the recipients of the **revelation** that God made to his people Israel; Gentiles have, as it were, been living in darkness. But now a **light** will shine on them; Jesus will be God's **revelation** to them. What God is doing through Jesus is foreshadowed in prophecies of Isaiah that speak of a servant of God who will be "a light to the nations / that my salvation may reach to the ends of the earth" (Isaiah 49:6; see also Isaiah 42:6).

The salvation brought by Jesus will be **glory for your people Israel.** God's people are included in what he is doing through Jesus. The **glory** Jesus brings for God's people is the presence and splendor of God (see 2:9). Again, prophecies of Isaiah foreshadow what Jesus will accomplish: "I will put salvation within Zion / and give to Israel my glory" (Isaiah 46:13; see also Isaiah 45:25).

Inspired by the Spirit (verse 25), Simeon praises God for sending Jesus as salvation for all peoples, Gentiles as well as Jews. What Isaiah foreshadowed is being fulfilled.

33 **The child's father and mother were amazed at what was said about him.** Luke refers to Joseph and Mary as Jesus' **father and mother.** Luke knows that Jesus was conceived in the virgin Mary through the Holy Spirit (1:27, 34–35) yet he does not hesitate to refer to Joseph as Jesus' **father** (and to Joseph and Mary as Jesus' parents—2:41). Joseph will act as a human father for Jesus. Joseph and Mary were amazed when shepherds reported that angels had announced Jesus' birth (2:17–18). Now they are again **amazed,** astonished by what they hear. A stranger has taken Jesus into his arms and spoken of him as God's agent of salvation for all peoples, Gentiles as well as Jews. Gabriel told Mary that Jesus would be given the throne of David and would rule over the house of Jacob forever (1:32–33), indicating that he is the Messiah. Most Jews expected that the

73

Messiah would conquer Gentiles, not be a light of revelation for them. **What** Simeon **said about** Jesus means that he will be and do more than was expected of the Messiah. Joseph and Mary, **amazed** by his words, must expand their understanding of their child.

> *For reflection: How have I grown in my understanding of Jesus? What about him most amazes me?*

34 **Simeon blessed them**: Simeon called down God's blessing upon Joseph and Mary, praying for their well-being during what lies ahead. God has shown great favor to them by sending Jesus as their child but has thereby called them to a great service. It will not always by easy for them. After Simeon blesses **them** he turns his attention to **Mary**, as if what he says now applies more to her than to Joseph. (Since Joseph never appears on the scene during Jesus' adult life, the common speculation is that he died before Jesus began his public ministry.) Simeon **said to Mary his mother, "Behold, this child is destined for the fall and rise of many in Israel."** Jesus will be God's salvation and glory for Israel (verses 30, 32), but not everyone in Israel will embrace him. He is **destined** for a mixed response. Some will **fall** because of him, some will **rise**; Jesus will be the downfall of those who reject him even as he is God's salvation for those who accept him. Simeon first mentions those who **fall**: Jesus may meet more rejection than acceptance. This is borne out in Simeon's next words: Jesus will **be a sign that will be contradicted**. Here the word **sign** might be best taken to mean an indicator, something that points the way. Jesus will point out the way of God (see 20:21), yet he will be **contradicted**, spoken against, opposed, rejected.

35 **Simeon** interrupts his prophetic words about Jesus to tell Mary what will happen to her: **and you yourself a sword will pierce**. Simeon's image is vivid but cryptic. It is commonly taken to mean that Mary will be pained when Jesus is rejected; Mary will suffer because of his sufferings. Luke will not recount Mary being present when Jesus is crucified, but she could hardly have remained ignorant of it and not been pained to the core of her being. Still, we can wonder whether there are other implications in Simeon's image of a sword piercing Mary. We will need to keep his words in mind as we encounter Mary again in Luke's Gospel (see 2:41–51).

For reflection: What implications do I find in Simeon's words to Mary?

Simeon finishes his prophetic words about Jesus: Jesus will be a sign that will be contradicted **so that the thoughts of many hearts may be revealed**. The Greek word for **thoughts** can be used for doubting and hostile thoughts (as it is at 5:22). The response made to Jesus will reveal the true condition of those who oppose him.

Simeon praised God for sending Jesus as salvation for all peoples, Gentiles as well as Jews (verses 28–32) but now warns that Jesus will receive a mixed response. Some will reject him; Mary will be pierced to her core. These are the first ominous notes in Luke's Gospel.

Anna Bears Witness to Jesus
³⁶ There was also a prophetess, Anna, the daughter of Phanuel, of the tribe of Asher. She was advanced in years, having lived seven years with her husband after her marriage, ³⁷ and then as a widow until she was eighty-four. She never left the temple, but worshiped night and day with fasting and prayer. ³⁸ And coming forward at that very time, she gave thanks to God and spoke about the child to all who were awaiting the redemption of Jerusalem.

OT: Isaiah 52:9
NT: Luke 2:22–35

36 The setting continues to be a Temple courtyard, where Joseph and Mary have brought Jesus and offered a sacrifice for Mary's purification (2:22–24). **There was also a prophetess, Anna.** Women prophets are mentioned in both the Old and New Testaments (Exod 15:20; Judges 4:4; 2 Kings 22:14; Neh 6:14; Isaiah 8:3; Acts 21:9; 1 Cor 11:5). As a **prophetess,** Anna is guided by the Holy Spirit in her perceptions and proclamations, as were Elizabeth (1:41–45), Zechariah (1:67–79), and Simeon (2:25–35). **Anna** is **the daughter of Phanuel, of the tribe of Asher**, one of the twelve tribes that made up ancient Israel (see Deut 33:24–25); she comes from good Israelite stock. **She was advanced in years**: the expression conveys she is very old (see Gen 18:11; Josh 13:1; 23:1). Anna **lived seven years with her husband after her marriage**, which might have taken place when she was around thirteen years old.

75

37 **and then as a widow until she was eighty-four.** The Greek words translated **until she was eighty-four** could also mean that she had been a widow for eighty-four years. In either case she has had a long life. **She never left the temple.** Luke's words should not be taken too literally; he will write that Jesus' disciples "were continually in the temple praising God" (24:53) without meaning that they lived there. Luke conveys that Anna was habitually at the Temple where she **worshiped night and day with fasting and prayer.** Along with almsgiving, **fasting and prayer** became customary practices for many pious Jews toward the end of the Old Testament era (see Tobit 12:8). **Fasting** meant abstaining from all food and drink for a period of time; Anna's **prayer** would have included participation in the public prayers offered each day at the Temple (see Acts 3:1). Anna is a devout Jew, totally committed to God.

Temple: See page 519

Fasting: See page 153

38 **And coming forward at that very time**: like Simeon (2:27), Anna is led by the Holy Spirit to come to the right place at the right time to encounter Jesus, identifying him among all the people present in the Temple courtyards. **At that very time** might indicate that she overheard Simeon's description of Jesus as the salvation sent by God for all peoples (2:29–32). But there was no need for her to eavesdrop: Anna is a prophetess, guided by the Spirit to recognize Jesus' significance. **She gave thanks to God.** The characteristic Jewish way to give **thanks** or praise to God is to acknowledge what God has done ("I will praise you, LORD, with all my heart; / I will declare all your wondrous deeds"—Psalm 9:2). The end of the verse indicates that Anna **thanks** God for sending Jesus as **the redemption of Jerusalem.** The word **redemption** means liberation or deliverance; many Jews expected that the Messiah would liberate Jerusalem from Roman rule (see Acts 1:6). Some Jews also expected that the Messiah would free God's people from their sinfulness; the *Psalms of Solomon* (not in the Bible) proclaim that the Messiah will "cleanse Jerusalem and make it holy as it was at the beginning." **Jerusalem** can represent all Israel, as a capital stands for a nation; Anna's praise echoes that of Zechariah, who blessed God for bringing "redemption to his people" (1:68). **The redemption of Jerusalem** has the same basic meaning as "the consolation of Israel" that Simeon awaited (2:25); both expres-

sions reflect a prophecy of Isaiah that speaks of God restoring Jerusalem after the exile (Isaiah 52:8–9). Anna perceives that God is carrying out a great restoration through Jesus and for this **she gave thanks to God**.

Jerusalem: See page 516

Jewish expectations at the time of Jesus: See page 69

Psalms of Solomon: See page 259

> Break out together in song,
>   O ruins of Jerusalem!
> For the LORD comforts his people,
>   he redeems Jerusalem.

> Isaiah 52:9

In addition to thanking God for what he is doing through Jesus, she **spoke about the child**. The word translated **spoke** could also be translated as kept speaking. After the Holy Spirit had led Simeon to recognize Jesus' significance, Simeon spoke about him to Mary and Joseph (2:27–35). Anna speaks about Jesus to a wider audience: **all who were awaiting the redemption of Jerusalem**. She tells those who are longing for God to liberate his people that Jesus is the one who brings this redemption.

Anna recognizes the significance of Jesus, thanks God for him, and bears witness to him. She is a model for disciples of Jesus.

For reflection: How is Anna specifically a model for me?

Jesus is destined to be the fall as well as the rise of many in Israel (2:34); not every Jew will accept him. Anna and Simeon represent devout Jewish women and men who do recognize and embrace Jesus. Even though Luke's two-volume work will end on a note of Jewish rejection of Jesus (Acts 28:17, 25–28), Luke begins his work by portraying Jesus as the fulfillment of Jewish expectations, welcomed by pious Jews like Zechariah and Elizabeth, Mary and Joseph, Simeon and Anna.

Jesus Grows up in Nazareth
³⁹ When they had fulfilled all the prescriptions of the law of the Lord, they returned to Galilee, to their own town of Nazareth.

⁴⁰ **The child grew and became strong, filled with wisdom; and the favor of God was upon him.**

NT: Luke 2:52

39 **When they had fulfilled all the prescriptions of the law of the Lord, they returned to Galilee:** during their sojourn in Judea, Joseph and Mary have obeyed all that civil edicts (2:1–5) and religious law (2:22–24, 27) required of them, and they are now free to return to **Galilee**. They went back **to their own town of Nazareth**, where they live (1:26–27).

Galilee: See page 114

Nazareth: See page 19

40 **The child grew and became strong.** Luke conveys that Jesus **grew** as any child would and gained strength; Luke said much the same of John the Baptist (1:80). Jesus became **filled with wisdom**. In the Old Testament **wisdom** ranges from practical skills necessary for success to a gift from God (Prov 2:6; Wisd 7:7; Sirach 1:1) that enables one to view things as God

---

COMMENT: MATTHEW AND LUKE ON THE BIRTH OF JESUS In telling how Jesus was conceived and born, Luke and Matthew agree on the essential elements. Jesus was conceived in the virgin Mary through the Holy Spirit; Jesus is the Son of God. Jesus is also the Son of David through Joseph's acceptance of him as his legal son. Jesus was born in Bethlehem but grew up in Nazareth. Yet Luke and Matthew differ when it comes to fleshing out the story of Jesus' birth. Each relates events not mentioned by the other; for example, magi pay homage in Matthew, shepherds in Luke. Sometimes the differences between their accounts are difficult to smooth over. One difference, for example, concerns the place of residence. Matthew portrays Joseph and Mary apparently living in Bethlehem for more than a year after Jesus is born, and then relocating to Nazareth after a sojourn in Egypt. Luke portrays Mary and Joseph living in Nazareth when Jesus is conceived, and on a visit to Bethlehem when Jesus is born; they return to Nazareth with no detour to Egypt. The differences between Luke's and Matthew's accounts remind us that neither Luke nor Matthew provides his readers with a video recording of events surrounding the birth of Jesus. Both accounts proclaim who Jesus is; both accounts link Jesus with what God has done in the past; and both accounts foreshadow what God will do through Jesus in the future. The Church accepts both accounts as inspired Scripture, despite the differences. In reading their accounts as Scripture, our primary focus should be on what they proclaim about Jesus. We should not try to force Luke's account into Matthew's mold, nor Matthew's account into Luke's mold—much less force the two of them into a mold of our own contriving.

---

views them (see Jer 9:11; Hosea 14:10). The full range may be implied here: Jesus grew in his life-skills and in his perception of God's will. **And the favor of God was upon him.** Mary enjoyed God's **favor** (1:28, 30) and so does her son; God looks upon him with fondness and esteem.

Luke provides no details about Jesus' early childhood and home life. The spectacular events surrounding Jesus' birth seem to fade away as Jesus grows up in an ordinary farming village.

ORIENTATION: *Luke recounts but a single incident that takes place between Jesus' infancy and the beginning of his public ministry thirty years later (see 3:23).*

Jesus in His Father's House
⁴¹ **Each year his parents went to Jerusalem for the feast of Passover,** ⁴² **and when he was twelve years old, they went up according to festival custom.** ⁴³ **After they had completed its days, as they were returning, the boy Jesus remained behind in Jerusalem, but his parents did not know it.** ⁴⁴ **Thinking that he was in the caravan, they journeyed for a day and looked for him among their relatives and acquaintances,** ⁴⁵ **but not finding him, they returned to Jerusalem to look for him.** ⁴⁶ **After three days they found him in the temple, sitting in the midst of the teachers, listening to them and asking them questions,** ⁴⁷ **and all who heard him were astounded at his understanding and his answers.** ⁴⁸ **When his parents saw him, they were astonished, and his mother said to him, "Son, why have you done this to us? Your father and I have been looking for you with great anxiety."** ⁴⁹ **And he said to them, "Why were you looking for me? Did you not know that I must be in my Father's house?"** ⁵⁰ **But they did not understand what he said to them.** ⁵¹ **He went down with them and came to Nazareth, and was obedient to them; and his mother kept all these things in her heart.** ⁵² **And Jesus advanced [in] wisdom and age and favor before God and man.**

OT: Exod 12:1–20, 24–27; 23:14–17; Lev 23:5–8
NT: Luke 2:19, 40; Heb 5:8

41 **Each year his parents went to Jerusalem for the feast of Passover.** The law of Moses required that three feasts be celebrated by pilgrimage

to Jerusalem: the springtime feast of Passover and Unleavened Bread, the feast of Weeks (or Pentecost) fifty days later, and the fall feast of Tabernacles (Exod 23:14–17). The law required only Jewish men to travel to Jerusalem (Exod 23:17; 34:23; Deut 16:16), but women and families went as well (Deut 16:14-15): the Passover meal was ideally a family meal (see Exod 12:3–4, 26–27). Joseph and Mary made the trip **each year.** They likely would have walked and it would have taken them five or more days to travel from Nazareth (2:39) to **Jerusalem.**

Jerusalem: See page 516
The feasts of Passover and Unleavened Bread: See page 577

42 **When he was twelve years old, they went up according to festival custom**, taking Jesus with them. There is no implication that this is the first time Jesus went with them to Jerusalem for Passover. Nor is the age **twelve years old** of significance in itself, other than telling the reader how old Jesus was went this incident took place. Rabbis will later hold that a Jewish male thirteen years or older was bound to observe the Mosaic law; the custom of a Bar Mitzvah ceremony, indicating that a boy is now undertaking to keep the law as a man, dates from the Middle Ages (Bar Mitzvah is Hebrew for "Son of the Law"—i.e., obligated to obey the law). Jesus did not go to Jerusalem because he was twelve years old; he went when he was twelve because it was the **custom** of his family to go every year and this particular year he was twelve.

43 **After they had completed its days**: the feast of Passover and Unleavened Bread lasted eight days (Lev 23:5–8). Pilgrims would normally come to Jerusalem several days early to be purified of anything that made them ritually unclean and prevented them from entering the Temple complex (John 11:55). Some Jews would leave after the second day of the feast, but Joseph and Mary remained until it was **completed**. Afterward, **as they were returning** home to Nazareth, **the boy Jesus remained behind in Jerusalem, but his parents did not know it**. Jesus did not tell Mary and Joseph that he was going to stay in Jerusalem.

Clean and unclean: See page 140

44 **Thinking that he was in the caravan, they journeyed for a day.** The word **caravan** means a traveling party. Jews traveling through Samaria

might encounter hostility (see 9:52–53); robbers preyed on travelers (see 10:30). Traveling in a group was safer as well as appropriate for a pilgrimage. Joseph and Mary traveled with their **relatives and acquaintances** from Nazareth. They assumed that Jesus was somewhere in the group on the return trip and did not become concerned until they stopped for the night. Then they **looked for him among their relatives and acquaintances,**

45 **but not finding him, they returned to Jerusalem to look for him.** They had traveled for a day before stopping, and it took them another day to get back to Jerusalem.

46 **After three days they found him**—presumably **three days** from the time they left Jerusalem: two days of travel and one day of searching. Jesus was **in the temple** precincts, **sitting in the midst of the teachers**. The colonnaded halls surrounding the perimeter of the Temple complex were used for a variety of purposes, including religious education and discussions (see 19:47; 20:1; 21:37–38; Acts 3:11–4:2; 5:25). **Teachers**—those who instructed in the law of Moses and its application—customarily sat while teaching (see 4:20–21), as did their students (see 10:39; Acts 22:3). Jesus is **sitting in the midst of the teachers, listening to them and asking them questions**. Jewish religious teachers relied more on dialogue than lectures, questioning their students and being questioned by them. Jesus behaves as any Jewish student of the time would, **listening** to **teachers** and **asking them questions**, and being in turn questioned by them.

Temple: See page 519

47 But Jesus is no ordinary student: **all who heard him were astounded at his understanding and his answers**. The **all** would have included the teachers and other students, and any who were eavesdropping on the discussion. They were amazed by Jesus' **understanding**, his intelligence and insight; his **answers** and observations were perceptive. Jesus grasped religious truths and issues astonishingly well for a twelve-year-old.

Luke summarized Jesus' early years in Nazareth by writing, "The child grew and became strong, filled with wisdom; and the favor of God was upon him" (2:40). His wisdom was a gift, a favor of God. Yet we should not neglect the role Mary and Joseph played in his upbringing:

he was raised by devout Jewish parents who spoke to him about God and God's ways.

48 Among those who were astounded by Jesus' interaction with teachers in the Temple precincts were his parents—but for an entirely different reason than others were astounded. **When his parents saw him, they were astonished, and his mother said to him, "Son, why have you done this to us?"** Why did you stay behind in Jerusalem without telling us? **Your father and I have been looking for you with great anxiety.** Mary refers to Joseph as Jesus' **father**; Joseph has the role of earthly father for Jesus. Jesus' apparent thoughtlessness caused Mary and Joseph to suffer **great anxiety**. The Greek word translated **great anxiety** has connotations of suffering pain or mental torment. Mary and Joseph have been worried about Jesus for the last two days, not sure what had happened to him. They are relieved to discover that he is fine, but they are distressed by what he has put them through. Simeon told Mary that she would be pierced by a sword (2:35), but she probably did not anticipate that Jesus himself would cause her pain.

In our speaking to one another, a lot depends on our tone of voice. What was Mary's tone when she said, **Son, why have you done this to us?** and spoke of the **great anxiety** she and Joseph experienced? Was she complaining and reproachful, or simply hurt and baffled?

For reflection: What do I imagine to be the tone of Mary's words?

49 **And he said to them, "Why were you looking for me? Did you not know that I must be in my Father's house?"** The implication of **did you not know** is, You should have known. But what should they have known? The Greek words translated **be in my Father's house** are literally "be in the of my Father," and translators must fill them out to make sense of them. Context suggests the sense, **be in my Father's house,** for Jesus is in the Temple, the dwelling place of God on earth. But the sense could also be, "be about my Father's affairs." The underlying meaning is the same: Jesus **must** be preoccupied with God and the service of God. **Must** conveys necessity, conformity to God's will. Jesus must put God first.

In the first words of Jesus recounted in Luke's Gospel, Jesus refers to God as **my Father:** he is aware that he enjoys a special relationship with God as his Father. Luke does not tell his readers how Jesus arrived at this knowledge. Yet Luke's readers know that Jesus' perception of himself is correct: he is the Son of God, conceived through the Holy Spirit (1:35).

Jesus tells Mary that she and Joseph should have known that he must devote himself to his Father's service; there was no reason for them to have been searching for him with anxiety. Yet the fact that they did so indicates that Jesus had never done anything like this before. They searched for him as any parents of a missing twelve-year-old would search for their child. Were they wrong to do so?

50 **But they did not understand what he said to them.** They are astonished by Jesus' remaining in Jerusalem without telling them and they do not understand his justification for doing so. They are baffled despite everything that has been said to one or both of them about Jesus: Gabriel's announcement that he would be conceived through the Holy Spirit and be the Son of God (1:31–35), Elizabeth's reference to him as her Lord (1:43), an angel's announcement that Jesus is savior, Messiah, and Lord (2:10–12, 17), and Simeon's recognition that Jesus would bring salvation to all peoples (2:26–32). Mary, and presumably Joseph as well, had taken these words to heart (2:19). Yet now they fail to understand Jesus when he says that he must make his Father his priority.

Their lack of understanding has a lesson for us: the identity of Jesus is a mystery beyond our comprehension. For Mary and Joseph the mystery surfaced in Jesus' dual relationships as a son: Son of his Father in heaven, and son of his mother and father in Nazareth. For us the mystery may be how Jesus can be both fully divine and fully human.

For reflection: What about Jesus is most a mystery for me?

51 **He went down with them and came to Nazareth, and was obedient to them.** God commanded that one honor one's father and mother (Exod 20:12): Jesus' obedience toward his heavenly Father included obedience toward his earthly parents. Perhaps Jesus learned from the anguish he caused Mary and Joseph by staying behind in Jerusalem and he took care to never cause them grief again. Perhaps the letter to the

Hebrews' statement that Jesus "learned obedience" (Heb 5:8) can apply to this incident and its aftermath.

Nazareth: See page 19

For reflection: Have I ever adjusted my behavior when I realized the grief I was causing others? What changes did I make?

Jesus' actions and words were matters for Mary to ponder. **His mother kept all these things in her heart**, as she had been doing since his birth (2:19), trying to understand the marvelous thing that God was doing through sending Jesus as her son.

For reflection: What do I imagine Mary's thoughts and ponderings to be at this point in Jesus' life?

52 Luke summarizes Jesus' growing up: **Jesus advanced [in] wisdom and age**. The word translated **age** can refer to height as well as age: Jesus grew taller as he got older, as we would expect any youth to do. He continued to grow in **wisdom** (see 2:40). He advanced in **favor before God and man**. Jesus continued to enjoy God's favor (see 2:40); his relatives and neighbors in Nazareth also looked upon him favorably. The Gospels give no indication, however, that the people of Nazareth realized the extraordinary nature of the boy growing up in their midst. When he is an adult they will think of him as the son of Joseph (4:22) and fail to realize that he is also the Son of God (see 4:28–29). Jesus, Mary, and Joseph apparently led what to all appearances were ordinary lives, not profoundly different from the lives of the several hundred others who lived in Nazareth.

The ordinariness of Jesus' life before he began his ministry deserves our reflection. For roughly thirty years (3:23) the Son of God lived as the son of Joseph and Mary, doing manual labor like his fellow villagers, observing God's laws and celebrating feasts, living a simple life in an unremarkable village, waiting for the time to arrive for him to set out on his life's mission.

For reflection: What lessons can I learn from the decades of Jesus' life before he began his ministry?

CHAPTER 3

ORIENTATION: *Luke began his work with an elegant sentence (1:1–4) and now employs another stately sentence to mark a new stage in God's unfolding plans.*

The Word of God Comes to John

¹ **In the fifteenth year of the reign of Tiberius Caesar, when Pontius Pilate was governor of Judea, and Herod was tetrarch of Galilee, and his brother Philip tetrarch of the region of Ituraea and Trachonitis, and Lysanias was tetrarch of Abilene, ² during the high priesthood of Annas and Caiaphas, the word of God came to John the son of Zechariah in the desert. ³ He went throughout [the] whole region of the Jordan, proclaiming a baptism of repentance for the forgiveness of sins, ⁴ as it is written in the book of the words of the prophet Isaiah:**

> **"A voice of one crying out in the desert:**
> **'Prepare the way of the Lord,**
> **make straight his paths.**
> ⁵ **Every valley shall be filled**
> **and every mountain and hill shall be made low.**
> **The winding roads shall be made straight,**
> **and the rough ways made smooth,**
> ⁶ **and all flesh shall see the salvation of God.' "**

Gospel parallels: Matt 3:1–3; Mark 1:2–4
OT: Isaiah 40:3–5
NT: Luke 1:13–17, 76–80; John 1:19–23

1   **In the fifteenth year of the reign of Tiberius Caesar**: ancient writers often used the reigns of emperors to date events, a practice found in the Old Testament (see Judith 1:1). The Roman emperor **Tiberius Caesar** assumed rule by stages; most scholars consider his **reign** to have begun during A.D. 14. The **fifteenth year** of his reign would be A.D. 28–29. At this time, **Pontius Pilate was governor of Judea**. After the death of Herod the Great in 4 B.C., Rome divided up his kingdom among three of his sons. One son, Archelaus, was made ruler over **Judea** and some adjacent

territories. He ruled so incompetently that Rome deposed him in A.D. 6, replacing him with a governor sent from Rome. **Pontius Pilate** was the **governor** from A.D. 26 to 36.

Roman Empire: See page 52
Pontius Pilate: See page 617
Judea: See page 40

The other two sons of Herod the Great who inherited parts of his kingdom enjoyed longer rules. **Herod** Antipas **was tetrarch of Galilee** from 4 B.C. until A.D. 39, when Rome removed him. The title **tetrarch** originally meant the ruler of a fourth part of a kingdom but came to be used for a ruler who was of lesser rank than king. **His brother Philip** was the **tetrarch of the region of Ituraea and Trachonitis** from 4 B.C. until his death in A.D. 34. This **region** lay northeast of Galilee and included the city of Bethsaida (see 9:10; 10:13).

Herod Antipas: See page 99
Galilee: See page 114

The fifteenth year of the reign of Tiberius Caesar was also the time when **Lysanias was tetrarch of Abilene,** a region to the west of Damascus. This is the only time **Lysanias** or **Abilene** are named in Scripture, and we do not know Luke's reason for mentioning them.

2 **During the high priesthood of Annas and Caiaphas**: only one high priest served at a time. **Annas** was high priest from A.D. 6 to 15 and may have been called high priest afterwards as an honorary title. He continued to be powerful even out of office and arranged for his son-in-law **Caiaphas** to be appointed high priest in A.D. 18. Caiaphas remained high priest until A.D. 36.

High priest, chief priests: See page 605

After indicating the year and the political and religious context, Luke announces that **the word of God came to John the son of Zechariah in the desert**. Luke has recounted how **John** was born to **Zechariah** and Elizabeth in fulfillment of Gabriel's promise (1:5-25, 57-80); John was to be a "prophet of the Most High" (1:76). Until the time came for John to begin his ministry, he lived in the **desert** (1:80).

The eastern portion of Judea around the Jordan River and Dead Sea lies far below sea level and is a hot, arid, and barren wilderness. In the fifteenth year of the reign of Tiberius Caesar, God calls John to begin his mission: **the word of God came to John**. The Old Testament uses this or similar expressions to describe the call of prophets, sometimes naming their fathers and telling who was king at the time (Jer 1:1–3; Hosea 1:1; Haggai 1:1; Zech 1:1). God called John to be a prophet—and more than a prophet (see 7:26).

For reflection: What mission has God given me? How did he make me aware of his call?

3 John heeded God's word and began his mission: **he went throughout [the] whole region of the Jordan, proclaiming a baptism of repentance for the forgiveness of sins**. The **whole region of the Jordan** means the land on both sides of the river. John attracted crowds who heard of him and came to him for baptism (see 3:7). John preached **a baptism of repentance for the forgiveness of sins**. The Greek word for "baptize" means to immerse or wash. Washing in water was one of the steps required to remove ritual uncleanness (see Lev 14:8–9; 15:5–27; 16:26–28; 17:15–16), and Jewish groups like the Pharisees and Essenes practiced additional ritual washings. John's washing, however, was **for**

BACKGROUND: CAIAPHAS He was high priest from A.D. 18 to 36—a long time for one man to hold this office. Caiaphas had good connections: his father-in-law was Annas, who served as high priest from A.D. 6 to 15, and who used his influence to obtain the high priesthood for five of his sons as well as for Caiaphas. More important, Caiaphas maintained a good relationship with the Roman prefects who governed Judea. These Roman governors appointed the high priest and could remove him from office at any time. In particular, Caiaphas seems to have cooperated with Pilate (who governed Judea from A.D. 26 to 35) despite Pilate's lack of sensitivity to Jewish religious concerns. Caiaphas may have been responsible for moving the sale of sacrificial animals into the Temple precincts. In any case, he profited from these commercial activities. Jesus' disruption of this commerce and talk of the Temple's destruction would have been reasons for Caiaphas to ask Pilate to get rid of Jesus. What are apparently the tomb and bones of Caiaphas were discovered by archaeologists in 1990; the bones are of a man who died in his sixties. *Related topics: Burial practices (page 646), High priest, chief priests (page 605).*

the forgiveness of sins. It was a **baptism of repentance**: John called men and women to reform their lives and seek God's forgiveness. Psalm 51 asks of God, "Wash away all my guilt; / from my sin cleanse me" (Psalm 51:4). John baptized or washed in water as a sign of God's washing away of sin. Unlike ritual washings that a person would do many times for himself or herself, John's washing was administered by John and was apparently a onetime event. John's practice was so distinctive that it gave him a nickname: the Baptist (7:20, 33; 9:19).

Repentance: See page 92

For reflection: Where am I most in need of washing from sin?

4 John's baptism of repentance is a fulfillment of what **is written in the book of the words of the prophet Isaiah: / "A voice of one crying out in the desert: / 'Prepare the way of the Lord, / make straight his paths.' "** Isaiah's prophecy was originally addressed to exiles in Babylon, telling them that their exile was nearing an end. The prophecy called for the preparation of a highway for God to use as he leads his people back to Jerusalem. John prepares **the way of the Lord** in a different sense. His father Zechariah prophesied that he would "go before the Lord to prepare his ways" by giving people "knowledge of salvation / through the forgiveness of their sins" (1:76-77). In Isaiah's prophecy, the way is prepared for the **Lord** God, but Zechariah's words indicate that John will prepare the way for the Lord Jesus.

Lord: See page 137

BACKGROUND: BAPTISM The Greek word *baptize* means to dip, plunge, immerse, drench, soak, or wash. Mark uses a variant of this word to describe the washing of dishes (Mark 7:4). There is some indication that John's baptism involved fully immersing a person in water: John 3:23 suggests that John needed ample water, and Mark 1:10 speaks of Jesus "coming up out of the water" after being baptized. In Matthew's Gospel, after his resurrection Jesus directs his disciples to "make disciples of all nations, baptizing them in the name of the Father, and of the Son, and of the holy Spirit" (Matt 28:19). In Acts, Peter exhorts the crowd that gathered on Pentecost to "repent and be baptized, every one of you, in the name of Jesus Christ for the forgiveness of your sins; and you will receive the gift of the holy Spirit" (Acts 2:38). Christian baptism is "the bath of rebirth / and renewal by the holy Spirit" (Titus 3:5) that allows one to enter the kingdom of God (John 3:5).

A voice cries out:
In the desert prepare the way of the LORD!
    Make straight in the wasteland a highway for
        our God!
Every valley shall be filled in,
    every mountain and hill shall be made low;
The rugged land shall be made a plain,
    the rough country, a broad valley.
Then the glory of the LORD shall be revealed,
    and all mankind shall see it together;
    for the mouth of the LORD has spoken.
Isaiah 40:3–5

5 Isaiah called for a level and smooth highway to be constructed between Babylon and Jerusalem: **every valley shall be filled / and every mountain and hill shall be made low. / The winding roads shall be made straight, / and the rough ways made smooth**. John's building materials are not rock but women and men. Filling in valleys can be an image for lifting up the lowly (see 1:52) and bringing mountains low an image for throwing down the proud. The word translated **winding** means crooked and can have the sense of corrupt (Luke uses the word in this sense in Acts 2:40). Straightening the crooked and smoothing the rough can be images for removing sin, which John does through his baptism of repentance, preparing a people fit for the Lord (see 1:17).

For reflection: What needs straightening out in my life?

6 Isaiah's prophecy ends with a promise: **and all flesh shall see the salvation of God**. The expression **all flesh** is an idiom for the human race. Isaiah spoke literally of all flesh seeing the glory of the Lord revealed through Israel's return from exile (Isaiah 40:5). Luke quotes a Greek translation of this prophecy that characterizes the return from exile as **salvation**—a rescue, a saving act of God. The salvation that John announces is not rescue from exile but from sin; salvation ultimately means being baptized with the Holy Spirit (see 3:16; Acts 2:38). In Luke's use of Isaiah's prophecy, **see** has the sense of experience: **all flesh** will experience God's salvation. This is the second time that Luke's Gospel

speaks of salvation being extended to everyone, including Gentiles (see 2:30–32).

The Fruit of Repentance

⁷ **He said to the crowds who came out to be baptized by him, "You brood of vipers! Who warned you to flee from the coming wrath?** ⁸ **Produce good fruits as evidence of your repentance; and do not begin to say to yourselves, 'We have Abraham as our father,' for I tell you, God can raise up children to Abraham from these stones.** ⁹ **Even now the ax lies at the root of the trees. Therefore every tree that does not produce good fruit will be cut down and thrown into the fire."**

¹⁰ **And the crowds asked him, "What then should we do?"** ¹¹ **He said to them in reply, "Whoever has two cloaks should share with the person who has none. And whoever has food should do like-wise."** ¹² **Even tax collectors came to be baptized and they said to him, "Teacher, what should we do?"** ¹³ **He answered them, "Stop collecting more than what is prescribed."** ¹⁴ **Soldiers also asked him, "And what is it that we should do?" He told them, "Do not practice extortion, do not falsely accuse anyone, and be satisfied with your wages."**

Gospel parallels: Matt 3:7–10
OT: Isaiah 13:9
NT: Luke 13:6–9; John 8:33

7   John **said to the crowds who came out to be baptized by him:** people **came out** from towns to the place along the Jordan River where John was baptizing (see 3:2–3). Although these **crowds** came **to be baptized by him**, John's greeting is harsh: **You brood of vipers!** To call some-one the children of venomous snakes is sure to get their attention, and that is apparently what John is trying to do. He asks those seeking his baptism, **Who warned you to flee from the coming wrath?** John's question presumes that his listeners know about **the coming wrath**. Old Testament prophecies foretold a "day of the Lord" when God would come in judgment and display his **wrath** against sin and sinners (Isaiah 13:9; Ezek 7:10–13, 19; Zeph 1:14–15; 2:2). The sense of John's question seems

to be, who told you that by being baptized you could escape God's wrath? Calling them a **brood of vipers** indicates that John believes that their repentance is feigned; they are seeking baptism merely as a ritual that will protect them from God.

> Lo, the day of the LORD comes,
> > cruel, with wrath and burning anger;
> To lay waste the land
> > and destroy the sinners within it!
>
> Isaiah 13:9

8 John tells them that if they are sincere in their repentance, then they should **produce good fruits as evidence of your repentance**. In biblical idiom, **fruits** means deeds. The word translated **as evidence** is literally "worthy" and has the sense of fitting or appropriate. **Repentance** means a change of mind and behavior. If those seeking John's "baptism of repentance" (3:3) have truly repented, then their deeds should show it.

BACKGROUND: THE DAY OF THE LORD Old Testament prophecy is filled with expectations that God will act to vanquish evil. Some expectations are expressed in terms of "the day of the Lord" or "that day" or "the day when" God will act, or similar expressions. Originally "the day of the Lord" meant a time when God would vindicate his people by defeating their enemies. But Amos proclaimed that it would be a time when God would judge his own sinful people (Amos 5:18–20). Other prophets issued similar warnings, sometimes with the promise that God would restore his people after punishing them. Some prophecies use cosmic imagery to convey how momentous "the day of the Lord" would be (Isaiah 13:9–10; Joel 2:10–11; 3:3–4). Isaiah prophesied that that day would have worldwide consequences, not only restoring Israel but bringing a reign of justice to all nations (Isaiah 2:2–4; 19:18–25; 25:6–9). Most prophecies envision "the day of the Lord" as a time when God will act directly; a few prophecies portray God raising up a descendant of David to rule God's people (Isaiah 11:10; Jer 23:5–6; 30:7–9; 33:14–18; Zech 3:8–10). "The day of the Lord" thus carries a range of meanings in the Old Testament, some of which influenced expectations of the Messiah and the establishment of the kingdom of God, although "the day of the Lord" prophecies do not use these terms. In the letters of the New Testament, "the day of the Lord" takes on the meaning of "the day of the Lord Jesus Christ," when he will judge the human race and establish the final reign of God (see 1 Cor 1:8; Phil 1:6, 10; 2:16). *Related topics: Cosmic signs (page 565), Jewish expectations at the time of Jesus (page 69), Judgment (page 327).*

There is no room for complacency; John warns the crowds, **do not begin to say to yourselves, "We have Abraham as our father."** Jews thought that descent from Abraham gave them special status (see John 8:33): they were God's chosen people (Deut 7:6–7; 14:2). John does not deny God's choice but proclaims that God is able to choose others as well: **for I tell you, God can raise up children to Abraham from these stones**. The Judean wilderness is rocky and John may have pointed to **these stones** as a visual aid. Nothing is impossible for God (1:37); God can make **stones** into **children**. John may have been punning: the Aramaic words for **children** and **stones** are similar. If God can turn stones into children of Abraham, then being a descendant of Abraham is no grounds for complacency.

It may have occurred to Luke's Gentile readers that they were in a sense the stones that John was talking about: God had turned them into his children. We may take John's words as an assurance that God can change our hearts, however stony (see Ezek 11:19; 36:26), into hearts of love.

9 John tells a parable about fruit trees to convey the urgency of repentance. It begins with an image: **even now the ax lies at the root of the trees**. A man about to chop down a tree might lay the head of his ax at the spot where he wanted to chop, measuring his stroke. Felling a tree is an image for God's judgment (Isaiah 32:19; Dan 4:11). John proclaims that **even now** the ax is in position; God is about to act. **Therefore every tree that does not produce good fruit will be cut down and thrown into the fire.** An olive or fig tree that does not yield **good fruit** is a

---

BACKGROUND: REPENTANCE In the Old Testament, the Hebrew word used for "repent" means to turn back or return: "Return, O Israel, to the LORD, your God" (Hosea 14:2). The New Testament expresses repentance differently: the Greek word translated "repentance" literally means "a change of mind." A change of mind means recognizing that one's views are wrong or inadequate. If wrong views lead to wrong actions, then a change of mind should result in a change of behavior. Summing up all of this is the notion of conversion, a profound reorientation of oneself. When John the Baptist and Jesus call for repentance, they are calling for an acceptance of the messages they proclaim and for life changes on the basis of their messages. Repentance is not simply a matter of feeling sorry but also of adopting new attitudes and new behavior.

waste of space and water and might as well **be cut down** (see 13:6–9) **and thrown into the fire**—used for firewood. So too, those who do not produce "good fruits" as evidence of their repentance (verse 8) will fare badly at God's coming judgment. **Fire** is used by prophets as a symbol of God's punishment (Isaiah 66:15, 24; Jer 11:16; Ezek 15:6–7; Zeph 1:18; 3:8). Jews have the privilege of being descendants of Abraham, but they will nonetheless be judged by God on the basis of their conduct—and punished if their lives have been fruitless.

For reflection: What fruit have I produced for God?

10 **And the crowds asked him, "What then should we do?"** The crowds seem moved by John's words and want to know what they should do to demonstrate repentance. What good fruit should they bear?

The crowd's question is one that we can pose to ourselves whenever we read Scripture. What should I **do** in light of what I read?

11 **He said to them in reply, "Whoever has two cloaks should share with the person who has none."** Although the New American Bible has John speaking of **cloaks,** the Greek word means "tunics" (which is how it is translated at 6:29 and 9:3). A tunic was an inner garment, worn under a cloak. Having **two** tunics means having a change of clothing— hardly an extravagance. Nevertheless, **whoever** has two tunics (and that would be just about everyone) should give one of them to a person who has no tunic. **And whoever has food should do likewise.** John doesn't specify the amount of food but indicates that **whoever** has something to eat should share it with whoever has nothing to eat. Food and clothing are the essentials of life (see 1 Tim 6:8); by mentioning them John conveys that those who have the means to survive should share with those who do not. John gives no justification for making this demand but could have cited a commandment ("You shall love your neighbor as yourself"—Lev 19:18; see also Deut 15:11).

Clothing: See page 175

It is worth noting what John does not say. He does not demand that the crowds wear sackcloth and sit in ashes to express their repentance.

He does not invite them to become his disciples. He does not tell them to offer more sacrifices in the Temple. Rather, he tells them to share what they have with those who are in need. This is the good fruit that is evidence of true repentance; this is how they will avoid being thrown into fire.

> *For reflection: How well do I live up to what John requires? How might I be more generous?*

12 **Even tax collectors came to be baptized.** Tax collectors were commonly viewed as sinners (see 5:30; 7:34; 15:1-2); the tax system fostered corruption. **They said to him, "Teacher, what should we do?"** They call John a **Teacher**—someone who is able to instruct them. They ask what they, as tax collectors, need to do beyond sharing what they have with those in need. They tacitly acknowledge that more may be required of them, given their profession.

13 **He answered them, "Stop collecting more than what is prescribed."** The occupational temptation of tax collectors was **collecting more** than was due in taxes and then pocketing the difference. John tells them to collect only the **prescribed** amount. John does not tell them to find another line of work (no occupation is free of temptations) but to behave honestly.

BACKGROUND: TAX COLLECTORS Those who collected taxes were almost universally scorned by Jews in Palestine at the time of Jesus and were spoken of in the same breath with sinners (Matt 11:19). They were despised for several reasons. First, the tax system lent itself to abuse. One arrangement was to auction off the right to collect taxes to the highest bidder and then allow the tax collector to keep anything he could collect over that amount. That was a license for greed and extortion, and many tax collectors took advantage of it. Second, there were many forms of taxation, and together they extracted a sizable portion of the income of ordinary people—up to 40 percent, by some estimates. Third, Jewish tax collectors were agents, directly or indirectly, of Rome. After about a century of Jewish self-rule, Rome had taken away Jewish independence in 63 B.C. and had imposed tribute or taxes. As a result of these factors, tax collectors were considered unscrupulous extortionists and were despised for working on behalf of a foreign power and draining people's livelihoods.

---

14 Soldiers also asked him, "And what is it that we should do?" Like the tax collectors, they ask what is required of them beyond sharing what they have. Luke does not say whether these **soldiers** are Jews or Gentiles; both served in the army of Herod Antipas, who ruled a region that encompassed Galilee and a portion of the area east of the Jordan River. John **told them, "Do not practice extortion, do not falsely accuse anyone."** The word translated **extortion** means to shake violently and has the connotation of extorting money by force—we would say, shake down someone. **Falsely accuse** has the sense of extorting money by lodging false charges. John tells the soldiers to **be satisfied with your wages**. The word for **wages** means provisions or money for rations. Soldiers were poorly paid but could supplement their income by strong arm tactics or blackmail. John forbids such extortion and tells them to be satisfied with what they have. Not wanting more is the first step toward sharing what we have with those who have less.

John's response to the crowd indicates that helping others is the repentance required of everyone; his responses to tax collectors and soldiers show that repentance has specific requirements in particular situations. Tax collectors and soldiers were tempted to enrich themselves at the expense of others—the opposite of helping others. Each situation has its own way in which the crooked must be made straight (see 3:5).

For reflection: What in my situation poses the most dangerous temptation for me?

John Announces the Coming One

15 Now the people were filled with expectation, and all were asking in their hearts whether John might be the Messiah. 16 John answered them all, saying, "I am baptizing you with water, but one mightier than I is coming. I am not worthy to loosen the thongs of his sandals. He will baptize you with the holy Spirit and fire. 17 His winnowing fan is in his hand to clear his threshing floor and to gather the wheat into his barn, but the chaff he will burn with unquenchable fire." 18 Exhorting them in many other ways, he preached good news to the people. 19 Now Herod the tetrarch, who had been censured by him because of Herodias, his brother's wife,

and because of all the evil deeds Herod had committed, **²⁰** added still another to these by [also] putting John in prison.

Gospel parallels: Matt 3:11–12; 14:3–4; Mark 1:7–8; 6:17–18;

John 1:19–20, 26–27, 33; 3:28

OT: Mal 3:2–3

NT: Luke 3:7–9

15 **Now the people were filled with expectation.** Many Jews expected that God would act once and for all to vanquish evil; John's preaching increased their **expectation**. He announced that "even now the ax lies at the root of the trees." God was about to judge his people and punish the unrepentant (3:7–9). They **all were asking in their hearts whether John might be the Messiah**. The **heart** was considered the seat of thought and willing and emotion; they pondered in their thoughts whether **John** might be **the Messiah**. John had not done the things expected of a messiah. He had, however, proclaimed that God was about to set things right, and many expected that God would do so by sending the Messiah. If the time was ripe for the coming of the Messiah, **might** John himself be the Messiah?

Jewish expectations at the time of Jesus: See page 69

Messiah, Christ: See page 257

16 **John answered them all, saying, "I am baptizing you with water."** The sense of John's words is, I am baptizing you *only* with water. **But one mightier than I is coming**—so much mightier that John proclaims **I am not worthy to loosen the thongs of his sandals**. Untying sandal straps was a lowly task that slaves did for their masters. John says that he is **not worthy** to carry out even a menial task for the one who is coming. To those who wonder whether John might be the Messiah, his response implies that the coming one, not John, is the Messiah. John does not name the coming one, but Luke's readers know that it is Jesus.

The one who is coming is **mightier** than John because, while John baptizes only with water, **he will baptize you with the holy Spirit and fire**. John's listeners would have understood **baptize . . . with the holy Spirit** to mean immersing or washing someone with the Holy Spirit. Prophecies spoke of the Spirit being poured out, as water is poured out, on God's people (Isaiah 32:15; 44:3; Ezek 39:29) and even upon all mankind (Joel 3:1). Prophecies also spoke of God washing or cleansing his people (Isaiah 4:4; Ezek 36:25). John may have coined the phrase, **baptize . . . with the holy Spirit,** but the notions of being washed over and cleansed by the Spirit would have been familiar to Jews. There was no previous expectation that the Messiah would wash and cleanse with the Holy Spirit, although Isaiah spoke of the Spirit of God resting on an ideal future ruler descended from David (Isaiah 11:1–9).

Baptism: See page 88

The Spirit: See page 100

What John proclaims about the coming one raises questions. What kind of person could have the power to baptize with the Holy Spirit? Who but God could send God's Spirit to wash and purify?

For reflection: What does it tell me about Jesus that he is able to baptize with the Holy Spirit?

The coming one will baptize with the Holy Spirit **and fire**. While John usually uses **fire** as an image for punishment (see 3:9, 17), a prophecy about "the day of the Lord" speaks of purification by fire, as impurities are refined out of precious metals (Mal 3:2–3; see also Zech 13:9). That is likely the sense when **fire** is spoken of in conjunction with the **Holy Spirit**. The coming one will wash God's people in the Holy Spirit and fire, burning out their impurities, cleansing them. **Fire** may also have another association for Luke. Jesus' disciples gathered together on Pentecost, and "there appeared to them tongues as of fire, which parted and came to rest on each one of them. And they were all filled with the holy Spirit" (Acts 2:3–4)—a fulfillment of Jesus' promise, "John baptized with water, but in a few days you will be baptized with the holy Spirit" (Acts 1:5).

> But who will endure the day of his coming?
> And who can stand when he appears?
> For he is like the refiner's fire,
>   or like the fuller's lye.
> He will sit refining and purifying [silver],
>   and he will purify the sons of Levi,

> *Refining them like gold or like silver*
> *that they may offer due sacrifice to the* LORD.
> Mal 3:2–3

For reflection: What has the Holy Spirit done to cleanse and purify me?

17 John continues to speak of the coming one: **his winnowing fan is in his hand to clear his threshing floor.** After a grain crop was harvested, it was laid on a **threshing floor** of rock or packed earth and beaten with flails to loosen the grain from the stalks. The mixture of grain and stalks was tossed into the air with a **winnowing fan** or forked shovel. The wind blew aside the lighter stalks; the heavier grain fell back onto the threshing floor to be collected and stored in a **barn.** The stalks or **chaff** were swept up and used as fuel for cooking fires. So too, John proclaims, the coming one would execute God's judgment, sorting out good from evil. He will **gather the wheat into his barn**, gathering the repentant to himself, **but the chaff he will burn with unquenchable fire**. Cooking fires burn out, but John speaks of **unquenchable fire**, echoing Scripture passages that use inextinguishable fire as an image for the finality of God's punishment (Judith 16:17; Isaiah 66:24).

18 **Exhorting them in many other ways, he preached good news to the people.** Luke summarizes John's preaching as an exhortation and a proclamation of good news. John warned of God's punishment, exhorting his listeners to turn away from their sins so the coming one could gather them to himself. His message is **good news** for them, if they heed it.

Gospel, good news: See page 59

For reflection: How do I respond to calls to repentance? Do I accept calls to repentance as good news for me?

19 Luke uses a flash forward to wrap up the incident with John the Baptist before beginning the next, as he does with other incidents (see 1:56, 80). **Now Herod the tetrarch, who had been censured by him because of Herodias, his brother's wife**: the word translated **censored** can refer to a public reprimand (which is how it is used at 1 Tim 5:20). John censored Herod Antipas **because of Herodias**, whom Herod had married in

A.D. 26 after she had previously been **his brother's wife**. Such marriages were forbidden by the law of Moses (Lev 18:16; 20:21). John reproved Herod Antipas for his illicit marriage and for **all the evil deeds Herod had committed**. Since many people esteemed John as a prophet (see 20:6), his denunciations could have turned people against Herod Antipas.

20 Herod Antipas **added still another** evil deed **to these by [also] putting John in prison**. John will not appear on the scene again in Luke's Gospel, although we will hear from him (7:18–19). We will learn that Herod Antipas beheaded John (9:9), but Luke will not recount the event. John has fulfilled his role as a prophet giving "knowledge of salvation / through the forgiveness of their sins," going before Jesus to prepare the way for him (1:76–77). Since John's mission is accomplished, Luke moves the spotlight from John to Jesus.

ORIENTATION: *The first glimpse Luke gives us of the adult Jesus is of him at prayer.*

Father, Son, Holy Spirit
²¹ After all the people had been baptized and Jesus also had been baptized and was praying, heaven was opened ²² and the holy Spirit descended upon him in bodily form like a dove. And a voice came from heaven, "You are my beloved Son; with you I am well pleased."
Gospel parallels: Matt 3:13–17; Mark 1:9–11
NT: Luke 1:31–35; 3:7, 16; 4:14–20; 9:35; Acts 10:37–38

BACKGROUND: HEROD ANTIPAS A son of Herod the Great, Herod Antipas ruled Galilee as Jesus was growing up and during his public ministry. Herod Antipas's mother, Malthace, one of his father's ten wives, was a Samaritan. After the death of Herod the Great in 4 B.C., Rome divided his kingdom among three of his sons. Herod Antipas was made tetrarch of Galilee and of a region east of the Jordan River called Perea; he is sometimes called Herod the Tetrarch in the Gospels and sometimes simply Herod. The title "tetrarch" originally meant the ruler of a fourth part of a kingdom but later was used for a ruler who was of lesser rank than king. Herod Antipas executed John the Baptist, but Galilee was generally tranquil during his more than forty years of rule. Herod Antipas was deposed by Rome for political intrigue and exiled in A.D. 39. *Related topic: Herod the Great (page 7).*

---

21 After a gap of roughly two decades from the time Jesus was twelve (see 2:42 and 3:23), Luke resumes his account of Jesus, picking it up **after all the people had been baptized** by John (see 3:7) **and Jesus also had been baptized.** Luke does not describe the baptism itself nor explain why Jesus sought John's baptism. Luke's interest is in what happened afterwards, when Jesus **was praying.** Luke will describe Jesus praying (5:16; 6:12; 9:18, 28-29; 11:1; 22:41-45), from the time he first appears on the scene as an adult until his dying words (23:34, 46). Jesus will instruct his followers to "pray always without becoming weary" (18:1), imitating his example.

For reflection: Where does prayer rank in my daily priorities? What might I do to become a more faithful person of prayer?

As Jesus was praying, **heaven was opened**. The Hebrew and Greek words translated **heaven** also mean sky, which was figuratively thought of as the dwelling place of God (11:13; see 1 Kings 8:30; 2 Macc 3:39; Psalm 2:4; 103:19; 123:1). The Old Testament speaks of heaven opening for God to act or reveal himself (Isaiah 63:19; Ezek 1:1; see also Acts 7:56). **Heaven was opened** while Jesus was at prayer so that God could do or reveal something.

BACKGROUND: THE SPIRIT The opening verses of the Old Testament speak of a "mighty wind" (Gen 1:2) that sweeps over the waters as God begins his work of creation. The phrase translated "mighty wind" might also be translated "Spirit of God," for the same Hebrew word means "wind," "breath," or "spirit," and the Hebrew word taken to mean "mighty" can be translated as "divine" or "of God." It is the breath of God breathed into humans that gives life (Gen 2:7). When the Old Testament speaks of the Spirit of God, it generally refers to God's influence or power at work, as in, for example, the inspiration of prophets (Isaiah 61:1). The Spirit of God is not yet thought of as a person in the Old Testament. The New Testament bears witness to a deeper experience and understanding of the Spirit. Paul speaks of the Spirit many times in his letters but writes more about what the Spirit does than who the Spirit is. In the Gospel of John, Jesus speaks of the Spirit as the Paraclete, or Advocate, who will carry on his work (John 14:16-17, 26; 15:26; 16:7-11). The Gospel of Matthew ends with Jesus' instruction that people be baptized "in the name of the Father, and of the Son, and of the holy Spirit" (Matt 28:19). The Council of Constantinople in A.D. 381 proclaimed the Spirit to be "the holy, the lordly and life-giving one, proceeding forth from the Father, co-worshiped and co-glorified with Father and Son, the one who spoke through the prophets."

---

22 **and the holy Spirit descended upon him.** Jesus was conceived through the Holy Spirit (1:35) so this is not his initial reception of the Spirit. In Jesus' first public pronouncement recounted in Luke's Gospel, he will interpret the Holy Spirit's coming upon him as an anointing and empowerment for ministry (4:14–21; see also Acts 10:37–38). He who will baptize with the Holy Spirit (3:16) preeminently possesses the Spirit. Luke writes that the Spirit descended upon Jesus **in bodily form,** emphasizing the reality of what happened. The Holy Spirit appearing **like a dove** is unique to Jesus' experience after his baptism; nowhere else in Scripture is the Spirit represented as a dove.

And a voice came from heaven, "You are my beloved Son." The angel Gabriel told Mary that Jesus would be conceived through the Holy Spirit and would be called the Son of God (1:35). Now God speaks from heaven and tells Jesus, **You are my beloved Son.** The word translated **beloved** can have the connotation of "only." Jesus is uniquely the Son of God. God tells Jesus, **with you I am well pleased**. God delights in Jesus. This is not Jesus' first realization that God is his Father (see 2:49). Yet God's words, coming with the descent of the Holy Spirit while Jesus is in prayer, mark a decisive point in Jesus' life. Led by the Spirit, Jesus will withdraw into the wilderness (4:1–13) and then, again led by the Spirit, he will set out on his life's mission (4:14–15). His mission will be rooted in his identity as the Son of God, and he will carry it out anointed by the Holy Spirit.

Son of God: See page 25

For reflection: What does this incident tell me about Jesus? About his relationship with the Father and the Spirit?

ORIENTATION: *Luke traces Jesus' genealogy back for seventy-seven generations. About half of his ancestors are mentioned only here in Scripture.*

Son of Adam, Son of God
23 **When Jesus began his ministry he was about thirty years of age. He was the son, as was thought, of Joseph, the son of Heli,**
24 **the son of Matthat, the son of Levi, the son of Melchi, the son**

of Jannai, the son of Joseph, ²⁵ the son of Mattathias, the son of Amos, the son of Nahum, the son of Esli, the son of Naggai, ²⁶ the son of Maath, the son of Mattathias, the son of Semein, the son of Josech, the son of Joda, ²⁷ the son of Joanan, the son of Rhesa, the son of Zerubbabel, the son of Shealtiel, the son of Neri, ²⁸ the son of Melchi, the son of Addi, the son of Cosam, the son of Elmadam, the son of Er, ²⁹ the son of Joshua, the son of Eliezer, the son of Jorim, the son of Matthat, the son of Levi, ³⁰ the son of Simeon, the son of Judah, the son of Joseph, the son of Jonam, the son of Eliakim, ³¹ the son of Melea, the son of Menna, the son of Mattatha, the son of Nathan, the son of David, ³² the son of Jesse, the son of Obed, the son of Boaz, the son of Sala, the son of Nahshon, ³³ the son of Amminadab, the son of Admin, the son of Arni, the son of Hezron, the son of Perez, the son of Judah, ³⁴ the son of Jacob, the son of Isaac, the son of Abraham, the son of Terah, the son of Nahor, ³⁵ the son of Serug, the son of Reu, the son of Peleg, the son of Eber, the son of Shelah, ³⁶ the son of Cainan, the son of Arphaxad, the son of Shem, the son of Noah, the son of Lamech, ³⁷ the son of Methuselah, the son of Enoch, the son of Jared, the son of Mahalaleel, the son of Cainan, ³⁸ the son of Enos, the son of Seth, the son of Adam, the son of God.

Gospel parallels: Matt 1:1–17
OT: Gen 5:1–32; 11:10–27; 1 Chron 1:1–34; 2:1–15; 3:1–5

23 When Jesus began his ministry he was about thirty years of age. Now Jesus **began** his life's mission, with the anointing of the Holy Spirit, carrying out his call as the Son of God (3:22). Luke writes that Jesus is **about thirty years of age**: Luke knows only approximately when Jesus was born.

While Jesus is the Son of God (3:22), he also has a human identity. Israelites used genealogies to specify one's descent from a particular line of ancestors and therefore one's identity (Gen 5; 10; 11:10–32; 1 Chron 1—3). Luke briefly indicated the ancestral identity of Zechariah and Elizabeth (1:5), but he lays out Jesus' family tree in detail. **He was the son, as was thought, of Joseph.** Luke qualifies Joseph's fatherhood with an **as was thought**: Joseph was commonly assumed to be the father of Jesus by those who did not know that Jesus was conceived through the Holy Spirit (see 4:22). From a legal point of view, however, Jesus was Joseph's son and heir and, like him (1:27; 2:4), a descendant of David. Joseph was **the son of Heli**, who is not otherwise mentioned in Scripture. Also otherwise unmentioned in Scripture are the ancestors that follow in Luke's list until we reach Zerubbabel in verse 27.

24 Heli, the father of Joseph, was **the son of Matthat, the son of Levi, the son of Melchi, the son of Jannai, the son of Joseph,**

25 **the son of Mattathias, the son of Amos, the son of Nahum, the son of Esli, the son of Naggai,**

26 **the son of Maath, the son of Mattathias, the son of Semein, the son of Josech, the son of Joda,**

27 **the son of Joanan, the son of Rhesa, the son of Zerubbabel, the son of Shealtiel.** We know that **Zerubbabel, the son of Shealtiel,** was among those who returned from exile and helped rebuild the Temple in Jerusalem (Ezra 3:2, 8; 5:2; Neh 12:1; Hag 1:14). Their ancestors, however, are otherwise unmentioned in Scripture until we come to Nathan in verse 31. Shealtiel was **the son of Neri,**

28 **the son of Melchi, the son of Addi, the son of Cosam, the son of Elmadam, the son of Er,**

29 **the son of Joshua, the son of Eliezer, the son of Jorim, the son of Matthat, the son of Levi,**

30 **the son of Simeon, the son of Judah, the son of Joseph, the son of Jonam, the son of Eliakim,**

> *For reflection: What might it tell me about Jesus that we know so little about many of his ancestors?*

31 **the son of Melea, the son of Menna, the son of Mattatha, the son of Nathan, the son of David.** With **Nathan** and **David** we begin to find familiar names; most of the remainder of Jesus' ancestors are mentioned

in the Old Testament. **Nathan** was the third son born to King **David** after he began to rule in Jerusalem (2 Sam 5:14; 1 Chron 3:4–5; 14:3–4). Luke has emphasized that Jesus is of the "house of David" (1:27, 69; 2:4; see also 1:32) and now has laid out his genealogy stretching back to **David** through Joseph's legal paternity.

32 David was **the son of Jesse** (1 Sam 16:1, 11–13; 1 Chron 2:13–15), **the son of Obed** (Ruth 4:17; 1 Chron 2:12), **the son of Boaz,** the husband of Ruth (Ruth 4:13–17; 1 Chron 2:12), **the son of Sala** (Salma in 1 Chron 2:11), **the son of Nahshon** (1 Chron 2:11), who helped Moses take a census of the Israelites in the wilderness (Num 1:1–7); Nahshon's sister Elisheba was Aaron's wife (Exod 6:23).

33 Nahshon was **the son of Amminadab** (1 Chron 2:10), **the son of Admin** (otherwise unknown), **the son of Arni** (otherwise unknown), **the son of Hezron,** who migrated from Canaan to Egypt with his great-grandfather Jacob (Gen 46:8, 12), **the son of Perez** (Gen 46:12; 1 Chron 2:5), **the son of Judah** (Gen 38:29; 1 Chron 2:3–4), whose descendants are the tribe of Judah, one of the twelve tribes of Israel.

34 Judah was **the son of Jacob** (Gen 29:35; 1 Chron 2:1); Jacob was given the name Israel (Gen 32:29). Jacob was **the son of Isaac** (Gen 25:26; 1 Chron 1:34), who was **the son of Abraham** (Gen 21:2–3; 1 Chron 1:28). God called **Abraham** to be the father of a great people (Gen 12:2); Jesus, as a descendant of Abraham and Jacob, is a member of the people God chose to be his own (Deut 7:6–8; 14:2). Abraham was **the son of Terah** (Gen 11:26), **the son of Nahor** (Gen 11:24),

35 **the son of Serug** (Gen 11:22), **the son of Reu** (Gen 11:20), **the son of Peleg** (Gen 11:18), **the son of Eber** (Gen 11:16), **the son of Shelah** (Gen 11:14),

36 **the son of Cainan** (not mentioned in the Hebrew text of Genesis but found in its Greek translation), **the son of Arphaxad** (Gen 11:12 calls him Arpachshad and lists him as the father of the Shelah of verse 35), **the son of Shem** (Gen 11:10), **the son of Noah** (Gen 5:32), **the son of Lamech** (Gen 5:28–29),

37 **the son of Methuselah** (Gen 5:25), **the son of Enoch** (Gen 5:21), **the son of Jared** (Gen 5:18), **the son of Mahalaleel** (called Mehalalel at Gen 5:15), **the son of Cainan** (called Kenan at Gen 5:12),

38 **the son of Enos** (called Enosh at Gen 5:9), **the son of Seth** (Gen 5:6), **the** third **son of Adam** (Gen 4:25). Luke traces Jesus' family tree all the way back to **Adam** to proclaim that Jesus shares a common ancestry with the entire human race. Jesus, of the house of David, will bring salvation to the descendants of Abraham, and will also be a "light for revelation to the Gentiles" (2:32), extending what God had begun in Abraham to all the descendants of Adam.

Luke concludes his genealogy by calling Adam **the son of God**, indicating that his origin was from God (Gen 1:26–27; 2:7). By calling Adam the son of God immediately after God has called Jesus his beloved Son (3:22), Luke conveys that Jesus has a dual heritage as a son of God. God created the human race; all women and men are his progeny, his children. Jesus fully shares the human condition as a son of Adam. Yet Jesus is also uniquely **the son of God**, conceived through the Holy Spirit (1:35), beloved by and pleasing to his Father (3:22).

Son of God: See page 25

For reflection: What is the significance of Jesus' genealogy for me?

CHAPTER 4

ORIENTATION: *Before Luke paused to provide Jesus' genealogy (3:23–38), he recounted the Holy Spirit's descending on Jesus and God's proclaiming him to be his beloved Son (3:22). Luke now tells what happened next.*

The Testing of the Son of God

¹ **Filled with the holy Spirit, Jesus returned from the Jordan and was led by the Spirit into the desert** ² **for forty days, to be tempted by the devil. He ate nothing during those days, and when they were over he was hungry.** ³ **The devil said to him, "If you are the Son of God, command this stone to become bread."** ⁴ **Jesus answered him, "It is written, 'One does not live by bread alone.'"** ⁵ **Then he took him up and showed him all the kingdoms of the world in a single instant.** ⁶ **The devil said to him, "I shall give to you all this power and their glory; for it has been handed over to me, and I may give it to whomever I wish.** ⁷ **All this will be yours, if you worship me."** ⁸ **Jesus said to him in reply, "It is written:**

'You shall worship the Lord, your God,
and him alone shall you serve.'"

⁹ **Then he led him to Jerusalem, made him stand on the parapet of the temple, and said to him, "If you are the Son of God, throw yourself down from here,** ¹⁰ **for it is written:**

'He will command his angels concerning you,
to guard you,'

¹¹ **and:**

'With their hands they will support you,
lest you dash your foot against a stone.'"

¹² **Jesus said to him in reply, "It also says, 'You shall not put the Lord, your God, to the test.'"** ¹³ **When the devil had finished every temptation, he departed from him for a time.**

Gospel parallels: Matt 4:1–11; Mark 1:12–13
OT: Deut 6:13, 16; 8:3; Psalm 91:11–12
NT: Luke 3:21–22; Heb 2:14–18; 4:15

1   **Filled with the holy Spirit**, who descended upon him while he was at prayer after being baptized (3:21–22), **Jesus returned from the Jordan River**. The word **returned** has the sense of departed; Jesus left the Jordan **and was led by the Spirit into the desert**, the rocky wilderness near the Jordan River and the Dead Sea. If we set aside Jesus' genealogy (3:23–38), Luke has mentioned the **Spirit** three times in two verses, all in conjunction with Jesus. This repetition emphasizes the presence of the Holy Spirit in Jesus; he is **filled with** and **led by** the **Spirit**. He will carry out his mission as the Son of God with the power and promptings of the Spirit of God.

The Spirit: See page 100

For reflection: How have I experienced the promptings and power of the Holy Spirit in my life?

Jesus **was led by the Spirit into the desert,**

2   **for forty days, to be tempted by the devil.** The number **forty** is a biblical round number (Gen 7:12; Exod 34:28; Num 14:34; Deut 25:3; 1 Kings 19:8). The **devil** is another name for Satan. Luke's statement might be translated "for forty days, Jesus was being led by the Spirit in the desert, tempted by the devil." The Spirit did not simply lead Jesus to the wilderness but **led** Jesus throughout his time there. And throughout these forty days, Jesus was **tempted by the devil;** Luke will only recount three temptations (verses 3–13). The wilderness was thought of as the haunt of evil spirits (see 8:29; 11:24; Lev 16:10; Tobit 8:3; Isaiah 13:21; 34:11, 14), so the devil's presence there is no surprise. The New American Bible translation reads that the Spirit led Jesus into the desert **to be tempted** by the devil, as if that was why Jesus was there. However, the Greek word literally means "being tempted": Jesus spent forty days in the wilderness being tempted. Did the Spirit lead Jesus into the wilderness simply to be tempted, or was that only one of the purposes for Jesus being there? Jesus' time in the wilderness comes immediately after the Spirit descended upon him and God proclaimed him to be his beloved Son (3:22), and immediately before he begins his public ministry (4:14–15). Jesus is a man of prayer (3:21; 5:16; 6:12; 9:18, 28–29; 11:1; 22:32, 41–45), and so we would expect him to spend time in prayer after experiencing a

dramatic manifestation of his Father and of the Spirit and in preparation for his mission as the Spirit-filled Son of God. Yet during this time when he was being "led by the Spirit" (verse 1), he was also being **tempted by the devil**. Jesus' faithfulness to his Father is put to the test.

For reflection: What does it mean for me that Jesus, even though led by the Spirit, was tempted?

He ate nothing during those days, and when they were over he was hungry. Luke does not write that Jesus fasted; he simply states that Jesus **ate nothing** without explaining why. (Jesus apparently will not fast during his public ministry; see 5:33–34; 7:34.) There is virtually no food to forage in the Judean wilderness; as long as the Spirit kept Jesus there he would have little if anything to eat. He would naturally become **hungry**.

3 **The devil said to him, "If you are the Son of God, command this stone to become bread."** The sense of the devil's **if** is "since": since you are **the Son of God**. It may not have been necessary for the devil to overhear God's proclamation of Jesus as his Son (3:22); evil spirits recognize who Jesus is (see 4:33–34, 41; 8:27–28). The devil tells Jesus to

---

BACKGROUND: SATAN In Hebrew, the word *satan* means "adversary" or "accuser." A figure called "the Satan," that is, "the accuser," appears in the book of Job as an angelic prosecuting attorney who puts humans to the test (Job 1:6–12; 2:1–7). In Job this accuser is a member of God's heavenly court, not an evil spirit opposed to God (see also Zech 3:1–2). In late Old Testament times, however, the term "Satan" began to be applied to an evil spirit (see 1 Chron 21:1). Nonbiblical writings from shortly before the time of Jesus describe the fall of some angels, the chief of whom is variously called Mastema, Satan, Belial, and Beliar. In the New Testament, this evil spirit is likewise called a variety of names, including "Satan," "the devil," "Beelzebul" (Matt 12:24–27; Mark 3:22; Luke 11:15–19), and "Beliar" (2 Cor 6:15), and is portrayed as the chief of evil spirits (Matt 12:24; Luke 11:15). While demons are inferior to God, they can influence or control individuals and events. The Gospels present Satan as having authority in this world but do not specify its extent (Matt 4:8–9; Luke 4:5–6; John 12:31; 14:30; 16:11; see also 1 John 5:19). The coming of God's kingdom abolishes the reign of Satan. *Related topics: Demons, unclean spirits (page 125), Nonbiblical writings (page 342).*

---

use his power as the Son of God to **command this stone** lying on the ground **to become** a loaf of **bread** for him to eat. The devil knows Jesus is hungry and uses his hunger as the basis of a suggestion.

Son of God: See page 25

4   The devil's suggestion seems innocent on the surface. What would be wrong with Jesus using his powers to feed himself when he will use them to feed others (9:12–17)? But there are deeper issues. Should Jesus use his powers to exempt himself from the inconveniences and suffering inherent in the human condition? The Spirit led Jesus to a place where there was no food; should Jesus second-guess the Spirit's guidance by turning the wilderness into a bakery? Should the Son of God take care of himself instead of waiting for his Father's provision for him? The last consideration seems to be the weightiest for Jesus. **Jesus answered him, "It is written in Scripture, 'One does not live by bread alone.'"** Jesus invokes Scripture as an expression of God's will for him. He quotes from a passage in Deuteronomy that speaks of God's allowing the Israelites to experience hunger in the wilderness so that they would learn to rely on his word and keep his commands (Deut 8:3). Jesus as the Son of God must rely on his Father's care and direction for him; he cannot forego reliance by removing all occasions for it.

> He therefore let you be afflicted with hunger, and then fed you with manna, a food unknown to you and your fathers, in order to show you that not by bread alone does man live, but by every word that comes forth from the mouth of the LORD.
>
> Deut 8:3

For reflection: To what extent do I rely on God for the things that are most important to me?

5   **Then he took him up and showed him all the kingdoms of the world in a single instant.** Luke writes that the devil **took** Jesus **up** without saying where. In any case, Luke pictures Jesus being given a vision of **all the kingdoms of the world in a single instant.** The word Luke uses here for **world** means the inhabited world; often referring to

the Roman empire (see 2:1) but here perhaps encompassing other **king-doms** as well. Jesus is, as it were, being shown the goods by a salesman.

6 **The devil said to him, "I shall give to you all this power and their glory."** In Luke's Greek, **to you** is emphatic; the devil tells Jesus, *You* can have authority over all these kingdoms and enjoy the glory that goes with it. The devil claims that he can **give** Jesus this authority **for it has been handed over to me**. The words **handed over** may imply handed over by God. The devil claims that he can dispose of it as he sees fit: **I may give it to whomever I wish**. How should we evaluate the devil's claims? Is he deluded in thinking that he has authority over the kingdoms of the world? Is he lying (he is "a liar and the father of lies"—John 8:44)? Or is he exaggerating: does God allow him some sway on this earth but not complete authority? The New Testament acknowledges that Satan wields authority but does not define its limits (John 12:31; 14:30; 16:11; 2 Cor 4:4; Eph 2:2; 1 John 5:19).

7 The devil tells Jesus, **All this will be yours**, all this authority and glory, **if you worship me**. We do not know whether the devil is able to—or would—deliver on his promise; we do know what he asks of Jesus in return. He wants Jesus to **worship** him—to bow down before him in an expression of allegiance to him. The devil asks Jesus to repudiate being the Son of God and to be subservient to him instead, in order to gain worldly power.

8 Jesus does not address the issue of whether the devil is able to deliver on his claims. **Jesus said to him in reply, "It is written: 'You shall worship the Lord, your God, / and him alone shall you serve.' "** Jesus again turns to Scripture as an expression of God's will and again quotes from Deuteronomy (Deut 6:13). The word translated **serve** can also be translated "worship" (as it is at 1:74 and 2:37). God alone is to be worshiped; God alone is to receive absolute allegiance. Jesus will not shift his allegiance from his Father to the devil, no matter the size of the promised payoff.

Lord: See page 137

> The LORD, your God, shall you fear; him shall you serve,
> and by his name shall you swear.
>
> Deut 6:13

The letter to the Hebrews states that Jesus is able to "sympathize with our weaknesses" because he was similarly "tested in every way" (Heb 4:15; see also Heb 2:14–18). We can be tempted to compromise our allegiance to God in order to gain worldly advantage; we can be tempted to go along to get along, even though it means going down the wrong path. Jesus' temptation is our temptations carried to their extreme.

For reflection: How am I tempted to compromise my allegiance to God?

9 **Then he led him to Jerusalem** and **made him stand on the parapet of the temple**. We cannot identify today what **the parapet of the temple** was. Herod the Great's massive reconstruction of the Temple complex created many high vantage points, a fall from any of which would normally have been fatal. The devil **said to him, "If you are the Son of God, throw yourself down from here."** Again, the sense of **if** is "since." Since you are the Son of God, capitalize on your sonship by jumping off this high perch.

Jerusalem: See page 516
Temple: See page 519

10 Jesus has twice rebuffed the devil's temptations by quoting Scripture (verses 4, 8), so the devil tries to use Scripture to sway Jesus, saying, **for it is written: "He will command his angels concerning you, / to guard you"** (Psalm 91:11). The devil quotes from a psalm that promises that God will protect those who put their trust in him.

Angels: See page 11

11 Psalm 91 continues, **With their hands they shall support you, / lest you strike your foot against a stone** (Psalm 91:12). If God promises protection even against stubbed toes, how much more will he preserve the life of his Son, especially when Jesus is at the Temple, the dwelling place of God. The devil tempts Jesus to do something that will force God's hand; Jesus is to jump off the pinnacle of the Temple so that God will have to demonstrate his care for him.

For God commands the angels
to guard you in all your ways.

> *With their hands they shall support you,*
> *lest you strike your foot against a stone.*
>
> Psalm 91:11–12

12 Jesus rejects the devil's application of Scripture and quotes words from Deuteronomy that provide a key for the proper interpretation of Psalm 91 (Deut 6:16): **Jesus said to him in reply, "It also says, 'You shall not put the Lord, your God, to the test.' "** Psalm 91 is an invitation to trust God, not to test God. Demanding God's miraculous protection is not trust but presumption. God has assured Jesus that he is his beloved Son (3:22); with this assurance Jesus does not need to make God demonstrate his loving care for him. To demand that God act to prove that he cares would be to doubt God's care. As the Son of God, Jesus will follow his Father's script, not try to impose one on him. His testing in the wilderness foreshadows his struggle on the night before he dies; his allegiance to his Father will mean accepting suffering and death (see 22:41–44).

> *You shall not put the LORD, your God, to the test, as you*
> *did at Massah.*
>
> Deut 6:16

For reflection: Do I demand that God act according to my script? Do I presume that God will rescue me from the consequences of my poor decisions or habits?

13 **When the devil had finished every temptation**: the sense of **every** is "all different sorts of" temptations, of which Luke has recounted three. The devil has proposed various temptations to Jesus, probing for weaknesses. Finding none, the devil for the moment admits defeat **and he departed from him for a time**. The Greek word used here for **time** can have the connotation of the opportune moment: the devil will attack again when the time is ripe. Jesus will vanquish Satan and evil spirits throughout his ministry (4:33–36, 41; 6:18; 7:21; 8:27–33; 9:1, 38–42; 10:17–19; 11:14–26; 13:11–14); Satan will counterattack particularly when the time draws near for Jesus to die (22:3, 31).

Jesus was tempted to use his status as the Son of God for his own advantage and agenda. Since he was uniquely the Son of God, there is a corresponding uniqueness to his temptations. But we pray to God as Father (11:2), and our sonship and daughtership will also be put to the test. Will we follow God's agenda or our own?

ORIENTATION: *Jesus returns to Galilee, which will be the setting for virtually all of his ministry until his journey to Jerusalem (9:51).*

Jesus Begins His Spirit-empowered Mission

¹⁴ **Jesus returned to Galilee in the power of the Spirit, and news of him spread throughout the whole region. ¹⁵ He taught in their synagogues and was praised by all.**

¹⁶ **He came to Nazareth, where he had grown up, and went according to his custom into the synagogue on the sabbath day. He stood up to read ¹⁷ and was handed a scroll of the prophet Isaiah. He unrolled the scroll and found the passage where it was written:**
¹⁸ **"The Spirit of the Lord is upon me,**
    because he has anointed me
        to bring glad tidings to the poor.
He has sent me to proclaim liberty to captives
    and recovery of sight to the blind,
        to let the oppressed go free,
¹⁹ **and to proclaim a year acceptable to the Lord."**
²⁰ **Rolling up the scroll, he handed it back to the attendant and sat down, and the eyes of all in the synagogue looked intently at him. ²¹ He said to them, "Today this scripture passage is fulfilled in your hearing."**

Gospel parallels: Matt 4:12, 23; Mark 1:14
OT: Isaiah 58:6; 61:1–11
NT: Luke 3:21–22; 4:1

14 **Jesus returned to Galilee in the power of the Spirit.** Jesus had grown up in the village of Nazareth in **Galilee** (2:39–40, 51–52), and after his forty days in the wilderness he **returned** to his native district. He had been led by **the Spirit** throughout his time in the wilderness (4:1), and

113

the Spirit continues to lead and empower him. Luke does not say what Jesus did through **the power of the Spirit** after coming to Galilee but implies that it was noteworthy, for **news of him spread throughout the whole region**. Luke will later recount Jesus doing things so extraordinary that news about him spreads widely (see 4:37; 5:15; 7:17).

The Spirit: See page 100

15 Luke does say that Jesus **taught in their synagogues**—the synagogues of Galilee. **Synagogues** were assemblies, or the places where Jews assembled, on the Sabbath for prayer, Scripture reading, instruction, and discussion (see Acts 17:1–3). Teaching was largely the interpretation of Scripture. That Jesus **taught** in **synagogues** was not out of the ordinary: any qualified layman could teach, and visitors might be invited to say a few words (see Acts 13:14–15). He made use of Sabbath assemblies to proclaim his message (see 4:16, 31–33, 44; 6:6; 13:10). Jesus' teaching in synagogues indicates that he is sufficiently well versed in the law of

---

BACKGROUND: GALILEE This was the northern region of ancient Palestine. Most of the Galilean sites mentioned in the Gospels were in what was considered lower Galilee in the time of Jesus: a roughly circular area twenty to twenty-five miles across, with the Sea of Galilee on the east and the coastal hills of the Mediterranean on the west. Nazareth was near the southern edge of lower Galilee, and Capernaum was in the northeast. The general character of Galilee was rural: the two most significant cities in lower Galilee—Sepphoris and Tiberias—seem to have had little cultural impact on those who did not live within them. Most of the inhabitants of Galilee made their living as farmers or fishermen and lived in villages or small towns. Galilee contained the estates of its ruler, Herod Antipas, and his wealthy supporters, and some Galileans worked as tenant farmers or day laborers on these estates. There was not much of a middle class in Galilee: there was a small, wealthy elite and many ordinary and rather poor people. The Galilee to which Jesus addressed himself was primarily the Galilee of ordinary people: while his message reached members of the upper class, the Gospels never describe him going into Sepphoris or Tiberias, even though Sepphoris lay only four miles from Nazareth, and Tiberias seven miles from Capernaum. Galilee during the ministry of Jesus has sometimes been described as a paganized area, a region of lax religious observance, and a hotbed of revolutionary nationalism, but none of these characterizations is accurate. In general, the Jews of rural Galilee were traditional in their religious practices, relatively uninfluenced by Greek culture, and slow to heed calls to revolution. *Related topic: Herod Antipas (page 99).*

Moses that he is able to instruct. Those who hear Jesus teach respond very favorably to him: he **was praised by all**.

16 **He came to Nazareth, where he had grown up.** The word translated **had grown up** could also be translated "had been reared." Jesus was brought up by Joseph and Mary in their home in **Nazareth**. Now, in the power of the Spirit (verse 14), Jesus returns to his hometown. He **went according to his custom into the synagogue on the sabbath day**. It would have been his custom since childhood to attend the synagogue every Sabbath, and now he has made it his **custom** to teach in synagogues on the Sabbath (verse 15). **He stood up to read**, the posture of someone proclaiming Scripture aloud to those assembled together.

Nazareth: See page 19
Sabbath: See page 158

17 Jesus **was handed a scroll of the prophet Isaiah**. It was customary in the Sabbath synagogue service to read a selection from the law of Moses followed by a selection from one of the prophets (see Acts 13:15, 27). Jesus does the prophetic reading. The books of Scripture were written on scrolls

---

BACKGROUND: SYNAGOGUE The original meaning of the Greek word *synagogue* was a gathering or an assembly, but it came to mean the place of assembly—the building that served as a Jewish community center and place of prayer and study. Synagogues may have originated during the exile in Babylonia, when Israelites were deprived of Temple worship. At the time of Jesus, synagogues, at least in the sense of assemblies, were common in Galilee, in Jerusalem, and wherever Jews resided outside of Palestine. Synagogues were used for Scripture reading and prayer; sacrifices were offered only in the Temple in Jerusalem. Synagogues were also used for religious education and community gatherings, which sometimes included communal meals. After the time of Jesus, synagogues became more exclusively used for religious activities and less as general-purpose community centers. Archaeologists have discovered the remains of a few first-century synagogues. They typically consisted of a large room with tiers of stone benches around the walls. Anything done in such a synagogue—such as Jesus' teachings, healings, and exorcisms—would have been visible to the whole congregation. Remains of a synagogue built of limestone around the fourth century can be seen in Capernaum today. Beneath it are what seem to be the remains of a first-century synagogue built of basalt blocks—apparently the synagogue in which Jesus taught and healed. Remains of another first-century synagogue have been found at the site of Magdala, home of Mary Magdalene.

---

made of parchment or papyrus. Judging from a scroll found among the Dead Sea Scrolls, a complete **scroll** of the book of **Isaiah** would be about twenty-four feet long. Locating a passage in a scroll requires unrolling it with one hand and rolling it up with the other until the desired page is found. This Jesus did, for he had in mind the passage he wished to read. **He unrolled the scroll and found the passage where it was written:**

Dead Sea Scrolls: See page 174

18 **The Spirit of the Lord is upon me, / because he has anointed me / to bring glad tidings to the poor.** The prophet is speaking of himself, proclaiming that **the Spirit of the Lord is upon** him and **has anointed** him. This prophecy was first delivered to those who had returned to Jerusalem from exile in Babylon. The Babylonian army had burned down Jerusalem a half-century earlier (2 Kings 25:9), and the city still lay in ruins. Many who had returned from exile had to struggle to survive and were **poor**. The Spirit empowered the prophet **to bring glad tidings to the poor**, to proclaim a message of good news for them.

For reflection: How has the Holy Spirit enabled me to bring good news to others?

The prophet announces the good news that he brings: **He has sent me to proclaim liberty to captives / and recovery of sight to the blind**. The Spirit has **sent** the prophet to tell **captives** that they are liberated. Those to whom the prophet speaks have been freed from captivity in Babylon but not freed yet from its aftereffects. Jerusalem is in ruins, and those who returned from exile are hungry because cropland has been unattended. But the prophet proclaims that the city will be rebuilt (Isaiah 61:4) and the hungry will feast (Isaiah 61:5–6). There will be **recovery of sight to the blind**: the Hebrew text of Isaiah reads "release to the prisoners" but Luke quotes a Greek translation of Isaiah that reads "recovery of sight to the blind." Both would have been good news for Isaiah's listeners. The prophet is sent **to let the oppressed go free**. These words, drawn from Isaiah 58:6, repeat the promise of **liberty to captives** for emphasis: God will release the oppressed from their oppression.

For reflection: How am I most in need of being set free?

> *The spirit of the Lord GOD is upon me,*
>   *because the LORD has anointed me;*
> *He has sent me to bring glad tidings to the lowly,*
>   *to heal the brokenhearted,*
> *To proclaim liberty to the captives*
>   *and release to the prisoners,*
> *To announce a year of favor from the LORD*
>
>   Isaiah 61:1–2

Liberty and **go free** both translate the same Greek word, a word that means release from captivity and can also be used for release from sin (it is translated as "forgiveness" at 1:77; 3:3; 24:47). Some of Luke's first readers may have associated the release Jesus brings with his freeing them from their sins.

19 The prophet is sent by the Spirit **to proclaim a year acceptable to the Lord**—probably an allusion to the jubilee year that came every fifty years (Lev 25:8–55). During the jubilee year, slaves were to be freed, property taken as security for unpaid debts was to be restored, and debts were to be forgiven (see also Deut 15:1–2). The jubilee year was a time of release; the note of release runs through Isaiah's prophecy. The prophecy goes

---

BACKGROUND: WHAT LANGUAGES DID JESUS SPEAK? The language of ancient Israel was Hebrew, and most of the Old Testament was written in Hebrew. Jesus would have had to have a reading knowledge of Hebrew in order to read aloud from the scroll of Isaiah in the synagogue in Nazareth (Luke 4:16–21). Aramaic, a related language, was the international language of the Babylonian and Persian empires. Jews adopted Aramaic as their ordinary language after the Exile, when they were under the rule of Persia. Some chapters of the books of Ezra and Daniel, written during or after this period, are in Aramaic. Jesus grew up speaking Aramaic, the ordinary language of Jews in Palestine in the first century. The Gospels preserve a few Aramaic words that Jesus used, such as *talitha koum* (little girl, arise—Mark 5:41) and *Abba* (Father—Mark 14:36). Following the conquests of Alexander the Great around 330 B.C., Greek became widely used throughout the eastern Mediterranean world, especially for commerce. Scholars debate whether Jesus knew any Greek. The common view is that he probably picked up some Greek words but taught in Aramaic, the language in which both he and the rural people of Galilee were most at home. *Related topic: Greek language and culture (page 5).*

---

on to refer to this release as "salvation" (Isaiah 61:10)—rescue from what oppresses God's people.

As an aside we can note that this incident indicates that Jesus had a reading knowledge of Hebrew; only two other Gospel passages might offer evidence of Jesus' literacy (John 7:15; 8:6–8).

20 **Rolling up the scroll, he handed it back to the attendant and sat down.** Scripture was proclaimed while standing, but teachers usually **sat** while teaching (see 5:3). **And the eyes of all in the synagogue looked intently at him,** waiting expectantly for what he had to say about the Scripture that had been read. News of Jesus had "spread throughout the whole region" (verse 14) and reached Nazareth (see also 4:23). Those in the synagogue had probably heard of the acclaim Jesus received for his teaching in other synagogues (verse 15). They look at him with rapt attention.

For reflection: How eager am I to hear Jesus' words?

21 **He said to them, "Today this scripture passage is fulfilled in your hearing."** In the Greek of Luke's Gospel, **today** is emphatic. **Today,** right now, even as you listen, **this scripture passage is fulfilled**. Jesus proclaims that he is the fulfillment of what Isaiah had prophesied. The Spirit of God is upon Jesus (3:21–22; 4:1, 14); the Spirit has anointed and empowered Jesus to bring good news to the poor and lowly. Jesus gives sight to the blind and opens eyes to God's salvation (see 2:29–32; 3:6). Jesus frees those who are in bondage to Satan or disease. Jesus brings release, liberating men and women from sin. Isaiah's prophecy serves as Jesus' job description as he begins his ministry. Jesus is the fulfillment of God's plans, bringing salvation to his people.

For reflection: What insights into Jesus and his mission does Isaiah's prophecy give me?

Acclaim Turns into Violent Rejection
²² **And all spoke highly of him and were amazed at the gracious words that came from his mouth. They also asked, "Isn't this the**

son of Joseph?" ²³ He said to them, "Surely you will quote me this proverb, 'Physician, cure yourself,' and say, 'Do here in your native place the things that we heard were done in Capernaum.' " ²⁴ And he said, "Amen, I say to you, no prophet is accepted in his own native place. ²⁵ Indeed, I tell you, there were many widows in Israel in the days of Elijah when the sky was closed for three and a half years and a severe famine spread over the entire land. ²⁶ It was to none of these that Elijah was sent, but only to a widow in Zarephath in the land of Sidon. ²⁷ Again, there were many lepers in Israel during the time of Elisha the prophet; yet not one of them was cleansed, but only Naaman the Syrian." ²⁸ When the people in the synagogue heard this, they were all filled with fury. ²⁹ They rose up, drove him out of the town, and led him to the brow of the hill on which their town had been built, to hurl him down headlong. ³⁰ But he passed through the midst of them and went away.

Gospel parallels: Matt 13:54–58; Mark 6:1–6

OT: 1 Kings 17:1–16; 2 Kings 5:1–14

NT: Luke 2:34; 4:14–21; John 4:44

22 Jesus has proclaimed that, in fulfillment of prophecy, he is anointed with the Spirit of God to bring good news to the poor and release to those in bondage (4:18–21). That is a claim that demands a response: one must accept Jesus as God's agent or reject him as deluded or a charlatan. The immediate reaction of those in the synagogue of Nazareth is positive. They had waited expectantly for Jesus to speak (4:20) and were not disappointed by what he said: **All spoke highly of him and were amazed at the gracious words that came from his mouth.** The sense of **gracious words** is not eloquent words but words expressing God's grace, God's favor. The people of Nazareth take Jesus' words as good news for them. **They also asked, "Isn't this the son of Joseph?"** Their remark is open to different interpretations. It could be a put-down: who does this local boy think he is? In the context of Luke's Gospel, however, it more likely conveys pride over one of their own being blessed by God with gracious words. The people of Nazareth are **amazed** by **the son of Joseph** and **spoke highly of him.**

Readers of Luke's Gospel know that Jesus is the son of Joseph only "as was thought" (3:23). Although the people of Nazareth do not realize it, Jesus is the Son of God (1:35; 3:22).

23 Jesus detects a dark side in their eagerness to claim him as one of their own. **He said to them, "Surely you will quote me this proverb, 'Physician, cure yourself.'"** Jesus uses a popular **proverb** to characterize what is on their minds. The sense of the proverb is, use your skills on yourself. Jesus spells out how this proverb applies to the thinking of the people of Nazareth: they want him to **do here in your native place the things that we heard were done in Capernaum**. Luke hasn't yet recounted a visit of Jesus to **Capernaum**, about eighteen miles away. However, Luke has told of Jesus coming to Galilee "in the power of the Spirit" and has implied that Jesus did extraordinary things, for "news of him spread throughout the whole region" (4:14). Jesus perceives that the people of Nazareth want him to do the extraordinary **things** here in his **native place** that he had **done in Capernaum**. Are they jealous that he did wonderful things in Capernaum before doing them in his hometown? In any case they want Jesus to put their needs first, just as the proverb would have a physician take care of himself.

Capernaum: See page 124

24 **And he said, "Amen, I say to you."** The word **Amen** is the only Hebrew or Aramaic word spoken by Jesus that Luke carries over untranslated into his Gospel. **Amen** means "truly." Used at the end of a prayer it expresses one's agreement with the prayer (see 1 Chron 16:36; Psalm 106:48). Jesus uses **amen** at the beginning of a statement to emphasize the importance of what he is saying. He tells the people of Nazareth, **no prophet is accepted in his own native place**. This might be another popular proverb. Yet the saying is found only in the Gospels (see Matt 13:57; Mark 6:4; John 4:44) and might simply be Jesus' observation about the fate of prophets. The Old Testament provides ample record of prophets being rejected and even killed (1 Kings 19:10; 2 Chron 24:19–21; Neh 9:26; Jer 2:30). By invoking this saying Jesus implicitly identifies himself as a **prophet**, as one who speaks for God under the impulse of the Holy Spirit. Jesus says in effect, "You people of Nazareth may be acclaiming me now, but the record of how prophets are treated indicates that your

acceptance will not last long." Those who speak for God often do not say what their listeners want to hear, and they end up being rejected along with their message. Indeed, that is what is happening in Nazareth even as Jesus speaks.

For reflection: If Jesus speaks for God, how seriously do I take his words?

25 Because Jesus will not be accepted in his "native place" (verse 24), he will go elsewhere. Jesus cites two precedents for prophets helping those who are not of the prophets' native place. **Indeed, I tell you, there were many widows in Israel in the days of Elijah when the sky was closed for three and a half years and a severe famine spread over the entire land.** Elijah lived in the ninth century B.C. and announced a drought that resulted in crop failure and **severe famine** (1 Kings 17:1). **Widows** who had no family to support them were in a precarious situation and would especially suffer during a famine. There were **many** such **widows in Israel** at the time of this famine.

26 Yes **it was to none of these** widows in Israel **that Elijah was sent** by God, **but only to a widow in Zarephath in the land of Sidon**. The town of **Zarephath** lay between Tyre and Sidon on the Mediterranean coast, in what is Lebanon today. The **widow** in Zarephath was presumably a Gentile, for Zarephath was a Phoenician town. Nonetheless, God **sent** Elijah to her with the promise that the little food she had would not run out before the famine ended (1 Kings 17:8–16). Elijah's words proved true; she and her son survived the famine.

Tyre and Sidon: See page 166

27 Jesus provides a second example of a prophet helping someone not of the prophet's native place: **Again, there were many lepers in Israel during the time of Elisha the prophet**, who also lived in the ninth century B.C. **Yet not one of them was cleansed, but only Naaman the Syrian**. Second Kings 5:1–14 recounts how **Naaman the Syrian** came to **Elisha** and was cleansed of his leprosy. Although the Syrian Naaman was healed, there were Israelites with leprosy who were not healed (see 2 Kings 7:3).

Leprosy: See page 458

Luke's Gentile readers would have noted Jesus' examples of God assisting the Gentiles, and taken them as foreshadowings of God's favor being extended to them through Jesus.

28 **When the people in the synagogue heard this, they were all filled with fury.** They wanted Jesus to use his powers for them—to "do here in your native place the things that we heard were done in Capernaum" (verse 23). Instead Jesus has pointedly spoken of prophets helping foreigners while people in the prophet's native place went unaided. Jesus even accented those who did not receive help, saying that "none" of the widows were fed and that "not one" of those who had leprosy was healed (verses 26, 27). This infuriates those who only moments earlier were thinking how fortunate they were to have a native son who could exercise God's power on their behalf. They take Jesus' words as a rebuff, and they **were all filled with fury**.

29 **They rose up, drove him out of the town, and led him to the brow of the hill on which their town had been built, to hurl him down headlong.** Their intent is to do Jesus great bodily harm, perhaps even kill him. The rolling hills surrounding Nazareth provide places where someone might be thrown down and suffer fatal injuries. Some of those who had gathered in the synagogue to celebrate the Sabbath by prayer and Scripture reading have become a lynch mob. Their acclaim for Jesus (verse 22) has turned into violent rejection. Their attitude seems to be that if Jesus won't help them, they will make sure he won't help anyone else either.

For reflection: What is my reaction to Jesus' rejection by the people of Nazareth?

30 **But he passed through the midst of them and went away.** Luke does not say *how* Jesus was able to pass through the **midst** of an angry mob unharmed; he simply states that it happened and that Jesus **went away** from Nazareth. Luke will not recount Jesus ever returning to Nazareth.

Luke's account of Jesus' visit to Nazareth begins on a high note and ends dismally. Jesus comes in the power of the Spirit (4:14), proclaims that he fulfills a prophecy of Isaiah (4:18–21), and receives a very positive response (4:22). But when he challenges the expectations of the people of Nazareth (4:23–27), they turn against him, even murderously so (4:28–29), and he leaves, never to return to his "native place," the village in which he had grown up.

For reflection: Have I ever turned away from or against Jesus because he did not satisfy my expectations?

Luke could have selected other incidents to present as the initial event in Jesus' public ministry (see 4:15, 23) but chose to use Jesus' visit to Nazareth with its unhappy ending. Luke probably intended it as an illustration of Jesus being "a sign that will be contradicted" and the cause of "the fall and rise of many in Israel," as Simeon prophesied after his birth (2:34). Luke probably also presents the incident as a foreshadowing of what lies ahead: Jesus will be embraced by some but rejected by others, culminating in his death. Yet death will have no more hold over him than the mob in Nazareth: he will, as it were, pass through the **midst** of the earth, rising from his tomb.

ORIENTATION: *After being rejected in Nazareth, Jesus goes to Capernaum. Luke recounts a day of Jesus' activities in Capernaum (4:31–41).*

The Authority of Jesus' Word

31 Jesus then went down to Capernaum, a town of Galilee. He taught them on the sabbath, 32 and they were astonished at his teaching because he spoke with authority. 33 In the synagogue there was a man with the spirit of an unclean demon, and he cried out in a loud voice, 34 "Ha! What have you to do with us, Jesus of Nazareth? Have you come to destroy us? I know who you are—the Holy One of God!" 35 Jesus rebuked him and said, "Be quiet! Come out of him!" Then the demon threw the man down in front of them and came out of him without doing him any harm. 36 They were all amazed and said to one another, "What is there about his word? For with authority and power he commands the unclean spirits, and they come out." 37 And news of him spread everywhere in the surrounding region.

Gospel parallels: Matt 4:13; Mark 1:21–28

31 **Jesus then went down** from Nazareth **to Capernaum,** a journey of roughly eighteen miles. This is not Jesus' first visit to Capernaum (see 4:23). Luke aptly writes that Jesus **went down** to Capernaum: Nazareth lies in the hills, over 1,200 feet above sea level; Capernaum is on the shore of the Sea of Galilee, 680 feet below sea level. Luke adds that Capernaum is **a town of Galilee** to help his readers situate it; they likely would never have heard of Capernaum if Jesus had not taken his ministry there. **He taught them on the sabbath** while they were gathered together in the synagogue (see verse 33); Jesus uses Sabbath assemblies as opportunities to teach and proclaim his message (4:15–21). Luke does not tell us what Jesus **taught;** later we will learn that Jesus proclaimed the good news of the kingdom of God in Capernaum (see 4:43).

Galilee: See page 114
Sabbath: See page 158

32 Luke does recount the reaction of those who heard Jesus teach: **they were astonished at his teaching,** just as the people in the synagogue in Nazareth had been amazed by Jesus' words (4:22). They were astonished at his teaching **because he spoke with authority,** literally, "because his

BACKGROUND: CAPERNAUM lay on the northwest shore of the Sea of Galilee, along a road that led from the Mediterranean to Bethsaida and ultimately to Damascus. Since Capernaum was near the border between the territory governed by Herod Antipas and the territory governed by Philip, there was a customs post there to collect taxes on goods being transported between the territories. Capernaum was a fishing and farming village covering about twenty-five acres, with a population estimated to have been between six hundred and fifteen hundred. Its houses were one story and small, with walls of unworked stones and flat thatched roofs. Archaeologists have not found signs of wealth in any of its houses; Capernaum was a village of ordinary rural Galileans. Nor have they found evidence of public buildings, other than what seem to be the remains of a synagogue, which probably served as a community center. Jesus moved from Nazareth to Capernaum and made Capernaum his base of operations for his public ministry; Mark and Matthew indicate that he stayed in the house of Peter. In later centuries there was a continuing Jewish-Christian presence in Capernaum, alongside its Jewish population. Capernaum was progressively abandoned after the seventh-century Islamic conquest of Palestine and an earthquake in 746. *Related topics: Farming (page 218), Fishing (page 135), Galilee (page 114), Peter's house in Capernaum (page 128).*

word was with authority." Jesus taught "in the power of the Spirit" (4:14), giving his words **authority**.

> *For reflection: Do I accept Jesus' words as authoritative for me? Do I take Jesus at his word?*

33 In the synagogue there was a man with the spirit of an unclean demon. In Greek culture, the word translated **demon** could mean either an evil spirit or a deity (Luke uses it for deities in Acts 17:18), so Luke specifies for his readers that this is an **unclean,** or evil, **demon.** Having the **spirit** of an unclean demon likely means being under its influence; Luke elsewhere characterizes this condition as being possessed by a demon (7:33; 8:27). Evil spirits do the work of Satan (see 11:14–15; 13:11, 16); Jesus contended with the devil in the wilderness (4:2–13) and will combat evil spirits throughout his ministry: Jesus has come to replace the reign of evil with the reign of God (see 11:20).

Synagogue: See page 115

The unclean demon, speaking through the man it possessed, **cried out in a loud voice,**

34 Ha!—a cry that expresses surprise or dismay. **What have you to do with us, Jesus of Nazareth?** The demon recognizes that the one teaching with authority is **Jesus of Nazareth,** the Jesus who grew up in Nazareth.

BACKGROUND: DEMONS, UNCLEAN SPIRITS The New Testament takes the existence of demons for granted but does not describe their origin and says little about their nature. The chief emphasis lies on their influence and effects on human beings. Both mental and physical illnesses, including epilepsy, blindness, deafness, muteness, and curvature of the spine, are sometimes ascribed to the influence of demons, and healing takes place through casting out the demon causing the illness. But not every illness is attributed to the influence of demons, and some healings are presented simply as healings. Likewise, some exorcisms are simply exorcisms, with no mention of any accompanying physical healing. Demons are also referred to as unclean spirits and evil spirits, and they are under the authority of Satan, also called Beelzebul. Jesus' casting out of demons was an assault on the kingdom of Satan and evidence that the kingdom of God was breaking into this world through the power of Jesus. *Related topic: Satan (page 108).*

What have you to do with us? is literally, "What to us and to you?" This is a Hebrew idiom that has the sense, "Why are you meddling in our affairs? Mind your own business!" Jesus has not yet done anything to the demon, but the demon is threatened by Jesus' very presence because of who Jesus is. The question, **have you come to destroy us?** is rhetorical. The demon knows that is Jesus' mission. The demon refers to **us**, to all evil spirits. Jesus will **destroy** the grip that evil has on men and women, releasing them from its power; he has been sent "to proclaim liberty to captives . . . to let the oppressed go free" (4:18). The demon shouts out, **I know who you are—the Holy One of God!** The devil recognizes that Jesus is the Son of God (4:3, 9); to call him **the Holy One of God** is a similar way of identifying him. Conceived through the Holy Spirit, Jesus is "holy, the Son of God" (1:35).

Nazareth: See page 19

35 **Jesus rebuked him and said, "Be quiet! Come out of him!"** While the word **rebuked** can simply mean reproached or reprimanded, the word was sometimes used for commanding evil spirits to depart (see Zech 3:2). **Be quiet** is literally "be muzzled," as an animal is muzzled (Deut 25:4). The demon was shouting loudly through the man (verse 33) and Jesus shuts it up. Jesus commands the demon, **come out of him**—relinquish your evil influence over him. **Then the demon threw the man down in front of them and came out of him without doing him any harm.** We might visualize what happened when the demon **threw the man down . . . without doing him any harm** as the man falling down in a faint. It happened **in front of them**, literally, "in the midst" of those gathered in the synagogue. Everyone present could see that as a result of Jesus' command the demon **came out** of the man, evident in his shouting ending in a silent faint.

36 **They were all amazed and said to one another, "What is there about his word? For with authority and power he commands the unclean spirits, and they come out."** They had been astonished by Jesus' teaching, for his word had authority (verse 32), and now they are **amazed** that his **word** even has the **authority and power** to command unclean spirits, expelling them. Jesus has the **power** of the Holy Spirit

(4:14) to teach and command with **authority**; there is power in Jesus' word.

> *For reflection: How have I experienced the transforming power of Jesus' word?*

37 **And news of him spread everywhere in the surrounding region.** The Greek word translated as **news** gives us the English word "echo": what Jesus did in the synagogue reverberated throughout Galilee. Luke earlier stated that "Jesus returned to Galilee in the power of the Spirit, and news of him spread throughout the whole region" (4:14). Now Luke has recounted what Jesus does that amazes and astonishes people and sets them talking. Word of Jesus' power-filled word **spread everywhere**.

Jesus Frees Those in the Grip of Evil

³⁸ **After he left the synagogue, he entered the house of Simon. Simon's mother-in-law was afflicted with a severe fever, and they interceded with him about her.** ³⁹ **He stood over her, rebuked the fever, and it left her. She got up immediately and waited on them.**

⁴⁰ **At sunset, all who had people sick with various diseases brought them to him. He laid his hands on each of them and cured them.** ⁴¹ **And demons also came out from many, shouting, "You are the Son of God." But he rebuked them and did not allow them to speak because they knew that he was the Messiah.**

Gospel parallels: Matt 8:14–16; Mark 1:29–34
NT: Luke 4:18

38 **After he left the synagogue** of Capernaum, where he taught and freed a man from a demon (4:31–36), **he entered the house of Simon.** This is the first time **Simon** (whom Jesus will name Peter—6:14) is mentioned in Luke's Gospel. Presumably Jesus and Simon became acquainted when Jesus previously visited Capernaum (see 4:23). Luke does not provide every detail of Jesus' ministry, preferring to concentrate on what is important. In the house is **Simon's mother-in-law**: Simon was married (see also 1 Cor 9:5, where he is called Cephas). His mother-in-law's presence

suggests that she lived with Simon and his wife, which would be expected if she was a widow without sons. She **was afflicted with a severe fever**: Luke's words **afflicted with** (or tormented by) and **severe** convey that she is seriously ill. Malaria was common in northern Palestine until modern times and might have been the cause of her high fever. **They interceded with him about her.** Luke does not say who **they** are who ask Jesus to heal her (were they Simon and his wife?) but their identity is less important than their request. Asking Jesus to heal her shows that they believe he can.

39 **He stood over her**—she was lying on a pallet or bedroll on the floor—and **rebuked the fever,** just as he rebuked the demon in the man in the synagogue (4:35) and will rebuke demons that evening (verse 41). Luke does not draw a sharp line between exorcisms and physical healings; both

---

BACKGROUND: PETER'S HOUSE IN CAPERNAUM In Capernaum, archaeologists have found the remains of an ancient neighborhood of houses clustered around courtyards. An octagonal church was erected over and in place of one of the houses in the fifth century; octagonal or circular churches were built to mark holy places. Beneath the center of the church are the remains of a small one- or two-room building that was constructed around 65 B.C. Its walls and floor were made of unworked basalt stones—the local black, volcanic rock—and would have supported a roof of beams and tree branches covered with thatch and earth. The interior of this building measured about twenty by twenty feet, and it shared a courtyard with other similar small buildings. Archaeologists have found fishhooks and broken kitchenware indicating that it was used as a family home at the time of Jesus. Later in the first century this room was set aside for special use. Its walls and floor were plastered (unlike other houses in Capernaum), and Christians began carving prayers in the plaster, which suggests that it was a venerated site used for Christian gatherings. An arch was added in the fourth century to support a tile roof. Egeria, a European nun who came on pilgrimage to the Holy Land sometime around 390, wrote in her travel notes, "In Capernaum a house church was made out of the house of Peter, and its walls still stand today." Egeria's words and the archaeological evidence make it very probable that the venerated room was the house of Peter. Subsequently the octagonal church was built over the site. This church was destroyed in the seventh century, perhaps during a Persian invasion. Capernaum went into a steady decline after an eighth-century earthquake and was abandoned in the eleventh century. A modern church was dedicated in 1992, with a glass floor that allows worshipers to gaze down on the remains of Peter's house.

---

are releases from the grip of evil. In Acts, Peter will proclaim that Jesus "went about doing good and healing all those oppressed by the devil" (Acts 10:38). See the comment on demons and sickness on page 377.

At Jesus' rebuke the fever **left her,** just as the demon came out of the possessed man (4:35). **She got up immediately and waited on them.** She recovered **immediately** from a life-threatening fever and was able to resume normal life. She **waited on them,** that is, she served them. By serving them a meal, Simon's mother-in-law becomes the first example of service in Luke's Gospel. She waited on **them**: Luke does not say who she fed along with Jesus—another unimportant detail.

For reflection: What can I learn from the example of Simon Peter's mother-in-law?

40 Jesus is in Simon's house on the Sabbath (4:31). According to Jewish reckoning, days run from sunset to sunset (see Lev 23:32) rather than from midnight to midnight. **At sunset, all who had people sick with various diseases brought them to him.** Carrying burdens was considered a work forbidden on the Sabbath (see John 5:10), so the people of Capernaum waited until the Sabbath was over to carry to Jesus those who were **sick with various diseases.** Perhaps word had gotten around that Jesus had healed Simon's mother-in-law; Jesus in any case is known as someone who has amazing power (see 4:14, 23, 36–38). **All** in Capernaum who have sick relatives or friends bring them to Jesus. **He laid his hands on each of them,** giving them his individual attention, touching them. Jesus can heal with a touch (5:13; 8:54; 22:51), which Luke sometimes describes as laying his hands on them (see also 13:13). The practice of laying hands on someone to heal him or her is not found in the Old Testament. However, the custom may have developed by the time of Jesus, for it is mentioned in one of the Dead Sea Scrolls. The early Church will continue Jesus' practice of laying on hands for healing (Acts 9:12, 17; 28:8). Jesus **cured them,** all whom he touched.

Dead Sea Scrolls: See page 174

41 **And demons also came out from many**: Luke apparently means out of many whom Jesus healed of various diseases. Luke sometimes associates physical maladies with the influence of evil spirits (see 11:14; 13:11, 16);

healing means being freed from their power. Jesus came to set free the oppressed, releasing them from every kind of evil (see 4:18).

> For reflection: What are my demons, addictions, afflictions? How have I experienced Jesus' setting me free of them?

The demons came out **shouting, "You are the Son of God."** Evil sprits recognize who Jesus is (see 4:3, 9, 34). Jesus will pray to God as his Father (10:21; 22:42; 23:34, 46) and speak of God as "my Father" (2:49; 10:22; 22:29; 24:49), but he is slow to claim the title **the Son of God** (see 22:70) because it is open to misinterpretation. It could be taken as a claim to divine privileges, which Jesus shunned as the devil's temptations (4:3–4, 9–12). **He rebuked them and did not allow them to speak because they knew that he was the Messiah.** If Jesus will not claim the title the Son of God, even less will he claim to be **the Messiah** at this point in his ministry. The most common understanding of **the Messiah** was that he would restore Jewish independence and usher in a golden age for God's people (see Acts 1:6). Jesus did not come to lead a rebellion against Rome; he will have to redefine what it means to be the Messiah in order for it to be an appropriate designation of him (see 9:20–22). Consequently, Jesus **did not allow** the demons to make it known that he is the Son of God and Messiah.

Demons, unclean spirits: See page 125
Son of God: See page 25
Messiah, Christ: See page 257

Jesus' day of ministry in Capernaum (4:31–41) has lasted until well into the evening. He has taught, and he has freed many who were in the grip of evil. This will be the daily rhythm of his life throughout his ministry.

Why God Sent Jesus

⁴² **At daybreak, Jesus left and went to a deserted place. The crowds went looking for him, and when they came to him, they tried to prevent him from leaving them. ⁴³ But he said to them, "To the other towns also I must proclaim the good news of the kingdom**

of God, because for this purpose I have been sent." ⁴⁴ And he was preaching in the synagogues of Judea.

Gospel parallels: Mark 1:35–39
NT: Matt 4:23; Luke 4:15, 18–19

42 **At daybreak, Jesus left and went to a deserted place.** Jesus had gone to the house of Simon in Capernaum the previous day (4:38); after sunset many people were brought to him to be freed of their afflictions (4:40). Although it may have been a long evening for Jesus, he nonetheless rises **at daybreak** so that he can go **to a deserted place,** presumably to have some time by himself. Luke elsewhere notes that Jesus "would withdraw to deserted places to pray" (5:16). **The crowds**—the people of Capernaum—**went looking for him,** searching him out, **and when they came to him, they tried to prevent him from leaving them**. They want to keep him and his healing powers for themselves. They are in awe of him (4:32, 36), but they are fans rather than disciples: their hunting him down when he evidently wants to be alone shows that they lack the respect that disciples should have for their master.

43 **But he said to them, "To the other towns also I must proclaim the good news of the kingdom of God, because for this purpose I have been sent."** Jesus cannot remain in Capernaum, however much its people would like him to, because he **must** bring his message to other towns as well. **Must** in this context indicates divine necessity (see also 2:49): it is God's will that Jesus go from town to town. Jesus says, **for this purpose I have been sent**—sent by God. Jesus is a man on a mission.

Jesus **must proclaim the good news of the kingdom of God**: this is what God sent Jesus to do. This is the first time that **the kingdom of God** is mentioned in Luke's Gospel. Although the expression **the kingdom of God** is not found in the Old Testament, Jesus' listeners would have been familiar with the idea of God reigning as king over his people and ultimately over the world. Psalms spoke of God reigning (Psalms 93:1; 96:10; 97:1), as did prophets (Isaiah 6:5; 33:22; 43:15; 52:7; Jer 8:19; Zeph 3:15); "The LORD shall become king over the whole earth" (Zech 14:9). That Jesus must **also** proclaim the kingdom of God to other towns implies that this was his message in Capernaum, when he taught in the synagogue (4:31).

Gospel, good news: See page 59
Kingdom of God: See page 381

Jesus must proclaim **the good news** of the kingdom of God. Jesus has been sent by God to bring good news to the poor, to proclaim liberty to captives, to heal the blind and let the oppressed go free (4:18–19). He freed the afflicted of Capernaum from diseases and demons (4:31–41). His ministry in Capernaum demonstrates that God's reigning over women and men means that they are released from the grip of evil. That is good news indeed!

> *For reflection: How have I experienced what Jesus does and teaches as good news for me?*

44 **And he was preaching in the synagogues of Judea.** Luke sometimes uses **Judea** to refer to all of Palestine (see 1:5) and sometimes to the region of Palestine called Judea (see 1:65; 2:4; 3:1); here he apparently means Palestine, for in his next verse Jesus is still in Galilee (5:1). Jesus has already been teaching in synagogues (4:15), and he continues this practice, going from town to town to bring the good news of God's reign to those gathered together on the Sabbath.

Synagogue: See page 115
Judea: See page 40

CHAPTER 5

Jesus Calls a Fisherman to Fish

¹ **While the crowd was pressing in on Jesus and listening to the word of God, he was standing by the Lake of Gennesaret.** ² **He saw two boats there alongside the lake; the fishermen had disembarked and were washing their nets.** ³ **Getting into one of the boats, the one belonging to Simon, he asked him to put out a short distance from the shore. Then he sat down and taught the crowds from the boat.** ⁴ **After he had finished speaking, he said to Simon, "Put out into deep water and lower your nets for a catch."** ⁵ **Simon said in reply, "Master, we have worked hard all night and have caught nothing, but at your command I will lower the nets."** ⁶ **When they had done this, they caught a great number of fish and their nets were tearing.** ⁷ **They signaled to their partners in the other boat to come to help them. They came and filled both boats so that they were in danger of sinking.** ⁸ **When Simon Peter saw this, he fell at the knees of Jesus and said, "Depart from me, Lord, for I am a sinful man."** ⁹ **For astonishment at the catch of fish they had made seized him and all those with him,** ¹⁰ **and likewise James and John, the sons of Zebedee, who were partners of Simon. Jesus said to Simon, "Do not be afraid; from now on you will be catching men."** ¹¹ **When they brought their boats to the shore, they left everything and followed him.**

> Gospel parallels: Matt 4:18–22; 13:1–2; Mark 1:16–20; 4:1
> OT: Isaiah 6:1–5
> NT: Luke 4:38–39; John 21:1–11

1   Word about Jesus has spread throughout Galilee (4:14, 37) and he attracts crowds (4:40, 42). **While the crowd was pressing in on Jesus and listening to the word of God, he was standing by the Lake of Gennesaret.** The setting is the shore of the **Lake of Gennesaret,** which is called the Sea of Galilee in other Gospels. The following verses suggest that Jesus is at or near Capernaum, where Simon lived (4:38). There is a **crowd** of people **pressing in on** him and **listening to the word of God.** Jesus' preaching and teaching conveys **the word of God;**

133

Jesus speaks for God. Luke does not say what Jesus proclaimed to the crowd on this occasion; presumably it was "the good news of the kingdom of God" (4:43).

For reflection: Do I listen to Jesus' words in the Gospels as God's word to me? How might I listen more attentively?

2 **He saw two boats there alongside the lake; the fishermen had disembarked and were washing their nets.** It will emerge that these commercial **fishermen** had fished through the night (verse 5). After fishing, it was necessary to wash **nets** clean of seaweed and anything else that fouled them and then hang them up to dry. The fishermen are finishing up their workday.

3 **Getting into one of the boats, the one belonging to Simon, he asked him to put out a short distance from the shore.** The crowd's pressing in on Jesus made it difficult for everyone to hear his teaching. By **getting into one of the boats** and having it go out **a short distance from the shore,** Jesus creates an excellent pulpit for himself: sound travels well over water. He chooses to use the boat of **Simon**: Jesus was in Simon's house and healed his mother-in-law (4:38–39), so Jesus and Simon are acquainted. Even though Simon is at the end of his workday and probably wants to go home and get some sleep, he complies with Jesus' request and lets him use his boat. **Then he sat down**—the natural

---

BACKGROUND: LAKE OF GENNESARET Luke refers to the Sea of Galilee as the Lake of Gennesaret (Luke 5:1). Gennesaret (1 Macc 11:67; Matt 14:34; Mark 6:53) is a fertile area on its northwest shore. Luke calls the body of water a "lake" (Luke 8:22), which is more apt than "sea," for it is a freshwater body thirteen miles long and seven miles wide at most, with a maximum depth of two hundred feet. The Jordan River empties into the northern end of the lake and flows out from its southern end. In the time of Jesus the lake was ringed with fishing villages, and it was still commercially fished until recent years. The Sea of Galilee lies seven hundred feet below sea level and is bordered by high hills that are cut by steep valleys. Strong winds can blow through these valleys and down onto the Sea of Galilee and stir up sudden storms. The Sea of Galilee is also called the Sea of Chinnereth, or Kinneret, in the Old Testament (Num 34:11) and the Sea of Tiberias by John (John 21:1).

thing to do in a boat, but also the customary posture for a teacher (see 4:20–21)—**and taught the crowds** along the shore **from the boat**.

4 **After he had finished speaking, he said to Simon, "Put out into deep water and lower your nets for a catch."** While Jesus tells **Simon** to take the boat out into deep water, his instruction **lower your nets** is addressed to others in Simon's boat as well: **your** is plural in the Greek of Luke's Gospel. Maneuvering a boat and deploying fishing nets is not a one-man job. The fishermen are to lower their nets **for a catch**: Jesus indicates that their efforts will be successful.

5 **Simon said in reply, "Master, we have worked hard all night and have caught nothing."** Simon addresses Jesus as **Master**, using a title for a person with some sort of authority, such as the authority of a teacher over a student. That **Simon** calls Jesus his **Master** is an acknowledgment of Jesus' authority and may indicate that Simon is already his disciple, even though Luke has not recounted Jesus calling Simon to follow him. Simon's response to Jesus is deferential but nonetheless pointed. He says that he and his crew have **worked hard**, toiling wearisomely. They did so **all night**, yet they **caught nothing**. As professional fishermen, they

---

BACKGROUND: FISHING In the first century, the Sea of Galilee was ringed with villages with harbors and was commercially fished, as it was until very recently. Commercial fishing, rather than sport-fishing, is reflected in the Gospels. There were about eighteen species of fish in the Sea of Galilee, with three categories making up the bulk of commercial catches: sardine, carp, and tilapia. Tilapia feed on plankton and must be caught with nets, not with hooks and bait. Tilapia weigh up to four pounds and swim in schools around the northern end of the Sea of Galilee during wintertime; the great nettings of fish reported in the Gospels were likely catches of tilapia. Fishermen used various forms of nets, including circular nets that were cast by hand and dragnets that were deployed from boats. Remains of a first-century fishing boat were discovered in 1986 buried in the mud near the shore of the Sea of Galilee at Ginnosar (ancient Gennesaret), an area Jesus visited (Matt 14:34; Mark 6:53). This boat, 26 1/2 feet long, 7 1/2 feet wide, and 4 1/2 feet deep, was apparently typical of the fishing boats mentioned in the Gospels. It had a rounded stern and may have had decks fore and aft. It would have had a small square sail and a crew of four rowers and a rudder man. It could have carried an additional ten to twelve passengers when it was not transporting nets and fish.

know that the odds of netting fish now that it is day are very low: the kind of fishing they do is most successful at night, which is why they fish at night. Jesus grew up in the farming village of Nazareth, not near a lake. Could he be expected to know more about fishing than those who had done it all their lives? Nevertheless, Simon tells Jesus **but at your command I will lower the nets**—or more literally, "on account of your word I will lower the nets." Simon has witnessed the authority of Jesus' word, in teaching (4:32), in commanding evil spirits (4:36), in healing his mother-in-law (4:39). Even if Simon may think that he knows more about fishing than Jesus, he acknowledges Jesus as his **Master** and follows his instructions.

> *For reflection: How readily do I follow Jesus' instructions? Do I second-guess Jesus when he asks something of me that does not make sense to me?*

6 **When they had done this, they caught**—literally, enclosed—**a great number of fish and their nets were tearing.** The catch is more than their nets can handle.

7 **They signaled to their partners in the other boat to come to help them.** There had been two boats on the shore (verse 2); the other boat belongs to their fishing **partners**. Nets were often deployed by two boats working together. The fishermen in Simon's boat need their partners in the other boat to **help them** handle the great catch of fish. **They came and filled both boats so that they were in danger of sinking.** Not only is the catch of fish more than their nets can handle; it is more than can be transported by two boats without overloading them dangerously.

8 Simon has already seen Jesus do astonishing things. He was presumably present when Jesus freed a man from a demon (4:33–36) and when he healed his mother-in-law instantly from a severe fever (4:38–39). Yet the huge catch of fish sweeps him off his feet. **When Simon Peter saw this, he fell at the knees of Jesus and said, "Depart from me, Lord, for I am a sinful man."** Luke calls him **Simon Peter**, adding the name that Jesus will give him (see 6:14). The great catch of fish gives Peter a sudden realization that Jesus is more than a man with extraordinary powers; God is somehow present in Jesus. Where before Simon called Jesus "Master"

(verse 5), he now calls him **Lord**. While the title "Lord" can simply be a polite form of address, it is also used for God, as it is seventeen times just in the first chapter of Luke's Gospel. Simon **fell** down before Jesus as one prostrates oneself in worship (see 4:7–8). Simon is aware of his sins and is overcome by a sense of unworthiness in the presence of Jesus. He tells him, **depart from me, Lord, for I am a sinful man**. His experience seems similar to that of Isaiah when he was given a vision of the glory of God. Isaiah exclaimed, "Woe is me, I am doomed! For I am a man of unclean lips, living among a people of unclean lips; yet my eyes have seen the King, the LORD of hosts!" (Isaiah 6:5).

For reflection: Have I ever been uncomfortable in the presence of Jesus? How do I feel knowing that he knows my sins?

9 **For astonishment at the catch of fish they had made seized him and all those with him** in his boat. Simon is not the only one who is astonished by the catch of fish, although his reaction is more than mere astonishment.

10 **and likewise James and John, the sons of Zebedee, who were partners of Simon** and had come in their boat to assist him. They too are stunned by the catch of fish. Jesus directs his attention to Simon and responds to his cry, "Depart from me, Lord, for I am a sinful man." **Jesus**

BACKGROUND: LORD The Greek word for "lord" is *kyrios*, familiar to many in the form in which it occurs in the petition *Kyrie, eleison* (Lord, have mercy)—Greek words in the Roman liturgy. A *kyrios*, or lord, is someone who has power and authority; thus the word has wide application. The owner of a property could be called its *kyrios* (the "owner of the vineyard" in Mark 12:9 is literally the "lord of the vineyard"). A master would be addressed as "lord" by his servants, but anyone could also use "lord" as a polite form of address to a man, much as the English word "sir" is used (see John 12:21). At the other extreme, Greek-speaking Jews used the word *kyrios*—"Lord"— as a title for God (Tobit 3:2, 11–12), as did New Testament writers (Luke 1:32; Rev 1:8). Because of this range of usage, when Jesus is called *kyrios* by someone in the Gospels, it can simply be a respectful form of address (translated as "sir" in John 4:19) or an acknowledgment that he is someone with authority (the meaning of "Lord" in Matt 8:21 and Luke 7:6) or a declaration that he can be called "Lord" as God is called "Lord" (the meaning of "Lord" in John 20:28 and Phil 2:11).

---

said to Simon, "Do not be afraid; from now on you will be catching men." Fear is a normal response to an encounter with the divine; angels reassuringly told those to whom they appeared, "Do not be afraid" (1:13, 30; 2:10). Jesus' words to Simon are similarly reassuring but carry a fuller meaning: Jesus tells Simon, **Do not be afraid** to be with me in your sinfulness. Jesus does not tell Simon that he is not sinful; he tells him that despite his sins, he should not be fearful to be in Jesus' presence.

For reflection: What reassurance do I find in Jesus' words, "Do not be afraid"?

Jesus also tells Peter, **from now on you will be catching men.** The words **from now on** signal the beginning of a new stage in Simon's life, and a new stage in Jesus' ministry as well: Jesus' teaching and healing have attracted such great crowds that he now must involve others in his mission. Jesus adopts the language of fishing to commission Simon to gather women and men into the reign of God. By saying that Simon **will be catching** (instead of "will catch"), Jesus indicates that this will be an ongoing task for Simon. Perhaps implicit in Jesus' words is the comparison, "If I can give you a huge catch of fish, I can also give you a huge catch of men and women." Simon will turn out to be a great fisherman of people: about three thousand will accept baptism in response to his Pentecost sermon (Acts 2:41).

When fishermen catch fish, it is good for the fishermen but highly detrimental for the fish: they die and are eaten. To counter any negative connotation in **catching men**, Luke uses a word for **catching** that is formed from Greek words for "catch" and "alive" and can mean to rescue from danger or to bring to life. Simon's catching of women and men will mean life for them.

For reflection: What can I learn from Jesus' words to Simon? What has Jesus commissioned me to do for him?

11 **When they brought their boats to the shore, they left everything and followed him.** To follow Jesus means to be his disciple. **They** who brought **their boats** to the shore and **followed** Jesus are Simon and James and John, who will be listed among Jesus' disciples (6:13–14).

Perhaps others in the boats also became Jesus' disciples; Luke will speak of Jesus having "a great crowd" of disciples (6:17). **They left everything,** even the huge catch of fish, in order to travel with Jesus as his disciples. It may have seemed to them a small price to pay to be with him whose words had such astonishing authority.

For reflection: What have I left behind in order to be Jesus' disciple? What do I still need to leave behind in order to follow him more closely?

Jesus Cleanses an Untouchable
¹² Now there was a man full of leprosy in one of the towns where he was; and when he saw Jesus, he fell prostrate, pleaded with him, and said, "Lord, if you wish, you can make me clean." ¹³ Jesus stretched out his hand, touched him, and said, "I do will it. Be made clean." And the leprosy left him immediately. ¹⁴ Then he ordered him not to tell anyone, but "Go, show yourself to the priest and offer for your cleansing what Moses prescribed; that will be proof for them." ¹⁵ The report about him spread all the more, and great crowds assembled to listen to him and to be cured of their ailments, ¹⁶ but he would withdraw to deserted places to pray.

Gospel parallels: Matt 8:2–4; Mark 1:40–45
OT: Lev 13—14
NT: Luke 4:43; 7:22

12 Jesus told the people of Capernaum that he must take the good news of the kingdom of God to other towns (4:43). **Now there was a man full of leprosy in one of the towns where he was.** What the Bible calls **leprosy** included a variety of disfiguring skin diseases (see Lev 13; 14:54–56). This man was **full of leprosy**: he had a severe case. Leprosy made one ritually unclean, and anyone who touched a leper also became unclean. Hence, lepers were forbidden to live with others (Lev 13:46), lest they spread their ritual defilement. The social consequences of leprosy were as bad as the disease itself. Yet this man who is **full of leprosy** is **in one of the towns** Jesus visits. He should not be there; perhaps he came into town because he heard that Jesus was visiting. He knows that Jesus heals, for word of what Jesus does has gotten around (4:14, 37). **When he**

saw Jesus, he fell prostrate, pleaded with him, and said, "Lord, if you wish, you can make me clean." He falls on his face before Jesus, a posture of reverence and supplication, and begs Jesus to help him. He calls him **Lord**, acknowledging Jesus' authority. He expresses his plea as an act of faith in Jesus: **If you wish, you can make me clean.** He wants to be healed and made ritually **clean** so that he can be restored to society, and he acknowledges that Jesus has the power to do so.

Leprosy: See page 458
Lord: See page 137

For reflection: Do I have faith that Jesus can cleanse me of all that defiles me? How do I seek his cleansing?

13 **Jesus stretched out his hand** and **touched him**. Jesus touches this untouchable man, expressing his tenderness and care, breaking through the barrier that separates him from society. Jesus reaches out to us no matter our condition. He **said, "I do will it. Be made clean."** I am

BACKGROUND: CLEAN AND UNCLEAN The Old Testament contains complex regulations regarding the ritually clean and the ritually unclean, for example, Leviticus 11—15. The ritually clean could come in contact with the holy; the ritually unclean could not. An unclean person could not worship in the Temple. A person could become unclean either through sin or through a variety of causes that had nothing to do with sin. Sexual intercourse, even if perfectly moral, rendered one unclean, as did menstruation or giving birth to a child. Uncleanness also resulted from certain diseases, contact with a corpse, or eating certain forbidden foods. In these cases, contact with an unclean person or object rendered a person unclean. An unclean person could be made clean through remedies that depended on the type of uncleanness. Washing with water and the passage of a certain amount of time were required, and, for more serious types of uncleanness, sacrifice in the Temple. Most Jews were probably ritually unclean much of the time but could remedy their condition in order to enter the Temple area. Maintaining or restoring cleanness was important for priests because they served in the Temple, and special rules pertained to them. Ritual cleanness was a particular concern for the Pharisees, and their program aimed at maintaining in everyday life the ritual purity required for Temple worship. Archaeologists have found widespread evidence of concern for ritual cleanness in Galilee and Judea (baths for ritual washing; cups and bowls carved from stone, which was impervious to uncleanness), but most Jews of Jesus' time did not observe the detailed traditions of the Pharisees. *Related topic: Pharisees (page 143).*

willing to cleanse you; be cleansed. **And the leprosy left him immediately.** The leprosy that had filled the man (verse 12) **left** him, almost
as if it was a demon departing (see 4:35, 41). The man is freed from his
leprosy **immediately,** just as Simon's mother-in-law was healed immediately (4:39). Jesus came to release those in the grip of evil (see 4:18) and
is able to do so with a touch or a word.

14 **Then he ordered him not to tell anyone, but "Go, show yourself
to the priest and offer for your cleansing what Moses prescribed."**
If the leper was to resume contact with others, they would have to know
that he had been cured of his leprosy and uncleanness. Yet Jesus **ordered
him not to tell anyone.** Jesus likely meant not to tell anyone he had
been cleansed of leprosy until a priest confirmed it and he was ritually
purified. When a skin condition considered to be leprosy went away, a
priest was to make an examination and certify that the person no longer
had the disease (Lev 14:1–3). Then the person underwent an eight-day
process of purification to become ritually clean, making sacrificial offerings on the first and eighth days (Lev 14:4–32). Jesus tells the man to
show himself to a priest and to **offer** the sacrifices **prescribed** in the law
of **Moses.** Jesus has removed the cause of the man's uncleanness, but his
restoration to society requires that he follow the procedures set down in
the Mosaic law. Jesus adds, **that will be proof for them.** By this Jesus
may mean that the man's undergoing examination by a priest and eight
days of purification will make it "manifest" that the man is in "a state of
cleanness" (Lev 14:57). There may be another meaning to Jesus words:
his ordering the man to fulfill the requirements of the law of Moses is
proof that Jesus respects the law. It will not be long before some accuse
Jesus of violating the law.

Priests and Levites: See page 302

15 Jesus was already widely known for his teaching and healing, and word
of his healing the man with leprosy adds to his reputation. **The report
about him spread all the more, and great crowds assembled to
listen to him and to be cured of their ailments.** Jesus enjoys considerable success in his mission. He has been sent to proclaim the good news
of the kingdom of God (4:43), and **great crowds assembled to listen to**

him. He has been sent to release those in the grip of evil (4:18), and large numbers of people come to him **to be cured of their ailments**.

16 **but he would withdraw to deserted places to pray.** Jesus habitually withdrew from the crowds to go to **deserted places** where he could be alone **to pray**. Jesus has a mission to carry out with the crowds, but his life cannot be reduced to his mission. Jesus knows that God is his Father (2:49; 3:22) and he makes time for communion with his Father, getting up early in the morning (4:42) or going off by himself to pray.

For reflection: How do I balance my obligations to others with my need to spend time in prayer?

ORIENTATION: *Apart from his rejection by the people of Nazareth (4:16–30), Jesus has received great acclaim (4:14–15). Luke now recounts five incidents where Jesus' words or actions are criticized (5:17—6:11).*

Jesus Releases a Man from His Paralysis

¹⁷ **One day as Jesus was teaching, Pharisees and teachers of the law were sitting there who had come from every village of Galilee and Judea and Jerusalem, and the power of the Lord was with him for healing.** ¹⁸ **And some men brought on a stretcher a man who was paralyzed; they were trying to bring him in and set [him] in his presence.** ¹⁹ **But not finding a way to bring him in because of the crowd, they went up on the roof and lowered him on the stretcher through the tiles into the middle in front of Jesus.** ²⁰ **When he saw their faith, he said, "As for you, your sins are forgiven."** ²¹ **Then the scribes and Pharisees began to ask themselves, "Who is this who speaks blasphemies? Who but God alone can forgive sins?"** ²² **Jesus knew their thoughts and said to them in reply, "What are you thinking in your hearts?** ²³ **Which is easier, to say, 'Your sins are forgiven,' or to say, 'Rise and walk'?** ²⁴ **But that you may know that the Son of Man has authority on earth to forgive sins"—he said to the man who was paralyzed, "I say to you, rise, pick up your stretcher, and go home."** ²⁵ **He stood up immediately before them,**

picked up what he had been lying on, and went home, glorifying God. **26** Then astonishment seized them all and they glorified God, and, struck with awe, they said, "We have seen incredible things today."

Gospel parallels: Matt 9:1–8; Mark 2:1–12
NT: Luke 4:18; 5:15

17 **One day as Jesus was teaching, Pharisees and teachers of the law were sitting there.** This is the first time **Pharisees** are mentioned in Luke's Gospel. **Pharisees** were a religious group intent on the careful observance of the law of Moses. Luke will elsewhere refer to **teachers of the law** as "scribes" (verse 21) or "scholars of the law" (7:30). Some scribes were Pharisees, but not all Pharisees were trained as scholars of the law. These Pharisees and teachers of the law **had come from every village of Galilee**, from **Judea**, eighty miles south of Galilee, and from **Jerusalem**, the center of Jewish worship and learning. Have they come,

---

BACKGROUND: PHARISEES were a group or movement, primarily of laymen, who developed particular traditions for how God's law was to be observed. Although they were influential, they were only one group within first-century Judaism. An ancient historian reports that there were about six thousand Pharisees at the time of Jesus, out of a total Jewish population estimated at a half-million to one million in Judea and Galilee. The Pharisees' traditions particularly spelled out how a Jew should observe the Mosaic law regarding food, tithing, the Sabbath, and ritual purity. Pharisees had their origin about 150 years before the birth of Jesus, and their rules for observing the law of Moses were handed on as "the tradition of the elders" (Mark 7:3, 5)—traditions established by earlier Pharisees. Pharisees accepted recent developments within Judaism, such as the belief in an afterlife (Acts 23:6–10). Jesus' outlook was closer to that of the Pharisees than to that of any other group we know of in first-century Judaism. Sadducees, for example, denied that there would be a resurrection of the dead, while Jesus affirmed it (20:27–38). But Jesus also had some serious disagreements with the Pharisees. These disagreements carried over into the early Church, which found itself in competition with the Pharisees for the allegiance of Jews. Since the Pharisees were concerned with daily life rather than Temple worship, their influence survived the destruction of the Temple in A.D. 70, and they were among those who shaped the future course of Judaism. The Judaism of today is not identical to that of the Pharisees of the time of Jesus, but the traditions of the Pharisees are part of the roots of modern Judaism.

---

like others in the crowd, to be instructed and healed by Jesus? Or have these **Pharisees and teachers** come to examine what Jesus is **teaching** and check him out?

Galilee: See page 114
Judea: See page 40
Jerusalem: See page 516

And the power of the Lord was with him for healing: Jesus is **healing** as well as **teaching**. People come to him for both: "great crowds assembled to listen to him and to be cured of their ailments" (5:15). Jesus heals because **the power of the Lord was with him**. Jesus is filled with and led by the Holy Spirit (4:1); he goes about his mission "in the power of the Holy Spirit" (4:14), which Luke here refers to as **the power of the Lord** God. The "Spirit of the Lord" is upon Jesus (4:18), empowering him to proclaim God's message and release men and women from evil.

Lord: See page 137

18 **And some men brought on a stretcher a man who was paralyzed; they were trying to bring him in and set [him] in his presence.** While Jesus was in Simon Peter's house in Capernaum, "all who had people sick with various diseases brought them to him" (4:40). Jesus is again in a house (verse 19) and a man who is **paralyzed** and unable to come to Jesus on his own is carried by others **on a stretcher** so that Jesus may heal him.

19 **But not finding a way to bring him** into the house **because of the crowd** gathered around the door, **they went up on the roof and low-ered him on the stretcher through the tiles**. The houses of ordinary people in Palestine were one or two stories high and had flat roofs. An outside stairway led to the roof, which was used for drying crops, for sleeping on warm nights (1 Sam 9:25–26), and as a place to have some privacy (Acts 10:9). Those trying to bring the paralyzed man to Jesus go up onto the roof and make an opening through it by removing roof **tiles**. Luke recounts what they did in terms of his readers' experience: houses in the Greek world were roofed with tiles. An ordinary house in Palestine would likely have had a roof of branches and thatch covered with packed earth. After making a hole in the roof, those carrying the paralyzed man

lowered him down **into the middle** of the room **in front of Jesus**. They go to great lengths to bring the paralyzed man to Jesus.

For reflection: What lengths have I gone to in order to bring others to Jesus?

20 **When he saw their faith**: Jesus sees **their faith** manifest in their actions. The paralyzed man and those carrying him have come to Jesus so that he may be healed. They refused to let anything keep them away from Jesus—not the crowd, not even a solid roof. Their determination is a reflection of their **faith**, their confidence that Jesus will heal the paralyzed man. Jesus responds to those who come to him in faith. **He said, "As for you, your sins are forgiven."** He addresses the paralyzed man, but instead of healing him of his paralysis, he pronounces that his sins have been **forgiven**.

For reflection: Where am I most paralyzed by sin? How does Jesus' forgiving of this man invite me to turn to Jesus in faith?

Jesus' words raise questions. Are the man's sins the cause of his paralysis? Sin can lead to sickness or infirmity (see 1 Cor 11:29–30), but sickness or afflictions are not infallible indicators of sin (see 13:1–5; John 9:2–3). By granting the man forgiveness rather than healing, Jesus indicates that the man's greatest need is release from the paralysis of sin, but Jesus does not indicate that the man's sins are the cause of his physical paralysis.

A second question is, Who forgives his sins, Jesus or God? Jesus' words, **your sins are forgiven**, could be taken to mean "Your sins are forgiven by God." Nathan told David, "The Lord . . . has forgiven your sin" (2 Sam 12:13). Is Jesus announcing what God has done, or is Jesus on his own authority pronouncing forgiveness?

21 Those who hear Jesus' words interpret them as Jesus' pronouncing the forgiveness of sins on his own authority. **Then the scribes and Pharisees began to ask themselves, "Who is this who speaks blasphemies? Who but God alone can forgive sins?"** Sin is an offense against God; therefore, **God alone can forgive sins**. For a human being to claim to

be able to forgive sins is to usurp God's authority, and the scribes and Pharisees consider this blasphemy. They **ask themselves** a crucial question: **who is this** who pronounces release from sin?

22 **Jesus knew their thoughts.** Does Jesus observe them muttering among themselves and deduce it was in response to his telling the man his sins were forgiven? Or does Jesus have greater-than-human insight? He is frequently aware of what people are thinking (4:23; 6:8; 9:47; 24:38). We might understand this as a work of the Holy Spirit in him, giving him perception "so that the thoughts of many hearts may be revealed" (2:35). He **said to them in reply, "What are you thinking in your hearts?"** He knows that they think he is a blasphemer because he told a man his sins were forgiven, but he asks the question to set up his response.

23 **Which is easier, to say, "Your sins are forgiven," or to say, "Rise and walk"?** It is **easier** to **say** or claim something that cannot be verified than to say or claim something that can be verified. Whether a person's sins have been forgiven cannot be observed, for it is a matter of how a person stands with God. Hence, it is **easier** to say **your sins are forgiven** than to say **rise and walk**, for whether the person rises and walks can be observed.

BACKGROUND: SCRIBES The scribes encountered in the Gospels are scholars and teachers of the law of Moses, but the profession of scribe included others as well. A scribe was literally someone who could write, a literate person in a largely illiterate society. Scribes ranged from village scribes who handled routine correspondence and record-keeping to high-ranking officials in governmental administrative positions. (Today we apply the title "secretary" both to a clerical assistant and to the Secretary of State.) In the Gospel accounts, scribes are men who specialize in studying and teaching the law of Moses and are centered in Jerusalem. Luke sometimes uses "scholars of the law" as an alternative name for scribes. When Jesus proclaimed interpretations of the law different from those of scribes, conflicts arose between scribes and Jesus. Some scribes (a professional group) were Pharisees (a religious group), but not all scribes were Pharisees, and not all Pharisees were scribes. Some Jerusalem priests were also scribes, and some scribes were Sadducees, an aristocratic elite that included some members of the high-priestly families. After the destruction of Jerusalem by Rome in A.D. 70, some scribes took part in the reshaping of Judaism and were among those who became known as rabbis. *Related topics: Pharisees (page 143), Sadducees (page 538).*

---

24 **But that you may know that the Son of Man has authority on earth to forgive sins**: Jesus for the first time in Luke's Gospel refers to himself as **the Son of Man**. This expression was not a title in common use before Jesus, although it was used to describe "One like a son of man" in Daniel (Dan 7:13) and it echoes the way Ezekiel was addressed by God (Ezek 2:1, 3, 6, 8, etc.). By calling himself **the Son of Man** and speaking of the **authority** he has, Jesus indicates that, although he is a human, he possesses extraordinary authority. He has **authority on earth to forgive sins**. God alone can forgive offenses against him (verse 21)—unless God shares his authority with someone. By proclaiming that he has the authority to forgive sins, Jesus makes the claim that God has given him such authority. The Pharisees and scribes asked themselves, "Who is this?" (verse 21). Jesus' response is bold indeed: I am one who can forgive sins as God forgives sins.

For reflection: What does Jesus' claim to forgive sins tell me about Jesus and about his relation to God?

As Jesus indicated, it is easy to say "your sins are forgiven" (verse 23), but how can anyone know that the person pronouncing forgiveness has the authority to do so? To demonstrate his authority to do what cannot be seen, Jesus exercises his authority to do what can be seen. **He said to the man who was paralyzed, "I say to you, rise, pick up your**

BACKGROUND: SON OF MAN Jesus uses the expression "Son of Man" more than eighty times in the four Gospels; it is found only four times in the rest of the New Testament. In its origin it is a Hebrew and Aramaic idiom that means "human being": Ezekiel, for example, is repeatedly addressed by God as "son of man" (Ezek 2:1; 3:1; 4:1). Jesus employs the expression as a way of referring to himself during his public ministry, even when he is doing things that by human standards are extraordinary, for example, forgiving sins (Mark 2:10). In other passages, Jesus uses the expression "Son of Man" when speaking of his coming suffering and death. In still other passages, the Son of Man is the risen Jesus returning in glory at the end of time. These last instances echo the use of "One like a son of man" in Daniel 7:13–14. Neither in Daniel nor in any other Jewish writing from before the time of Jesus is "Son of Man" used as a title for the Messiah. Jesus' referring to himself as the Son of Man was distinctive: others did not call him the Son of Man. It is also enigmatic: scholars have endlessly debated the complexities of this title.

---

stretcher, and go home." A **paralyzed** man getting up and walking is certainly observable.

25 **He stood up immediately before them, picked up what he had been lying on, and went home.** The man who had been paralyzed is **immediately** able to obey Jesus' commands. There can be no doubt that he is free of his paralysis, and his physical healing testifies to his release from sin as well. Those who wonder, "Who is this?" should know that Jesus has the authority from God to forgive sins just as he has the authority to heal. The man whom Jesus released from his paralysis recognizes this: he goes home **glorifying God**, who has cured him of sin and sickness through Jesus.

26 **Then astonishment seized them all and they glorified God, and, struck with awe, they said, "We have seen incredible things today."** The Greek words translated **astonishment** and **awe** have connotations of fear—the normal reaction to an encounter with the divine (1:12, 65; 2:9). Those who heard Jesus' words and saw the paralyzed man walk recognize that God is at work through Jesus, and for this they **glorified God.** They said, **We have seen incredible things today.** The word translated **incredible** means contrary to expectations. No one expects a paralyzed man to walk; no one expects a man to forgive sins. Truly amazing things happened that day.

> *For reflection: Am I astonished by what God does through Jesus? How might I rekindle my awe and praise?*

Jesus Feasts with Sinners

²⁷ After this he went out and saw a tax collector named Levi sitting at the customs post. He said to him, "Follow me." ²⁸ And leaving everything behind, he got up and followed him. ²⁹ Then Levi gave a great banquet for him in his house, and a large crowd of tax collectors and others were at table with them. ³⁰ The Pharisees and their scribes complained to his disciples, saying, "Why do you eat and drink with tax collectors and sinners?" ³¹ Jesus said to them in reply, "Those who are healthy do not need a physician, but the

sick do. ³² I have not come to call the righteous to repentance but sinners."

Gospel parallels: Matt 9:9–13; Mark 2:13–17
NT: Luke 5:8–11; 7:34; 15:2

27 **After this he went out** from the house in which he had forgiven and healed a paralyzed man (5:17–26) **and saw a tax collector named Levi sitting at the customs post.** Luke does not provide the location of the **customs post**; duties or **customs** were collected on goods being transported between territories. Jesus **saw** a tax collector named Levi: the Greek word Luke uses for **saw** means looking intently, singling **Levi** out. While others might see only **a tax collector** at work, Jesus sees who Levi can become. **He said to him, "Follow me."** To **follow** Jesus is to be his disciple, traveling with him, sharing his life. Some who were already Jesus' disciples had been commercial fishermen (5:4–11), a respectable occupation. Tax collectors, however, were widely scorned as extortionists. Yet Jesus calls **a tax collector named Levi** to be his disciple.

Tax collectors: See page 94

For reflection: When Jesus looks intently at me, what does he see? How have I heard his call, "Follow me"? How am I responding?

BACKGROUND: DISCIPLE Generally, a first-century Jewish disciple was someone who studied for a period of time under a teacher. Once this training was complete, the disciple could in turn become a teacher, gathering disciples and passing on to them what he had learned. However, Jesus' call of men and women to follow him involved more than their studying under him. Jesus invited them not into a temporary apprenticeship but into a lifelong personal relationship with him. Being a disciple of Jesus meant sharing his life and accompanying him as he traveled about, taught, and healed. Hence Jesus issued his invitations to discipleship by saying, "Come after me" (Mark 1:17) or "Follow me" (Mark 2:14). At the same time, some of Jesus' disciples did not accompany him in his travels: the Gospels portray Martha, Mary, and Lazarus as remaining at home and extending hospitality to Jesus. Matthew, Mark, and Luke show Jesus taking the initiative in inviting men and women to become his disciples, rather than would-be followers taking the first step toward discipleship. Becoming a disciple of Jesus could involve not only some break with one's family and livelihood, but potentially even giving up one's life. That was the cost of sharing the life of the one who would lay down his life for the sake of others.

---

28 **And leaving everything behind, he got up and followed him.** Levi accepts Jesus' invitation to become his disciple. **Followed him** is literally, "was following him," indicating that Levi's following of Jesus was ongoing. Being a disciple of Jesus is a continuing process. Luke writes that Levi left **everything behind,** including his lucrative job, to become Jesus' disciple, just as Peter, James, and John "left everything" when they followed Jesus (5:11). The next verse indicates that Luke may be presenting a simplified account of Levi's transition into his new life. Levi is apparently a man of some means, and disposing of his property and settling his affairs would take some time.

29 **Then Levi gave a great banquet for** Jesus **in his house.** The word translated **then** does not mean "right away." It would take a few days to make arrangements for a **great banquet**—procuring food and sending out invitations ahead of time (see 14:16–17). A **large crowd** attends the banquet; it is indeed a **great banquet.** It is held in Levi's **house,** which must be of sufficient size to accommodate a **large crowd** reclining at a banquet. Some tax collectors became quite wealthy (see 19:2), and Levi is apparently one of them. Perhaps as part of his disposing of his wealth, Levi gives what must be a costly banquet **for** Jesus: Jesus is the guest of honor. **A large crowd of tax collectors and others were at table with them**—with Levi and Jesus. The next verse indicates that the **others** include Jesus' disciples. Levi, now a disciple of Jesus, invites fellow **tax collectors** to the banquet in honor of Jesus. A disciple is to be, like Peter, a fisher of men and women (5:10). Levi fishes in the waters he knows best, among his business associates and friends, and brings them into contact with Jesus. The word translated **at table** literally means lying down; guests at banquets reclined.

Banquets: See page 386

For reflection: What example does Levi set for me by giving a banquet for Jesus and inviting his friends to it? What might I concretely do to imitate his example?

30 **The Pharisees and their scribes complained to his disciples, saying, "Why do you eat and drink with tax collectors and sinners?"** In the context of a banquet, **drink** means drink wine. The sense of **tax collec-**

tors and sinners is, tax collectors and other sinners. The complaint of the **Pharisees and their scribes** (scribes who were also Pharisees) indicates that they did not take part in Levi's banquet. Perhaps they heard about it and later accosted Jesus' **disciples**, who had been at the banquet. The name "Pharisee" may come from a word that means "separated"; Pharisees tried to separate themselves from sin and sinners. Obeying the Mosaic food laws and maintaining ritual purity were high on their list of concerns. They would not **eat and drink with tax collectors and sinners,** lest they be associated with and contaminated by them. They criticize Jesus' disciples for the company they keep.

Pharisees: See page 143

Scribes: See page 146

Luke does not record the disciples' response to the Pharisees and their scribes, but they could well have said, "We eat and drink with sinners because, as Jesus' disciples, we do what our master does." Jesus had no hesitations about attending a banquet in his honor and fully enjoying it; he will later be accused of being "a glutton and a drunkard" (7:34). Jesus also had no hesitation in associating with and eating with **tax collectors and sinners**, resulting in the charge "This man welcomes sinners and eats with them" (15:2). In the culture of the time, a shared meal meant shared lives; eating together expressed mutual acceptance, fellowship, even intimacy. While Pharisees sought salvation through separation, Jesus brings salvation through association.

For reflection: How does Jesus' willingness to associate with sinners and outcasts give me encouragement? What does his example ask of me?

31 Although the Pharisees' complaint is made to the disciples, Jesus provides the response. **Jesus said to them in reply, "Those who are healthy do not need a physician, but the sick do."** Jesus compares himself to a **physician**. Sin is not so much a crime to be punished as a disease to be cured. Jesus brings healing of body and spirit, cleansing a man of leprosy (5:12–13) and forgiving the sins of a paralytic (5:17–20). Jesus must associate with those who are in **need** of spiritual healing, just as he attends to those who need physical healing.

32 **I have not come to call the righteous to repentance but sinners.**
Jesus provides another statement of his mission, of why he has **come**
(see also 4:18–21, 43). The **righteous** by definition are those who have
no need to repent and be forgiven. Jesus has come for the sake of those
who are not righteous but are **sinners**; his eating with sinners is part
of his mission. He does not simply preach to them but associates with
them and draws them into fellowship with himself. He has come to **call**
sinners **to repentance**—to profoundly reformed lives, a reorientation
of their thinking and behavior. **Repentance** is not a precondition for
associating with Jesus but a consequence of it. Jesus commissions sinful
Peter to catch men (5:8, 10); he eats with sinners; he calls a tax collector
to be his disciple. Jesus wants sinners to repent and become righteous,
and they are able to do so because he is a physician who heals them of
their sins.

Repentance: See page 92

*For reflection: How is Jesus calling me to repentance? How have I
experienced his giving me the strength to repent?*

The Old and the New

33 **And they said to him, "The disciples of John fast often and offer
prayers, and the disciples of the Pharisees do the same; but yours
eat and drink." 34 Jesus answered them, "Can you make the wedding guests fast while the bridegroom is with them? 35 But the days
will come, and when the bridegroom is taken away from them,
then they will fast in those days." 36 And he also told them a parable. "No one tears a piece from a new cloak to patch an old one.
Otherwise, he will tear the new and the piece from it will not
match the old cloak. 37 Likewise, no one pours new wine into old
wineskins. Otherwise, the new wine will burst the skins, and it
will be spilled, and the skins will be ruined. 38 Rather, new wine
must be poured into fresh wineskins. 39 [And] no one who has been
drinking old wine desires new, for he says, 'The old is good.' "**

Gospel parallels: Matt 9:14–17; Mark 2:18–22
NT: Luke 18:12

33 **And they said to him, "The disciples of John fast often and offer prayers, and the disciples of the Pharisees do the same."** Although this verse follows Jesus' exchange with some Pharisees (5:30–32), **they** who now address Jesus are apparently not Pharisees, for they speak of what **Pharisees do** rather than of what "we do." Some whom **John** baptized became his **disciples** (see 7:18; 11:1). John lived an ascetical life, "neither eating food nor drinking wine" (7:33), and in imitation of him his disciples **fast often**. For Jews, fasting meant abstaining from food and drink for a period of time, usually a day. Those who followed the teachings of the **Pharisees** (here referred to as **the disciples of the Pharisees**) also fasted, often two days of the week (see 18:12). Fasting accompanied by **prayers** had become a common pious practice among Jews (see Tobit 12:8). But while devout Jews fast, the disciples of Jesus **eat and drink**. Jesus is being taken to task for not requiring his disciples to fast. Presumably Jesus did not fast either (see 7:34), or he would have had his disciples imitate his practice.

Disciple: See page 149

Pharisees: See page 143

BACKGROUND: FASTING In both the Old and New Testaments, fasting means abstaining from all food for a period of time. In its origins, fasting may have been a sign of mourning: David fasted following the deaths of Saul, Jonathan, and Abner (2 Sam 1:12; 3:31–35), and Judith fasted after the death of her husband as part of her mourning (Judith 8:2–6). Fasting out of grief was not necessarily a religious practice but a mark that one was so deeply sorrowful that he or she had lost all appetite for food. Fasting as an expression of sorrow may have evolved to include fasting as an expression of sorrow for sin (Joel 2:12–13). The Day of Atonement is the only annual fast day prescribed in the law of Moses (Lev 16:29). Fasts could also be called in times of national crisis, as part of prayers of supplication (Joel 1:14). Prophets such as Isaiah warned that fasting was no substitute for upright and merciful conduct (Isaiah 58). Eventually fasting became a pious act, done not only in times of sorrow or crisis but also simply as an act of devotion. The book of Tobit, written about two centuries before Jesus, lists fasting, prayer, and almsgiving as three pious Jewish practices (Tobit 12:8). Different Jewish groups at the time of Jesus had their own traditions of fasting. The *Didache,* a Christian writing dating from about a century after Jesus, speaks of Jews fasting on Mondays and Thursdays and advises Christians to fast instead on Wednesdays and Fridays.

34 Jesus answered them, "Can you make the wedding guests fast while the bridegroom is with them?" A **wedding** was celebrated with a banquet at the home of the groom (see 14:8). How could anyone **make the wedding guests fast**? The point of having a banquet is to feast! Jesus implicitly compares himself to a **bridegroom** and his disciples to **wedding guests**. His presence with his disciples should make them as joyful as guests at a wedding banquet. They cannot be expected to fast and mourn while he is **with them**.

For reflection: How am I aware of the presence of Jesus? How have I experienced joy at his presence?

Marriage practices: See page 540

35 But the days will come, and when the bridegroom is taken away from them, then they will fast in those days. Bridegrooms were normally not **taken away** from wedding feasts; when the feast was over, the guests left and the groom remained with his bride in his home. But Jesus speaks of himself as a **bridegroom** who will be **taken away from** his disciples. He does not explain when or how this will happen but only says that **the days will come** when it will happen. When those days come, then his disciples **will fast in those days**, out of grief over his being taken away from them. Jesus does not say how long **those days** will last in which his followers fast. The early Church will continue the practice of fasting (Acts 13:2–3; 14:23).

This is Jesus' first allusion to his coming death. Luke does not record his disciples' reaction to it. Perhaps they were puzzled (see 9:44–45; 18:31–34).

36 And he also told them a parable, "No one tears a piece from a new cloak to patch an old one. Otherwise, he will tear the new and the piece from it will not match the old cloak." No one who has an **old** and worn cloak with a hole in it would cut a patch from a **new cloak** to sew on the old cloak, for that would ruin the new cloak. Nor would it provide a satisfactory repair for the old cloak, since the patch from the new would **not match the old cloak**. Jesus appeals to the common sense of his listeners: **no one** would commit such folly. Luke characterizes Jesus' words as a **parable**, which means they provide some kind of comparison. But what is being compared to what?

Parables: See page 217

37 Jesus continues with another parable or implied comparison: **Likewise, no one pours new wine into old wineskins.** The hides of small animals, such as sheep or goats, could be dehaired and sewn up so that they could hold liquids such as water (Gen 21:14–15, 19) or wine. As these skins got **old** they became brittle. **New wine** is wine that is not completely fermented and is still producing carbon dioxide as a fermentation byproduct. **No one** stores **new wine** in **old wineskins** because the pressure from the gas produced by the **new wine will burst the skins, and** the wine **will be spilled, and the skins will be ruined**. Jesus again appeals to the common sense of his listeners: **no one** who knows anything about wine-making would put new wine in to old skins; doing so would ruin both.

38 New and still-supple wineskins are able to accommodate the pressure of the gas given off by new wine, and therefore **new wine must be poured into fresh wineskins**.

In these parables, something that is new cannot be sacrificed for or contained by something that is old. A new cloak cannot provide a patch for an old cloak; new wine cannot be put in to old wineskins. To try to do so would harm both the old and the new.

By telling these parables as a response to those who question why his disciples do not fast, Jesus indicates that he is about something new that cannot be subordinated to or contained by old Jewish practices such as fasting. Jesus does not condemn Jewish practices: in both parables there is a concern for the well-being of what is old. But neither can the old place a limit on what Jesus is doing: the new wine of his mission requires new wineskins, new responses to what God is doing through him. Jesus is certainly doing new things: touching a leper (5:13), forgiving sins (5:20), eating with sinners (5:29–30), and not requiring fasting. What Jesus is doing is rooted in what God has done for his people in the past but cannot be limited by it.

39 Jesus concludes with a somewhat cryptic remark: **[And] no one who has been drinking old wine desires new, for he says, "The old is good."** Aged wine tasted better than newly fermented wine (see Sirach 9:10). Those who have been **drinking old wine** have no desire for **new** wine, for they think that **the old is good**. Jesus hardly intends this to mean that the new wine of his mission is inferior to old Jewish practices. Rather, Jesus is making a wry comment on why some are closing their minds to him without giving him a fair hearing. They are unwilling to taste his new wine because they think that **the old is good** and must be better than anything Jesus has to offer. They are missing out on the greatest wine ever!

> *For reflection: Does my respect for the past prevent me from appreciating what is new? What new thing might Jesus want to do in my life?*

CHAPTER 6

The Lord of the Sabbath
¹ While he was going through a field of grain on a sabbath, his disciples were picking the heads of grain, rubbing them in their hands, and eating them. ² Some Pharisees said, "Why are you doing what is unlawful on the sabbath?" ³ Jesus said to them in reply, "Have you not read what David did when he and those [who were] with him were hungry? ⁴ [How] he went into the house of God, took the bread of offering, which only the priests could lawfully eat, ate of it, and shared it with his companions." ⁵ Then he said to them, "The Son of Man is lord of the sabbath."

Gospel parallels: Matt 12:1–8; Mark 2:23–28
OT: Exod 20:8–11; 34:21; Lev 24:5–9; Deut 5:12–15; 23:26; 1 Sam 21:2–7
NT: Luke 5:24

1 **While he was going through a field of grain on a sabbath, his disciples were picking the heads of grain, rubbing them in their hands** to separate the hulls from the kernels, **and eating them**. Grain crops, chiefly wheat and barley, were planted during the winter rainy season and ripened during spring and early summer. The law of Moses allowed anyone passing through a field to handpick some of the grain; full-fledged harvesting was forbidden (Deut 23:26). Jesus and his disciples are walking through a field on a **sabbath**, and as they walk the disciples pluck some grain for a meal on the run.

> When you go through your neighbor's grainfield, you may pluck some of the ears with your hand, but do not put a sickle to your neighbor's grain.
>
> Deut 23:26

2 **Some Pharisees said, "Why are you doing what is unlawful on the sabbath?"** God commanded that no work be done on the seventh day of the week, the **sabbath** (Exod 20:8–11; Deut 5:12–15). Pharisees developed detailed interpretations of what constituted work and was therefore **unlawful** on the Sabbath. Reaping and threshing were clearly forbidden

157

(see Exod 34:21). **Some Pharisees** considered the disciples' picking of heads of grain to be reaping; they may have considered the disciples' rubbing off the hulls from the kernels to be threshing. They held that the disciples were doing what was **unlawful on the sabbath**.

Pharisees: See page 143

> *For six days you may work, but on the seventh day you shall rest; on that day you must rest even during the seasons of plowing and harvesting.*
>
> Exod 34:21

3 Although the Pharisees' accusation is directed at Jesus' disciples, Jesus responds to it, defending his disciples. He could have gotten into a debate with the Pharisees over what constituted work forbidden on the Sabbath: does casual plucking of grain qualify as harvesting? But Jesus takes a different tack in order to address a more fundamental issue. **Jesus said to them in reply, "Have you not read what David did when he and those [who were] with him were hungry?"** Jesus asks the Pharisees if they have **read** what **David did**—read about it in 1 Samuel (1 Sam 21:2–7). David and his companions were **hungry**: hunger is not explicit in 1 Samuel but implied.

BACKGROUND: SABBATH The Sabbath is the seventh day of the week in the Jewish calendar, our Saturday. "Sabbath" comes from a Hebrew verb that means to stop or cease, indicating an essential note of the Sabbath: it was a day on which all work was to cease. The third of the Ten Commandments spells this out: "Remember to keep holy the sabbath day. Six days you may labor and do all your work, but the seventh day is the sabbath of the LORD, your God. No work may be done then either by you, or your son or daughter, or your male or female slave, or your beast, or by the alien who lives with you" (Exod 20:8–10). Eventually the Sabbath became a day for prayer and study of Scripture as well as a day of leisure. By the time of Jesus, complex interpretations had been developed of what constituted work forbidden on the Sabbath, for example, walking more than roughly one thousand yards (the "sabbath day's journey" of Acts 1:12). Different Jewish groups had different interpretations of what constituted forbidden work, with the Essenes and some Pharisees taking a very rigorous approach. Jesus rejected rigorous Sabbath regulations as burdensome and instead emphasized the original meaning of the Sabbath, as a day of rest that God had given to his people. *Related topics: Essenes (page 395), Pharisees (page 143).*

4   David **went into the house of God**, which at the time was a sanctuary
at the town of Nob (1 Sam 21:2), a little north of Jerusalem. He **took the
bread of offering**: twelve loaves of **bread** were placed on a table in front
of the Holy of Holies as an **offering** to God (Exod 25:23–30). Freshly
baked loaves were set out each Sabbath and replaced with new loaves
the following Sabbath (Lev 24:5–8). **Only the priests could lawfully
eat** bread that had been offered (Lev 24:9). Nevertheless, David took **the
bread of offering** and **ate of it, and shared it with his companions**.
David did what only priests could **lawfully** do, yet there is no hint in 1
Samuel that David was wrong to do so. Jesus presents it as an example
of David justifiably doing something that the law of Moses declared
unlawful.

Priests and Levites: See page 302

5   **Then he said to them, "The Son of Man is lord of the sabbath."**
David had been anointed by Samuel and "from that day on, the spirit
of the LORD rushed upon David" (1 Sam 16:13). So too, but in a far
more profound sense, Jesus is God's anointed: he is begotten through
and filled with the Holy Spirit (1:35; 3:22; 4:1, 14, 18). Jesus proclaims
that he, **the Son of Man, is lord of the sabbath**: the Greek of Luke's
Gospel emphasizes the word **lord**, stressing Jesus' authority over the
Sabbath. He can interpret how the law regarding Sabbath observance is
to be interpreted or overridden; he can allow his disciples to pick heads
of grain.

Son of Man: See page 147
Lord: See page 137

Jesus does not defend his disciples' actions by defining what constitutes work but by saying that satisfying hunger takes precedence over
Sabbath law, and by proclaiming his authority as **lord of the sabbath**.
The **Son of Man** can forgive sins as God forgives sins (5:24); he can
rule how the Sabbath established by God is to be observed. God is doing
something radically new through Jesus; God is providing new wine that
cannot be contained in old wineskins (5:37).

For reflection: What does Jesus' response tell me about him?

Doing Good on the Sabbath

⁶ **On another sabbath he went into the synagogue and taught, and there was a man there whose right hand was withered. ⁷ The scribes and the Pharisees watched him closely to see if he would cure on the sabbath so that they might discover a reason to accuse him. ⁸ But he realized their intentions and said to the man with the withered hand, "Come up and stand before us." And he rose and stood there. ⁹ Then Jesus said to them, "I ask you, is it lawful to do good on the sabbath rather than to do evil, to save life rather than to destroy it?" ¹⁰ Looking around at them all, he then said to him, "Stretch out your hand." He did so and his hand was restored. ¹¹ But they became enraged and discussed together what they might do to Jesus.**

Gospel parallels: Matt 12:9–14; Mark 3:1–6
NT: Luke 4:15–16, 31, 44; 6:5; 13:14

6 **On another sabbath he went into the synagogue and taught:** Jesus regularly makes use of gatherings in village synagogues on the **sabbath** as occasions to proclaim his message (4:15–16, 31–33, 44). **There was a man there whose right hand was withered**—paralyzed and atrophied. Since most men made their living in occupations that involved manual labor (farming, for example), having a crippled **right hand** was a serious disability.

Sabbath: See page 158
Synagogue: See page 115

7 **The scribes and the Pharisees watched him closely**: there have been verbal skirmishes between Jesus and some **scribes** and **Pharisees** (5:20–25, 30–32, 33–39; 6:1–5). Now they have him under surveillance **to see if he would cure on the sabbath so that they might discover a reason to accuse him**. Perhaps they heard reports of Jesus freeing a man from a demon and healing Simon Peter's mother-in-law on the Sabbath (4:31–35, 38–39); they lie in wait for Jesus to **cure** someone this **sabbath** so that they can charge him with violating Sabbath law. They consider medical treatment to be work forbidden on the Sabbath except in life-threatening situations (see 1 Macc 2:41 for an example of preserving life taking precedence over Sabbath regulations). A withered hand was not a

life-threatening condition, and its healing could be postponed until the Sabbath was over (see 13:14). The scribes and Pharisees acknowledge that Jesus has the power to heal people but think that his healing should be subject to Sabbath regulations.

Scribes: See page 146
Pharisees: See page 143

8 **But he realized their intentions**: Jesus knows their thoughts (see 5:22) and realizes that they are out to get him. Instead of backing away from a confrontation with them, he **said to the man with the withered hand, "Come up and stand before us."** The words translated **before us** are literally "in the middle"; Jesus asks the man to stand up in the middle of the synagogue so that everyone can witness what will happen. The man does as Jesus asks: **he rose and stood there.**

9 **Then Jesus said to them**—the scribes and Pharisees—**"I ask you, is it lawful to do good on the sabbath rather than to do evil, to save life rather than to destroy it?"** By prefacing his two sets of alternatives with an **I ask you**, Jesus forces those scrutinizing him to face the alternatives. Jesus frames the issue not in terms of what constitutes work forbidden on the Sabbath but in terms of whether it is **lawful to do good on the sabbath**. God would want his people to **do good** always, and especially on the **sabbath**, a day consecrated to him. By having the alternative to doing good, not to do nothing, but **rather** to **do evil,** Jesus implies that failure to do the good one could is to do evil. Doing evil is never **lawful**. Jesus, the "lord of the sabbath" (6:5), conveys that doing good is always **lawful** on the Sabbath.

For reflection: What good do I do on the Lord's Day?

Jesus' second set of alternatives narrows the focus from the broad categories of good and evil to whether one can **save life** on the Sabbath **rather than destroy it**. To **save** means to rescue from danger and distress or to deliver from death. **Life** here means a person's life. If Jesus heals the man's crippled hand, he is saving him in the sense that he is enabling him to live a normal life again. The alternative to saving life is

rather to **destroy it**; failure to rescue someone from distress is to destroy that person by leaving him or her in his or her distress.

Before Jesus was born, Zechariah blessed God for raising up "a horn for our salvation / within the house of David" (1:69), referring to Jesus. At his birth, an angel announced to shepherds that "a savior has been born for you" (2:11); and when Simeon held the infant Jesus, he said to God, "my eyes have seen your salvation" (2:30). Jesus will save the man with a crippled hand by healing him; he will also save by rescuing women and men from eternal death.

10 **Looking around at them all**: Jesus looked at **all** present in the synagogue, for everyone has to decide whether to do good and help others, or to do evil and destroy them by not doing good. **He then said to him**, directing his words to the man with the crippled hand, **"Stretch out your hand."** As before (verse 8), the man does what Jesus asks of him: **he did so and his hand was restored**. Through his hand being **restored** he was restored to normal life.

For reflection: Who do I know that is in distressed circumstances? What can I do to help them be restored to normal life?

11 A healing is cause for rejoicing, **but they**—the scribes and Pharisees who have Jesus under surveillance—**became enraged**. They are furious because Jesus has publicly healed a man on the Sabbath while frustrating their desire to charge him with violating Sabbath law. They would be hard-pressed to point out exactly what he did that was work on the Sabbath: he only told a man to stretch out his hand and when the man did so, his hand was healed. They **discussed together what they might do to Jesus**. Tensions have been growing between them and Jesus, over his claim to forgive sins (5:20–25), over his associating with sinners (5:30), over his not requiring fasting (5:33), and over his activities on the Sabbath and claiming authority over the Sabbath (6:1–10). The tensions have reached the point that they are now discussing **what they might do to Jesus**. Simeon warned that Jesus would be "a sign that will be contradicted" (2:34); there are now stirrings of organized opposition to Jesus.

Jesus Chooses the Twelve
¹² **In those days he departed to the mountain to pray, and he spent the night in prayer to God. ¹³ When day came, he called his disciples to himself, and from them he chose Twelve, whom he also named apostles: ¹⁴ Simon, whom he named Peter, and his brother Andrew, James, John, Philip, Bartholomew, ¹⁵ Matthew, Thomas, James the son of Alphaeus, Simon who was called a Zealot, ¹⁶ and Judas the son of James, and Judas Iscariot, who became a traitor.**

Gospel parallels: Matt 10:1–4; Mark 3:13–19
NT: Matt 16:18; Luke 5:1–11; 9:1–6; 22:29–30; John 1:42; Acts 1:13

12 After a series of confrontations with Jesus (5:17—6:10), some scribes and Pharisees are discussing what they might do to him (6:11). Jesus is surely aware of their intentions (see 5:22; 6:8). **In those days**, as he begins to face organized opposition, **he departed to the mountain to pray.** Jesus often takes time to pray (5:16), particularly at critical points in his life (3:21; 9:18, 28; 22:39–46). He now has much to pray about. His mission has produced mixed results. Some have become his disciples, but others are now plotting against him. Jesus knows that eventually he will be "taken away" (5:35). His mission is to "proclaim the good news of the kingdom of God" (4:43); how will this message be proclaimed after he is gone? Jesus **spent the night in prayer to God**, seeking God's will for him.

For reflection: What have been the most significant occasions when I sought God's will for me? How has my response in these situations shaped the course of my life?

13 **When day came, he called his disciples to himself, and from them he chose Twelve, whom he also named apostles.** Jesus has attracted a number of disciples, even "a great crowd" of them (6:17). After spending all night communing in prayer with his Father, Jesus **chose Twelve** of his disciples for a special role. What their role includes will emerge in the course of Luke's two-volume work. Here we are told that Jesus **named** them to be his **apostles**. An apostle was an authorized representative sent on a mission. Jesus will not send the Twelve out on their first mission (9:1–6) until he has had more opportunity to instruct them. His choice of **Twelve** (and not, say, ten) is not arbitrary. It recalls the twelve sons

163

of Jacob (Gen 35:23–26), whose descendants formed the twelve tribes of Israel (Gen 49:1, 28). The choice of **Twelve** indicates that they will be the nucleus of a renewed or restored Israel. Jesus will later tell the Twelve that they will judge the twelve tribes of Israel (22:29–30). In the first half of Acts, Luke will recount how members of the Twelve provided leadership for the early Church.

Disciple: See page 149

14 First on the list of the Twelve is **Simon, whom he named Peter.** Luke recounted Simon's call to be a disciple at greater length than he devoted to the call of any other disciple (5:1–11), foreshadowing Simon's role as first among the disciples. Jesus gave the name **Peter** to Simon. "Peter" comes from the Greek word for "rock"; it was not used as a person's name before Jesus applied it to Simon. (Paul usually refers to him as "Cephas," a form of the Aramaic word for "rock"—1 Cor 1:12; 3:22; 9:5; 15:5; Gal 1:18; 2:9, 11, 14.) Luke does not explain why Jesus gave the name Rock to Simon. However, a rock is something stable and solid; Jesus will speak of a house withstanding a flood because it was built on rock (6:48). Jesus will ask Simon Peter, despite his failings, to be a source of stability and strength for the other disciples (22:31–32).

Along with Simon Peter, Jesus chose **his brother Andrew** to be one of the Twelve. Andrew's name will appear again in Acts, when Luke provides another list of the apostles (Acts 1:13), but Andrew will not appear on the scene again in Luke's Gospel. The next two of the Twelve are **James** and **John,** sons of Zebedee and fishing partners of Simon Peter; they became disciples after the great catch of fish (5:9–11). Luke then lists **Philip** and **Bartholomew;** like Andrew, they will be mentioned in Acts (Acts 1:13) but will not appear again in Luke's Gospel.

BACKGROUND: APOSTLE The English word "apostle" is derived from a Greek word meaning to send out. In secular usage, an apostle was an ambassador or a messenger. Jesus was sent by God (Mark 9:37; John 20:21), and so the letter to the Hebrews calls Jesus an apostle (Heb 3:1). Jesus in turn sent out twelve specifically chosen followers as his envoys, commissioned to bear his message and carry out his work. The Gospels often refer to this group as "the Twelve"; their significance lay in their being a symbol of Jesus' restoration of all Israel, which was made up of twelve tribes (see Luke 22:29–30). The early Church used the term "apostle" for a select few of those who went out on mission for Christ (Rom 1:1; 16:7).

15 Also chosen are **Matthew, Thomas, James the son of Alphaeus,** and **Simon who was called a Zealot.** They too will be listed in Acts (Acts 1:13) but not named again in Luke's Gospel. **James** is called **the son of Alphaeus** to distinguish him from James the son of Zebedee (verse 14), and this **Simon** is identified as the **Simon who was called a Zealot** to distinguish him from Simon Peter. Calling Simon a **Zealot** was once taken to mean that he belonged to a political group known as the Zealots who took part in the Jewish rebellion again Roman rule in A.D. 66–70. However, it now appears that these Zealots only formed in the course of the revolt. It is likely that this **Simon** is **called a Zealot** because he is religiously zealous. Luke uses forms of the word in Acts in referring to those who are "zealous observers of the law" (Acts 21:20) or "zealous for God" (Acts 22:3). We might wonder what zealous Simon initially thought of Jesus' free association with tax collectors and sinners (see 5:30).

16 The last two of the Twelve that Luke lists are both named Judas: **Judas the son of James, and Judas Iscariot**. The word **Iscariot** likely means a man from Kerioth, a town in southern Judea (see Joshua 15:25). **Judas the son of James** will not be mentioned again by Luke save in his list in Acts (Acts 1:13). We will hear of **Judas Iscariot** again, for he **became a traitor**. We think of **Judas** as the one whose betrayal led to Jesus' death, but we should keep in mind that he was chosen by Jesus to be among the Twelve after Jesus had spent a night in prayer. Judas **became** a traitor, but that is not how he started out.

For reflection: What lesson might there be for me in what Judas was and what Judas became?

It is worth noting how little Luke tells us about most of the Twelve; he mentions eight of them only here and in his list in Acts. The other four—Simon Peter, James, John, and Judas Iscariot—will play roles as individuals, but otherwise the significance of the Twelve lies more in their collectively symbolizing a renewed or restored Israel than in what they do as individuals.

For reflection: What significance do I find in the relative anonymity of most of the Twelve?

ORIENTATION: *Jesus has taught on a number of occasions without Luke recounting what he taught (4:15, 44; 5:3, 17; 6:6). Luke will now present an extended teaching of Jesus, addressed first of all to his disciples (6:20–49). As a prelude to this teaching, Luke describes the setting.*

The Sermon on the Plain

17 And he came down with them and stood on a stretch of level ground. A great crowd of his disciples and a large number of the people from all Judea and Jerusalem and the coastal region of Tyre and Sidon 18 came to hear him and to be healed of their diseases; and even those who were tormented by unclean spirits were cured. 19 Everyone in the crowd sought to touch him because power came forth from him and healed them all.

Gospel parallels: Matt 4:24–25; Mark 3:7–10
NT: Luke 5:15

17 **And he came down** from the mountain where he had appointed the Twelve (6:12–16) **with them** and his other disciples **and stood on a stretch of level ground**. This **level** setting for what Jesus will teach (6:20–49) gives rise to the popular name for this teaching: the Sermon on the Plain. With Jesus is **a great crowd of his disciples**: Jesus has many disciples in addition to the Twelve (see also 19:37). Presumably not all of his disciples travel with him all the time; Martha and Mary, for example, receive him as a guest in their home (10:38–42). Also gathered on the stretch of level ground is **a large number of the people from all Judea and Jerusalem**. Here (as at 4:44) Luke uses **Judea** to stand for all of Palestine, including Galilee. Some have also come from **the coastal**

BACKGROUND: **TYRE AND SIDON** were the largest cities in southern Phoenicia, the Mediterranean coastal region northwest of Galilee. Both cities, lying in what is today's Lebanon, were seaports and trading centers. Tyre was about 35 miles northwest of the Sea of Galilee; Sidon lay about 22 miles up the coast from Tyre. Lands under the control of Tyre and Sidon extended east and south toward Galilee. Galilee provided grain and other crops to Tyre and Sidon in both Old and New Testament times (see Ezek 27:17; Acts 12:20). The populations of Tyre and Sidon were predominantly Gentile with a Jewish minority. The Church took root in Tyre and Sidon within a few decades of the resurrection of Jesus (see Acts 21:3–6; 27:3).

region of Tyre and Sidon, on the Mediterranean. **Tyre** and **Sidon** were predominantly pagan cities; Luke does not say whether those who came from this region were Jews or Gentiles. **A large number** of people from different areas are waiting for Jesus when he comes down the mountain.

Disciple: See page 149
Judea: See page 40
Jerusalem: See page 516

18 They **came** from distances **to hear him and to be healed of their diseases.** Luke previously noted that news of what Jesus does has gotten around (4:14), and as a result "great crowds assembled to listen to him and to be cured of their ailments" (5:15). They again have come to **hear** his teaching and to be **healed** of their afflictions. Jesus does not disappoint them. He will teach at length, but first he heals those who need healing. Jesus might have several reasons for healing before teaching. Those who are well are better able to absorb his teachings than those who are plagued by sickness. More significantly, Jesus' healings and exorcisms release men and women from the grip of evil and free them to accept the good news of the kingdom of God that he proclaims (see 4:43; 11:20). **Even those who were tormented by unclean spirits were cured.** The word translated **tormented** can connote sickness; **even** those afflicted by evil spirits were **cured**.

Demons, unclean spirits: See page 125

19 **Everyone in the crowd sought to touch him because power came forth from him.** People crowd to Jesus to receive his healing touch, even straining to **touch him** to experience his healing **power**. Jesus **healed them all**: he has the **power** to heal (4:14; 5:17) and he heals everyone who comes to him.

For reflection: How have I sought and experienced the healing power of Jesus?

The Fortunate and the Unfortunate
²⁰ **And raising his eyes toward his disciples he said:**
 "Blessed are you who are poor,
  for the kingdom of God is yours.

²¹ Blessed are you who are now hungry,
   for you will be satisfied.
Blessed are you who are now weeping,
   for you will laugh.
²² Blessed are you when people hate you,
   and when they exclude and insult you,
   and denounce your name as evil
   on account of the Son of Man.
²³ Rejoice and leap for joy on that day! Behold, your reward will
be great in heaven. For their ancestors treated the prophets in the
same way.
²⁴ But woe to you who are rich,
   for you have received your consolation.
²⁵ But woe to you who are filled now,
   for you will be hungry.
Woe to you who laugh now,
   for you will grieve and weep.
²⁶ Woe to you when all speak well of you,
   for their ancestors treated the false prophets in
      this way."

Gospel parallels: Matt 5:3–12
NT: Luke 1:53; 4:18; 21:17

20 **And raising his eyes toward his disciples he said:** along with his disciples there are "a large number of the people" present who came to Jesus
"to hear him and to be healed" (6:17–18). Although Jesus addresses his
words to **his disciples**, he knows that the crowd is listening (see 6:27; 7:1),
and his words bear a message for them as well. Jesus proclaims, **Blessed
are you who are poor**. Proclaiming someone **blessed** or happy is a biblical pattern of speech used for congratulating or praising someone (see
11:27–28); today we call these pronouncements "beatitudes." Greek uses
different words for different degrees of poverty; the word used here for
poor means those who are utterly destitute and reduced to begging. The
same word is used in Jesus' later parable: "Lying at his door was a poor
man named Lazarus, covered with sores, who would gladly have eaten his
fill of the scraps that fell from the rich man's table" (16:20–21). Being in
abject poverty hardly seems good fortune, but Jesus says **blessed are you**

who are poor. Even if we do not fully understand how the poor are in a blessed condition, unless we accept Jesus' declaration to be true, some of the things he will go on to teach will not make sense.

Disciple: See page 149
The poor and the rich: See page 198

Beatitudes explain why a person is fortunate; the poor are blessed because **the kingdom of God is yours.** Jesus' mission is to "bring glad tidings to the poor" (4:18, using the word for "poor" that means utterly destitute). These "glad tidings" are "the good news of the kingdom of God" (4:43). Jesus proclaims to the **poor** the good news that **the kingdom of God is yours.** God's kingdom, or reign, will not be fully established until some future time (21:25–31), but it is being inaugurated even now through Jesus (11:20; 17:21), and those who are poor are able to enter it: Jesus tells them the kingdom of God **is** yours. In the Greek of Luke's Gospel, **yours** is emphatic, conveying that the kingdom of God belongs particularly to the very poor. Some of Jesus' disciples have left everything, including their jobs, to become his disciples (5:11, 28). Although their following him may mean being destitute and dependent on the generosity of others, it is also bringing them into God's reign, making them indeed **blessed** and fortunate.

Kingdom of God: See page 381

BACKGROUND: BEATITUDES A beatitude praises or congratulates someone for being fortunate, telling why or how they are fortunate. "A woman from the crowd called out and said to him, 'Blessed is the womb that carried you and the breasts at which you nursed.' He replied, 'Rather, blessed are those who hear the word of God and observe it'" (Luke 11:27–28). There are about sixty beatitudes in the Old Testament and, by one count, twenty-eight beatitudes in the New Testament. Psalm 1 is an extended beatitude. It begins with an exclamation, "Happy the man," or "the person," and then lays out the basis of the person's happiness: he or she avoids bad company and spends time meditating on Scripture (Psalm 1:1–2). By explaining why the person is fortunate, the beatitude usually encourages the behavior that is the basis of the person's happiness. Beatitudes may also describe the nature of the person's happiness. Psalm 1, for example, speaks of flourishing even in difficult circumstances (Psalm 1:3). Beatitudes are sometimes translated "Blessed is so and so," but a beatitude does not call down God's blessing on a person; it declares that the person is already fortunate in the eyes of God because of what the beatitude praises him or her for being or doing.

---

21 **Blessed are you who are now hungry.** Jesus continues to address the abjectly poor, for they often are **hungry** (in Jesus' parable, poor Lazarus longs for scraps—16:20–21). Jesus speaks to the hungry and says **you will be satisfied**. The word translated **satisfied** has the connotation of eating one's fill. Those who are **now hungry** are blessed and fortunate for they **will be satisfied**—implying, satisfied by God. Theirs is the kingdom of God (verse 20), and they will "recline at table in the kingdom of God" (13:29), sharing in the heavenly banquet (see Isaiah 25:6–9).

　　Blessed are you who are now weeping. Jesus continues to address the poor. Jesus does not glamorize poverty; the poor are **now weeping** because of their destitution and hunger. Jesus tells them that the time will come when **you will laugh**. Banquets are festive occasions, occasions for rejoicing; those who enter the kingdom of God and take part in the heavenly banquet (verses 20–21) will have eternal joy. Their future prospects enable them to be called **blessed** even in their present misery.

　　For reflection: How do I understand Jesus' first three beatitudes at this point in my reading?

22 **Blessed are you when people hate you, / and when they exclude and insult you, / and denounce your name as evil / on account of the Son of Man.** Jesus presumes that his disciples will be hated **on account of the Son of Man**—on account of him, because they are his disciples (see also 21:17). He tells them that they are nonetheless **blessed** and fortunate. Their good fortune does not lie in their being hated but in their being his disciples. He tells them that they are fortunate even **when they exclude and insult you**. Being excluded likely means being ostracized by relatives and associates because one is a follower of Jesus. This may have an economic impact: in the highly interdependent society of the time, being shunned by one's family and business associates could leave one poor—the condition addressed in the previous beatitudes. **Insult you** means revile you face-to-face. **Denounce your name as evil on account of the Son of Man** means denunciation because one is Jesus' follower and perhaps betrayal to the authorities during a persecution (see 21:16). For Luke it might have meant being denounced for bearing the name Christian (see Acts 11:26). Jesus proclaims that those who suffer these adversities are **blessed**.

Son of Man: See page 147

23 Because they are blessed, Jesus tells them to **Rejoice and leap for joy on that day**—on the day when they experience hatred and exclusion, insult and denunciation. Jesus provides two reasons for their rejoicing. He tells them, **Behold, your reward will be great in heaven.** The Greek word for **reward** literally refers to a wage paid a worker (it is used for a laborer's "hire" at 10:7). Jesus' disciples will receive a **great** reward for what they endure for his sake. Their reward will be **in heaven**: those who endure suffering for him will receive a great reward in the presence of God. Jesus adds a second reason for his followers to rejoice when they are hated and denounced: **For their ancestors treated the prophets in the same way.** Prophets had been ill-treated (4:24; 11:47–51; 13:33–34; see also 1 Kings 19:10; Jer 26:20–24; 38:6–13). Mistreated disciples of Jesus are in the good company of God's **prophets**, and that is reason for them to rejoice.

For reflection: Have I experienced rejection or scorn because of my loyalty to Jesus? How did I respond? Am I able to rejoice in the midst of such adversity?

24 **But woe to you who are rich**: while pronouncing someone blessed extols their fortunate condition, a **woe** laments their misfortune. Jesus tells any in the crowd who are **rich** that they are in a woeful state, **for you have received your consolation**. The word translated **received** has the meaning of "received in full": the rich cannot expect anything more than they already have.

Jesus will have much to say about riches in the course of Luke's Gospel, and his later teachings throw light on his proclaiming a woe upon the rich. Money in itself is not evil and should be used to help the

BACKGROUND: WOES A woe is the opposite of a beatitude. While a beatitude congratulates someone as fortunate, a woe laments and reproaches someone for his or her unfortunate condition. Just as a beatitude encourages the behavior that is being praised, a woe warns against the behavior that is being lamented. There are about fifty woes in the Old Testament, mostly as prophetic denunciations of those who do evil. Chapter 5 of Isaiah pronounces six woes: "Woe to those who call evil good, and good evil" (Isaiah 5:20; see also 5:8, 11, 18, 21–22). The New Testament has thirty-seven woes. Luke's Gospel pairs four beatitudes with four woes (Luke 6:20–26). A woe is a cry of grief and alarm over a course of action that will bring God's punishment (see Matt 11:20–24). Woes are warnings and expressions of sorrow, not curses.

poor (11:41; 12:33; 16:9; 18:22; 19:8). But being rich can entice one to use one's wealth to indulge oneself (12:13–21) and be an obstacle to entering the kingdom of God (18:18–27). No one can serve both God and wealth (16:13); those who put their wealth ahead of God are in a woeful condition. Jesus' woe warns his disciples about the dangers of wealth. Even those who have left everything to follow Jesus can be tempted by the lure of wealth and the prestige and comforts and security it brings.

For reflection: What are my temptations to self-indulgence?

25 **But woe to you who are filled now, for you will be hungry.** Those who are wealthy can eat well; the rich man in Jesus' later parable "dined sumptuously each day" (16:19). Those who **now** eat well until they are **filled** are in a woeful state for they **will be hungry**: they will experience a reversal of their condition. Luke's readers can recall that Mary proclaimed about God, "The hungry he has filled with good things; / the rich he has sent away empty" (1:53). Jesus continues, **Woe to you who laugh now**, referring to laughter as an expression of a rich person's carefree contentment with the present. It will not last forever: **you will grieve and weep**. While the poor can enter into the eternal banquet of the kingdom (verses 20–21; 13:29), it is hard for those who are rich to enter the kingdom of God (18:24). They will be left out of the banquet, hungry and grieving: "There will be wailing and grinding of teeth when you see Abraham, Isaac, and Jacob and all the prophets in the kingdom of God and you yourselves cast out" (13:28).

26 **Woe to you when all speak well of you, for their ancestors treated the false prophets in this way.** People might **speak well** of the wealthy in the hope of getting something from them; those with wealth had influence and could act as patrons. **False prophets** told people what they wanted to hear (Isaiah 30:10–11; Jer 5:31; 14:14–15; 23:16–17; Micah 2:11) and consequently were popular. Being praised by others was no index of a prophet's standing with God, and neither is it for those whose wealth has made them popular.

Jesus' four woes balance his four beatitudes and show the reverse sign of the coin. They shed light on why those who are poor and rejected are blessed. Jesus' disciples have no wealth to tempt them to self-reliance and self-indulgence; they can more easily realize that they must rely on God (see 12:22–34). The rich may consider themselves filled and have little need of God (see Rev 3:17); the poverty and emptiness of Jesus' disciples allows God to fill them with good things.

Some of Luke's first readers (including Theophilus—1:3) were probably wealthy. This will not be the last time that Luke's Gospel challenges them to examine their attitude toward wealth—and challenges us as well.

For reflection: On balance, am I among the poor or among the wealthy? How fortunate am I in the eyes of God?

The Gospel of Love

27 "But to you who hear I say, love your enemies, do good to those who hate you, 28 bless those who curse you, pray for those who mistreat you. 29 To the person who strikes you on one cheek, offer the other one as well, and from the person who takes your cloak, do not withhold even your tunic. 30 Give to everyone who asks of you, and from the one who takes what is yours do not demand it back. 31 Do to others as you would have them do to you. 32 For if you love those who love you, what credit is that to you? Even sinners love those who love them. 33 And if you do good to those who do good to you, what credit is that to you? Even sinners do the same. 34 If you lend money to those from whom you expect repayment, what credit [is] that to you? Even sinners lend to sinners, and get back the same amount. 35 But rather, love your enemies and do good to them, and lend expecting nothing back; then your reward will be great and you will be children of the Most High, for he himself is kind to the ungrateful and the wicked. 36 Be merciful, just as [also] your Father is merciful."

Gospel parallels: Matt 5:38–48; 7:12

OT: Exod 34:6; Lev 19:18

NT: Luke 6:20–23; Rom 12:14

27 But to you who hear I say: Jesus is still speaking to his disciples (6:20) but knows that a large crowd is also listening (6:17–18; 7:1). He has a message for everyone who will **hear** his words. He tells them, **I say** to you,

love your enemies. Loving enemies goes beyond what is demanded in the law of Moses. The command, "You shall love your neighbor as yourself" (Lev 19:18) required one to love fellow Israelites; it was presumed that one could hate one's enemies (see Psalm 137:8–9; 139:21–22). One of the Dead Sea Scrolls—the library of a Jewish community of Jesus' time—urges community members to "love all the sons of light" (members of the community) and "hate all the sons of darkness" (enemies of the community). They were hardly alone in their view: almost everyone believes they are justified in hating those who would do them harm. But Jesus proclaims, **I say, love your enemies**. It is a radical demand upon every disciple in every age and setting. Not hating enemies is insufficient; a follower of Jesus must **love** her or his **enemies**.

For reflection: Who are my enemies? What is my attitude toward them?

The **love** that Jesus commands is borne out in action; he tells those listening to **do good to those who hate you**. Jesus has spoken of those who will **hate** and exclude, insult and denounce his disciples (6:22); his disciples must love and **do good** to them in return. To **do good** to them

---

BACKGROUND: DEAD SEA SCROLLS In 1947, a Bedouin shepherd boy came across some clay jars in a cave overlooking the Dead Sea. The jars contained seven ancient scrolls, including the book of Isaiah. Over the next nine years more scrolls were found in ten other caves in the area. Over nine hundred different scrolls have been discovered, virtually all of them incomplete and decayed, in more than one hundred thousand fragments. The process of assembling and translating the fragments has taken scholars many years. The scrolls were copied between roughly 200 B.C. and A.D. 68 and represent an entire library. About two hundred of the scrolls were copies of books of the Old Testament, including thirty-six copies of the Psalms. Also discovered were copies of nonbiblical religious writings, including about ten copies of 1 Enoch and fifteen copies of Jubilees, as well as scrolls of religious writings that had been previously unknown to modern scholars. Along with these works, which had been in general circulation among Jews at the time of Jesus, were a number of works that pertained to the religious community that owned the library. Some of these scrolls were community rules, hymns used in the community, and commentaries on books of the Old Testament written from the community's perspective. The community that owned this library is commonly identified as the Essenes, a sect headquartered at Qumran, on the shore of the Dead Sea, where the scrolls were found. *Related topics: Essenes (page 395), Nonbiblical writings (page 342).*

---

means doing things that benefit or assist them. This is the opposite of how we might normally treat those who hate us.

28 Jesus tells those listening to **bless those who curse you**. To **bless** someone is not to declare them to be blessed or fortunate but to invoke God's favor upon them. A **curse** is the opposite; to **curse** means to call down God's harm upon a person. Disciples are not to retaliate in kind; when someone curses a disciple of Jesus, the disciple is to ask God to show favor to the person. Paul will echo Jesus' teaching: "Bless those who persecute [you], bless and do not curse them" (Rom 12:14; see also 1 Pet 3:9). Similarly, Jesus tells his followers to **pray for those who mistreat you**, interceding with God on their behalf. Jesus sets the example: from the cross he will pray for those responsible for his crucifixion, "Father, forgive them, they know not what they do" (23:34; see also the example of Stephen—Acts 7:59–60).

For reflection: When have I done something good for a person who hated me? When have I prayed to God on that person's behalf?

29 Jesus provides some vivid illustrations of what it means to love those who harm you. **To the person who strikes you on one cheek, offer the other one as well.** Being struck on the **cheek** is insult and humiliation rather than grave bodily harm. If a person abuses and degrades a disciple of Jesus, he or she is to remain vulnerable to such abuse. **From the person who takes your cloak** by force or intimidation, **do not withhold even your tunic.** If someone **takes your cloak**, your outer garment, freely give them **even your tunic**, your inner garment. That

---

BACKGROUND: CLOTHING The two basic items of clothing at the time of Jesus were the tunic and the cloak (see Luke 6:29; Acts 9:39). The tunic was an inner garment often made by folding a rectangle of cloth, sometimes linen, over on itself and stitching the sides, with openings for the head and arms. The cloak, often wool, was an outer garment, perhaps a loose-fitting robe or a rectangular cloth that one draped around oneself. These garments were worn by both men and women, with only color and decoration distinguishing them. A Jewish man's cloak would have tassels (Num 15:37–40; Deut 22:12). Belts were used to cinch tunics and cloaks. A head covering could be simply a cloth draped or tied around the head; leather sandals protected the feet. The upper class could afford imported silk and dyes, and their clothing proclaimed their status.

---

would leave one naked if Jesus' words are followed literally, but he is providing dramatic examples to induce his disciples to face up to the requirements of love.

30 Give to everyone who asks of you. Beggars were common; giving indiscriminately to **everyone who asks of you** could leave one poor oneself. Jesus would consider this good fortune; he proclaimed, "Blessed are you who are poor" (6:20). **And from the one who takes what is yours** by stealth or force **do not demand it back.** Anyone would naturally want to reclaim what is rightfully theirs; Jesus instructs his disciples to forgo their rights. This is again a prescription that could lead to poverty.

Jesus' illustrations of the radical call to love one's enemies have a common thread of making oneself completely vulnerable to others, even at the price of losing one's dignity and possessions. Loving others, even one's enemies, takes precedence over preserving oneself. This would seem to be too much for Jesus to ask of his followers, except that he set the example by giving up his body and blood for them on the cross (see 22:19–20).

For reflection: What is my reaction to Jesus' illustrations of his call to love?

31 Do to others as you would have them do to you. Teachers before Jesus had advised treating people as one wanted to be treated, or not doing to others what one would not want done to oneself (see Tobit 4:15). The law of Moses commanded, "You shall love your neighbor as yourself" (Lev 19:18). Jesus' formulation of the maxim puts the accent on doing: **do to others**. Since Jesus has just commanded, "Love your enemies" (verse 27), **others** means all others, including enemies. Jesus' disciples are to "do good to those who hate you" (verse 27); the standard Jesus invokes here for doing good is what **you would have them do to you**. This is a high standard for conduct, as is loving others as one loves oneself.

For reflection: How much do I love others, as measured by what I do for them?

32 It is clear that Jesus includes all others, even enemies, within the scope of those whom his followers must love. **For if you love those who love you, what credit is that to you?** The sense is, if you *only* love those who

176

love you. The word translated **credit** literally means "favor" and here has the implication of favor in the sight of God (1 Pet 2:20 uses the word for "grace" before God). We receive no credit from God for loving only those who love us. Everyone, **even sinners love those who love them;** it is hardly a noteworthy achievement to behave as everyone else does.

33 **And if you do good to those who do good to you, what credit is that to you?** Jesus again indicates that to love others (verse 32) means to **do good** to others (see verse 27): the accent throughout the Sermon on the Plain is on doing. **Even sinners do the same**: it is only human to reciprocate love in order to be loved.

34 **If you lend money to those from whom you expect repayment, what credit [is] that to you?** Jesus taught, "Give to everyone who asks of you" (verse 30). Giving money away is quite different from lending money to those who will repay it. **Even sinners lend to sinners, and get back the same amount,** but Jesus' disciples are to give without the prospect of receiving any return other than **credit** with God.

35 **But rather** than follow the usual standards for loving and lending, **love your enemies and do good to them.** Jesus again pairs **love** with **do good,** and again proclaims that one's love and good deeds must be extended to one's **enemies,** to those who may return love with hate and harm. The Greek words for **love** and **do good** are in a tense that indicates repeated or habitual action: habitually **love your enemies** and repeatedly **do good to them.** Loving one's enemies implies that one loves everyone, regardless of whether they love in return. Likewise, while people lend expecting a return (verse 34), followers of Jesus are habitually to **lend expecting nothing back**—again a prescription for ending up in blessed poverty. Jesus abolishes reciprocity as the standard for his followers' conduct. They are to "do to others as you would have them do to you" (verse 31), not taking into account what others actually do to them.

For reflection: How well do I live up to Jesus' standards for love?

Jesus promises his disciples that if they love their enemies and do good and lend freely, **then your reward will be great**—their reward from God. Jesus told those who were poor and hungry and hated, "your reward will be great in heaven" (6:23), and he gives the same assurance to those who love and do good to those who hate them. Their reward **will be great**: others may take advantage of the disciples and return hate for their love, but their reward from God will far outweigh their losses. Jesus tells them, **you will be children of the Most High** God. Jesus will speak about God to his disciples as "your Father" (verse 36; see also 12:30, 32); he will teach them to pray to him as "Father" (11:2). Jesus, the Son of God (1:32, 35), will enable his disciples to be sons and daughters of God (Paul will refer to God's "adoption" of us as his children—Rom 8:14–15; Gal 4:5–6). Being **children**—literally, sons—of God has a second meaning. In Hebrew idiom, to be a "son of" someone or something meant to reproduce their characteristics (the words translated as "a peaceful person" at 10:6 are literally "a son of peace"). In loving those who do not love them, the disciples are like God and reproduce his characteristics, **for he himself is kind to the ungrateful and the wicked**. God sets the example, being kind and loving to everyone, even **the ungrateful** who do not return his love and **the wicked** who commit evil. Those who are children of God imitate his love.

We can now better understand why Jesus tells the poor and hated that they are blessed (6:20–23) and requires them to love with an extravagant love (verses 27–36). They are blessed and fortunate because their **reward will be great**; they have the good fortune to be **children of the Most High**. Jesus is indeed bringing "glad tidings to the poor" (4:18): the "good news of the kingdom of God" (4:43) is the good news of the ultimate triumph of love.

36 Jesus exhorts his disciples to live as children of God: **Be merciful, just as [also] your Father is merciful.** At Mount Sinai, God proclaimed that he is a "merciful and gracious God, slow to anger and rich in kindness and fidelity" (Exod 34:6; see also Deut 4:31; Joel 2:13; Jonah 4:2). The twenty-six verses of Psalm 136 have the refrain, "God's love endures forever" ("his mercy endures forever" in some translations). God's mercy is to be the measure of the disciples' mercy. This is a higher standard than doing to others what we would have them do to us (verse 31); followers of Jesus are to do to others as their **Father** does for them. If the Father is **merciful** and kind even to the ungrateful and the wicked (verse 35), how

much more merciful and kind is he to his children. They in turn are to **be merciful** just as he is merciful.

For reflection: How has God had mercy on me? What am I doing to show mercy to others?

Judge Oneself, Not Others

³⁶ "**Be merciful, just as [also] your Father is merciful.** ³⁷ **Stop judging and you will not be judged. Stop condemning and you will not be condemned. Forgive and you will be forgiven.** ³⁸ **Give and gifts will be given to you; a good measure, packed together, shaken down, and overflowing, will be poured into your lap. For the measure with which you measure will in return be measured out to you.**" ³⁹ **And he told them a parable, "Can a blind person guide a blind person? Will not both fall into a pit?** ⁴⁰ **No disciple is superior to the teacher; but when fully trained, every disciple will be like his teacher.** ⁴¹ **Why do you notice the splinter in your brother's eye, but do not perceive the wooden beam in your own?** ⁴² **How can you say to your brother, 'Brother, let me remove that splinter in your eye,' when you do not even notice the wooden beam in your own eye? You hypocrite! Remove the wooden beam from your eye first; then you will see clearly to remove the splinter in your brother's eye.**"

Gospel parallels: Matt 7:1–5; 10:24–25; 15:14; Mark 4:24
NT: Matt 6:12, 14–15; Luke 6:27–36; 11:4

36 **Be merciful, just as [also] your Father is merciful.** This verse concluded the previous section of the Sermon on the Plain but is printed again here because it also introduces the following section. It is a hinge, as it were, joining two parts of Jesus' teachings.

37 **Stop judging:** the Greek literally reads "and stop judging," linking the prohibition of judging with the command to be merciful as the Father is merciful. The Greek word for **judging** can mean to reach a decision (see 7:43; 12:57) or to pass judgment, whether favorable or unfavorable. It can also mean to condemn (it is translated "condemn" at 19:22), and

what follows indicates this is its meaning here. God is kind to the wicked (6:35), and disciples of Jesus are to imitate God's mercy (verse 36) by not being judgmental fault-finders. Jesus tells his disciples that if they do not judge others, **you will not be judged**—judged by God. Jesus does not mean that his disciples will be exempt from the final judgment (referred to at 10:14; 11:31–32); he means that if they refrain from condemning others, then God will be lenient with them. Jesus repeats his admonition for emphasis: **stop condemning and you will not be condemned** by God. If Jesus' followers imitate God's mercy, God will be all the more merciful to them.

For reflection: How critical am I of others for their faults?

Jesus tells his disciples, **Forgive and you will be forgiven**. The word translated **forgive** means to release. Disciples of Jesus may be the victims of mistreatment and theft (6:27–29); they are to release those who harm them from any obligation to make recompense. If they forgive and grant amnesty to others, they **will be forgiven** by God. Jesus will teach his disciples to pray, "Forgive us our sins / for we ourselves forgive everyone in debt to us" (11:4): release us from the debt of our sins as we release others of their debts to us. Jesus' disciples are to be slow to condemn but quick to forgive.

For reflection: How completely have I forgiven those who have harmed me?

38 **Give and gifts will be given to you.** To forgive wipes out debts and balances the books; to **give** goes further and makes a deposit in another's account, as it were. Jesus told his disciples to give to everyone who asks (6:30) and to lend expecting nothing back, promising that they would receive a great reward from God (6:35). He repeats his admonition to **give** and promises that in turn **gifts will be given to you**—given, that is, by God. Jesus invokes an image drawn from commerce to convey how generous God's reward will be: **a good measure, packed together, shaken down, and overflowing, will be poured into your lap.** Merchants used measuring containers in selling grain; a "bushel basket" (11:33) held a peck (roughly two gallons) of grain when filled and leveled. Jesus uses the image of a **good measure** of grain that is **packed together**

and **shaken down**, with the container topped off until it is **overflowing** and can hold no more. The grain is **poured** into the customer's **lap**, literally, into the fold of a garment. A cloak could be pulled up above the belt to form a temporary pocket. Jesus compares God to a merchant who generously favors the buyer; God will use a **good measure** for the **gifts** he gives to those who **give**.

For reflection: What does Jesus' image convey to me about God's generosity?

Jesus applies the image to his followers: **For the measure with which you measure will in return be measured out to you.** If his disciples are like a merchant who uses a dishonest measure to shortchange a buyer (see Amos 8:5), then God will shortchange them. But if the disciples are generous in their dealings with others—not condemning them, but forgiving them and giving to them—then God will be generous. God will do to them in good measure what they do to others.

For reflection: Is God's treating me as I treat others an unsettling prospect for me? If so, what can I do about it?

39 **And he told them a parable, "Can a blind person guide a blind person?"** Jesus' **parable** compares someone to **a blind person** trying to guide a second **blind person**. He rhetorically asks whether this will work, inviting a no answer. A second rhetorical question invites a yes answer: **Will not both fall into a pit?** If someone who is blind tries to lead another person who is blind, both will end up badly. But who is Jesus comparing to a blind would-be guide?

Parables: See page 217

40 Jesus does not immediately explain his parable but notes that **no disciple is superior to the teacher**. This is true because of the nature of their relationship. A **disciple** studies under a **teacher** to learn from him or her. If anyone is already **superior** to a teacher, then there is no reason to become a disciple of the teacher. Jesus adds, **but when fully trained, every disciple will be like his teacher.** After a disciple has been **fully trained** by a teacher and absorbed all that the teacher has to offer, then

181

the **disciple** will be on equal footing with the **teacher**. The disciple will even **be like** his teacher: disciples were to imitate their teacher's lifestyle as well as learn from him.

Disciple: See page 149

> *For reflection: Over the course of the last year, have I become more like Jesus? What might I do to better imitate him?*

41 Jesus returns to the seeing-impaired, now addressing his disciples directly. **Why do you notice the splinter in your brother's eye, but do not perceive the wooden beam in your own?** Jesus uses an outlandish comparison to characterize the behavior of his disciples. It is as if a disciple has a **wooden beam**—a hewn log—in his or her eye. Although the disciple has a sizable beam in one eye, the disciple does not **perceive** it. Yet this disciple is able, or thinks she or he is able, to **notice** a **splinter** of wood in a **brother's** eye—in the eye of another disciple.

Jesus' imagery suggests that his disciples should adopt the perspective, "My faults are big logs; the faults of others are splinters in comparison."

42 The disciple not only notices the splinter in the eye of another disciple but wants to do something about it. Jesus asks, **how can you say to your brother, "Brother, let me remove that splinter in your eye,"** **when you do not even notice the wooden beam in your own eye?** How can a disciple see a splinter clearly if he or she cannot see a log? Removing a splinter from an eye is a delicate affair; how can a disciple profess to be competent to do so when his or her vision is obscured by a beam? It would be like the blind trying to lead the mildly nearsighted! Jesus exclaims, **You hypocrite!** The Greek word **hypocrite** means an actor who plays a part on a stage. As Jesus uses it here, the word refers to those whose lives betray a disconnect between appearance and reality. The beam-in-the-eye disciple professes to be able to see and remove a splinter in the eye of another, but in reality is incapable of doing so.

Helping another is not wrong, only so-called help that may do harm, like a blind person trying to guide another blind person. Those who want to remove a splinter from the eye of another should first make sure that their own vision is up to it. Jesus tells his disciples, **remove the wooden**

beam from your eye first; then you will see clearly to remove the splinter in your brother's eye. Removing the beam requires being aware of it: a disciple's first task is self-examination. If the **beam** represents whatever impairs our ability to help others, then how do we rid ourselves of our impairments? Perhaps this is the point of Jesus speaking of disciples who are "fully trained" by a teacher and have become like their teacher (verse 40). Jesus' teachings and example will form his disciples to become like him, purging them of their impairments, equipping them to help others.

For reflection: What impairs my ability to help others? What am I doing to remove my impairments?

For Self-Examination
⁴³ "A good tree does not bear rotten fruit, nor does a rotten tree bear good fruit. ⁴⁴ For every tree is known by its own fruit. For people do not pick figs from thornbushes, nor do they gather grapes from brambles. ⁴⁵ A good person out of the store of goodness in his heart produces good, but an evil person out of a store of evil produces evil; for from the fullness of the heart the mouth speaks."
Gospel parallels: Matt 7:16–18; 12:33–35
NT: Luke 3:8; 6:40–42

43 Jesus continues to speak in parables (see 6:39). **A good tree does not bear rotten fruit**—literally, *for* **a good tree** . . . This "for," or "because," indicates that what Jesus says now is giving a cause or reason for what he has just said. In Palestine, olive, fig, and palm trees are cultivated for their **fruit.** Almost by definition, a **good** fruit **tree does not bear rotten** or bad **fruit**; if it bore **rotten** fruit it could not be considered to be a **good** tree. Likewise, **a rotten tree** does not **bear good fruit.** Fruit is only as good as the tree that produces it.

44 **For every tree is known by its own fruit:** Jesus invokes further agricultural images. **For people do not pick figs from thornbushes, nor do they gather grapes from brambles.** Figs grow on fig trees, grapes

grow on grapevines; no one would expect to find them growing on **thornbushes** or **brambles.** Just as you cannot harvest good fruit from bad trees, so you cannot harvest figs or grapes from thornbushes and brambles. In the same way, you cannot get good guidance from poor guides, or good teaching from poor teachers (see verses 39–42).

45 Jesus applies his parable about trees and fruit, making it clear that the parable refers to humans and human conduct. **A good person out of the store of goodness in his heart produces good.** In biblical idiom, the **heart** is the core of one's being, the source of thoughts, decisions, and emotions. The word translated **store** means a place where something is kept or that which is stored up (it is translated "treasure" in 12:33–34). A **good person** has an interior **store of goodness**, and from that store **produces good** conduct, just as a good tree produces good fruit. **But an evil person out of a store of evil produces evil**, just as a bad tree produces bad fruit. Jesus adds a specific way in which good or evil flow from the inner self: **for from the fullness of the heart**—from the abundance of what is within us—**the mouth speaks**. The mouth expresses what the heart contains.

Before speaking of fruit trees, Jesus spoke of logs and splinters in eyes, and urged his disciples to remove the unnoticed logs in their own eyes so that they could attend to the splinters in the eyes of others (6:41–42). His parable about fruit trees and the application he makes of it call for his disciples to examine their interior condition and to judge it on the basis of their conduct. The wooden beam in their eyes represented whatever impaired their ability to help others. The message of his fruit-tree parable is that the root of their impairments lies within them, in what is in their hearts. They can evaluate their hearts—their spiritual condition—by examining their conduct, their words and deeds. Their goal is to become like their teacher (6:40). That will require self-examination and repentance, until their inner **fullness** is a **store of goodness** that produces **good**.

For reflection: What do my words and actions reveal to me about my inner condition? What changes might I need to make?

ORIENTATION: *Jesus concludes his Sermon on the Plain with an exhortation to live according to his teachings.*

Acting on Jesus' Words

⁴⁶ **"Why do you call me, 'Lord, Lord,' but not do what I command? ⁴⁷ I will show you what someone is like who comes to me, listens to my words, and acts on them. ⁴⁸ That one is like a person building a house, who dug deeply and laid the foundation on rock; when the flood came, the river burst against that house but could not shake it because it had been well built. ⁴⁹ But the one who listens and does not act is like a person who built a house on the ground without a foundation. When the river burst against it, it collapsed at once and was completely destroyed."**

Gospel parallels: Matthew 7:21, 24–27
NT: Luke 8:21; 11:28; Rom 2:13; James 1:22–25

46 **Why do you call me, "Lord, Lord," but not do what I command?** The word **Lord** has a range of applications. Jesus' disciples and others who respect him call him **Lord** in acknowledgment of his authority (5:8, 12). In a more profound use of the word, Luke's first readers called Jesus **Lord** as God is called Lord (see Rom 10:9; 1 Cor 12:3; Phil 2:11). Doubling the title—**Lord, Lord**—adds emphasis (see 8:24; 10:41; 13:34; 22:31). Jesus addresses those who acknowledge his authority as their Lord **but [do] not do what I command.** Jesus characterizes his teachings as a **command**: he does not speak merely to inform and enlighten his followers but to tell them what they are to do. Jesus may particularly have in mind what he teaches in the Sermon on the Plain (6:20–49), but his words apply to all of his teachings. He stresses the importance of not only hearing but acting, for his words are the words of God (see 8:21; 11:28).

Lord: See page 137

For reflection: How well am I living up to what Jesus requires in his Sermon on the Plain, for example, loving and forgiving those who harm me?

47 **I will show you what someone is like who comes to me, listens to my words, and acts on them.** Many have come to Jesus, some to be his

disciples, some to hear his teachings and be healed (6:18). Jesus singles out **someone** who **comes** to him and **listens** to his **words,** and then **acts on them**. He tells what this person **is like:**

48 **That one** who comes and hears and acts **is like a person building a house, who dug deeply and laid the foundation on rock**. This builder does a thorough job, excavating **deeply** until reaching bedrock, so that **the foundation** of the house rests **on rock**. Then, **when the flood came, the river burst against that house but could not shake it because it had been well built**. Jesus might have had in mind heavy rains filling a ravine in the hills of Galilee with a torrent of water that surges down upon a house. Luke may have imagined the scene based on his own experience. An ancient writing portrays Luke as a native of Antioch, which was built on the banks of the Orontes River. Perhaps Luke imagined runoff from the mountains above Antioch swelling the Orontes River and flooding the city. A house **well built**, solidly anchored on rock, withstands floodwaters. Jesus says that the one who comes to him, listens to his teachings, and then acts on them is like the owner of a well-built house; she or he will withstand whatever adversity comes along. In the context of the Sermon on the Plain, there may also be an implication of withstanding God's judgment (see 6:37).

49 **But the one who listens and does not act is like a person who built a house on the ground without a foundation.** It is much easier

---

BACKGROUND: HOUSES First-century Palestinian houses ranged from the very small to the truly sumptuous. Ordinary people often lived in one-room houses that usually shared an open courtyard with other one-room houses. Much of life was lived outdoors; cooking was done in the courtyard. Rooms were dark and sometimes windowless and used for sleeping and shelter from the elements. In eastern Galilee (in Capernaum, for example), houses were built of basalt, a dark volcanic stone common in the area. Floors were made of basalt cobblestones; roofs were made of beams overlaid with thatch and clay. In Jericho, a city in the lower Jordan River valley, mud brick was used for the walls of ordinary dwellings. The wealthy elite lived in fine houses with mosaic floors, frescoed (painted plaster) walls, and elegant columns. The remains of several mansions belonging to the wealthy have been excavated in Jerusalem. One of these houses had several stories and more than six thousand square feet under its roof; it probably belonged to a member of a high-priestly family.

to build **a house on the ground without** digging down and laying a solid **foundation**. Such a house might look no different from a house with a foundation laid on bedrock: below-ground foundations are not visible. But in a time of testing the difference becomes apparent: **when the river burst against it, it collapsed at once and was completely destroyed**. Jesus emphasizes its utter ruin: **it collapsed at once** and **was completely destroyed**. So too, ruin lies in store for those who do not act on Jesus' teachings. It does them no good to come to him and listen to him and hail him as their Lord if they do not do as he commands.

For reflection: How solidly have I rooted my life on the bedrock of Jesus? Am I doing all that he commands me?

CHAPTER 7

A Gentile's Amazing Faith

¹ When he had finished all his words to the people, he entered Capernaum. ² A centurion there had a slave who was ill and about to die, and he was valuable to him. ³ When he heard about Jesus, he sent elders of the Jews to him, asking him to come and save the life of his slave. ⁴ They approached Jesus and strongly urged him to come, saying, "He deserves to have you do this for him, ⁵ for he loves our nation and he built the synagogue for us." ⁶ And Jesus went with them, but when he was only a short distance from the house, the centurion sent friends to tell him, "Lord, do not trouble yourself, for I am not worthy to have you enter under my roof. ⁷ Therefore, I did not consider myself worthy to come to you; but say the word and let my servant be healed. ⁸ For I too am a person subject to authority, with soldiers subject to me. And I say to one, 'Go,' and he goes; and to another, 'Come here,' and he comes; and to my slave, 'Do this,' and he does it." ⁹ When Jesus heard this he was amazed at him and, turning, said to the crowd following him, "I tell you, not even in Israel have I found such faith." ¹⁰ When the messengers returned to the house, they found the slave in good health.

Gospel parallels: Matt 8:5–13
NT: John 4:46–54; Acts 10

1 **When he had finished all his words to the people, he entered Capernaum.** Jesus has just given the teachings popularly known as the Sermon on the Plain (6:20–49). Although he directed his **words** to his disciples (6:20), there was a large crowd present (6:17–19), and his teaching was meant for these **people** as well. After Jesus **finished** his teaching, **he entered Capernaum,** a village he had previously visited (4:23, 31). Verse 9 indicates that the crowd accompanies him.

Capernaum: See page 124

2 **A centurion there had a slave who was ill and about to die.** A **centurion** was an army officer, normally in command of one hundred sol-

diers. Although centurion was a rank in the Roman army, other armies also had centurions. It is unlikely this centurion was a Roman; Roman soldiers were not stationed in Galilee during Jesus' public ministry. Galilee was ruled by Herod Antipas, who had his own army. His soldiers were recruited locally or in Syria, and included both Jews and Gentiles. Verse 9 indicates this **centurion** is a Gentile. He may be stationed in Capernaum because it lay near a border and had a customs post; soldiers facilitated the collection of taxes. This centurion owned a **slave who was ill and about to die, and he was valuable to him**. Some slaves held important administrative positions; this slave could have been **valuable** to the centurion in the sense of being highly useful. However, the word translated **valuable** can have the connotation of precious (as it is translated in 1 Pet 2:4) and that is likely its connotation here: the centurion is concerned for his slave as someone who is dear to him.

Herod Antipas: See page 99

Servant, slave: See page 454

3 **When he heard about Jesus**—heard that Jesus who heals the sick (4:31–39; 5:12–15) is coming into town—**he sent elders of the Jews to him.** The centurion does not go to Jesus but sends others on his behalf; the significance of this will emerge later. He sends **elders of the Jews**— those who are the village leaders of Capernaum. He wants Jesus to **come and save the life of his slave**. The slave is at the point of death (verse 1), too sick to be brought to Jesus.

4 **They approached Jesus and strongly urged him to come**: the elders of Capernaum do what the centurion asks of them and more:

BACKGROUND: ELDERS The Greek word for "elder" (*presbyteros*) literally means someone who is older (Luke 15:25), and it was used to refer to someone with authority within a family or clan, or within a group such as a synagogue or village (Luke 7:3). Religious scholars of the past could also be called elders (Mark 7:3). In the Gospels, the word "elders" usually refers to wealthy and influential Jewish laymen, particularly those who are part of the Sanhedrin in Jerusalem (Mark 15:1). In the early Church, the word "elders," or "presbyters," was used for local Church leaders (Acts 14:23), and the Greek word came through Latin into English as the word "priest." *Related topic: Sanhedrin (page 611).*

---

they **strongly urged** Jesus to come and heal the centurion's slave. They explain to Jesus that **he deserves**—literally, "he is worthy"—**to have you do this for him**.

5 The elders tell Jesus why the centurion is worthy of Jesus' coming to him: **for he loves our nation**—the Jewish people—**and he built the synagogue for us.** Some Gentiles were attracted by the monotheism and high moral code of Judaism but stopped short of converting and accepting circumcision. It is uncertain how fully this Gentile centurion embraced Jewish beliefs and morality, but he **loves** the Jewish people he is stationed among. As a demonstration of his love, **he built the synagogue** in Capernaum, where Jesus taught and cast out a demon (4:31–35). What may be the remains of the foundation of this synagogue can be seen today in Capernaum, beneath a later synagogue built on the same site. The centurion likely provided funds for the building of the synagogue, acting as a benefactor or patron for the people of Capernaum. He was not the only benefactor to pay for a synagogue. A first-century inscription discovered in Jerusalem states that a priest and synagogue leader named Theodotus "built this synagogue for the reading of the law and the teaching of the commandments" and as a hostel for pilgrims visiting Jerusalem. Centurions were well paid, far more than ordinary soldiers; this centurion must have been reasonably well off in order to pay for a synagogue. In the ancient world, patrons received loyalty and respect in exchange for what they did for others. The elders of Capernaum readily carried out their benefactor's wishes by going to Jesus on his behalf and **strongly** urging Jesus to help him.

Synagogue: See page 115
Patrons: See page 216

6 **And Jesus went with them,** indicating his willingness to help a Gentile, **but when he was only a short distance from the house, the centurion sent friends** to intercept Jesus. That Jesus was **only a short distance from the** centurion's **house** might suggest that the centurion saw Jesus approaching. The centurion gave his **friends** a message to convey to Jesus. They were **to tell him, "Lord, do not trouble yourself, for I am not worthy to have you enter under my roof."** His message addresses Jesus as **Lord,** acknowledging his authority. The message is

surprising on two counts. The centurion sent the elders of Capernaum to implore Jesus to come to his house to save the life of his slave (verse 3) but now he sends a second set of messengers to tell Jesus **do not trouble yourself** to come. Why his change of mind? Second, the elders told Jesus that the centurion is worthy of Jesus' attention (verse 4), but the centurion's message to Jesus is **I am not worthy** to have you enter **my** house. Why would the centurion view himself differently than the elders view him?

Lord: See page 137

7 **Therefore, I did not consider myself worthy to come to you.** If he is not worthy to have Jesus enter his house, neither does he **consider** himself **worthy to come to** Jesus in person, which is why he sends elders and friends on his behalf. The centurion believes that it is not necessary for Jesus to come into his house and have physical contact with his slave in order to heal him. It will be sufficient for Jesus to remain where he is and **say the word and let my servant be healed.** He refers to his slave as his **servant** (the Greek word can also mean "son") perhaps indicating his affection for him. The centurion recognizes the power of Jesus' **word**; he believes that at Jesus' command, his slave will **be healed.**

8 The centurion explains the basis for his belief in the power of Jesus' word. **For I too am a person subject to authority**: he works for Herod Antipas, the ruler of Galilee, and must carry out his orders. He says that in turn he has **soldiers subject to me**: as an officer in Herod's army, he has Herod's authority to command soldiers. **And I say to one, "Go," and he goes; and to another, "Come here," and he comes**: his soldiers carry out his orders. **And to my slave, "Do this," and he does it**: slaves must obey their owners. All it takes is a word from the centurion, and his soldiers and slave do what he wants. He believes that it is correspondingly the same with Jesus. By saying **for I too am a person subject to authority** he conveys his belief that Jesus is subject to authority and carries out works on behalf of another—by implication, on behalf of God. Since Jesus has God's authority, Jesus needs only to say a word and what he commands will be accomplished (verse 7). There is no need for Jesus to enter his house to heal his slave; a mere word from Jesus will be sufficient.

The elders of Capernaum may view the centurion as a worthy person, but he recognizes that he is not worthy compared with Jesus—not worthy to have him enter his house, not worthy to speak with him in person. Perhaps his sense of unworthiness became more acute when he caught sight of Jesus approaching his house, leading him to send friends to intercept Jesus and ask him simply to speak a healing word.

For reflection: When have I drawn back from Jesus out of a sense of my unworthiness?

9 **When Jesus heard this he was amazed at him and, turning, said to the crowd following him, "I tell you, not even in Israel have I found such faith."** Jesus is so **amazed** by the centurion's **faith** that, **turning** from the messengers, he makes an exclamation to the **crowd**, implicitly inviting them to learn from the centurion's example. **Not even in Israel**—that includes his own disciples—has Jesus **found such faith**. The word translated **such** means so great, so much. What is this great faith? Not simply belief that Jesus can cure the sick: many had come to him with such faith (4:40; 5:12, 18–20; 6:17–19). What sets the centurion apart is his faith that Jesus is so invested with the authority of God that it takes only a word from Jesus, spoken even at a distance, to save the life of someone at the point of death. The centurion believes that Jesus is God's agent, empowered by God to command sickness and spiritual forces as the centurion commands soldiers and slaves. Jesus is **amazed** by this centurion and his **faith,** and perhaps by his humility as well.

For reflection: Am I likewise amazed by the centurion's faith? How strong is my own faith in Jesus as compared with that of the centurion?

10 **When the messengers returned to the house, they found the slave in good health.** Luke skips ahead to the outcome, not recounting Jesus' healing word or what he said to the **messengers** that sent them back to the centurion. **When** they **returned to the** centurion's **house**, they **discovered** the **slave in good health**, healed before they arrived. Jesus did what the centurion had faith he could do.

This centurion, who has faith in Jesus without meeting him face-to-face, foreshadows another Gentile centurion in Luke's two-volume work.

In Acts 10, Luke recounts the baptism of the centurion Cornelius along with his relatives and friends, the first Gentiles to enter the Church. Luke's Gentile readers could look upon these two centurions as their ancestors in faith; all who have not met Jesus face-to-face can consider the centurions as models for their own faith.

For reflection: How is the centurion a model for me?

Jesus Has Compassion on a Widow

¹¹ Soon afterward he journeyed to a city called Nain, and his disciples and a large crowd accompanied him. ¹² As he drew near to the gate of the city, a man who had died was being carried out, the only son of his mother, and she was a widow. A large crowd from the city was with her. ¹³ When the Lord saw her, he was moved with pity for her and said to her, "Do not weep." ¹⁴ He stepped forward and touched the coffin; at this the bearers halted, and he said, "Young man, I tell you, arise!" ¹⁵ The dead man sat up and began to speak, and Jesus gave him to his mother. ¹⁶ Fear seized them all, and they glorified God, exclaiming, "A great prophet has arisen in our midst," and "God has visited his people." ¹⁷ This report about him spread through the whole of Judea and in all the surrounding region.

OT: 1 Kings 17:17–24
NT: Luke 1:78–79

11 **Soon afterward**—after being in Capernaum (7:1–10)—**he journeyed to a city called Nain,** a journey of about twenty-five miles. **Nain** lay six miles southeast of Nazareth and is today the Arab village of Nein. **His disciples and a large crowd accompanied him.** If Jesus walked ahead and his disciples and the large **crowd** followed behind him, we might envision a procession led by Jesus making its way along the roads between Capernaum and Nain.

12 **As he drew near to the gate of the city, a man who had died was being carried out.** As the procession led by Jesus is about to enter Nain, a funeral procession is leaving the city. A corpse is being **carried out** of

193

the city to be buried: Jewish burial grounds were always located outside towns. Funerals are sad affairs and this one particularly so, for the **man** who had died was young (verse 14) and **the only son of his mother.** The untimely death of one's only child is devastating. Compounding the mother's grief, **she was a widow**, and in losing her son, she lost her means of support. Widows without children or relatives to provide for them were in a precarious position, which is why the Old Testament made special provisions for them and for others without means of support (Deut 14:28–29; 24:19–22; 27:19). As she made her way out of Nain to bury her son, **a large crowd from the city was with her**, mourning her loss.

Burial practices: See page 646

13 **When the Lord saw her, he was moved with pity for her.** While three people—Peter, a leper, and a centurion—have called Jesus **Lord** (5:8, 12; 7:6), this is the first time that Luke as the narrator of his Gospel refers to him as **the Lord**. Early Christians called Jesus **Lord** as God is called the Lord (Rom 10:9; 1 Cor 12:3; Phil 2:11), and Luke will occasionally use this title to refer to Jesus. Jesus **saw her**—saw the widow in her sorrow and grasped the tragedy that had befallen her through the death of her only son. The Greek verb translated **moved with pity** is formed from a Greek word that means internal organs. **Moved with pity** has the connotation of moved from one's inner depth, profoundly moved—we might say a gut reaction of compassion. Jesus came to bring good news to the poor; he has a special concern for the poor and the mourning (4:18; 6:20–21). He **said to her, "Do not weep."** Another translation would be, "Stop weeping"; she is mourning the death of her son.

Lord: See page 137

For reflection: What does Jesus' being profoundly moved with compassion at the sight of the grieving widow tell me about him? About his compassion for me?

14 **He stepped forward and touched the coffin; at this the bearers halted.** The word translated **coffin** does not here mean a closed coffin such as are used today, but an open bier or pallet used for transporting a corpse. Jesus **stepped forward and touched the coffin** in order to bring the burial procession to a halt, and at his gesture **the bearers**

halted. Then **he said, "Young man, I tell you, arise!"** Jesus issues a command on his own authority: **I tell you.** He orders the dead young man to **arise!**

15 **The dead man sat up** on the bier **and began to speak**, obeying Jesus' command and demonstrating that he was no longer a **dead man** but fully alive. At Jesus' word, the centurion's slave who had been at the point of death was restored to health (7:1–10); at Jesus' word, a man who was dead and on the way to burial is restored to life. **Jesus gave him to his mother**: the mother rather than the son is the focus of Jesus' attention and mercy. Jesus sees her in her sorrow and need, and by restoring her son to life he restores her life as well: she again has her son to take care of her.

Luke's words, **gave him to his mother**, echo those of an account of the prophet Elijah bringing back to life the only son of a widow (1 Kings 17:17–24). Luke probably intends his readers to compare what Jesus did with what Elijah did. Elijah repeatedly prayed to God to restore the boy's life, and God heard his prayer. Jesus, however, exercises his own authority, bringing the widow's son back to life with the command "Arise!"

> Taking the child, Elijah brought him down into the house from the upper room and gave him to his mother.
> 1 Kings 17:23

16 **Fear seized them all**, the crowd following Jesus and the crowd in the funeral procession. A profound sense of awe is a natural response to a manifestation of the divine or divine power (see 1:12, 65; 2:9; 5:26). The crowds **glorified God**, recognizing that God was at work through Jesus, just as the centurion recognized that Jesus bore God's authority (7:7–8). They were **exclaiming, "A great prophet has arisen in our midst."** The prophets Elijah and Elisha each brought a dead person back to life (1 Kings 17:17–24; 2 Kings 4:18–37), leading the crowds to conclude that Jesus is a **prophet**, even **a great prophet.** Luke's readers know that Jesus is more than a prophet (see 1:26–38; 3:21–22), but, like a prophet, Jesus does speak and act on behalf of God. The crowds also exclaim, **God has visited his people.** The word **visited** means more than dropped in on; it means that God has come to the aid of his people. Zechariah in his

195

prophetic prayer of praise proclaimed that God "has visited and brought redemption to his people" (1:68) and spoke of "the tender mercy of our God / by which the daybreak from on high will visit us / to shine on those who sit in darkness and death's shadow" (1:78–79). God has visited his people through Jesus' visit to Nain; God has shown tender mercy through Jesus' heartfelt compassion; God has reached out to those in the shadow of death through Jesus' touching a coffin and commanding the one lying in it to arise.

For reflection: What does this incident teach me about who Jesus is?

17 **This report about him spread through the whole of Judea and in all the surrounding region.** Jesus' fame continues to spread (see 4:14, 37). Luke here uses **Judea** to refer to all of Palestine. The **surrounding region** would include Tyre and Sidon to the northwest; people have already come to Jesus from this region (6:17).

Is Jesus the One Who Is Expected?
¹⁸ **The disciples of John told him about all these things. John summoned two of his disciples ¹⁹ and sent them to the Lord to ask, "Are you the one who is to come, or should we look for another?" ²⁰ When the men came to him, they said, "John the Baptist has sent us to you to ask, 'Are you the one who is to come, or should we look for another?' " ²¹ At that time he cured many of their diseases, sufferings, and evil spirits; he also granted sight to many who were blind. ²² And he said to them in reply, "Go and tell John what you have seen and heard: the blind regain their sight, the lame walk, lepers are cleansed, the deaf hear, the dead are raised, the poor have the good news proclaimed to them. ²³ And blessed is the one who takes no offense at me."**
Gospel parallels: Matt 11:2–6
OT: Isaiah 26:19; 29:18–19; 35:4–6; 61:1
NT: Luke 3:15–20; 4:18–21

18 **The disciples of John told him about all these things.** John the Baptist is in prison (3:19–20) but has disciples (5:33) who tell him what

Jesus is doing and teaching. Reports about Jesus have circulated widely (4:14, 37; 7:17), so it is no surprise that John's disciples are well informed about Jesus. They tell John **about all these things**, which would include recent events such as the Sermon on the Plain (6:20–49), Jesus' healing of the centurion's slave (7:1–10), and his raising a dead man to life (7:11–16), as well as his earlier deeds and teachings. Their reports raise a question in John's mind, so he **summoned two of his disciples** to come to him in prison.

19 John **sent them to the Lord to ask, "Are you the one who is to come, or should we look for another?"** Luke again refers to Jesus as **the Lord** (see 7:13). John had proclaimed that "one mightier than I is coming. I am not worthy to loosen the thongs of his sandal" (3:16). Now John wonders whether Jesus is this mightier **one who is to come**. If not, then John and his disciples should **look for another**. John had leaped in Elizabeth's womb at the presence of Jesus in the womb of Mary (1:41); why is John now uncertain about Jesus? Luke's Gospel suggests two factors. First, although Jesus and John are related (see 1:36), they may have had minimal contact with each other because John lived in the wilderness (1:80). Luke does not recount any exchange between John and Jesus when Jesus is baptized, nor indicate that John witnesses heaven opening and the Spirit descending on Jesus (see 3:21–22). Second and more important, John had definite expectations of what the one coming after him would do, and Jesus is not living up to these expectations. John expected the coming one to execute God's judgment: "His winnowing fan is in his hand to clear his threshing floor and to gather the wheat into his barn, but the chaff he will burn with unquenchable fire" (3:17; see also 3:9). Rather than burning those who are chaff, Jesus embraces them. He shares meals and fellowship with "tax collectors and sinners" (5:30) and speaks of God being "kind to the ungrateful and the wicked" (6:35). John has heard about "all these things" (verse 18), and they give him pause. Is Jesus the one he expected? He sends two of his disciples to find out.

20 They carry out their mission. **When the men came to him, they said, "John the Baptist has sent us to you to ask, 'Are you the one who is to come, or should we look for another?'"**

197

21 Luke interrupts his account to describe what Jesus is doing when John's messengers arrive: **At that time he cured many of their diseases, sufferings, and evil spirits; he also granted sight to many who were blind.** Jesus cured **many**; his healings are not rare occurrences but a constant part of his mission (see 4:38–41; 5:12–15, 24–25; 6:17–19). The word translated **granted** means to give graciously as a favor: Jesus heals out of compassion, as he raised the widow's son to life out of compassion (7:13–14).

For reflection: What has Jesus graciously granted me?

22 John's disciples ask Jesus whether he is the one who is to come (verse 20), but he does not give them a yes or no answer. **He said to them in reply, "Go and tell John what you have seen and heard":** they are to give John eyewitness testimony about what Jesus is doing. Jesus asks them to report the ways in which he is curing "many of their diseases,

---

BACKGROUND: THE POOR AND THE RICH In first-century Galilee, few were well enough off to be what we would consider middle class and very few were wealthy. Most supported themselves by farming, usually on small plots of land. They were able to raise enough to pay taxes and feed their families, but barely. Bad harvests could mean going into debt, losing one's land, and becoming a day laborer. Herod Antipas controlled the prime farmland, entrusting some of it to his key supporters. The minority who did not farm commonly worked as craftsmen (carpenters, potters, tanners), merchants, fishermen, servants, shepherds, or tax collectors. Some Jews were slaves, although slavery was not as common as in other parts of the Roman Empire. Most Galileans could be thought of as the working poor. At the bottom of the working poor were day laborers, dependent on being hired each day. Worst off were those unable to work: the blind, the crippled, the leprous. Unless they had relatives to support them, the non-working poor survived by begging. Jesus' followers mirrored the composition of Galilean society: most were working poor, very few were wealthy. Jesus' ministry was marked by concern for the non-working poor: "the blind regain their sight, the lame walk, lepers are cleansed, the deaf hear, the dead are raised, the poor have the good news proclaimed to them" (Luke 7:22). Being wealthy posed the danger of using one's wealth only for oneself (Luke 12:16–21; 16:19–31). Wealth was properly used to help those who could not provide for themselves (Luke 12:33; 14:12–14; 18:22; 19:8). *Related topics: Farming (page 218); Herod Antipas (page 99); Servant, slave (page 454).*

---

sufferings, and evil spirits" (verse 21): **the blind regain their sight, the lame walk, lepers are cleansed, the deaf hear, the dead are raised**. They can also tell John that **the poor have the good news proclaimed to them**. The word translated **poor** means abjectly poor and reduced to begging. Luke does not recount that Jesus preached to the **poor** on this occasion. However, in the society of the time almost all those who were **blind**, **lame**, **lepers**, or **deaf** and dumb would have been **poor** because their disabilities limited their ability to support themselves. In healing them, Jesus proclaims the **good news** of God's reign (4:43) to them by deed rather than by word.

Gospel, good news: See page 59

For reflection: What witness do I give to what Jesus does and teaches?

There is a second and more important level of meaning in Jesus' response to John's disciples. Jesus singles out afflictions—blindness, lameness, leprosy, deafness—that are mentioned in prophecies of Isaiah that foretell God's coming to save his people (Isaiah 29:18–19; 35:4–6). The **dead** being raised is also foreshadowed in Isaiah (Isaiah 26:19). **The poor have the good news proclaimed to them** echoes Isaiah's "He has sent me to bring glad tidings to the lowly" (Isaiah 61:1); Jesus earlier proclaimed that he fulfilled this prophecy (4:18–21). Jesus crafts his response to John's disciples so that it conveys that Jesus' deeds and words are the fulfillment of what Isaiah prophesied. Through Jesus, God is visiting his people (see 7:16), coming to them to save them. John the Baptist would be sufficiently familiar with Isaiah's prophecies to grasp the implications of Jesus' choice of words.

> *Here is your God,*
> *he comes with vindication;*
> *With divine recompense*
> *he comes to save you.*
> *Then will the eyes of the blind be opened,*
> *the ears of the deaf be cleared;*
> *Then will the lame leap like a stag,*
> *then the tongue of the dumb will sing.*

Isaiah 35:4–6

> *The spirit of the Lord* GOD *is upon me,*
> *because the* LORD *has anointed me;*
> *He has sent me to bring glad tidings to the lowly,*
> *to heal the brokenhearted.*

Isaiah 61:1

23 By his allusions to Isaiah's prophecies, Jesus claims that he is God's agent to heal and save his people. Will his claim be accepted or rejected? Jesus pronounces a beatitude that contains a challenge: **blessed is the one who takes no offense at me.** The words translated **takes no offense** mean not be tripped up, as by an obstacle. **Blessed** and fortunate is the woman or man who accepts Jesus for who he is, not stumbling over what Jesus does or does not do. Blessed is the person who does not let precon-ceived notions about what God's agent must be like stand in the way of accepting Jesus as God's agent. If Jesus is not matching up to John's expectations, then John needs to revise his expectations.

Beatitudes: See page 169

This will not be the last time in Luke's Gospel that preconceived notions stand in the way of accepting Jesus for who he is; popular expec-tations of the Messiah will also be a stumbling block (see 9:20–22). Jesus' beatitude remains a challenge for all disciples of all times. Blessed is the one who does not try to make Jesus conform to his or her expecta-tions and desires, but conforms his or her thinking to the teachings and example of Jesus.

For reflection: How does Jesus' beatitude apply to me? Have I ever been put off or shocked by what Jesus said or did?

Jesus' View of John
²⁴ When the messengers of John had left, Jesus began to speak to the crowds about John. "What did you go out to the desert to see—a reed swayed by the wind? ²⁵ Then what did you go out to see? Someone dressed in fine garments? Those who dress luxuri-ously and live sumptuously are found in royal palaces. ²⁶ Then

what did you go out to see? A prophet? Yes, I tell you, and more
than a prophet. ²⁷ This is the one about whom scripture says:
'Behold, I am sending my messenger ahead of you,
he will prepare your way before you.'
²⁸ I tell you, among those born of women, no one is greater than
John; yet the least in the kingdom of God is greater than he."

Gospel parallels: Matt 11:7–11; Mark 1:2
OT: Exod 23:20; Mal 3:1
NT: Luke 1:13–17, 76–77; 3:1–20; 7:18–23

24 **When the messengers of John,** who were sent to ask Jesus whether he
is the one who is to come (7:18–23), **had left, Jesus began to speak to
the crowds about John.** Jesus uses the messengers' visit as an occasion
to say something about John the Baptist. He asks the crowd, **What did
you go out to the desert to see—a reed swayed by the wind?** Tall
marsh grass grows along the banks of the Jordan as it flows through the
wilderness. But it is not worth a trip into the **desert** just to see a **reed**
of grass swaying in the wind. If Jesus' words are taken figuratively, he is
asking whether crowds went into the desert to seek out a man who is
easily **swayed** by winds of expediency. John is hardly a weak or wavering person: he is in prison because he stood up to Herod Antipas and
denounced his illicit marriage and evil deeds (3:19–20).

25 **Then what did you go out to see? Someone dressed in fine garments?**
Those who live in the wilderness wear durable and practical clothing, not
fine (literally, soft) **garments.** If anyone is looking for a fashion show, the
wilderness is not the place to **go.** Rather, **those who dress luxuriously
and live sumptuously are found in royal palaces.** The connotation of
sumptuously is corrupt self-indulgence. **Royal palaces** belonged to rulers
such as Herod Antipas, and Jesus' audience might have taken his words as
a subtle dig at Herod. If people want to see someone who spends too much
money on himself, they should look for Herod Antipas in one of his fine
palaces; they will not find him roughing it in the desert.

26 If people did not go into the wilderness to watch the grass sway or to find
someone luxuriously clothed, **then,** Jesus asks them, **what did you go**

out to see? Was it **a prophet?** Jesus answers his question: **yes, I tell you**, you went to John (3:1–18) because the word of God had come to him (3:2) and he was a **prophet** (1:76; 20:6). That in itself would make John very important. God had not sent a prophet to his people for centuries (see 1 Macc 4:46; 9:27; 14:41) but sent John to give them "knowledge of salvation / through the forgiveness of their sins" (1:77). John is a prophet, but Jesus proclaims that he is **more than a prophet**. His role in God's plans is greater than the role of any previous prophet.

27 Jesus explains why John is more than a prophet: **this is the one about whom scripture says**—literally, about whom it is written. John fulfills what is written in Scripture. A prophecy of Malachi (Mal 3:1) echoes a passage in Exodus (Exod 23:20); Jesus quotes Malachi, adding some words from Exodus. **Behold, I am sending my messenger ahead of you, / he will prepare your way before you.** In Jesus' application of the prophecy, God is speaking to Jesus, addressing him as **you**. God refers to John as **my messenger.** God tells Jesus that he is **sending** John **ahead of you** to **prepare your way before you.** John is more than a prophet because he is the forerunner of Jesus, sent to prepare people for Jesus. John's being a prophet and more than a prophet was foreshadowed at his circumcision when his father Zechariah prophesied that John would "be called prophet of the Most High" and would "go before the Lord to prepare his ways" (1:76).

> Lo, I am sending my messenger
> to prepare the way before me.
>
> Mal 3:1

> See, I am sending an angel before you, to guard you on the
> way and bring you to the place I have prepared.
>
> Exod 23:20

28 Jesus solemnly proclaims, **I tell you, among those born of women, no one is greater than John.** The expression **born of women** is a biblical idiom for a human being (Job 15:14; Sirach 10:18). **Greater** here means considered greater by God; the angel Gabriel told Zechariah that "[John] will be great in the sight of [the] Lord" (1:15). No one **is greater than**

John, because of the role John plays in God's plans: God sent John to prepare the way for Jesus.

> *For reflection: If John has such greatness because of his role in preparing for Jesus, what does this tell me about Jesus?*

Jesus adds that while none greater than John has ever been born, **yet the least in the kingdom of God is greater than he**. The **kingdom of God** is God's complete reign over all of creation. Jesus is establishing God's reign by his preaching and by overthrowing the forces of evil (11:20), but the fullness of God's reign lies in the future (21:25–31). By saying that the **least** significant person who is part of God's reign is **greater** than the greatest man ever born, Jesus contrasts life in God's reign with natural human life. The **kingdom of God** so far surpasses the life we experience on earth that the least in God's kingdom is incomparably better off than the greatest in the present life. Jesus is not saying that John will not enter God's kingdom; John will presumably be among the prophets who join with Abraham, Isaac, and Jacob in the kingdom of God (13:28). Jesus is simply putting John in perspective. John is the greatest ever born because of his role in preparing for Jesus and the coming of God's kingdom, but what John prepares for far overshadows him. Entering the kingdom of God is more important than being the greatest person on earth.

Kingdom of God: See page 381

> *For reflection: Do I yearn to enter the kingdom of God? What am I doing to surrender myself to God's reign?*

Responding to God's Plan

²⁹ **(All the people who listened, including the tax collectors, and who were baptized with the baptism of John, acknowledged the righteousness of God; ³⁰ but the Pharisees and scholars of the law, who were not baptized by him, rejected the plan of God for themselves.)**
³¹ **"Then to what shall I compare the people of this generation? What are they like? ³² They are like children who sit in the marketplace and call to one another,**

'We played the flute for you, but you did not dance.
We sang a dirge, but you did not weep.'
³³ For John the Baptist came neither eating food nor drinking wine, and you said, 'He is possessed by a demon.' ³⁴ The Son of Man came eating and drinking and you said, 'Look, he is a glutton and a drunkard, a friend of tax collectors and sinners.' ³⁵ But wisdom is vindicated by all her children."

Gospel parallels: Matt 11:16–19
OT: Sirach 4:11
NT: Matt 21:31–32; Luke 1:15; 3:3, 12–13; 5:30–34

29 After recounting Jesus' words about John (7:24–28), Luke in an aside provides background for what Jesus will go on to say. **All the people who listened, including the tax collectors, and who were baptized with the baptism of John, acknowledged the righteousness of God.** Luke speaks of those who **listened** to the preaching of John the Baptist and took it seriously, including some **tax collectors** (see 3:12). John proclaimed "a baptism of repentance for the forgiveness of sins" (3:3); those who heeded John's message **were baptized with the baptism of John**. By repenting and being baptized, they **acknowledged the righteousness of God**: they embraced God's way as the right way and submitted themselves to God's will. By accepting the **baptism of John**, they acknowledged that he had been sent by God and they embraced "the plan of God for themselves" (verse 30).

Tax collectors: See page 94

30 Not everyone responded to John's message. Among those who didn't, Luke mentions **Pharisees and scholars of the law, who were not baptized by him**. Luke sometimes refers to scribes as **scholars of the law**, meaning experts in the law of Moses. By their failure to repent and accept baptism, they **rejected the plan of God for themselves**. The **plan of God** is God's will and purpose. God sent John to carry out his plan of salvation; those who reject John's call to repentance and baptism thwart God's plan **for themselves**.

Pharisees: See page 143
Scribes: See page 146

For reflection: How fully have I embraced God's plan for me? What do I need to do to become more aware of God's will for me?

31 Luke resumes recounting what Jesus said to the crowd after the visit of John's disciples (7:24–28). John was a prophet (7:26), but some rejected his message (verse 30). In light of that, Jesus asks the crowd **then to what shall I compare the people of this generation?** The expression, **the people of this generation** could simply mean those who are alive at the time of Jesus. However, Jesus will also use **generation** to designate those who have no faith (see 9:41; 11:29–32; 17:25), and that is its reference here. Jesus asks, **to what shall I compare** those who did not have faith in John and accept his message? **What are they like?**

32 Jesus provides a comparison: **they are like children who sit in the marketplace and call to one another, / "We played the flute for you, but you did not dance. / We sang a dirge, but you did not weep."** Jesus may be quoting a children's rhyme or ditty. **We played the flute for you** at a play wedding celebration, **but you did not dance;** you refused to join in the festivities. **We sang a dirge** at a play funeral, **but you did not weep** with the mourners. No matter whether it is a happy or sad game, you refuse to play. There's no pleasing you!

33 Jesus explains how the children and the ditty provide a comparison for "the people of this generation" (verse 31). **For John the Baptist came neither eating food nor drinking wine, and you said, "He is possessed by a demon."** John fasted (implied at 5:33) and abstained from wine (1:15), and some took this as evidence that he was a deranged fanatic, **possessed by a demon** ("possessed and out of his mind"—John 10:20). Therefore, they could ignore his call to repentance: no one need heed a madman.

Demons, unclean spirits: See page 125

34 John was to prepare the way for Jesus (7:27) and did so in an ironic sense: some who reject John also reject Jesus. Jesus, however, is criticized for behaving in an opposite way from John. **The Son of Man came eating and drinking and you said, "Look, he is a glutton and a drunkard,**

a friend of tax collectors and sinners." Jesus does not require his disciples to fast (5:33) and by implication does not fast himself. Rather, he is seen **eating** food and **drinking** wine, enjoying meals as if he were the groom at a wedding celebration (see 5:34). The next scene in Luke's Gospel will find him reclining at a banquet (7:36). Because Jesus seems to relish **eating and drinking**, he is accused of being **a glutton and a drunkard**. Even worse, he is **a friend of tax collectors and sinners**. Jesus not only eats and drinks too much; he does so with the wrong people! He even becomes their **friend**. Jesus has been criticized before for sharing meals and fellowship with outcasts and **sinners** (5:30) and he will be so criticized again (15:2). Jesus' critics believe that those who associate with the disreputable must be disreputable themselves, and whatever they have to say can be ignored.

Son of Man: See page 147

For reflection: What does Jesus' eating and drinking, and his choice of table companions, tell me about him? Do I consider Jesus to be a friend, even if he is more than a friend for me?

In the ditty (verse 32), neither a sad nor a happy tune satisfied the petulant children. So too with John and Jesus: some reject both John's stern warning of God's impending judgment and Jesus' demonstration of God's compassion for outcasts and sinners. But those who reject God's messengers and messages "rejected the plan of God for themselves" (verse 30).

35 Others "acknowledged the righteousness of God" (verse 29) and embraced his plan for them. Jesus now speaks of them, although cryptically: **But wisdom is vindicated by all her children**. By **wisdom** Jesus refers to the wisdom of God, who is the source of all wisdom (Prov 2:6; Sirach 1:1). Those whom wisdom instructs can be called her children: "Wisdom instructs her children / and admonishes those who seek her" (Sirach 4:11; see also Prov 8:32). They are called "her" children because wisdom is spoken of as a woman (Prov 1:20). Against this background of associations, **wisdom** is the mind or plan of God, and **her children** are those who align themselves with God's plan. Saying that **wisdom is vindicated by all her children** conveys the message that God's plan is

shown to be right by those who embrace it: the results of accepting God's way show that God's way is the right way. Those who listened to John and Jesus and heeded their messages are a living demonstration of the righteousness of God (verse 29).

For reflection: How has my following of God's way shown that his way is the right way? What fruit has it borne in my life?

ORIENTATION: *The following scene makes the most sense if there had been a previous encounter between Jesus and the woman who was a sinner.*

A Forgiven Woman's Gratitude

³⁶ A Pharisee invited him to dine with him, and he entered the Pharisee's house and reclined at table. ³⁷ Now there was a sinful woman in the city who learned that he was at table in the house of the Pharisee. Bringing an alabaster flask of ointment, ³⁸ she stood behind him at his feet weeping and began to bathe his feet with her tears. Then she wiped them with her hair, kissed them, and anointed them with the ointment. ³⁹ When the Pharisee who had invited him saw this he said to himself, "If this man were a prophet, he would know who and what sort of woman this is who is touching him, that she is a sinner." ⁴⁰ Jesus said to him in reply, "Simon, I have something to say to you." "Tell me, teacher," he said. ⁴¹ "Two people were in debt to a certain creditor; one owed five hundred days' wages and the other owed fifty. ⁴² Since they were unable to repay the debt, he forgave it for both. Which of them will love him more?" ⁴³ Simon said in reply, "The one, I suppose, whose larger debt was forgiven." He said to him, "You have judged rightly." ⁴⁴ Then he turned to the woman and said to Simon, "Do you see this woman? When I entered your house, you did not give me water for my feet, but she has bathed them with her tears and wiped them with her hair. ⁴⁵ You did not give me a kiss, but she has not ceased kissing my feet since the time I entered. ⁴⁶ You did not anoint my head with oil, but she anointed my feet with ointment. ⁴⁷ So I tell you, her many sins have been

forgiven; hence, she has shown great love. But the one to whom little is forgiven, loves little." ⁴⁸ He said to her, "Your sins are forgiven." ⁴⁹ The others at table said to themselves, "Who is this who even forgives sins?" ⁵⁰ But he said to the woman, "Your faith has saved you; go in peace."

NT: Matt 26:6–13; Mark 14:3–9; Luke 5:20–24, 28–32; John 12:1–8

36 **A Pharisee invited him to dine with him.** Although some Pharisees are critical of Jesus (5:21, 30, 33; 6:2, 7, 11), other Pharisees are favorably disposed toward him (13:31); some invite him into their homes for meals (11:37; 14:1). This particular **Pharisee** views Jesus as a religious teacher (verse 40) and possibly even a prophet (verse 39). He may want to hear Jesus' views, and one customary setting for discussions is a leisurely meal together. He **invited** Jesus **to dine with him**, taking the initiative. Jesus accepts his invitation: Jesus will eat with anyone, the respectable as well as the unrespectable (7:34). **And he entered the Pharisee's house and reclined at table.** Jews had adopted the Greek custom in which diners at banquets reclined on their left sides on couches arranged in a U around low tables. Banquets could be the occasion for philosophical and religious discussions (the setting for the Greek philosopher Plato's dialogue *Symposium* is a banquet). That the Pharisee can afford to give a banquet indicates he is several cuts above the working poor.

Pharisees: See page 143
Banquets: See page 386

37 **Now there was a sinful woman in the city**: that is, there was a woman who was known in the city to be **sinful**. Luke does not specify her sins but they are commonly assumed to be sexual in nature, almost as if women are capable of no other sins worth consideration. She **learned that** Jesus **was at table in the house of the Pharisee.** She goes to the house of the Pharisee **bringing an alabaster flask of ointment—** perfumed olive oil, used for anointing. **Alabaster,** a stone that can be carved into a **flask,** was used to preserve perfumes. It does not take much reading between Luke's lines to suspect that the woman's **bringing an alabaster flask of ointment** with her to the Pharisee's house indicates that she wants to anoint Jesus.

38 **She stood behind him at his feet weeping.** We would be upset if
we had guests over for dinner and a stranger wandered in uninvited.
Scholars believe it would have been more acceptable at the time of Jesus,
particularly at banquets: some might come to listen to the discussions.
The woman **stood behind** Jesus **at his feet**. Since Jesus was reclining
with his head toward a food table, anyone approaching him from **behind**
would be **at his feet**—his bare feet, for sandals were left at the door so
dirt wasn't tracked in. It was customary to anoint a person's head (Psalm
23:5; 133:2), but she cannot reach Jesus' head without thrusting herself
into the middle of the banquet—something a woman with a bad reputation might hesitate to do. Her emotions get the better of her, and as she
stood above Jesus' feet she **began to bathe his feet with her tears.** The
word translated **bathe** means to wet and is used for rain: her tears fall
on Jesus' feet. Perhaps embarrassed that she got his feet wet, **she wiped
them with her hair** as a makeshift towel. Some scholars think that her
letting her hair down in public would have been scandalous, but would
it have been less scandalous for her to dry Jesus' feet with her clothing?
Drying Jesus' feet with her hair brings her head near his feet, and she
kissed them: the feelings that brought her to tears are gratitude and
love for Jesus (verse 47). Her actions seem spontaneous, with one thing
leading to another. Since she cannot reach Jesus' head, she **anointed** his
feet **with the ointment.** Feet were not usually anointed; her action must
have struck others as odd. She may have realized that she was making a
spectacle of herself, but she didn't care: her affection for Jesus overrode
her concerns about herself.

*For reflection: When have I tried to do something for Jesus that didn't turn
out the way I planned? Does my love for him outweigh my self-concerns?*

39 Jesus does nothing to stop the woman; he allows her to express her
affection. **When the Pharisee who had invited him saw this he
said to himself, "If this man were a prophet, he would know who
and what sort of woman this is who is touching him, that she is
a sinner."** Some think of Jesus as a **prophet** (7:16; 9:18–19; 24:19), and
the Pharisee had entertained this view. Now he has his doubts. Surely a
prophet would have the perception to know **what sort of woman this**

is—that she is a sinner—and would not allow her to keep **touching him**. The Pharisee might be concerned that she is ritually unclean and a source of uncleanness, but more likely he is put off by a sinful woman publicly and affectionately touching a supposedly devout man. As a Pharisee he tried to distance himself from sinners and he does not understand why Jesus does not do the same.

40 What the Pharisee "said to himself" (verse 39) was wrong on several counts. The first is doubting that Jesus has prophetic perception, for Jesus knows what is going through the Pharisee's mind and responds to it. **Jesus said to him in reply, "Simon, I have something to say to you."** Jesus calls him **Simon**, addressing him by name: Jesus has a personal message for him and wants him to pay attention to it. Simon is willing to listen: **"Tell me, teacher," he said.** Simon acknowledges that Jesus is a **teacher**, someone competent to instruct about God's laws and ways.

41 Jesus tells Simon a parable. **Two people were in debt to a certain creditor**, or money lender. **One owed five hundred days' wages and the other owed fifty.** By **days' wages** is meant the wages for an ordinary worker, such as a farm hand.

42 Jesus' parable takes a surprising turn: **since they were unable to repay the debt, he forgave it for both.** Moneylenders do not stay in business by writing off debts; they do everything they can to recover at least a portion of what they are owed. This creditor, however, **forgave** the debts owed him: the word translated **forgave** also means to give graciously as a favor. **Since they were unable to repay** what was owed, the creditor graciously canceled their entire debts. Had Jesus told this parable in another setting, he could have used it to teach about God's graciously forgiving the debt of our sins. But he has a different application of the parable in mind for Simon. He asks him, **which of them will love him more?** In context, **love** has the connotation of gratitude: which debtor will be the most grateful to the moneylender?

43 **Simon said in reply, "The one, I suppose, whose larger debt was forgiven."** Simon is a little wary in his response; perhaps he suspects that Jesus' parable bears a message that he does not want to hear. But

there is no way Simon can avoid saying that the one owing the **larger debt** was the more grateful when both debts were **forgiven**, even though he hedges it with an **I suppose**. Jesus gets the answer he wants and **said to him, "You have judged rightly."** Perhaps implied is an unspoken, Keep on judging rightly.

44 **Then he turned to the woman and said to Simon, "Do you see this woman?"** Jesus turns his attention to the woman at his feet and directs Simon's attention to her as well. Although she is the focus, Jesus' words are addressed to Simon as he applies the parable to the woman. He asks Simon, **Do you see this woman?** Do you really see her as she is, or do you only see what you are predisposed to see? **When I entered your house, you did not give me water for my feet.** Sandaled feet became dusty on unpaved paths and streets; a considerate host might provide **water** for a guest to wash up. Simon gave Jesus no water for his feet, **but she has bathed them with her tears and wiped them with her hair.** Her spontaneous acts made up for Simon's omission.

45 **You did not give me a kiss**, an expression of affection between relatives and friends. Welcoming guests with a kiss was not obligatory but would be natural if there was any bond or warmth between host and guest. While Jesus received no kiss from Simon, **she has not ceased kissing my feet since the time I entered**. Jesus speaks as if she is still kissing his feet and has been doing so for some time.

46 **You did not anoint my head with oil**: anointing the head with olive oil was refreshing but not a normal part of hospitality. Simon behaved correctly toward Jesus but only correctly, omitting any of the little extras or special acts of kindness. **But she anointed my feet with ointment**, an unusual anointing to be sure, but nonetheless an expression of her affection for Jesus. He puts a favorable interpretation on all of her acts, even her drying his feet with her hair (verse 44). Jesus sees into her heart, just as he knew what Simon was thinking (verses 39–40).

47 Simon doubted that Jesus was a prophet because Jesus did not perceive that the woman was a sinner, but Simon turns out to be wrong about her as well: she is no longer a sinner. (Even had she been, Jesus would not

211

have turned her away.) Jesus solemnly proclaims, **So I tell you, her many sins have been forgiven; hence, she has shown great love.** The two Greek words translated here as **so** mean "for this reason" and refer to the women's acts that Jesus has just mentioned (verses 44–46). Her behavior is evidence that **her many sins have been forgiven.** The implication of **have been forgiven** could be, have been forgiven by God. The Greek verb for **have been forgiven** is in a tense that signifies the present result of a past act: the woman's sins, **many** as they were, have been forgiven and she is in a state of forgiveness. We are not told the circumstances in which she was forgiven, but the **great love** she has shown for Jesus indicates that he was the agent of God's forgiveness for her. Presumably she was among the sinners he befriended (5:30; 7:34) and called to repentance (5:32). She heeded his call and is now a changed woman. Her many sins have been forgiven; **hence, she has shown great love.** Her love for Jesus, demonstrated by her acts of affection, is the result of her being forgiven.

For reflection: In what ways can this woman serve as an example for me? How do I express my gratitude to and love for Jesus?

Some translations of the Bible interpret this verse, "her many sins have been forgiven *because* she has shown great love." While the word in question can be translated either as "hence" or as "because," the logic of Jesus' parable about the two debtors indicates that the woman's love is the consequence and evidence of her forgiveness, not the grounds for it.

If one who has received great forgiveness is filled with great love, then the other side of the coin is that **the one to whom little is forgiven, loves little.** Does this general principle have pointed application to Simon? Did Simon demonstrate **little** love for Jesus (verses 44–46) because Simon has received **little** forgiveness and stands in need of greater forgiveness? That is certainly something for Simon to ponder.

For reflection: What is the connection between my own failures to love and the sins to which I cling?

48 Jesus' gaze is still on the woman at his feet (verse 44). He wants to say some things to reassure her in her new life. **He said to her, "Your sins are forgiven."** The Greek word translated here as **are forgiven** is the

same word that is translated "have been forgiven" in the previous verse, conveying the continuing effect of a past act. Jesus is not forgiving the woman's sins as he speaks but reassuring her that she has already been forgiven and continues to be in a state of forgiveness.

49 Luke interrupts what Jesus is saying to recount the reaction of those at the banquet to Jesus' words. **The others at table said to themselves, "Who is this who even forgives sins?"** They understand Jesus' words to be a pronouncement of forgiveness, made as if he had the authority to do so. There was a similar reaction when Jesus told a paralyzed man, "your sins are forgiven" (5:20–21); Jesus responded by demonstrating that "the Son of Man has authority on earth to forgive sins" (5:24). Jesus makes no response now but leaves the question hanging: **Who is this who even forgives sins?** Who is this man, pronouncing that one is forgiven as if he had God's authority?

For reflection: How is Jesus God's agent of forgiveness for me?

50 Jesus continues his words to the woman: **But he said to the woman, "Your faith has saved you; go in peace."** She is in a state of forgiveness (verse 48), and her **faith** has saved her. Jesus does not indicate the content of her faith. It could have been her believing that Jesus was God's agent and her heeding his call to repentance (see 5:32). It may have included her confidence that God was willing to forgive her despite her many sins. Her faith **saved** her: **saved** is also in the Greek tense that conveys the continuing effect of a past action. To be **saved** means to be rescued from danger or delivered from death. Her faith led to her sins being forgiven, rescuing her from their consequences. Therefore Jesus tells her, **go in peace.** This is a farewell used in the Old Testament (Exod 4:18; 1 Sam 1:17; 20:42; 2 Kings 5:19; Tobit 10:12–13; 12:5; Judith 8:35) but has special meaning as Jesus' words to the woman. The Hebrew notion of peace is not simply absence of conflict but wholeness, harmony, well-being. The woman is in a state of wholeness through having been forgiven and saved, and Jesus' farewell to her bids her to **go** and live in this state of well-being.

For reflection: What do Jesus' parting words to the woman convey about what Jesus wants to do for me?

CHAPTER 8

The Women Who Followed and Supported Jesus

¹ **Afterward he journeyed from one town and village to another, preaching and proclaiming the good news of the kingdom of God. Accompanying him were the Twelve** ² **and some women who had been cured of evil spirits and infirmities, Mary, called Magdalene, from whom seven demons had gone out,** ³ **Joanna, the wife of Herod's steward Chuza, Susanna, and many others who provided for them out of their resources.**

NT: Mark 15:40–41; Luke 4:43; 24:10

1   **Afterward he journeyed from one town and village to another, preaching and proclaiming the good news of the kingdom of God.** Jesus has been on the road throughout his public ministry (4:14–15, 43–44), going from **town** to town and **village** to village. He will later comment that he has nowhere to lay his head (9:58), no fixed abode. His mission is to proclaim **the good news of the kingdom of God** (4:43), the news that God is about to establish his rule. **Accompanying him** as he travels about are **the Twelve** disciples whom he has chosen to be apostles (6:13–16).

Gospel, good news: See page 59

Kingdom of God: See page 381

2   Also accompanying Jesus are **some women who had been cured of evil spirits and infirmities**. Luke names three of these women, beginning with **Mary, called Magdalene, from whom seven demons had gone out**. This **Mary** is **called Magdalene** because she comes from the town of Magdala, on the shore of the Sea of Galilee. Luke does not identify her with the sinful woman who anointed Jesus' feet (7:36–50); popular piety was mistaken in making Mary Magdalene a repentant prostitute. Being afflicted by **seven demons** does not mean that one is a sinner; demons can cause mental or physical sickness (9:39; 11:14; 13:11, 16) but not wickedness. Mary is a woman whom Jesus freed of **evil spirits** and whatever **infirmities** she suffered, and she became his follower.

Demons, unclean spirits: See page 125

214

Married women were often identified in terms of their husbands ("Joanna, the wife of Herod's steward Chuza"—verse 3), but Mary is identified with the town of Magdala. This likely indicates she is not married. It might also indicate that she was prominently involved in the dominant industry of Magdala, preserving and selling fish. Some merchants were women: food containers found in the storerooms of Masada, Herod the Great's fortress by the Dead Sea, name three women among the suppliers. Mary of Magdala was in any case apparently a woman of some means (see verse 3).

3 Also traveling with Jesus was **Joanna, the wife of Herod's steward Chuza.** Herod Antipas ruled Galilee on behalf of Rome (3:1). **Chuza,** as his **steward,** would have been his chief administrator and manager of his vast estates—a position of considerable importance and income. **Joanna** and **Chuza** probably lived in Tiberias, the capital city Herod Antipas built on the western shore of the Sea of Galilee. None of the Gospels recount Jesus going into Tiberias; presumably Joanna heard of Jesus and came to him with her afflictions, as did many (6:17–18). Joanna was part of the wealthy elite, but she did not allow her social status to keep her from coming to Jesus and becoming his follower. Luke next names **Susanna** among the women whom Jesus freed from evil spirits and infirmities, and who then traveled with him. This is the only mention of Susanna in the New Testament.

Herod Antipas: See page 99

Along with the three women whom Luke names, there were **many others**—many other women who traveled with Jesus. For first-century

---

BACKGROUND: MAGDALA was a town on the western shore of the Sea of Galilee, about three miles north of Tiberias and seven miles south of Capernaum. It was a center for processing and selling fish caught in the Sea of Galilee. Later Jewish writings call it *Migdal Nunayya*, meaning "fish tower"—likely referring to a tower used for smoking fish. In Greek it was known as *Taricheae*, from a word that means dried or smoked fish. Smoking or salting fish preserved them and allowed them to be exported. Magdala had a harbor and shipyard, making it a center for commerce and trade. One ancient writer characterized Magdala as a place of wealth. There is no record in the Gospels of Jesus visiting Magdala, but at least one of his followers came from there: Mary of Magdala, better known as Mary Magdalene.

Jews it would have been unusual for women to travel for extended periods of time with a man who was not a relative. However, the new wine of the kingdom of God cannot be kept in old wineskins (5:37–38). Jesus invites women as well as men to follow him, even if this involves breaking with conventional behavior.

Mary of Magdala, Joanna, Susanna, and many other women not only traveled with Jesus and the Twelve; they also **provided for them out of their resources**. Whether they had much or little to contribute, they supported Jesus and his disciples as they traveled, buying food and other essentials. Luke will recount in Acts how the members of the early Church in Jerusalem shared resources with one another (Acts 2:44–45; 4:32–37).

Luke's first readers may have interpreted his naming of Mary Magdalene, Joanna, and Susanna as a signal that they were the most prominent and wealthy of Jesus' supporters, and understood them to be Jesus' patrons. Joanna was certainly a wealthy, upper-class woman, and Mary and Susanna may have been as well. But they did not behave as patrons normally behaved toward their clients. The three women were Jesus' disciples, subordinating themselves to him. They were grateful to Jesus for releasing them from evil spirits and infirmities, and they expressed their gratitude by using their resources to provide for him. In

---

BACKGROUND: PATRONS There was a great disparity in the ancient Mediterranean world between the few who were wealthy and powerful and the many who were poor and powerless. A patron was a person of wealth and influence to whom a person of lesser status turned for help. Patrons provided financial assistance or used their influence to benefit their clients. Doing favors brought honor and prestige for patrons and the loyalty and praise of their clients. Wealthy people often functioned as patrons of their city by paying for public buildings or projects; today we call someone who endows a concert hall a "patron of the arts." An ancient inscription found in Corinth speaks of an Erastus who paid out of his own funds for the paving of a street; this is likely the same Erastus who was a Christian and city treasurer (Rom 16:23). Women as well as men could be patrons. Paul converted a woman named Lydia in Philippi (Acts 16:14–15). As a dealer in expensive purple cloth, she was wealthy and in charge of a household. Lydia acted as Paul's patron, having him stay in her home and supporting him. She made her house available as a place where the Church could meet (Acts 16:40). Recourse to patrons continues today in the form of supplication to patron saints.

this they were like the other women (many presumably from the working poor) who followed Jesus and supported him as they could. Jesus is creating a new family around himself (see 8:19–21), where sisters and brothers are equals.

For reflection: What example do these women set for me? How do I express in action my gratitude for what Jesus has done for me?

ORIENTATION: *Jesus is going about "preaching and proclaiming the good news of the kingdom of God" (8:1). The following section of Luke's Gospel (8:4–21) deals with the response to be made to Jesus' preaching.*

The Parable of the Seed

⁴ **When a large crowd gathered, with people from one town after another journeying to him, he spoke in a parable. ⁵ "A sower went out to sow his seed. And as he sowed, some seed fell on the path and was trampled, and the birds of the sky ate it up. ⁶ Some seed fell on rocky ground, and when it grew, it withered for lack of moisture. ⁷ Some seed fell among thorns, and the thorns grew with it and choked it. ⁸ And some seed fell on good soil, and when it**

BACKGROUND: PARABLES Jesus did not invent the idea of conveying a message by means of a parable (see 2 Sam 12:1–7 for an Old Testament example). The Greek word for parable means "setting beside, placing two things side by side" for comparison. The Hebrew word translated parable has a broader range of meanings, including "proverb," "riddle," "metaphor," "story," "fable," and "allegory." Jesus' parables range from pithy sayings ("No one pours new wine into old wineskins"—Mark 2:22) to miniature stories (the parable of the loving father—Luke 15:11–32). Jesus' parables often use examples from everyday life as comparisons that throw light on what God is doing through him or how one should respond to what God is doing. Jesus' parables are vivid but sometimes enigmatic. They are meant to be thought-provoking, to stimulate the listener's reflection. Sometimes they confront the listener with a decision: Make up your mind—where do you stand? Some scholars have claimed that each parable makes only one point, but that is an artificial restriction. Some parables are like diamonds, revealing new facets of meaning when examined from different angles.

---

grew, it produced fruit a hundredfold." After saying this, he called out, "Whoever has ears to hear ought to hear."

Gospel parallels: Matt 13:1–9; Mark 4:1–9

4 **When a large crowd gathered, with people from one town after another journeying to him**: Jesus continues to attract crowds (4:42; 5:1, 15; 7:11), with people traveling distances to listen to his teaching and be healed (6:17–18). **He spoke in a parable**, addressing not only the crowd but also his disciples (8:1–3). A **parable**, often based on ordinary experience, provides a comparison to make a point. Jesus has used parables before (5:36–39; 6:39, 41–44, 47–49; 7:41–42).

5 **A sower went out to sow his seed.** Jesus' audience would have had no difficulty imagining the scene; most Galileans farmed. Grain crops such as wheat were sown in the late fall, before the beginning of the winter rainy season. **Seed** was cast by hand and later plowed under. **And as he sowed, some seed fell on the path** that ran alongside or through his field. The sower does not deliberately sow his seed on the path, but casting seed by hand is a somewhat hit-or-miss affair. The seed that landed on the path **was trampled** and crushed by those walking on the path, **and the birds of the sky ate it up**. This seed was wasted, but not sowing seed near a path would waste the land adjacent to the path, and cropland was precious.

BACKGROUND: FARMING Farmers made up most of the population of rural Galilee. Unlike American farmers, who tend to live in isolated houses on their farms, Galilean farmers lived together in small towns and villages and went out to work their fields. They grew grain crops, including wheat and barley; fruits, such as grapes, olives, and figs; and vegetables, such as lentils, beans, peas, and cucumbers. Galilee contained some prime farmland in its valleys, including the broad valleys north and south of Nazareth. Much of the prime land had been expropriated by rulers, such as Herod Antipas at the time of Jesus, who either had it managed for them or entrusted it to their influential supporters. Some farmers worked as tenant farmers or day laborers on these estates. Most farmers owned their own plots of land, which were often small and were sometimes on a rocky hillside that had to be terraced to support crops. Farmers were subject to tithes and taxes on their crops, which by some estimates added up to 40 percent of their harvests. These farmers were better off than day laborers, but a few bad harvests could lead to indebtedness and loss of land.

---

6   The limestone hills of Galilee are covered with an uneven layer of soil, and sometimes rock pokes through the soil. **Some seed fell on rocky ground**, literally, fell on the rock. For farmers with rocky fields, hand-sowing inevitably meant that some seeds would land on rocks or on very thin soil over rock. **And when it grew, it withered for lack of moisture.** Any seeds that sprouted on rock soon died.

7   **Some seed fell among thorns.** As the grain **seed** he planted grew, so did whatever weeds and thorns were in the soil, and in the competition for survival, the thorns won out: **the thorns grew with** the seed the sower sowed **and choked it** out.

8   It might seem as if farming is a futile occupation, doomed to failure. But **some seed fell on good soil, and when it grew, it produced fruit a hundredfold.** A **hundredfold** harvest is an extraordinarily good harvest (see Gen 26:12). The abundant harvest on some of the farmer's land more than makes up for the seed that was trampled or eaten by birds or withered or choked out. A farmer is usually able to reap a harvest that will feed his family until the next harvest, with some left over to be used as seed for the next crop. That is how farmers can survive to farm year after year. Jesus' parable describes a realistic and seemingly unexceptional situation.

   After saying this, he called out, "Whoever has ears to hear ought to hear." Jesus exhorts his disciples and the crowd to **hear** what he has just said and to perceive its significance. But what is it that they **ought to hear**? Jesus has told a story about seed falling in various places and producing a good harvest despite some seed being wasted. The story is a parable (verse 4), providing a comparison. But what is being compared to what? Is the comparison to be found in the various places the seed landed, or in the various fates of the seed, or in the ultimate good harvest, or in some other element of the parable? And what is being compared to it? Jesus urges his listeners to ponder the parable and perceive its point. He does not explain its significance to the crowd but challenges them to discover its significance for themselves: **whoever has ears to hear ought to hear.**

   For reflection: Why do I think that Jesus challenged his listeners to figure out the point of the parable themselves? If I were among those hearing Jesus tell this parable, what would I have taken to be its significance?

Jesus Explains the Parable of the Seed

⁹ Then his disciples asked him what the meaning of this parable might be. ¹⁰ He answered, "Knowledge of the mysteries of the kingdom of God has been granted to you; but to the rest, they are made known through parables so that 'they may look but not see, and hear but not understand.'

¹¹ "This is the meaning of the parable. The seed is the word of God. ¹² Those on the path are the ones who have heard, but the devil comes and takes away the word from their hearts that they may not believe and be saved. ¹³ Those on rocky ground are the ones who, when they hear, receive the word with joy, but they have no root; they believe only for a time and fall away in time of trial. ¹⁴ As for the seed that fell among thorns, they are the ones who have heard, but as they go along, they are choked by the anxieties and riches and pleasures of life, and they fail to produce mature fruit. ¹⁵ But as for the seed that fell on rich soil, they are the ones who, when they have heard the word, embrace it with a generous and good heart, and bear fruit through perseverance."

Gospel parallels: Matt 13:10–23; Mark 4:10–20
OT: Isaiah 6:9
NT: Luke 5:1; 7:50; 8:1–8

9 Jesus has been speaking to a large crowd (8:4) with his disciples present (8:1–3). He told a parable about a farmer sowing seed that falls on different kinds of ground (8:5–8). He concluded by exhorting his listeners, "Whoever has ears to hear ought to hear" (8:8), inviting them to grasp the point of the parable. His disciples are unable to do so: **then his disciples asked him what the meaning of this parable might be**. They realize that the parable provides some sort of comparison, but they do not understand what is being compared to what.

10 Instead of immediately explaining the meaning of the parable to his disciples, Jesus addresses their failure to understand it. **He answered, "Knowledge of the mysteries of the kingdom of God has been granted to you."** The **mysteries** of the kingdom of God are God's hidden purposes and plans (see Dan 2:18–19, 27–30; 1 Cor 2:1, 7; Eph 3:2–10; Col 1:26–27). **Knowledge** of these mysteries **has been granted**

to the disciples—implied, granted by God (see also 10:21). Therefore, his disciples should not need to ask him to explain the parable of the seed; they should be able to figure out its meaning themselves on the basis of the knowledge they have been given. Yet they fail to understand (see also 9:44–45). Jesus' words are an implicit rebuke.

Kingdom of God: See page 381

For reflection: Do I have a sense that God has granted me an understanding of his word to me in Scripture? Where does my understanding fail?

But to the rest, they are made known through parables—literally, "but to the rest in parables." Jesus' words are cryptic. He does not mean that his parables are meant only for those who are not disciples; he has addressed his parables to his disciples as well as to the crowds (see 6:17, 20, 39), just as he has proclaimed the kingdom of God to crowds as well as to his disciples (4:43–44; 8:1; 9:11). Rather, his meaning seems to be that for those who do not have knowledge of the mysteries of the kingdom, his parables remain only parables—enigmas. Consequently **"they may look but not see, and hear but not understand."** They do not **see** the significance of and **understand** the parables they **hear**. Jesus borrows words from a prophecy in which Isaiah is to proclaim that his words will fall on uncomprehending ears (Isaiah 6:9). Clearly, Jesus wants everyone to understand and accept his proclamation of what God is doing to establish his kingdom. It is also clear that some reject Jesus and his message (6:11; 7:31–35), thereby blocking the understanding God would give them. By invoking words from Isaiah's prophecy, Jesus categorizes their incomprehension as being of a piece with a long history of God's people not comprehending his words to them.

> Go and say to this people:
> Listen carefully, but you shall not understand!
> Look intently, but you shall know nothing!
> Isaiah 6:9

11 Jesus provides the explanation his disciples requested. **This is the meaning of the parable. The seed is the word of God.** In his preaching,

Jesus proclaims **the word of God** (see 5:1), the message from God addressed to women and men. Jesus' **parable** compares the word of God to a **seed**. Seeds have life within them but cannot produce a harvest unless they are received into good soil.

> *For reflection: What does comparing the word of God to a seed tell me about the word of God?*

12 In the parable, seed falls on four kinds of ground with four different outcomes. In Jesus' interpretation of the parable, these different outcomes represent different results when the word of God is proclaimed. **Those on the path are the ones who have heard, but the devil comes and takes away the word from their hearts** before it gets a chance to really sink in. These give the word of God no real hearing. Consequently, the **devil**—Satan—has no difficulty snatching it away so **that they may not believe and be saved**. To **believe** means to accept the word of God, trusting it. To **be saved** means to be rescued from the consequences of our sins and from eternal death (see 7:50). Those who give the word of God no hearing and do not believe it miss their offer of salvation.

Satan: See page 108

13 **Those on rocky ground are the ones who, when they hear, receive the word with joy.** They **hear** the word of God and accept it with **joy** and enthusiasm. **But they have no root.** Their acceptance of God's word is superficial; they do not allow it to penetrate deep within them, transforming them. **They believe only for a time**: unlike those in the previous group, who did not believe at all (verse 12), these do **believe** in God's word, but **only for a time**. They **fall away in time of trial**: it is taken for granted that every follower of Jesus will face a **time of trial** and testing. When a test comes, those who did not root their lives in God's word fail the test and **fall away**. They are like a house built on the ground with no foundation, easily destroyed by a flood (6:49).

14 **As for the seed that fell among thorns, they are the ones who have heard** the word of God and accepted it, **but as they go along**, living out their lives, **they are choked by the anxieties and riches and pleasures of life**. In Luke's Gospel, to have **anxieties**, to worry, has the

connotation of having unnecessary concerns (see 10:41-42), particularly about one's well-being (see 12:22, 25-26). Anxious self-concern crowds out allegiance to God's word and trust in his care. **Riches** can also choke out living for God. Jesus will teach, "You cannot serve God and mammon" (16:13); wealth can be an obstacle to entering the kingdom of God (18:24). Note, though, that the women who provide for Jesus (8:2–3) show that riches can be put to good use. The **pleasures of life** are the enjoyments life offers, which, since they are pleasurable, tempt us to go to excess and make "eat, drink, be merry" the motto of our lives (see 12:19). What began as a wholehearted response to God's word is gradually choked out by the pleasures of the moment. Whether the downfall is due to **anxieties** or **riches** or the **pleasures of life**, the result is the same: **they fail to produce mature fruit.** Only **mature fruit** can be harvested; it does a farmer no good to have a crop that only half-ripens.

For reflection: Do I see any of myself in the various responses and outcomes Jesus has described so far?

15 **But as for the seed that fell on rich soil, they are the ones who, when they have heard the word, embrace it with a generous and good heart.** The connotation of **embrace** is to hold fast, as to a prized possession; this group **heard the word** of God, welcomed it, and retained it. They did so **with a generous and good heart**. In biblical idiom, the heart represents the inner self, the core of one's being. They wholeheartedly embrace God's word **and bear fruit through perseverance**. Of all who heard the word of God, only they **bear fruit**, a harvestable crop, and they do so only **through perseverance**. The word translated **perseverance** conveys patience, endurance, fortitude, steadfastness, constancy in the face of adversity. They are faithful in a time of testing (verse 13); they withstand the allures of self-concern and riches and pleasures (verse 14); they persevere in living fruitful lives.

For reflection: How might I embrace God's word more wholeheartedly? Am I persevering in bearing fruit for God?

Jesus' interpretation of the parable of the seed explains why his preaching has had mixed results: some have not given him a hearing, some have responded only superficially, some have fallen by the wayside, and some have persevered as his disciples. For Luke's first readers, Jesus' interpretation would explain why the Church's preaching of the word of God has had mixed results. It would also be an exhortation to perseveringly embrace God's word and not to get discouraged in proclaiming God's word to others.

Jesus' explanation of the parable puts the accent on how men and women respond to God's word; persevering in it takes effort. This balances what Jesus had previously said to his disciples, where the accent was on God's granting understanding (verse 10). Both God's grace and our efforts are necessary if we are to embrace and live by God's word.

ORIENTATION: *To emphasize the importance of properly responding to the word of God, Jesus invokes three sayings. Luke recounts Jesus' also using these sayings in other contexts.*

Take Care How You Listen

⁶ "No one who lights a lamp conceals it with a vessel or sets it under a bed; rather, he places it on a lampstand so that those who enter may see the light. ⁷ For there is nothing hidden that will not become visible, and nothing secret that will not be known and come to light. ⁸ Take care, then, how you hear. To anyone who has, more will be given, and from the one who has not, even what he seems to have will be taken away."

Gospel parallels: Matt 5:15; 10:26; 13:12; Mark 4:21–25
NT: Luke 8:10; 11:33; 12:2; 19:26

16 After explaining the parable of the seed (8:11–15), Jesus tells another parable. **No one who lights a lamp conceals it with a vessel or sets it under a bed.** A **lamp** was a small pottery container filled with olive oil; a wick dipped in the oil burned with a candle-like flame. Anyone who **lights a lamp** does so for its light. **No one,** having lit a lamp, **conceals it with a vessel** (literally, covers it with a pot), blocking out its light. Even less would anyone put a lit lamp **under a bed,** which would not only block its light but might set fire to the bed. **Rather, he places it on a lampstand so that those who enter** the room it is in **may see the light.** Elevating a lamp on a stand allows its light to shine in all directions, making maximum use of the lamp.

What Jesus says is common sense, but what is the point he wants to make? This parable about a lamp can have different lessons in different contexts (see 11:33). In the present context, the lamp most likely represents those who "when they have heard the word, embrace it with a generous and good heart, and bear fruit through perseverance" (8:15). They have been enkindled with the light of the word of God, and they are meant to shine forth this light, not hide it. They are to shine **so that those who enter may see the light**—so that those becoming Jesus' disciples or entering the Church may be enlightened by the word of God.

17 **For there is nothing hidden that will not become visible, and nothing secret that will not be known and come to light.** This saying of Jesus, like the parable of the lamp, can have different lessons in different contexts (see 12:2). In the present context, Jesus' prefacing his statement with a **for** indicates that his words continue the lesson of the parable of the lamp. The notions of something being **hidden** and **secret** echo his speaking of the mysteries or secrets of the kingdom of God (8:10). These mysteries must **come to light**: they have been made known to Jesus' disciples (8:10), and the disciples must make them **visible** and **known** to others. Jesus' disciples are to proclaim publicly the word of God that has been revealed to them, radiating it as a lamp on a stand radiates light.

18 Since his disciples are to bring the word of God to others, Jesus exhorts them to **take care, then, how you hear** God's word. In his explanation of the parable of the seed (8:11–15), those represented by different kinds of soil all heard the word of God. Where they differed was in **how** they heard it. Only those who embraced God's word in their hearts and persevered bore fruit (8:15). Jesus' disciples are therefore to **take care** to listen to God's word properly, retaining and treasuring it. **How** they listen makes all the difference.

For reflection: How is responding to God's word part of my listening to it?

Jesus' final saying also has different lessons in different contexts (see 19:26). He invokes what might be a proverbial bit of wisdom: **To anyone who has, more will be given, and from the one who has not, even what he seems to have will be taken away.** A modern counterpart would be, The rich get richer and the poor get poorer. In this context in Luke's Gospel, **anyone who has** represents anyone who has listened properly to the word of God, embracing and retaining it. To them, **more will be given** by God: their embrace of God's word means that God can make even more known to them. But **from the one who has not, even what he seems to have will be taken away.** The word translated **seems** also means "thinks": **the one who has not** listened properly to the word of God, **even what he** thinks he understands, but really doesn't, **will be taken away.** His illusions will be shattered.

By his three sayings and his exhortation to be careful how they hear (verses 16–18), Jesus tells his followers to listen carefully to the word of God he proclaims, so that they can grow in understanding it and be able to proclaim it to others. Jesus wants them to bear the fruit (8:15) of being a light for others (verse 16).

For reflection: What is the most important lesson for me in these words of Jesus?

Hearing and Acting on the Word of God
¹⁹ Then his mother and his brothers came to him but were unable to join him because of the crowd. ²⁰ He was told, "Your mother and your brothers are standing outside and they wish to see you." ²¹ He said to them in reply, "My mother and my brothers are those who hear the word of God and act on it."
Gospel parallels: Matt 12:46–50; Mark 3:31–35
NT: Luke 1:38; 2:19, 51; 5:1; 6:47–48; 8:15, 18; 11:27–28

19 **Then his mother and his brothers came to him.** Mary the **mother** of Jesus has not been on the scene since Jesus was twelve (2:41–52), and she will not appear again in this Gospel. This is Luke's only mention of Jesus' **brothers** in his Gospel. However, "Mary the mother of Jesus, and his brothers" will be present in the upper room after Jesus' ascension, awaiting the outpouring of the Holy Spirit (Acts 1:13–14). The word **brothers** indicates relatives of Jesus without necessarily specifying that they are his siblings. They came to Jesus to visit him **but were unable to join him because of the crowd.** A large crowd of people from many

towns is present (8:4), along with Jesus' disciples (8:9). The crush of the crowd around Jesus prevents his relatives from reaching him.

20 Word of his relatives' arrival reaches Jesus: **He was told, "Your mother and your brothers are standing outside and they wish to see you."** Their **standing outside** would apparently imply that Jesus is at this point in a house. The sense of **see you** can be visit you (see Acts 16:40).

21 **He said to them in reply, "My mother and my brothers are those who hear the word of God and act on it."** Jesus has been speaking about hearing and responding to the word of God (8:4–18), and he uses the arrival of his **mother** and **brothers** to make an observation about them. He proclaims that they **hear the word of God and act on it**. They do what Jesus has been exhorting his disciples and the crowd to do: listen carefully to the word of God (8:18), "embrace it with a generous and good heart, and bear fruit through perseverance" (8:15). Jesus previously emphasized the importance of acting on his words (6:47–48), which

---

BACKGROUND: BROTHERS AND SISTERS OF JESUS Brothers of Jesus are mentioned in the Gospels as well as in Acts 1:14, 1 Corinthians 9:5, and Galatians 1:19. Four brothers are listed by name in Matthew 13:55 and Mark 6:3: James, Joses (or Joseph), Simon, and Judas; unnamed sisters are mentioned in Matthew 13:56 and Mark 6:3. While these references might be interpreted to mean that Mary and Joseph had children after Jesus' birth, other passages seem to indicate a different Mary as the mother of James and Joses (Matt 27:56; Mark 15:40), and the Church from early times has held to the perpetual virginity of Mary. One explanation, circulated in the second-century books *Protoevangelium of James* and *Infancy Gospel of Thomas,* is that the brothers and sisters of Jesus were children of Joseph from a previous marriage; this is the accepted view in the Byzantine and Orthodox tradition. St. Jerome (342-420) proposed that the brothers of Jesus were his cousins, since the Hebrew word for brother can also mean "cousin." Jerome's explanation became widely but not universally accepted (Greek has a word for cousin, used in Col 4:10: "Mark the cousin of Barnabas"). Some of the Gospels present the brothers of Jesus as having no faith in him during his public ministry (Mark 3:21; John 7:3-7). But "Mary the mother of Jesus, and his brothers," awaited Pentecost in the upper room (Acts 1:13–14). Paul lists a James, apparently the James called "the brother of the Lord" (Gal 1:19), who was not one of the twelve apostles, as among those to whom Jesus appeared after his resurrection (1 Cor 15:7). "James the brother of the Lord" (Gal 1:19) emerged as the leader of the Christian community in Jerusalem (Acts 12:17; 15:13-21; 21:18; Gal 2:9, 12).

---

are the word of God (5:1). Jesus does not go into the specifics of how his mother and brothers have heard and acted on the word of God. Readers of Luke's Gospel know that Mary pondered the events surrounding Jesus' birth (2:19) and his staying behind in the Temple (2:51). She is a model for taking care how one hears the word of God (8:18). She is also a model for acting on God's word: she responded to God's messenger, "May it be done to me according to your word" (1:38).

For reflection: How do I go about hearing the word of God? What have I done to act on it?

ORIENTATION: *In what Luke seems to recount as the events of a single day, Jesus demonstrates his authority and then shares his authority with the Twelve (8:22—9:5).*

Who Is This?

22 One day he got into a boat with his disciples and said to them, "Let us cross to the other side of the lake." So they set sail, 23 and while they were sailing he fell asleep. A squall blew over the lake, and they were taking in water and were in danger. 24 They came and woke him saying, "Master, master, we are perishing!" He awakened, rebuked the wind and the waves, and they subsided and there was a calm. 25 Then he asked them, "Where is your faith?" But they were filled with awe and amazed and said to one another, "Who then is this, who commands even the winds and the sea, and they obey him?"

Gospel parallels: Matt 8:23–27; Mark 4:35–41
OT: Psalm 65:8; 89:10; 107:28–29
NT: Luke 5:21; 7:49

22 **One day he got into a boat with his disciples.** By beginning his account with **one day,** Luke creates the impression that some time may have passed since Jesus told parables about responding to the word of God (8:4–18). That there is a **boat** handy for Jesus may indicate that his fishermen disciples still had access to a boat, even after leaving everything to follow him (5:11). Jesus got into a boat **with his disciples**: Jesus

has been accompanied by the Twelve and women whom he had healed (8:2). There would be no reason why some of these women would not go with him in the boat. Jesus **said to them, "Let us cross to the other side of the lake."** In Luke's Gospel, the Sea of Galilee is referred to as a **lake** (see also 8:33), the Lake of Gennesaret (5:1). The **other side** of the lake will turn out to be on the eastern or southeastern side (8:26), which implies that they are setting out from the west coast, where Capernaum and Magdala lay. **So they set sail.**

Disciple: See page 149
Lake of Gennesaret: See page 134

23 **And while they were sailing he fell asleep.** Jesus is not immune to fatigue. There are often crowds coming to him with their needs (4:40, 42; 6:17-19; 8:4), which can be wearying; crossing the Sea of Galilee in a boat provides an opportunity for Jesus to take a nap. **A squall blew over the lake**: the word translated **squall** means a fierce storm or whirlwind. A storm **blew over the lake**, literally, came down to the lake. The Sea of Galilee lies seven hundred feet below sea level; ravines in the hills around the lake funnel wind down onto the lake, causing sudden and violent storms. Because of the storm, **they were taking in water and were in danger**. The boat was swamping, and those in it were **in danger** of drowning.

24 That Jesus is able to sleep through a storm even as the boat fills with water is perhaps an indication of how tired he was. **They came and woke him saying, "Master, master, we are perishing!"** Calling Jesus **master** acknowledges his authority; doubling the title—**master, master**—conveys urgency. The disciples are in a panic and tell Jesus **we are perishing!** They wake Jesus because the boat is about to go under and they will probably drown. They do not necessarily expect him to do something about it (they are astonished when he does—verse 25); they may simply think he ought to be aware of what is happening. **He awakened** and **rebuked the wind and the waves**. Whether or not the disciples expected Jesus to rescue them, he does. He **rebuked** the wind and waves as he had rebuked demons (4:35, 41) and a fever (4:39). Whatever threatens human life is evil, and Jesus overcomes the forces of evil in establishing the reign of God. At Jesus' word (see 7:7), the wind

and the waves **subsided and there was a calm**. His disciples are safe again.

25 **Then he asked them, "Where is your faith?"** Jesus does not accuse them of having no **faith** in him but asks them why they have not been relying on it. By following him they have entrusted their lives into his hands. Their faith in his care for them should sustain them when storms or other challenges arise. Anyone would naturally experience fear when their boat begins to sink far from shore, but disciples of Jesus should have a faith that overrides fears.

For reflection: How has my faith in Jesus sustained me through the storms of life?

But they were filled with awe and amazed, natural reactions to a manifestation of divine presence or power (see 1:12; 2:9; 5:9; 7:16). They **said to one another, "Who then is this, who commands even the winds and the sea, and they obey him?"** God, certainly, could command **the winds and the sea**, as he did when he brought order to the chaos of the seas at creation (Gen 1:1–2, 9–10; see Psalm 65:8; 89:10; 107:28–29). But **who then is this** who commands wind and sea as God commands them? People wondered "who is this" when Jesus pronounced the forgiveness of sins (5:21; 7:49); people could have also asked "who is this" when he raised a dead man to life (7:14–15). Who is this who exercises God's authority over sea and sins and death? Jesus will shortly raise the question himself (9:18, 20).

For reflection: What answer do I give to the question, "Who is this?"

Jesus Saves a Man from Demons
²⁶ **Then they sailed to the territory of the Gerasenes, which is opposite Galilee. ²⁷ When he came ashore a man from the town who was possessed by demons met him. For a long time he had not worn clothes; he did not live in a house, but lived among the tombs. ²⁸ When he saw Jesus, he cried out and fell down before him; in a loud voice he shouted, "What have you to do with me,**

Jesus, son of the Most High God? I beg you, do not torment me!" ²⁹ For he had ordered the unclean spirit to come out of the man. (It had taken hold of him many times, and he used to be bound with chains and shackles as a restraint, but he would break his bonds and be driven by the demon into deserted places.) ³⁰ Then Jesus asked him, "What is your name?" He replied, "Legion," because many demons had entered him. ³¹ And they pleaded with him not to order them to depart to the abyss.

³² A herd of many swine was feeding there on the hillside, and they pleaded with him to allow them to enter those swine; and he let them. ³³ The demons came out of the man and entered the swine, and the herd rushed down the steep bank into the lake and was drowned. ³⁴ When the swineherds saw what had happened, they ran away and reported the incident in the town and through-out the countryside. ³⁵ People came out to see what had happened and, when they approached Jesus, they discovered the man from whom the demons had come out sitting at his feet. He was clothed and in his right mind, and they were seized with fear. ³⁶ Those who witnessed it told them how the possessed man had been saved. ³⁷ The entire population of the region of the Gerasenes asked Jesus to leave them because they were seized with great fear. So he got into a boat and returned. ³⁸ The man from whom the demons had come out begged to remain with him, but he sent him away, say-ing, ³⁹ "Return home and recount what God has done for you." The man went off and proclaimed throughout the whole town what Jesus had done for him.

Gospel parallels: Matt 8:28–34; Mark 5:1–20

26 **Then,** after the violent storm (8:22–25), **they sailed to the territory of the Gerasenes, which is opposite Galilee.** Luke calls the region east and south of the Sea of Galilee **the territory of the Gerasenes,** identi-fying it with the city of Gerasa (today's Jerash, in northern Jordan), even though Gerasa lay thirty-three miles from the Sea of Galilee. This **ter-ritory** had a predominantly Gentile, pagan population; it was **opposite Galilee** not only geographically but ethnically and religiously.

Galilee: See page 114

27 **When he came ashore a man from the town who was possessed by demons met him.** Luke leaves **the town** unnamed; his account unfolds as if it were a town near the Sea of Galilee. A man, presumably a Gentile, was **from** the town but no longer lived there because he **was possessed by demons** and behaved in a deranged manner. **For a long time he had not worn clothes**, living as wild animals do. **He did not live in a house, but lived among the tombs.** He was estranged from society, keeping company with the dead rather than the living. When Jesus **came ashore**, this possessed man **met him**.

Demons, unclean spirits: See page 125

28 **When he saw Jesus, he cried out and fell down before him.** He screams and falls down before Jesus because the demons in him recognize that Jesus is stronger than they are. **In a loud voice he shouted, "What have you to do with me, Jesus, son of the Most High God?"** The idiom **what have you to do with me** (literally, what to me and to you) conveys, Mind your own business and leave me alone!—the same idiom used by the demon that Jesus expelled in Capernaum (4:34). The demons, speaking through the man, recognize Jesus to be **son of the Most High God,** just as Satan and demons have previously known that Jesus is the Son of God (4:3, 9, 41). The demons call God **the Most High God.** While this is the way a Gentile might refer to the God of Israel (see Acts 16:17), Gabriel and Zechariah have also called God the Most High (1:32, 35, 76). The demons, speaking in the first-person singular, plead with Jesus **I beg you, do not torment me!** The demons recognize that Jesus has power over them and **beg** Jesus not to expel them from the man and consign them to the abyss (verse 31), which would be **torment** for them.

Son of God: See page 25

29 Luke explains why the demons beg Jesus to leave them alone: **for he had ordered the unclean spirit to come out of the man.** When Jesus got out of the boat and saw the naked man, he knew that his derangement was demonic and he commanded the **unclean spirit** or spirits to depart from him. Luke continues his aside to his readers, providing background information about the man. The demons **had taken hold of him many times**: the man's bizarre behavior periodically became worse. **He used to be bound with chains and shackles as a restraint**, because he was

a menace to others and to himself. **But he would break his bonds**: in his possessed condition he exhibited great strength, even to the point of breaking **chains and shackles**. He was uncontrollable. He would **be driven by the demon into deserted places**—into the wilderness, away from others. He was not in control of his life and was in desperate need of Jesus' compassion and deliverance.

For reflection: Are there any areas in my life in which I lack self-control? Where am I most in need of Jesus' compassion and deliverance?

30 **Then Jesus asked him,** addressing the demon or demons, **"What is your name?"** Why Jesus wishes to know this—or why he does not already know it—is unclear. The reply Jesus receives does, however, enlighten Luke's readers about the man's condition. **He replied, "Legion."** Jesus is not given a name but a number. A **legion** in the Roman army had up to six thousand soldiers; **many demons had entered** the man. Jesus freed Mary Magdalene of seven demons (8:2); this unfortunate man is plagued by thousands.

31 **And they pleaded with him not to order them to depart to the abyss.** In an Old Testament view of the world, the **abyss** is a deep ocean beneath the surface of the earth (Gen 7:11; 8:2; Tobit 13:2; Job 38:16; Sirach 1:3; Ezek 26:19; 31:15); sometimes, though, the **abyss** is simply the depths of the earth. In some nonbiblical writings from before the time of Jesus, fallen angels are imprisoned in the abyss, awaiting God's judgment—a view echoed in the letters of Jude (Jude 6) and Peter (2 Pet 2:4) as well as in the book of Revelation (Rev 17:8; 20:1–3). The demons beg Jesus not to imprison them in the abyss.

Nonbiblical writings: See page 342

32 **A herd of many swine was feeding there on the hillside.** This indicates that Jesus is in a Gentile region. Jews did not raise pigs because they were unclean and their flesh could not be eaten (Lev 11:6–8; Deut 14:8), making them worthless to Jews. The demons **pleaded with him to allow them to enter those swine** after they were expelled from the man. The demons apparently consider this preferable to being cast into the abyss. **And he let them**: Jesus gives the demons permission to enter the pigs.

33 **The demons came out of the man and entered the swine, and the herd rushed** in a panicked stampede **down the steep bank into the lake and was drowned.** The demon's presence in pigs is destructive, as it had been in the man. The demons wanted to avoid the abyss, but they end up in watery depths anyway; did Jesus foresee this happening when he gave them permission to enter the pigs? Nothing more is said about the fate of the demons after the pigs had drowned. What is important is that the demons **came out of the man** at the command of Jesus, freeing him from them.

34 Luke shifts his focus to those who witnessed the scene. **When the swineherds saw what had happened, they ran away and reported the incident in the town and throughout the countryside.** The **swineherds** were responsible for the pigs and had to explain their loss. More importantly, they had seen something awesome take place: a demonically deranged man stopped screaming, and their pigs stampeded into the Sea of Galilee. They would not need to have overheard Jesus' giving permission to the demons to enter the pigs to suspect that demons had left the man and gone into their pigs. **They ran away** in panic and told everyone they could **what had happened.**

35 **People came out to see what had happened,** wanting to see for themselves. Nothing like this had ever happened before! **When they approached Jesus, they discovered the man from whom the demons had come out sitting at his feet.** Previously he had been lying on the ground screaming; now he is calmly sitting at Jesus' feet, the posture of a disciple (10:39; Acts 22:3). Previously he had gone around naked; now **he was clothed.** Previously he was deranged and uncontrollable; now he is **in his right mind** and exercising self-control. **The man from whom the demons had come out** has been utterly transformed by their departure.

For reflection: How has Jesus freed and transformed me, so that I can be his disciple?

The people who came to see what had happened **were seized with fear.** They know what this man has been like, and they realize that it would have taken someone or something very powerful to so utterly change him. The presence of such power in their neighborhood fills them with **fear.**

36 **Those who witnessed it told them how the possessed man had been saved.** Those who had been present during Jesus' encounter with the possessed man reported what had happened, telling how the possessed man **had been saved.** To be **saved** means to be rescued from distress or death; the man has been rescued from demons and given wholeness of life. Luke's readers can find a fuller meaning in the word **saved:** Jesus rescues from eternal death and gives eternal life. If Jesus can free and transform a man afflicted by a legion of demons, he can free and transform anyone.

37 Those who came to find out what had happened learn that it was Jesus who freed the man and sent his demons into the herds of pigs. This focuses their fears on Jesus. **The entire population of the region of the Gerasenes asked Jesus to leave them because they were seized with great fear.** Their fear (verse 35) became **great fear** of him and they **asked Jesus to leave them.** Jesus is present to do good and not harm, but he does not force himself on anyone and he complies with their request. **So he got into a boat and returned** to Galilee.

38 Prior to his departure, **the man from whom the demons had come out begged to remain with him.** His life restored, he wishes to go in the boat with Jesus and **to remain with him** as his disciple. He has been given a new life and now wants to give himself to the one who saved him. He even **begged** Jesus for permission to accompany him, as Mary Magdalene accompanied Jesus after he had freed her of demons (8:1–2). However, Jesus **sent him away, saying,**

39 **Return home and recount what God has done for you.** Jesus does not spurn his allegiance but has something different in mind for him from what the man wants to do. Not all of Jesus' disciples travel with him (see 10:38–42), nor will all his disciples be assigned the same roles. This Gentile man would not be as suitable as Jesus' Jewish disciples to proclaim the kingdom of God to Jews (see 9:1–2). He is, however, well suited to bring a message to fellow Gentiles. Hence Jesus tells him to

return home, going back to where he lived before demons drove him to live among tombs and in the wilderness. He is to **recount what God has done for** him. The word **recount** could also be translated "narrate." Luke earlier used the noun form of this word to describe his Gospel: it is a "narration of the events that have been fulfilled among us" (1:1). Luke and the formerly possessed man have the same task: to tell others **what God has done.** The man obeys Jesus, even though Jesus' plans for him are different from his own: **the man went off and proclaimed throughout the whole town what Jesus had done for him.** Freed by Jesus from all that estranged him from society, he returns to his **town.** Although Jesus told him, "recount what God has done for you" (verse 39), the man proclaimed **what Jesus had done for him.** He recognized that God worked through Jesus to save him. He becomes the first evangelist to tell others about Jesus.

For reflection: What example does this man set for me? What am I able to say to others about what God has done for me through Jesus?

Modern readers might have questions about this incident. One concern might be for the owners of the pigs and the economic loss they suffered. This concern might not have occurred to Jesus' first followers. Jews would have looked upon the drowning of pigs much as Americans view the drowning of rats, even though rat meat is eaten as normal fare in a number of countries.

Rather than raise questions that Luke's account does not address, it is better to focus on its main points. Jesus displays extraordinary power, vanquishing a legion of demons; Jesus saves a man and restores his life. The man in turn responds wholeheartedly to Jesus, doing what Jesus asks of him.

This is the only time Luke will recount Jesus going into a Gentile area. Jesus' visit foreshadows the mission of the Church to Gentiles, and also the mixed response it will receive to its proclamation of what God has done through Jesus. Some will spurn its messengers, but others, like the man Jesus saved, will find new life.

Jairus's Request and a Woman with a Hemorrhage

⁴⁰ When Jesus returned, the crowd welcomed him, for they were all waiting for him. ⁴¹ And a man named Jairus, an official of the synagogue, came forward. He fell at the feet of Jesus and begged him to come to his house, ⁴² because he had an only daughter, about twelve years old, and she was dying. As he went, the crowds almost crushed him. ⁴³ And a woman afflicted with hemorrhages for twelve years, who [had spent her whole livelihood on doctors and] was unable to be cured by anyone, ⁴⁴ came up behind him and touched the tassel on his cloak. Immediately her bleeding stopped. ⁴⁵ Jesus then asked, "Who touched me?" While all were denying it, Peter said, "Master, the crowds are pushing and pressing in upon you." ⁴⁶ But Jesus said, "Someone has touched me; for I know that power has gone out from me." ⁴⁷ When the woman realized that she had not escaped notice, she came forward trembling. Falling down before him, she explained in the presence of all the people why she had touched him and how she had been healed immediately. ⁴⁸ He said to her,

"Daughter, your faith has saved you; go in peace."

Gospel parallels: Matt 9:18–22; Mark 5:21–34
OT: Lev 15:25–27; Num 15:37–40; Deut 22:12
NT: Luke 4:14; 5:17; 6:17–19; 7:50

40 **When Jesus returned** to Galilee, sailing from the territory of the Gerasenes (8:26–39), **the crowd welcomed him**. The "entire population of the region of the Gerasenes" had asked Jesus to leave them (8:37), but this crowd **welcomed** Jesus, **for they were all waiting for him**. Crowds come to Jesus to "to hear him and to be healed of their diseases" (6:18). Presumably this crowd included those who had seen Jesus sail away earlier in the day (8:22); in their needs, they waited for him to return.

41 Among those waiting for Jesus is **a man named Jairus, an official of the synagogue**. Each local **synagogue** had an **official** who supervised its functioning. The role involved administrative responsibilities rather than conducting religious services. Jairus **came forward** and **fell at the feet of Jesus**. Falling at the feet of someone is a posture of supplication; Jairus **begged** Jesus **to come to his house**. Prostrating himself before

Jesus took some humility: as an **official of the synagogue**, Jairus was a notable man in his town.

Synagogue: See page 115

42 Luke explains why Jairus wanted Jesus to come to his house: **he had an only daughter, about twelve years old, and she was dying**. She was dear to him as his **only** daughter. In the culture of the time, her being **about twelve years old** meant she was approaching marriageable age. She was on the brink of her life but it was being tragically cut short: **she was dying**. By asking Jesus to go to her, Jairus demonstrates that he has faith that Jesus can heal her. Jesus complies with his request and sets out with Jairus for his house. **As he went, the crowds almost crushed him.** Those who had waited for Jesus now go with him, a crowd so dense that it makes it difficult for Jesus to walk. Jairus might be concerned that Jesus will not reach his house in time to save his **dying** daughter.

For reflection: In what ways is Jairus an example for me in his pleading with Jesus for someone he loves?

43 Another person in the crowd who awaited Jesus' return was **a woman** who was **afflicted with hemorrhages for twelve years**. By **hemorrhages**, literally, flow of blood, is most likely meant continual vaginal bleeding. This would make her constantly ritually unclean (Lev 15:25) and furniture she sat on or people she touched unclean as well (Lev 15:19, 26–27). There were remedies for uncleanness (Lev 15:27–30), but some Jews went to lengths to maintain ritual purity and would have avoided contact with her if they were aware of her condition. Her flow of blood had gone on for **twelve years**: she has been **afflicted** for as long as Jairus' daughter has been alive. She of course wanted to be healed and sought medical help. Some ancient manuscripts of Luke's Gospel read that she **[had spent her whole livelihood on doctors]**—words that the New American Bible encloses in brackets because they are not found in other manuscripts. If she had **spent her whole livelihood**, then she was poor as well as **afflicted** and unclean. Despite her efforts, she **was unable to be cured by anyone**: doctors of the time had no remedy for her condition. In her need, she comes to Jesus.

For reflection: What needs do I bring to Jesus?

44 Making her way through the crowd surrounding Jesus, she **came up behind him and touched the tassel on his cloak**. Her approach from **behind** seems furtive, as if she wants to be as inconspicuous as possible. She seems to be aware that touching or being touched by Jesus brings healing; on another occasion "everyone in the crowd sought to touch him because power came forth from him and healed them all" (6:19). In her unclean condition she tries to minimize her physical contact with Jesus; she **touched** only **the tassel on his cloak**. As a law-observant Jew, Jesus wore four tassels on his cloak as visual reminders to keep God's commandments (Num 15:37–40; Deut 22:12). She touched a **tassel** and **immediately her bleeding stopped:** she was cured instantaneously.

Clothing: See page 175

45 Jesus is aware of the touch. **Jesus then asked, "Who touched me?"** This was less a question than an invitation for the person to step forward and identify herself. No one did so: **all were denying it**, apparently including the woman who had been healed. While the crowd is pressing on Jesus, almost crushing him (verse 42), no one will own up to a deliberate touch. Peter thinks that Jesus' question is unreasonable: **Peter said, "Master, the crowds are pushing and pressing in upon you."** Peter addresses Jesus respectfully, calling him **Master**. But Peter points out to Jesus that a lot of people are **pushing and pressing in upon you**. How could any one of them be singled out?

46 **But Jesus said, "Someone has touched me; for I know that power has gone out from me."** Jesus is not concerned with the crowd jostling him; he has just one person in mind, **someone** who **touched** him in a way that drew forth healing power from him. He says **I know that power has gone out from me.** The **power** Jesus has is the power of the Holy Spirit (4:14), the power of God through which he heals (5:17; 6:19). His power is not like a charge of static electricity that arcs between two people when they touch; a crowd has been pushing and pressing in on Jesus without anything happening to them. The healing power of Jesus is activated not by physical contact but by faith. Jesus knows that someone touched him with faith that heals, and this faith-filled touch drew his

healing power. He wants the person publicly identified so that he can correct any misunderstandings about his power.

For reflection: How have I experienced the healing power of Jesus?

47 **When the woman realized that she had not escaped notice**: she **realized** that Jesus had taken **notice** of her and that she could not preserve her anonymity. **She came forward trembling,** probably afraid to admit that she had touched Jesus despite her unclean condition, perhaps uncomfortable being in the spotlight after twelve years in the shadows. **Falling down before him** in submission to him, **she explained in the presence of all the people why she had touched him.** Her words are primarily directed to Jesus, explaining to him **why she had touched him,** but **all the people** in the crowd around Jesus hear what she says. She tells Jesus that she touched the tassel of his cloak so that she could be cured of her flow of blood **and how she had been healed immediately**. Her words proclaim what Jesus has done for her, just like the testimony of the man whom Jesus freed from demons (8:39).

48 **He said to her, "Daughter, your faith has saved you."** Jesus calls her **daughter**, an affectionate term, assuring her of his acceptance of her. It was not her touching him in itself that healed her but her **faith** expressed by the touch. Her faith **has saved** her, rescuing her from her twelve-year condition. He tells her, **go in peace**. Jesus' words mean more than stop trembling and relax; the Hebrew notion of **peace** is well-being and wholeness. Her faith in Jesus has saved her and made her whole. Jesus spoke the same words to the woman whose sins had been forgiven: "Your faith has saved you; go in peace" (7:50).

Just as the woman's words to Jesus were spoken in the presence of "all the people" (verse 47), so are Jesus' words to the woman. He made her come forth so that he could make it clear that it is faith that heals and saves. He implicitly invites the crowd to come to him not merely physically but with faith, so that they too can be saved and know peace.

For reflection: What example does the woman's faith set for me?

Jesus Raises Jairus' Daughter to Life

⁴⁹ **While he was still speaking, someone from the synagogue official's house arrived and said, "Your daughter is dead; do not trouble the teacher any longer."** ⁵⁰ **On hearing this, Jesus answered him, "Do not be afraid; just have faith and she will be saved."** ⁵¹ **When he arrived at the house he allowed no one to enter with him except Peter and John and James, and the child's father and mother.** ⁵² **All were weeping and mourning for her, when he said, "Do not weep any longer, for she is not dead, but sleeping."** ⁵³ **And they ridiculed him, because they knew that she was dead.** ⁵⁴ **But he took her by the hand and called to her, "Child, arise!"** ⁵⁵ **Her breath returned and she immediately arose. He then directed that she should be given something to eat.** ⁵⁶ **Her parents were astounded, and he instructed them to tell no one what had happened.**

Gospel parallels: Matt 9:23–26; Mark 5:35–43

49 **While he was still speaking** with the woman he had healed of her flow of blood (8:47–48), **someone from the synagogue official's house arrived and said** to the official, **"Your daughter is dead."** Jairus asked Jesus to come to his house because his only daughter was dying (8:41–42), but "as he went, the crowds almost crushed him" (8:42), slowing him down. Jesus' **speaking** with the woman meant more delay, and before Jesus reached the house of Jairus, the girl died. The messenger bringing the sad news that his daughter is **dead** suggests to Jairus that there is now no reason to **trouble the teacher any longer** by having him come to the house. Calling Jesus a teacher is respectful but reveals a limited understanding of Jesus and what he has the power to do. It also misreads Jesus to think that asking for his help is to **trouble** or bother or annoy him: he came among us to serve (see 22:27).

50 **On hearing this, Jesus answered him**, addressing Jairus, **"Do not be afraid; just have faith and she will be saved."** Here **afraid** may have the connotation of timid and wavering; Jairus is to boldly **have faith** that Jesus can restore his daughter to life. If Jairus has faith, **she will be saved**—delivered from death. Jairus came to Jesus with faith that Jesus could preserve his daughter's life when she was dying (8:41–42); he was present when Jesus told the woman he healed, "your faith has saved you"

(8:48). It takes a greater act of faith to believe that a dead person can be given life than to believe that a dying girl will get well or a hemorrhage will be cured, but Jairus should **not be afraid** to have such faith. Jairus may well have heard that Jesus raised the only son of the widow of Nain to life, for it was reported "through the whole of Judea and in all the surrounding region" (7:17). Now Jairus must have **faith** that Jesus can do the same for his only daughter.

> For reflection: What does Jesus' invitation, "Do not be afraid; just have faith" mean for me? How firm is my faith that Jesus can give me life after death?

51 **When he arrived at the house** of Jairus **he allowed no one to enter with him except Peter and John and James, and the child's father and mother.** The first disciples called by Jesus were **Peter and John and James** (5:1–11), and they were named, along with Andrew, first in the list of apostles (6:13–14). No explanation is given why Jesus wants these three disciples to enter with him, but presumably Jesus wants some of his disciples to witness what will happen. Allowing the **child's father and mother** to enter with him acknowledges their special relationship with her as her parents. Jesus prevents a crowd of mourners (verses 52–53) from entering; their wailing would not contribute to what he will do.

52 This and the following verse are best understood as describing what happened before Jesus entered the room where the daughter lay; Luke does not always recount things in strict chronological order (see 8:28–30; 37–38). **All were weeping and mourning for her**: family and friends have learned of the death of the girl and have gathered at Jairus's house. The word for **mourning** means to beat one's breast as an expression of sorrow. Their response to her death is natural, but Jesus tells them **do not weep any longer, for she is not dead, but sleeping**. Taken literally, Jesus' words convey that she is still alive and in a sound sleep; there is therefore no reason to mourn for her. But **sleeping** can also mean dead, when death is seen as a preliminary to being given new life. The book of Daniel proclaims, "Many of those who sleep / in the dust of the earth shall awake; / Some shall live forever" (Dan 12:2; see also 1 Cor 15:51; 1

Thess 4:13–15; 5:10). Jesus intends this meaning of **sleeping**: the girl has died, but Jesus can awaken her from the sleep of death.

53 Those mourning the death of the girl miss the implication of Jesus' words. **And they ridiculed him**—laughed derisively at him—**because they knew that she was dead.** They had seen her corpse; how could Jesus claim that she was only sleeping? They **knew** she was dead but did not know the power of Jesus.

54 After Jesus entered the room where the girl lay (verse 51), **he took her by the hand,** touching her, helping her up, **and called to her, "Child, arise!"** The word **arise** is used in various situations. Spoken to a sleeping person, it means to wake up or get up (a form of it is translated "woke" at 8:24). It can also be used for rising from the dead (see 9:7; 24:6; Eph 5:14). Jesus' command combines these two uses. He addresses the one he said was sleeping and tells her to arise, wake up, get up out of bed. But her sleep is the sleep of death, and he calls her to arise from the dead.

55 **Her breath returned and she immediately arose.** The Greek word translated **breath** also means spirit—as does the Hebrew word for breath. The book of Genesis describes God's creation of the first human being in this way: "the LORD God formed man out of the clay of the ground and blew into his nostrils the breath of life, and so man became a living being" (Gen 2:7). Psalm 104 proclaims to God, "When you take away their breath, they perish / and return to the dust from which they came" (Psalm 104:29; see also Job 34:14–15; Eccl 12:7). The girl was dead, but at Jesus' command **her breath returned** and she was restored to life. Jesus told her "arise!" **and she immediately arose,** waking from the sleep of death, getting up. **He then directed that she should be given something to eat.** Was Jesus concerned that she might be hungry? More likely, Jesus wanted a tangible demonstration that she was not a ghost or apparition; eating would be evidence that she was really alive again (see 24:36–43). Jairus' faith has been rewarded; his daughter has been saved.

For reflection: How is Jesus' taking the girl by the hand and bidding her to arise an image for what he will do for me?

56 **Her parents were astounded** by their daughter's coming back to life at the command of Jesus. It was surely the most amazing thing they would ever experience on this earth, and they were beside themselves with joy. But **he instructed them to tell no one what had happened.** It would be difficult for them to keep quiet: those who knew that their daughter had died and who mourned her death (verses 52–53) would surely want an explanation of **what had happened** that had brought her back to life. Jesus' reason for making this request of her parents is not clear. Luke does not recount Jesus giving a similar instruction to the widow whose son he raised from the dead (7:11–16), and a report of that spread widely (7:17). One conjecture might be that Jesus is already so besieged by crowds (8:4, 40, 42) that he does not want publicity that will attract even larger crowds. If that was his motive, his desire will be frustrated. Luke will shortly recount a crowd of more than five thousand people coming to Jesus at a time when he wants privacy (9:10–14).

CHAPTER 9

ORIENTATION: *Luke's Gospel was not divided into chapters until the Middle Ages. The beginning of chapter 9 continues Luke's account of a day in the life of Jesus (8:22—9:5), a day in which Jesus demonstrated his power to save people from sickness and evil. Now Jesus shares his authority with the Twelve and sends them out on mission.*

Jesus Shares His Power and Mission with the Twelve

¹ He summoned the Twelve and gave them power and authority over all demons and to cure diseases, ² and he sent them to proclaim the kingdom of God and to heal [the sick]. ³ He said to them, "Take nothing for the journey, neither walking stick, nor sack, nor food, nor money, and let no one take a second tunic ⁴ Whatever house you enter, stay there and leave from there. ⁵ And as for those who do not welcome you, when you leave that town, shake the dust from your feet in testimony against them." ⁶ Then they set out and went from village to village proclaiming the good news and curing diseases everywhere.

Gospel parallels: Matt 10:1, 5–15; Mark 6:7–13
NT: Luke 6:12–16; 8:22–56

1 **He summoned the Twelve:** earlier Jesus had "called his disciples to himself, and from them he chose Twelve, whom he also named apostles" (6:13). Along with other disciples, the Twelve have traveled with Jesus (8:1) but have played no special role to this point in Luke's Gospel. Now this changes. Jesus **summoned** them and **gave them power and authority over all demons and to cure diseases**. Jesus set out on his public ministry "in the power of the Spirit" (4:14) and has used his power and authority to free men and women from demons and diseases (4:36; 5:17; 6:19; 8:46). In Luke's account, this very day Jesus has calmed a storm at sea, rid a man of a legion of demons, cured a woman of a bleeding disorder, and raised a dead girl to life (8:22–56)—demonstrations of a power and authority that fill his disciples with awe and amazement (8:25). Now Jesus shares his power with the Twelve, so that they can do what he does.

245

They are given authority over **all** demons; they are empowered to **cure diseases** of every kind.

Demons, unclean spirits: See page 125

For reflection: How has Jesus empowered me?

2 The Twelve are given power and authority to carry out a mission: **he sent them to proclaim the kingdom of God and to heal [the sick]**. Jesus said, "I must proclaim the good news of the kingdom of God, because for this purpose I have been sent" (4:43). Now the Twelve are also **sent** with the same purpose. When Jesus chose the Twelve, he named them apostles (6:13); the Greek word for "apostle" comes from the verb **sent**. Jesus sends out the Twelve to **proclaim** the good news of **the kingdom of God,** the message that God is establishing his reign. "Knowledge of the mysteries of the kingdom of God has been granted" to Jesus' disciples (8:10); now they must make the kingdom known to others (see 8:17). As they proclaim the kingdom of God, they are to **heal** those who are sick. God's reign vanquishes evil; the Twelve must demonstrate the good news of the kingdom of God by freeing women and men from their afflictions, as Jesus has done (6:18; 7:22; 8:1–2). Jesus told his disciples that their work would be "catching men" (5:10); the Twelve are sent out on their first fishing trip.

Kingdom of God: See page 381

For reflection: What is the purpose of my life? What have I been sent to do?

3 Jesus gives the Twelve traveling instructions as they go out on their mission. **He said to them, "Take nothing for the journey."** Travelers normally carried essentials with them, but the Twelve are to take **nothing** as they go about proclaiming God's reign and healing the sick. Jesus lists five things that travelers often carried, explicitly prohibiting them: the Twelve are to take **neither walking stick, nor sack, nor food,** literally, bread, **nor money, and let no one take a second tunic**. Those journeying on foot used a **walking stick** to cross uneven terrain and as a defense against robbers and wild animals. A **sack** or knapsack held **food** and other items. **Money** enabled one to buy provisions. A **tunic** was an

inner garment; taking a **second tunic** gave one a change of clothing. All of these things the Twelve are to leave behind; they are to take **nothing** with them. This will force them to put their trust in God rather than in their own resources, and to depend on the hospitality of others for their food and lodging. They have been given great power and authority, but must exercise it in a state of dependence and vulnerability so that they do not mistake God's power for their own. (Paul will write, "We hold this treasure in earthen vessels, that the surpassing power may be of God and not from us"—2 Cor 4:7). By traveling with nothing, they will be imitating the example of Jesus, who has nowhere to lay his head (9:58) and is dependent on others for his needs (8:1–3).

Clothing: See page 175

For reflection: How have I experienced God's power working through my weaknesses?

4 The Twelve will receive hospitality, for the customs of the time dictated that travelers, even strangers, should be welcomed into homes. **Whatever house you enter** that offers hospitality, **stay there and leave from there.** By instructing the Twelve to **stay,** or remain, in the same house, Jesus prohibits them from upgrading their accommodations should they receive better offers. They are to be content with sufficiency and not lust after luxury. **Leave from there,** literally, go out from there, can be interpreted in two ways. It may mean that the Twelve are to use the house that provides them with hospitality as their base and go out from there to proclaim the kingdom of God and to heal. Or it may simply mean that they are to stay in the same house until they leave town.

Hospitality: See page 314

5 **And as for those who do not welcome you:** the rest of the verse indicates that **those** refers to the people of a town as a whole (see also 10:10). **Welcome** has the connotation of receive the Twelve and accept their message (the word is translated "receive" in 9:48). In their missionary travels, the Twelve will encounter rejection, just as Jesus was rejected by the people of Nazareth (4:28–30). They are not to waste their time in such a town but are to go on to the next. **When you leave that town, shake the dust** of the town **from your feet.** Shaking the dust off one's

feet was a symbolic act expressing disassociation (see Acts 13:51), similar to shaking the dust from one's garments (Acts 18:6). It conveyed, "We want nothing to do with you; we don't even want your dust on us." The Twelve are to do this as a **testimony against them**: shaking the dust from their feet will serve as the Twelve's bearing witness that the people of the town have rejected the message of the kingdom of God and have thereby "rejected the plan of God for themselves" (7:30).

6 **Then they set out and went from village to village proclaiming the good news,** just as Jesus had "journeyed from one town and village to another, preaching and proclaiming the good news of the kingdom of God" (8:1). As they went about, they were **curing diseases everywhere,** as Jesus has done and has now empowered them to do. Their **curing diseases** demonstrates that the kingdom of God is indeed arriving, freeing men and women from the grip of evil (see 11:20). The Twelve's going **everywhere** likely means everywhere in Galilee, but foreshadows the Gospel being proclaimed "to the ends of the earth" (Acts 1:8).

Gospel, good news: See page 59

For reflection: How do I demonstrate by my deeds the saving power of the gospel message?

Who Is Jesus?
7 **Herod the tetrarch heard about all that was happening, and he was greatly perplexed because some were saying, "John has been raised from the dead"; 8 others were saying, "Elijah has appeared"; still others, "One of the ancient prophets has arisen." 9 But Herod said, "John I beheaded. Who then is this about whom I hear such things?" And he kept trying to see him.**

Gospel parallels: Matt 14:1–2; Mark 6:14–16
OT: 2 Kings 2:11; Sirach 48:9–10; Mal 3:23–24
NT: Mark 6:17–29; Luke 3:1, 19–20; 13:31–33; 23:6–12

7 **Herod the tetrarch heard about all that was happening.** Virtually all of Jesus' ministry has been carried out in Galilee (4:14), which is ruled by **Herod** Antipas (3:1), who was made **tetrarch** by Rome. The title **tetrarch**

literally means ruler of a fourth of a kingdom, but was used more loosely for someone who ruled only a small domain. Herod Antipas **heard about all that was happening**. Reports have circulated about Jesus' proclaiming the kingdom of God, curing the afflicted, and raising the dead (4:14; 5:15; 6:17–18; 7:17), and as a shrewd ruler Herod kept himself informed about what was happening in his realm. He may have asked his steward Chuza about Jesus, since Chuza's wife, Joanna, was a follower of Jesus (8:1–3). He may also have heard that twelve of Jesus' disciples were going around proclaiming the kingdom of God and healing the sick (9:6). Herod is not interested in the kingdom of God; his concern is preserving the kingdom of Herod. Who is this Jesus, and how much of a threat is he? **He was greatly perplexed because** of what people were saying about Jesus. **Some were saying, "John has been raised from the dead."** Herod Antipas had imprisoned **John** the Baptist (3:19–20) and last we heard of him, he was still in prison (7:18–19). Now, however, he is dead, beheaded on Herod's orders (verse 9). Some think that Jesus is John **raised from the dead**. This is an odd speculation, for Jesus began his public ministry while John was still alive (see 7:18): how could he be John come back to life?

Herod Antipas: See page 99

8 **Others were saying, "Elijah has appeared."** This made more sense. Elijah had been taken up alive into heaven (2 Kings 2:11); Malachi prophesied that God would send him back to earth before the "day of the LORD" (Mal 3:23–24; see also Sirach 48:9–10). Could Jesus be Elijah? **Still others** said, **one of the ancient prophets has arisen**—one of the great prophets of the past. Jesus was popularly viewed as a prophet; after he raised a dead man to life people exclaimed, "A great prophet has arisen in our midst" (7:16). But was he John the Baptist (a prophet—7:26) or the prophet Elijah or one of the **ancient prophets** come back to life? People could only speculate. Clearly, Jesus is someone extraordinary, and Herod is not the only person who is perplexed (verse 7) about who Jesus is.

9 **But Herod said, "John I beheaded."** Herod knows that John is dead and rejects the idea that John has come back to life: Jesus is not John. But **who then is this about whom I hear such things?** Anyone who can do **such things** as Jesus does is clearly no ordinary man. **And he kept trying to see him**: Herod wants to find out for himself who Jesus

is. It will emerge that he is curious about Jesus' reported powers and wants Jesus to demonstrate them for him (23:8). He will also come to view Jesus as a threat to his rule and want to do away with him (13:31), as he did away with John.

The question Herod asks—and many others ask as well—is the key question: Who *is* Jesus? Who is it that forgives sins (5:21; 7:49), commands the winds (8:24), and raises the dead (7:14–15; 8:54–55)? Luke's Gospel repeatedly poses the question for its readers, for it is the all-important question.

For reflection: Who is Jesus for me?

The Feeding of More Than Five Thousand

¹⁰ **When the apostles returned, they explained to him what they had done. He took them and withdrew in private to a town called Bethsaida.** ¹¹ **The crowds, meanwhile, learned of this and followed him. He received them and spoke to them about the kingdom of God, and he healed those who needed to be cured.** ¹² **As the day was drawing to a close, the Twelve approached him and said, "Dismiss the crowd so that they can go to the surrounding villages and farms and find lodging and provisions; for we are in a deserted place here."** ¹³ **He said to them, "Give them some food yourselves." They replied, "Five loaves and two fish are all we have, unless we ourselves go and buy food for all these people."** ¹⁴ **Now the men there numbered about five thousand. Then he said to his disciples, "Have them sit down in groups of [about] fifty."** ¹⁵ **They did so and made them all sit down.** ¹⁶ **Then taking the five loaves and the two fish, and looking up to heaven, he said the blessing over them, broke them, and gave them to the disciples to set before the crowd.** ¹⁷ **They all ate and were satisfied. And when the leftover fragments were picked up, they filled twelve wicker baskets.**

Gospel parallels: Matt 14:13–21; Mark 6:30–44; John 6:1–13
NT: Luke 9:1–6; 22:19; 24:29–31, 35

10 **When the apostles returned** to Jesus after traveling from village to village (9:6), **they explained to him what they had done** to proclaim the

kingdom of God and to heal the sick through the power and authority he had given them (9:1–2, 6). **He took them and withdrew in private to a town called Bethsaida.** Jesus attracted large crowds in Galilee (8:4, 40), crowds that "almost crushed him" by their "pushing and pressing in upon" him (8:42, 45). Jesus wants to have some time **in private** to pray and to instruct his disciples (9:18–27), so he **withdrew** from the crowds and sought privacy with his disciples in the region of **Bethsaida**, a town just outside Galilee.

Apostle: See page 164

11 Jesus' desire for privacy is frustrated: **the crowds, meanwhile, learned of this and followed him**, gathering around him again. Rather than reacting irritably, as we might in a similar situation, **he received them**: another translation would be, "he welcomed them." The crowds are intruding on Jesus' privacy, but he does not turn them away. Instead he is faithful to his mission from God and addresses their needs: he **spoke to them about the kingdom of God, and he healed those who needed to be cured**. Jesus is sent to proclaim the good news of **the kingdom of God** (4:43); this has been his message throughout his ministry, accompanied by healing **those who needed to be cured** (6:17–19; 7:22; 8:1). He sent out the Twelve with the same mission (9:2), and they have just returned from "proclaiming the good news and curing diseases everywhere" (9:6). Jesus continues to do God's work, whether convenient

BACKGROUND: BETHSAIDA Remains of what archaeologists believe was Bethsaida were found four miles northeast of Capernaum, lying in the territory ruled by Philip (a son of Herod the Great) during Jesus' public ministry. Bethsaida was built on a hilltop near where the Jordan River flows into the northern end of the Sea of Galilee, allowing boats to be moored below the village. Archaeologists estimate that the population of Bethsaida at the time of Jesus was several hundred people. The village may have had a mixed pagan and Jewish population, with Greek commonly spoken. Some first-century houses have been discovered, several with evidence that their occupants were wealthy. Fishhooks and other fishing gear were found; the name "Bethsaida" may mean "house of the fisher." John's Gospel tells us that one of Jesus' disciples, named Philip, "was from Bethsaida, the town of Andrew and Peter" (John 1:44). The other Gospels portray Peter and Andrew living in Capernaum during Jesus' public ministry; perhaps they moved from Bethsaida to Capernaum. Bethsaida was apparently destroyed by an earthquake in A.D. 115; it was never rebuilt.

or inconvenient; his example is a lesson for disciples, who share in his mission.

Kingdom of God: See page 381

For reflection: What can I learn from Jesus' response to the crowds who intrude on his privacy?

12 Jesus spoke to the crowds about the kingdom of God and healed until **the day was drawing to a close** and it was time for the evening meal. **The Twelve approached him and said, "Dismiss the crowd so that they can go to the surrounding villages and farms and find lodging and provisions; for we are in a deserted place here."** That the Twelve **approached** Jesus with a recommendation indicates that he is approachable and does not discourage suggestions. They **are in a deserted place**: they are somewhere outside Bethsaida (verse 10), which had no open space large enough to accommodate the thousands (verse 14) who have come to Jesus. The suggestion the **Twelve** make is sensible. Some in the crowd are likely within walking distance of home; Capernaum and Chorazin are about four miles away. Those who had come from distances could **find lodging and provisions**—hospitality—in nearby **villages and farms.** Hence the Twelve tell Jesus to **dismiss the crowd** so that they can get a meal and lodging for the night. The Twelve show sensitivity to the needs of the crowd and offer a practical solution for meeting those needs.

Hospitality: See page 314

13 **He said to them, "Give them some food yourselves,"** literally, "you give to them," with "you" emphatic. Jesus acknowledges that the crowd needs to eat, but pointedly tells the Twelve to provide for their needs. **They replied, "Five loaves and two fish are all we have, unless we ourselves go and buy food for all these people."** Jesus did not let the Twelve take food with them when he sent them on their mission (9:3), but now that they are back with him they are carrying a few provisions—**five loaves and two fish.** Bread was the staple food for ordinary people; dried or salted fish were eaten with bread as a condiment. **Five loaves and two fish** might provide a sparse evening meal for the Twelve, but they point out to Jesus that they cannot feed the crowd **unless we our-**

selves go and buy food for all these people. Some women, at least one of them wealthy, provided for the needs of Jesus and the Twelve (8:1–3); there might have been funds to purchase simple fare for the crowd, if that is what Jesus wants.

For reflection: How has Jesus said to me, "You give to them," asking me to meet the needs of others?

14 Luke notes that the crowd that came to Jesus is very large: **now the men there numbered about five thousand**, with women presumably present as well. The Twelve raised the possibility of buying food for the crowd, but Jesus does not address it. Instead **he said to his disciples, "Have them sit down in groups of [about] fifty."** Jesus wants the crowd to **sit down**, literally, to recline, as at a banquet. They are to do so in **groups**: the Greek word Luke uses has the connotation of groups of people eating together. **Fifty** diners would be a large banquet. Jesus tells the Twelve to divide the crowd into dining groups, as if the countryside is about to be covered with banquets.

Banquets: See page 386

BACKGROUND: DIET Bread was the basic food of ordinary people in Palestine at the time of Jesus and provided a substantial part of their daily calorie intake. Most families baked their own bread daily in an outdoor oven and ate bread at every meal. Bread was usually made from wheat; barley bread was cheaper but less desirable. Bread made up so much of the diet that the word "bread" could be used to refer to food in general. Grain was also eaten parched ("roasted"—Ruth 2:14). Vegetables such as beans, lentils, cucumbers, and onions rounded out meals, along with fruits such as grapes, figs, dates, and pomegranates. Grapes could be processed into wine or raisins. Olives were crushed for oil, which was used in cooking as well as in oil lamps. Goats and sheep provided milk, yogurt, and cheese. Fish were usually dried or salted to preserve them and were eaten more often as a condiment for bread than as a main course. Herbs, spices, and salt added taste to even simple meals. Ordinary people ate meat only on special occasions, such as feasts. Meals were eaten with the fingers, with pieces of bread used as edible spoons to scoop up porridges and soak up sauces (Ruth 2:14; John 13:26), as is still the custom in some Middle Eastern cultures today. Members of the upper class ate much better than ordinary people: imported wines graced their tables, along with ample meat. *Related topic: Banquets (page 386).*

---

15 Jesus' instructions may have puzzled the Twelve, but **they did** as he asked **and made them all sit down** in groups of fifty.

16 **Then taking the five loaves and the two fish**: Jesus takes what the Twelve are able to put at his disposal, however little it seems, compared with the size of the crowd. **And looking up to heaven**—a posture of prayer (see 18:13)—**he said the blessing over them.** Jesus acts as would the host at any Jewish meal, saying a **blessing** over the food (see 24:30; Acts 27:35). The traditional Jewish blessing for bread praises God for supplying it: "Blessed are you, O Lord our God, King of the universe, who bring forth bread from the earth." Then Jesus **broke them,** dividing up the loaves and fishes, **and gave them to the disciples to set before the crowd**. Jesus acts as if putting five loaves and two fish in the hands of his **disciples** will enable them to feed the **crowd**.

17 The disciples distribute to the crowd what Jesus gave them, and **they all ate**. In the Greek of Luke's Gospel, **all** is emphatic: **all** in the crowd **ate and were satisfied**—ate their fill. Luke does not describe the mechanics of how five loaves and two fish became sufficient to satisfy a crowd of more than five thousand people. Nor does he recount there being amazement over what Jesus has done, as there was on other occasions (4:36; 5:9, 26; 7:16; 8:25, 37, 56). Luke instead concludes by noting that **when the leftover fragments were picked up, they filled twelve wicker baskets**, as if this is of greater significance than how Jesus fed so many with so little or how people reacted to it. That there were **twelve** baskets of leftovers suggests that the incident has a lesson for the Twelve. They should realize that Jesus empowers them to do what he asks them to do, even if it seems beyond their abilities—like feeding more than five thousand people with five loaves and two fish. The leftovers are proof that his power is more than ample for them.

For reflection: When has Jesus empowered me to do something for him that was beyond my ability?

Luke recounts Jesus' actions—taking bread, saying a blessing, breaking the bread, and giving it to his disciples—in a way that foreshadows what he will do on the night before he dies: "Then he took the bread, said the blessing, broke it, and gave it to them, saying, 'This is my body, which will be given for you; do this in memory of me' " (22:19). The feeding of a large crowd near Bethsaida foreshadows countless women and men, Gentile and Jewish, gathering to break the bread of the Eucharist in memory of him (Acts 2:42, 46; 20:7, 11). After his resurrection, two of his disciples will come to recognize him "in the breaking of the bread" (24:30–31, 35). Luke narrates Jesus' feeding of the crowd just after Herod wonders who Jesus is (9:7–9) and just before Jesus asks his disciples who they say he is (9:18–20). Luke wants his readers to recognize who Jesus is, gaining insight into him from his feeding of the crowd as a foreshadowing of his giving his body and blood in the Eucharist.

For reflection: What does Jesus' feeding of the crowd tell me about him?

What God's Messiah Must Undergo

¹⁸ Once when Jesus was praying in solitude, and the disciples were with him, he asked them, "Who do the crowds say that I am?" ¹⁹ They said in reply, "John the Baptist; others, Elijah; still others, 'One of the ancient prophets has arisen.' " ²⁰ Then he said to them, "But who do you say that I am?" Peter said in reply, "The Messiah of God." ²¹ He rebuked them and directed them not to tell this to anyone.

²² He said, "The Son of Man must suffer greatly and be rejected by the elders, the chief priests, and the scribes, and be killed and on the third day be raised."

Gospel parallels: Matt 16:13–23; Mark 8:27–33
NT: Luke 1:32–33; 2:11, 26; 4:41; 9:7–9

18 **Once when Jesus was praying**: the beginning of this verse could also be translated, "And while Jesus was praying." There is not necessarily much of a lapse of time between the crowd being fed (9:10–17) and Jesus' praying. He is **praying in solitude**, that is, away from the crowds, **and the disciples** are **with him**. Jesus prays in the presence of his disciples, as he does on other occasions (9:28; 11:1; 22:39–41). Jesus is a man of prayer (5:16), particularly at critical points in his life (3:21–22; 6:12–13). **Jesus was praying** and **he asked** his disciples, **"Who do the crowds**

255

say that I am?" His question might indicate that he was praying about who he is and about God's will for him. The Twelve have gone "from village to village" (9:6) and would have heard opinions about Jesus, since he was widely discussed (4:14, 37; 5:15; 7:17). Jesus asks what they have heard about him: **who do the crowds say that I am?**

Disciple: See page 149

19 **They said in reply, "John the Baptist; others, Elijah; still others, 'One of the ancient prophets has arisen.' "** The disciples heard the speculations that also reached the ears of Herod Antipas (9:7–8). Jesus is viewed as a prophet, someone who speaks for God. His deeds indicate that he is an extraordinary person, and so people try to match him up with an extraordinary person of the past. Some, rather inexplicably, think Jesus is **John the Baptist,** raised from the dead. **Others** identify Jesus with **Elijah,** who was expected to return to earth (Mal 3:23–24; Sirach 48:9–10). Still others think that **one of the ancient prophets has arisen.** We can note that the disciples do not report any speculations that Jesus is the Messiah.

20 **Then he said to them, "But who do you say that I am?"** By prefacing his question with **but,** Jesus indicates that the popular views of him are inadequate and that he is hoping his disciples have greater insight into him. In Jesus' question, **you** is emphatic and plural; he asks his disciples who *they* think he is. They have been with him for some time, hearing his words and observing his deeds. After he calmed a storm at sea "they were filled with awe and amazed and said to one another, 'Who then is this, who commands even the winds and the sea, and they obey him?' " (8:25). Do they now have an answer? Jesus asks them, **who do you say that I am?**

> *For reflection: Had I been among Jesus' first disciples, how would I have answered his question, based on what I had seen him do and heard him say?*

Peter said in reply, "The Messiah of God." Peter, the first to be called by Jesus (5:10), answers on behalf of the disciples. **The Messiah of**

God means the Messiah sent by God, God's anointed one. At the time of Jesus, there were differing expectations of who the **Messiah** would be and what he would do. The most commonly held view expected the Messiah to be a descendant of David who would "restore the kingdom to Israel" (Acts 1:6), winning independence from Rome and ushering in a golden age for God's people. Jesus' disciples realize that Jesus is more than the prophet that others perceive him to be. Jesus has proclaimed

BACKGROUND: MESSIAH, CHRIST There is a temptation to define the title "Messiah," or "Christ," in terms of who Jesus is, and to presume that this is the meaning that the word *messiah* had for Jews at the time of Jesus. The situation was more complex, however. The Hebrew word *messiah* is a noun meaning "anointed one," that is, a person anointed, or smeared, with oil—usually olive oil. Israelite kings were ceremonially anointed, as were high priests. Thus a king could be referred to as God's "anointed" (Psalm 2:2). Based partly on a prophecy of the prophet Nathan, an expectation developed that an anointed descendant of David would play a decisive role in God's plans for his people; Nathan had prophesied to David that his throne would "stand firm forever" (2 Sam 7:16). David's dynasty came to an end with the Babylonian conquest of 586 B.C., and Jews were under foreign rule for the next four centuries. In the two centuries before Jesus, there was a resurgence of hope for rule by a descendant of David—a messiah. Alongside various expectations for a kingly messiah, nonbiblical Jewish writings from this period spoke of other messianic figures; there was no single clearly defined picture of a messiah. One Jewish group, the Essenes, expected God to send two messiahs: a kingly messiah descended from David and a priestly messiah descended from Aaron. Most messianic hopes had a political dimension: God would bring an end to Roman domination. Some expected God to bring the present age to an end and to usher in a new age. There was no expectation that a messiah would suffer: the "servant" of Isaiah 52:13—53:12 was not identified with the Messiah before the time of Jesus. Jesus was ambivalent about being called the Messiah. On the one hand, he could accept it, because he *was* establishing the reign of God as God's agent. On the other hand, popular understandings of what a messiah would do usually included the overthrow of Roman rule, and that was not Jesus' mission. Jesus clarified what it meant for him to be called the Messiah through his teachings, death, and resurrection. The New Testament, written in Greek, uses the Greek word for "anointed," christos, which gives us the word "Christ." The early Church embraced the word "Christ" as its most common title for Jesus, so much so that it evolved from being a title (Jesus the Christ) to being virtually a second name (Jesus Christ). *Related topics: The age to come (page 487), Essenes (page 395), Jewish expectations at the time of Jesus (page 69), Kingdom of God (page 381), Nonbiblical writings (page 342), Psalms of Solomon (page 259).*

"the good news of the kingdom of God" (4:43): God is establishing his reign. The disciples perceive Jesus to be God's agent for establishing his reign, overcoming the evils of disease, demon-possession, and death. For the disciples, the title that best matches up with Jesus' role as God's agent inaugurating his kingdom is **Messiah:** Jesus is **the Messiah of God.**

That Jesus is the Messiah is no surprise for readers of Luke's Gospel. Gabriel told Mary that God would give Jesus the throne of David, and "of his kingdom there will be no end" (1:32–33). At Jesus' birth, an angel told shepherds that "today in the city of David a savior has been born for you who is Messiah and Lord" (2:11). It was revealed to Simeon that he would not die "before he had seen the Messiah of the Lord" (2:26), and that is what Simeon recognized Jesus to be (2:29–32). Jesus did not allow demons to speak, "because they knew he was the Messiah" (4:41). Jesus is the Messiah—but how will he carry out his role?

21 Jesus' response to Peter's words probably startled the disciples: **he rebuked them and directed them not to tell this to anyone.** Jesus does not say to the disciples, "You are wrong. I am not the Messiah." He does use strong language to command them not to tell anyone that he is the Messiah, and he goes on to say what is behind his command.

22 Although the New American Bible renders verse 22 as a new sentence beginning a new paragraph, in the Greek of Luke's Gospel verses 21 and 22 are one sentence. **He said** is better translated as "saying"; Jesus rebuked them and directed them not to tell this to anyone, saying **the Son of Man must suffer greatly and be rejected by the elders, the chief priests, and the scribes, and be killed and on the third day be raised**. Jesus speaks of himself as **the Son of Man**. Because of what will happen to him, the disciples are not to tell anyone that he is the Messiah. Jesus **must** undergo four things; **must** refers to divine necessity (see 4:43). If Jesus is to remain faithful to God's purpose and will, then he must **suffer greatly**; he does not explain the nature of this suffering. Jesus must **be rejected by the elders, the chief priests, and the scribes**, the

three types of leaders who make up the Sanhedrin (22:66), the Jewish governing body in Jerusalem. Jesus must **be killed**. He does not say how or why he will die; he says only that he **must** be killed, conveying that this is part of God's plan for him. Finally, Jesus must **on the third day be raised**—implied is, raised by God. Jesus must suffer and be rejected and killed, but God will raise him from the dead. Jesus alluded to his death when he spoke of himself as a bridegroom who will be taken away (5:35), but this is the first time in Luke's Gospel that he speaks directly of his suffering and dying and being raised—and he speaks of them as the reason why his disciples are not to tell anyone that he is the Messiah. The Messiah was popularly expected to be a warrior king empowered by God to defeat the enemies of God's people. A Jewish hymn written less than a century earlier hailed "the Lord Messiah" who would "cleanse Jerusalem from Gentiles"—from its Roman rulers (*Psalms of Solomon*, 17—not in the Bible). Jesus will establish God's reign, but by suffering, dying, and being raised, not by force of arms. For the disciples to publicly proclaim Jesus to be the Messiah would be misleading, because popular

---

BACKGROUND: PSALMS OF SOLOMON Eighteen hymns called the *Psalms of Solomon* were written around 50 B.C., probably in Jerusalem. While not part of Scripture, they shed light on the messianic expectations of some Jews around the time of Jesus. One psalm speaks of a messiah who will deliver Jews from Roman rule and lead them into holiness: "See, Lord, and raise up for them their king, the son of David, to rule over your servant Israel in the time you have chosen, O God. Gird him with strength to shatter unrighteous rulers, to cleanse Jerusalem from gentiles who trample and destroy it . . . to destroy their sinful pride like a clay pot, to smash their plan with an iron rod . . . He will have gentile nations serving under his yoke . . . and he will cleanse Jerusalem and make it holy as it was in the beginning. . . . For all shall be holy, and their king shall be the Lord Messiah. He will not trust in horse and rider and bow; he will not multiply gold and silver for war. . . . He himself will be free from sin so as to rule over a great people. He will put officials to shame and drive out sinners by the strength of a word. And he will not weaken during his days, because of his God, for God has made him powerful with a holy spirit. . . . This is the majesty of the king of Israel, whom God knew, to raise him over the house of Israel" (Psalms of Solomon 17:21–24, 30, 32–33, 36–37, 42). The "Lord Messiah" of this psalm, while sinless, is a human being, and his rule takes place on this earth. *Related topics: Jewish expectations at the time of Jesus (page 69), Messiah, Christ (page 257), Nonbiblical writings (page 342), Son of David (page 493).*

---

understandings of the Messiah do not match up with who Jesus is and what he must endure.

Son of Man: See page 147

Elders: See page 189

High priest, chief priests: See page 605

Scribes: See page 146

Sanhedrin: See page 611

Jesus has met with rejection (4:28–29; 6:11), but his telling his disciples that he must suffer and die has to be a shock for them. Jesus has demonstrated amazing powers—expelling demons, calming storms, raising the dead. How could a man with such powers suffer defeat? How could his suffering and dying be God's will for him? The disciples could well rephrase their earlier question (see 8:25): Who then is this, who must suffer and be rejected, be killed and be raised?

For reflection: In light of his suffering, dying, and being raised, who do I say that Jesus is?

Finding Life by Following Jesus

²³ Then he said to all, "If anyone wishes to come after me, he must deny himself and take up his cross daily and follow me. ²⁴ For whoever wishes to save his life will lose it, but whoever loses his life for my sake will save it. ²⁵ What profit is there for one to gain the whole world yet lose or forfeit himself? ²⁶ Whoever is ashamed of me and of my words, the Son of Man will be ashamed of when he comes in his glory and in the glory of the Father and of the holy angels. ²⁷ Truly I say to you, there are some standing here who will not taste death until they see the kingdom of God."

Gospel parallels: Matt 16:24–28; Mark 8:34—9:1

NT: Luke 9:22; 12:8–9; 14:27; 17:33; John 12:25

23 **Then he said to all**: Jesus has been speaking with his disciples (9:18–22), but now he directs his words **to all**—to everyone who would become his disciple. He proclaims that **if anyone wishes to come after me**, following him as his disciple, then **he** or she **must deny himself** or

herself. To **deny** oneself is to renounce self-centeredness, relinquishing what one is for what one can become as a disciple of Jesus. Saying no to selfish desires frees one to become a new person whose life is centered on Jesus.

For reflection: What self-centeredness is Jesus asking me to deny?

Second, to be Jesus' disciple one must **take up his** or her **cross daily** (see also 14:27). Luke's readers would have heard that Jesus was crucified, and would have understood taking up a **cross** in light of his crucifixion: his disciples must be willing to accept suffering and death in imitation of him. But what meaning would taking up a cross have had for his first disciples? Even if they did not know how Jesus would die, they were familiar with how crucifixions were carried out. After being sentenced, a condemned person carried a crossbeam to the place of execution, where it was affixed to an upright beam already in place. Carrying a cross is often interpreted as bearing a burden or affliction for the sake of Jesus, but there is also another meaning. In the first century, to **take up** a **cross** meant one was on the way to crucifixion and hence in the final hours of one's life. To take up a cross **daily** can mean to live each day as if it is one's last, focusing on the most important thing to do in one's remaining hours: unite oneself with Jesus as his follower.

Crucifixion: See page 626

For reflection: How can I better live each day as if it were my last?

Jesus says, thirdly, that **if anyone wishes to come after me**, then she or he must **follow me**—actually do it, putting one's desire to be his disciple into action. In the Greek of Luke's Gospel, **follow** is in a tense that conveys continuing action. Jesus has spoken of those who hear the word of God and "bear fruit through perseverance" (8:15); being a disciple of Jesus requires perseverance, following him wherever he leads, remaining faithful to him. Disciples must pattern their lives on their teacher: "every disciple will be like his teacher" (6:40). Jesus "must suffer greatly and be rejected by the elders, the chief priests, and the scribes, and be killed and on the third day be raised" (9:22). Following Jesus means being willing to share in his rejection and suffering.

For reflection: What do my actions and habits reveal about my willingness to imitate Jesus?

24 Jesus goes on to provide reasons why following him is the best course, despite what is required. In the Greek of Luke's Gospel, each reason begins with **for**, connecting it with what preceded it. **For whoever wishes to save his life will lose it, but whoever loses his life for my sake will save it.** Jesus will make the same observation on another occasion (17:33). The word translated **life** could also be translated "self." Trying to cling to who we are or what we have is futile; only through relinquishing can we attain. Jesus has yet to speak in Luke's Gospel about God's final judgment (see 10:14; 11:31–32) or about eternal life (see 10:25–28; 16:9; 18:18–30), but his words about saving and losing life envision life in eternity as well as life on earth. **Whoever wishes to save his life** by not denying himself and taking up his cross **will lose it**—will have diminished life here and now, and will not fare well at the final judgment. **But whoever loses his life**, denying himself **for my sake will save it**—will enjoy fuller life now and eternal life in the age to come (see 18:29–30). **For my sake** means on account of him, in his service. Denying ourselves and following Jesus preserves our lives.

For reflection: What hope am I given by Jesus' words, "whoever loses his life for my sake will save it"?

25 In the Greek of Luke's Gospel, this verse and the next begin with a "for": *For* **what profit is there for one to gain the whole world yet lose or forfeit himself?** Jesus' question is framed in commercial terms of **profit** and **gain** and loss. In a business transaction, what would one demand in exchange for oneself? Even if one was offered **the whole world**, would one come out ahead if forfeiting one's life was part of the deal? No matter what one might **gain** or retain by not denying oneself in order to follow Jesus, it is a poor bargain. The devil offered Jesus power over "all the kingdoms of the world" to sway him from service of God (4:5–6); we are

offered far less to compromise our discipleship, but whatever the offer, there is no **profit** for us in accepting it.

26 *For* **whoever is ashamed of me and of my words, the Son of Man will be ashamed of when he comes in his glory and in the glory of the Father and of the holy angels.** This is the first time in Luke's Gospel that Jesus speaks of himself, the Son of Man, coming in glory; he will say more about it later (see 21:25–28). The general sense of Jesus' words here (and his similar words in 12:8–9) is sufficiently clear. He speaks of those who are **ashamed** of him and of his **words**, referring to those who refuse to publicly acknowledge their relationship with him and their acceptance of his message. One example will be Peter, who will deny that he knows Jesus (22:54–62). Jesus will be **ashamed** of those who are **ashamed** of him: he will not acknowledge them as his disciples. Jesus will refuse this acknowledgment when he **comes in his glory**, which is **the glory of the Father**, shared by **the holy angels**. The **glory** of God was manifest when an angel appeared to shepherds at the birth of Jesus (2:9); this glory will also be manifest when Jesus comes at some future time. (Three of Jesus' disciples will shortly be given a foretaste of Jesus in glory—9:28–32.) His coming will mean that the eternal destiny of men and women is in the balance; whether one's life is saved or lost will be determined by whether one acknowledges Jesus before others (12:8) or is **ashamed** of him and denies him before others (12:9).

Son of Man: See page 147

For reflection: When have I acknowledged Jesus in circumstances where it would have been easier to remain silent?

27 Jesus concludes on a note of reassurance and encouragement for his disciples. **Truly I say to you, there are some standing here who will not taste death until they see the kingdom of God.** The expression **taste death** is an idiom for experience death (see John 8:52; Heb 2:9). **Some** who are **standing here** with Jesus and listening to his words will not die **until they see**—experience—**the kingdom of God.** Jesus seems to presume that some may die beforehand; he does not seem to be referring to the reign of God as it is already being inaugurated during his public ministry (11:20; 17:21). Nor is it evident that Jesus' words mean

that the end of this age is coming soon. Rather, by speaking about **the kingdom of God** as it will be experienced during the lifetime of his listeners, Jesus seems to be referring to the growth and success of the Church after his resurrection (Paul will refer to the kingdom of God as a present reality: Rom 14:17; 1 Cor 4:20). Those who persevere in following Jesus will enjoy fellowship with other disciples and experience the reign of God in their midst.

Kingdom of God: See page 381

The Exodus of the Son into Glory

²⁸ **About eight days after he said this, he took Peter, John, and James and went up the mountain to pray. ²⁹ While he was praying his face changed in appearance and his clothing became dazzling white. ³⁰ And behold, two men were conversing with him, Moses and Elijah, ³¹ who appeared in glory and spoke of his exodus that he was going to accomplish in Jerusalem. ³² Peter and his companions had been overcome by sleep, but becoming fully awake, they saw his glory and the two men standing with him. ³³ As they were about to part from him, Peter said to Jesus, "Master, it is good that we are here; let us make three tents, one for you, one for Moses, and one for Elijah." But he did not know what he was saying. ³⁴ While he was still speaking, a cloud came and cast a shadow over them, and they became frightened when they entered the cloud. ³⁵ Then from the cloud came a voice that said, "This is my chosen Son; listen to him." ³⁶ After the voice had spoken, Jesus was found alone. They fell silent and did not at that time tell anyone what they had seen.**

Gospel parallels: Matt 17:1–9; Mark 9:2–10
OT: Isaiah 42:1
NT: Luke 3:21–22; 9:22–27, 51

28 **About eight days after he said this**—after Jesus foretold his suffering, being killed and being raised, and required his followers to deny themselves and lose their lives for his sake (9:22–27)—**he took Peter, John, and James and went up the mountain to pray.** Jesus allowed **Peter, John, and James** to be present when he raised the daughter of Jairus to life (8:51–55), and he has them accompany him up the **mountain**. Luke

does not name the mountain; a Christian tradition identifies it as Mount Tabor, a majestic hill rising about 1,500 feet above the Jezreel Valley, six miles east of Nazareth. Jesus goes up the mountain **to pray**: "he would withdraw to deserted places to pray" (5:16), and mountains provided solitude. He previously spent a night in prayer on a mountain before naming twelve of his disciples to be apostles (6:12–13); he will remain on this mountain all night (see 9:37). Eight days earlier Jesus apparently prayed about what lay ahead as God's will for him (9:18–22), and he ascends the mountain to pray about it again, as what happens there will indicate.

29 **While he was praying, his face changed in appearance and his clothing became dazzling white.** The word **dazzling** has the connotation of flashing like lightning. Scripture portrays God (Dan 7:9) and angels (24:4) wearing white or dazzling clothing; Jesus while **praying** is bathed with the divine. Luke does not describe how Jesus' **face changed in appearance**, but Luke will write that his disciples "saw his glory" (verse 32) when they looked at him. Jesus spoke of his coming in glory (9:26); in prayer he experiences a foretaste of that glory.

30 **And behold, two men were conversing with him, Moses and Elijah.** God gave his law through **Moses** at Mount Sinai; **Elijah** is the first great prophet in the Old Testament. Their presence with Jesus is thus often interpreted to represent the law and the prophets, or the totality of God's prior revelation. Their presence may carry additional significance. The covenant God made with the Israelites through Moses formed them into his people; **Moses** marks a beginning. **Elijah**, taken up into heaven (2 Kings 2:11), was expected to return before "the day of the LORD" (Mal 3:23–24), when God would purify his people (Mal 3:1–3); Elijah's coming will mark a culmination. **Moses** and **Elijah** can thus signify the broad sweep of God's plan, now entering a decisive phase in Jesus.

The day of the Lord: See page 91

31 Moses and Elijah **appeared in glory**, sharing some of the glory of God. They **spoke of his exodus that he was going to accomplish in Jerusalem**. The Greek word *exodos*, transliterated as **exodus**, means going out, or departure, and is used for the Israelites' departure from Egypt (Heb 11:22). It is also used as a euphemism for death (translated as

"passing away" at Wisd 3:2 and as "departure" at 2 Pet 1:15). Are Moses and Elijah simply talking about Jesus' departure from this life? More likely they are discussing his entire transit into glory, his being "taken up" (9:51) to God through suffering, dying, and being raised. This **exodus** Jesus **was going to accomplish**, literally, was going to fulfill. Jesus "must" suffer, die, and be raised (9:22) in order to fulfill God's plan (see 24:25–27) and enter into glory. His suffering and dying will take place **in Jerusalem**. Jesus will shortly set out for Jerusalem so that he may be "taken up" and God's plan fulfilled. Jesus went to the mountain to pray about what lay ahead, and while he is praying Moses and Elijah confirm that he is on the right course in fulfillment of God's will. Jesus experiences a foretaste of the glory that awaits him on the other side of death.

Jerusalem: See page 516

For reflection: What are the most important things God has asked me to accomplish? How has he confirmed that I am on the right course?

32 **Peter and his companions had been overcome by sleep.** This is understandable if Jesus is spending the night in prayer, as he has done previously (6:12). The three disciples dozed off **but becoming fully awake, they saw his glory and the two men standing with him**. The disciples slept through Jesus' exchange with Moses and Elijah and awoke as it concluded (verse 33). They **saw his glory** in his changed appearance and shining garments (verse 29), and they also saw and recognized **the two men standing with him**.

33 **As** Moses and Elijah **were about to part from him, Peter said to Jesus, "Master, it is good that we are here."** Peter respectfully addresses Jesus as **Master**, as he has done previously (5:5; 8:45), but the title hardly seems adequate for someone radiant in glory. Peter says **it is good that we are here**, literally, it is good for us to be here. Peter would like Jesus, Moses, and Elijah to remain in their glory, prolonging the disciples' experience of their glorious presence. Peter suggests to Jesus, **let us make three tents, one for you, one for Moses, and one for Elijah.** Does Peter think that figures robed in glory needed **tents** to shelter them from the elements and enable them to remain on the mountain? Luke comments, **but he did not know what he was saying**. Waking up from a sound

sleep and finding oneself in the presence of figures radiant in glory can be disorienting.

34 **While he was still speaking, a cloud came and cast a shadow over them.** The **cloud** both manifests and conceals God's presence, as on Mount Sinai (Exod 19:9, 16; 24:15–18), over the tent that was God's desert dwelling (Exod 40:34–38), and in the Temple built by Solomon (1 Kings 8:10–12). The cloud **cast a shadow over them**, that is, overshadowed and enveloped them. **They became frightened when they entered the cloud**: fear is a natural reaction in the presence of God and of manifestations of the divine (1:11–12, 65; 2:9; 7:16; 8:35, 37; see also Exod 19:16; 20:18–20).

35 **Then from the cloud came a voice that said, "This is my chosen Son; listen to him."** When Jesus was praying after his baptism, a voice from heaven told him, "You are my beloved Son; with you I am well pleased" (3:21–22). Now God speaks **from the cloud**, not to Jesus but to his disciples, telling them **this is my chosen Son**, literally, this is my Son, the chosen. God proclaims Jesus to be his **Son**: Jesus was conceived in Mary through the Holy Spirit and is the Son of God (1:35). Jesus is also God's **chosen** one: God has chosen him to carry out a mission (see 4:18–19, 43). The word **chosen** is an echo of a prophecy of Isaiah in which God speaks of "my servant . . . my chosen one" (Isaiah 42:1). Luke's Gospel has repeatedly raised the question of Jesus' identity (5:21; 7:20, 49; 8:25; 9:7–9, 18–20). Now God proclaims to Peter, John, and James that Jesus is his **Son**, his **chosen** one.

Son of God: See page 25

For reflection: What do I learn from Jesus' transfiguration? From God's words about Jesus?

After proclaiming **this is my chosen Son**, the voice from the cloud commands the disciples to **listen to him**. In Old Testament idiom, to **listen**, or hear, includes obeying what one hears (see, for example, Deut 6:4–9). Because Jesus is the Son of God, it is of utmost importance to **listen to him** and to heed all that he says. In the context of Luke's Gospel, **listen to him** refers specifically to what Jesus says about his coming suffering and death (9:22, 44) and the necessity for his followers to deny themselves and take up their crosses daily (9:23–26).

For reflection: How carefully do I listen to Jesus' words? What do I find the hardest to hear and obey?

36 **After the voice had spoken, Jesus was found alone.** The cloud of God's presence lifts, revealing that Moses and Elijah are gone. **Jesus is alone** with his disciples and no longer in glory. The disciples **fell silent**, apparently stunned by what they had witnessed. They **did not at that time tell anyone what they had seen.** The Greek words translated **at that time** are literally *in those days* and most likely refer to the time before Jesus' resurrection and ascension. Luke does not explain why Peter, John, and James waited until after Jesus' ascension to **tell anyone what they had seen,** leaving his readers to wonder whether they were so stunned by what they experienced that they could not talk about it.

ORIENTATION: *Jesus is about to embark on his exodus (9:31, 51), but will his disciples be able to carry on after his ascension? Luke recounts four incidents (9:37–50) that show they are woefully unprepared.*

The Disciples' Failure to Expel a Demon
37 On the next day, when they came down from the mountain, a large crowd met him. 38 There was a man in the crowd who cried out, "Teacher, I beg you, look at my son; he is my only child. 39 For a spirit seizes him and he suddenly screams and it convulses him until he foams at the mouth; it releases him only with difficulty, wearing him out. 40 I begged your disciples to cast it out but they could not." 41 Jesus said in reply, "O faithless and perverse generation, how long will I be with you and endure you? Bring your son here." 42 As he was coming forward, the demon threw him to the ground in a convulsion; but Jesus rebuked the unclean spirit, healed the boy, and returned him to his father. 43 And all were astonished by the majesty of God.
Gospel parallels: Matt 17:14–18; Mark 9:14–27
NT: Luke 9:1, 28–36

37 **On the next day, when they came down from the mountain:** Jesus, along with Peter, John, and James, remained on the mountain all night after Jesus was transfigured (9:28-36). Perhaps Jesus again spent an entire night in prayer (see 6:12). Now there is enough light for them to make their way **down from the mountain**. When Jesus does so, **a large crowd met him**. Crowds come to Jesus to hear his teaching and be healed (5:15; see also 4:42; 5:1; 6:17-19; 7:11; 8:4, 40; 9:11). This crowd may have followed him to the foot of the mountain on the previous day and waited for him.

38 **There was a man in the crowd who cried out, "Teacher, I beg you, look at my son."** Because he teaches God's ways, Jesus is commonly addressed as **teacher** (7:40; 10:25; 11:45; 18:18; 19:39; 20:21, 28, 39). The man begs Jesus, **look at my son.** The word translated **look** means more than glance; it has the connotation of looking intently with concern. The man tells Jesus, **he is my only child.** Not only does this father love his son, but the boy is the father's only hope for his family line and name to be continued.

39 The man explains why he is begging Jesus to be concerned about his son: **for a spirit seizes him and he suddenly screams and it convulses him until he foams at the mouth**. The **spirit**—unclean spirit, or demon—causes the boy to have seizures. Today the boy might be diagnosed as having a form of epilepsy; at the time of Jesus, some physical or mental afflictions were understood to be caused by evil spirits (see 13:11, 16). The boy's periodic seizures were severe; the spirit thought to be their cause **releases him only with difficulty, wearing him out**. Such an affliction would have prevented the boy from living a normal life and, as evidence of demonic possession, would have cut him off from others. Out of love and concern for his only son, the man begs Jesus to see his condition and release him from it.

Demons, unclean spirits: See page 125
Demons and sickness: See page 377

For reflection: On whose behalf do I implore Jesus, asking him to release them from evil and suffering?

40 The father tells Jesus, **I begged your disciples to cast it out**. Jesus gave the Twelve "power and authority over all demons and to cure diseases" (9:1), and they had gone about "curing diseases everywhere" (9:6). The father apparently knew that Jesus' disciples expelled demons and healed, and he asked them to do so for his son, even begging them, **but they could not**: they tried but failed. No explanation is given for the disciples' failure. The father turns to Jesus, begging him to do what his disciples could not.

Disciple: See page 149

41 **Jesus said in reply, "O faithless and perverse generation, how long will I be with you and endure you?"** Jesus' tone of voice seems one of exasperation. The words **faithless and perverse generation**, echo an Old Testament passage that refers to the Israelites' failures to live up to what God expected of them after their exodus from Egypt (Deut 32:5). Jesus' words do not seem to be directed at the crowd or at all those living at the time but at his disciples. The Twelve have been given "power and authority over all demons and to cure diseases" (9:1) but nonetheless failed to free the boy from the unclean spirit. Jesus calls them **faithless**: they had not put their trust in him and in his power working through them. Jesus' question **how long will I be with you and endure you?** echoes Old Testament passages that ask how long an unfortunate situation will continue (Num 14:11, 27; 1 Kings 18:21; Psalm 4:3; Prov 1:22–23; Jer 4:14; 13:27; 31:22). Asked the morning after Moses and Elijah spoke about his exodus or departure (9:31), Jesus' question is rhetorical. He knows he will not be **long** with his disciples, enduring their shortcomings. Jesus is exasperated because his disciples are like slow learners on the eve of an exam. It is vitally important for them to be prepared for what lies ahead, and they are not.

For reflection: Where am I slowest to learn and follow God's ways for me?

Jesus turns his attention to the father of the boy and tells him, **bring your son here**.

42 **As he was coming forward, the demon threw him to the ground in a convulsion.** It is not clear whether this was simply one of the boy's periodic seizures or whether the demon recognized the threat Jesus posed

to his influence over the boy and launched a preemptive attack against Jesus' power. **But Jesus rebuked the unclean spirit, healed the boy, and returned him to his father.** Luke recounts the boy's deliverance rather tersely, as if there could be no other outcome than Jesus vanquishing the unclean spirit and healing the boy. Jesus **returned him to his father,** just as he had returned a widow's only son to her after raising him from the dead (7:12, 15).

43 **And all were astonished by the majesty of God.** God demonstrates his greatness and majesty by his deeds (Exod 15:7; Deut 3:24; 32:3–4; Ezek 38:18–23). Those who witnessed Jesus freeing the boy from the demon were **astonished** at this display of God's power, manifested through Jesus as God's agent (for similar reactions, see 5:26; 7:16).

The Disciples' Failure to Understand Jesus' Words

⁴³ **While they were all amazed at his every deed, he said to his disciples,** ⁴⁴ **"Pay attention to what I am telling you. The Son of Man is to be handed over to men."** ⁴⁵ **But they did not understand this saying; its meaning was hidden from them so that they should not understand it, and they were afraid to ask him about this saying.**

Gospel parallels: Matt 17:22–23; Mark 9:31–32
NT: Luke 9:22, 35

43 The first half of verse 43 concluded the previous section of Luke's Gospel; the second half of the verse begins a new section, closely tied to what precedes. Those who witnessed Jesus' healing of the demon-possessed boy were astonished, and **while they were all amazed at his every deed, he said to his disciples**: Jesus speaks to his disciples in the context of the crowd's amazement. They are **amazed at his every deed,** astonished not only by his freeing the boy from a demon but by everything he is doing. People have previously been amazed by Jesus' teachings (4:22) and by his forgiving sins and healing (5:26); amazement is a natural reaction to Jesus' displays of authority and power. In reaction to such amazement, Jesus **said to his disciples,**

Disciple: See page 149

For reflection: Am I properly amazed by Jesus?

44 **Pay attention to what I am telling you**: literally, place these words in your ears—a vivid and emphatic way of telling his disciples to listen carefully to what he is going to say and let his words sink in. God spoke from a cloud to Peter, John, and James on the mountain, telling them, "This is my chosen Son; listen to him" (9:35). Now Jesus tells all his disciples to listen carefully.

For reflection: How carefully do I pay attention to Jesus' words?

Jesus tells his disciples, **the Son of Man is to be handed over to men.** Jesus refers to himself as **the Son of Man**. He **is to be handed over.** Another translation would be, "is about to be handed over": it will happen sooner rather than later. **Handed over** can imply, handed over by God, but it can also mean that he will handed over, betrayed, by a human or humans. He is to be handed over **to men**, literally, into the hands of men, meaning into their power. Jesus does not spell out what will happen to him when he is in the power of others, but he has told his disciples that he must "be rejected by the elders, the chief priests, and the scribes, and be killed and on the third day be raised" (9:22). Jesus may amaze the crowds (verse 43), but he knows that his "exodus" (9:31) is approaching, when he will be jeered rather than cheered and will be put to death. Jesus wants his disciples to realize this and not let his popularity with the crowds lull them into thinking that he will be preserved from suffering and death.

Son of Man: See page 147

45 **But they did not understand this saying**: the disciples cannot grasp what Jesus is telling them. **Its meaning was hidden from them so that they should not understand it.** Luke's words might imply that the **meaning** of Jesus' statement **was hidden from them** by God, but why would God want them to **not understand** something that Jesus told them to pay close attention to (verse 44)? Perhaps the significance of Jesus' words can really be grasped only after what he foretells happens (see 24:4–8, 25–27). In any case, **they were afraid to ask him about this saying**. They did not understand and were **afraid** to ask Jesus to explain his words. Were they ashamed to admit their incomprehension to Jesus? Did they catch the ominous tone of Jesus' words and not want to

face up to what he was telling them? Were they fearful of what the consequences might be for them of Jesus' being handed over (see 9:22–23)? Whatever their motive, they make no attempt to grow in understanding.

For reflection: When do I shy away from facing up to what Jesus teaches?

The Disciples' Failure to Understand Greatness

⁴⁶ An argument arose among the disciples about which of them was the greatest. ⁴⁷ Jesus realized the intention of their hearts and took a child and placed it by his side ⁴⁸ and said to them, "Whoever receives this child in my name receives me, and whoever receives me receives the one who sent me. For the one who is least among all of you is the one who is the greatest."

Gospel parallels: Matt 18:1–5; Mark 9:33–37
NT: Matt 25:31–40; Luke 9:44–45; 22:24–27; John 13:20

46 The Greek of Luke's Gospel would allow this verse to be translated with an "instead" as its first word, linking it with the previous verses. Jesus foretold being handed over; his disciples did not understand his statement but didn't ask him about it (9:44–45); *instead* **an argument arose among the disciples about which of them was the greatest**. Jesus directs their attention to his coming death, but they argue among themselves over their relative importance. Their minds should be on what awaits Jesus; instead they are concerned about themselves, each wanting the prestige of being recognized as **the greatest** among the disciples. Jesus' words about denying themselves (9:23) seem to have made no impression.

Disciple: See page 149

For reflection: When have my self-concerns distracted me from Jesus and the path of discipleship?

47 **Jesus realized the intention of their hearts**: Luke's account reads as if their argument was out of Jesus' earshot but he nevertheless **realized** what was on their **hearts** (see 5:22; 6:8; 7:39–40). In light of their self-concern, Jesus **took a child and placed it by his side**. Jesus responds

273

to his disciples with an act and not just a word. But what should taking a **child** and placing it by **his side** convey to the disciples? Children were the weakest members of society, with no claims to greatness. On another occasion the disciples will try to shield Jesus from contact with infants (18:15), apparently thinking that Jesus should not bother himself with insignificant children. Yet here is Jesus, taking a **child** and placing it **by his side**, the place of honor.

48 Jesus intends his esteem for the child to be an example and lesson for his disciples. He tells them, **whoever receives this child in my name receives me**. The expression **in my name** means on my behalf, for my sake, in imitation of me. Jesus tells his disciples that whoever receives **this child** receives **me**: Jesus identifies himself with this child, and by extension with all weak and unimportant people. What his disciples do for this child, they do for Jesus.

This is a startling reality. The nobodies of this world usually do not strike us as Jesus in disguise; they simply seem like unimportant or unfortunate people. Yet Jesus tells us that our response to them is our response to him (see also Matt 25:31–40).

For reflection: What are the implications for me of Jesus' words, "whoever receives this child in my name receives me"?

Jesus adds, **and whoever receives me receives the one who sent me**. The response made to a messenger is a response to the one the messenger represents. Jesus has been sent on a mission by God (see 4:18, 43); receiving Jesus means receiving God, who sent him. Jesus' words take on additional significance in the context of his speaking about receiving a child as equivalent to receiving him. The response we make—or do not make—to even the most seemingly insignificant person is ultimately our response to God.

Jesus' setting a child at his side and his words about receiving the child are in response to the disciples' arguing over which of them is greatest. Jesus now tells them who is greatest: **the one who is least among all of you is the one who is the greatest**. In context, being **least** means being willing to receive a child—becoming a nobody in order to accept and care for a nobody. Self-important people seek the company of important people; Jesus' disciples are to make themselves **least**, setting aside dignity and pride, so that they can receive and accept all who are least in this world. To do so is to attain true **greatness** in the eyes of God.

For reflection: How do I try to achieve greatness?

The Disciples' Narrowness

⁴⁹ **Then John said in reply, "Master, we saw someone casting out demons in your name and we tried to prevent him because he does not follow in our company."** ⁵⁰ **Jesus said to him, "Do not prevent him, for whoever is not against you is for you."**

Gospel parallels: Mark 9:38–40
NT: Luke 9:47–48

49 Jesus taught his disciples that they must accept those who are least important, like the child Jesus placed at his side (9:47–48). **Then John said in reply: "Master, we saw someone casting out demons in your name and we tried to prevent him."** John reports an instance in which the disciples did not accept someone. Along with his brother James, **John** was one of the first disciples called by Jesus (5:9–11) and one of the Twelve apostles (6:13–14). John acts here as a spokesman for the disciples. He calls Jesus **Master**, acknowledging his authority. **Someone** had been **casting out demons**: Jesus and his disciples are not the only Jews who drive out demons (see 11:19). A man had been casting out demons **in** the **name** of Jesus: he invoked Jesus' name in order to draw on Jesus' power. Later some disciples will report to Jesus, "Even demons are subject to us because of your name" (10:17; see also Acts 16:18). John tells Jesus that the reason why **we tried to prevent him** from casting out demons in your name is **because he does not follow in our company**: he is not one of the disciples who accompany Jesus as he travels. He may simply be a man who knows of Jesus' power over demons and who tries to draw upon it (see Acts 19:13). Because he is not one of Jesus' disciples, John and other disciples tried to prevent him from invoking Jesus' name.

Demons, unclean spirits: See page 125

275

50 **Jesus said to him, "Do not prevent him."** Jesus is not upset that someone who is not one of his disciples is invoking his name to cast out demons. Whoever the man might be, he is overcoming evil and human affliction; the fruit of his efforts is good. The Twelve have been given power over demons (9:1) but not a monopoly; they should not try to restrict Jesus' powers to themselves. Jesus tells them not to stop the man, **for whoever is not against you is for you**. The disciples are to accept and embrace **whoever** does not oppose them. Being **not against** them means that they are **for** them: neutrality is to be viewed positively. Jesus' disciples are to accept nobodies (9:47–48) and outsiders as well.

> *For reflection: How might I grow in tolerance, so that I become as tolerant toward others as Jesus would have me be?*

ORIENTATION: *Luke's Gospel reaches a turning point, with Jesus setting out for Jerusalem, where he will be put to death. Luke devotes about ten chapters to the journey to Jerusalem (9:51—19:44).*

Jesus Sets His Face toward Jerusalem
⁵¹ **When the days for his being taken up were fulfilled, he reso-lutely determined to journey to Jerusalem,**
  NT: Luke 9:22, 31

51 **When the days for his being taken up were fulfilled**: Luke's choice of the word **fulfilled** indicates that what is happening is in fulfillment of God's plans (see also 1:1, 20, 45; 4:21). The time has come for Jesus' "exodus that he was going to accomplish in Jerusalem" (9:31), his depar-ture from this life and his being **taken up** by God into heaven. Jesus must "be rejected by the elders, the chief priests, and the scribes, and be killed and on the third day be raised" (9:22); elders, chief priests, and scribes make up the Jewish governing body in Jerusalem (see 22:66). Knowing what lies ahead for him, **he resolutely determined to jour-ney to Jerusalem**. The words translated **he resolutely determined** are literally, "he set his face," an Old Testament idiom conveying resolve (Isaiah 50:7). Jesus is resolved to do his Father's will, even if it means

276

suffering and dying, and he sets out for Jerusalem so that God's plan may be fulfilled.

For reflection: How determined am I to do God's will?

The Disciples' Reaction to Inhospitality
⁵² and he sent messengers ahead of him. On the way they entered a Samaritan village to prepare for his reception there, ⁵³ but they would not welcome him because the destination of his journey was Jerusalem. ⁵⁴ When the disciples James and John saw this they asked, "Lord, do you want us to call down fire from heaven to consume them?" ⁵⁵ Jesus turned and rebuked them, ⁵⁶ and they journeyed to another village.

OT: 2 Kings 1:9–12
NT: Luke 6:27–29; 9:5, 51

52 When Jesus set out for Jerusalem from Galilee (9:51), **he sent messengers ahead of him. On the way they entered a Samaritan village to prepare for his reception there**—to make arrangements for him. The most direct route from Galilee to Jerusalem is through the heart

---

BACKGROUND: SAMARIA, SAMARITANS A region called Samaria lay south of Galilee, separating the predominantly Jewish areas of Galilee and Judea. In Old Testament times it was part of the northern kingdom of Israel after its split from the southern kingdom of Judah. The split between the kingdoms was religious as well as political: the northern kingdom established shrines as rivals to the Temple in Jerusalem. The northern kingdom was conquered by Assyria around 721 B.C.; some of its inhabitants were deported, and foreigners settled in their place (see 2 Kings 17). The Samaritans of New Testament times were considered by the Jews of Judea and Galilee to be the descendants of the foreigners and Israelites left by the Assyrians, mixed in race and religion and ritually unclean. Sirach, writing around 180 B.C. called Samaritans "degenerate folk" whom he loathed with his whole being (Sirach 50:25–26). Samaritans, on the other hand, thought of themselves as true Israelites who rigorously followed the law set down in the five books of Moses (Genesis through Deuteronomy). They erected a temple to God in the heart of Samaria on Mount Gerizim, the place they believed God wanted to be worshiped (see John 4:20). A Jewish ruler invaded and tore down the Samaritan temple in 128 B.C., increasing tensions between Samaritans and Jews.

of Samaria, a journey of at least three days on foot. Travelers relied on the hospitality of people along the way for lodging and food. A sizable number of disciples are traveling with Jesus (see 10:1), making it advisable to send **messengers ahead** as an advance party to arrange accommodations. There were tensions between Jews and Samaritans, but Jesus does not avoid Samaria on his way to Jerusalem. Nor does he assume the worst of Samaritans and presume they will be inhospitable. Rather, he gives a Samaritan village an opportunity to receive him.

Hospitality: See page 314

For reflection: What can I learn from Jesus' not assuming the worst of Samaritans?

53 But they would not welcome him because the destination of his journey was Jerusalem. The first-century Jewish historian Josephus recounts Samaritan hostility and even violence directed at Galilean pilgrims making their way to **Jerusalem** to celebrate feasts such as Passover at the Temple. Samaritans believed that God's choice of place for his temple was not Jerusalem but Mount Gerizim in Samaria. Deuteronomy 12:11 speaks of God, choosing a place for the Temple, but does not say what place he chooses; the Samaritans had a version of Deuteronomy that identified the place as Mount Gerizim. Samaritans built a temple on Mount Gerizim, but a Jewish ruler destroyed it, fanning Samaritan hostility toward Jews. This Samaritan village **would not welcome** and extend hospitality to Jesus **because the destination of his journey was Jerusalem**. Jews prevented Samaritans from worshiping at their temple on Mount Gerizim; why should Samaritans provide lodging and food for Jews on their way to their Temple in Jerusalem?

Jerusalem: See page 516

54 When the disciples James and John saw this they asked, "Lord, do you want us to call down fire from heaven to consume them?" Reacting to the Samaritans' inhospitality, **James and John** want to wipe out their village. They apparently think that they have the power **to call down fire from heaven**, as did Elijah (2 Kings 1:9–12). They do address Jesus as **Lord**, acknowledging his authority, and they do seek his will for them: **do you want us to . . . ?** Nevertheless, their reaction is completely misguided for disciples who heard Jesus teach, "love your enemies, do good to those who hate you, bless those who curse you, pray for those who mistreat you" (6:27–28)—especially for two disciples who also heard God tell them, "This is my chosen Son; listen to him" (9:28, 35). Furthermore, Jesus has instructed them how to respond to an inhospitable village: shake the dust from your feet as you leave (9:5). Hardly a license to turn a village into cinders!

Lord: See page 137

55 **Jesus turned and rebuked them.** Luke does not recount Jesus' words of correction, but Jesus is obviously displeased with James and John wanting to incinerate the village. It is one more example of the disciples' failure to understand the way of Jesus (see 9:45, 46, 49), which is now the way to Jerusalem, where he will suffer, die, and be taken up (9:51).

For reflection: How well do I understand the way of Jesus? How well do I follow it?

56 Luke concludes his account of the incident by noting that **they journeyed to another village**—perhaps another Samaritan village. Luke does not say whether Jesus and his disciples received hospitality there.

The Cost of Discipleship

⁵⁷ **As they were proceeding on their journey someone said to him, "I will follow you wherever you go." ⁵⁸ Jesus answered him, "Foxes have dens and birds of the sky have nests, but the Son of Man has nowhere to rest his head." ⁵⁹ And to another he said, "Follow me."**
But he replied, "[Lord,] let me go first and bury my father." ⁶⁰ But he answered him, "Let the dead bury their dead. But you, go and proclaim the kingdom of God." ⁶¹ And another said, "I will follow you, Lord, but first let me say farewell to my family at home." ⁶² [To him] Jesus said, "No one who sets a hand to the plow and looks to what was left behind is fit for the kingdom of God."

Gospel parallels: Matt 8:19–22
NT: Luke 5:27; 14:26; 18:29

57 **As they were proceeding on their journey**: Jesus is leading his disciples to Jerusalem (9:51), where he will suffer, be killed, and be raised (9:22; see also 9:31, 44). Along the way, **someone said to him, "I will follow you wherever you go."** The word **someone** could refer either to a man or a woman. This person volunteers to become Jesus' disciple: **I will follow you.** The offer is unconditional and open-ended: the person promises to follow Jesus **wherever you go**. Does the person realize that Jesus is on the way to his death, and that his followers must deny themselves and take up their crosses if they are to follow him (9:23)? Many might be attracted to giving themselves wholeheartedly to Jesus, but not realize the cost of doing so.

> *For reflection: When I gave my life to Jesus, how much did I foresee of what he would ask of me?*

58 **Jesus answered him, "Foxes have dens and birds of the sky have nests, but the Son of Man has nowhere to rest his head."** Jesus, traveling "from one town and village to another" (8:1), depended on the hospitality of others for lodging. He was recently turned away by a Samaritan village (9:52–53) and may have had **nowhere to rest his head** that night. Jesus warns the would-be disciple that following him means sharing the hardships he endures for the sake of his mission; those who travel with him must leave their homes behind (see 18:29). Jesus could have spoken about the suffering and death that lie ahead for him, but he only mentions homelessness: perhaps he wishes to acquaint the would-be follower with the cost of discipleship by stages.

Son of Man: See page 147

59 **And to another he said, "Follow me."** While the previous person volunteered to become Jesus' disciple (verse 57), Jesus takes the initiative with **another** person, saying **follow me**, just as he called Levi to be his disciple (5:27). This person is willing to accept Jesus' call; if he overheard Jesus' previous words, he is willing to share Jesus' homelessness. Yet there is something he must take care of first: **"[Lord,] let me go first and bury my father."** He addresses Jesus as **Lord**, acknowledging his authority (the New American Bible puts **Lord** in brackets because it is not found in all ancient manuscripts of Luke's Gospel). Burying the dead

was a religious duty (Tobit 1:18; 2:3–8), and particularly a son's obligation toward his parents (Tobit 4:3–4; 6:15; 14:12–13). It is unlikely that this man's **father** has already died: Jewish burials took place on the day of death (see 23:52–53; Acts 5:5–6, 10), and the man would not be walking with Jesus on the way to Jerusalem (verse 57) if his father was dead and awaiting burial. Rather, the sense of the man's words seems to be, "Allow me to first go home and remain with my father until he has died, and then I will be free to follow you." He is willing to be Jesus' disciple, but only after his family obligations have been satisfied.

Lord: See page 137

For reflection: Are there any obligations that are holding me back from wholeheartedly living as Jesus' disciple? What is Jesus asking of me concerning these obligations?

60 **But he answered him, "Let the dead bury their dead."** Jesus' response seems harsh, but it is a wakeup call conveying the urgency of making an immediate response to his invitation, "Follow me." God is establishing his kingdom through Jesus (see 11:20); those who are not becoming part of God's reign are, as it were, **dead**. (Jesus will tell a parable in which a son who rejects his father is spoken of as dead—15:24, 32.) Jesus is gathering a family around himself made up of those who are coming into God's reign by hearing the word of God and acting on it (8:21). Becoming part of Jesus' family may require leaving one's biological family behind (14:26). Family obligations, like burying one's parents, can be left to those who remain behind: **let the dead bury their dead**. Jesus' call, "Follow me," is a call to take part in what God is doing: **but you, go and proclaim the kingdom of God**. Jesus sent out the Twelve to "proclaim the kingdom of God" (9:2), and he will shortly send out other disciples to announce that "the kingdom of God is at hand" (10:1, 9). He calls this man to follow him immediately so that he can be part of this mission.

Kingdom of God: See page 381

61 **And another said, "I will follow you, Lord,"** volunteering to be Jesus' disciple. Like the previous man, he asks Jesus to allow him to address family obligations: **but first let me say farewell to my family at home.**

281

Asking to say goodbye to one's family before joining Jesus on his journey seems like a reasonable request. Nevertheless, the man is making a conditional offer of discipleship: **I will follow you . . . but**. If the man truly acknowledges Jesus as his **Lord**, then his response to Jesus must be unconditional. Even a seemingly innocent request to take leave of one's family can indicate divided loyalties or a hedged response to Jesus.

For reflection: How in my own way do I tell Jesus, "I will follow you, but . . ."?

62 **[To him] Jesus said, "No one who sets a hand to the plow and looks to what was left behind is fit for the kingdom of God."** The word translated "looks" has the connotation of continuing to look. Jesus uses an agricultural image to convey the necessity of making a wholehearted response to him and to what God is doing to establish his reign. Plowing a field demanded a farmer's full attention. With one hand the farmer steered a plow; the other hand held a goad to guide the animal pulling the plow, keeping it on course. If the farmer kept looking back, the furrow quickly went awry. Once a farmer **sets a hand to the plow** he cannot pay attention to **what** is **behind**. So too, once one sets out to follow Jesus, there can be no looking back on **what** one **has left behind**—in this case, one's family. Doing so means one is not **fit for the kingdom of God**: entering into God's reign demands full attention and absolute commitment, the kind of resolve Jesus exhibited when he "resolutely determined to journey to Jerusalem" (9:51), knowing what awaited him there.

For reflection: Am I resolutely determined to follow Jesus, not looking back on what I leave behind?

Luke recounts Jesus' words to three would-be disciples about the requirements of discipleship but does not report how they responded. Luke thereby invites us, his readers, to put ourselves in the place of these three and to take Jesus' words as his words to us. How willing are we to pay the price of discipleship?

CHAPTER 10

Jesus Involves More Disciples in His Mission
¹ After this the Lord appointed seventy[-two] others whom he sent ahead of him in pairs to every town and place he intended to visit. ² He said to them, "The harvest is abundant but the laborers are few; so ask the master of the harvest to send out laborers for his harvest. ³ Go on your way; behold, I am sending you like lambs among wolves. ⁴ Carry no money bag, no sack, no sandals; and greet no one along the way. ⁵ Into whatever house you enter, first say, 'Peace to this household.' ⁶ If a peaceful person lives there, your peace will rest on him; but if not, it will return to you. ⁷ Stay in the same house and eat and drink what is offered to you, for the laborer deserves his payment. Do not move about from one house to another. ⁸ Whatever town you enter and they welcome you, eat what is set before you, ⁹ cure the sick in it and say to them, 'The kingdom of God is at hand for you.' ¹⁰ Whatever town you enter and they do not receive you, go out into the streets and say, ¹¹ 'The dust of your town that clings to our feet, even that we shake off against you.' Yet know this: the kingdom of God is at hand. ¹² I tell you, it will be more tolerable for Sodom on that day than for that town.

Gospel parallels: Matt 9:37–38
OT: 2 Kings 4:29
NT: Matt 10:7–16; Mark 6:8–11; Luke 9:1–5, 51–52

1 **After this the Lord appointed seventy[-two] others whom he sent ahead of him.** Luke uses the title **Lord** to refer to Jesus (see 7:13). Just as Jesus appointed the Twelve to correspond to the twelve tribes of Israel (6:13; 22:30), so he appoints a larger group of disciples whose number is significant. But what is that number? About half the ancient manuscripts of Luke's Gospel read that Jesus appointed seventy, and half read seventy-two; hence the New American Bible prints the number as **seventy [-two].** Either number can have the same association. The Hebrew text of Genesis 10 lists seventy non-Israelite nations; the Greek version of this

chapter has seventy-two nations. Jesus' sending of seventy or seventy-two disciples foreshadows the gospel being proclaimed to all nations.

Lord: See page 137

As Jesus is traveling to Jerusalem (9:51, 57), he sends those he appointed **ahead of him in pairs**. Sending them **in pairs** allowed mutual support. He sent them **to every town and place he intended to visit** to make arrangements for him, as was the task of the messengers he sent to a Samaritan village (9:52). They are also to cure the sick and to proclaim the good news of the kingdom of God (verse 9), which is Jesus' mission (4:43; 6:18–19; 7:22; 8:1–2) and the mission he gave the Twelve (9:1–2). Jesus now involves a larger number of disciples in his mission. They are to prepare people to receive him and to enter into the reign of God.

For reflection: To whom has Jesus sent me, to prepare them to meet him?

2 **He said to them, "The harvest is abundant but the laborers are few."** Jesus uses ripened crops awaiting **harvest** as an image for God's plan reaching a critical stage. Crops were harvested quickly once they ripened, lest they spoil or be stolen. Extra farm workers were needed to bring in the harvest (Jesus' parable about workers hired at various times of the day likely has a harvest setting—Matt 20:1–16). The **harvest** of those who can be brought into the kingdom of God **is abundant, but the laborers** to bring them in **are few**. Jesus has been establishing God's reign by his preaching and by freeing men and women from evil (see 11:20), and he has involved first twelve and now seventy or seventy-two others in this work. More people could be brought into the kingdom of God if there were more **laborers** to preach and heal. Therefore Jesus tells his disciples to **ask the master of the harvest to send out laborers for his harvest**. The **master of the harvest** is God; those who serve the kingdom of God are to pray that God will **send** more women and men to serve with them. Disciples of Jesus are not to treat their mission as a personal prerogative but are to pray that many others are likewise called.

For reflection: How often do I pray for vocations to ministry?

3 Jesus tells those he has appointed: **go on your way**; he sends them as he previously sent the Twelve (9:1–2). He tells them, **behold, I am sending you like lambs among wolves**. Sheep are rather defenseless animals, easy prey for wolves. Jesus' disciples will meet opposition as they carry out the mission Jesus is giving them. They will not be strong enough to prevail on their own over opponents; they will be **like lambs** vulnerable to **wolves**.

4 How are the disciples to survive if they are so vulnerable? Jesus tells them, **carry no money bag, no sack** for provisions, **no sandals**—normal gear for travelers. Jesus gave similar instructions to the Twelve when he sent them on mission, so that they would rely on God and the hospitality of others rather than on their own resources (9:1–4). The disciples he is sending now are similarly to rely on God, trusting in his care for them as they go like lambs among wolves. Their strength lies in acknowledging their weakness and their dependence on God (see 2 Cor 12:9). They are to **greet no one along the way**. This does not mean that they are to be rude but that they are to forgo the elaborate and time-consuming greetings that were customary. When the prophet Elisha sent his servant Gehazi on an urgent mission, he told him, "Take my staff with you and be off; if you meet anyone, do not greet him, and if anyone greets you, do not answer" (2 Kings 4:29). The harvest is abundant and ready to be brought in (verse 2); there is no time to waste exchanging pleasantries. Jesus' disciples must be single-minded as they carry out the mission he has given them.

5 **Into whatever house you enter, first say, "Peace to this household."** Jesus' disciples are to seek hospitality in the villages they enter, but their **first** act is to be one of giving rather than receiving. Wishing someone **peace** is a customary greeting (24:36; Acts 15:33) but rich in significance. The Hebrew notion of peace is not simply an absence of conflict but a state of wholeness. Peace is a blessing from God (Num 6:24–26), the consequence of God's favor and mercy and salvation (see 1:78–79; 2:14, 29–32; 7:50; 8:48). Jesus' disciples are envoys bringing God's **peace** to those whom they visit.

For reflection: How have I been able to bring peace?

6 **If a peaceful person lives there**—a person who is open to receiving God's peace—**your peace will rest on him; but if not, it will return to you.** God's peace is viewed as an almost tangible reality, like a letter one sends. If a person refuses delivery of a letter, it is returned to the sender. So too, if a greeting of peace is rejected: it returns to the one making the greeting so that it can be given to someone more receptive.

7 **Stay in the same house** that welcomes you **and eat and drink what is offered to you.** Jesus' disciples are to accept the hospitality that is offered them, **for the laborer deserves his payment**. Those whom Jesus sends out are laborers for God's harvest (verse 2), and like any laborer they deserve payment for their work (see Deut 24:14–15). The **payment** they will receive is room and board, and they are to be content with **what is offered** to them. Jesus tells them, as he earlier told the Twelve (9:4), **do not move about from one house to another,** seeking better accommodations and meals.

8 **Whatever town you enter and they welcome you, eat what is set before you.** Jesus seems to repeat what he just said. However, his words can have additional meaning since he speaks of **whatever town** his disciples may enter. Jesus recently sought hospitality in a Samaritan village (9:52), and some of those whom he is now sending may also go to Samaritan villages. Many Jews considered Samaritans to be ritually unclean along with their dishes and food (see John 4:9). Jesus' words convey that his disciples need have no scruples about accepting hospitality and food from Samaritans: **eat what is set before you**. A related issue will arise when the early Church begins to incorporate Gentiles: can Jewish Christians who follow the Mosaic food laws share meals, and therefore the Eucharist, with Gentile Christians, who do not follow these laws? The question and its ramifications will be hotly debated (see Gal 2:11–14). By including this verse Luke may indicate to his readers that followers of Jesus can eat whatever their hosts, whether Jews or Gentiles, set before them (see 1 Cor 10:27 for Paul's similar resolution of a food question).

9 The disciples Jesus sends ahead of him to villages he will visit are to **cure the sick in it and say to them, "The kingdom of God is at hand for**

you." Before Jesus sent out the Twelve "to proclaim the kingdom of God and to heal" (9:2), he "gave them power and authority over all demons and to cure diseases" (9:1). Jesus shares his power and authority to **cure** with the seventy or seventy-two as well (see 10:17–19). They are to tell those they visit, **the kingdom of God is at hand for you**. God's reign will not be established in its fullness until the end of this age (21:25–31), yet it is **at hand for you:** it is beginning to be present in the lives of women and men through the healing and preaching of Jesus' disciples. As they **cure the sick**, they release those who are in the grip of evil and bring them under the reign of God, just as Jesus does (4:18; 11:20). The healing and preaching of Jesus' disciples makes a tangible difference in the lives of those who accept it; **the kingdom of God** becomes a reality for them.

Kingdom of God: See page 381

For reflection: How am I empowered to make God's reign a reality in the lives of others?

10 Not everyone, however, will welcome Jesus' disciples and accept their message. He tells them how to deal with rejection: **whatever town you enter and they do not receive you, go out into the streets and say,**

11 **The dust of your town that clings to our feet, even that we shake off against you.** Jesus gave a similar instruction to the Twelve when he sent them to proclaim the kingdom of God and to heal (9:2, 5). Shaking off the **dust** of a **town** from one's **feet** as one is leaving town conveys that one wants to have nothing more to do with the town and its people (see Acts 13:51). The disciples are to add as their final word, **Yet know this: the kingdom of God is at hand.** Even if the people of a town reject the disciples' proclamation of God's kingdom, God is establishing his kingdom nonetheless. Humans can refuse to cooperate with God's reign, but they cannot prevent God from reigning.

12 Rejecting God's reign has dire consequences: **I tell you, it will be more tolerable for Sodom on that day than for that town.** The town of **Sodom** was infamous for its wickedness and for its destruction by God (Gen 13:13; 18:20–21; 19:1–29; Isaiah 3:9; Ezek 16:49–50). The people of

Sodom, along with everyone else, will face judgment on **that day**, the day when God will pass final judgment on the human race (see 10:14; 11:31–32). Jesus solemnly pronounces that those who reject his disciples and their message will find themselves worse off at the final judgment than the people of proverbially wicked Sodom. A sobering prospect indeed!

The Woeful Condition of the Unrepentant
¹³ "Woe to you, Chorazin! Woe to you, Bethsaida! For if the mighty deeds done in your midst had been done in Tyre and Sidon, they would long ago have repented, sitting in sackcloth and ashes. ¹⁴ But it will be more tolerable for Tyre and Sidon at the judgment than for you. ¹⁵ And as for you, Capernaum, 'Will you be exalted to heaven? You will go down to the netherworld.' " ¹⁶ Whoever listens to you listens to me. Whoever rejects you rejects me. And whoever rejects me rejects the one who sent me."

Gospel parallels: Matt 11:20–24
OT: Isaiah 14:12–15
NT: Luke 9:48; 10:1–12

13 Jesus is instructing disciples he is sending on mission (10:1), and he has told them that Sodom will be better off on the day of judgment than towns that reject their proclamation of the kingdom of God (10:10–12). He expands on the fate of unresponsive towns, mentioning places he has visited. He exclaims, **Woe to you, Chorazin! Woe to you, Bethsaida! For if the mighty deeds done in your midst . . .** A **woe** laments someone's unfortunate condition (see 6:24–26). **Chorazin** was a village two miles from Capernaum. It is not mentioned elsewhere in the Gospel of Luke, but Luke does not provide a record of everything Jesus did everywhere. **Bethsaida** was four miles from Capernaum; Jesus fed a crowd of more than five thousand in its vicinity (9:10–17). Jesus refers to the **mighty deeds**, or works of power, he performed in Chorazin and

---

BACKGROUND: CHORAZIN was a small farming village built on a hill two miles north of Capernaum. Although excavated by archaeologists, no significant remains from the time of Jesus have been discovered. Chorazin was destroyed by an earthquake in the fourth century, rebuilt in the fifth century, and abandoned in the ninth century.

Bethsaida—perhaps expelling demons and curing the sick (see 4:36; 5:17; 6:19). Jesus singles out Chorazin and Bethsaida as privileged beneficiaries of his ministry.

Woes: See page 171
Bethsaida: See page 251

Jesus says to Chorazin and Bethsaida that **if the mighty deeds done in your midst had been done in Tyre and Sidon, they would long ago have repented, sitting in sackcloth and ashes**. Lying on the Mediterranean coast, **Tyre** and **Sidon** were prosperous Phoenician seaports. Prophets condemned them for their wantonness and pride (Isaiah 23; Ezek 28). **Repented** means changed course, turning from wickedness to God. **Sackcloth** was a coarse fabric woven from goat hair. **Sitting in sackcloth and ashes**—wearing sackcloth, and sitting in or covering oneself with ashes—were ways of mourning (Gen 37:34; 2 Sam 3:31; Esther 4:1, 3), and of humbling oneself before God (Neh 9:1; Judith 4:9–11; 1 Macc 3:47; Isaiah 58:5). If mighty deeds had been done in Tyre and Sidon like the mighty deeds Jesus performed in Chorazin and Bethsaida, then Tyre and Sidon **would long ago have repented**. Jesus' words imply that the people of Chorazin and Bethsaida have not **repented** despite the **mighty deeds** he did in these villages.

Tyre and Sidon: See page 166
Repentance: See page 92

14 Jesus tells Chorazin and Bethsaida that **it will be more tolerable for Tyre and Sidon at the judgment than for you**. At the end of the present age (see 18:30), the dead will rise to face **the judgment** of God (11:31–32). Jesus does not say that the people of **Tyre** and **Sidon** will not be punished for their sins but that the people of **Chorazin** and **Bethsaida** will fare even worse. They did not repent despite the mighty deeds Jesus worked on their behalf, making their failure to respond to his teaching all the more serious. As Jesus will observe in another context, "Much will be required of the person entrusted with much" (12:48).

Judgment: See page 327

For reflection: How have I been graced by God? Have I responded to him accordingly?

15 **And as for you, Capernaum, "Will you be exalted to heaven? You will go down to the netherworld."** Jesus taught and healed many people in the village of **Capernaum** (4:23, 31–41; 7:1–10). In response, its people "tried to prevent him from leaving them" (4:42). They may have thought that Jesus' presence gave Capernaum an exalted status. This seems to lie behind the sentiment Jesus attributes to them, adapting words from Isaiah: **will you be exalted to heaven?** (see Isaiah 14:13–14). Isaiah was taunting the pretensions of the king of Babylon (Isaiah 14:4), who considered himself so exalted that his throne should be in the heavens. Isaiah told him that his place was not in the heavens but under the earth: "down to the nether world you go" (Isaiah 14:15). Jesus applies Isaiah's words to Capernaum: **you will go down to the netherworld**. In the Old Testament, the **netherworld**, or depths of the earth, is called Sheol and is the abode of the dead (Job 17:13–16; Psalms 49:15; 89:49). By New Testament times the netherworld was viewed as place of punishment (16:23). Jesus tells Capernaum that instead of being exalted to heaven it will be brought low. The context suggests that, like the neighboring villages of Chorazin and Bethsaida, it will be punished for not repenting in response to Jesus' teachings and mighty deeds.

Capernaum: See page 124

> *You said in your heart:*
> *"I will scale the heavens;*
> *Above the stars of God*
> *I will set up my throne . . ."*
> *Yet down to the nether world you go*
> *to the recesses of the pit!*
>
> Isaiah 14:13, 15

Jesus has drawn crowds wherever he has gone (4:42; 5:1, 15; 6:17–18; 7:11; 8:4, 40; 9:11, 37), and his mighty deeds have generated amazement (5:26; 7:16; 8:56; 9:43). Yet coming to Jesus to be healed and being amazed at his deeds are not the same as changing one's life in response to his teachings. Jesus' woes indicate that while many in Chorazin, Bethsaida, and Capernaum may have been amazed, few have repented.

For reflection: What warning do Jesus' woes have for me?

16 Jesus concludes his instructions to the disciples he is sending on mission (10:1) by authorizing them to be his representatives, speaking on his behalf. He tells them, **whoever listens to you listens to me**. In Old Testament idiom, to listen includes accepting and obeying what one hears (see 6:47; Deut 6:4). When the disciples proclaim the kingdom of God (10:9), **whoever listens to** them and accepts their message **listens to** Jesus as the one who sent them. Jesus tells them that conversely, **whoever rejects you rejects me**. Rejecting Jesus has serious consequences, for, as he tells his disciples, **whoever rejects me rejects the one who sent me**. Jesus has been sent by God (see 4:18, 43). Whoever receives Jesus receives the one who sent him (9:48), and whoever rejects Jesus has "rejected the plan of God for themselves" (7:30). Hence Jesus' warning that it will be more tolerable for Sodom on the day of judgment than for towns that reject the disciples Jesus sends them (10:10–12). Those whom Jesus sends bear a message of eternal consequence.

> For reflection: Do I accept Jesus' words as God's word to me? Do I accept those who speak on Jesus' behalf as bringing me "the words of eternal life" (John 6:68)?

Written in the Book of Life

¹⁷ **The seventy[-two] returned rejoicing, and said, "Lord, even the demons are subject to us because of your name."** ¹⁸ **Jesus said, "I have observed Satan fall like lightning from the sky.** ¹⁹ **Behold, I have given you the power 'to tread upon serpents' and scorpions and upon the full force of the enemy and nothing will harm you.** ²⁰ **Nevertheless, do not rejoice because the spirits are subject to you, but rejoice because your names are written in heaven."**

OT: Psalm 91:13
NT: Luke 10:1, 9

17 Jesus sent disciples ahead of him to towns he will visit on his journey to Jerusalem (10:1), instructing them to cure the sick and announce that the kingdom of God is at hand (10:9). Luke does not recount how long they were away on their mission or what Jesus did during their absence; he simply jumps ahead to their return. **The seventy[-two] returned** to Jesus **rejoicing**. The significance of **seventy[-two]** is discussed in the

exposition of 10:1. They come back **rejoicing**, beside themselves with joy over the success of their mission. They address Jesus as **Lord**, acknowledging his authority. They exclaim in amazement that **even the demons are subject to us because of your name**. Jesus sent them out with a mandate to heal the sick (10:9); they found that they were also able to expel **demons** when they invoked the **name** of Jesus. He has authority over demons (4:36, 40–41; 6:18; 8:2, 29; 9:42), and those who invoke his name draw on his authority (see 9:49; Acts 16:18).

Lord: See page 137

Demons, unclean spirits: See page 125

For reflection: When have I been amazed over what I was able to do because of Jesus?

18 **Jesus said, "I have observed Satan fall like lightning from the sky."** Some prophets had visions that contained symbols of what God was doing (Jer 1:11–16; Ezek 2:9–10; Amos 8:1–3), and Jesus has such a vision. Old Testament writings portray **Satan** as a heavenly prosecuting attorney who tests humans (Job 1:6–12; 2:1–7; Zech 3:1) or as a spiritual being that leads them astray (1 Chron 21:1; see also Wisd 2:24). Jesus has a vision of Satan (previously referred to in Luke's Gospel as the devil—4:2–13; 8:12) falling from the sky, symbolizing his being defeated and deposed. The vision reveals the significance of the disciples' success: their casting out demons signals the downfall of Satan, the chief evil spirit. The vision does not mean that Satan has been completely conquered (see 22:3, 31; Acts 5:3; 26:18). Rather, Jesus sees the ultimate outcome of the struggle against Satan that he and his disciples are engaged in. The defeat of Satan is sure; it is as evident to Jesus as a bolt of **lightning** piercing the sky.

Satan: See page 108

19 Jesus tells the disciples why demons are subject to them: **Behold, I have given you the power "to tread upon serpents" and scorpions and upon the full force of the enemy.** For those who worked outdoors or who traveled off the beaten paths, **serpents** and **scorpions** were deadly hazards. They served as symbols for what was malignant and dangerous (see 11:11–12). Jesus has **given** his disciples **power** over the forces of evil, figuratively expressed as **serpents** and **scorpions**; they will **tread upon**

and crush them. Jesus invokes Psalm 91, which is an assurance of God's protection: **to tread upon serpents** echoes "You shall tread upon the asp and the viper" (Psalm 91:13). Jesus has given his disciples power over **the full force of the enemy**: the **enemy** is Satan. They are assured of ultimate victory in their struggle against Satan and the forces of evil. Jesus assures his disciples, **nothing will harm you**. Jesus does not promise that they will never suffer; as the next verse indicates, he is speaking of their being preserved for eternal life (see also 18:30).

> You shall tread upon the asp and the viper,
> trample the lion and the dragon.
>
> Psalm 91:13

20 **Nevertheless, do not rejoice because the spirits are subject to you, but rejoice because your names are written in heaven.** Names **written in heaven** implies, written by God. Behind the idea of God keeping a list of names was the practice of cities keeping a registry of their citizens. This developed into the idea of God having a book of the names of his people (Exod 32:32–33; Psalm 87:6; Isaiah 4:3; Dan 12:1; Mal 3:16), which in New Testament writings is called the book of life—the registry of those destined for eternal life (Phil 4:3; Rev 3:5; 13:8; 17:8; 20:12, 15; 21:27; see also Heb 12:23). The sense of Jesus' pronouncement is, rejoice more over your names being written in heaven than over evil spirits being subject to you. Evil must be overcome as God's reign is established, but what is most important is the inclusion of women and men in God's reign. Jesus tells his disciples to **rejoice** because of the great destiny to which they are called: their **names are written in heaven** in the registry of citizens of God's kingdom.

> For reflection: How often does my hope to be eternally with God fill me with joy?

God's Revelation and Its Recipients

²¹ **At that very moment he rejoiced [in] the holy Spirit and said, "I give you praise, Father, Lord of heaven and earth, for although you have hidden these things from the wise and the learned you have**

revealed them to the childlike. Yes, Father, such has been your gracious will. ²² All things have been handed over to me by my Father. No one knows who the Son is except the Father, and who the Father is except the Son and anyone to whom the Son wishes to reveal him."

²³ Turning to the disciples in private he said, "Blessed are the eyes that see what you see. ²⁴ For I say to you, many prophets and kings desired to see what you see, but did not see it, and to hear what you hear, but did not hear it."

Gospel parallels: Matt 11:25–27; 13:16–17
NT: Luke 3:22; 9:35; 10:17–20

21 **At that very moment he rejoiced [in] the holy Spirit.** Jesus' joy flows from what was happening **at that very moment.** His disciples reported their success in casting out demons; he saw Satan fall and he knew his disciples' names were written in heaven (10:17–20). The mission God gave him was being accomplished: evil was being overcome, and men and women were entering into the reign of God. Jesus **rejoiced [in] the holy Spirit**—was filled with joy by the Holy Spirit. Jesus was led and empowered by the Spirit (4:1, 14), and now the **Spirit** moves him to rejoice over his mission's success, just as his mother, Mary, rejoiced over what God was doing through her (1:47–48). Luke rarely describes Jesus' emotions, making this instance all the more significant.

The Spirit: See page 100

For reflection: When has an awareness of what God was doing through me filled me with joy?

Jesus expresses his joy in an outburst of prayer: he **said, "I give you praise, Father, Lord of heaven and earth."** Jesus acknowledges God to be **Lord of heaven and earth**. God is "the creator of heaven and earth" (Gen 14:22) and **Lord** or master over all he created (Judith 9:12). Jesus addresses God, the Lord of the universe, as **Father**, just as God addresses Jesus as his Son (3:22; see also 9:35). Jesus is uniquely the Son of God, as the following verse makes explicit. Jesus tells his Father, **I give you praise**. The Greek word translated **give praise** means to acknowledge or confess (see Acts 19:18; Phil 2:11), but has the sense of praise when addressed to

God (see Rom 14:11; 15:9). Jesus praises God by acknowledging what he has done: **for although you have hidden these things from the wise and the learned you have revealed them to the childlike**. What are **these things** that have been **revealed**? They could be "knowledge of the mysteries of the kingdom of God" (8:10): a recognition that God was establishing his reign through the healings and exorcisms and preaching of Jesus and of his disciples (10:9–11, 17–20). But what Jesus goes on to say indicates that **these things** include his relationship with God as his Father, a relationship that enables him to make God known (verse 22). God has **hidden these things from the wise and the learned**. The **wise** and the **learned** would include "scholars of the law" (7:30). God has not make known to them **these things** that he is doing through Jesus but has **revealed them to the childlike**. The **childlike** are those without status or pretensions, and are elsewhere referred to as the lowly (see 1:48, 52) and the poor (see 4:18; 6:20; 7:22). Jesus' disciples are among the child-like: they are blessed recipients of God's revelation (verses 23–24).

Lord: See page 137

Jesus concludes his prayer by saying, **Yes, Father, such has been your gracious will**—more literally, it was well-pleasing to you. God has chosen some to receive his revelation because it has pleased him to do so. No one has a claim to receive God's revelation, no matter how wise they are (see 1 Cor 1:18–31); God chooses "those on whom his favor rests" (2:14). Jesus praises God for his graciousness in sending his revelation to those to whom he sends it.

22 Jesus proclaims that **All things have been handed over to me by my Father**. Jesus makes an extraordinary claim about himself: God is his **Father** and has **handed over** and entrusted to him **all things**. Luke's Gospel has shown that Jesus exercises God's authority and power to expel demons and cure the sick, to forgive sins and raise the dead. **All things** also includes an intimate knowledge of God and the ability to make God known, as Jesus makes clear: **No one knows who the Son is except the Father, and who the Father is except the Son and anyone to whom the Son wishes to reveal him.** Luke's Gospel has repeatedly raised the question, Who is Jesus? (5:21; 7:20, 49; 8:25; 9:9, 18, 20). Only **the Father** has full knowledge of **who the Son is**, and only **the Son**

knows **the Father.** Just as a human father and son have an intimate knowledge of each other shared by no one else, so God and Jesus know each other as **Father** and **Son.** Because Jesus is uniquely the Son of God and has a privileged intimacy with the Father, he can make him known to **anyone to whom the Son wishes to reveal him.** What Jesus is able **to reveal** about his Father goes beyond the knowledge that humans can have of God through creation (Rom 1:19–20) or through God's previous revelation (Heb 1:1–2). **All things have been handed over** to Jesus so that, as **the Son,** he can make known **the Father.**

Son of God: See page 25

For reflection: What are the most important truths that Jesus' words reveal about him?

Jesus will not again in Luke's Gospel speak so directly about his relationship with God. A major theme of John's Gospel is Jesus' relationship with and revelation of God (John 1:18; 3:35; 5:20; 7:29; 10:15; 13:3; 14:9–11; 15:15; 16:15; 17:2, 6, 25–26).

23 **Turning to the disciples in private he said, "Blessed are the eyes that see what you see."** After his joyful prayer, Jesus turns his attention to his disciples and tells them that they are indeed fortunate. They have been "eyewitnesses from the beginning" (1:2) and **see** what God is doing through Jesus. To **see** can have the connotation of experience (see 2:26; 3:6; 9:27). The disciples are blessed to be among the childlike whom God has graciously favored with his revelation (verse 21; see also 8:10). Jesus is making his Father known to them (verse 22; see also 6:36; 11:2, 13; 12:30–32). They are very fortunate and **blessed.**

Disciple: See page 149
Beatitudes: See page 169

Jesus does not tell his disciples, Blessed are you who see what you see; he says, Blessed are the eyes seeing what you see. The blessed state of his disciples extends to those of all time who receive Jesus' revelation of God as his Father and their Father, who are released from the grip of evil, who hear and respond to the good news that Jesus proclaims.

For reflection: How have I been blessed by God's revelation?

24 Jesus tells his disciples that they have been given what many others desired: **For I say to you, many prophets and kings desired to see what you see, but did not see it, and to hear what you hear, but did not hear it.** Jesus may single out **prophets** and **kings** as being the most significant figures in what God had done for his people in the past. **Prophets** spoke for God; many of them foretold God coming to the rescue of his people. **Kings** were responsible for leading God's people. But even the most important people of the past **did not see** and experience what God is doing through Jesus; they **did not hear** Jesus' teachings and his revelation of his Father. Fortunate indeed are the disciples—and all who experience and hear Jesus.

What Must I Do to Inherit Eternal Life?

²⁵ **There was a scholar of the law who stood up to test him and said, "Teacher, what must I do to inherit eternal life?" ²⁶ Jesus said to him, "What is written in the law? How do you read it?" ²⁷ He said in reply, "You shall love the Lord, your God, with all your heart, with all your being, with all your strength, and with all your mind, and your neighbor as yourself." ²⁸ He replied to him, "You have answered correctly; do this and you will live."**

Gospel parallels: Matt 22:34–40; Mark 12:28–34
OT: Lev 18:5; 19:18; Deut 6:4–5
NT: Luke 18:18–20

25 **There was a scholar of the law who stood up to test him.** Jesus spoke of God hiding things from "the wise and the learned" (10:21); now he is confronted by a **scholar of the law**, or scribe, learned in the law of Moses. Scribes have been critical of Jesus (5:21, 30; 6:7), and this scribe wishes **to test him.** He addresses Jesus as **Teacher,** someone who should know about religious matters. He asks Jesus, **What must I do to inherit eternal life?** This is the first explicit mention of **eternal life** in Luke's Gospel. Some Jews believed that God would give **eternal life** to martyrs and the upright in the age to come (see 2 Macc 7; Dan 12:2). The scholar asks what he must **do** to **inherit** eternal life. Linking doing and inherit-

ing can seem puzzling. One does not necessarily do anything to obtain an inheritance; one is simply named in a will. Yet the scholar's question is not meaningless. Even though eternal life is a bequest or gift from God, there can be conditions attached to receiving it. As a comparison, we might think of a woman leaving behind a trust fund that gives each of her grandchildren $5,000 if they graduate from college. The scholar asks what he must do—what conditions he must meet—in order to inherit eternal life. He asks his question to **test** Jesus, hoping that Jesus' response can be used against him (see 6:7).

Scribes: See page 146

26 **Jesus said to him, "What is written in the law?"** Jesus does not answer the scholar's question but directs him to Scripture as the revelation of God's will. The **law** of Moses, that is, the first five books of the Old Testament, contains many commands (613 by a later count), some with promises or threats attached. Jesus asks the scholar, **How do you read it?** How do you, as a scholar of the law, understand what the law requires you to do to inherit eternal life?

BACKGROUND: LIFE AFTER DEATH For the ancient Israelites, a human being was living flesh, and meaningful life apart from the flesh was inconceivable. There was no belief in an immortal soul; the Hebrew word that is sometimes translated as "soul" can mean the livingness of a body but not something that can enjoy existence apart from a body. What survived death was at best a shadow or a ghost of one's former self, consigned to a netherworld beneath the surface of the earth (Num 16:31–33). The netherworld was a place of darkness and silence; those in the netherworld were cut off from the living and from God (Job 14:20–21; Sirach 17:22–23). Good and bad alike languished in the netherworld, sharing the same fate (Eccl 9:2–6). It was only near the end of the Old Testament era that hopes arose that there would be meaningful life after death. These hopes were often expressed in terms of bodily resurrection from the dead (2 Macc 7; Dan 12:2). However, the book of Wisdom, written around the time of Jesus, drew on Greek thinking and taught that after death, "the souls of the just are in the hand of God" (Wisd 3:1). Greek philosophers thought of souls as immortal and as temporarily imprisoned in bodies (see Wisd 9:15); death meant the release of the soul from this imprisonment. Some nonbiblical Jewish writings presumed that there would be life in the age to come but were vague about its nature. *Related topics: The age to come (page 487), Nonbiblical writings (page 342), Resurrection (page 401).*

For reflection: What are the implications for me of Jesus' sending the scholar to Scripture for an answer to his question?

27 **He said in reply, "You shall love the Lord, your God, with all your heart, with all your being, with all your strength, and with all your mind, and your neighbor as yourself."** The scholar quotes two passages of Scripture, joining them together. In Deuteronomy is the command **You shall love the Lord, your God, with all your heart, with all your being, with all your strength** (Deut 6:5). In the biblical view of the human person, the **heart** represents the core of oneself and the seat of emotions. The word translated as **being** can also be translated as "life," or as "soul" in the Hebrew sense of soul as one's livingness. **Strength** means one's might and energy. The scholar adds a fourth clause: **and with all your mind**, with all one's thinking and planning. Heart, being, strength, and mind are not four separate components of the human person so much as the whole person viewed from different angles. The point of the command is that one is to love God completely and totally, with all one has and all one is, with absolute loyalty and devotion. The scholar joins to this command a command found in Leviticus: you shall love **your neighbor as yourself** (Lev 19:18). We are to act as if we were on the receiving end of our actions, helping others as we would want them to help us, not inflicting on others what we would not want inflicted on us. The scholar joins the two commands by having the word **love** govern both our stance toward God and our stance toward our neighbor: You shall **love the Lord, your God . . . and your neighbor**.

> *Hear, O Israel! The LORD is our God, the LORD alone! Therefore, you shall love the LORD, your God, with all your heart, and with all your soul, and with all your strength.*
>
> Deut 6:4–5

> *Take no revenge and cherish no grudge against your fellow countrymen. You shall love your neighbor as yourself.*
>
> Lev 19:18

For reflection: How do I understand the link between loving God and loving others? What steps can I take to increase my love for God and others?

Why might the scholar connect inheriting eternal life with loving God and neighbor? Perhaps he has in mind God's promise of life for those who keep his commands: "Keep . . . my statutes and decrees, for the man who carries them out will find life through them" (Lev 18:5; see also Deut 6:1–2, 24). God's promise of life originally meant a long life in the promised land (Deut 4:40; 5:16, 33; 11:8–9; 25:15) but by extension could mean life in the age to come. The scholar proposes that loving God and neighbor is the vitally important command to keep in order to receive God's gift of life.

28 Jesus agrees with the scholar's answer, even if the scholar wanted to test him. **He replied to him, "You have answered correctly; do this and you will live."** Loving God and neighbor is necessary in order to inherit eternal life. One must actually **do** as the command requires, loving God without reserve and treating others as well as one treats oneself. This is no light demand, but those who **do** what God asks will **live** eternally.

For reflection: What must I do to inherit eternal life?

The Example of the Compassionate Samaritan
²⁹ But because he wished to justify himself, he said to Jesus, "And who is my neighbor?" ³⁰ Jesus replied, "A man fell victim to robbers as he went down from Jerusalem to Jericho. They stripped and beat him and went off leaving him half-dead. ³¹ A priest happened to be going down that road, but when he saw him, he passed by on the opposite side. ³² Likewise a Levite came to the place, and when he saw him, he passed by on the opposite side. ³³ But a Samaritan traveler who came upon him was moved with compassion at the sight. ³⁴ He approached the victim, poured oil and wine over his wounds and bandaged them. Then he lifted him up on his own animal, took him to an inn and cared for him. ³⁵ The next day he took out two silver coins and gave them to the innkeeper with the instruction, 'Take care of him. If you spend more than what I have given you, I shall repay you on my way back.' ³⁶ Which of these three, in your opinion, was neighbor to the

robbers' victim?" ³⁷ He answered, "The one who treated him with mercy." Jesus said to him, "Go and do likewise."

OT: Lev 19:18, 34
NT: Luke 10:25–28

29 A scholar's attempt to test Jesus was frustrated when Jesus had him answer his own question and then told him to do what he knew he should do: love God wholeheartedly and his neighbor as himself (10:25–28). **But because he wished to justify himself, he said to Jesus, "And who is my neighbor?"** To vindicate himself and show that the matter is not as simple as Jesus would make it, he questions the scope of what God requires. In the Old Testament, a neighbor was a "fellow countryman" (Lev 19:18), another Israelite. But who were neighbors in the mixed ethnic and religious situation of first-century Palestine? Were Roman soldiers stationed near the Temple neighbors? The scholar challenges Jesus, **who is my neighbor?** The implication of his question is, Who is not my neighbor? If I have to love my neighbor as I love myself, I want as few neighbors as possible!

For reflection: How many neighbors do I want?

30 In response to his question Jesus tells a story. **Jesus replied, "A man fell victim to robbers as he went down from Jerusalem to Jericho."** Jesus' parable has a realistic setting: those traveling **from Jerusalem to Jericho** were sometimes waylaid by **robbers.** The road ran through the Judean wilderness, full of ravines and caves that provided hideouts for highwaymen. Jesus speaks of a certain **man** traveling this route, but does not specify whether he is Jew or Gentile, rich or poor, righteous or sinner. He is going **down** from Jerusalem to Jericho, a descent of thirty-three hundred feet over the course of seventeen miles. He **fell victim to robbers,** overpowered by a gang. **They stripped and beat him and went off leaving him half-dead.** The Greek word for **half-dead** is used for those at the point of death; the man will die unless someone comes along to help him. He is unconscious, for Jesus does not recount him crying out for help when people pass by. Being **stripped** of his clothes and unable to speak made him unidentifiable, for clothing indicated social status (see

16:19) and accent betrayed one's place of origin (see Judges 12:5–6; Matt 26:73). The man's appearance is reduced to his mere humanity.

Jerusalem: See page 516

Jericho: See page 496

31 **A priest happened to be going down that road.** Most priests lived outside of Jerusalem, but came in rotating divisions to Jerusalem twice a year to serve in the Temple (see 1:8, 23). That this **priest** was **going down that road** indicates that he was traveling from Jerusalem to Jericho, perhaps returning home after completing his week's service in the Temple. He comes within sight of the robbers' victim, **but when he saw him, he passed by on the opposite side.** Some suggest that since contact with a corpse would have made the priest unclean (Lev 21:1–4; Num 19:11–16) he **passed by on the opposite side** in case the unconscious man was dead. However, he was not on the way to Jerusalem, where ritual uncleanness would have prevented him from serving in the Temple; he was on his way home and could have accepted uncleanness for the sake of helping the man. Others suggest that he hurried past the man out of fear that he too might be beaten and robbed if he lingered in what was obviously a dangerous area. We can also wonder whether he rationalized to himself that if the man was not yet dead, he would soon die anyway, and trying to help him would be a waste of time. But Jesus

---

BACKGROUND: PRIESTS AND LEVITES Priests in the time of Jesus were primarily responsible for offering sacrificial worship in the Temple. During the Old Testament era, priests also instructed the people in the law of Moses, but in time this function largely passed to scribes, that is, professional scholars and teachers, although some priests were also scribes. The office of priesthood was hereditary. All priests were members of the tribe of Levi and descendants of Aaron (Exod 28:1; 29:9; Num 18:1, 7); those who were of the tribe of Levi but not descended from Aaron served in the Temple in secondary roles as Levites (Num 1:47–53; 8:5–26; 18:2–6). At the time of Jesus there were perhaps seven thousand priests and ten thousand Levites, out of a total Jewish population in Palestine of a half-million to a million. Some priests, especially those from high-priestly families, lived in Jerusalem and were in charge of the Temple. Most priests lived in other towns and served in the Temple only a week at a time on a twenty-four-week rotation. There was a considerable gap in income and influence between the Jerusalem high-priestly families and ordinary priests living outside Jerusalem.

---

does not say why he avoided coming near the man. He simply says that a priest, a man dedicated to the service of God, failed to help him.

For reflection: When have I had an opportunity to assist someone in serious need but did not do so? What were my reasons for not helping?

32 **Likewise a Levite came to the place.** Levites also served in the Temple in rotating divisions, assisting priests in offering sacrifice. A **Levite** catches sight of the nearly dead man **and when he saw him, he passed by on the opposite side.** Again, Jesus does not say why he did not stop to assist the man. Whatever his reasons, **he passed by on the opposite side** and continued on his journey. A second man dedicated to the service of God fails to help the robbers' victim.

33 **But a Samaritan traveler who came upon him**: the scholar of the law may have anticipated Jesus saying that a layman next came upon the victim, for the Jewish people were commonly thought of as made up of priests, Levites, and lay people (see Ezra 8:15; 9:1). But in a surprising turn it is not a Jew but a **Samaritan** who comes upon the half-dead man (Luke constructs his Greek sentence to emphasize the word **Samaritan**). The road from Jerusalem to Jericho was a major thoroughfare, used by Gentiles and Samaritans as well as Jews. This Samaritan might be a merchant, a commercial **traveler.** There was hostility between Samaritans and Jews (see 9:52–54), and they usually avoided contact with each other (see John 4:9). Since the Samaritan is traveling through heavily Jewish Judea, he might figure the odds are that the unidentifiable injured man is a Jew and give him an even wider berth than did the priest and the Levite. But this **Samaritan** who came upon the robbery victim **was moved with compassion at the sight.** What did he see that filled him with **compassion**? He could see only a wounded and unconscious naked man by the road, and **at the sight** of a person in dire straits he **was moved with compassion.** The Greek word Luke uses for **compassion** has the connotation of being moved from the depths of one's being.

Samaria, Samaritans: See page 277

For reflection: When have I been most deeply moved with compassion for a person in distress? What did my compassion lead me to do?

303

34 The Samaritan puts his compassion into action. **He approached the victim** whom others had gone out of their way to avoid, **poured oil and wine over his wounds and bandaged them.** He performs first aid with what he has on hand. **Wine** was used as an antiseptic; anointing with olive **oil** soothed wounds. If the Samaritan was a merchant, he may have been transporting **oil** and **wine**, both of which were exported from Samaria; otherwise he used his own provisions. He **bandaged** the man's wounds, perhaps tearing up some of his clothes for bandages. Dressing the wounds took some time, exposing him to the risk that those who beat and robbed the man might return and set upon him. But transporting a nearly dead man without first bandaging his bleeding wounds might have been fatal. **Then he lifted him up on his own animal** and **took him to an inn.** The Samaritan gives up his seat on the animal and walks so that a man who cannot walk can ride. A commercial **inn** offered shelter for the night but minimal amenities. At the inn the Samaritan **cared for him**, perhaps redressing his wounds with more proper bandages and giving him something to drink and eat if he regained consciousness. The Samaritan does as much as he can for a nearly dead stranger he came upon by accident.

35 **The next day he took out two silver coins and gave them to the innkeeper with the instruction, "Take care of him."** The Samaritan may have cared for the robbers' victim through the night but now must be on his way. He pays the **innkeeper** to **take care** of the injured man until he has recovered sufficiently to travel; the man had been robbed and could not pay for his care himself. **Two silver coins** are literally two denarii, representing two days of wages for an ordinary laborer (see Matt 20:2). Two denarii would pay for the injured man's lodging for a week or more, depending on how much food and care the innkeeper gave him. The Samaritan tells the innkeeper, **If you spend more than what I have given you, I shall repay you on my way back.** His travels will take him **back** to the inn. He makes an open-ended commitment, telling the innkeeper that he will repay him for whatever care he gives the man. He makes the wounded man's needs the criteria for the amount of help he provides.

For reflection: What lessons does the Samaritan teach me?

36 Jesus asks the scholar of the law, **Which of these three, in your opinion, was neighbor to the robbers' victim?** The word translated **was** could be more literally translated "became": which of the three became a neighbor to the victim? The scholar asked, "Who is my neighbor?" (verse 29) but Jesus turns his question around and asks which of the three acted as a neighbor. It is clear that the Samaritan and the victim were not neighbors in any conventional sense: they did not know each other. But the Samaritan became a neighbor to a stranger in need, treating him as he would have wished to be treated if he had been left half-dead by robbers.

37 **He answered, "The one who treated him with mercy."** The scholar must acknowledge that the Samaritan alone showed **mercy** toward the victim, although he apparently cannot bring himself to say the word "Samaritan." **Jesus said to him, "Go and do likewise."** Go and show **mercy**, imitating the example of the compassionate Samaritan, becoming a neighbor to whomever you find in need. There are no racial or religious boundaries that determine who is a neighbor; to love your neighbor as yourself (10:27) means to have mercy on whoever needs mercy, even an enemy (6:27–36). The wounded man by the road, stripped of his identity, stands for everyone in need.

For reflection: How am I able to do likewise, becoming a neighbor to those who need my help?

The One Thing Necessary

38 As they continued their journey he entered a village where a woman whose name was Martha welcomed him. 39 She had a sister named Mary [who] sat beside the Lord at his feet listening to him speak. 40 Martha, burdened with much serving, came to him and said, "Lord, do you not care that my sister has left me by myself to do the serving? Tell her to help me." 41 The Lord said to her in reply, "Martha, Martha, you are anxious and worried about many things. 42 There is need of only one thing. Mary has chosen the better part and it will not be taken from her."

NT: Luke 10:25–28

38 Jesus and his disciples are traveling to Jerusalem (9:51), and **as they con‐ tinued their journey he entered a village where a woman whose name was Martha welcomed him**. Luke does not name the **village**. The word translated as **welcomed** means to receive as a guest, offering hospitality. Jesus is dependent on others for his meals and lodging (see 9:52, 58), as are his disciples while on mission (9:4; 10:5–8). A woman named **Martha** welcomed Jesus into her house and set about preparing a meal for him. A large number of disciples are traveling with Jesus (see 10:1); she perhaps took some of them into her home as well.

Hospitality: See page 314

39 **She had a sister named Mary [who] sat beside the Lord at his feet listening to him speak.** Mary **sat** herself by Jesus; she takes the initia‐ tive to be near him. She sat **at his feet,** the posture of a disciple studying under a master (Paul will say, "At the feet of Gamaliel I was educated strictly in our ancestral law"—Acts 22:3). Jewish religious teachers did not accept women as disciples, but Jesus does. Mary was **listening to him**, literally, listening to his word. Jesus' words are the word of God (5:1); those who "hear the word of God and act on it" become his new family (8:21).

40 **Martha** was **burdened with much serving.** As a hostess, she wanted to prepare a first-rate meal for Jesus; true hospitality demanded nothing less (see the example set by Abraham—Gen 18:1–8). If she was also hosting some of Jesus' disciples, then **much** food preparation and **serving** might be required. But her tasks, however necessary, **burdened** her. The literal meaning of the word translated as **burdened** is to be pulled or dragged away; its figurative meaning is distracted or burdened. Martha may have liked to sit at Jesus' feet as her sister Mary is doing, but she is preoccupied with her duties as hostess. She is also put out that all the work is falling on her. She **came to** Jesus **and said, "Lord, do you not care that my sister has left me by myself to do the serving?"** While she addresses Jesus as **Lord**, acknowledging his authority, she also challenges what she considers to be his insensitivity to her needs: **do you not care . . . ?** She does not name Mary but refers to her as **my sister**, perhaps out of pique. She complains that Mary **has left me by myself to do the serving**. She

says to Jesus, **tell her to help me**, virtually ordering Jesus to order Mary to assist her.

Lord: See page 137

For reflection: At this point in Luke's account, am I identifying more with Martha or with Mary?

41 **The Lord said to her in reply, "Martha, Martha,"** gently chiding her. He tells her, **you are anxious and worried about many things**—the **things** she is doing to provide hospitality for him. Extending hospitality is commendable; Martha's problem lies in her being **anxious and worried**. Anxiety and worry are symptoms of something being amiss, perhaps a breakdown in one's trust in God (see 12:22–34). In this case they manifest Martha's misplaced priorities. The most important requirement of hospitality is to pay attention to the guest, but Martha's fretting over the things she is doing for Jesus distracts her from Jesus and makes her petulant.

For reflection: Have I let my service for Jesus distract me from my personal relationship with him?

42 Jesus tells Martha that **there is need of only one thing**. Jesus is not saying a casserole will do so don't bother preparing a seven-course meal. Rather, what **one thing** refers to is implied by what he says next: **Mary has chosen the better part**. Mary has chosen the **one** necessary **thing**; she has given Jesus her undivided attention, listening to him. The Father has handed all things over to Jesus so that he can reveal the Father (10:22); whoever receives Jesus receives the one who sent him (9:48). Mary wholeheartedly received Jesus and the God he reveals; Martha let her service of Jesus pull her away from him. Mary made the **better** choice, and what Mary has chosen **will not be taken from her**: Jesus will not turn away anyone who is eager to embrace him and his words.

For reflection: What can I learn from Jesus' words about Mary?

Martha and Mary also interact with Jesus in John's Gospel, with Martha serving a meal (John 11:1–44; 12:1–3). John's Gospel tells us that they live in Bethany (John 11:1), a village on the outskirts of Jerusalem. In Luke's Gospel, Jesus will not arrive in Bethany (19:29) until he completes his travels "through Samaria and Galilee" (17:11). Luke recounts events "in an orderly sequence" (1:3), but an orderly sequence may not necessarily be chronological. Luke places Jesus' encounter with Martha and Mary at this point in his Gospel because it illustrates something that Jesus has just taught. To inherit eternal life we must love God wholeheartedly and our neighbor as ourselves (10:25–28). The parable of the compassionate Samaritan (10:29–37) shows what love of neighbor involves. The better part chosen by Mary demonstrates how to love God: go to Jesus to receive his revelation of his Father. It is the one thing necessary for eternal life (see John 5:24; 17:3).

CHAPTER 11

ORIENTATION: *Jesus' disciples ask him to teach them how to pray. In response, Jesus provides them with a model prayer (11:2–4) and instructs them about prayer (11:5–13).*

The Lord's Prayer
¹ He was praying in a certain place, and when he had finished, one of his disciples said to him, "Lord, teach us to pray just as John taught his disciples." ² He said to them, "When you pray, say:
Father, hallowed be your name,
your kingdom come.
    ³ Give us each day our daily bread
    ⁴ and forgive us our sins
for we ourselves forgive everyone in debt to us,
and do not subject us to the final test."
    Gospel parallels: Matt 6:9–13
    OT: Sirach 28:2–4; Ezek 36:22–32
    NT: Mark 14:36; Luke 10:21–22; John 12:28; Rom 8:15; Gal 4:6

1 **He was praying in a certain place**: Jesus often spent time in prayer (3:21; 5:16; 9:28; 10:21), even an entire night (6:12). Sometimes he prayed in presence of his disciples (9:18), which is the case here, for **when he had finished, one of his disciples said to him, "Lord, teach us to pray just as John taught his disciples."** Those who are **disciples** look to their master, or **Lord**, for instruction. **John** the Baptist **taught his disciples** how they were to pray, presumably teaching them to pray as he prayed, just as they fasted as he fasted (5:33; 7:33). Now **one of** Jesus' **disciples** asks him to **teach us to pray**. As devout Jews, Jesus' disciples prayed the Psalms as well as other Jewish prayers. Yet they still ask Jesus to teach them how to pray. They apparently noticed something distinctive about Jesus' prayer and wish to imitate their master in their prayers, just as the disciples of John imitated John. We call the prayer that Jesus

teaches them the "Lord's Prayer," and it is literally that—a prayer rooted in the prayer of the Lord Jesus.

Disciple: See page 149
Lord: See page 137

For reflection: How did I learn how to pray? What would I like to learn now so that I could pray more like Jesus?

2 **He said to them, "When you pray, say . . ."** The word translated **when** can also be translated "whenever." The prayer that Jesus teaches his disciples is for every time they pray. They are to say **Father**, addressing God as Father just as Jesus addresses God as Father when he prays (10:21; 22:42; 23:34, 46). Jesus is speaking to his disciples in their native language of Aramaic, and the Aramaic word he uses to address his Father is *Abba* (Mark 14:36). *Abba* is an informal and affectionate word that might best be translated as "Dad." Grown children as well as children just learning to speak would address their father as *Abba*. Jesus prayed to God with the intimacy of the Son speaking to his Father. He spoke of God as "my Father" (2:49; 22:29; 24:49) and proclaimed that as the Son he was able to make his Father known (10:22). He is doing so now, teaching his disciples that they can address God as *Abba* just as he addresses God as *Abba* (see also John 20:17), approaching him with the intimacy that a daughter or son has for a loving human father. The practice of addressing God as *Abba* continued in the early Church, even for those whose native language was not Aramaic (see Rom 8:15; Gal 4:6).

> *As proof that you are children, God sent the spirit of his Son into our hearts, crying out, "Abba, Father!"*
>
> Gal 4:6

For reflection: In my prayers, how do I address God? How might I enter into greater intimacy with him?

After calling God **Father**, Jesus' disciples are to pray **hallowed be your name**. To be **hallowed** is to be made holy or sanctified. Implied by **hallowed be** is, hallowed by God; hallowed by humans in the sense of being reverenced would also be entailed. In the biblical view, a person's **name** is not an arbitrary label but reveals a person's identity. God's **name** can be tantamount to his reputation, which he establishes by his deeds on behalf of his people (see Ezek 36:22–32). Praying **hallowed be your name** asks God to demonstrate his holiness so that everyone recognizes who God is. Similarly, in John's Gospel Jesus prays, "Father, glorify your name" (John 12:28).

Jesus' disciples are to pray to their Father, **your kingdom come**. Jesus was sent by his Father to "proclaim the good news of the kingdom of God" (4:43; see also 8:1; 9:11), the good news that God is establishing his reign. Jesus sent out his disciples to proclaim the same message (9:2, 60; 10:9, 11). Praying **your kingdom come** asks God to establish his reign, vanquishing all of the world's evil, strife, and suffering. God's reign will not be complete until Jesus comes in glory (21:25–31), but it has already begun to be a reality in and through Jesus (11:20; 17:21). Jesus' disciples ask both for its present flowering and its ultimate fulfillment when they pray **your kingdom come**. The first two petitions of the Lord's prayer are related: God will hallow his name, manifesting who he is, by establishing his reign.

Kingdom of God: See page 381

For reflection: What do I have in mind when I pray the first two petitions of the Lord's prayer?

3   The remaining petitions of the prayer that Jesus teaches his disciples deal with their needs as God is establishing his reign. They are to ask, **give us each day our daily bread**. In biblical times, **bread** was the staple food, providing a substantial portion of daily nourishment. **Bread** therefore could stand for food in general (the Greek word for "bread" is translated as "food" at 7:33 and 9:3). **Daily bread** is thus best interpreted as daily nourishment, whatever is necessary to sustain us each day. The Greek word translated **give** is in a tense that conveys repeated action; Jesus' disciples are to ask the Father to give them **each day** the necessities they need. Jesus sent his disciples out on mission without provisions (9:3; 10:4) so that they would rely on God's care for them. He will tell them, "do not seek what you are to eat and what you are to drink, and do not

worry anymore . . . Your Father knows that you need them" (12:29–30). Rather than worry, they are to ask their Father, **give us each day our daily bread,** confident that he will hear their prayer (see 11:5–13).

Diet: See page 253

For reflection: What are the daily cares I bring to my Father? How has he provided me with what I need to sustain me?

Jesus teaches his disciples to pray, "give *us* each day *our* daily bread" rather than "give *me* each day *my* daily bread." Jesus' disciples are to pray for each other's needs as well as their own. The final petitions in the prayer Jesus teaches are phrased in terms of "us" and "our."

4 **and forgive us our sins**: Jesus realizes that his disciples will commit sins and need forgiveness as much as they need daily bread. They are to ask their Father to **forgive us,** praying for each other's forgiveness as well as their own. They ask forgiveness, **for we ourselves forgive everyone in debt to us**. Someone being **in debt to us** might mean that he or she has harmed us in some way and owes us damages. Jesus' disciples can pray for forgiveness because they **forgive everyone,** with no exceptions, who is in any way in need of their forgiveness. Jesus promised, "Forgive and you will be forgiven" (6:37). Our forgiving others does not earn God's forgiveness but puts us in the position of being able to ask for God's forgiveness. We must be willing to do for others what we ask God to do for us: "Should a man refuse mercy to his fellows, / yet seek pardon for his own sins?" (Sirach 28:4).

For reflection: What are the sins for which I need God's forgiveness? Is there anyone I am refusing to forgive?

Finally, disciples of Jesus are to pray, **do not subject us to the final test**, literally, "do not bring us into temptation." The sense of this petition is, "preserve us from yielding to temptation." The Greek word translated **final test** can mean either temptation (it is translated as "temptation" at 4:13) or trial or test (it is translated as "trial" at 8:13 and as "test" at 22:40, 46). The New American Bible interprets the test to be the **final test**, the difficulties and persecution expected before the end of this age (see 21:10–19; Rev 3:10). However, while the Lord's Prayer has the culmination of God's plans as its ultimate perspective ("your kingdom come"), it is also concerned about daily needs. The final petition can cover the recurring temptations and testing we experience as well as the **final test**. Jesus' disciples are to ask God to spare them and each other from what is beyond their strength to withstand.

For reflection: What do I have in mind when I pray, "lead us not into temptation"?

A Midnight Plea

⁵ **And he said to them, "Suppose one of you has a friend to whom he goes at midnight and says, 'Friend, lend me three loaves of bread, ⁶ for a friend of mine has arrived at my house from a journey and I have nothing to offer him,' ⁷ and he says in reply from within, 'Do not bother me; the door has already been locked and my children and I are already in bed. I cannot get up to give you anything.' ⁸ I tell you, if he does not get up to give him the loaves because of their friendship, he will get up to give him whatever he needs because of his persistence.**

5   One of Jesus' disciples asked him, "Teach us to pray" (11:1). After providing a model prayer (11:2–4), Jesus continues to teach them about prayer. **And he said to them, "Suppose one of you has a friend to whom he goes at midnight."** Jesus is asking for a reaction to an imagined situation. In his scenario, you go a **friend** at **midnight** and say to him, **Friend, lend me three loaves of bread.** Bread was the staple of daily diet, often baked fresh each day. You have run out and want your friend to **lend** you **three loaves** that you will replace the next time you bake.

Diet: See page 253

6   You explain to your friend why your need for bread is so urgent that you wake him in the middle of the night: **for a friend of mine has arrived at my house from a journey and I have nothing to offer him**. Summer travel was sometimes done at night to avoid the heat of the day. Travelers normally lodged with relatives or friends; hospitality was an

almost sacred duty. You have a **friend** who has arrived at your house that night and you **have nothing to offer him** to eat. So you go to another friend who lives nearby to borrow some bread.

7 In Jesus' imagined situation your neighbor **says in reply from within, "Do not bother me; the door has already been locked and my children and I are already in bed."** He lives, as many do, in a one-room house, used mainly for sleeping and shelter from the weather. At night, mats would be unrolled on the floor for the family to sleep on. Since it is midnight, they went to bed some time ago, after having **locked** the door with a bar. Getting up and opening the door would wake the family, so he tells you **Do not bother me** and adds **I cannot get up to give you anything.** Of course, he *can* get up, although it would wake his family; his meaning is, "I won't get up for you; it's not convenient."

Houses: See page 186

Jesus asks his listeners, "Which of you would go to a friend, even in the middle of the night, in need of food to offer hospitality, and be turned away?" The response could only be, "That would be unthinkable!" In a first-century setting, no one—certainly not a friend—would refuse to provide bread: hospitality was obligatory even if inconvenient.

Jesus is conveying a message to his disciples about prayer. If it is unimaginable that a friend would refuse to provide bread for a guest, so

---

BACKGROUND: HOSPITALITY The practice of welcoming guests, including strangers, into one's home for meals and lodging is common in the Old and New Testaments. Abraham provides an example of generous hospitality when he begs three traveling strangers to accept a snack from him but then serves them a banquet (Gen 18:1–8). Abraham's nephew Lot pleads with passing strangers to spend the night in his house rather than sleep in the town square (Gen 19:1–3). Job lists hospitality among his upright deeds: "No stranger lodged in the street, / but I opened my door to wayfarers" (Job 31:32). Those who traveled usually had to rely on the hospitality of others. Caravan inns on main routes provided shelter for travelers and animals (Luke 10:34–35), but there were no inns in ordinary towns and villages. Jesus depended on the hospitality of his followers, including Peter (Mark 1:29–34; 2:1) and Martha and Mary (Luke 10:38–42). Jesus included hospitality among his concerns on judgment day: "I was . . . a stranger and you welcomed me" (Matt 25:35). The practice of hospitality is evident in Acts (Acts 10:21–23; 16:15; 28:7), and the letters of the New Testament hold hospitality in high regard (Rom 12:13; 1 Tim 3:2; 5:10; Titus 1:8; Heb 13:2).

too, it is unimaginable that your Father will refuse to answer your prayer, "Give us each day our daily bread" (11:3).

For reflection: Who is my best friend? Can I count on her or him to help me out in a pinch? Do I accept that God is even more concerned for me?

8   Jesus makes the point explicit by telling how the midnight request would have been fulfilled: **I tell you, if he does not get up to give him the loaves because of their friendship, he will get up to give him whatever he needs because of his persistence.** The neighbor will provide him with not only three loaves of bread but **whatever he needs** to present a decent meal for the traveler. If he is not willing to do so out of **friendship**, as unthinkable as that might be, he will certainly do so **because of his persistence.**

Biblical scholars are divided over who **his** refers to and what the word translated as **persistence** means. Some interpret it as the boldness and insistence of the man coming at midnight to ask for bread. The lesson is then about praying, and is similar to the point of Jesus' parable about the widow and the judge (18:1–8): we can approach God boldly and persistently with our needs.

Other scholars note that the word translated as **persistence** has as its root a word for shame, and they maintain that it applies to the man who was asleep with his family. Even if he will not provide bread out of friendship, he will do so to avoid the shame and dishonor that would befall him when it became known that he had refused to help offer hospitality. Jesus' message would then be, If a friend can be counted on to act honorably, how much more will your Father hear your prayers and give you whatever you need.

For reflection: How do I understand Jesus' words? What lessons do they convey to me about prayer? About my heavenly Father?

The Father's Trustworthiness

⁹ "And I tell you, ask and you will receive; seek and you will find; knock and the door will be opened to you. ¹⁰ For everyone who asks, receives; and the one who seeks, finds; and to the one who

knocks, the door will be opened. ¹¹ What father among you would hand his son a snake when he asks for a fish? ¹² Or hand him a scorpion when he asks for an egg? ¹³ If you then, who are wicked, know how to give good gifts to your children, how much more will the Father in heaven give the holy Spirit to those who ask him?"

Gospel parallels: Matt 7:7–11
OT: Deut 4:29
NT: Luke 11:1–8; 12:22–32; 1 John 5:14–15

9   In teaching his disciples how they should pray (11:1), Jesus uses a friend's willingness to help provide hospitality as a comparison for God's willingness to provide for his disciples' needs (11:5–8). He continues, **And I tell you, ask**: the Greek may have the connotation, And *so* I tell you. Because of God's willingness to answer prayer, the disciples are to **ask**—to turn to God and present their needs. **Ask** is in a tense that conveys, keep on asking. Jesus is exhorting his disciples to **ask** and adds the assurance **you will receive**, literally, it will be given you, implying given you by God. His disciples are to prayerfully **seek**—to keep on seeking. **Seek** can cover seeking whatever one needs; Scripture encourages people specifically to seek God (Deut 4:29; Psalm 105:4; Isaiah 55:6; Jer 29:13–14) and to seek to live under his reign (12:31). Jesus assures his disciples that seeking means **you will find**. They are to **knock**—to keep on knocking—**and the door will be opened to you** by God. The image is of gaining entrance, as to the kingdom of God (13:24–29; 16:16; 18:17, 24–25). Because God is willing to provide for the disciples, they are to continually **ask, seek**, and **knock**, bringing their needs to him in prayer.

> *You shall seek the LORD, your God; and you shall indeed find him when you search after him with your whole heart and your whole soul.*
>
> Deut 4:29

For reflection: How steadfast am I in asking and seeking God? What are my greatest needs?

10 Jesus has already assured his disciples that their prayerful asking, seeking, and knocking will not be in vain, but he repeats his assurances to emphasize God's trustworthiness. **For everyone who asks, receives**: Jesus' promise covers **everyone**. Likewise, **the one who seeks, finds; and to the one who knocks, the door will be opened** by God. Jesus' disciples can have absolute confidence that their prayers will be heard.

> *For reflection: Do I think that Jesus promises too much? How have my prayers been answered?*

11 Jesus compared God to a friend whom one goes to with one's needs (11:5–8); now he compares God to a father, in order to demonstrate why his disciples can have confidence that God will answer their prayers. **What father among you would hand his son a snake when he asks for a fish?** By **a snake** (translated as serpent at 10:19) Jesus means a venomous snake. No **father** among his disciples would give his **son** a deadly serpent when his son is hungry and asks for a **fish**. Whatever their failings as fathers might be, they are not malicious men.

12 **Or** which father among them would **hand him a scorpion when he asks for an egg?** Snakes and scorpions were paired as dangerous hazards (10:19; Deut 8:15). Certainly none of Jesus' disciples would ever be so cruel as to hand a son a stinging **scorpion** when he asks for an **egg** to eat. Unthinkable!

13 **If you then, who are wicked, know how to give good gifts to your children**: the disciples are **wicked** compared with the goodness of God, but they nevertheless **give good gifts,** not deadly snakes and scorpions, to their **children.** Then **how much more will the Father in heaven give the holy Spirit to those who ask him?** If human fathers can be counted on to provide their children with nourishment, how much more can the heavenly **Father** be counted on to provide for his children's needs (see 12:22–32)? If the disciples know how to give **good gifts** to their children, bringing them joy, how much more will their **Father in heaven** give them good gifts? The best gift of all is **the holy Spirit**, whom the Father will send **to those who ask him**. The Holy Spirit descended

upon Jesus after his baptism by John (3:21–22) and led and empowered him (4:1, 14, 18; 10:21); the Father of Jesus will give the same Holy Spirit to Jesus' followers (12:12; 24:49; Acts 1: 4–5, 8; 2:1–4). The Spirit is the Father's ultimate good gift to his children.

The Spirit: See page 100

For reflection: When have I prayed to receive the power and guidance of the Holy Spirit in my life? How was my prayer answered?

Jesus assures his disciples that his Father will give them good things in answer to their asking, seeking, knocking. But what if they ask for the wrong thing, perhaps like a young child asking for a scorpion for a pet? What if they are misguided in their seeking? What if the door they are knocking on is not the door that leads to eternal life (13:24)? Just as loving human fathers and mothers will not give their children anything harmful, so too the heavenly Father gives his children only what is good and nourishing for them. Some prayers may not be answered in the way they were intended but they will nevertheless be answered. We pray to a loving God whom we can address as Abba (see exposition of 11:2), who wills our best interests (see 1 John 5:14–15) and gives only good gifts.

ORIENTATION: *Even as some acclaim Jesus, he begins to meet with mounting opposition (11:14–54).*

Two Kingdoms at War

[14] **He was driving out a demon [that was] mute, and when the demon had gone out, the mute person spoke and the crowds were amazed. [15] Some of them said, "By the power of Beelzebul, the prince of demons, he drives out demons." [16] Others, to test him, asked him for a sign from heaven. [17] But he knew their thoughts and said to them, "Every kingdom divided against itself will be laid waste and house will fall against house. [18] And if Satan is divided against himself, how will his kingdom stand? For you say that it is by Beelzebul that I drive out demons. [19] If I, then, drive out demons by Beelzebul, by whom do your own people drive them out? Therefore they will be your judges. [20] But if it is by the**

finger of God that [I] drive out demons, then the kingdom of God has come upon you. ²¹ When a strong man fully armed guards his palace, his possessions are safe. ²² But when one stronger than he attacks and overcomes him, he takes away the armor on which he relied and distributes the spoils. ²³ Whoever is not with me is against me, and whoever does not gather with me scatters."

Gospel parallels: Matthew 12:22–30; Mark 3:22–27
OT: Exod 8:15
NT: Matt 12:38; 16:1; Mark 8:11; Luke 17:21

14 The scene shifts to a time when Jesus **was driving out a demon [that was] mute**—a demon that caused a person to be mute. **And when the demon had gone out, the mute person spoke.** Luke passes over Jesus' expulsion of the demon rather quickly; he has already recounted instances of Jesus' freeing men and women from the grip of demonic evil (4:33–36, 41; 6:18; 8:2, 26–36; 9:37–43). Luke's interest is in how people react to what Jesus did and in Jesus' responses to their reactions. **The crowds were amazed** at Jesus' display of power over demons, as they have been amazed on previous occasions (4:36; 9:43). Yet amazement can be little more than a puzzled "I wonder how he did that?" Being amazed by Jesus is not the same as having allegiance to him.

Demons, unclean spirits: See page 125
Demons and sickness: See page 377

15 Some in the crowd have a malevolent explanation of Jesus' power to expel demons: **Some of them said, "By the power of Beelzebul, the prince of demons, he drives out demons."** They acknowledge that Jesus exercises authority over demons but attribute his authority to **Beelzebul**, another name for Satan (see verse 18). Satan as **the prince of demons** has authority over demons; if Jesus **drives out demons**, he does so as Satan's agent.

Satan: See page 108

16 **Others** in the crowd have not made up their minds about the source of Jesus' power. It might be from Satan or it might be from God: those seem to be the only sources for power over demons. **To test him,** they **asked him for a sign from heaven**—a sign that would prove that his power

319

comes from God. What kind of sign might satisfy them is uncertain. But if Jesus could not produce a sign that his authority came from God, then by default his authority must come from Satan.

17 **But he knew their thoughts and said to them**: Jesus is aware of what those in the crowd are thinking and saying (see 5:22; 6:8), and he addresses it. He first responds to those who attribute his power to Satan; he will address the demand for a sign in due course (11:29–32). To show the illogic of attributing his power to expel demons to Satan, Jesus begins with a general truth: **Every kingdom divided against itself will be laid waste and house will fall against house.** No **kingdom** relishes a civil war that lays **waste** to its cities. The sense of **house will fall against house** seems to be that in the ravages of war, one building collapses against another.

18 **And if Satan is divided against himself, how will his kingdom stand?** Jesus speaks of those under the sway of Satan as **his kingdom**. It would be illogical for Satan to be **divided against himself**—to work against himself by encouraging a rebellion in his realm. How could **his kingdom stand** if Satan empowered agents to free people from his rule? But that is what Jesus has been doing: he has been releasing people from the power of Satan, removing them from his kingdom. Yet, Jesus tells his critics, **you say that it is by Beelzebul that I drive out demons.** That is absurd; Satan wants to enlarge his kingdom, not depopulate it.

19 Jesus proposes a second reason why his power over demons should not be attributed to Satan. **If I, then, drive out demons by Beelzebul, by whom do your own people drive them out?** Jesus points out that he is not the only one who casts out evil spirits; some of **your own people**—fellow Jews—also **drive them out** (see 9:49; Acts 19:13). Are they also to be accused of being agents of Satan? **Therefore they will be your judges**: they will repudiate any charge you make that their power comes from Satan, and maintain instead that they are relying on the power of God. Jesus' critics have no basis for attributing his power to Satan any more than they have for attributing the power of other exorcists to Satan.

20 **But if it is by the finger of God that [I] drive out demons**: the expression **the finger of God**, is an Old Testament image for the power of God at work (Exod 8:15; see also Psalm 8:4). If Jesus' power does not come from Satan, then it must come from God: no one else has power over evil spirits. And, Jesus tells his accusers, if it is by the power of God that I cast out demons, **then the kingdom of God has come upon you**. Jesus was sent to proclaim the good news of the kingdom of God (4:43; 8:1; 9:11), the news that God was going to vanquish evil and establish his active rule over his creation. Jesus not only proclaims this message but accomplishes it: he is God's agent establishing God's rule. Jesus' mission is "to let the oppressed go free" (4:18), releasing men and women from the grip of evil and enabling them to live under the reign of God. Jesus proclaims that through his exorcisms and healings **the kingdom of God has come upon you** and is in your midst (see 10:9; 17:21). The kingdom of Satan (verse 18) is being replaced by the kingdom of God. The full establishment of God's reign lies in the future (21:25–31), but it is being inaugurated now through Jesus. It is all important that women and men recognize what God is doing through Jesus and embrace it.

Kingdom of God: See page 381

For reflection: How has the kingdom of God come upon me? What are the signs that I am now living under God's rule?

21 Far from being Satan's agent, Jesus is Satan's opponent and will overcome him, freeing those he holds captive. Jesus expresses this by means of a comparison. **When a strong man fully armed guards his palace, his possessions are safe**. By speaking of a **palace**, Jesus may imply that the **strong man** is a prince or king. As long as he has his strength and is **fully armed**, he can guard his palace and **possessions**.

22 **But when one stronger than he attacks and overcomes him, he takes away the armor on which he relied and distributes the spoils.** If someone **stronger**, perhaps another king, **attacks and overcomes him**, the victor will strip him of his **armor** and possessions and give them as **spoils** of war to others. History is full of kings overthrowing kings, to say nothing of warlords jockeying for power. Jesus uses such conflicts as a comparison for what is going on between him and Satan.

Satan is like a strong man guarding his possessions—those possessed by evil spirits. Jesus is the **stronger** one who **attacks and overcomes him**, stripping him of his power and possessions. Jesus **distributes the spoils** in the sense of releasing those whom Satan held captive, so that they can enter into the kingdom of God.

23 In the context of a battle between the kingdom of God and the kingdom of Satan, Jesus proclaims that **whoever is not with me is against me**. There is no safe neutral corner in the front line of a war. Before Joshua laid siege to Jericho, he saw someone holding a sword and asked him, "Are you one of us or of our enemies?" (Joshua 5:13). **Whoever** is not **with** Jesus in his battle against Satan is by default **against** him. Yet in another context Jesus taught his disciples, "whoever is not against you is for you" (9:50). Neither statement is an absolute rule in all circumstances; both find their significance in the context in which Jesus uttered them. In the context of the clash between the kingdom of God and the kingdom of Satan, each person must side with one or the other: there are ultimately no other kingdoms. Jesus adds, **and whoever does not gather with me scatters**. The image is of a shepherd gathering sheep; sheep without a shepherd scatter. The Old Testament uses shepherding imagery for God gathering his people to himself (Isaiah 40:11; Ezek 34:11–16). Ultimately one is either gathered to Jesus and brought into the kingdom of God, or cast out and scattered (see 13:28).

> For reflection: Where does my ultimate allegiance lie? What am I doing to be among those Jesus gathers to himself?

The Return of an Unclean Spirit
²⁴ **"When an unclean spirit goes out of someone, it roams through arid regions searching for rest but, finding none, it says, 'I shall return to my home from which I came.' ²⁵ But upon returning, it finds it swept clean and put in order. ²⁶ Then it goes and brings back seven other spirits more wicked than itself who move in and dwell there, and the last condition of that person is worse than the first."**

Gospel parallels: Matt 12:43–45
NT: Luke 11:14–23

24 Jesus has just taught that in his battle against Satan, "Whoever is not with me is against me" (11:23). He goes on to illustrate why there is no neutrality in this conflict. **When an unclean spirit goes out of someone**: since demons do not leave their victims willingly (see 8:26-33; 9:38-40), this **unclean spirit** was apparently driven **out of someone** by an exorcism, such as Jesus performed only a short while ago (11:14). After an unclean spirit is exorcized, **it roams through arid regions searching for rest.** Wilderness **regions** were considered the haunt of demons (Tobit 8:3; Isaiah 13:21; 34:11, 14). The homeless unclean spirit is **searching for** a place of **rest. But, finding none, it says, "I shall return to my home from which I came."** The spirit speaks of the person it once possessed as **my home from which I came,** literally, came out.

Demons, unclean spirits: See page 125

25 **But upon returning, it finds it swept clean and put in order**, like a house that has been refurbished after an undesirable tenant had been evicted. It has been prepared for a new occupant, but none has moved in yet.

26 **Then it goes and brings back seven other spirits.** Perhaps the unclean spirit thought that there would be safety in numbers, making it more difficult for them to be evicted. We can recall that Jesus freed Mary Magdalene of seven demons (8:2.) The other spirits that the first spirit brings back are **more wicked than itself**—even more undesirable as tenants. They **move in and dwell there**, settling down, **and the last condition of that person is worse than the first** (see 2 Pet 2:20). Instead of hosting just one evil spirit, the person is victimized by an additional seven.

Unguarded empty houses do not stay empty forever; if they are not rented to good tenants, squatters will take them over. So too, those who have been delivered of evil spirits cannot remain spiritually empty. If the void within them is not filled by the Holy Spirit (see 11:13), then evil spirits can return. One is ultimately part of the kingdom of God or the kingdom of Satan (11:18-20); one is either with Jesus or against him, either gathering with him or scattering (11:23).

For reflection: What lesson do I find in these words of Jesus?

True Blessedness
²⁷ While he was speaking, a woman from the crowd called out and said to him, "Blessed is the womb that carried you and the breasts at which you nursed." ²⁸ He replied, "Rather, blessed are those who hear the word of God and observe it."

NT: Luke 1:26–55; 2:19, 51; 5:1; 6:47–48; 8:11, 15, 21

27 **While he was speaking**, responding to those who accused him of driving out demons by the power of Satan (11:14–26), he is interrupted by **a woman from the crowd** who **called out and said to him, "Blessed is the womb that carried you and the breasts at which you nursed."** Speaking of **womb** and **breasts** is a poetic way of referring to a woman (see 23:29). A woman proclaims the mother of Jesus to be **blessed** and fortunate, pronouncing a beatitude on her. In the culture of the time, a mother was honored for the accomplishments of her sons. The **woman from the crowd** is full of admiration for Jesus. To praise him, she extols his mother, telling Jesus that his mother is blessed to have him as her son: "How fortunate to be the mother of such a great son!" Her positive response to Jesus contrasts with those who think he is an agent of Satan (11:15) or who demand a sign from heaven to authenticate him (11:16). She echoes Elizabeth's proclamations of Mary's blessedness: "Most blessed are you among women, and blessed is the fruit of your womb" (1:42). The woman in the crowd fulfills Mary's prophecy, "From now on will all ages call me blessed" (1:48).

Beatitudes: See page 169

28 **He replied, "Rather, blessed are those who hear the word of God and observe it."** Jesus responds to the woman's beatitude with a beatitude of his own. The Greek word translated **rather** has various nuances. Here it is best taken as having the connotation that the woman's praise of his mother is correct as far as it goes, but that more needs to be said. Jesus' mother is blessed and fortunate to be his mother, but even more **blessed are those who hear the word of God and observe it**. The Greek words for **hear** and **observe** are in a tense that conveys ongoing action: blessed are those who continue to hear God's word and continue to observe it. Jesus proclaims **the word of God** (see 5:1), and he teaches the importance of not only hearing it but acting on it (6:47–49; 8:11, 15). **Blessed are**

those: Jesus' beatitude applies to all **those** of all time who hear and obey, but it also has particular application to Mary. She responded to the word that God sent her through Gabriel and said to him, "I am the handmaid of the Lord. May it be done to me according to your word" (1:38). She pondered in her heart what God was doing in sending Jesus as her son (2:19, 51). Jesus said, "My mother and my brothers are those who hear the word of God and act on it" (8:21). Mary is blessed not simply because she is the mother of Jesus but because she is preeminent among **those who hear the word of God and observe it.**

For reflection: What do Jesus' words tell me about his mother, Mary? What do his words invite me to do in order to be among the blessed?

Jesus' Response to the Demand for a Sign

²⁹ **While still more people gathered in the crowd, he said to them, "This generation is an evil generation; it seeks a sign, but no sign will be given it, except the sign of Jonah. ³⁰ Just as Jonah became a sign to the Ninevites, so will the Son of Man be to this generation. ³¹ At the judgment the queen of the south will rise with the men of this generation and she will condemn them, because she came from the ends of the earth to hear the wisdom of Solomon, and there is something greater than Solomon here. ³² At the judgment the men of Nineveh will arise with this generation and condemn it, because at the preaching of Jonah they repented, and there is something greater than Jonah here."**

Gospel parallels: Matt 12:38–42
OT: 1 Kings 10:1–13; Jonah 3:1–10
NT: Mark 8:11–12; Luke 7:31–35; 10:13–16; 11:16

29 **While still more people gathered in the crowd** that witnessed Jesus driving out a demon (11:14), **he said to them, "This generation is an evil generation."** The expression **this generation** can simply refer to those who are alive at the time of Jesus (see 21:32), but it often has the connotation of those who respond negatively to him (see 7:31-34; 17:25), as is the case here. This generation is **an evil generation** because **it seeks a sign.** After seeing Jesus free a man from a demon, some, "to test

him, asked him for a sign from heaven" (11:16) to prove that he expelled demons by the power of God. It should be evident that Jesus is on God's side, if he frees men and women from the grip of evil. It should also be evident that God has endowed Jesus with power, if he is overcoming the forces of Satan and healing afflictions. To demand anything more to authenticate Jesus reveals a hostile skepticism, a refusal to believe. Jesus calls these hostile skeptics **an evil generation** and says that **no sign will be given it, except the sign of Jonah**. Jesus goes on to speak of **Jonah** as a **sign**.

30 **Just as Jonah became a sign to the Ninevites**: God sent **Jonah** to the city of Nineveh, the capital of the Assyrian empire (see 2 Kings 19:36). Jonah wanted to have nothing to do with **the Ninevites**, since Assyrians had destroyed the northern kingdom of Israel (2 Kings 15:29), but in the end he proclaimed God's message to them: "Forty days more and Nineveh shall be destroyed" (Jonah 3:4). After the Ninevites repented in sack-cloth and ashes, God spared them (Jonah 3:5–10). The "sign of Jonah" (verse 29) is best interpreted as Jonah's proclaiming God's judgment on the people of Nineveh. Just as Jonah became a sign to the Ninevites, **so will the Son of Man be to this generation**: Jesus, **the Son of Man**, proclaims God's judgment on those who reject him.

Son of Man: See page 147

31 Jesus provides two comparisons that make it clear what judgment awaits those who reject him. **At the judgment** that will come at the end of this age, **the queen of the south will rise with the men of this generation.** The **queen of the south** is the queen of Sheba (1 Kings 10:1), who ruled a region in southern Arabia, today's Yemen. Like all who die, she **will rise** to face judgment along **with the men of this generation.** And **she will condemn them**, those who reject Jesus, **because she came from the ends of the earth to hear the wisdom of Solomon, and there is something greater than Solomon here.** The expression **the ends of the earth** means regions lying a great distance away (see Psalm 2:8; 22:28; 46:10). She came to Jerusalem **to hear the wisdom of Solomon** (1 Kings 10:1) and was left "breathless" by his "great wisdom" (1 Kings 10:4–5). Yet **there is something greater than Solomon here**: although God gave Solomon wisdom (1 Kings

3:12), God gave even more to Jesus, handing over all things to him so that he could make God known (10:22) and inaugurate God's kingdom (11:20). The queen of the south will reproach and **condemn** those who refuse to perceive the **greater** things Jesus is doing right there in their midst, while she had traveled **from the ends of the earth** just to hear Solomon.

32 **At the judgment the men of Nineveh will arise with this generation and condemn it, because at the preaching of Jonah they repented, and there is something greater than Jonah here.** God sent **Jonah** as his spokesman, but Jesus accomplishes **something greater than Jonah**. By his preaching, exorcisms, and healings, Jesus is establishing the kingdom of God (11:20). The people of **Nineveh** took Jonah seriously and changed their lives in response to his message; **this generation,** however, rejects Jesus, dismissing him as "a glutton and a drunkard" (7:34). They will be condemned by the people of Nineveh **at the judgment**: the Ninevites responded to Jonah, but some of Jesus' contemporaries reject the **greater** work of God carried out by Jesus.

Jesus issued a similar warning to the people of Chorazin, Bethsaida, and Capernaum, comparing them unfavorably to the pagan cities of Tyre and Sidon (10:13–16).

BACKGROUND: JUDGMENT For much of the Old Testament era, Israelites did not expect a meaningful life after death but only a shadowy existence in the netherworld for good and bad alike. As expectations arose that there would be life after death, there also arose the expectation that God would judge individuals after death, rewarding those who had led good lives and punishing those who had done evil. God's judgment is implicit in the book of Daniel, written about 164 B.C.: "Many of those who sleep / in the dust of the earth shall awake; / Some shall live forever, / others shall be an everlasting horror and disgrace" (Dan 12:2). The book of Judith, written after Daniel, speaks of judgment: "The LORD Almighty will requite them; / in the day of judgment he will punish them: / He will send fire and worms into their flesh, / and they shall burn and suffer forever" (Judith 16:17). In some nonbiblical writings of the era, God's judgment marks the transition between this age and the age to come. Some of these writings portray Gehenna as the place of fiery punishment. *Related topics: The age to come (page 487), Gehenna (page 343), Life after death (page 298), Nonbiblical writings (page 342), Resurrection (page 401).*

Jesus again invokes pagans—the queen of the south and the Ninevites—as comparisons for judging the conduct of **this generation.** Jesus' words are meant to wake them up to the consequences of their behavior so that they will change it, just as the Ninevites repented and escaped God's punishment.

For reflection: How has Jesus tried to wake me up to the consequences of my destructive patterns of behavior? How have I responded to him?

Be Enlightened

³³ **"No one who lights a lamp hides it away or places it [under a bushel basket], but on a lampstand so that those who enter might see the light. ³⁴ The lamp of the body is your eye. When your eye is sound, then your whole body is filled with light, but when it is bad, then your body is in darkness. ³⁵ Take care, then, that the light in you not become darkness. ³⁶ If your whole body is full of light, and no part of it is in darkness, then it will be as full of light as a lamp illuminating you with its brightness."**

Gospel parallels: Matt 5:15; 6:22–23
NT: Luke 2:32; 8:16; 11:29–32

33 Jesus has warned that some—"this generation"—will be condemned at the judgment because they do not perceive what God is doing through him (11:29–32). Now Jesus addresses the cause of their blindness. He begins with an observation he invoked on another occasion: **No one who lights a lamp hides it away or places it [under a bushel basket], but on a lampstand so that those who enter might see the light** (see 8:16). A **lamp** was a small pottery container filled with olive oil; a wick dipped in the oil burned with a candle-like flame. Lamps are lit to provide light; no one would light a lamp and then hide it away or put it under a basket, shrouding its light. A lamp is instead placed **on a lampstand so that those who enter** the room **might see** and be guided by **the light**. Jesus previously used this observation about lamps to make the point that his disciples should let their light shine by proclaiming his message to others (see 8:16–17). Here, however, Jesus uses the observation to make a different point. Jesus is comparing himself and the revelation

328

he brings to a lamp on a lampstand; he is "a light for revelation" (2:32) for all to see. There is nothing hidden about what Jesus has been doing; he has proclaimed his message to crowd after crowd (5:3, 15; 6:17–18; 7:9, 24; 9:11; 11:29).

34 If Jesus is a light shining for all to see, why has "this generation" not perceived him correctly? He offers an explanation, playing on the idea of a lamp: **The lamp of the body is your eye.** Comparing an **eye** to a **lamp** would have made more sense to Jesus' audience than it might to us. Some ancient peoples, including Jews, thought of eyes as having a light or fire within them; eyes were not only like windows that let in light but also like lamps that gave light. Eyes could even be imagined to be like "fiery torches" (Dan 10:6) or a "fiery flame" (Rev 1:14; 2:18; 19:12). In this understanding of how an eye worked, **when your eye is sound**—when it is healthy—**then your whole body is filled with light**: the eye is like a light shining into one's body, filling it with light. **But when it is bad, then your body is in darkness.** A **bad** or unhealthy eye provides no light for the body, leaving it in **darkness**. We would think of an unhealthy eye as not letting in light, but in either understanding of eyesight the point is the same: a bad eye leaves one in darkness.

Jesus is implicitly communicating that "this generation"—those who reject him or demand signs—do not perceive who he is and what he is accomplishing because their eyes are **bad**. In a medical sense, the word **bad** means unhealthy. But in a moral sense, the word translated as **bad** means "evil"; it is the word used Jesus used when he said that "This generation is an evil generation" (11:29). Jesus is like a lamp on a lampstand, shining for all to see. If any do not perceive and accept him, it is because their willful blindness leaves them in **darkness**.

35 Jesus is less interested in condemning those who reject him than in opening their eyes. He exhorts them, **Take care**—more literally, see to it—**then, that the light in you not become darkness.** The sense of Jesus' words seems to be, safeguard the vision you have lest you be left in darkness. Open your eyes to what I am doing; recognize that "if it is by the finger of God that [I] drive out demons, then the kingdom of God has come upon you" (11:20).

For reflection: How intent am I on perceiving the full significance of Jesus? What might I do to open my eyes more fully to him?

36 Jesus concludes with words of encouragement, continuing to use lamp and light imagery: **If your whole body is full of light, and no part of it is in darkness, then it will be as full of light as a lamp illuminating you with its brightness.** Jesus' words are somewhat cryptic. I suggest that their sense is: If you allow the light I shine forth to enlighten you, then I will be for you **a lamp illuminating you with its brightness**; you will not be left **in darkness** but will be **full of light**. Jesus reveals his Father (10:22) and makes known "the mysteries of the kingdom of God" (8:10). Blessed are those who hear and embrace the word of God that he proclaims (11:28); they will be **full of light**—enlightened by God's revelation through Jesus.

For reflection: How have I been enlightened by Jesus' teachings? How has he opened my eyes to who God is?

Woe to You Pharisees!

37 After he had spoken, a Pharisee invited him to dine at his home. He entered and reclined at table to eat. 38 The Pharisee was amazed to see that he did not observe the prescribed washing before the meal. 39 The Lord said to him, "Oh you Pharisees! Although you cleanse the outside of the cup and the dish, inside you are filled with plunder and evil. 40 You fools! Did not the maker of the outside also make the inside? 41 But as to what is within, give alms, and behold, everything will be clean for you. 42 Woe to you Pharisees! You pay tithes of mint and of rue and of every garden herb, but you pay no attention to judgment and to love for God. These you should have done, without overlooking the others. 43 Woe to you Pharisees! You love the seat of honor in synagogues and greetings in marketplaces. 44 Woe to you! You are like unseen graves over which people unknowingly walk."

Gospel parallels: Matt 23:6–7, 23–28
OT: Tobit 12:9; Sirach 3:29
NT: Mark 7:3–4; 12:38–40; Luke 20:46

37 **After he had spoken, a Pharisee invited him to dine at his home.**
Possibly the Pharisee had been in the crowd that Jesus spoke to about the
judgment awaiting "this generation" (11:29–36). Inviting Jesus to **dine at
his home** indicates some degree of openness to Jesus: shared meals express
fellowship. Some Pharisees have been critical of Jesus (5:17–21, 30; 6:2,
7; 7:39), but Jesus nonetheless dines with Pharisees (7:36; 14:1), just as he
dines with tax collectors and sinners (5:28–30): Jesus does not turn down
anyone's invitation. **He entered and reclined at table to eat.** That Jesus
reclined to eat indicates that it was a formal meal or banquet. There are
others present at the meal along with Jesus and the Pharisee (11:45)

Pharisees: See page 143
Banquets: See page 386

38 **The Pharisee was amazed to see that he did not observe the prescribed washing** of hands **before the meal**. Nowhere does the law of
Moses require that Jews must ritually wash their hands before eating.
Pharisees, who were very concerned about maintaining ritual purity, had
adopted the practice in imitation of priests washing their hands before
offering sacrifices (Exod 30:17–21; see Mark 7:3–4). While the **Pharisee**
had ritually purified his hands in preparation for the meal, Jesus had
come into his house and reclined at table without doing so. This **amazed**
the Pharisee: even if Jesus normally did not ritually wash his hands before
eating, as a respectful guest he might be expected to observe the practices
customary in the host's house.

39 Jesus is aware of his amazement and uses it as an occasion to address the
relative unimportance of ritual washings. **The Lord said to him, "Oh
you Pharisees! Although you cleanse the outside of the cup and the
dish, inside you are filled with plunder and evil."** Luke sometimes
refers to Jesus as **the Lord** (7:13; 10:1). Jesus shifts from washing hands to
washing a **cup** or **dish**, and uses the image of washing only the **outside** of
a cup or dish as a comparison for washing oneself externally while being
interiorly **filled with plunder and evil**. The word translated **plunder**
means what has been stolen, but it can also mean greed, which is its sense
here. It makes no sense to wash the outside of a cup or dish and leave
the inside filthy, since the inside comes in contact with what one drinks

and eats. So too, ritual washing is pointless if one is filled with greed and wickedness. Filth in the heart is far more serious than filth on fingers.

Lord: See page 137

40 Jesus says **You fools!** to those who are preoccupied with externals and ignore their inner condition. The Psalms and the wisdom books of the Old Testament use the word **fools** for senseless people who spurn wisdom and do not comprehend God's ways (Psalm 92:7; 94:8; Prov 1:7, 30; 17:24). **Did not the maker of the outside also make the inside?** A potter in forming a cup or dish creates its **inside** as well as its **outside**. God is the **maker** of men and women, forming them as a potter forms vessels: "We are the clay and you the potter: / we are all the work of your hands" (Isaiah 64:7). Just as a potter is concerned for the inside of vessels as well as their exterior, so God is concerned for the inner condition of the women and men he created. Those who are full of greed and evil but think that God is placated by their ritual washings are **fools**.

41 Just as hands can be cleansed, so can hearts. **But as to what is within, give alms, and behold, everything will be clean for you.** Giving **alms**—giving money to the poor—is the antidote for the greed and wickedness that is **within** a person. Giving to others is the opposite of plundering; generosity is the opposite of greed. The Old Testament teaches that "almsgiving saves one from death and expiates every sin" (Tobit 12:9) and that "alms atone for sins" (Sirach 3:29). Jesus proclaims that **everything will be clean** for those who help the poor: giving alms cleanses inner

---

BACKGROUND: ALMS is money given to help those in need. A clue to the meaning of "alms" is found in the Greek word used in the Gospels for "alms," for it is derived from the verb that means to show mercy (the English word "alms" is derived from the same Greek word). There is no mention of giving alms in the early Old Testament era, because money had not yet been invented. In a farming economy, mercy could be exercised by feeding the hungry with what one raised or letting the poor glean crops from one's fields (Lev 19:9–10; Deut 15:11). As coins came into use, the hungry could be also helped by giving them money to buy food and to meet their other needs. Almsgiving—the showing of mercy by giving money—is praised in the books of Tobit (Tobit 4:7–11, 16; 12:8–9) and Sirach (Sirach 3:29; 7:10), among the last books of the Old Testament to be written.

---

defilement and accomplishes what ritual washings cannot. Jesus invites the Pharisee to **give alms** so that **everything will be clean for you**.

For reflection: How high a value do I place on helping the poor? How might I become more generous in giving alms?

42 Jesus judges that Pharisees are in a woeful state because of misplaced priorities: **Woe to you Pharisees!** A **woe** laments someone's unfortunate condition and reproaches them for it. **You pay tithes of mint and of rue and of every garden herb.** The law of Moses required farmers to give **tithes**—ten percent—of their harvests for the support of Levites and priests: "Each year you shall tithe all the produce that grows in the field you have sown" (Deut 14:22; see also Num 18:21–32). Pharisees applied this law even to **mint** and **rue** and **every garden herb** grown as a seasoning. We might compare it to someone today filing a tax return that included as income a dollar found on the street. Although Pharisees are meticulous in tithing garden herbs, Jesus tells them that **you pay no attention to judgment and to love for God**. The word translated as **judgment** has the sense here of justice (it is translated as "justice" at Acts 8:33). Having **love for God** and treating others justly corresponds to the commandment to love God wholeheartedly and one's neighbor as oneself (10:27)—the fundamental requirement for inheriting eternal life (10:25, 28). Jesus tells the Pharisees that they are in a woeful condition because, although they are scrupulous about minor matters, they **pay no attention** to the most important things that God requires. **These you should have done**—acting justly toward others and loving God—**without overlooking the others**. Jesus does not tell them not to tithe herbs; he does tell them that there are far more important matters they should be concerned about.

Woes: See page 171

For reflection: In light of my call to love God and act justly, does my use of my time and money indicate any misplaced priorities in my life?

43 **Woe to you Pharisees! You love the seat of honor in synagogues and greetings in marketplaces.** The **seat of honor** is literally the first seat, at the front of a synagogue. **Synagogues** and **marketplaces** were places where people gathered. The **greetings** Jesus speaks about were not

casual hellos but respects paid to people of high status; Pharisees enjoyed being honored for their strict observance of the law. Jesus tells Pharisees that they **love** to be the center of attention and be shown deference: they are driven by self-love instead of love of God (verse 42). They are therefore in a woeful condition, even if they do not realize it.

Synagogue: See page 115

44 Others may be ignorant of their woeful condition and be misled by them. **Woe to you! You are like unseen graves over which people unknowingly walk.** Contact with a grave rendered one ritually unclean: anyone "who touches a human bone or a grave . . . shall be unclean for seven days" (Num 19:16). Jews therefore marked graves, sometimes whitewashing them (see Matt 23:27), lest anyone **unknowingly walk** on them and become unclean. Because Pharisees appear to be very law-observant, others can mistake them for holy men and try to imitate them. Yet they are "filled with plunder and evil" (verse 39), which makes imitating them dangerous. They are like the hazard posed by unmarked **graves** that can contaminate without the person being aware of it.

Jesus' words to his Pharisee host are harsh, but they should be understood in light of the strong denunciations spoken by Old Testament prophets. Isaiah called the leaders of Jerusalem "princes of Sodom" and its citizens "people of Gomorrah" (Isaiah 1:10) to wake them up to the perilous condition they were in. Amos addressed the upper-class women of Samaria as "you cows" (Amos 4:1) to shake them out of their complacent self-centeredness. So too, Jesus compares Pharisees who are concerned about ritual cleanness to graves, the ultimate in unclean places. He accuses them of being scrupulous about tithing herbs while ignoring justice and love of God; he calls them fools for focusing on hand washing while harboring greed and wickedness. He came to save the lost (19:10), even those who are lost in their own religious observances. He speaks bluntly so that his words might get through to those who have become spiritually hard of hearing. His hope is that those whom he addresses will "hear the word of God and observe it" (11:28), so that "everything will be clean" for them (verse 41).

For reflection: What message do Jesus' words to his Pharisee host have for me? How are the failings of the Pharisees reflected in my own life?

Woe to You Scholars of the Law!

⁴⁵ **Then one of the scholars of the law said to him in reply, "Teacher, by saying this you are insulting us too." ⁴⁶ And he said, "Woe also to you scholars of the law! You impose on people burdens hard to carry, but you yourselves do not lift one finger to touch them. ⁴⁷ Woe to you! You build the memorials of the prophets whom your ancestors killed. ⁴⁸ Consequently, you bear witness and give consent to the deeds of your ancestors, for they killed them and you do the building. ⁴⁹ Therefore, the wisdom of God said, 'I will send to them prophets and apostles; some of them they will kill and persecute' ⁵⁰ in order that this generation might be charged with the blood of all the prophets shed since the foundation of the world, ⁵¹ from the blood of Abel to the blood of Zechariah who died between the altar and the temple building. Yes, I tell you, this generation will be charged with their blood! ⁵² Woe to you, scholars of the law! You have taken away the key of knowledge. You yourselves did not enter and you stopped those trying to enter." ⁵³ When he left, the scribes and Pharisees began to act with hostility toward him and to interrogate him about many things, ⁵⁴ for they were plotting to catch him at something he might say.**

Gospel parallels: Matt 23:4, 13, 29–36
OT: Gen 4:8–10; 2 Chron 24:20–21
NT: Luke 6:7, 11; 11:37–44

45 **Then one of the scholars of the law** present at the meal in the Pharisee's house (11:37) **said to him in reply, "Teacher, by saying this you are insulting us too."** Luke sometimes refers to scribes (see verse 53) as **scholars of the law**. Pharisees relied on **scholars** as their legal experts, trained in interpreting and applying the **law** of Moses. This scholar respectfully addresses Jesus as **Teacher** but finds his words about the practices of the Pharisees (11:39–44) to be **insulting** to **us too**. By criticizing Pharisees, Jesus is insulting the **scholars of the law** who guide Pharisees in their practices.

Scribes: See page 146

46 Jesus makes no apologies for his blunt words. Rather, he now includes scholars of the law in his laments over those who are in a woeful condition. **And he said, "Woe also to you scholars of the law! You impose**

335

on people burdens hard to carry." In order to apply the law of Moses to everyday situations, **scholars of the law** developed detailed interpretations, for example, about what kinds of activities qualified as work forbidden on the Sabbath (see 6:1–2). In later times these interpretations and applications would be spoken of as a "fence around the law"—regulations, which if kept, ensured that one did not come even close to breaking the law. These regulations they tried to **impose on people**, virtually equating the regulations with the law itself. As regulations multiplied, they became **burdens hard to carry**: ordinary people found it difficult to abide by all the imposed restrictions and obligations. Jesus accuses the scholars of the law of having no sympathy for those whom they have burdened: **you yourselves do not lift one finger to touch them**—you do not lift a finger to help them carry the burdens you have imposed upon them.

Woes: See page 171

For reflection: When have I placed obligations on others without helping them carry out the obligations?

47 **Woe to you! You build the memorials of the prophets whom your ancestors killed.** Jesus does not explicitly address this **woe** to scholars of the law, for Jews in general built **memorials**—commemorative tombs—as a way of venerating **prophets** or other great figures (see 1 Macc 13:27–30; Acts 2:29). **Prophets** often got a poor reception from the **ancestors** of Jews (Jer 7:25–27), even to the point of being **killed** (1 Kings 19:10; 2 Chron 24:19–21; Neh 9:26; Jer 2:30; 26:20–24; Acts 7:52).

48 Jesus turns the logic of building memorial tombs on its head. Rather than being a sign of veneration, it is evidence of complicity in the murder of prophets: **Consequently, you bear witness and give consent to the deeds of your ancestors, for they killed them and you do the building.** Jesus accuses them of being in solidarity with their ancestors and having in effect the stance, "You kill them, we bury them."

49 Jesus proclaims how God will deal with them: **Therefore, the wisdom of God said, "I will send to them prophets and apostles."** Here **the wisdom of God** is best understood as meaning God in his wisdom. God will send **prophets** and **apostles** as his envoys and messengers, even though

he knows that **some of them they will kill and persecute,** continuing a long history of God's messengers being persecuted and killed.

50 God sends envoys who will be rejected and killed **in order that this generation might be charged with the blood of all the prophets shed since the foundation,** or beginning, **of the world**. By killing those whom God sends, **this generation** demonstrates that they are no different from their ancestors (verse 47). And since they are no different, they can be **charged** with responsibility for earlier shedding of **blood**: they take the guilt of their ancestors upon themselves by continuing the bloodshed. It is as if, by joining a criminal gang, one assumes responsibility for the crimes the gang committed in the past.

51 The blood shed from the foundation of the world runs **from the blood of Abel to the blood of Zechariah who died between the altar and the temple building**. The first murder recorded in the first book of the Bible is Cain's slaying of **Abel** (Gen 4:8–10). In the Jewish ordering of their Scriptures, 2 Chronicles is the final book. The last murder recorded in 2 Chronicles is that of a **Zechariah**, who was stoned to death in a courtyard of the Temple (2 Chron 24:20–21), here specified as **between the altar and the temple building**. Abel and Zechariah symbolize all those who were murdered in the Old Testament era. Jesus assures his listeners, **Yes, I tell you, this generation will be charged with their blood**: because **this generation** has blood on its hands, it will share the guilt of all who have shed blood.

Temple: See page 519

Certainly not all who were alive at the time of Jesus took part in slaying prophets and apostles. **This generation** has the connotation of those who reject Jesus (see 11:29–32). Jesus knows that he will "suffer greatly and be rejected by the elders, the chief priests, and the scribes, and be killed" (9:22). He will not be the only one who is killed; Acts will recount the deaths of Stephen (Acts 7:58–60) and James the brother of John (Acts 12:2). Jesus' words about those of his time joining with their ancestors in the killing of God's envoys will be born out. God in his justice does not allow murder and the shedding of blood to go unpunished (see Gen 4:10–11; 9:5–6; Num 35:16–34). Jesus' words of warning to those who harbor murderous thoughts are an invitation to repentance. At least one Pharisee with blood on his hands will change course: Saul of Tarsus (see Acts 7:58—8:1; 22:4, 20; 26:10).

52 **Woe to you, scholars of the law! You have taken away the key of knowledge.** The **key of knowledge** means the key that gives access to knowledge, unlocking its secrets. The knowledge in question is knowledge of the **law** of God, which reveals how God's people are to behave and relate to him. The role of **scholars of the law** is to explain God's law and help people to live by it. But, Jesus tells them, **"You yourselves did not enter and you stopped those trying to enter."** You have not entered into a proper understanding of God and God's law, and your teachings have therefore been an obstacle to others who are trying to enter into such understanding. You have burdened people with your interpretations of the law (verse 46); you are a hindrance instead of a help. Just as Jesus compared Pharisees who are concerned about ritual cleanness to graves, the ultimate in unclean places (11:44), so he tells scholars whose role is to help people live by God's law that they are preventing people from living by it. There could be no worse charge that Jesus could level against them in their profession.

> For reflection: By my words and actions, do I make it easier or more difficult for those I encounter to know God's love for them?

53 **When he left** the Pharisee's house (see verse 37), **the scribes and Pharisees began to act with hostility toward him,** apparently following him out so that they could continue to protest what he said. By his blunt words Jesus has aroused their **hostility,** and they **interrogate him about many things:** they question him as a hostile lawyer might badger a witness in a courtroom,

54 **for they were plotting to catch him at something he might say.** They want to use his words to entrap him; they hope to **catch** him saying **something** that can be used against him. Luke earlier recounted how scribes and Pharisees became enraged at Jesus and discussed what they might do about him (6:7, 11). Now Jesus' words about them (11:39–52) have made them all the more determined in their opposition to him.

Jesus must have realized that his words would arouse their hostility but judged that he must say them nonetheless, lest his silence make him complicit with their woeful condition.

For reflection: When has Jesus spoken words to me that I did not want to hear? How did I respond?

CHAPTER 12

Do Not Be Afraid, My Friends

¹ Meanwhile, so many people were crowding together that they were trampling one another underfoot. He began to speak, first to his disciples, "Beware of the leaven—that is, the hypocrisy—of the Pharisees.

² "There is nothing concealed that will not be revealed, nor secret that will not be known. ³ Therefore whatever you have said in the darkness will be heard in the light, and what you have whispered behind closed doors will be proclaimed on the housetops. ⁴ I tell you, my friends, do not be afraid of those who kill the body but after that can do no more. ⁵ I shall show you whom to fear. Be afraid of the one who after killing has the power to cast into Gehenna; yes, I tell you, be afraid of that one. ⁶ Are not five sparrows sold for two small coins? Yet not one of them has escaped the notice of God. ⁷ Even the hairs of your head have all been counted. Do not be afraid. You are worth more than many sparrows."

Gospel parallels: Matt 10:26–31; 16:6
OT: Prov 1:7
NT: Luke 8:17; 11:37–54; John 15:13–15

1 **Meanwhile,** after Jesus left the house of the Pharisee (11:37, 53), **so many people were crowding together that they were trampling one another underfoot.** Jesus attracts crowds (4:42; 5:1, 15; 6:17–18; 8:4, 40; 9:11, 37; 11:29); this one is so huge that people are **trampling one another underfoot** to be near Jesus. **He began to speak, first to his disciples**: Jesus instructs his **disciples** in the hearing of the crowd, as he has done previously (see 6:19–20; 7:1). His teaching is meant **first** of all for the disciples but also bears a message for the others. He tells them, **Beware of the leaven—that is, the hypocrisy—of the Pharisees**. At the time of Jesus, **leaven** was a bit of leavened dough left unbaked from a previous batch of bread and used to leaven a new batch (see 13:21). **Leaven** permeates and transforms, and can therefore represent a pervading influence. Jesus warns his disciples and all who are listening to be on their guard against being influenced by the **hypocrisy** of the

Pharisees. **Hypocrisy** is a disconnect between appearance and reality. Jesus lamented the woeful condition of those Pharisees who appear to be scrupulous about observing God's law but are filled with greed and evil (11:39) and ignore justice and love (11:42). Jesus' disciples are to **beware** lest they indulge in the same hypocrisy, hiding serious failings behind a pious exterior.

Disciple: See page 149
Pharisees: See page 143

For reflection: Where are the disconnects in my life between who I appear to be and who I really am? What should I do about them?

2   Jesus invokes a saying that he used on another occasion (8:17): **There is nothing concealed that will not be revealed, nor secret that will not be known.** The significance of this saying depends on the context in which it is used. In light of Jesus' warning about hypocrisy (verse 1), the saying indicates that hypocrisy is futile because one's inner condition will be shown to be what it is. The implication of **revealed** and **made known** is that what is secret will be revealed and made known by God. Jesus has God's judgment in mind, as will shortly be clear (verse 5).

3   Jesus makes an application of the saying to his disciples: **Therefore whatever you have said in the darkness will be heard in the light.** The image of saying something **in the darkness** conveys saying it secretly; words said in secret will be brought to **light**. Jesus repeats his message for emphasis, clothing it in different imagery: **and what you have whispered behind closed doors will be proclaimed on the housetops.** The word translated **behind closed doors** means in the innermost rooms, places where one might whisper in another's ear and think it will not be overheard. Such whisperings **will be proclaimed on the housetops**: houses usually had flat roofs, accessible by an exterior staircase or ladder, that made fine platforms for shouting out announcements. There are no secrets from God, no innermost rooms where he is not present. At God's judgment, what the disciples have said in private will be as if shouted from the housetops, and they will be judged for their words. Any hypocrisy (verse 1) will be unmasked by God. Jesus next addresses what their attitude should be to God's judgment.

4 **I tell you, my friends**: Jesus looks upon his disciples as **my friends**. The Greek word Luke uses for **friends** has the same root as a word for love and could be translated "beloved ones." By calling his disciples **my friends,** Jesus manifests his love for them.

For reflection: What does it mean for me that Jesus calls me his friend?

Jesus tells his friends, **do not be afraid of those who kill the body but after that can do no more.** Jesus knows that his disciples will face legal proceedings (see 12:11); some will be persecuted and killed (see 11:49). Yet Jesus tells them, **do not be afraid**. They are to have no fear of those who can **kill the body** but can do nothing **more**. Death puts one beyond the reach of what humans can do.

5 Jesus' disciples are not to fear their persecutors, but there is someone whom they should fear. **I shall show you whom to fear. Be afraid of the one who after killing has the power to cast into Gehenna.** God is able bring a human's life on earth to an end. Afterward, at the resurrection of the dead, "those who sleep / in the dust of the earth shall

BACKGROUND: NONBIBLICAL WRITINGS Other religious writings besides the books of the Old Testament were in circulation among Jews at the time of Jesus. Many of these texts had been written in the previous two centuries. Two of these writings, *1 Enoch* and the *Assumption of Moses,* are quoted in the letter of Jude (Jude 6, 9, 14–15). Other writings included *Jubilees, Psalms of Solomon,* and some of the *Testaments of the Twelve Patriarchs,* as well as other writings found among the Dead Sea Scrolls. Some of these writings claim to be revelations of how God will act to overcome evil and begin a new age. They differ considerably over what lies ahead. Various ideas about messianic figures, angels, the present age and the age to come, judgment, the resurrection of the dead, and life in the age to come are found in these writings, in more developed forms than they are found in the books of the Old Testament. It is uncertain how popular each of these writings was at the time of Jesus or how familiar the average Jew was with them. Yet at least some of their ideas and imagery, such as of Gehenna as a place of fiery punishment, were sufficiently familiar to first-century Jews for Jesus to invoke them in his teachings without having to explain them as if his listeners were hearing of them for the first time. These writings form part of the background for the Gospels and help bridge the Old and the New Testaments, even though they are not part of inspired Scripture. *Related topics: Dead Sea Scrolls (page 174), Revelations of the end (page 555).*

awake; / some shall live forever, / others shall be an everlasting horror and disgrace" (Dan 12:2). Some Jewish writings used **Gehenna** (the Hinnom Valley on the southern and western sides of Jerusalem) as a symbol for punishment in the age to come. Jesus' disciples should not fear what humans can do to them, but they should **fear** and **be afraid of** God, who **has the power to cast into Gehenna.** Jesus repeats his admonition for emphasis: **yes, I tell you, be afraid of that one.** The **fear** of God that Jesus is speaking of is not terror but an awe of God, a reverence and respect for who God is and what God can do. This is "the fear of the LORD" that "is the beginning of knowledge" (Prov 1:7)—a recognition that we are utterly and eternally in the hands of the one in whom "we live and move and have our being" (Acts 17:28). Jesus solemnly proclaims, **yes, I tell you,** be filled with fear and awe of God, who will decide your eternal destiny at a final judgment.

For reflection: Do I fear God? What word best describes my fundamental attitude toward God?

6   Recognizing who God is should result not only in fear and awe but also in trust of God. Jesus demonstrates this with a comparison. **Are not five sparrows sold for two small coins?** Small birds were a cheap source of food for the poor. The **small coins** in question were perhaps comparable to today's dimes. **Five sparrows** could be purchased very cheaply, **yet not one of them has escaped the notice of God.** The implication, which Jesus will soon make explicit, is that if even the least significant

---

BACKGROUND: GEHENNA This word is a transliteration of the Greek form of the Hebrew name for the Hinnom Valley, a steep ravine on the western and southern sides of Jerusalem. In Old Testament times the Hinnom Valley was the setting for idolatrous worship (called "Ben-hinnom"—Jer 7:31; 19:1–6) which took place at sites that may have been considered entrances to the underworld. The Hinnom Valley was also used for burials and as a refuse dump. As the ideas of judgment after death and punishment of the wicked developed, some nonbiblical writings portrayed the Hinnom Valley as a place of fiery punishment, perhaps because of its smoldering refuse and associations with death and idolatry. When Jesus spoke of Gehenna as a place of everlasting punishment, he was using imagery familiar to his listeners. *Related topics: Judgment (page 327), Nonbiblical writings (page 342).*

among God's creatures are not neglected by him, how much more does God take **notice** of the women and men he has created.

7 God's notice extends to every aspect of every person. Jesus tells his disciples, **even the hairs of your head have all been counted**—counted by God. Hair can symbolize the least significant part of a person; to say that not even a hair from someone shall fall to the ground is to express that person's complete safety (1 Sam 14:45; 2 Sam 14:11; see also Luke 21:18; Acts 27:34). If **the hairs** on a person's head have **all been counted** by God, then God knows that person intimately and completely. Jesus tells his disciples, **do not be afraid**: they can entrust themselves to God, who knows them thoroughly. Jesus assures his disciples, **You are worth more than many sparrows**. If God takes notice of sparrows (verse 6), how much more does he take notice of Jesus' friends! Even as Jesus three times told his disciples to be afraid of God (verse 5) in the sense of having an awe-filled respect for God, so he also tells them **do not be afraid** of God: God is their merciful Father (6:36), who gives the best in gifts to his children (11:13). They can confidently and serenely entrust themselves into the hands of such a God, even as they face persecution, and even as they await God's judgment.

> For reflection: Am I unafraid of God in the sense in which Jesus tells me, "Do not be afraid"? What might I do to entrust myself more completely to him?

Bearing Confident Witness

⁸ **"I tell you, everyone who acknowledges me before others the Son of Man will acknowledge before the angels of God. ⁹ But whoever denies me before others will be denied before the angels of God.**

¹⁰ **"Everyone who speaks a word against the Son of Man will be forgiven, but the one who blasphemes against the holy Spirit will not be forgiven. ¹¹ When they take you before synagogues and before rulers and authorities, do not worry about how or what your defense will be or about what you are to say. ¹² For the holy Spirit will teach you at that moment what you should say."**

Gospel parallels: Matt 10:17–20, 32–33; 12:31–32; Mark 3:28–29; 8:38; 13:11
NT: Luke 9:26; 11:13; 12:2–7; 21:12–15

8 Jesus has spoken about everything being brought to light, and he has alluded to God's judgment (12:2–7). He is preparing his disciples to bear witness to him in times of persecution. **I tell you, everyone who acknowledges me before others the Son of Man will acknowledge before the angels of God.** To **acknowledge** Jesus is to proclaim who he is and declare one's allegiance to him. Doing so **before others** can mean any public witness to him; in context it specifically means his disciples acknowledging him when they are brought "before synagogues and before rulers and authorities" (verse 11) to be interrogated about their relationship with him. Referring to himself as **the Son of Man,** Jesus promises that he will **acknowledge before the angels of God** in the court of heaven those who acknowledge him before others in human courts. The implied setting is the final judgment, when each person's eternal fate is determined (see 9:26, 12:5). Jesus will testify on behalf of those who have testified on behalf of him.

Son of Man: See page 147

Angels: See page 11

For reflection: What do I do to publicly acknowledge my allegiance to Jesus?

9 The reverse is also true: **But whoever denies me before others will be denied before the angels of God.** If anyone denies having any relationship with Jesus, then at the judgment Jesus will deny having any relationship with that person. The vivid example in Luke's Gospel of denying Jesus is when Peter says, "I do not know him," responding to the claim that he was with Jesus (22:57). So then, will Jesus deny Peter at the final judgment? Jesus goes on to teach that forgiveness is always available.

10 **Everyone who speaks a word against the Son of Man will be forgiven**—forgiven by God at the judgment. Those who speak against Jesus or deny any association with him can be forgiven. Peter wept bitterly over his denials (22:62), and his tears were accepted; Jesus appeared to Peter after his resurrection (24:34), and Peter led the early Church (Acts 1–15). But there may be some who refuse to accept forgiveness, and Jesus addresses their situation: **but the one who blasphemes against the holy Spirit will not be forgiven.** In this context, the **holy Spirit**

345

represents the saving power of God, and **blasphemes** means reviling or opposing. Those who reject God's power to save them **will not be forgiven** by God: those who refuse forgiveness will remain unforgiven.

The Spirit: See page 100

For reflection: How have I experienced God's forgiveness? Is there any area of my life that I am hesitant to let the power of God touch and heal?

11 Jesus knows that his followers will face opposition, and he prepares them for it. **When they take you before synagogues and before rulers and authorities**: opposition will come both from Jews, who will put disciples on the stand in **synagogue** assemblies, and from Gentile **rulers and authorities**, who will conduct civil hearings (see 21:12). Paul will recount his persecuting Jesus' followers: "Many times, in synagogue after synagogue, I punished them in an attempt to force them to blaspheme"—to revile Jesus (Acts 26:11; see also Acts 22:19). Paul himself will be repeatedly examined by **rulers and authorities** regarding his relationship with Jesus (Acts 24–26). Jesus tells his disciples that when they must testify before religious and civil authorities, **do not worry about how or what your defense will be or about what you are to say**. Here **defense** means a defendant's testimony. Jesus' disciples should **not worry** about how they will defend themselves when they are put on trial for their allegiance to Jesus.

Synagogue: See page 115

12 Jesus tells them that they do not need to worry, **for the holy Spirit will teach you at that moment what you should say**, literally, what it is necessary to say. Their having to testify will be an opportunity for them to bear witness to Jesus, and the Holy Spirit will **at that moment** give them the right words to say (see also 21:13–15). The Holy Spirit filled and empowered Jesus (3:22; 4:1, 14, 18; 10:21), and Jesus promised that his Father would give the same Holy Spirit to those who ask him (11:13). The Holy Spirit will **teach** and guide those who are facing persecution for the sake of Jesus. Consequently, Jesus' disciples are not to worry about their defense (verse 11), nor are they to be afraid of what the authorities might do to them. Persecutors may "kill the body but after that can do no more" (12:4). Jesus' disciples can face God's judgment knowing that

the testimony they gave to Jesus "will be proclaimed on the housetops" (12:3)—an image for being made public at the judgment—and that Jesus himself will testify on their behalf (verse 8). They can therefore confidently bear witness to Jesus using the words that the Holy Spirit will give them. In his Acts of the Apostles, Luke will recount examples of followers of Jesus being inspired by the Holy Spirit to boldly proclaim Jesus (Acts 4:8–13, 29–31; 5:27–32; 6:8–10; 7:55–56).

For reflection: How have I experienced the Holy Spirit guiding me in bearing witness to Jesus?

ORIENTATION: *In response to an interruption, Jesus warns against greed and anxiety (12:13–34).*

Guard Against All Greed

¹³ **Someone in the crowd said to him, "Teacher, tell my brother to share the inheritance with me." ¹⁴ He replied to him, "Friend, who appointed me as your judge and arbitrator?" ¹⁵ Then he said to the crowd, "Take care to guard against all greed, for though one may be rich, one's life does not consist of possessions."**

OT: Exod 2:14; Deut 21:15–17

13 **Someone in the crowd** that was listening to Jesus instruct his disciples about bearing witness (12:1–12) **said to him, "Teacher, tell my brother to share the inheritance with me."** The man's demand has nothing to do with what Jesus has been speaking about; the man is preoccupied with his own affairs and wants Jesus to intervene on his side in a family dispute. The dispute is over an **inheritance**, and since the law of Moses dealt with inheritances (Deut 21:15–17), the man turns to Jesus as a religious **teacher** to rule on the matter. The man provides no details about the nature of the inheritance (money? the family farm?) or why he thinks his **brother** is not giving him his fair share. He simply demands that Jesus **tell** his brother **to share the inheritance**. Earlier Martha had demanded that Jesus tell Mary to help her with the serving (10:40). Jesus did not get in the middle of that family dispute, and he will not intervene in this one either.

14 **He replied to him, "Friend, who appointed me as your judge and arbitrator?"** The word translated **friend** literally means a human being; another translation of it would be "man." Jesus' response echoes words directed at Moses when he took it upon himself to intervene in the affairs of others: "Who has appointed you ruler and judge over us?" (Exod 2:14). Jesus rebuffs the man's attempt to enlist him on his side of his dispute with his brother. Jesus' mission is not to settle family disputes, especially when they arise from greed. Jesus detects avarice in the man's request, and that is what needs addressing rather than whatever legal issues may be at stake in dividing the inheritance.

15 **Then he said to the crowd**: Jesus addresses his words to the man, to his disciples, to the crowd, to all who can hear him. He admonishes them, **Take care to guard against all greed**, every kind or form. **Greed** is an insatiable desire to have more. Jesus urges his listeners to **take care** and be on **guard against** all forms of wanting more. He will go on to teach why greed and anxiety over possessions are misguided and destructive (12:16–34); he begins by showing the pointlessness of greed. **For though one may be rich, one's life does not consist of possessions**. The word translated **rich** means having more than enough (it is translated "surplus wealth" at 21:4). Even if one has far more than one needs, still **one's life does not consist of possessions**. One exists and is alive independent of what one owns. The wealthiest person on earth and the poorest person on earth, while they differ in many ways, are the same in having **life**. And if one's being alive is not derived from even an abundance of possessions, then obtaining more possessions does not confer any more **life**. Greed is futile, for getting more adds nothing to life itself.

For reflection: In what ways do I yearn for more? How have I learned that possessing more does not make me anything more than I am?

A Rich Fool
16 **Then he told them a parable. "There was a rich man whose land produced a bountiful harvest.** 17 **He asked himself, 'What shall I do, for I do not have space to store my harvest?'** 18 **And he said, 'This is what I shall do: I shall tear down my barns and build larger ones.**

There I shall store all my grain and other goods ¹⁹ and I shall say to myself, "Now as for you, you have so many good things stored up for many years, rest, eat, drink, be merry!" ' ²⁰ But God said to him, 'You fool, this night your life will be demanded of you; and the things you have prepared, to whom will they belong?' ²¹ Thus will it be for the one who stores up treasure for himself but is not rich in what matters to God."

> OT: Psalm 49:18; Wisd 15:8; Sirach 11:18–19
> NT: Luke 9:25; 12:15

16 **Then he told them a parable** to illustrate that "one's life does not consist of possessions" (12:15). **There was a rich man whose land produced a bountiful harvest.** The man is already **rich**, and now his fields have **produced a bountiful harvest** of grain (verse 18), a bumper crop.

> Parables: See page 217
> The poor and the rich: See page 198
> Farming: See page 218

17 **He asked himself, "What shall I do, for I do not have space to store my harvest?"** His wondering **What shall I do?** is a proper reaction. He needs to do something with the grain, for it would be irresponsible to leave it exposed to the weather and to rodents. Yet the man's thinking is narrowly self-centered throughout the parable, constantly framed in terms of **I** and **my**. He seems to take it as a given that he must **store** the harvest, hoarding it, and does not consider other options.

18 **And he said, "This is what I shall do: I shall tear down my barns"**—he has more than one barn—**"and build larger ones"** to hold the large harvest. **There I shall store all my grain and other goods.** What the **other goods** might be is left unspecified. The important point is that he will store **all** that he has harvested and owns, keeping it for himself.

19 **and I shall say to myself, "Now as for you, you have so many good things stored up for many years."** The man congratulates himself on his increased prosperity and on the security and pleasure he thinks it will bring him. He has so **many** goods **stored up** for himself that they

349

will last **for many years**. Consequently he will **rest, eat, drink, be merry!** By **rest** he means that he will enjoy a life of leisure. **Eat, drink, be merry** is biblical shorthand for enjoying the good things of life (Tobit 7:10; Eccl 8:15). Such pleasures can be received as a gift from God (Eccl 2:24; 3:13), but this man looks upon them as satisfactions that his wealth provides. As is the case throughout his monologue with himself, the man's thoughts are completely on himself; thought of others never enters his mind.

> *For reflection: How do I use the income and possessions that are at my disposal? What would I do if I received an unexpected windfall?*

20 **But God said to him, "You fool."** The Old Testament sometimes uses the word **fool** for those who do not understand things from God's point of view (Psalm 92:6–9; 94:8–10; Prov 1:7). This man certainly doesn't. He is sure that he has many years of earthly enjoyments ahead of him (verse 19), but God knows that he has only a few hours to live and informs him that **this night your life will be demanded of you**. The word **demanded** has the connotation of demanded back (which is how it is translated at 6:30). The man's earthly **life** is a loan from God; at death "the life that was lent him is demanded back" (Wisd 15:8). Clearly, one's life is not guaranteed by what one owns, for this man's abundance of possessions cannot prolong his life past **this night**. And, God asks him, **the things you have prepared, to whom will they belong** after your death? Certainly not to him. When humans die, "they take nothing with them, / their wealth will not follow them" (Psalm 49:18; see also 1 Tim 6:7). Jesus' parable echoes verses from the book of Sirach that speak of a rich man's wealth passing to others at his death (Sirach 11:18–19; see also Eccl 2:18–21).

> *A man may become rich through a miser's life,*
> *and this is his allotted reward:*
> *When he says: "I have found rest,*
> *now I will feast on my possessions,"*
> *He does not know how long it will be*
> *till he dies and leaves them to others.*
> Sirach 11:18–19

21 **Thus will it be for the one who stores up treasure for himself but is not rich in what matters to God.** Implicit in Jesus' words is the judgment that this man, who stored up treasure **for himself** and his own enjoyment, and had no thought of the needs of others, is poverty-stricken in what matters to God. Jesus earlier made the point that there is no profit in gaining the whole world but losing or forfeiting oneself in the process (9:25). This rich man has lost his life, perhaps eternally. **Rich in what matters to God** is literally, rich toward God, or rich in God. The only lasting riches are those that one has on deposit, as it were, with God. And what are these lasting riches? What should the man have done with his wealth and bountiful harvest? Jesus will go on to explain how one stores up "treasure in heaven" (12:33). Meanwhile, Jesus has used a parable to dramatize the folly of greed: "though one may be rich, one's life does not consist of possessions" (12:15).

For reflection: What lesson does Jesus' parable have for me?

Seek and Receive the Kingdom
²² **He said to [his] disciples, "Therefore I tell you, do not worry about your life and what you will eat, or about your body and what you will wear. ²³ For life is more than food and the body more than clothing. ²⁴ Notice the ravens: they do not sow or reap; they have neither storehouse nor barn, yet God feeds them. How much more important are you than birds! ²⁵ Can any of you by worrying add a moment to your lifespan? ²⁶ If even the smallest things are beyond your control, why are you anxious about the rest? ²⁷ Notice how the flowers grow. They do not toil or spin. But I tell you, not even Solomon in all his splendor was dressed like one of them. ²⁸ If God so clothes the grass in the field that grows today and is thrown into the oven tomorrow, will he not much more provide for you, O you of little faith? ²⁹ As for you, do not seek what you are to eat and what you are to drink, and do not worry anymore. ³⁰ All the nations of the world seek for these things, and your Father knows that you need them. ³¹ Instead, seek his kingdom, and these other things will be given you besides. ³² Do not be afraid any longer, little flock, for your Father is pleased to give you the kingdom. ³³**

**Sell your belongings and give alms. Provide money bags for your-
selves that do not wear out, an inexhaustible treasure in heaven
that no thief can reach nor moth destroy. ³⁴ For where your treasure is, there also will your heart be."**

Gospel parallels: Matt 6:19-21, 25-33

OT: Tobit 4:7-11; Sirach 29:8-12

NT: Luke 12:15-21; 18:29-30

22 **He said to [his] disciples**: Jesus had been instructing his **disciples** before
he was interrupted by a man concerned about an inheritance (12:1-13).
He resumes instructing them, but now addresses attitudes toward the
necessities of life and exhorts them to have faith in God's care for them.
He had made the point that "one's life does not consist of possessions"
(12:15) and illustrated it with a parable about a man who hoarded his
wealth instead of becoming "rich in what matters to God" (12:21). Now he
says to his disciples, **Therefore I tell you,** because life does not consist of
possessions, **do not worry about your life and what you will eat, or
about your body and what you will wear.** The sense is, **do not worry**
about not having enough to **eat** to preserve your **life**, or about not having
anything to **wear** on your **body.** Jesus knows that food and clothing are
necessary, but his disciples are to **not worry** about them. For some of Jesus'
disciples—and for some in the crowd listening in (12:1)—having sufficient
food and clothing were likely a real concern. Most Galileans were among
the working poor, barely getting by; some were very poor and reduced to
begging. How could they **not worry** about not having enough to survive?

Disciple: See page 149

*For reflection: How much do I worry about not being able to provide for
my needs?*

23 Jesus gives his disciples a variety of reasons why they should not worry
about their needs. He begins by restating in more specific terms his assertion that "life does not consist of possessions" (12:15): **For life is more
than food and the body more than clothing**. A person's **life** cannot
be reduced to what she or he eats and wears. Even if food and clothing
are necessary, obtaining them is not the purpose of life. There are more
important things to be concerned about, which Jesus will speak of shortly.

24 Jesus tells his disciples, **Notice** and draw a lesson from **the ravens: they do not sow or reap; they have neither storehouse nor barn, yet God feeds them**. Ravens (crows) were unclean birds (Deut 14:11–12, 14), yet God responds to their cries for food (Job 38:41; Psalm 147:9). Even though ravens neither grow crops nor have means of storing them, **God** has so arranged his creation that it **feeds them**. Ravens can eat just about anything, including seeds and insects, and so they survive. Jesus tells his disciples, **How much more important are you than birds!** If God provides for birds, **how much more** will he provide for Jesus' disciples! They do not need to worry about what they will eat (verse 22).

25 Jesus gives another reason why his disciples do not need to worry. He asks them, **Can any of you by worrying add a moment to your lifespan?** We can cut our lifespans short by bad habits, and generally prolong our lives by healthful diet and exercise, but our **worrying** cannot in itself lengthen our lives even by a minute. The contrary is true: anxieties can raise blood pressure and lead to shorter lives.

> For reflection: Do I worry about how long I will live? What am I doing that might either extend or shorten my life?

26 Jesus asks his disciples, **If even the smallest things**—like adding a moment to your lives through worry—**are beyond your control, why are you anxious about the rest?** If worry cannot lengthen your life, why worry about anything else? Not being in complete control over **even the smallest things** means that you cannot control greater matters, and it is pointless to be **anxious** about them.

27 Jesus provides another reason not to worry, this time addressed to concerns about clothing. He tells his disciples, **Notice** and take a lesson from **how the flowers grow. They do not toil or spin**; they simply grow. **But I tell you, not even Solomon in all his splendor was dressed like one of them.** Solomon's court was a monument to luxurious pomp and conspicuous consumption; he reigned from an ivory throne overlaid with gold (1 Kings 10:4–5, 16–21). Presumably his royal robes had corresponding **splendor**, but they did not match up to the dazzling display of wildflowers in bloom.

28 **If God so clothes the grass in the field that grows today and is thrown into the oven tomorrow**: flowers and **grass** are proverbially short-lived (Job 8:11-12; 14:2; Psalm 37:2; 90:5–6; 102:12; 103:15–16; Isaiah 40:6–8). They can radiate beauty **today** and be fuel for cooking fires **tomorrow**. Despite their brief lives and ultimate destiny, God **clothes** them in such fashion that the splendor of Solomon pales in comparison. Jesus tells his disciples, if God so clothes flowers, **will he not much more provide for you, O you of little faith?** Do they think that God cares more for plants than for them? Anxiety over what they will wear is evidence that they have **little faith** that God will **provide** for them. If God can array flowers in beauty, surely he will not leave the disciples naked; they should have confidence in God's care for them.

   When Jesus sent the Twelve and other disciples out on mission, he instructed them to take no money or provisions with them (9:3; 10:4); they were to trust in God's care for them, exercised through the hospitality of people along the way. Their experience was meant to strengthen their **faith** that God would provide them with what they needed.

For reflection: In what ways do I rely on God to take care of me?

29 Jesus returns to concerns about food (verse 22), again explicitly addressing his disciples: **As for you, do not seek what you are to eat and what you are to drink, and do not worry anymore.** What Jesus will go on to say indicates that not to **seek** what they eat and drink has the sense of not making the quest for food their top priority. Jesus does not expect that meals will drop out of the sky for his followers; he knows that they will normally have to work to support themselves. But satisfying their needs is not the goal of their lives. They are to have faith that God will make provision for them, including through their own efforts, and **not worry** about their survival. Worry is evidence of weak faith (verse 28).

30 **All the nations of the world seek for these things**, for food and drink and the necessities of life. While the word translated **nations** can mean Gentiles, speaking of **all the nations of the world** may be a way of referring to the human condition. Men and women around the world **seek** and strive for what they need to keep themselves alive. Jesus tells his

disciples, **your Father knows that you need them**, that is, the things necessary for their survival. His disciples share the human condition and have the same basic needs as anyone else, but they differ from others in their relationship with God. They can turn to God as their **Father**, asking him for their daily bread (11:3), confident that he hears their prayers (11:5–13). They do not need to be anxious about food and clothing, or make striving for survival their goal in life, because they can rely on their Father to care for his children.

31 **Instead, seek his kingdom**: instead of worrying about their needs, Jesus' disciples are to **seek** and strive for the **kingdom** of God. They are to pray, "your kingdom come" (11:2). They are to **seek** to live under God's reign by accepting and acting upon the teachings of Jesus (see 6:20–49; 8:21; 11:28). They are to announce the good news of the kingdom and free others from afflictions (9:2, 6; 10:9). Seeking God's **kingdom** is to be their preoccupation, their number-one priority. Jesus exhorts them to put first things first.

Kingdom of God: See page 381

For reflection: What have I made my highest priority? What do I do to seek the kingdom of God?

Jesus tells his disciples that if they seek the kingdom of God, **these other things will be given you besides**. They will not need to be preoccupied with obtaining the necessities of life or be anxious about their survival. Their lives are in the hands of their Father, and he provides for those who are committed to his reign. Jesus will assure his disciples that those who give up everything "for the sake of the kingdom of God" will receive "an overabundant return in this present age and eternal life in the age to come" (18:29–30).

For reflection: How has God made provision for my needs?

32 **Do not be afraid any longer, little flock.** The Old Testament uses a **flock** of sheep as an image for the Israelite people under the care of God as their shepherd (Psalm 74:1–2; 77:21; Isaiah 40:11; Jer 13:17). The disciples are a **little flock**, not very numerous. Sheep are vulnerable to

355

attack by predators, but Jesus tells his followers **do not be afraid**, because **your Father is pleased to give you the kingdom**. The word **pleased** conveys God's favor or gracious will (see 2:14; 3:22; 10:21). For God to **give** the disciples the kingdom means that they receive it as a gift. To **give** them his **kingdom** means to make them part of it, to bring them into his reign, beginning now through their association with Jesus. This is a great gift indeed! Because of what God is graciously giving them, they are to **not be afraid** for their survival. Fear, like worry, is a symptom of lack of faith. They are to embrace God's gift of the kingdom with confidence, trusting that they are in his care now and eternally.

> For reflection: How do I experience the reign of God in my life? How has my confidence in God quieted my fears?

33 Jesus tells his disciples, **Sell your belongings and give alms**. To **give alms** means to provide financial or other assistance to those in need. Because their faith in God's care frees them from fears and worries about their own survival, the disciples can **sell** their **belongings** and use the proceeds to help the poor. Those whom God cares for do not need bigger storage facilities to hoard their possessions (see 12:16–19). Seeking God's reign (verse 31) involves caring for others, imitating the mercy shown by the Samaritan to the half-dead man (10:33–37). Jesus began speaking about possessions with a warning to "take care to guard against all greed" (12:15) and now he has reached the opposite pole: generosity is the converse of greed. Because of God's care for them, Jesus' disciples have no reason to be greedy; because of God's care for them, they can care for others, giving alms.

Alms: See page 332

> For reflection: How generous am I in helping those in need? What might I do to free up money so that I can give it away?

Jesus exhorts his disciples to **provide**—literally, make—**money-bags for yourselves that do not wear out**. Anything manufactured by humans eventually becomes old and wears out. How then are Jesus' disciples to make **money bags** for themselves that **do not wear out**? Since Jesus has just told them to **give alms**, the implication is that by giving their money away to the poor, the disciples will be putting it in

money bags that will permanently preserve it for them. What they give away will be **an inexhaustible** and unfailing **treasure in heaven**. The book of Tobit speaks of almsgiving as "storing up a goodly treasure for yourself" (Tobit 4:9); Sirach advises, "Store up almsgiving in your treasure house" (Sirach 29:12). The alms one gives will be a treasure in heaven **that no thief can reach nor moth destroy**. The fine garments of the wealthy are prey to moths, but moths cannot destroy, and thieves cannot steal, treasure kept in heaven. The way to become "rich in what matters to God" (12:21) is to use one's resources to help those in need. In the divine economy, we retain what we give away—and only that.

> *For reflection: If alms given are deposits, what is the balance in my heavenly bank account?*

34 **For where your treasure is, there also will your heart be.** Today we are advised, "Follow the money," in order to discover what is really going on. Jesus says much the same thing. If your **treasure** is in heaven, then your **heart** is set on the things of heaven: you are seeking the kingdom of God (verse 31). If one's treasure is in ever bigger barns, then one's heart is earthbound, like the rich man of Jesus' parable (12:16–21). What we treasure reveals our priorities, our goals, and ultimately our final end. Jesus invites his disciples to seek and receive the kingdom of God, making it what we most treasure.

> *For reflection: What do I treasure most? How firmly is my heart set on seeking and receiving the kingdom of God?*

ORIENTATION: *Jesus exhorts his disciples to be ready for what is going to happen. He begins with what lies in the future (12:35–48) and then addresses more immediate circumstances (12:49–59).*

Be Prepared
35 **"Gird your loins and light your lamps** 36 **and be like servants who await their master's return from a wedding, ready to open immediately when he comes and knocks.** 37 **Blessed are those servants whom the master finds vigilant on his arrival. Amen, I say to you,**

he will gird himself, have them recline at table, and proceed to wait on them. ³⁸ And should he come in the second or third watch and find them prepared in this way, blessed are those servants. ³⁹ Be sure of this: if the master of the house had known the hour when the thief was coming, he would not have let his house be broken into. ⁴⁰ You also must be prepared, for at an hour you do not expect, the Son of Man will come."

Gospel parallels: Matt 24:43–44
NT: Mark 13:33–37; Luke 22:27–30; John 13:4–5

35 Jesus tells his disciples, **Gird your loins and light your lamps**. The word translated **loins** also means waist. The ankle-length robe customarily worn by men and women could be cinched up with a belt around the waist to make walking or working easier. The Israelites were told to eat the first Passover meal ready to depart from Egypt, "with your loins girt, sandals on your feet and your staff in hand, you shall eat like those who are in flight" (Exod 12:11). **Gird your loins** was an expression meaning "get prepared" (Job 38:3; 40:7; Jer 1:17; 1 Pet 1:13). **Lamps** burning olive oil were used to illuminate rooms (see 8:16; 11:33), allowing activity at night. **Light your lamps** in combination with **gird your loins** means be prepared at night as well as during the day; be ready around the clock.

36 Before telling his disciples what they are to be prepared for, Jesus uses two comparisons, or parables, to emphasize the importance of preparedness. In the first comparison, Jesus tells his disciples that they are to **be like servants who await their master's return from a wedding, ready to open immediately when he comes and knocks**. The word translated **wedding** can also be translated "wedding banquet" (as it is at 14:8). Wedding banquets could last for several days or longer: "They celebrated Tobiah's wedding feast for seven happy days" (Tobit 11:18). It was difficult to know when someone might return from a wedding celebration. Therefore those inside a house **who await their master's return from a wedding** must be constantly prepared for his arrival, **ready to** unlock and **open** the door **immediately when he comes and knocks**.

37 **Blessed are those servants whom the master finds vigilant on his arrival.** The word translated as **servants** is literally "slaves"; the word translated as **master,** meaning owner of the slaves, can in other contexts be translated as "lord." Jesus pronounces a beatitude upon those found by their **master** to be **vigilant**; they are **blessed** and fortunate. Because they were watchful and alert, they were able to answer their master's knock when he returned from the wedding. Their blessedness, or good fortune, is found in what their master will do for them in response to their vigilance. Jesus tells his disciples, **Amen, I say to you, he will gird himself,** cinching up his robe around his waist to free him for action, **have them recline at table,** as guests do at formal meals and banquets, **and proceed to wait on them**. The master makes himself the servant of his slaves. Jesus solemnly assures his disciples—**Amen, I say to you**—that this is what will happen. Yet it is highly improbable that any **master** or slave owner would treat his servants or slaves in such a manner. Jesus will paint a more realistic picture in another parable (see 17:7–9). Servants and slaves wait on their masters, not vice versa. Why then does Jesus speak of a **master** who will **wait on** those who were **vigilant** for his return? Rather than try to answer this question now, let us listen to what Jesus goes on to say, hoping that it will bring clarification.

Beatitudes: See page 169
Servant, slave: See page 454

38 **And should he come in the second or third watch**: Jews divided the night into three watches; the **second** watch ran from roughly 10 p.m. to 2 a.m., and the **third watch** from roughly 2 to 6 a.m. If the master should return from the wedding feast in the middle of the night or just before daybreak **and find them prepared in this way,** vigilantly awaiting his return, **blessed are those servants**. They did not fall asleep even though it was late at night but were prepared for their master's return. Consequently he had them recline at table and waited on them; **blessed are those servants** who receive such reward from their master.

39 Jesus proposes a second comparison or parable: **Be sure of this: if the master of the house had known the hour when the thief was coming, he would not have let his house be broken into.** Like the previous parable, a key element in the story is an unexpected arrival: a **thief** does not make an appointment to burgle a house. Since a homeowner has no way of knowing the **hour** when someone will try to break into his house, he must be ever vigilant and alert.

40 Jesus tells his disciples, **You also must be prepared**, vigilant like the slaves awaiting their master's return, alert like a homeowner on guard against thieves, **for at an hour you do not expect, the Son of Man will come.** Jesus speaks of himself as **the Son of Man** and tells his disciples to **be prepared** for his coming. He spoke previously of himself as the Son of Man coming "in his glory and in the glory of the Father and of the holy angels" (9:26), referring to what will happen at the end of this age, and he will say more about it on another occasion (see 21:25–28). For the moment he tells his disciples about one aspect of his coming: it will be **at an hour you do not expect.** Like the slaves who had no idea when their master would return from the wedding feast, like the homeowner who did not know the hour that a thief would try to break in, the disciples cannot know when Jesus will come: it will happen at a time they **do not expect.** Consequently they **must be prepared**, constantly ready, loins girt and lamps lighted in round-the-clock vigilance.

Son of Man: See page 147

For reflection: When do I expect Jesus to come? What am I doing so that I will be prepared for his coming?

Now that Jesus has made it clear that the disciples' vigilance is for his coming, some elements in his first parable take on meaning. The master or lord of the slaves (verses 36–38) stands for the Lord Jesus. While it is unthinkable that a slave owner would provide a banquet for his slaves and wait on them, Jesus does so for his disciples: "I am among you as the one who serves" (22:27; see also John 13:4–5). He will promise his disciples that they will "eat and drink at my table in my kingdom" (22:30), alluding to the banquet of heaven (see 13:29; 14:15). Blessed and eternally fortunate are the vigilant whom Jesus serves!

For reflection: Do I accept the fact that Jesus is willing to serve me? What does this tell me about him?

What Is Expected of Me?

⁴¹ Then Peter said, "Lord, is this parable meant for us or for everyone?" ⁴² And the Lord replied, "Who, then, is the faithful and prudent steward whom the master will put in charge of his servants to distribute [the] food allowance at the proper time? ⁴³ Blessed is that servant whom his master on arrival finds doing so. ⁴⁴ Truly, I say to you, he will put him in charge of all his property. ⁴⁵ But if that servant says to himself, 'My master is delayed in coming,' and begins to beat the menservants and the maidservants, to eat and drink and get drunk, ⁴⁶ then that servant's master will come on an unexpected day and at an unknown hour and will punish him severely and assign him a place with the unfaithful. ⁴⁷ That servant who knew his master's will but did not make preparations nor act in accord with his will shall be beaten severely; ⁴⁸ and the servant who was ignorant of his master's will but acted in a way deserving of a severe beating shall be beaten only lightly. Much will be required of the person entrusted with much, and still more will be demanded of the person entrusted with more."

Gospel parallels: Matt 24:45–51
OT: Num 15:27–31
NT: Luke 12:35–40

41 **Then Peter said, "Lord, is this parable meant for us or for everyone?"** Jesus has been speaking to his disciples with a crowd present (12:1, 13, 22). Peter addresses Jesus as **Lord**, acknowledging his authority, and asks whether the **parable** of the servants awaiting their master's return from a wedding (12:35–40) is **meant** for Jesus' disciples **or for everyone**.

Lord: See page 137
Parables: See page 217

42 Jesus does not answer Peter's question directly but tells another parable. **And the Lord replied, "Who, then, is the faithful and prudent steward**: the sense of Jesus' words is, who will prove to be a **faithful and prudent steward**. A **steward** is a manager; **faithful** means reliable, and **prudent** means sensible and wise. Who will prove to be a good manager **whom the master will put in charge of his servants to distribute [the] food allowance at the proper time?** What follows indicates that

the **master** is going away for a while; in his absence he puts his **steward** (who is his slave—verse 43) **in charge of his** other **servants** and makes him responsible for distributing their rations of **food**. There would have been nothing unusual in giving such authority to a slave; some slaves served as managers and in other important positions. This steward is given charge of the other servants so that he can care for them, making sure they receive their rations **at the proper time**.

Servant, slave: See page 454

43 **Blessed is that servant**—literally, slave—**whom his master on arrival** back home **finds doing so**. The servant who faithfully and prudently carries out the responsibilities his master entrusted to him will be **blessed** and fortunate when the master returns and finds him doing so.

Beatitudes: See page 169

44 Jesus tells how the servant will be blessed and fortunate: **Truly, I say to you, he will put him in charge of all his property.** The steward had been temporarily in charge of the master's servants and food pantry while the master was away; now he is given permanent **charge of all his property**, his entire estate. His proper discharge of his duties earns him a major promotion.

For reflection: How has my faithfulness enabled me to be entrusted with greater responsibilities?

45 Not everyone proves to be faithful and prudent in carrying out their responsibilities, so Jesus provides an alternative middle and ending for his parable that takes this into account. **But if that servant says to himself, "My master is delayed in coming"**: he does not expect his master to return any time soon. Believing he can get away with abusing his powers, he **begins to beat the menservants and the maidservants**, harming them instead of providing for their well-being. He also begins **to eat and drink and get drunk**, indulging himself instead of distributing food rations to others.

46 Should a steward behave in such an irresponsible manner, **then that servant's master will come on an unexpected day and at an unknown**

hour. He will discover what his servant has been doing in his absence **and will punish him severely and assign him a place with the unfaithful.** The word translated **punish severely** literally means, "cut in half," a vivid way of expressing severe punishment. The steward had not been faithful (verse 42), and now he is consigned to a **place with the unfaithful.** The parable does not spell out where those who are unfaithful end up. Clearly, though, a steward who is found irresponsible is demoted, just as a steward who carries out his responsibilities is promoted (verse 44).

47 Jesus sketches two other ways that a servant might behave and the consequences. **That servant**—literally, slave—**who knew his master's will but did not make preparations nor act in accord with his will**: unlike a steward who mistreats those in his charge and gets drunk, this servant might do nothing horribly wrong. Rather, his failure is that through deliberate neglect he does not do what is right. He ignores the instructions he has been given, making no **preparations** to carry them out. He does not **act** according to **his master's will** and accordingly **shall be beaten severely.** Physical punishment of slaves was common in the world of Jesus and of Luke.

48 The law of Moses made allowances for inadvertent violations of God's commandments (Num 15:27–31), and Jesus also takes inadvertence into account. Unlike a servant who knows his master's will but fails to do it (verse 47), there can be a **servant who was ignorant of his master's will but acted in a way deserving of a severe beating.** He may behave the same as the servant who knew what his master wanted and didn't do it, but because he acted out of ignorance he **shall be beaten only lightly**—receive a light punishment.

Peter asked Jesus if a parable about servants awaiting their master's return applied specifically to the disciples (verse 41), and Jesus responded with a parable about four ways that a servant might behave and what the outcomes would be. Because Peter might not understand how the last parable answers his question, Jesus adds, **Much will be required of the person entrusted with much.** It is implicit in Jesus' words that God is the one who entrusts and requires: **much will be required** by God **of the person entrusted** by God **with much.** The word translated **person** could be more literally translated as "everyone": much will be required of everyone to whom much is given. For emphasis, Jesus repeats his statement in heightened terms: **and still more will be demanded of the person entrusted with more**—again, entrusted and demanded by God.

Jesus' words indicate that the parables of the servants awaiting their master's return (12:35–38) and of the homeowner who doesn't know when the burglar will come (12:39) apply to everyone but have pointed application to his disciples, who have been **entrusted with much**. "Knowledge of the mysteries of the kingdom of God" has been granted to them (8:10; see also 10:21–24); they are servants who know their master's will (verse 47). They have been given authority by Jesus to proclaim the kingdom of God and to heal (9:1–2; 10:8–9). They are like stewards who are to care for those put in their charge, providing them with the physical (9:13) and spiritual nourishment they need until their master comes. They are to vigilantly await their master's arrival (12:36), even if it seems delayed (verse 45). Jesus will come at a time they do not expect (12:40); their vigilance consists in faithfully carrying out the duties he has assigned them. If they do so, they will be blessed (verse 43); if they do not carry out his will, they will be punished in accordance with their culpability (verses 46–48). Jesus' disciples have been **entrusted with much** by God, and **much will be required** of them.

For reflection: With what has God entrusted me? What does he expect of me?

ORIENTATION: *After telling his disciples to be prepared for his coming (12:35–48), Jesus turns to what lies in the present and in the immediate future (12:49–59).*

Jesus' Mission

⁴⁹ **"I have come to set the earth on fire, and how I wish it were already blazing!** ⁵⁰ **There is a baptism with which I must be baptized, and how great is my anguish until it is accomplished!** ⁵¹ **Do you think that I have come to establish peace on the earth? No, I tell you, but rather division.** ⁵² **From now on a household of five will be divided, three against two and two against three;** ⁵³ **a**

father will be divided against his son and a son against his father, a mother against her daughter and a daughter against her mother, a mother-in-law against her daughter-in-law and a daughter-in-law against her mother-in-law."

Gospel parallels: Matt 10:34–36

OT: Micah 7:6

NT: Mark 10:38; Luke 2:34; 3:16; 14:26; 21:16

49 **I have come to set the earth on fire.** Jesus has spoken on other occasions about why he was sent (4:18–19, 43; see also 5:32); now he alludes to another aspect of his mission. He has **come to set the earth on fire**; another translation would be, throw fire on the earth. **Fire** can represent different things, making Jesus' words a bit cryptic. When James and John wanted to "call down fire from heaven" to consume inhospitable Samaritans, Jesus rebuked them (9:54–55), so Jesus is presumably not speaking of a destroying fire now. John the Baptist used **fire** as an image for punishment after judgment (3:9, 17), but Jesus has stressed mercy as well as judgment (see 5:30–31; 6:35–36; 7:34), leading John to wonder whether Jesus was the one who was to come (7:18–19). **Fire** can also refine and purify (Num 31:22–23; Jer 6:29; 9:6; Ezek 22:17–22; Zech 13:9; Mal 3:2–3), and that is most likely its significance here. A purifying **fire** will accompany being baptized in the Holy Spirit (3:16; see Acts 2:3). Jesus' mission is to release men and women from the grip of evil (4:18; 7:22), bringing them to repentance (5:32), purifying them. Jesus exclaims, **how I wish it were already blazing!** He is eager for his mission to be accomplished.

50 **There is a baptism with which I must be baptized, and how great is my anguish until it is accomplished!** Like fire (verse 49), **baptism** can signify different things, and Jesus' words are again cryptic. The verb for baptize means to immerse, soak, or wash, and does not have a specifically religious meaning. A **baptism** is an immersion, soaking, or washing. John's "baptism of repentance" (3:3) was a washing of the body to symbolize the washing away of sin, but that can hardly be the significance of **baptism** here. Rather, Jesus likely uses **baptism** as a symbol for the suffering and death that await him in Jerusalem. Knowing that "the days for his being taken up" were at hand, he had set out for Jerusalem (9:51), first

warning his disciples what would happen to him there (9:22, 44). Jesus will be immersed or plunged into suffering and death: **there is a baptism with which I must be baptized**. He **must be baptized** because it is his Father's will for him: "The Son of Man must suffer greatly . . . and be killed" (9:22; see also 13:32; 22:37; 24:26). **And**, Jesus exclaims, **how great is my anguish until it is accomplished!** Although Jesus is resolutely determined to carry out his Father's will (9:51), he experiences normal human **anguish** at the prospect of suffering and death (see also 22:44). And like any woman or man facing an extremely difficult time, he wants to get it over with: **how great is my anguish until it is accomplished!** He is eager for his baptism in suffering to be **accomplished**.

Baptism: See page 88

For reflection: What insight into Jesus do his words give me?

Jesus' sayings in verses 49 and 50 each convey eagerness for his mission to be accomplished, but these sayings may also have a deeper connection with one other. Jesus has come to set the earth ablaze in a purifying fire (verse 49); he faces a baptism of suffering in which he must be baptized. It will it be through his baptism of suffering and death that he will baptize with the Holy Spirit and fire (3:16). John's Gospel will connect the outpouring of the Holy Spirit with Jesus' glorification through death and resurrection (John 7:39).

51 Jesus continues to speak about his mission. He asks, **Do you think that I have come to establish peace on the earth?** The seemingly obvious answer is "Yes, you came to bring peace." Zechariah prophesied that Jesus would "guide our feet into the path of peace" (1:79). Jesus' birth was heralded by angels who proclaimed, "Glory to God in the highest / and on earth peace to those on whom his favor rests" (2:14). Jesus tells those he frees from sin and affliction, "Go in peace" (7:50; 8:48). He sends out his disciples to proclaim, "Peace to this household" (10:5). Jesus' answer to his question is therefore startling: **No, I tell you, but rather division**, disunity, discord. Jesus is able to give this startling answer because he refers to the *results* of his mission rather than its *purpose*: he has not **come** with the mission of causing **division**, but as a result of his coming people will become divided from each other. As Simeon prophesied after his birth,

Jesus is "destined for the fall and rise of many in Israel, and to be a sign that will be contradicted" (2:34). Those who fall as a result of his coming will be divided from those who rise; those who contradict and oppose him will be divided from those who accept him. There has already been division because of Jesus: some have left everything to become his disciples (5:11), while others are plotting against him (6:11; 11:54).

52 Jesus gives an example of the division that will occur because of him: **From now on a household of five will be divided, three against two and two against three.** The words **from now on** mean from the time of Jesus' ministry. A **household** was the basic unit of society, a family with its servants or slaves. A household of **five** will be split **three against two and two against three**, divided between those who accept him and those who reject him.

53 Echoing Micah 7:6, Jesus spells out a division that falls along generational lines: **a father will be divided against his son and a son against his father, a mother against her daughter and a daughter against her mother.** In Jewish culture, a grown son's primary relationship with his parents was with his father, and a grown daughter's was with her mother. These primary relationships will be shattered because of Jesus, with **father** and **son** divided against each other, **mother** and **daughter** opposed to each other. In Jesus' example, the son is married and living with his wife in his father's house (a common arrangement), and **mother-in-law** is divided **against her daughter-in-law and a daughter-in-law against her mother-in-law.** A married woman's primary relationship with her in-laws was with her **mother-in-law**, and this relationship is strained because of Jesus. The household of five—father, mother, son, daughter, son's wife—is divided three against two and two against three (verse 52), with the parents alienated from their children and their daughter-in-law because of Jesus.

> For the son dishonors his father,
> the daughter rises up against her mother,
> The daughter-in-law against her mother-in-law,
> and a man's enemies are those of his household.
>
> Micah 7:6

Jesus does not specify which generation accepts him and which generation rejects him; he simply paints a picture of a fractured family. Jesus did not come to break up families, but the divisions that will arise because of the different responses people make to him will tear apart even the most close-knit unit of Jewish society, the family (see also 14:26; 21:16).

For reflection: Who am I divided from because of Jesus? How might I go about trying to repair the breach?

Interpreting the Time

⁵⁴ He also said to the crowds, "When you see [a] cloud rising in the west you say immediately that it is going to rain—and so it does; ⁵⁵ and when you notice that the wind is blowing from the south you say that it is going to be hot—and so it is. ⁵⁶ You hypocrites! You know how to interpret the appearance of the earth and the sky; why do you not know how to interpret the present time?"

Gospel parallels: Matt 16:2–3
OT: 1 Kings 18:43–45
NT: Luke 7:31–35; 10:13–15; 11:14–16, 20, 29–32

54 **He also said to the crowds**: Jesus has been instructing his disciples in the presence of **crowds** (12:1, 13), and he now directs his words to the crowds. **When you see [a] cloud rising in the west you say immediately that it is going to rain—and so it does.** The Mediterranean Sea lies to the **west** of Palestine, and storms blow in from the sea. In 1 Kings a man observes "a cloud as small as a man's hand rising from the sea"—appearing on the western horizon—which produces a "heavy rain" once it sweeps inland (1 Kings 18:43–45). Spotting a **cloud rising in the west** is a signal to get ready for **rain**.

55 **and when you notice that the wind is blowing from the south you say that it is going to be hot—and so it is.** Winds that come **from the south** blow across the Arabian and Negev deserts, bringing scorching heat to Palestine in the summer. A **wind** that is blowing **from the south** is a sign that it is going to be a very **hot** day.

56 **You hypocrites!** Hypocrisy is a disconnect between appearance and reality. Jesus tells the crowd, **You know how to interpret the appearance of the earth and the sky**, the physical world. Since people lived much of their lives outdoors and many were farmers, they were concerned about the weather. They knew how to **interpret** the signs that told them whether it was going to be dry or rainy, hot or cold. He asks them, **Why do you not know how to interpret the present time?** The crowds fail to perceive something important that is going on right now in their midst. They are **hypocrites** in that there is a disconnect between their ability to interpret the weather and their inability to **interpret the present time**.

What is happening that people fail to perceive? Jesus is proclaiming the good news of the kingdom of God (4:43; 8:1; 9:11), and he has commissioned his disciples to do the same: "The kingdom of God is at hand for you" (10:9; see also 9:2, 60). Jesus is freeing women and men from the grip of evil so that they can be part of God's reign: "If it is by the finger of God that [I] drive out demons, then the kingdom of God has come upon you" (11:20; see also 17:21). Yet "this generation" (7:31) does not embrace what God is doing through Jesus, just as they did not accept what God was doing through John (7:32–35). Villages where Jesus performed mighty deeds have not repented (10:13–15). Some ascribe Jesus' power to Satan, and others demand a sign from heaven to authenticate him (11:15–16). They fail to perceive that someone greater than Solomon and Jonah is in their midst (11:29–32). Even as Jesus is eager to "set the earth on fire" and is in anguish until his baptism of suffering is accomplished (12:49–50), many go on with life as usual, unable to **interpret** the significance of what they can see Jesus do and hear him proclaim (see 7:31–34). They are missing out on "the plan of God for themselves" (7:30), their salvation (1:69; 2:30; 19:9).

For reflection: What are the signs pointing to what Jesus is doing in my time?

Seize the Moment
⁵⁷ **"Why do you not judge for yourselves what is right? ⁵⁸ If you are to go with your opponent before a magistrate, make an effort to**

settle the matter on the way; otherwise your opponent will turn
you over to the judge, and the judge hand you over to the constable, and the constable throw you into prison. ⁵⁹ I say to you, you
will not be released until you have paid the last penny."

Gospel parallels: Matt 5:25–26
NT: Luke 12:54–56

57 Jesus has just criticized the crowds gathered around him for not recognizing that they are living in a critical time (12:54–56): the kingdom of God
is being made present to them through Jesus' preaching and healing, but
they are oblivious to it. Now he urges them to discern the right thing to
do: **Why do you not judge for yourselves what is right?** Instead of
going along with the indifference of those around them, **judge for yourselves what is** the **right** course of action. Think for yourselves; decide
how you will respond to the good news of the kingdom of God.

58 Jesus tells a parable to illustrate the urgency of seizing the moment and
making a response. **If you are to go with your opponent before a
magistrate:** the parable will go on to make it evident that **your opponent** is someone to whom you owe money, who is taking you to court
so that a **magistrate**, or judge, will force payment. If you find yourself
in such a situation, then it is far preferable to **make an effort to settle
the matter on the way** to court rather than face a judge's certain ruling against you. Jesus does not say how you might **settle the matter**
(promise periodic payments?); he simple conveys that it is urgent to do
so. **Otherwise your opponent will turn you over to the judge**, or
magistrate, **and the judge hand you over to the constable, and the
constable throw you into prison**. The word translated **constable** is a
term used for, among others, an official in charge of a debtors' **prison.**
Debtors were imprisoned until their property was sold or family or friends
provided the funds to repay the debt. In practice, those who ended up in
debtors' prisons often had no way of raising money to repay their debt.
They consequently languished in prison, unable to work and earn money
as they could if they were free.

59 **I say to you, you will not be released until you have paid the last
penny.** The copper coin denoted by **penny** was the smallest coin in

circulation. Jesus assures his listeners that if they do not reach an out-of-court settlement and are imprisoned, they will not get out until they have repaid every **last penny** that they owe—an unlikely prospect once they are in prison.

Jesus' parable could be applied to different situations to convey the urgency of taking decisive action before it is too late. In the context of Jesus' speaking about the crowd's inability to "interpret the present time" (12:56), the parable is a prod to "judge for yourselves" (verse 57) about Jesus and his message and to respond to him while there is the opportunity. Jesus will go on to speak about the need for repentance (13:1–9), filling in what it means to "settle the matter" (verse 58).

For reflection: What is the lesson of Jesus' parable for me? What do I need to do to settle my accounts with God?

CHAPTER 13

ORIENTATION: *Jesus is speaking to a crowd about the critical time in which they live and inviting them to set matters right with God before it is too late (12:54–59). In response to an interruption, he uses two recent incidents to emphasize the need for repentance.*

Calls to Repentance

¹ At that time some people who were present there told him about the Galileans whose blood Pilate had mingled with the blood of their sacrifices. ² He said to them in reply, "Do you think that because these Galileans suffered in this way they were greater sinners than all other Galileans? ³ By no means! But I tell you, if you do not repent, you will all perish as they did! ⁴ Or those eighteen people who were killed when the tower at Siloam fell on them—do you think they were more guilty than everyone else who lived in Jerusalem? ⁵ By no means! But I tell you, if you do not repent, you will all perish as they did!"

NT: Luke 12:54–59; John 9:1–3

1   **At that time some people who were present there**: the Greek word translated **who were present** could also be translated, "who had just arrived," and that is likely its sense here. Jesus is speaking to a crowd (12:54–59), and **at that time** some arrive **there** who **told him about the Galileans whose blood Pilate had mingled with the blood of their sacrifices**. The word translated **told** means announced and is used for reporting news. Pontius **Pilate** was the Roman governor of Judea and some adjacent territories. The **Galileans** would have been killed in Jerusalem, for its Temple was the only place where **sacrifices** could be offered. That Pilate **mingled** their blood with the blood of their sacrifices is a dramatic way of saying that he had them killed as they were offering their animal sacrifices. The incident is not otherwise reported in the Gospels or by ancient historians. It would not have been anything extraordinary for Pilate's soldiers to kill a few Galileans; historians recount occasions when Pilate's orders led to the deaths of Judeans

and Samaritans. **Some people** may have told Jesus about the incident to solicit his condemnation of Pilate; on another occasion Jesus will be questioned about paying taxes to trap him into saying something seditious (20:20–22).

Galilee: See page 114
Pontius Pilate: See page 617

2   If there was a political agenda behind telling Jesus what Pilate did, Jesus ignores it. He uses the incident to accent the importance of getting right with God (see 12:57–59). **He said to them in reply, "Do you think that because these Galileans suffered in this way they were greater sinners than all other Galileans?"** Many in the crowd may well have thought so; it was commonly believed that sickness, untimely death, or other calamities were punishments for sin (see Job 4:7; Psalm 1:6; 37:20; Ezek 18:26; John 9:1–2). Therefore, if some Galileans **suffered in this way**, hacked down by Pilate's soldiers, that was a sign that they were sinners. If punishment is proportionate to sinfulness, then the gruesomeness of their fate indicates that **they were greater sinners** than were **other Galileans**.

For reflection: What connection do I see between sin and suffering?

3   Jesus emphatically answers his own question: **By no means!** The way in which these Galileans died does not indicate that they were more sinful than others. Job challenged the notion that his suffering was a sign of his sinfulness; he protested that "I have not transgressed the commands of the Holy One" (Job 6:10). Jesus also rejects the notion that misfortune is always a sign of sin (see John 9:3); no one can gauge the sinfulness of the Galileans Pilate killed by the manner of their death. There is a lesson to be found in their deaths, however, Jesus proclaims. **But I tell you, if you do not repent, you will all perish as they did!** To **repent** is to change course, adopting new thinking and behavior, reforming one's life and orienting oneself to God. To perish **as they did** does not necessarily mean die by the sword; its sense is die suddenly and unexpectedly (like the rich man in Jesus' parable—12:20). In light of what Jesus has been teaching, **perish** includes perishing eternally—"cast into Gehenna" (12:5) without hope of release (12:59). The deaths of the Galileans whom

Pilate killed should be a wake-up call; every man and woman faces death and judgment (see 11:31–32; 12:8–10). Each person needs to "settle the matter on the way" (12:58): to set themselves right with God in this life through repentance, lest they perish eternally.

Repentance: See page 92

4 Jesus invokes another example of sudden and unexpected death, citing an incident that his listeners were apparently familiar with: **Or those eighteen people who were killed when the tower at Siloam fell on them**. The pool of Siloam (John 9:7, 11) lay on the southern side of Jerusalem, and the adjacent area was called **Siloam** because of the pool (today it is the site of the Palestinian neighborhood of Silwan). Archaeologists have found the remains of an ancient tower in the area, but whether it is the **tower** that Jesus is referring to cannot be established. A tower collapsed, killing **eighteen people**. The Galileans died at the hands of humans; these eighteen died in an accident. By using this as his second example, Jesus covers death through natural catastrophes or so-called "acts of God." Jesus asks, **Do you think they were more guilty than everyone else who lived in Jerusalem?** Again, some might answer yes, thinking that God does not allow anyone to be struck down without cause.

Jerusalem: See page 516

For reflection: How do I understand lives being cut short by accidents and natural disasters? How does God's love encompass tragedies?

5 Jesus again gives an emphatic answer to his question: **By no means!** Sudden deaths, however tragic, are not infallible signs of sinfulness. Those who are good die in accidents no less than those who are evil. But sudden deaths can remind us of our own precarious hold on life, and Jesus uses them as a call to repentance: **But I tell you, if you do not repent, you will all perish as they did!** Jesus is again speaking of perishing eternally, and urging his listeners to **repent** so that they will not perish.

For reflection: What warning do Jesus' words have for me? What is the repentance he is asking of me?

One Last Chance

⁶ **And he told them this parable: "There once was a person who had a fig tree planted in his orchard, and when he came in search of fruit on it but found none,** ⁷ **he said to the gardener, 'For three years now I have come in search of fruit on this fig tree but have found none. [So] cut it down. Why should it exhaust the soil?'** ⁸ **He said to him in reply, 'Sir, leave it for this year also, and I shall cultivate the ground around it and fertilize it;** ⁹ **it may bear fruit in the future. If not you can cut it down.' "**

NT: Matt 21:18–19; Mark 11:12–14; Luke 3:8–9; 8:15; 13:1–5

6   After exhorting the crowd gathered around him to repent (13:1–5), Jesus **told them this parable: "There once was a person who had a fig tree planted in his orchard."** Fig trees were common, and figs a favorite fruit. **When he came in search of fruit on** his fig tree he **found none**. Fig trees produced one crop a year, in late summer, but this tree is barren.

Parables: See page 217

7   **He said to the gardener, "For three years now I have come in search of fruit on this fig tree but have found none."** A fig tree does not bear fruit for the first few years after it is planted. But although this tree apparently reached maturity **three years** ago and should have been producing **fruit**, it has yet to do so. Its continued barrenness indicates that it will likely never bear fruit. The orchard owner tells his gardener, **[So] cut it down. Why should it exhaust the soil?** There is no point in allowing a barren fruit tree to take up space and soil and water in an orchard; it should be replaced with a tree that does bear fruit.

8   The gardener **said to him in reply, "Sir, leave it for this year also, and I shall cultivate the ground around it and fertilize it."** The word translated **sir** is in other contexts translated as "lord" or "master." The gardener will **cultivate the ground around** the tree to allow water to reach its roots more easily. The words translated **fertilize it** are literally "throw manure" on it; dung was used as a fertilizer. The gardener asks the owner to spare the fig tree for a **year**, during which time he will give the tree special care.

9   The gardener expresses the hope that **it may bear fruit in the future**, next fruit season. **If not you can cut it down.** The gardener asks the owner to give the tree one last chance; if the tree remains fruitless, then the owner can have him **cut it down.**

Jesus concludes his parable with the outcome left hanging. Will the fig tree produce a harvest next year? That is uncertain. The tree is given extra care and a last chance, but it is up to the tree to bear fruit.

For reflection: How have I been given special care and extra chances by God?

What does Jesus convey to his listeners by telling this parable? He told the crowd that the time is critical and they need to get right with God before it is too late (12:54–59); he twice called for them to repent (13:1–5). The orchard owner represents the Lord God, graciously allowing a last chance to bear fruit despite a history of unfruitfulness. John the Baptist exhorted, "Produce good fruits as evidence of your repentance" (3:8), and warned that "every tree that does not produce good fruit will be cut down" (3:9). Fruit is a biblical idiom for behavior; God is offering a chance to produce the fruit of repentance—changed behavior. In Jesus' parable of the seed, the seed that fell on good soil and "produced fruit a hundredfold" (8:8) represented those "who, when they have heard the word, embrace it with a generous and good heart, and bear fruit through perseverance" (8:15). God is sending his word through Jesus (see 5:1), providing an opportunity to bear fruit; but it is the last chance. Now is the time to repent and be fruitful.

For reflection: What fruit am I bearing for God? What opportunities is he giving me now to bear more fruit?

Jesus Frees a Woman on the Sabbath

¹⁰ He was teaching in a synagogue on the sabbath. ¹¹ And a woman was there who for eighteen years had been crippled by a spirit; she was bent over, completely incapable of standing erect. ¹² When Jesus saw her, he called to her and said, "Woman, you are set free of your infirmity." ¹³ He laid his hands on her, and she at once stood up straight and glorified God. ¹⁴ But the leader of the

synagogue, indignant that Jesus had cured on the sabbath, said to the crowd in reply, "There are six days when work should be done. Come on those days to be cured, not on the sabbath day." ¹⁵ The Lord said to him in reply, "Hypocrites! Does not each one of you on the sabbath untie his ox or his ass from the manger and lead it out for watering? ¹⁶ This daughter of Abraham, whom Satan has bound for eighteen years now, ought she not to have been set free on the sabbath day from this bondage?" ¹⁷ When he said this, all his adversaries were humiliated; and the whole crowd rejoiced at all the splendid deeds done by him.

OT: Exod 20:8–11; Deut 5:12–15
NT: Matt 12:11; Luke 4:18–19; 6:6–11; 14:5

10 **He was teaching in a synagogue on the sabbath.** Jesus frequently taught in synagogues, (4:15–21, 31–33, 44; 6:6), and he does so again as he is making his way to Jerusalem (9:51–53; 13:22). The **sabbath** was a day of rest when no work was to be done (Exod 20:8–11; Deut 5:12–15). Jews

---

COMMENT: DEMONS AND SICKNESS It was taken for granted in the world of Jesus that the influence of demons could be experienced in everyday life. Evil spirits were sometimes understood as the cause of physical and mental illnesses, perhaps epilepsy and schizophrenia; hence curing these illnesses required the expulsion of such spirits. In the Gospels of Matthew, Mark, and Luke, Jesus' casting out of demons is sometimes associated with healings, such as the healing of a woman with curvature of the spine (Luke 13:11–16). The line between healings and exorcisms in the Gospels is not always clear. How should we understand Jesus' actions? Some points to keep in mind: First, the Catholic Church teaches that Satan exists and can cause spiritual harm and even, indirectly, physical harm (*Catechism of the Catholic Church*, 395), but the Church urges care in distinguishing between demonic activity and physical or mental illness (*Catechism*, 1673). Second, although we understand more about the natural causes of sickness than people did in the first century, this does not change the effect that Jesus had on the sick people who came to him: they were healed. Jesus remains a healer. And even if we understand the effects of Satan differently from how they were understood in the first century, Jesus is the stronger one who overcomes him (Mark 3:27). Third, Jesus' exorcisms and healings were not merely done out of compassion for afflicted individuals but were also assaults on the forces of evil. Evil is still manifestly present in the world, and Jesus' overcoming of evil is no less a part of establishing God's reign today than it was in the first century.

---

gathered in synagogues on the sabbath for prayer and Scripture reading, providing an audience for Jesus' **teaching**.

Synagogue: See page 115
Sabbath: See page 158

11 **And a woman was there who for eighteen years had been crippled by a spirit.** The Gospels sometimes ascribe physical infirmities to the influence of an evil **spirit** or demon (8:2; 9:39, 42; 11:14). This **woman** has been **crippled** for **eighteen years**, a long time. **She was bent over** with a severe curvature of the spine, **completely incapable of standing erect.**

Demons, unclean spirits: See page 125

12 **When Jesus saw her, he called to her.** The woman does not approach Jesus and ask to be healed; she is simply present that day in the synagogue. **Jesus saw her** and her condition. He takes the initiative to free her from her affliction, as he had taken the initiative to relieve the suffering of others (6:8; 7:13–14). He **called to her and said, "Woman, you are set free of your infirmity."** The implication is, **set free** by God. The word translated **set free** is used for the release of a prisoner (which is how it is used at 23:16, 18). The woman had been held captive, as it were, by her infirmity, and now she is **set free**.

For reflection: From what do I most need to be set free? What can I do to help bring about my release?

13 **He laid his hands on her**, just as he had laid hands on or touched others to heal them (4:40; 5:13; 8:54). Jesus can heal by a word (7:7; see 4:39; 5:24–25), but his touch conveys his personal concern. **She at once stood up straight**, immediately released from her infirmity. She **glorified God**, recognizing that she was healed by God's power at work through Jesus. Some have attributed Jesus' powers to Satan or have demanded a sign from heaven to prove that Jesus' powers come from God (11:15–16), but this woman recognizes that Jesus is God's agent and praises God for what he has done for her.

For reflection: How often do I glorify and praise God for what he has done for me?

14 **But the leader of the synagogue,** who supervised its operation, was **indignant that Jesus had cured on the sabbath.** On a previous occasion, some religious leaders "became enraged" when Jesus healed a person **on the sabbath** (6:6–11). They maintained that medical treatment and healing were works forbidden on the Sabbath except when a life was in danger. This synagogue leader also considers healing to be a work forbidden on the Sabbath, and is **indignant** that Jesus has done such work in his synagogue. He does not direct his indignation to Jesus but takes it out on members of his synagogue. He **said to the crowd in reply, "There are six days when work should be done. Come on those days to be cured, not on the sabbath day."** He is being petulant. Those assembled in the synagogue had not come **to be cured** but to pray and study Scripture. Not even the woman whom Jesus healed had sought healing. The synagogue leader seems to make it the responsibility of the congregation to turn down healing should it be offered **on the sabbath day.** The proper thing for him to have done would be to confront Jesus directly with his concerns about violating the Sabbath. Another synagogue official had a quite different attitude toward Jesus: Jairus begged Jesus to save his daughter's life (8:41–42).

For reflection: When have I taken out my anger or frustration on those who had done nothing wrong?

15 **The Lord said to him in reply, "Hypocrites!"** Luke refers to Jesus as **the Lord,** perhaps as a subtle allusion to Jesus as "lord of the sabbath" (6:5). Jesus does not call everyone in the synagogue congregation **hypocrites** but addresses his words to the synagogue leader and those who think and behave like him. There is hypocrisy in the synagogue leader's browbeating the congregation about healing on the Sabbath instead of directing his concern to Jesus as the source of healing. Jesus goes on to provide a second instance of hypocrisy. He begins by asking, **Does not each one of you on the sabbath untie his ox or his ass from the manger and lead it out for watering?** Even though they do not do farm work on the Sabbath, they at least make sure their animals do not go the

whole day without water. They **untie** their animals from where they are tethered in the manger so that they can be led to a watering trough.

Lord: See page 137

16 **This daughter of Abraham, whom Satan has bound for eighteen years now**: she is a **daughter of Abraham**, a member of God's people and far more important than an ox or an ass. **Whom Satan has bound**: Satan, the "prince of demons" (11:15), rules the spirit that crippled her (verse 11). **Ought she not to have been set free**: the word translated **set free** is the same word that is translated "untie" in the previous verse; it echoes the same word, in a slightly different form, translated "set free," in verse 12. If an animal may be set free on the Sabbath so that it does not go without water for a single day, how much more should this woman be set free on the Sabbath from what has **bound** her for eighteen years! There is hypocrisy (verse 15) in not treating humans as well as one treats animals. The words translated **ought . . . not** literally mean "was it not necessary." Jesus proclaims that it is not only permissible but necessary that she be **set free on the sabbath day from** her **bondage**. The **sabbath** was established by God as a weekly release from work. It is fitting that bonds be broken on the Sabbath, and women and men be set free, especially those **whom Satan has bound**. Jesus has been sent by God "to proclaim liberty to captives" and "to let the oppressed go free" (4:18), and it is necessary—it is God's will—that he release this woman from the bondage of Satan.

Satan: See page 108

For reflection: How has Jesus freed me from bondage?

17 **When he said this, all his adversaries were humiliated**: those who oppose Jesus are put to shame by his words. **The whole crowd rejoiced at all the splendid deeds done by him**, rejoicing not only over his freeing this woman from her affliction but also over **all the splendid deeds** he has **done**. Jesus continues to be a source of division (see 2:34), with some admiring him and others becoming his **adversaries**. He is on his way to Jerusalem (13:22), where opposition to him will come to a head (9:22, 44).

What Is the Kingdom of God Like?

¹⁸ **Then he said, "What is the kingdom of God like? To what can I compare it? ¹⁹ It is like a mustard seed that a person took and planted in the garden. When it was fully grown, it became a large bush and 'the birds of the sky dwelt in its branches.' "**

²⁰ **Again he said, "To what shall I compare the kingdom of God? ²¹ It is like yeast that a woman took and mixed [in] with three measures of wheat flour until the whole batch of dough was leavened."**

> Gospel parallels: Matt 13:31–33; Mark 4:30–32
>
> OT: Ezek 17:22–23; 31:3–6; Dan 4:7–9, 17
>
> NT: Luke 13:10–17

18 **Then he said**—literally, "Therefore he said." Jesus set a woman free from a crippling affliction (13:10–17) and now is commenting on the significance of what he did. He asks, **What is the kingdom of God like? To what can I compare it?** Jesus has spoken often of **the king-**

BACKGROUND: KINGDOM OF GOD The central theme of Jesus' preaching was that God was establishing his kingly rule: "The kingdom of God is at hand" (Mark 1:15). (Matthew's Gospel usually refers to it as the kingdom of heaven, reflecting the Jewish practice of avoiding using the name "God" out of reverence.) When Jesus spoke of the kingdom of God, he invoked Old Testament images of God reigning as king (Psalm 97:1; Isaiah 52:7), and so his listeners would have had some grasp of what he was talking about. Yet the expression "the kingdom of God" never occurs in the Hebrew Scriptures and is rarely found in the New Testament except on the lips of Jesus. The coming of the kingdom of God means the coming of God's final triumph over evil; it means the coming of God's direct, manifest reign over everyone and everything. Jesus' listeners would not necessarily have understood it to mean the end of space and time, but they would at least have understood it as the end of the world as they knew it, the end of a world shot through with evil and suffering, a world in which God's people were in bondage to their sins and to foreign domination. The kingdom of God was anticipated as the fulfillment of hopes engendered by Old Testament prophecies and by nonbiblical writings of the two centuries before Jesus. But because of the richness and diversity of these prophecies and writings, Jesus' listeners had no single blueprint in mind for what the reign of God would be like. Some expected God to free them from Roman rule; others expected God to accomplish a great deal more. Jesus used parables to convey what the reign of God was like. *Related topics: Jewish expectations at the time of Jesus (page 69), Nonbiblical writings (page 342).*

---

dom of God (4:43; 6:20; 7:28; 9:11, 27, 62; 11:20; 12:31–32) and sent out disciples to proclaim it (9:2, 60; 10:9, 11), but Luke has not recounted him explaining what the kingdom of God is. His listeners would have had a general notion that it meant God ruling over his people and over the whole world, but they may have had widely different views about how this would happen. Jesus does not try to define **the kingdom of God** but indicates what it is **like**. He will provide something to which he can **compare it**.

19 In his comparison, or parable, Jesus says that the kingdom of God **is like a mustard seed that a person took and planted in the garden**. A **mustard seed** is very small, about .075 inches in diameter. It was used as a proverbial example of something tiny (see 17:6), comparable to our speaking of a "speck of dust." Jesus' listeners were likely startled that he would say that the kingdom of God is **like** something so minute as **a mustard seed**. They may have expected him to say that God's kingdom could be compared to the heavens being torn apart and mountains quaking as God comes in power to destroy evil and establish his reign (see Isaiah 63:19; Micah 1:3–4). But like a mustard seed? That is unexpected.

Parables: See page 217

Jesus' comparison is not simply to a **mustard seed** but also to what became of it: **a person took** the seed **and planted in the garden**. A mustard plant was grown for its seeds, which could be crushed and the oil used as a seasoning. **When it was fully grown, it became a large bush**, literally, it grew and became a tree. It is an exaggeration to call a mustard plant a tree, even though it can grow to ten feet high. However, the image of a tree fits with what Jesus goes on to say: **and "the birds of the sky dwelt in its branches."** Jesus' words echo Old Testament prophecies that use a tree as an image for a world empire and birds nesting in its branches as an image for peoples finding security within the empire (Ezek 17:22–23; 31:3–6; Dan 4:7–9, 17–19).

Jesus healed a woman who was crippled, setting her free from her bondage to Satan (13:10–17). While this made a great difference for the woman, it did not amount to much in comparison with all the evil and suffering there is in the world. By freeing her from Satan (13:16), however,

Jesus was bringing about the reign of God: "If it is by the finger of God that [I] drive out demons, then the kingdom of God has come upon you" (11:20). What begins as a seed will grow and become a tree that provides shelter for birds: the mustard seed of Jesus' ministry will produce great results and benefit many. However modest its beginning, God is establishing a reign that will encompass the whole world.

Jesus' parable should reassure and comfort us today. It may appear that God has a long way to go in establishing his reign, vanquishing evil and suffering. But as surely as the tiny mustard seed became a great plant, so God's kingdom will come.

For reflection: Where do I see God establishing his reign in the world today?

20 **Again he said, "To what shall I compare the kingdom of God?"** Jesus provides a second comparison for **the kingdom of God**.

21 **It is like yeast:** a better translation would be "leaven." Yeast as we buy it in stores today was unknown; fresh dough was leavened with a bit of leavened dough left unbaked from a previous batch of bread. The kingdom of God is like leaven **that a woman took and mixed [in] with three measures of wheat flour until the whole batch of dough was leavened**. The word translated mixed is literally "hid"; the leaven disappears into the new batch of dough. **Three measures of wheat flour** would amount to forty to fifty pounds of flour; the woman is making a very large batch of bread, capable of feeding over one hundred people. Yet despite the size of her batch, the **whole** of it is leavened.

Like the previous parable, the parable of the leaven conveys that something great results from modest beginnings. It was proverbial that it took only a little yeast to leaven a whole batch of dough (1 Cor 5:6; Gal 5:9). The woman "hid" the leaven in the dough: leaven works unobserved, permeating and transforming the dough. Jesus does not compare the coming of the kingdom of God to a mighty army invading a country but to hidden leaven quietly at work. He will teach that "the coming of the kingdom of God cannot be observed" (17:20). Yet it is coming and is transforming the world, as surely as leavened dough rises.

For reflection: What does the kingdom of God being like leaven imply about how God is at work in the world today?

ORIENTATION: *In response to a question, Jesus tells a parable involving a door leading into a banquet. The significance of the parable only becomes explicit toward its end, requiring that some of its later elements be taken into consideration in interpreting the parable.*

Strive Hard to Be Saved!

22 He passed through towns and villages, teaching as he went and making his way to Jerusalem. 23 Someone asked him, "Lord, will only a few people be saved?" He answered them, 24 "Strive to enter through the narrow door, for many, I tell you, will attempt to enter but will not be strong enough. 25 After the master of the house has arisen and locked the door, then will you stand outside knocking and saying, 'Lord, open the door for us.' He will say to you in reply, 'I do not know where you are from.' 26 And you will say, 'We ate and drank in your company and you taught in our streets.' 27 Then he will say to you, 'I do not know where [you] are from. Depart from me, all you evildoers!' 28 And there will be wailing and grinding of teeth when you see Abraham, Isaac, and Jacob and all the prophets in the kingdom of God and you yourselves cast out. 29 And people will come from the east and the west and from the north and the south and will recline at table in the kingdom of God. 30 For behold, some are last who will be first, and some are first who will be last."

Gospel parallels: Matt 7:13–14, 23; 8:11–12; 19:30; 20:16; Mark 10:31
OT: Psalm 6:9; 107:2–3; Isaiah 25:6–9
NT: Luke 12:54–59; 13:1–9

22 **He passed through towns and villages, teaching as he went.** Jesus is **making his way to Jerusalem** (see 9:51, 53), where suffering and death await him (9:22, 44; 13:33). He was sent by God to proclaim the good news of the kingdom of God (4:43), and he has done so throughout Galilee, traveling "from one town and village to another, preaching and

proclaiming the good news of the kingdom of God" (8:1). He continued to carry out his mission on his final journey to Jerusalem, **teaching** as he **passed through towns and villages** along the way. He is faithful to his mission to the end.

Jerusalem: See page 516

23 **Someone asked him, "Lord, will only a few people be saved?"** Jesus warned that those who do not repent will perish (13:3, 5). To be **saved** broadly means to be rescued from danger or death; here it means being rescued from perishing (see also 2 Cor 2:15). It will later be clear that to be **saved** means to enter the kingdom of God and inherit eternal life (see 18:18, 24–26). Someone wants to know whether **only a few people** will **be saved**: Will most people perish? Jesus **answered them**, addressing everyone present as well as the one who asked the question.

Lord: See page 137

24 Jesus does not provide the numbers of those who are saved and those who perish. Instead he issues a warning: **Strive to enter through the narrow door**. As Jesus will go on to indicate, the **door** leads into a house (verse 25) that represents the kingdom of God; inside, the heavenly banquet takes place (verse 29). The **door** is **narrow** and difficult to pass through: entering into the reign of God takes determination and effort. Jesus urges his listeners, **strive to enter**. The word translated **strive** has the connotation of an intense effort, as in an athletic contest or fight (it is translated as "struggle" at Col 1:29 and 1 Tim 4:10). Jesus' message to his listeners is, "The question to be concerned about is not whether only a few people will be saved but whether *you* will be saved. Therefore, strive to enter into the heavenly banquet of the kingdom of God; strive hard and struggle with all your might." **For many, I tell you, will attempt to enter but will not be strong enough.** Many who try to enter the kingdom of God will fail to do so because they do not have the strength or determination to do what is required. Eternal life is a gift from God, but a gift that we must strive to obtain by repenting (13:3, 5) and turning away from evildoing (see verse 27).

For reflection: How hard am I striving to enter heaven?

25 The door to the heavenly banquet, however narrow, now stands open. It will not remain open indefinitely; it is urgent to seize the opportunity and enter—a point that Jesus made in his parable of the person on the way to court (12:58–59). **After the master of the house has arisen and locked the door**: what follows indicates that we should picture a man giving a banquet in his house, and after all the invited guests arrived he **locked the door** so that they could dine undisturbed. What follows also indicates that the **master of the house** is Jesus (verse 26), **arisen** from the dead. Jesus will welcome those who are saved (verse 23) into the heavenly banquet and lock the door of the kingdom. Jesus addresses those who have missed their opportunity to repent and are excluded: **then will you stand outside knocking and saying, "Lord, open the door for us."** They will call upon Jesus as **Lord** and ask him to admit them to the banquet. **He will say to you in reply, "I do not know where you are from."** Saying **I do not know where you are from** has the sense, I don't know you; you are no friend of mine.

26 **And you will say, "We ate and drank in your company and you taught in our streets"**—surely you know us! Jesus **ate and drank** with many people, ranging from tax collectors and sinners (5:29–30; 7:34) to Pharisees (7:36; 11:37). Shared meals expressed fellowship, and Jesus also

---

BACKGROUND: BANQUETS played important social and religious roles at the time of Jesus. Banquets were not only a chance for ordinary people to enjoy ample food and wine, which they otherwise rarely did, but also a form of entertainment in a world that offered few diversions compared with the modern world. Banquets marked special occasions, such as weddings (Matt 22:2; John 2:1–3) or the homecoming of a wayward son (Luke 15:23). Those who were wealthy could feast every day (Luke 16:19). Banquets were also used to celebrate religious feasts, such as Passover (Exod 12:1–28). It was the custom at Greek banquets for diners to recline on their left side on cushions or couches arranged in a U shape. Servants served the food on low tables inside the U. Jews adopted the custom of reclining during banquets, as John portrays in his account of the Last Supper (John 13:12, 23–25). The prophets spoke of God providing a banquet for his people (Isaiah 25:6), and Jesus used a feast as an image for the reign of God (Matt 8:11; 22:1–14; Luke 13:24–29; 14:15–24). Having plenty of good food to eat would have sounded heavenly to Jesus' listeners. *Related topic: Diet (page 253).*

---

used meals as occasions for inviting those he dined with to repentance (5:31–32; 11:39–42). Jesus **taught in** the **streets** of many towns and villages (verse 22; see also 8:1) and many heard his teachings. Some of those who ate with him and listened to him now plead with him, asking to be admitted to the heavenly banquet on the basis of their acquaintance with him.

27 **Then he will say to you, "I do not know where [you] are from."** He again denies knowing them, their acquaintance with him notwithstanding. He invokes words from Psalm 9 that indicate why he disavows them: **Depart from me, all you evildoers!** Although they may have listened to his teachings, they did not act on them (see 6:47; 8:15, 21). They are **evildoers** who did not repent when there was time to do so (12:54—13:9). Therefore Jesus does not acknowledge them to be his friends, and they are not among those invited into the heavenly banquet.

> *Away from me, all who do evil!*
>
> Psalm 6:9

> *For reflection: Does my conduct allow Jesus to call me his friend? What needs changing?*

28 Those denied admission to the heavenly banquet are left stranding outside, peering in through the window, as it were. **And there will be wailing and grinding of teeth,** a biblical idiom for mourning, rage, despair (Matt 8:12; 13:42, 50; 22:13; 24:51; 25:30), **when you see Abraham, Isaac, and Jacob and all the prophets in the kingdom of God and you yourselves cast out.** The faithful of the Old Testament era will be welcomed into **the kingdom of God,** but some who dined with Jesus and listened to his teachings will be **cast out**—excluded from the kingdom at the judgment. Their awareness that others are enjoying that from which they are excluded will fill them with anguish.

Kingdom of God: See page 381

29 Along with the righteous from the Old Testament era, **people will come from the east and the west and from the north and the south.** Jesus invokes a Psalm that speaks of "the LORD's redeemed" being gathered "from east and west, from north and south" (Psalm 107:2–3). Naming the

four directions conveys that those who are saved (verse 23) will come from all over the world. Jesus' witnesses will go out "to the ends of the earth" (Acts 1:8); Gentiles as well as Jews will hear and act on the message of salvation. At the end of this age they will **recline at table in the kingdom of God**. Isaiah used a banquet as an image for what was in store for those whom God saved (Isaiah 25:6–9), and Jesus adopts this imagery (see also 12:36–37). Will only a few people be saved (verse 23)? God wants "all peoples" to take part in the "feast of rich food and choice wines" (Isaiah 25:6) in the kingdom of God; God wants everyone to "rejoice and be glad that he has saved us" (Isaiah 25:9). All are invited to the banquet and the door is still open; it is up to each woman and man to respond.

> On this mountain the LORD of hosts
> > will provide for all peoples
> A feast of rich food and choice wines,
> > juicy, rich food and pure, choice wines. . . .
> > he will destroy death forever.
> The Lord GOD will wipe away
> > the tears from all faces. . . .
> > On that day it will be said:
> "Behold our God, to whom we looked to save us!
> > This is the LORD for whom we looked;
> > let us rejoice and be glad that he has saved us!"
> > > > Isaiah 25:6, 8–9

For reflection: What do I imagine heaven will be like?

30 **For behold, some are last who will be first, and some are first who will be last.** This observation can have different applications in different situations. Here it can mean that some who will be among the **last** to hear the message of Jesus and respond to it—Gentiles—will be among the **first** in the kingdom of God, while some who have been among the **first** to hear his message—Jews in whose villages he taught (verses 22, 26)—will be **last** or left out. Jesus' words convey a warning: Don't take entrance into the kingdom of God for granted; strive earnestly to enter it, lest you be left on the outside looking in.

For reflection: What is the significance for me of Jesus' response to the question about whether only a few people will be saved?

Jesus' Lament over Jerusalem

³¹ **At that time some Pharisees came to him and said, "Go away, leave this area because Herod wants to kill you." ³² He replied, "Go and tell that fox, 'Behold, I cast out demons and I perform healings today and tomorrow, and on the third day I accomplish my purpose. ³³ Yet I must continue on my way today, tomorrow, and the following day, for it is impossible that a prophet should die outside of Jerusalem.**

³⁴ **"Jerusalem, Jerusalem, you who kill the prophets and stone those sent to you, how many times I yearned to gather your children together as a hen gathers her brood under her wings, but you were unwilling! ³⁵ Behold, your house will be abandoned. [But] I tell you, you will not see me until [the time comes when] you say, 'Blessed is he who comes in the name of the Lord.' "**

Gospel parallels: Matt 23:37–39
OT: Psalm 118:26; Jer 12:7
NT: Luke 13:22–30; 19:37–44; 21:5–6, 20–24

31 **At that time,** as Jesus is speaking about striving to enter the kingdom of God (13:23–30), **some Pharisees came to him and said, "Go away, leave this area because Herod wants to kill you."** Although some **Pharisees** oppose Jesus (5:21, 30; 6:2, 7, 11; 11:53–54), other Pharisees seem concerned for his well-being. After **some Pharisees** learned that **Herod** Antipas, the ruler of Galilee (3:1), wanted **to kill** Jesus, they **came to him,** taking the initiative to warn Jesus of Herod's intent. They advise him to **go away** and **leave this area** that Herod rules, where he has the authority to execute those whom he considers a threat. John the Baptist censored Herod Antipas "because of all the evil deeds Herod had committed" (3:19); Herod responded by having John beheaded (9:9). Herod had wanted to see Jesus (9:9) and watch him perform a wonder (23:8), but now his intentions are murderous. Jesus is already on his way to Jerusalem (9:51; 13:22), but these Pharisees think that he should get out of Galilee immediately.

Pharisees: See page 143

Herod Antipas: See page 99

32 **He replied, "Go and tell that fox"**: Jesus is not asking them to become
his messengers as much as conveying, "This is my response to Herod." He
unflatteringly calls Herod a **fox**. In Greek literature and in later Jewish
writings, a fox is characterized as a sly, crafty animal, and this may have
been the connotation in the world of Jesus as well. His response to Herod
Antipas is, **Behold, I cast out demons and I perform healings today
and tomorrow, and on the third day I accomplish my purpose**.
Throughout his ministry, Jesus has **cast out demons** and performed
healings to free men and women from evil and bring them into the
reign of God (see especially 4:40–41; 6:17–19; 7:22; 11:20). The sense of
today and tomorrow is day by day: Jesus continues to cast out demons
and heal day by day as he makes his way to Jerusalem. The sense of **on
the third day** is shortly. **I accomplish my purpose** is literally, "I am
finished" or "I am completed." The day is coming soon when Jesus will
reach the goal of his life and his mission will be accomplished.

Demons, unclean spirits: See page 125

*For reflection: What is my mission from God? How am I, day by day,
accomplishing the purpose of my life?*

33 Jesus adds, **Yet I must continue on my way today, tomorrow, and
the following day**. Jesus is on his way out of Herod's realm, but not
because of Herod. Rather, Jesus **must** travel to Jerusalem as a matter
of divine necessity (see 4:43); it is God's will for him. There he "must
suffer greatly . . . and be killed and on the third day be raised" (9:22),
accomplishing his "exodus" (9:31), his "being taken up" (9:51). That is
his purpose (verse 32), and it will be fulfilled in Jerusalem. **For it is impossible that a prophet should die outside of Jerusalem.** Saying that
it is **impossible** that a prophet die—be killed—outside of Jerusalem is
intended rhetorically rather than literally: while some prophets were put
to death in Jerusalem (see, for example, Jer 26:20–23), others died elsewhere (Jezebel murdered prophets far north of Jerusalem—1 Kings 18:4).
But since Jerusalem was the religious center for God's people, and since
they had a long history of rejecting and killing the prophets God sent
to them (see 6:22–23; 11:47–51), Jesus rhetorically ascribes their deaths

to Jerusalem. Jesus is a **prophet** in that he speaks on behalf of God; his words are "the word of God" (5:1; see also 4:24; 7:16). Therefore he has nothing to fear from Herod Antipas: he must and will die in Jerusalem.

Jerusalem: See page 516

34 Although Jesus will die in Jerusalem, he is filled with compassion for its inhabitants. He utters a prophetic lament over the city: **Jerusalem, Jerusalem, you who kill the prophets and stone those sent to you**. Calling out twice to the city—**Jerusalem, Jerusalem**—can convey a note of sadness, as over a death (see 2 Sam 19:1, 5), or of reproach (see 10:41; 22:31). Jesus has alluded to **prophets** dying in Jerusalem (verse 33); **those sent to you** also refers to prophets (see Isaiah 6:8; Jer 1:7). God **sent** prophets to his people to guide them along his way, keeping them off paths that lead to destruction. Jesus exclaims, **How many times I yearned to gather your children together**: the inhabitants of Jerusalem were spoken of as its **children** (Isaiah 66:8; Baruch 5:5; Joel 2:23). Jesus **yearned** to gather the inhabitants of Jerusalem to himself **as a hen gathers her brood under her wings**. Jesus uses an example of maternal care, of a **hen** sheltering her chicks **under her wings** to protect them, as an image for the care and protection he wants to give the people of Jerusalem. **Many times** Jesus wanted to care for them, **but**, he tells them, **you were unwilling!** That Jesus speaks of **many times** need not imply that Jesus has visited Jerusalem many times. We can best understand Jesus to be prophetically speaking on behalf of God, expressing God's continual desire to gather and protect his people. God wants to gather his people into his kingdom through Jesus, but many are **unwilling.**

For reflection: What does the image of a hen gathering her chicks under her wings convey to me about Jesus' care for me?

35 Because the people of Jerusalem were unwilling to accept God's protective care, Jesus prophetically pronounces, **Behold, your house will be abandoned**—abandoned by God. Jesus invokes a prophecy of Jeremiah in which God says, "I abandon my house" (Jer 12:7), referring either to the Temple or to his people. The same two senses are possible in Jesus' use of the word **house**. He may be referring to the Temple, the **house**

of God, for he will predict its destruction (21:5–6). More likely, however, Jesus is using **house** in the sense of household and referring to all of Jerusalem. Jerusalem will be destroyed by a besieging army (21:20–24) and **abandoned** because it did not recognize "what makes for peace" (19:41–44). Jesus concludes, **[But] I tell you, you will not see me until [the time comes when] you say, "Blessed is he who comes in the name of the Lord."** The quotation is from Psalm 118. Jesus' words can be interpreted in different ways. At the conclusion of his journey, as he is making his way down the Mount of Olives into Jerusalem, crowds will hail him, proclaiming, "Blessed is the king who comes / in the name of the Lord" (19:38). However, there would be little point in Jesus telling Jerusalem, "You will not see me until I arrive." Jesus may therefore be referring to his not being seen by the people of Jerusalem after his resurrection until he comes at the end of this age (9:26; 12:35–48; see also Acts 1:11). Then it will be evident that he **comes in the name of the Lord**—"comes in his glory and in the glory of the Father and of the holy angels" (9:26).

> Blessed is he
> who comes in the name of the LORD.
> Psalm 118:26

CHAPTER 14

ORIENTATION: *Jesus dines in a Pharisee's house and uses the occasion to invite Pharisees and scribes to new attitudes and behavior (14:1–24).*

Some Pharisees Refuse to Engage with Jesus

¹ **On a sabbath he went to dine at the home of one of the leading Pharisees, and the people there were observing him carefully.** ² **In front of him there was a man suffering from dropsy.** ³ **Jesus spoke to the scholars of the law and Pharisees in reply, asking, "Is it lawful to cure on the sabbath or not?"** ⁴ **But they kept silent; so he took the man and, after he had healed him, dismissed him.** ⁵ **Then he said to them, "Who among you, if your son or ox falls into a cistern, would not immediately pull him out on the sabbath day?"** ⁶ **But they were unable to answer his question.**

NT: Matt 12:11; Luke 6:6–11; 13:10–17

1   **On a sabbath he went to dine at the home of one of the leading Pharisees.** Jesus is willing to dine with everyone, no matter if they are tax collectors (5:29; 7:34) or **Pharisees**, who are often critical of him (5:21, 30; 6:2, 7, 11; 7:36, 39; 11:37, 53–54). His host this day is **one of the leading Pharisees**. It was the custom on the **sabbath** to eat a midday meal after synagogue services, often inviting guests. The meal would have been prepared the previous day to keep the Sabbath a day of rest. During this meal, religious topics often were discussed. **The people there were observing him carefully**: the connotation of **observing him carefully** is scrutinizing him. On a previous occasion "the scribes and the Pharisees watched him closely to see if he would cure on the sabbath so that they might discover a reason to accuse him" (6:7).

Sabbath: See page 158

Pharisees: See page 143

For reflection: What does Jesus' willingness to dine with Pharisees despite their opposition to him tell me about Jesus?

2 **In front of him there was a man suffering from dropsy.** Today **dropsy** is more commonly called edema. It is a swelling of tissue, often in the limbs, due to retained fluid, possibly caused by congestive heart failure or kidney disease. The man suffering from this condition is right **in front of him**; Jesus cannot fail to notice the man.

3 **Jesus spoke to the scholars of the law and Pharisees in reply**: Jesus is aware that he is being watched closely by **scholars of the law** (Luke sometimes refers to them as scribes: see 11:52–53) and **Pharisees**. Jesus knows that they consider his healings a work forbidden on the Sabbath (see 6:6–11; 13:10–17). **Jesus spoke to** them, in response to their watching to see whether he would heal the man with dropsy. He asked them, **Is it lawful to cure on the sabbath or not?** Jesus is not raising an abstract issue but asking, "In your view, does the law of Moses permit me to heal this man today?"

Scribes: See page 146

4 They should have had no difficulty answering Jesus' question; as scholars of the law they were trained to interpret and apply the law of Moses. They could have replied that in their interpretation, while preserving life took precedent over Sabbath regulations (see 1 Macc 2:41), medical treatment for non-life-threatening conditions cannot be performed on the Sabbath (see 13:14). Since dropsy was not a life-threatening condition, in their view it would not be lawful for Jesus to cure this man until the Sabbath was over. **But they kept silent.** Jesus gave them the opportunity to express their understanding of what the law of Moses required, which would have allowed him to address their reasoning and concerns. **But they kept silent** and would not engage with Jesus. **So he took the man and, after he had healed him, dismissed him.** Jesus does not allow their silence to prevent him from healing the man. He is carrying out his mission from God, performing healings today and tomorrow as he makes his way to Jerusalem (13:32). He **took** hold of the man, grasping him, and **healed him**. The word translated **dismissed** is translated "set free" at 13:12 and that is likely its connotation here. Like the woman he set free from curvature of the spine (13:12), Jesus sets the man free of his dropsy. Luke does not dwell on the healing because his main interest is in Jesus' interaction with the Pharisees and their scholars of the law.

5   Even though they declined to enter into a discussion of Sabbath law with Jesus (verses 4–5), he does not stop trying to reason with them. **Then he said to them, "Who among you, if your son or ox falls into a cistern, would not immediately pull him out on the sabbath day?"** Jesus knows that Pharisees would pull a **son or ox** out of a **cistern on the sabbath day**, and do so **immediately**, without waiting until the Sabbath was over. In this the Pharisees and their scholars of the law differed from another Jewish group, the Essenes. Essenes allowed that a human being could be pulled out of a well or pit on the Sabbath as long as no ropes or ladders or other implements were used, but that animals could not be pulled out on the Sabbath.

6   **But they were unable to answer his question**—unable in the sense of unwilling. They could have answered his question, acknowledging that they would indeed pull not only a son but also an ox out of a cistern on the Sabbath. But they realized that if they made this admission, then Jesus

---

BACKGROUND: ESSENES Although not mentioned in the Bible, ancient writers described Essenes as a sect of Jews. Pliny the Elder (a Roman who lived from A.D. 23 to 79) wrote, "On the west side of the Dead Sea is the solitary tribe of the Essenes, which is remarkable beyond all the other tribes in the whole world, as it has no women and has renounced all sexual desire, has no money, and has only palm trees for company" (*Natural History,* 5:73). The first-century Jewish historian Josephus described the Essenes as celibate men who lived at the Dead Sea and owned everything in common; he added that there were also Essenes, some married, who lived throughout the land. Josephus numbered the Essenes at four thousand, several hundred of whom lived at their headquarters by the Dead Sea, in all likelihood at the site known today as Qumran. Most scholars identify the Essenes as the group who collected or wrote the Dead Sea Scrolls. Some scrolls show that the Essenes rejected the current high priests in Jerusalem as illegitimate and Temple worship as corrupt. Essenes determined religious feasts by a calendar different from the one used by the Temple. They expected God to act soon to vindicate them in a cosmic battle that would bring the end of this age; God would send two messiahs, one priestly and one royal. The Essenes carefully studied and rigorously observed the law of Moses and made daily ritual washings and communal meals part of their life. The Gospels describe no encounters between Jesus and the Essenes, but Jesus was likely aware of them. Jesus and the Essenes would have agreed that God was about to act but would have differed over how. Rome destroyed Qumran in A.D. 68, and the Essenes disappeared from history. *Related topics: Dead Sea Scrolls (page 174).*

could retort, "If an ox can be set free from a cistern on the Sabbath, then how much more should a man be set free of his sickness on the Sabbath!" Jesus used similar reasoning in a previous situation to show the unreasonableness of their interpretation of Sabbath law (13:15–16). They are **unable** to refute Jesus' argument, and so refuse to **answer his question**.

Jesus has no interest in an academic debate about fine points of the law. His interest is in opening the minds of those he encounters to what God is doing through him. The time is critical (12:54–59); Jesus is calling men and women to repentance (13:1–9) so that they may enter through the narrow door of the kingdom of God and enjoy the heavenly banquet (13:23–30). He is setting free those in bondage to evil (verse 4; 13:10–17, 32). He accepted the Pharisee's invitation to dine in his home so that he could bring his message to Pharisees and scholars of the law. They have witnessed him set a man free from dropsy—surely a sign that God is at work through him. Yet they have refused to respond to him.

For reflection: How am I failing to engage with Jesus and respond to him?

A Parable about Being Exalted

⁷ He told a parable to those who had been invited, noticing how they were choosing the places of honor at the table. ⁸ "When you are invited by someone to a wedding banquet, do not recline at table in the place of honor. A more distinguished guest than you may have been invited by him, ⁹ and the host who invited both of you may approach you and say, 'Give your place to this man,' and then you would proceed with embarrassment to take the lowest place. ¹⁰ Rather, when you are invited, go and take the lowest place so that when the host comes to you he may say, 'My friend, move up to a higher position.' Then you will enjoy the esteem of your companions at the table. ¹¹ For everyone who exalts himself will be humbled, but the one who humbles himself will be exalted."

OT: Prov 25:6–7; Sirach 3:18
NT: Matt 23:6, 12; Luke 11:43; 18:14; 20:46

7   Jesus is in the house of a Pharisee for a Sabbath-day meal (14:1). **He told a parable to those who had been invited, noticing how they were**

choosing the places of honor at the table. The words **at the table**
are not in the Greek of Luke's Gospel but the translation adds them
to indicate that **the places of honor** are in seating arrangements at a
meal. Verse 8 indicates that it is a formal meal or banquet, which guests
ate while reclining on couches or cushions arranged in a U shape. The
food was served on low tables inside the U. Jesus notices that the guests
were choosing the places of honor. The **places of honor** at a banquet would have been to the right and left of the host, reclining on the
couch or cushions that formed the bottom of the U. Since the host is
"one of the leading Pharisees" (14:1), it is probable that some of his guests
are also prominent. Seating arrangements at banquets reflected social
standing; those concerned about their status would want to sit in **the
places of honor.** Jesus criticized Pharisees for loving "the seat of honor
in synagogues" (11:43) and will warn against scribes who love "seats of
honor in synagogues, and places of honor at banquets" (20:46). He uses
the competition for places of honor at this banquet as a springboard for
a **parable**.

Parables: See page 217
Banquets: See page 386

8 Jesus tells them, **When you are invited by someone to a wedding
banquet**—or by extension any banquet—**do not recline at table in
the place of honor.** The **place of honor** is literally the first place,
next to the host. It is risky to assign the place of highest honor to yourself, because **a more distinguished guest than you may have been
invited by him**: you can't be sure who is on the invitation list.

9 Distinguished guests tend to arrive late so that they can make a grand
entrance. If one does show up after you have reclined in the place of
honor, then **the host who invited both of you may approach you
and say, "Give your place to this man."** The **host** has final say in the
assignment of the place of highest honor. If someone more distinguished
than you arrives, then you will be bumped from the place of honor and
proceed with embarrassment to take the lowest place. All the
intermediate places at the banquet will have been filled, leaving only
the lowest place for you. Everyone present at the banquet will see your

public demotion, to your great **embarrassment**. You wanted honor but achieved disgrace.

10 **Rather,** to prevent this from happening, **when you are invited, go and take the lowest place so that when the host comes to you he may say, "My friend, move up to a higher position."** He will call you his **friend**, publicly acknowledging you. He will assign you a **higher** place carrying greater honor. **Then you will enjoy the esteem of your companions at the table**, literally, "all the ones reclining with you." The way to achieve the **esteem** of others is by letting the host honor you rather than by trying to grab a place of honor for yourself. Jesus echoes counsel given in Proverbs: do not claim honors, let others honor you (Prov 25:6–7).

> Claim no honor in the king's presence,
> nor occupy the place of great men;
> For it is better that you be told, "Come up closer!"
> than that you be humbled before the prince.
>
> Prov 25:6–7

Is Jesus merely giving shrewd advice? It may be a better strategy to pursue honors indirectly rather than directly, but in either case the goal is to be honored. Is Jesus advising those he condemns as honor-loving (11:43; 20:46) how to best obtain honors?

For reflection: How at this point do I understand Jesus' words?

11 Jesus is not giving shrewd advice but using shrewd advice as a parable (verse 7). He uses a principle that he will invoke on another occasion (18:14) to draw the lesson of the parable: **For everyone who exalts himself will be humbled**—it is implied, humbled by God—**but the one who humbles himself will be exalted**—exalted by God. Being in an exalted place of honor at a banquet is of no interest to Jesus (see 12:37; 22:27); what is of importance is being **exalted** by God. The word for **be exalted** literally means to be lifted up or raised up; its figurative meaning is to be honored. Jesus uses being raised up to a higher place and honored at an earthly banquet as an image for God raising someone

up and honoring them at the banquet of heaven (13:28–29; 14:15–24). God will exalt **the one who humbles himself** or herself before him. Jesus echoes the counsel of Sirach: those who humble themselves will find favor with God.

> *Humble yourself the more, the greater you are,*
> *and you will find favor with God.*
>
> Sirach 3:18

A human host might be taken in by a ploy of appearing humble, but God is not fooled. God knows what is in our hearts (16:15); those who exalt themselves will be brought down and humbled; those who are truly humble, and not play-acting, will be exalted by God. Human honors are empty and fleeting; those who seek them should turn their efforts to attaining heavenly honors by being truly humble.

For reflection: How concerned am I about my reputation and prestige? What does it mean for me to be humble before God?

Whom to Invite?
¹² **Then he said to the host who invited him, "When you hold a lunch or a dinner, do not invite your friends or your brothers or your relatives or your wealthy neighbors, in case they may invite you back and you have repayment. ¹³ Rather, when you hold a banquet, invite the poor, the crippled, the lame, the blind; ¹⁴ blessed indeed will you be because of their inability to repay you. For you will be repaid at the resurrection of the righteous."**
NT: Luke 6:32–36; 14:1

12 Jesus is dining in the house of a leading Pharisee (14:1). **Then he said to the host who invited him, "When you hold a lunch or a dinner"**: it was apparently customary to eat two basic meals a day, a late morning breakfast or **lunch,** and a late afternoon or early evening **dinner.** When you are having guests at a meal, **do not invite your friends or your brothers or your relatives or your wealthy neighbors.** It is natural to invite such people in for meals. **Friends** are those whom you enjoy being

with. **Brothers** and other **relatives** are your family. **Neighbors** who are **wealthy** would have influence and power; you might invite them to gain their goodwill. Yet Jesus says **do not invite** friends or family or the wealthy, **in case they may invite you back**. The customs of the time called for reciprocity—responding in kind, returning hospitality for hospitality, repaying favors. Jesus, however, teaches, **do not invite** those who will **invite you back**, for then you will have received **repayment** for your hospitality. Jesus' words may leave his host wondering, "What's wrong with being repaid for my hospitality? That's how society operates! If I shouldn't invite those I normally invite to dine with me, whom then should I invite?"

13 Jesus tells him, **Rather, when you hold a banquet, invite the poor, the crippled, the lame, the blind**. The Greek word translated **poor** means the abjectly poor, those reduced to begging. Those who are **crippled** or **lame** or **blind** would likely be among the abjectly poor because of their inability to earn a living in an economy where most supported themselves by some kind of manual labor. One might have a poor friend, or a crippled relative, or a blind neighbor whom one might naturally invite for a meal but Jesus is referring to the poor and disabled with whom one has no ties. Poor strangers are not normally invited into one's home for a **banquet,** yet Jesus instructs his host to invite them **rather** than those he normally invites. Jesus overturns the practice of reciprocity, of helping only those who help you (see 6:32–36).

Banquets: See page 386

14 Jesus pronounces a beatitude upon his host if he invites the poor and disabled to his table, telling him **blessed indeed will you be because of their inability to repay you**. Those who are unable to work and are abjectly poor do not have the means to **repay** anyone for what they receive. Jesus proclaims that those who assist them will be **blessed indeed** because they will receive nothing in return—nothing immediate, that is: **For you will be repaid at the resurrection of the righteous.** The connotation of **will be repaid** is repaid by God. This is the first mention of **resurrection** in Luke's Gospel. At **the resurrection** of the dead, the **righteous** or upright will awaken to eternal life (see Dan 12:2–3). Those who feed the poor will be **repaid** by God for their gen-

erosity; God will repay those whom the poor cannot. Those who invite the poor into their banquets on earth—and by extension, help the poor in any way—will be admitted to the banquet in the kingdom of God (see 13:29; 14:15).

Beatitudes: See page 169

For reflection: How am I helping those who cannot pay me back? Who is in need that I am able to assist?

Who Will Dine in the Kingdom of God?

¹⁵ One of his fellow guests on hearing this said to him, "Blessed is the one who will dine in the kingdom of God." ¹⁶ He replied to him, "A man gave a great dinner to which he invited many. ¹⁷ When the time for the dinner came, he dispatched his servant to say to those invited, 'Come, everything is now ready.' ¹⁸ But one by one, they all began to excuse themselves. The first said to him, 'I have purchased a field and must go to examine it; I ask you, consider me excused.' ¹⁹ And another said, 'I have purchased five yoke

---

BACKGROUND: RESURRECTION While there was apparently no belief in an afterlife worth living during most of the Old Testament era, various hopes for the resurrection of the dead arose in the two centuries before Jesus. These hopes were associated with expectations that God would transform the world, ending the present age and inaugurating a new one. One of the first hopes was that martyrs who had given up their lives for their faith would be raised to new life so that they could be part of God's new creation (2 Macc 6—7). The book of Daniel went a step further: not only would the righteous be raised to be part of God's reign, but the wicked would be raised as well, to be punished (Dan 12:2). How Jews conceived of resurrected bodies depended on how they conceived of God's reign in the age to come. If the age to come would be like the present age except that God would be in charge, then a person's body in the age to come would be like that person's present body (2 Macc 14:46). Some conceived of the age to come in less earthly terms and thought that resurrected bodies would be heavenly bodies, making humans like angels. At the time of Jesus, some Jews, including Pharisees, believed in the resurrection of the dead, but other Jews, including Sadducees, did not (Acts 23:7–8). *Related topics: The age to come (page 487), Jewish expectations at the time of Jesus (page 69), Judgment (page 327), Life after death (page 298).*

---

of oxen and am on my way to evaluate them; I ask you, consider me excused.' ²⁰ And another said, 'I have just married a woman, and therefore I cannot come.' ²¹ The servant went and reported this to his master. Then the master of the house in a rage commanded his servant, 'Go out quickly into the streets and alleys of the town and bring in here the poor and the crippled, the blind and the lame.' ²² The servant reported, 'Sir, your orders have been carried out and still there is room.' ²³ The master then ordered the servant, 'Go out to the highways and hedgerows and make people come in that my home may be filled. ²⁴ For, I tell you, none of those men who were invited will taste my dinner.' "

OT: Isaiah 25:6–9

NT: Matt 22:1–14; Luke 13:22–30; 14:1–14

15 Jesus, together with some Pharisees and scholars of the law, is dining in the house of a leading Pharisee (14:1, 3). He told those at the meal that if they invited the poor and disabled to their banquets, they would "be repaid at the resurrection of the righteous" (14:14). **One of his fellow guests on hearing this said to him, "Blessed is the one who will dine in the kingdom of God."** Isaiah used a feast or banquet as an image for God's ultimate salvation; death will be destroyed and God "will provide for all peoples / A feast of rich food and choice wines" (Isaiah 25:6–9). Jesus drew on this image when he spoke of those who "will recline at table in the kingdom of God" (13:29). One of the **guests** dining with Jesus correctly understands that to be "repaid at the resurrection of the righteous" (14:14) means to **dine in the kingdom of God**. He pronounces a beatitude upon those whose good fortune it will be to take part in the heavenly banquet: **blessed is the one who will** be raised by God to **dine in the kingdom of God**.

Beatitudes: See page 169

Kingdom of God: See page 381

16 Jesus agrees that those who will be at God's eternal banquet are blessed and fortunate indeed, but this raises a question: who will dine in the kingdom of God? Jesus addresses this question with a parable. **A man gave a great dinner to which he invited many.** The word translated

dinner is used for the late afternoon or early evening meal. It is a **great** dinner to which **many** are invited; the **man** is a person of some means, able to give a large banquet. For such banquets, invitations were sent out some days in advance with the ancient equivalent of an RSVP. After those who were **invited** accepted their invitations, the host would know how many people were coming and how much food to prepare.

Parables: See page 217

Banquets: See page 386

17 **When the time for the dinner came, he dispatched his servant**—literally, his slave—**to say to those invited, "Come, everything is now ready."** This too was standard practice; those who had already been invited were summoned when the food was prepared and everything was in place for the banquet.

Servant, slave: See page 454

18 **But one by one, they all began to excuse themselves.** After accepting an invitation to a banquet, it is rude not to attend, especially when one waits until after the food is prepared to **excuse** oneself. It would be unheard of for **all** those invited to back out, but this is what happens in the parable. Jesus provides the excuses of three of the non-attendees as a sampling. **The first said to him, "I have purchased a field and must go to examine it; I ask you, consider me excused."** The man's excuse is absurd. No farmer or estate owner would purchase a **field**—farmland—without first examining it for the quality of its soil, seeing whether there was a spring or other source of water for crops, and weighing all the factors that must be taken into account in determining its desirability and value. And even if the man had in fact bought a field without first seeing it, surely the examination could wait until the following morning; there is no reason why he **must** go immediately. One thing is clear: the man chooses to go to his field rather than to the banquet.

19 **And another said, "I have purchased five yoke of oxen and am on my way to evaluate them; I ask you, consider me excused."** Again, the excuse makes no sense. **Five yoke of oxen**—ten oxen linked two by

403

two for plowing—would have been sufficient to work well over a hundred acres of crop land, a large farm by the standards of the time (the average farmer might have five to ten acres). A man who needed ten oxen for his farm was at least moderately wealthy. It is unlikely that he could retain his wealth if he was so foolhardy as to buy oxen without first evaluating them. Were they young, well-fed, and strong, or sickly and on their last legs? And even if the man had bought ten oxen unseen, evaluating them could easily wait until the next day. Again, clearly the man chooses his oxen over the banquet.

20 **And another said, "I have just married a woman, and therefore I cannot come."** The previous two non-attendees at least made a pretense of politeness by asking to be excused; this man responds with a brusque **I cannot come**. His reason, like the previous reasons, is absurd: **I have just married a woman**. He certainly knew that he was or would be recently married when he accepted the invitation to the banquet; marriage is hardly an unforeseen circumstance. Nor does being recently married mean that a husband cannot be away from his wife for a few hours (banquets were normally male affairs, and she would not have been invited). Nor in the culture of the time did a wife have authority over her husband, such that she could prevent him from honoring an invitation he had accepted. Yet he says **I cannot come** because of his wife, choosing to remain with her rather than attend the banquet.

> *For reflection: At this point in the parable, what do I make of the three excuses?*

21 **The servant went and reported this to his master.** The word translated here as **master** is in some contexts translated as "lord." The servant conveys the excuses and refusals to his master; no one invited to the banquet is going to show up. **Then the master of the house in a rage commanded his servant, "Go out quickly into the streets and alleys of the town and bring in here the poor and the crippled, the blind and the lame."** The **streets** and **alleys** of the **town** are where beggars and the unemployed hang out. The Greek word translated **poor** means those reduced to begging, the abjectly poor. Among the abjectly

poor would be those who are **crippled** or **blind** or **lame** and unable to earn a living. None of these people were on the original invitation list; a man wealthy enough to provide a large banquet (verse 16) would invite others of similar wealth, such as the man who could afford five yoke of oxen. He would not invite **poor** people off the street. But in his **rage** over being rudely, almost contemptuously treated by all those he originally invited, the man turns to those who are available on a moment's notice, the unemployed. His banquet is prepared and ready, and he is determined that it not go to waste. He tells his servant to go **quickly**, for the food is on the table, and **bring in** those he finds on the streets and alleys of the town—**the poor and the crippled, the blind and the lame**.

22 **The servant** did so and then **reported, "Sir, your orders have been carried out and still there is room."** The man has prepared a great banquet, able to accommodate many (verse 16), and there are not enough poor and disabled in the town to fill it; **still there is room** for more.

23 **The master then ordered the servant, "Go out to the highways and hedgerows and make people come in."** The slave is told to go out of the town to expand his search for guests, going to the **highways** and to the **hedgerows**—hedges grown around vineyards and fields as fences ("A man planted a vineyard, put a hedge around it"—Mark 12:1). He is to invite everyone he can find, whoever they are. He is to **make** them come to the banquet: the word translated **make** can mean to persuade, to urge with compelling speech. The man tells his slave to do so in order **that my home may be filled**.

24 Jesus does not say that the servant was able to persuade enough people to come; as the parable ends, the banquet is still in the process of being filled, with room for more. The man giving the banquet exclaims, **For, I tell you, none of those men who were invited will taste my dinner**. In one sense, this is a banal observation: those who refused to attend the banquet will of course not taste it. But there is a quirk in the host's words. Although he has been speaking only to his servant (verses 21, 23), his final declaration is addressed to a broader audience: the **you** in **I tell**

you is plural in Greek. It is as if the host steps out of the parable and addresses those whom Jesus is dining with, pointing out an implication of the parable for them.

What is that implication—and more broadly, what is the significance of the parable? Jesus told this parable about a banquet in response to someone proclaiming the blessedness of those who will dine in the kingdom of God (verses 15–16). The banquet in the parable corresponds to the heavenly banquet, with the "master," or lord, in the parable (verse 21) corresponding to the Lord God. Those who were first invited correspond to those whom God invited first to the heavenly banquet: the people with whom he made a covenant at Mount Sinai and whom he is now summoning into his kingdom through his servant Jesus. Some are refusing the invitation, not being willing to set aside their preoccupations with possessions (see 8:14; 14:33; 16:13; 18:22–30) or family ties (see 9:59–62; 14:26; 18:29) or whatever they think excuses them from heeding the invitation. The final words of the parable are addressed to them and implicitly convey a warning that time for them to respond is running out (see 12:54–59; 13:1–9). They should reconsider before it is too late for them to enter the banquet of heaven (see 13:23–30). Whatever excuses they might offer for not responding are absurd when their eternal destiny is at stake.

For reflection: How are my concerns about possessions or personal relationships or other matters inhibiting me from making a wholehearted response to Jesus?

In the parable, the host may have invited the poor and disabled because of their availability, but their being brought into a banquet representing the heavenly banquet has significance. Many considered wealth to be a sign of God's favor and approval, basing their view on Scripture (Deut 28:1–14; Job 1:9–10; 42:10; Sirach 11:21–22). Such a view would make the poor less favored in the sight of God and in the sight of others. The disabled were likewise usually marginalized. One Jewish group, the Essenes, excluded those who were crippled, lame, or blind from their community assemblies and communal meals. Jesus has shown special compassion for the marginalized and excluded: "the blind regain their sight, the lame walk . . . the poor have the good news proclaimed to them" (7:22). Jesus invites others to likewise have special compassion on the poor and excluded: "when you hold a banquet, invite the poor, the crippled, the lame, the blind" (14:13). They are welcome in the heavenly banquet; they should be welcomed now by disciples of Jesus.

Essenes: See page 395

For reflection: Who are the excluded today? What am I able to do to overcome their exclusion?

Those who come into the banquet last, brought in from outlying areas (verse 23), represent those who will be brought into the banquet of the kingdom of God through the worldwide mission of the Church (see Acts 1:8), Gentiles as well as Jews. There is still room in the kingdom for more (verse 22); God is eager for his heavenly banquet hall to be filled (verse 23) and makes repeated efforts to draw men and women in.

Who will dine in the kingdom of God? Those who accept and act on God's invitation. Blessed are they (verse 15), blessed and fortunate indeed!

For reflection: Have I accepted all that God offers me? What can I do to more fully respond to his invitation to me?

Counting the Cost of Commitment

25 Great crowds were traveling with him, and he turned and addressed them, 26 "If any one comes to me without hating his father and mother, wife and children, brothers and sisters, and even his own life, he cannot be my disciple. 27 Whoever does not carry his own cross and come after me cannot be my disciple. 28 Which of you wishing to construct a tower does not first sit down and calculate the cost to see if there is enough for its completion? 29 Otherwise, after laying the foundation and finding himself unable to finish the work the onlookers should laugh at him 30 and say, 'This one began to build but did not have the resources to finish.' 31 Or what king marching into battle would not first sit down

and decide whether with ten thousand troops he can successfully oppose another king advancing upon him with twenty thousand troops? ³² But if not, while he is still far away, he will send a delegation to ask for peace terms. ³³ In the same way, everyone of you who does not renounce all his possessions cannot be my disciple.

³⁴ "Salt is good, but if salt itself loses its taste, with what can its flavor be restored? ³⁵ It is fit neither for the soil nor for the manure pile; it is thrown out. Whoever has ears to hear ought to hear."

Gospel parallels: Matt 5:13; 10:37–38; 16:24; Mark 8:34; 9:50
NT: Luke 9:23–24, 59–62; 13:25–27

25 **Great crowds were traveling with him**: Jesus is on his way to Jerusalem (9:51, 53; 13:22), where he knows suffering and death await him (9:22, 44; 13:33). **Great crowds** of people constantly gather around Jesus (4:42; 5:1, 15; 6:17–18; 7:11; 8:4, 40; 9:11, 37; 12:1); that they are **traveling with him** does not mean that all of them have become his disciples. Some have heard him teach and have shared meals with him but have not acted on his teachings (see 13:25–27). **He turned and addressed them**: Jesus paused in his journey and **turned** to the crowd so that he can tell them what is required to follow him as a disciple and not simply travel with him.

26 **If any one comes to me**: being a disciple of Jesus is possible for **any one**. Jesus speaks of the person who **comes** to him, wishing to become his disciple, but does so **without hating his father and mother, wife and children, brothers and sisters, and even his own life**. In biblical idiom, to hate can mean to love less. Genesis says that Jacob loved Rachel more than Leah, characterizing Leah as hated (Gen 29:30–31; the word in Gen 29:31 that the New American Bible translates as "unloved" is literally "hated"). Jesus will uphold the commandment to honor one's father and mother (18:20; Exod 20:12; Deut 5:16), so when he speaks of **hating** one's **father** and **mother** the sense is loving them less (see Matt 10:37). Jesus says that anyone who loves his parents or **wife** or **children** or **brothers** or **sisters** more than they love him **cannot be my disciple**. As deeply as one might love a parent or sibling, a spouse or child, one must love Jesus even more. One's commitment to him must take precedence over one's commitment to family (see also 9:59–62). This was a

radical demand in the society of the time, which placed great importance on family ties and loyalty. Jesus foresaw that some of his disciples would face opposition from family members (see 12:51–53; 21:16); he makes it clear that his disciples' first allegiance must be to him.

> *For reflection: Who is the one person on earth that I most love? What do I do out of love for that person? Do I have even greater love for Jesus? What do I do out of love for him?*

A disciple must love Jesus more than **even his** or her **own life**. Jesus taught, "If anyone wishes to come after me, he must deny himself . . . For whoever wishes to save his life will lose it, but whoever loses his life for my sake will save it" (9:23–24). If someone is unwilling to put Jesus above **even his** or her **own life**, if someone is unwilling to deny himself or herself and lose their life for the sake of Jesus, then Jesus says that he or she **cannot be my disciple**. The door to the banquet of heaven stands open (see 14:21–23), but it is a narrow door (see 13:24, 29), and there is a cost to enter. The price of admission is one's very self, given to Jesus in order to be his disciple.

Disciple: See page 149

> *For reflection: What are the indications that I love Jesus more than I love myself? What are the indications that I love myself more than I love Jesus?*

27 **Whoever does not carry his own cross and come after me cannot be my disciple.** Those listening to Jesus were well aware of how Romans carried out crucifixions. A condemned person was stripped of his clothes and forced to carry a crossbeam to the place of execution, where it was affixed to an upright beam already in place. Jesus previously taught that anyone wanting to be his disciple must "take up his cross daily and follow me" (9:23). Here Jesus says that a disciple must **carry** his or her cross: the verb for **carry** is in a tense that conveys an ongoing process rather than a onetime event. Those who wish to be Jesus' disciples must continually live as though they were on the way to crucifixion, stripped of all status and possessions, wrenched away from their former life. That is the only way to **come after** Jesus, who is himself on the way to crucifixion. Those who do not continually set aside all things for the sake of Jesus, casting

them off as rigorously as they would be divested of them by crucifixion, **cannot be** his **disciples**.

Crucifixion: See page 626

For reflection: What does it mean for me to carry my cross in order to come after Jesus?

28 Jesus wants those listening to him to face up to the cost of following him, and he tells two parables to make the point. He begins the first by asking, **Which of you wishing to construct a tower**: the **tower** might be for a vineyard, so that a guard could keep watch over the ripened grapes until they were harvested (see Isaiah 5:1–2; Mark 12:1). Anyone intending to build a tower will **first sit down and calculate the cost to see if there is enough for its completion**—to see if he or she has enough cash to pay all the construction costs. That is the common-sense thing to do.

Parables: See page 217

29 **Otherwise, after laying the foundation and finding himself unable to finish the work**: if someone begins building a tower without having the funds to complete it, construction will stop when the money runs out. The tower's **foundation** sitting in the abandoned construction site will be a monument to the foolishness of the builder. Those who see it, **the onlookers**, will **laugh at him**, ridiculing and deriding him.

30 They will **say, "This one began to build but did not have the resources to finish."** The unfinished tower will be a reminder that its builder did not have enough common sense to make sure he had **the resources to finish** before beginning to **build**. It will be a continuing source of amusement for the neighborhood and embarrassment for him. To avoid such embarrassment, one should calculate the cost before laying the first stone.

31 Jesus follows his parable about building a tower with a parable about a king in a time of war. **Or what king marching into battle**: things have already been set in motion and the king is on his way to a **battle**. A king in such a situation would **first sit down** before reaching the battle site **and decide whether with** his **ten thousand troops he**

can successfully oppose another king advancing upon him with twenty thousand troops. The two kings are **advancing** toward each other; some kind of confrontation is inevitable. The first king must consider whether his army can defeat the other king's army.

32 **But if not**, if he calculates that the other king will defeat him, **while he is still far away** from the battle site **he will send a delegation** to the other king **to ask for peace terms**. There is no guarantee that he will receive favorable terms, but the alternative is sure defeat, with thousands of his soldiers and perhaps he himself losing their lives. Only a foolish king would go into a war he cannot win.

Jesus tells these two parables after placing high demands on those who would be his disciples. They must love him more than they love their families and more than they love themselves; they must be willing to live as though on the way to crucifixion (verses 26–27). Jesus' parables convey that any would-be disciples should carefully count the cost of discipleship before setting out to follow him. Don't start what you are not prepared to finish.

For reflection: What is Jesus asking of me as his disciple? Am I committed to following him to the end, despite the cost?

33 Jesus seems to take it for granted that his listeners will understand the parables in light of his demands to put him above their families and above themselves. He applies the parables to a further demand: **In the same way, everyone of you who does not renounce all his possessions cannot be my disciple**. The word translated **renounce** also means to say farewell to (which is how it is translated at 9:61); Jesus is telling those who would be his disciples that they need to say goodbye to their possessions. **Renounce** is in a tense that conveys ongoing action. **Possessions** means what is at one's disposal. Jesus here requires his disciples to give up **all** of their belongings, to dispose of everything that is at their disposal. The two parables indicate that this too is one of the costs of discipleship that one must take into account before setting out to follow Jesus.

For reflection: What is my reaction to Jesus' asking those who would follow him to renounce all of their possessions?

This is not the first time that possessions or wealth have come up in the Gospel of Luke, nor will it be the last (see 5:11, 28; 6:20, 24, 30, 35; 8:3, 14; 9:3; 10:4; 12:33; 14:13; 16:9–13; 18:22–30; 19:8–10). Sometimes Jesus requires giving up everything; sometimes he seems satisfied with great generosity; he will commend Zacchaeus for giving away half of his possessions to the poor (19:8–10). Perhaps the key to understanding Jesus' teaching here is that his words end with the same refrain he used twice earlier: anyone who does not renounce all possessions **cannot be my disciple**, just as anyone who puts family first **cannot be my disciple** (verse 26) and anyone who does not carry his or her cross **cannot be my disciple** (verse 27). Renouncing possessions is not an isolated requirement but an aspect of what a person must do in order to be Jesus' disciple. Setting aside family, self, and possessions are three facets of the complete commitment that Jesus requires of his disciples. Whatever gets in the way of following Jesus, whether it be relationships with others or self-love or possessions or anything else, must be renounced. Jesus wants his followers to face up to what it means to follow him, and to get rid of whatever prevents them from wholeheartedly being his disciples.

For reflection: What impedes me from following Jesus wholeheartedly? What is he asking me to renounce for his sake?

34 Jesus adds another parable or comparison. **Salt is good**: the word translated **good** can have the connotation of "useful." Salt is useful for flavoring or preserving food. **But if salt itself loses its taste, with what can its flavor be restored?** It is pointless to speculate about how **salt** could lose its **taste** without ceasing to be salt; Jesus is proposing a hypothetical situation. Should all your salt lose its taste, its saltiness, how could you restore it? You have nothing to salt it with, so you are left with useless salt.

35 **It is fit neither for the soil nor for the manure pile.** Being **fit . . . for the soil** is cryptic; salt is not normally used as a soil conditioner or fertilizer. There is some evidence, though, that when dried dung was used in cooking fires, salt could serve as a catalyst to make it burn better; this might be the meaning of being fit **for the manure pile**. The general sense of Jesus' words is clear: salt that loses its saltiness is good for nothing and **it is thrown out**, disposed of as useless.

Jesus concludes by saying, **Whoever has ears to hear ought to hear**: Whoever has ears should perceive the significance of what Jesus said about salt. Since Jesus speaks of salt to conclude his teachings about the requirements of discipleship, salt that is good presumably stands for disciples who meet the requirements: those who, after recognizing the cost of complete commitment to Jesus, are renouncing everything that would keep them from following him wholeheartedly. Salt that loses its flavor represents disciples who have compromised or lost their commitment. They have become useless as disciples; they are good for nothing and may be cast out of the band of disciples.

For reflection: Have I lost any of my saltiness, my commitment to Jesus, my usefulness to him? What can I—or Jesus—do to restore my saltiness?

CHAPTER 15

ORIENTATION: *In response to being criticized for associating with sinners, Jesus tells parables that convey the message that God seeks out the lost and is filled with great joy when they are found (15:1–32).*

Searching, Finding, Rejoicing

¹ **The tax collectors and sinners were all drawing near to listen to him,** ² **but the Pharisees and scribes began to complain, saying, "This man welcomes sinners and eats with them."** ³ **So to them he addressed this parable.** ⁴ **"What man among you having a hundred sheep and losing one of them would not leave the ninety-nine in the desert and go after the lost one until he finds it?** ⁵ **And when he does find it, he sets it on his shoulders with great joy** ⁶ **and, upon his arrival home, he calls together his friends and neighbors and says to them, 'Rejoice with me because I have found my lost sheep.'** ⁷ **I tell you, in just the same way there will be more joy in heaven over one sinner who repents than over ninety-nine righteous people who have no need of repentance.**

⁸ **"Or what woman having ten coins and losing one would not light a lamp and sweep the house, searching carefully until she finds it?** ⁹ **And when she does find it, she calls together her friends and neighbors and says to them, 'Rejoice with me because I have found the coin that I lost.'** ¹⁰ **In just the same way, I tell you, there will be rejoicing among the angels of God over one sinner who repents."**

Gospel parallels: Matt 18:12–14
OT: Psalm 23; Isaiah 40:10–11; Ezek 34:11–12
NT: Luke 3:12–13; 5:27–32; 7:29, 34; 19:10

1 **The tax collectors and sinners were all drawing near to listen to him.** By **sinners** Luke does not mean those who were a little lax in their religious observances but those who seriously violated God's laws—habitual thieves, for example. **Tax collectors** were lumped together with sinners because they often extorted more than the prescribed taxes (see

3:12–13). They were **all drawing near to** Jesus: Luke describes a general pattern rather than a specific incident. Jesus concluded his previous teaching by exhorting, "Whoever has ears to hear ought to hear" (14:35). By drawing near to Jesus **to listen to him**, tax collectors and sinners are taking the first step toward transformed lives. They were among those who accepted John's baptism of repentance (3:12; 7:29); now many of them are making a positive response to Jesus.

Tax collectors: See page 94

For reflection: What steps can I take to draw near to Jesus to listen to him?

2 **But the Pharisees and scribes began to complain**: the Greek verb translated **began to complain** is in a tense that can equally well have the sense, "kept complaining." **Pharisees** and **scribes**, or scholars of the law, are grumbling, **This man welcomes sinners and eats with them**, a complaint they have made in the past (5:30; 7:34). They refer to Jesus as **this man**, literally, "this one," an expression with a slightly contemptuous ring. They charge that Jesus **welcomes sinners**, willingly receiving and accepting them. Pharisees and their scribes believed that sinners should be shunned in disapproval of their sinfulness. They complain that Jesus even **eats with them**. In the culture of the time, sharing a meal with others meant entering into fellowship with them; shared food signified shared lives. By eating with sinners, Jesus unequivocally demonstrates his acceptance of them. Sharing meals with them gave him an opportunity to bring his message to them, just as he addressed his words to Pharisees and scribes when he ate with them (7:36–50; 11:37–54; 14:1–24).

Pharisees: See page 143
Scribes: See page 146

For reflection: How has Jesus demonstrated his acceptance of me?

3 **So to them**, Pharisees and scribes, **he addressed this parable**—a series of parables, in fact (15:4–32). Each parable deals with the complaint that Jesus welcomes sinners and eats with them.

Parables: See page 217

4 Jesus asks his critics, **What man among you having a hundred sheep and losing one of them**: not everyone in Jesus' audience would have had the means to own **a hundred sheep**, a moderately sizable flock by the standards of the time, but each of them could imagine owning such a flock. They could likewise easily imagine **losing one of them**: sheep tend to wander as they graze. Should that happen, Jesus asks, **would** the owner who is shepherding his sheep **not leave the ninety-nine in the desert and go after the lost one until he finds it?** By **desert** Jesus refers to a wilderness region that is too arid for farming, but where sheep and goats can graze on wild vegetation. Leaving **the ninety-nine in the desert** simply means allowing the ninety-nine to continue to graze, presumably in someone's care, so that the shepherd can **go after the lost one**. The shepherd is determined to find his lost sheep and keeps on searching for it **until he finds it**. He devotes more attention and effort to the one lost sheep than to the ninety-nine that are still safely in the flock.

Those listening to Jesus' parable might already perceive that the shepherd stands for God, for this is a common image for God in the Old Testament. Psalm 23 begins, "The LORD is my shepherd" (Psalm 23:1). In a prophecy of Ezekiel, God promised to gather his scattered people as a shepherd gathers his scattered sheep (Ezek 34:11–12). In Jesus' parable, the shepherd's persistence in searching for his lost sheep conveys God's persistence in searching out those who have strayed from him.

> Thus says the Lord GOD: I myself will look after
> and tend my sheep.
> As a shepherd tends his flock when he finds himself among
> his scattered sheep, so will I tend my sheep. I will rescue
> them from every place where they were scattered.
> Ezek 34:11–12

5 **And when he does find it**, as he surely will, since he will keep searching until he does, **he sets it on his shoulders with great joy**. He may carry the sheep back to the flock **on his shoulders** because that is the most practical way to transport it, but the image is also reminiscent of a prophecy of Isaiah that uses a shepherd carrying his sheep as an image for God's tender care for his people (Isaiah 40:10–11). The shepherd in Jesus'

parable carries his sheep **with great joy**, relieved that he found it before it fell prey to predators, happy that it is now safe.

> Like a shepherd he feeds his flock;
>> in his arms he gathers the lambs,
> Carrying them in his bosom,
>> and leading the ewes with care.
>
> Isaiah 40:11

For reflection: How has God come looking for me when I have strayed? What does the image of a shepherd carrying his sheep convey to me about God's care for me?

6 The shepherd is filled with such great joy that **upon his arrival home**, presumably at the end of the workday, **he calls together his friends and neighbors and says to them, "Rejoice with me because I have found my lost sheep."** He is so filled with joy that he must share it, telling his friends and neighbors to **rejoice with me**.

7 Jesus makes it explicit that the shepherd in the parable stands for God: **I tell you, in just the same way there will be more joy in heaven over one sinner who repents than over ninety-nine righteous people who have no need of repentance**. The Old Testament spoke of **repentance** as a return to God, and that notion is present here. Through **repentance** one adopts new ways of thinking and behaving (see 3:8); through **repentance** one turns away from sin and turns to God. Jesus knows what fills God with **joy**: the **repentance** and return to him of even **one sinner**. Just as a shepherd rejoices over a lost sheep being found and restored to the flock, so God rejoices over someone lost in sin being rescued and restored. That does not mean that God is any less concerned about those **who have no need of repentance**, any more than the shepherd is unconcerned about the ninety-nine sheep that were not lost. Rather, God is concerned for every woman and man, just as the shepherd is concerned for every one of his sheep. Because of that concern, God seeks out those who become lost, and is filled with joy when they are found. God sought out the lost and invited them to repentance through John the Baptist (3:1–14) and is now doing so through Jesus.

Jesus welcomes sinners to himself, explaining "I have not come to call the righteous to repentance but sinners" (5:32). If Jesus devotes special attention and effort to sinners, it is because they are in need of it.

Repentance: See page 92

8 Jesus tells a second parable: **Or what woman having ten coins and losing one**. The word translated **coins** is literally "drachmas"; the value of a drachma varied over time but was roughly equivalent to a day's wage for an ordinary laborer (see Tobit 5:15, which refers to a drachma). The sheep owner in the previous parable was moderately well off; this woman is rather poor, having savings of only ten drachmas. If she lost one of them, she would **light a lamp and sweep the house, searching carefully** for her coin. Most ordinary people lived in one-room houses, used mainly for sleeping and shelter from the elements. Such houses had few if any windows and were dark; one searching for a small coin would **light** an oil **lamp**. Floors were packed earth or cobblestone, sometimes strewn with straw; the woman will **sweep the house** and search through the sweepings for her coin, **searching carefully until she finds it.** She is persistent in her search; she cannot afford to lose even one of her coins.

Houses: See page 186

9 **And when she does find it, she calls together her friends and neighbors**: in the Greek of Luke's Gospel, the words for **friends** and **neighbors** are both feminine. After finding her coin, she **calls together** the women who are her friends and neighbors **and says to them, "Rejoice with me because I have found the coin that I lost."** She must share her great joy with those to whom she is close.

There are obvious parallels between Jesus' two parables: a lost possession (sheep/coin); a search until it is found; friends and neighbors invited to rejoice with the finder. In using a shepherd to represent God, the first parable has ample precedents in Scripture. Jesus' second parable, however, is unprecedented in its use of a woman to stand for God—and an ordinary, rather poor woman at that and not, say, a queen. It is striking that Jesus pairs a male image for God with a female image for God. Both images portray God as one who searches persistently for those who are lost and rejoices when they are found.

For reflection: What significance do I find in Jesus' using a woman to represent God?

10 **In just the same way, I tell you, there will be rejoicing among the angels of God over one sinner who repents.** The second parable concludes as does the first: heaven is filled with rejoicing when the lost is found. Jesus has the same attitude toward sinners as does God, and his mission from God is to search for and restore the lost: "The Son of Man has come to seek and to save what was lost" (19:10). Consequently Jesus "welcomes sinners and eats with them" (verse 2), calling them to repent (see 13:1–5). Rather than complain and grumble about Jesus' association with sinners, the Pharisees and scribes should join in the heavenly rejoicing over the success of Jesus' mission.

Angels: See page 11

ORIENTATION: *Although Jesus' parable in verses 11 to 32 is traditionally called the Parable of the Prodigal Son, its main character is a loving father who has two wayward sons.*

A Loving Father and His Younger Son
" **Then he said, "A man had two sons,** " **and the younger son said to his father, 'Father, give me the share of your estate that should come to me.' So the father divided the property between them.** " **After a few days, the younger son collected all his belongings and set off to a distant country where he squandered his inheritance on a life of dissipation.** " **When he had freely spent everything, a severe famine struck that country, and he found himself in dire need.** " **So he hired himself out to one of the local citizens who sent him to his farm to tend the swine.** " **And he longed to eat his fill of the pods on which the swine fed, but nobody gave him any.** " **Coming to his senses he thought, 'How many of my father's hired workers have more than enough food to eat, but here am I, dying from hunger.** " **I shall get up and go to my father and I shall say to him, "Father, I have sinned against heaven and against you.** " **I no longer deserve to be called your son; treat me as you would treat one of your hired workers."'** " **So he got up and went back**

419

to his father. While he was still a long way off, his father caught sight of him, and was filled with compassion. He ran to his son, embraced him and kissed him. ²¹ His son said to him, 'Father, I have sinned against heaven and against you; I no longer deserve to be called your son.' ²² But his father ordered his servants, 'Quickly bring the finest robe and put it on him; put a ring on his finger and sandals on his feet. ²³ Take the fattened calf and slaughter it. Then let us celebrate with a feast, ²⁴ because this son of mine was dead, and has come to life again; he was lost, and has been found.' Then the celebration began.

OT: Deut 21:17; Sirach 33:19–24
NT: Luke 15:1–10

11 Jesus is responding to Pharisees and scribes who criticize him for welcoming sinners and eating with them (15:1–2). After telling them two parables about the lost being found (15:3–10), **he said, "A man had two sons."** Jesus begins a new parable by saying that a certain **man** had **two sons**, indicating that the man and his two sons are the focal points of the parable.

Parables: See page 217

12 **and the younger son said to his father, "Father, give me the share of your estate that should come to me."** It will become evident in the course of the parable that the father's **estate** includes farmland and cattle, and that, in addition to his slaves and servants, he hires day laborers. This indicates that he is reasonably well off and that his **estate** is not insignificant. According to the law of Moses, if there are two male heirs, the **younger son** would receive one-third of an estate upon his father's death, with a double share, two-thirds, going to the firstborn son (Deut 21:17). Normally the estate would be distributed to the sons only after the father's death, but it was legally possible for a man to make a distribution while he was still alive (see Tobit 8:21), even though it was considered unwise for him to do so (Sirach 33:19–24). There was no provision in the law that allowed a son to demand his share of the estate while his father was living. Yet the younger son does so. He does not tell his father why he wants his share immediately; he simply asks his father to **give** it to him.

The implication of the son's words is, "I can't wait around for you to die; give me my share now." How would a father respond to such a request? In the culture of the time, a father might be expected to indignantly refuse the demand and to beat his son for his impudence and disrespect (see Prov 13:24; 22:15; 23:13–14; 29:15).

> *For reflection: If I had a child who made such a request of me, how would I respond?*

Surprisingly, though, this father complies with his younger son's request; **the father divided the property between them**. We are not told his reasoning in doing so; it is something to ponder as the parable unfolds. The word translated **property** literally means "life" and has the sense here of that which supports life, the means of livelihood. The legal details of what took place when the father **divided the property between** his two sons are not completely clear because it was possible to transfer title to a property to someone while retaining the income the property produced (see Gen 25:5–6). It seems that the father made an outright transfer of a third of his estate to his younger son, and transferred title to two-thirds of his estate to his older son while retaining the right to the income. The father will continue to manage the two-thirds as his means of livelihood.

13 **After a few days, the younger son collected all his belongings.** The word translated **collected** can have the connotation of converted into cash, which is its implication here. The younger son sold his share of the estate, as he was apparently legally able to do so, selling **all**. After selling everything, he **set off to a distant country**. That he did so **after** only **a few days** indicates that this was his plan all along. He wanted to get what he could from his father and then move far away, distancing himself from his father. Perhaps his father knew that this was his intention; parents can often discern their children's desires. In the distant country the younger son **squandered his inheritance on a life of dissipation**. The word translated **dissipation** does not necessarily mean immorality; it conveys that he spent his money carelessly and recklessly. There

were many ways to waste money in the ancient world, as there are today. Whatever the son's desires, he indulged them.

14 The son's spending spree came to an end when his money ran out, and the timing could not have been worse: after **he had freely spent everything, a severe famine struck that country**. Ancient economies were based on agriculture, and a **severe famine** would cause a deep recession along with widespread hunger. Having wasted his money, **he found himself in dire need**. Families provided a safety net in difficult times, but he had moved far away from his family and was on his own.

15 To survive he needed to find a job, but good jobs are scarce in a recession. The young man is forced to take what is available, **so he hired himself out to one of the local citizens who sent him to his farm to tend the swine.** His employer is a Gentile, for **swine** were unclean according to the law of Moses (Lev 11:6–7; Deut 14:8), and Jews did not eat or raise them. The young man, although Jewish, must **tend**, literally, feed, **swine**; his repudiation of his family and reckless spending has reduced him to taking a disagreeable menial job.

16 Along with being disagreeable, feeding swine did not pay a lot. **And he longed to eat his fill of the pods on which the swine fed, but nobody gave him any.** Scholars debate the precise meaning of this verse, but the general sense is clear: the swine are eating better than he is. The **pods** that he fed the swine may have been from the carob tree (barely edible by humans unless processed) or from a wild bush (inedible by humans). His hunger was so great that **he longed** to be able **to eat his fill** of the pods, but they were not something he could stomach. **Nobody gave him any**—literally, no one was giving to him—may not refer to not giving him pods but may mean that no one was giving him alms or other assistance. There was a severe famine, affecting all, and he was a foreigner, at the bottom of the list of those needing help.

17 **Coming to his senses**: the young man begins to realize the folly of his actions. **He thought, "How many of my father's hired workers have more than enough food to eat."** The word translated **hired workers** refers to day laborers, hired each day and paid each evening (see Lev

19:13; Matt 20:1–8). Unlike slaves and servants, day laborers did not have steady employment but depended on someone hiring them anew each day. Housing and food were usually provided for slaves and servants, but day laborers had to take care of themselves. Day laborers were among the worst off of the working poor, but even so, his **father's hired workers** had **more than enough food to eat**. The young man realizes that, in contrast to them, **here am I, dying from hunger**. He is at the point of perishing.

> *For reflection: In what area of my life do I most need to come to my senses?*

18 He resolves, **I shall get up**, arising from dying, as it were, and I will **go to my father and I shall say to him, "Father, I have sinned against heaven and against you."** The sense of **sinned against heaven** is, sinned against God. He has sinned against his father by the shamelessly selfish and callous way he treated him, and he has thereby also sinned against God. He is prepared to acknowledge this, taking responsibility for his actions.

> *For reflection: In what circumstances do I find it hardest to take responsibility for what I have done? To admit to God and to others that I have sinned against them?*

19 He will tell his father, **I no longer deserve to be called your son.** He took everything he could from his father so that he could move far away from him, deliberately cutting himself off from his father. He recognizes that he has repudiated his sonship by his actions and does not **deserve** to have his father consider him a **son**. He will not ask to be reinstated as a son but will tell his father, **treat me as you would treat one of your hired workers**, literally, make me as one of your day workers. The son will not ask to live at home again but only that his father hire him when he needs day laborers. That is the most he thinks he deserves, but it will be sufficient for him to survive, and better than dying of hunger in a distant country.

20 **So he got up and went back to his father.** The journey would have taken him some time, for he is penniless and must walk from the distant country (verse 13) back to his father (and walk barefoot at that—see verse 22). He likely had to forage for food and sleep in the open at night. Nonetheless he persevered in trudging along day after day and eventually he drew near to the town where his father lived. Then, **while he was still a long way off, his father caught sight of him.** In the book of Tobit, "Anna sat watching the road by which her son was to come," enabling her to see him coming (Tobit 11:5–6). This father apparently is likewise watching for his son's return, for he is able to catch sight of him **while he was still a long way off**. He has not given up hope for his son; despite the passing of time, he has been watching for his return. When he sees him in the distance he is **filled with compassion.** The Greek word translated **filled with compassion** has the connotation of being moved from the depths of one's being. It is the compassion the Samaritan had for the half-dead robbers' victim in Jesus' earlier parable (10:33); it is the profound pity Jesus felt for the widow whose only son had died (7:13). The father's immediate reaction when he sees his son in the distance is not anger over the way his son has treated him but profound **compassion** for his son.

> *For reflection: What is the most profound compassion I have ever felt for another? What is the most profound compassion I have ever experienced from another?*

He ran to his son. He did not walk to meet him halfway; he **ran** to him. The word translated **ran** is used for foot races in athletic competitions and conveys an all-out effort. In the culture of the time, grown men of substance never ran; they walked slowly, with dignity. A man's gait along with his clothing proclaimed who he was (Sirach 19:26). The sight of a prosperous, middle-aged man hitching up his robe and running would have filled everyone with amazement, and brought derision on him. But heedless of this, the father **ran** to his son. He **embraced him**, hugging him. For a comparison, we might think of pictures we see of military personnel returning home from a lengthy deployment in a war zone, being reunited with their families, embracing their spouses, lifting up their children in their arms and hugging them. That is the kind of welcome the father gave his son, hugging him to himself. He **kissed him,** wholeheartedly welcoming his son, enveloping him in his love.

> *For reflection: If the father in Jesus' parable represents God the Father, what does the way he welcomes his son tell me about God's attitude toward me?*

21 The father embraced his son before the son had a chance to speak, but the son is eventually able to recite the speech he composed in the distant country and probably rehearsed over and over as he walked back to his father. **His son said to him, "Father, I have sinned against heaven and against you,"** acknowledging that he has wronged his father and sinned in the sight of God. He tells his father, **I no longer deserve to be called your son.**

> *For reflection: Do I deserve to be a daughter or son of God? How do I approach my Father when I have sinned?*

22 Before he can finish his set speech his father cuts him off by giving orders to his household staff. **But his father ordered his servants**—literally, slaves—**"Quickly bring the finest robe and put it on him."** The **finest robe** would be the best robe the father owned, worn on special occasions. The son's clothes are likely in tatters, but he is to be garbed in his father's finest clothing. The father orders, **put a ring on his finger**: scholars debate whether this might be the father's signet ring, used as his personal seal on documents. In any case being given a **ring** represents a restoration of his status as the son of a wealthy landowner; those who are destitute cannot afford fine rings. He orders, put **sandals on his feet**, for the son has walked home barefoot. Although wearing sandals was not a sign of wealth, those who were wealthy did not go barefoot, while those who were extremely poor often did. The son arrived home destitute because he had wasted his inheritance, but his father showers material comforts on him as a sign that he is restored to his place as a son.

Servant, slave: See page 454

23 He orders his slaves, **Take the fattened calf and slaughter it. Then let us celebrate with a feast**. Ordinary people rarely ate meat, save when a

feast or banquet was held to **celebrate** a special occasion like a wedding (see 14:8). The father treats his son's return as a special occasion indeed, for not only will they feast on meat but it will be the meat of a **fattened calf**. The Greek word for **fattened** is formed from the word for grain. A **calf** would be kept in a fattening pen (see 1 Sam 28:24; Amos 6:4) and fed grain in order to make its meat as delectable as possible—high grade veal. A **fattened calf** was reserved for the most special of occasions. A whole **calf** would provide meat for far more people than a family; friends and neighbors will be invited so that they can **celebrate** his son's home-coming.

Diet: See page 253

Banquets: See page 386

24 The father explains that he is throwing a feast **because this son of mine was dead, and has come to life again**. He refers to him as **this son of mine:** he still considers him to be his **son**. He may not deserve to be his son (verse 21), but his father claims him as his son anyway. He **was dead**, at the point of perishing from hunger in a distant country (verse 17), and as good as dead to his father, but he **has come to life again**, not simply to physical life but to the life of his family. He has also come alive spiritually by taking responsibility for his conduct and admitting his sin. **He was lost, and has been found**: the father has regained the son that he **lost**. After the fattened calf is slaughtered and preparations made, **then the celebration began**. As in Jesus' previous two parables (15:4–10), something that was **lost** has been **found**: a lost sheep, a lost coin, a lost son. The finding of what was lost calls for a **celebration** so that others can share the joy (see 15:6, 9).

Jesus' parable does not end here, but before proceeding to the next scene it is worth reflecting on the father and his younger son.

The father could have denied his son's request for his share of the estate but he did not; he allowed him to leave home and to waste his inheritance. Although he longed for his son's return, he did not travel to the distant country and kidnap him. He allowed his son to return to him freely, just as he allowed him to leave. He was no less filled with compassion for his son when his son left than he was when he returned. Compassion can forgive all failings, but compassion cannot compel the seeking of reconciliation. The father gave his son more than he asked for or deserved; his compassion knew no bounds. He threw a great feast to celebrate his lost son coming back to life.

> *For reflection: What insights does the father in the parable give me into God as my Father? How have I experienced his compassion for me?*

The son was very selfish and foolish. He had no regard for his father's feelings, but exploited him to indulge himself. He comes to his senses only when he has hit bottom. He thinks that he has irrevocably lost his sonship and he is reconciled to living as a lowly day laborer. The parable does not tell us what went through his mind and heart when his father embraced him as his son; we can imagine that it was a combination of stunned surprise, profound gratitude, and great love for his father.

> *For reflection: What do I see of myself in the behavior of the younger son? What can I learn from his example?*

A Loving Father and His Older Son

²⁵ **"Now the older son had been out in the field and, on his way back, as he neared the house, he heard the sound of music and dancing. ²⁶ He called one of the servants and asked what this might mean. ²⁷ The servant said to him, 'Your brother has returned and your father has slaughtered the fattened calf because he has him back safe and sound.' ²⁸ He became angry, and when he refused to enter the house, his father came out and pleaded with him. ²⁹ He said to his father in reply, 'Look, all these years I served you and not once did I disobey your orders; yet you never gave me even a young goat to feast on with my friends. ³⁰ But when your son returns who swallowed up your property with prostitutes, for him you slaughter the fattened calf.' ³¹ He said to him, 'My son, you are here with me always; everything I have is yours. ³² But now we must celebrate and rejoice, because your brother was dead and has come to life again; he was lost and has been found.' "**

NT: Luke 15:1–24; 19:10

25 **Now the older son had been out in the field** when his father called for a feast to celebrate his younger son's return (15:23–24). Since the family estate makes use of slaves (15:22), servants (verse 26), and day laborers (15:19), the **older son** has presumably been **out in the field** supervising farm workers. Now the workday is over, and he is returning home for the evening meal. **On his way back, as he neared the house, he heard the sound of music and dancing.** The celebration has already begun (15:24), and it is an exuberant, noisy affair. A band would have been hired for the occasion, with flutes and lyres to provide **music** to accompany singing and **dancing**.

26 The older son is puzzled: nothing like this was planned when he left for work earlier that day. **He called one of the servants and asked what this might mean.** What's going on here? Why the party?

27 **The servant said to him, "Your brother has returned and your father has slaughtered the fattened calf because he has him back safe and sound."** The older son can scarcely believe what he is hearing. His **brother has returned**—unthinkable! After running off to a distant country with his share of the family fortune, for him to show his face again was shocking. Equally unthinkable and shocking was his **father** having **slaughtered the fattened calf** to celebrate his return. How could his father be happy that this good-for-nothing son of his was **back** home **safe and sound**? He should have beaten him within an inch of his life and sent him on the road again.

Servant, slave: See page 454

For reflection: Who are the outcasts in my family? What kind of a reception would I give them if they wanted to patch things up?

28 **He became angry**, probably growing angrier by the minute the more he thought about it. He certainly was not going to celebrate his brother's return! He was not even going to go into the house, although everyone would note his absence from the celebration. **When he refused to enter the house, his father came out and pleaded with him.** His **father** learns that his older son is outside and will not come in. He takes the initiative to bring him in: he **came out and pleaded with him** to join

the celebration. The word translated **pleaded** can have the connotation of spoke kindly.

29 The older son's response to his father is anything but kindly. **He said to his father in reply, "Look, all these years I served you and not once did I disobey your orders."** He does not address him as "father" but begins with a rather brusque **look** or "see here" (the younger son, despite no longer deserving to be considered a son, nevertheless began his words with a respectful "father"—15:21). The older son reminds his father of **all these years I served you**, literally, slaved for you. He boasts, **not once did I disobey your orders**. He draws an implicit contrast between himself and his younger brother, who has not worked for or submitted to his father. Yet the older son's self-image seems to be one of a dutiful slave rather than a son. The older son feels unappreciated and says that although he slaved, **yet you never gave me even a young goat to feast on with my friends**. A **young goat** from the herd would have been far less expensive than the fattened calf that the father slaughtered for his brother; he complains that his father did not do even that little thing for him. His complaint may reveal that he does not particularly enjoy being with his father: his choice of companions for a nice meal would be **friends**, not family.

For reflection: Is my relationship with God primarily one of obedience and service, or primarily one of love?

30 The older son becomes accusatory, telling his father, **But when your son returns who swallowed up your property with prostitutes, for him you slaughter the fattened calf**. He cannot bring himself to call him "my brother" but speaks of him as **your son**, literally, this son of yours, a rather contemptuous way to refer to him. He charges that he **swallowed up your property**: the word translated as **property** has the sense of that which supports life, the means of livelihood (see 15:12). He speaks as if his brother has devoured his father's means of support, ignoring that his father freely bestowed his share of the estate on him and that there was ample left over to support the family. He alleges that his brother wasted his father's property on **prostitutes**. It is improbable that he had any way of knowing this; his brother had been living in a distant country (15:13), and communications in the ancient world were difficult.

429

It is more likely that he is imagining the worst about his brother. It is also possible that he is attributing his own temptations and fantasies to his brother: we sometimes project onto others the sins we wrestle with ourselves. In any case, he views his brother, whom he will not acknowledge as his brother, in the worst possible light, making it incomprehensible to him that his father would **slaughter the fattened calf** for him. He resents the welcome his father is giving him.

For reflection: When have I thought the worst of someone, without having any real basis for doing so?

31 His father could not fail to notice his resentment, and that he justifies himself while disparaging his brother. Yet the father glosses over his disrespectful tirade so that he can reassure his son of his love for him. It pains the father to have his son think of himself as a slave. **He said to him, "My son, you are here with me always."** The word translated **my son** is an affectionate term for a child; the father warmly affirms his son to be his son. He tells him, **you are here with me always**. Since their relationship as father and son is the primary bond between them, it is their being together and not the son's work that the father prizes most. He tells his son, **everything I have is yours**. The father divided his estate between his two sons (15:12); the two-thirds of the estate that remained after the younger son received his share is the older son's, although his father apparently retained the right to manage and derive income from it. There is nothing more for the father to pass on to his older son. He shouldn't be upset about not being given a goat when he has been given everything!

32 Having reassured his older son of his place as his son, the father directs his attention to his younger brother, saying, **But now we must celebrate and rejoice, because your brother was dead and has come to life again; he was lost and has been found**. The father speaks to his older son about **your brother**, even though the older son pointedly avoided calling him his brother (verse 30). The father wants to restore not only his relationship with his older son, but also the relationship between the two brothers. There **must** be a celebration because the **brother** who was **dead** has now **come to life again** (15:24): if coming

back from the dead does not call for a celebration, what does? **He** who **was lost** has now **been found**, a cause for rejoicing (see 15:6, 9).

Jesus' parable ends with the father pleading with his older son to come into the house and join the celebration and be reconciled with his brother. We do not know whether the older son did so, or whether he persisted in his self-righteous hardness of heart. We do know that his father will persevere in his love for his older son, just as he had for his younger son.

As with the earlier parables of the lost sheep and the lost coin (15:4–10), Jesus addresses the parable about a loving father and his two wayward sons to Pharisees and scribes who criticize him for welcoming sinners and eating with them (15:1–3). The man searching for his lost sheep, the woman searching for her lost coin, and the father each represent God. The parables convey the message that God is concerned for the lost. He seeks them out and rejoices when they are found; he welcomes home the wayward; he is constant in his compassion. Jesus is God's agent to "seek and save what was lost" (19:10). Therefore he welcomes sinners and eats with them, entering into fellowship with them. He invites them to repent and lead reformed lives (5:32), but he takes the first step toward them, like the father running to his younger son, like the father going out to his older son. He embraces them in his compassion so that they can come to life.

For reflection: What do the parables in chapter 15 tell me about God's fundamental attitude toward me? About why he sent his Son?

Just as the younger son represents the tax collectors and sinners whom Jesus welcomes to himself, the older son represents Pharisees and scribes who criticize him for doing so. They may serve God and scrupulously obey all his commandments, but they have their blind spots. They are missing out on God's compassion extended to them through Jesus; they fail to join in the rejoicing when tax collectors and sinners are embraced by that compassion. The open-ended conclusion of Jesus' parable is an invitation to them to allow their Father to draw them into the heavenly celebration (15:7, 10).

For reflection: Am I missing what God celebrates today? What blind spots prevent me from seeing what God is doing?

CHAPTER 16

ORIENTATION: *As Jesus continues on his way to Jerusalem (9:51–53; 13:22,*
33), he increasingly devotes his time to instructing his disciples.
Among his concerns are their attitudes toward, and use of,
possessions (16:1–13, 19–31).

The Parable of the Shrewd Steward
**¹ Then he also said to his disciples, "A rich man had a steward
who was reported to him for squandering his property. ² He summoned him and said, 'What is this I hear about you? Prepare a
full account of your stewardship, because you can no longer be
my steward.' ³ The steward said to himself, 'What shall I do, now
that my master is taking the position of steward away from me? I
am not strong enough to dig and I am ashamed to beg. ⁴ I know
what I shall do so that, when I am removed from the stewardship, they may welcome me into their homes.' ⁵ He called in his
master's debtors one by one. To the first he said, 'How much do
you owe my master?' ⁶ He replied, 'One hundred measures of
olive oil.' He said to him, 'Here is your promissory note. Sit down
and quickly write one for fifty.' ⁷ Then to another he said, 'And
you, how much do you owe?' He replied, 'One hundred kors of
wheat.' He said to him, 'Here is your promissory note; write one
for eighty.' ⁸ And the master commended that dishonest steward
for acting prudently."**

1   **Then he also said to his disciples**, telling them a parable (verses 1–8)
as a springboard for teachings (16:8–13). **A rich man had a steward**: a
landowner who was **rich** would usually employ a **steward** to manage his
estate. A **steward** functioned as an administrator, property manager, and
business agent. A steward could buy and sell, make loans, rent property,
and enter into contracts on behalf of his employer. This steward **was
reported to** his employer **for squandering his property**. He may have
mismanaged the estate through incompetence or neglect, or he may
have embezzled from what was entrusted to him. In any case, the result

was the same: instead of increasing his employer's wealth, he reduced it. Accusations about his conduct reached his employer.

Disciple: See page 149
Parables: See page 217

2   **He summoned him and said, "What is this I hear about you?"** His employer takes seriously the accusations made against his steward. He tells him, **Prepare a full account of your stewardship, because you can no longer be my steward**. The employer has decided to terminate the steward's service and appoint someone else to manage his estate. As his final duty, the steward is to prepare a **full account** of what has been under his management, likely including inventory, transactions, accounts due, and loans outstanding. It will be a final audit (to use a modern term) of the steward's performance, and it will provide his successor with an overview of the estate.

> *For reflection: If at this point in my life God called me to make an accounting of how I have used what he has entrusted to me, what would the record show?*

3   **The steward** makes no effort to defend his performance or to try to retain his position; he accepts that he is being fired. He **said to himself, "What shall I do, now that my master is taking the position of steward away from me?"** He will lose his source of income; he will probably lose his housing as well, since room and board were usually provided for estate and household staff (see 12:42, which refers to a steward giving servants their food allowance). The prospects that another wealthy person will hire him are not very good, since word will get around that he was fired for squandering his employer's property. He has apparently squandered his own money as well and is broke. He considers his alternatives. He realizes, **I am not strong enough to dig**. He had a white-collar job, as it were, and was not **strong enough** to do strenuous physical labor like digging all day. He also recognizes, **I am ashamed to beg**. As the steward of a rich man, he had enjoyed the esteem of others. Beggars were at the bottom of the social order; no one begged unless the alternative was starvation. Sirach even advised, "My son, live not the

life of a beggar, / better to die than to beg" (Sirach 40:28). The shame of begging is more than the steward can accept.

4 A course of action occurs to him. He tells himself, **I know what I shall do so that, when I am removed from the stewardship, they may welcome me into their homes**. At present he is still his master's steward, but he knows he will shortly be **removed** from his stewardship. It will become clear that the **they** he refers to are the people he had dealings with on behalf of his employer. His goal is to have them **welcome** him **into their homes**, one after another, providing him with extended hospitality. This may not be a long-term solution, but it will buy him time and prevent him from becoming homeless.

5 He sets his plan into action while he is still able to function as a steward. **He called in his master's debtors one by one**, arranging a private meeting with each of then. Their debts could have been incurred in a number of ways. They may be tenant farmers who owe a share of the harvest, or they may have borrowed from his master, or they may be merchants who bought produce from the estate and have yet to pay for it. The steward handled such transactions on behalf of his master. **To the first he said, "How much do you owe my master?"**

6 **He replied, "One hundred measures of olive oil."** The word translated **measure** was a liquid measure of about ten gallons; the man owed around a thousand gallons of **olive oil**, which would have been the annual produce of an olive grove with about one hundred fifty trees. This is a sizable debt, indicating that the debtor dealt in large quantities and was sufficiently well off to be an attractive host for an out-of-work steward. **He said to him, "Here is your promissory note."** When the debtor incurred the debt, he would have written a **promissory note**, or IOU, in his own hand, for the steward to hold for his master. The steward produces the note and tells the debtor to **sit down and quickly write one for fifty**. He must act **quickly** while the steward is still in office. The old promissory note will be destroyed and the new one substituted, with the debt half the original amount. There will be no way for the steward's master to prove that the debt had been written down, for the only written record will be for the smaller amount. Having his debt cut

in half would naturally please the debtor, but put him in debt, as it were, to the steward for reducing the amount he owed.

7   **Then to another he said, "And you, how much do you owe?" He replied, "One hundred kors of wheat."** A **kor** was a dry measure equivalent to about eleven modern bushels. This debtor owes over a thousand bushels of wheat, which would have been the annual yield of about one hundred acres of farmland. Since the average farmer had only about five to ten acres, this debtor was also a man of some means. The steward **said to him, "Here is your promissory note; write one for eighty."** Not as great a discount, but nevertheless large enough to have the debtor owe the steward a favor.

While the parable only describes how the steward reduced the debts of two debtors, it is implied that he did so for all who were in debt to his master (see verse 5). Since social norms called for reciprocity, for returning a favor with a favor (see 6:32–34; 14:12), the steward has ensured that a number of well-off people will welcome him into their homes for extended stays after he loses his job.

Did the steward defraud his master by writing down the debts? Scholars have debated this but not reached a consensus. Among their different interpretations are two simple ones. Some suggest that the amounts written off represented the steward's commission, and that his master would still receive all that was owed to him. Others reject this and maintain that the steward falsified accounts and defrauded his master. As it will turn out, the point of the parable is the same no matter how legally or illegally he acted.

8   Jesus concludes his parable by saying that **the master commended that dishonest steward for acting prudently**. Jesus characterizes the steward as **dishonest**, perhaps referring to his squandering his master's property (verse 1), or perhaps to his reducing what his master was owed (verses 5–7), or perhaps both. However, the point of the parable does not lie in his being dishonest but in his acting **prudently**, which has the connotation here of "shrewdly" (a form of the word is translated as "shrewd" at Matt 10:16). The master found out what his steward did and **commended**, or praised, him for acting shrewdly when he was going to lose his job. He does not praise him for squandering his property or for

435

being dishonest. Rather, the master commends him only for reacting **prudently** in a time of crisis. The steward may be a scoundrel, but he showed foresight and took decisive action. There is nothing to admire about the steward save for his cunning in providing for his future. Jesus will draw a lesson from his shrewdness (see the last part of verse 8, which is the beginning of the next reading).

For reflection: Although Jesus has yet to draw a lesson from his parable, what do I think the lesson might be for me?

The Shrewd Use of Money
8 "For the children of this world are more prudent in dealing with their own generation than are the children of light. 9 I tell you, make friends for yourselves with dishonest wealth, so that when it fails, you will be welcomed into eternal dwellings. 10 The person who is trustworthy in very small matters is also trustworthy in great ones; and the person who is dishonest in very small matters is also dishonest in great ones. 11 If, therefore, you are not trustworthy with dishonest wealth, who will trust you with true wealth? 12 If you are not trustworthy with what belongs to another, who will give you what is yours? 13 No servant can serve two masters. He will either hate one and love the other, or be devoted to one and despise the other. You cannot serve God and mammon."

Gospel parallels: Matt 6:24
OT: 1 Chron 29:14; Psalm 24:1; Sirach 31:5–7
NT: Luke 12:33–34; 16:1–8

8 After saying, in the beginning of verse 8, "And the master commended that dishonest steward for acting prudently," Jesus draws a lesson: **For the children of this world are more prudent in dealing with their own generation than are the children of light.** The expression **the children of this world** refers to those whose frame of reference is this world, this life. **Their own generation** means their kind of people. The dishonest steward in Jesus' parable (16:1–8) is an example of the way that worldly people are **prudent** and shrewd in their dealings with each other. They are **more prudent than are the children of light**. The expression

children of light means those who are enlightened by God; to walk in the light means to follow God's ways (see John 12:35–36; Eph 5:8–9; 1 Thess 5:5). Jesus does not endorse the amoral behavior of **the children of this world**, but says they act more expediently in obtaining what they want than do **the children of light** in attaining the goal God has for them. The implicit lesson is that those whose allegiance is to God should be as prudent and farsighted in acting in godly ways as the worldly are in acting in worldly ways.

For reflection: Which has a greater sense of urgency for me, serving God or securing my well-being?

9 Jesus goes on to apply this lesson to an area in which it is important for his followers to act shrewdly: **I tell you, make friends for yourselves with dishonest wealth**. The word translated **dishonest** means unrighteous or wicked; **dishonest wealth** is not wealth acquired dishonestly but wealth that by its very nature can corrupt and lead to wickedness. Jesus urges his followers to **make friends for yourselves** by your use of money, however corrupting money can be, **so that when it fails, you will be welcomed into eternal dwellings**. Jesus does not spell out who these **friends** are, or how his disciples are to **make** them their friends, or when their money will **fail**. But since Jesus is drawing lessons from his parable about a shrewd steward (16:1–8), we are justified in seeing a parallel between the steward using what is in his stewardship to obtain the friendship and hospitality of others and disciples of Jesus using their money to make friends who will welcome them. Jesus elsewhere teaches that the proper use of money and possessions is to help the poor: "Sell your belonging and give alms" (12:33; see also 11:41; 18:22). Jesus' disciples are to make the poor their **friends** by assisting them. Eventually all wealth will **fail**; if it is not lost during the course of life, it will be lost at the time of death (see 12:20). Jesus' disciples are to use their resources while they have them to help the poor, so that they **will be welcomed into eternal dwellings**, into the eternal kingdom of God. The welcome can come both from God and from the poor they have helped who have entered the kingdom ahead of them (see 6:20). Jesus previously taught his disciples to store up treasure in heaven through almsgiving, so that they would end up with their heavenly treasure (12:33–34); his present

teaching makes much the same point. The prudent and shrewd use of money is to help the poor.

For reflection: How eternally shrewd am I in my use of money? How much of my income do I use to help those in need?

10 Jesus invokes a general principle: **The person who is trustworthy in very small matters is also trustworthy in great ones**. This is true in all spheres of life. A person who proves trustworthy in **very small matters** may safely be entrusted with greater responsibilities. A complementary principle is also true: **the person who is dishonest in very small matters is also dishonest in great ones**. It would be foolhardy to choose a pickpocket to manage one's retirement account.

11 Jesus applies the principles to the use of wealth: **If, therefore, you are not trustworthy with dishonest wealth, who will trust you with true wealth?** In Jesus' view, **wealth** is a small matter (verse 10); there are many things that are more important for his disciples. The **trustworthy** way to use **dishonest wealth**—wealth that can corrupt—is to assist the poor (see verse 9). Those who fail to do so, who use their wealth only for their own benefit (see 12:16–19), will not be entrusted **with true wealth**. The only **true wealth** is "inexhaustible treasure in heaven that no thief can reach nor moth destroy" (12:33); all other wealth will eventually fail (verse 9). God will not entrust **true wealth** to those who **are not trustworthy** in the small matter of their use of **dishonest wealth**.

12 Jesus invokes a second line of reasoning to make the same point. **If you are not trustworthy with what belongs to another, who will give you what is yours?** Jesus characterizes resources and wealth as **what belongs to another**, that is, to God. The world and all that is in it belongs to God: "The earth is the LORD's and all it holds" (Psalm 24:1). David acknowledged to God, "Everything is from you, and we only give you what we have received from you" (1 Chron 29:14). All of one's resources are a loan from God. Jesus tells his disciples, if you are **not trustworthy** in using what has been loaned to you, **who will give you what is yours?** Who will give you something as your permanent possession? The only truly permanent possession is treasure in heaven

(see 12:33). Jesus' disciples are to use what has been entrusted to them temporarily to obtain what will be given to them eternally.

For reflection: How have I proved trustworthy in what has been entrusted to me? How might I become more trustworthy?

13 Jesus observes that **no servant can serve two masters.** The word translated **serve** literally means "to be the slave of"; the word **masters** is used for slave owners. No **servant** can be wholeheartedly devoted to two different masters. **He will either hate one and love the other, or be devoted to one and despise the other.** Here **hate** has the connotation of neglect, and **love** means to prefer; **devoted** conveys loyalty, and **despise** conveys disregard. A slave with two masters will inevitably give allegiance to one master over the other when conflicts of interest arise. And just as a slave cannot **serve two masters,** Jesus tells his disciples, **you cannot serve God and mammon.** The word **mammon** is the English form of a Hebrew and Aramaic word whose root meaning may be "that in which one puts one's trust." The word came to be used for money and wealth (it is translated as "wealth" in verses 9 and 11). Jesus tells his disciples that they cannot give their ultimate allegiance both to God and to wealth. They must choose whether they will serve God as their master or will serve and be mastered by wealth—"choked by the anxieties and riches and pleasures of life" (8:14). Sirach warned that "The lover of gold will not be free from sin, / for he who pursues wealth is led astray by it" (Sirach 31:5). Jesus exhorts his followers to choose God over wealth and to use their resources to help the poor, thereby obtaining treasure in heaven.

Servant, slave: See page 454

For reflection: When have I compromised my allegiance to God for the sake of material gain? When have I rejected an opportunity for gain because of my allegiance to God?

Jesus Tries to Open the Eyes of Those Who Ridicule Him

¹⁴ **The Pharisees, who loved money, heard all these things and sneered at him.** ¹⁵ **And he said to them, "You justify yourselves**

in the sight of others, but God knows your hearts; for what is of human esteem is an abomination in the sight of God.

¹⁶ "The law and the prophets lasted until John; but from then on the kingdom of God is proclaimed, and everyone who enters does so with violence. ¹⁷ It is easier for heaven and earth to pass away than for the smallest part of a letter of the law to become invalid.

¹⁸ "Everyone who divorces his wife and marries another commits adultery, and the one who marries a woman divorced from her husband commits adultery."

Gospel parallels: Matt 5:18, 32; 11:12–13; Mark 10:11–12
OT: Exod 20:14; Lev 20:10; Deut 5:18; 22:22
NT: Matt 19:3–9; Mark 10:2–12; Luke 11:39; 13:24; 16:1–13

14 Although Jesus is speaking to his disciples about money (16:1–13), others are present. **The Pharisees, who loved money, heard all these things and sneered at him.** Luke characterizes **Pharisees** as people **who loved money**. There is little evidence in ancient documents that Pharisees were any more greedy than people in general. The reason why Luke mentions that they **loved money** is that this is why they **sneered** at Jesus when they **heard all these things**—heard Jesus teach about wealth and say, "you cannot serve God and mammon" (verse 13). Pharisees, along with many other Jews, viewed wealth as a sign of God's favor and approval, basing their view on Scripture (see Deut 28:1–14; Job 1:9–10; 42:10; Sirach 11:21–22). They thought their love of money and love of God were compatible, and they **sneered** at Jesus for thinking otherwise.

Pharisees: See page 143

15 Jesus is aware of their sneering **and he said to them, "You justify yourselves in the sight of others"**—you try to appear just and righteous in the sight of others. Since the issue is their attitude toward money, the implied sense of Jesus' words is, you love money because you want people to esteem you. Wealth confers high status in virtually every culture; wealth especially bestows high status when it is seen as a sign of God's favor. **But God knows your hearts**: God knows your secret thoughts and desires (see 1 Sam 16:7; 1 Kings 8:39; Prov 21:2; 24:12). Jesus previously spoke of what was in the Pharisees' hearts, saying, "inside you are filled with plunder and evil" (11:39; "plunder" has the sense of "greed"). **For what is of human**

esteem is an abomination in the sight of God. The Old Testament uses the word **abomination** for something that is loathsome or detestable. What humans can see and **esteem** can be an **abomination**, something detestable, to **God**, since God sees what is in the heart. Jesus apparently has in mind God's detesting of lust for wealth and esteem (see 6:24, 26). Pharisees may sneer at Jesus' words about wealth, but God considers their attitude toward wealth to be an **abomination.**

For reflection: What are my deepest desires? What does God see when he looks into my heart?

16 Jesus turns his attention to a more fundamental matter than love of wealth, however important a proper attitude toward wealth may be. By sneering at Jesus and disdaining his message, Pharisees are missing out on what God is doing through Jesus. He proclaims, **The law and the prophets lasted until John**—literally, the law and the prophets until John. The New American Bible translation adds the word **lasted** to bring out the sense of Jesus' words, but **lasted until John** should not be interpreted to mean lasted *only* until John (see verse 17). Another way to bring out the sense of Jesus' words would be to add "were proclaimed": the law and the prophets were proclaimed until John. The **law** of Moses and the words of the **prophets** expressed God's will for his people. God's word then came to John the Baptist (3:2). John prepared the way for one to come after him (3:4, 16–17) who would inaugurate a new era in God's dealings with his people. **From then**—from the time of John—**on the kingdom of God is proclaimed.** God sent Jesus to "proclaim the good news of the kingdom of God" (4:43). Jesus **proclaimed** and brought about God's rule through his exorcisms and healings, and he authorized his disciples to do the same (9:2; 10:9). The kingdom of God is being proclaimed, **and everyone who enters** it **does so with violence.** The sense of enters **with violence** is, enters through determined striving and rigorous effort (see 13:24). Following Jesus and entering into God's reign requires a wholehearted commitment of all that one has and all that one is (see 9:23–25; 14:26–33).

Kingdom of God: See page 381

For reflection: When have I had to strive rigorously in order to follow God's way for me? Where have I held back from making the necessary effort?

17 What God is accomplishing through Jesus builds on what God has done in the past and does not abolish it. Jesus proclaims, **It is easier for heaven and earth to pass away than for the smallest part of a letter of the law to become invalid**. Here **heaven and earth** represent the entire universe; **the smallest part of a letter** refers to a tiny stroke made by a scribe in writing a single letter in a word in **the law**. It is **easier** for the entire universe to **pass away** than for even the least significant detail in God's law **to become invalid**. The word translated **invalid** literally means to fall: nothing in God's revelation will fall away. God is now making his will known through Jesus (verse 16), but that does not mean that God's earlier revelation is annulled. Rather, what God required in the past is being augmented by Jesus—and will continue to be augmented and applied to new situations by the Church under the guidance of the Holy Spirit (see Acts 15:1–29).

18 Jesus provides an example of the law being augmented, an instance in which the standard for entering God's kingdom is higher than the standard set by the law of Moses. He proclaims, **Everyone who divorces his wife and marries another commits adultery**. The law of Moses allowed men to **divorce** their wives (see Deut 24:1–4). A man having sexual relations with someone else's wife committed **adultery** against her husband, a violation of his rights (Exod 20:14; Lev 20:10; Deut 5:18; 22:22). A married woman having sexual relations with another man committed adultery against her husband, but a husband did not commit adultery against his wife by having relations with another woman. Jesus proclaims that any husband who divorces his wife and remarries commits **adultery** against his divorced wife. This goes beyond the law of Moses on two counts. First, since divorce was normally done in order to remarry, Jesus effectively prohibits husbands from divorcing their wives. Second, Jesus teaches that a husband is able to commit adultery against his wife just as a wife is able to against her husband. Jesus adds, **and the one who marries a woman divorced from her husband commits adultery** against her husband. This effectively prohibited women from seeking a divorce. Jesus gives husbands and wives equal rights to a permanent marriage.

Jesus, in responding to sneering (verse 14), has challenged his critics to look into their hearts (verse 15) and to open their eyes to what God is doing through him (verse 16). The new era that has dawned in God's relationship with his people does not abolish the past (verse 17) but does require great striving (verse 16) and a higher standard of conduct (verse 18), if men and women are to enter into the kingdom of God.

The Parable of the Rich Man and Lazarus

¹⁹ "There was a rich man who dressed in purple garments and fine linen and dined sumptuously each day. ²⁰ And lying at his door was a poor man named Lazarus, covered with sores, ²¹ who would gladly have eaten his fill of the scraps that fell from the rich man's table. Dogs even used to come and lick his sores. ²² When the poor man died, he was carried away by angels to the bosom of Abraham. The rich man also died and was buried, ²³ and from the netherworld, where he was in torment, he raised his eyes and saw Abraham far off and Lazarus at his side. ²⁴ And he cried out, 'Father Abraham, have pity on me. Send Lazarus to dip the tip of his finger in water and cool my tongue, for I am suffering torment in these flames.' ²⁵ Abraham replied, 'My child, remember that you received what was good during your lifetime while Lazarus likewise received what was bad; but now he is comforted here, whereas you are tormented. ²⁶ Moreover, between us and you a great chasm is established to prevent anyone from crossing who might wish to go from our side to yours or from your side to ours.' ²⁷ He said, 'Then I beg you, father, send him to my father's house, ²⁸ for I have five brothers, so that he may warn them, lest they too come to this place of torment.' ²⁹ But Abraham replied, 'They have Moses and the prophets. Let them listen to them.' ³⁰ He said, 'Oh no, father Abraham, but if someone from the dead goes to them, they will repent.' Then Abraham said, 'If they will not listen to Moses and the prophets, neither will they be persuaded if someone should rise from the dead.' "

OT: Lev 19:9–10; 23:22; Deut 14:28–29; 15:1–11; 24:10–22; 26:12–13; Isaiah 32:6–7; 58:6–7, 10; Ezek 18:14–17; Zech 7:9–10
NT: Luke 1:53; 6:20–26; 12:16–21, 33–34; 13:28–30; 16:9–14

19 Jesus continues to instruct his disciples about the proper use of wealth (16:9–13), addressing his words as well to Pharisees who ridicule him

because they love money (16:14). He begins a parable: **There was a rich man who dressed in purple garments and fine linen**. He is **rich** indeed if he can afford **purple garments**. Purple dye was exceedingly expensive because it was extracted from the murex sea snail, with each snail yielding only an infinitesimal amount. **Purple garments** were worn by royalty (Judg 8:26; 1 Macc 10:62; 11:58; 14:43–44) and by those who could live like royalty. **Fine linen** undergarments, although less expensive than purple cloth, were favored by those who could afford them. This rich man **dined sumptuously each day**, undoubtedly inviting his upper class friends as guests (see 14:12). In another parable, a man slaughtered a fattened calf and threw a feast to celebrate a special occasion (15:23); in this parable, a rich man throws a feast for himself every single day. Expensive clothing and dining were favorite means of conspicuous consumption in the ancient world.

Parables: See page 217
Clothing: See page 175
Banquets: See page 386

20 **And lying at his door was a poor man named Lazarus.** The **door** was the gated entry into the rich man's walled estate. The word translated **poor** means abjectly poor and reduced to begging. A beggar takes up his post outside the rich man's door, hoping that those going in and out of the estate will give him alms. That he is **lying** by the entrance may mean that he is sick or paralyzed and cannot sit as beggars normally do (see 18:35; John 9:8). The word translated **lying** could also be translated, "having been laid," as if Lazarus had to be carried by others to his begging post. He is **covered with sores**, open ulcers on his skin. His name is **Lazarus**. In the biblical mentality, names were not arbitrary labels but revealed the nature and identity of a person. Since **Lazarus** is the only person named in any of Jesus' parables, his name likely carries significance for the parable. **Lazarus** comes from a Hebrew word meaning "God helps." His name would indicate that Lazarus relies on God to help him in his poverty and affliction.

The poor and the rich: See page 198

For reflection: What is the significance of the meaning of Lazarus' name for me?

21 Lazarus **would gladly have eaten his fill of the scraps that fell from the rich man's table**. That he **would gladly have eaten his fill** implies that he is not eating his fill (see 15:16); the rich man is not sharing his food with Lazarus, not even the leftovers and **scraps**. Customary practice would have been to throw scraps and garbage over the wall of the estate for wild scavenging dogs to consume (see Exod 22:30; 1 Kings 21:23–24; 2 Kings 9:33–36; Psalm 59:7, 15–16). Lazarus is in no shape to compete with wild dogs for the scraps. Rather, **dogs even used to come and lick his sores**. Lazarus is too feeble to drive away dogs attracted to the seepage from his open sores.

22 **When the poor man died, he was carried away by angels to the bosom of Abraham.** God's **angels** are agents of his care (see Psalm 34:8; 91:11–12). They take Lazarus **to the bosom of Abraham**—an expression that occurs only here in Scripture. In the next verse, the New American Bible translates the word for "bosom" as "side." The image is that of Lazarus being in the place of honor next to Abraham at the heavenly banquet (see 13:28–29), reclining at his side so that he can lean back against **the bosom** or chest **of Abraham** (see John 13:23–25). **The rich man also died and was buried** (probably in a fine tomb, for all the good it will do him).

Angels: See page 11

23 **and from the netherworld, where he was in torment**: Jewish ideas about life after death were evolving at the time of Jesus. In the Old Testament, the **netherworld** (called Sheol—Psalm 16:10; 30:4; 49:15; 89:49) was a place of darkness and silence beneath the surface of the earth (Num 16:31–33) where good and bad alike went when they died (Eccl 9:2–6). As Jews began to believe in reward or punishment in the next life, some began to think of a region of the netherworld as a place of punishment for the wicked. The rich man goes to the **netherworld** after he dies, and it is for him a place of **torment**: he is being punished by God for the life he led while on earth. Yet from his place in the netherworld he is able to see the heavenly banquet: **he raised his eyes and saw Abraham far off and Lazarus at his side**, literally, at his bosom. Jesus spoke of those who would wail and grind their teeth when they "see Abraham, Isaac, and Jacob and all the prophets in the kingdom of God"

enjoying the heavenly banquet while they are excluded (13:28), and the scene is similar here.

Life after death: See page 298

24 **And he cried out, "Father Abraham, have pity on me."** The rich man is a descendant of **Abraham** and calls upon him as his **Father**. John the Baptist proclaimed that the mere fact of descent from Abraham does not count for much: "Do not begin to say to yourselves, 'We have Abraham as our father,' for I tell you, God can raise up children to Abraham from these stones" (3:8). The rich man pleads with Abraham, **have pity on me**. There is irony in his asking for **pity** even though he never showed any pity to Lazarus. He certainly saw Lazarus lying by his door; it was the only way in and out of his estate. He even knew that the beggar's name was Lazarus, for he now recognizes him and tells Abraham, **Send Lazarus to dip the tip of his finger in water and cool my tongue, for I am suffering torment in these flames**. Some Old Testament books used **flames** or fire as an image for punishment after death (Judith 16:17; Sirach 21:9–10; Isaiah 66:24). The rich man does not ask Abraham to release him from his place in the netherworld or to bring him into the heavenly banquet; he seems to realize that he is permanently consigned to **torment.** But he does ask that his **suffering** be alleviated by Abraham sending **Lazarus to dip the tip of his finger in water and cool my tongue**. He apparently still considers Lazarus to be a virtual nobody, someone who can be expected to perform tasks for their social superiors.

25 **Abraham replied, "My child, remember that you received what was good during your lifetime."** Abraham calls him **my child**, acknowledging their kinship (the same word is translated as "my son" at 15:31). The rich man certainly had enjoyed **what was good**, indeed, the very best, during his lifetime. At the same time, **Lazarus likewise received what was bad**. Those whose afflictions reduced them to begging were among the worst off in life. **But now he is comforted here, whereas you are tormented.** Their deaths have brought about a reversal of their fortunes. Mary prophetically spoke of God bringing about such reversals: "The hungry he has filled with good things; / the rich he has sent away empty" (1:53). Jesus indicated what would happen to those like Lazarus, saying, "Blessed are you who are poor, / for the kingdom of God is yours. /

Blessed are you who are now hungry, / for you will be satisfied" (6:20–21). Lazarus would gladly have eaten discarded scraps but now is **comforted** by God and enjoying the eternal banquet in his kingdom. Jesus also said, "But woe to you who are rich, / for you have received your consolation. / But woe to you who are filled now, / for you will be hungry" (6:24–25). The rich man "dined sumptuously each day" (verse 19) and **received what was good during** his **lifetime**, but now is **tormented** and in a truly woeful condition.

The reversals that the rich man and Lazarus experienced after death were not simply due to their having been rich and poor during their lifetimes. It is clear that the rich man had callous disregard for Lazarus, despite the clear call of Scripture to show mercy to those in need (see the references given in the exposition of verse 29). Likewise, Lazarus is not rewarded simply for being poor but for relying on God, as his name implies. Wealth can be an obstacle to allegiance to God (16:13), an obstacle the rich man tripped over but that Lazarus in his poverty was spared.

For reflection: What are the lessons for me in the reversals of fortune that the rich man and Lazarus experienced?

26 What the rich man asks Abraham to do is not only inappropriate but impossible. Abraham tells him, **Moreover, between us and you a great chasm is established**—implied, established by God—**to prevent anyone from crossing who might wish to go from our side to yours or from your side to ours.** We should not try to construct a geography of the next life on the basis of this parable, for that was not Jesus' intent in teaching it. The **great chasm** simply signifies that God's final judgment is indeed final. Jesus has spoken about human life on earth as a not-to-be-missed opportunity to live in a way that allows women and men to enter into God's eternal kingdom (12:54–59; 13:1–9, 23–30). The **great chasm** between those who follow God's ways and those who do not is a visual image reinforcing his message: one's eternal fate is eternal.

27 **He said, "Then I beg you, father, send him to my father's house."** Although Lazarus cannot cross from where he is to where the rich man is, perhaps he can go to the rich man's **father's house**. His father's **house** might be literally his dwelling, or the expression **father's house** might

have the sense of the father's family (the "house of David" means the family of David—1:27; see also 2:4).

28 **for I have five brothers, so that he may warn them, lest they too come to this place of torment.** The rich man's **five brothers** are apparently living as he lived, enjoying the luxuries their wealth provides but being heedless of the needs of others. The rich man realizes that they, like him, will end up in **this place of torment** if they continue in their ways. The rich man wants Abraham to send Lazarus to **warn** his brothers to begin to help the poor lest they suffer the same eternal **torment** that he is suffering. The rich man does have consideration for his brothers and a sober appraisal of their prospects, but he still looks upon Lazarus as someone who can be sent on errands for the wealthy.

29 **But Abraham replied, "They have Moses and the prophets."** The law of **Moses** and the books of **the prophets** made up a substantial part of Scripture and revealed God's will for his people. The law and the prophets make it abundantly clear that God requires that special care be given to those in need (Lev 19:9–10; 23:22; Deut 14:28–29; 15:1–11; 24:10–22; 26:12–13; Isaiah 32:6–7; 58:6–7, 10; Ezek 18:14–17; Zech 7:9–10). **Let them listen to them** as they are read aloud in the synagogue every Sabbath (see Acts 13:14–15). To **listen** has the sense of heeding and obeying as well as hearing (see Deut 4:1; 5:1; 6:3–9). The rich man's five brothers should be well aware of what God requires of them through the law and the prophets. They simply need to do what God asks and use their wealth to help the poor and vulnerable.

For reflection: How well am I showing the special concern that God requires for those in need? What specific things might I begin doing?

30 **He said, "Oh no, father Abraham, but if someone from the dead goes to them, they will repent."** The rich man speaks as if his brothers are aware of what God requires of them through the law and the prophets but ignore it. It will take more than the revelation God has made to his people to move them to **repent** and change their behavior; something extraordinary would have to happen. The rich man believes that **if someone from the dead goes to them,** if Abraham sends Lazarus to warn them where they will end up if they continue on their present course, then **they will repent.**

Repentance: See page 92

31 **Then Abraham said, "If they will not listen to Moses and the prophets, neither will they be persuaded if someone should rise from the dead."** Abraham soberly pronounces that not even someone rising from the dead would persuade those who **will not listen to Moses and the prophets**. Minds defiantly closed to God's revelation will remain closed no matter what signs are given them or wonders performed for them.

Jesus' parable ends with the rich man in torment, and his brothers on the way to the same torment unless they begin to heed the law and the prophets. The parable poses a challenge to Jesus' audience: will you heed the law and the prophets? (See also 16:17.) Will you spend your money only on yourself, or will you help the poor outside your door? Will you end up in torment or in the bosom of Abraham?

For reflection: What is the most important message of Jesus' parable for me?

While the rich man spoke of someone from the dead going to his brothers, Abraham in his response used the phrase rise from the dead. Luke's readers would naturally think of Jesus' rising from the dead. The resurrection of Jesus will not convince everyone that he is God's Son and Messiah, Lord and savior. In the Acts of the Apostles, Luke will tell how the Gospel message is accepted by some and disbelieved by others; Abraham's words foreshadow such disbelief.

CHAPTER 17

ORIENTATION: *Jesus continues to instruct his followers, addressing different aspects of discipleship (17:1–10).*

The Faith to Do What Jesus Requires
¹ **He said to his disciples, "Things that cause sin will inevitably occur, but woe to the person through whom they occur. ² It would be better for him if a millstone were put around his neck and he be thrown into the sea than for him to cause one of these little ones to sin. ³ Be on your guard! If your brother sins, rebuke him; and if he repents, forgive him. ⁴ And if he wrongs you seven times in one day and returns to you seven times saying, 'I am sorry,' you should forgive him."**

⁵ **And the apostles said to the Lord, "Increase our faith." ⁶ The Lord replied, "If you have faith the size of a mustard seed, you would say to [this] mulberry tree, 'Be uprooted and planted in the sea,' and it would obey you."**

Gospel parallels: Matt 17:20; 18:6–7, 15, 21–22; 21:21; Mark 9:42; 11:22–23
OT: Lev 19:17–18
NT: Luke 11:4

1 **He said to his disciples, "Things that cause sin will inevitably occur."** The word translated **things that cause sin** means that which trips one up and causes one to fall. It can cover a range of harmful influences, including scandals that weaken faith as well as temptations to sin. Jesus realistically acknowledges that there **will inevitably** be things that can trip up his disciples. **But woe to the person through whom they occur**: woe to the one who leads a disciple away from Jesus and into sin. Even if temptations and scandal are inevitable, the person responsible for them will be held accountable. **Woe to** that **person!**

Disciple: See page 149
Woes: See page 171

2 **It would be better for him if a millstone were put around his neck and he be thrown into the sea than for him to cause one of these**

little ones to sin. Grain was commercially milled between a lower stone set in place and an upper **millstone** that rotated on an axel—a heavy stone disk with a hole in its center. To have a millstone **put around** one's **neck** like a collar and **be thrown into the sea** guaranteed swift descent to the bottom and drowning. Yet such a fate is **better** than what will befall those who **cause one of these little ones to sin.** By **little ones** Jesus means not only children but disciples who have become as children (see 9:47–48; 10:21; 18:16–17) and, more broadly, any who are weak and vulnerable. **Cause . . . to sin** is literally cause to stumble, and includes leading others to disbelief as well as leading them into sin. It is preferable to be forcibly drowned rather than remain alive to lead even a single **one** of the **little ones** astray. Jesus does not spell out what will befall those who cause a little one to fall, but he has just used imagery of suffering torment in flames (16:22–24). Even if that is only an image for punishment in the next life and not a literal description of it, it is certainly a far more dreadful prospect than a rather quick death by drowning.

For reflection: Who are the "little ones," the weak and vulnerable people, in my life? What effects have my words and example had on them?

3 Jesus adds, **Be on your guard** against leading any little ones astray. If tempted to do so, keep a millstone in mind.

Jesus has just addressed sinning against others by leading them into sin or disbelief (verses 1–2). Now he addresses being sinned against by others. **If your brother sins:** by **brother** Jesus means a fellow disciple. **Sins** might be sins in general, but the next verse deals with wrongs committed against oneself, and that also seems to be the sense here. If a fellow disciple sins against you, **rebuke him**. The sense of **rebuke** is reprove and admonish—perhaps pointing out how his or her behavior harms you, and asking him or her to behave differently. Instead of bearing a grudge, seek to work things out; instead of talking behind a person's back, confront the person. The spirit in which one rebukes another is found in the passage of Leviticus where God commands love of neighbor: one must reprove a brother or sister in love (Lev 19:17–18). Admonish the person who sins against you, **and if he repents, forgive him**. In this context, **repents** means that the person admits that his or her behavior was wrong and promises to change. In response to repentance, the one who was harmed must **forgive** the one who did the harm.

Repentance: See page 92

> *You shall not bear hatred for your brother in your heart.*
> *Though you may have to reprove your fellow man, do not*
> *incur sin because of him. Take no revenge and cherish no*
> *grudge against your fellow countrymen. You shall love*
> *your neighbor as yourself.*
>
> Lev 19:17–18

For reflection: Do I find it difficult to deal directly with those who have harmed me? How might I prepare myself to approach them in love?

4 **And if he wrongs you seven times in one day and returns to you seven times saying, "I am sorry," you should forgive him.** The word translated **I am sorry** is literally, "I repent." In biblical idiom, **seven times** may stand for many times (Psalm 119:164; Prov 24:16). Being wronged by someone **seven times in one day** means he or she habitually wrongs you even in the course of a single day. Yet if the person says **I am sorry**—I repent—**you should forgive him**, forgiving even **seven times** a day, which means to forgive constantly. It may strain our goodwill to be repeatedly wronged and nonetheless be expected to repeatedly forgive a chronic offender, but this is what Jesus requires.

For reflection: Who do I have the hardest time forgiving for the way they treat me? Who stands right now in need of my forgiveness?

Jesus may demand that we forgive more than we seem capable of doing, but there is a silver lining: we are given hope that God will forgive us for our chronic offenses. How many times have we resolved to change—perhaps seven times a day, day after day—and then fallen back into our habitual patterns of behavior? Jesus taught his disciples to pray, "Forgive us our sins / for we ourselves forgive everyone in debt to us" (11:4). Since we hope to receive the forgiveness we extend, we can be glad that Jesus requires us to forgive repeatedly!

5 **And the apostles said to the Lord, "Increase our faith."** Jesus chose twelve disciples to be **apostles** (6:13). Luke sometimes refers to Jesus as **the Lord**. The apostles ask Jesus to **increase our faith**. This presumes that they already have faith and want greater faith. It is a request that they could have made of Jesus at many points during his public ministry, for example, when he sent them on mission without provisions and charged them to cure the sick (9:1–3). Surely that took faith! But in the present context in Luke's Gospel, the apostles ask Jesus to **increase our faith** after he warns against leading others astray and requires them to forgive seven times a day (verses 1–4). They recognize that Jesus is demanding a lot of them, and they ask to have the power to do what he requires. **Faith** in this context is lived-out faith, belief in action. We might paraphrase their request as, "Give us a greater ability to live according to what we believe."

Apostle: See page 164

Lord: See page 137

6 **The Lord replied, "If you have faith the size of a mustard seed":** a **mustard seed** was considered the smallest of seeds (see 13:19; Matt 13:32; Mark 4:31). The sense of Jesus' words is, even if your faith is very small, **you would** be able **say to [this] mulberry tree, "Be uprooted and planted in the sea," and it would obey you.** The **mulberry tree** had very deep roots, making it extremely difficult for it to **be uprooted**. The idea of a mulberry tree being **planted in the sea** is perplexing: mulberry trees grow on land, not in the sea. Nor do people usually speak to trees, or have any success in telling trees what to do. It would seem that what Jesus portrays is thoroughly impossible: a deeply rooted tree being uprooted and planted in the sea at the apostles' command. Yet Jesus assures them that with the faith they have, if they were to **say** to a mulberry tree, **be uprooted and planted in the sea**, then **it would obey you.** Jesus uses an outlandish example to convey to his apostles, you have sufficient faith to live according to my teachings; you simply need to do what I ask, even if it may seem impossible.

For reflection: How did I discover that I had faith by acting in faith? When have I been able to accomplish what at first seemed to me impossible?

The Proper Attitude of a Slave

⁷ "Who among you would say to your servant who has just come in from plowing or tending sheep in the field, 'Come here immediately and take your place at table'? ⁸ Would he not rather say to him, 'Prepare something for me to eat. Put on your apron and wait on me while I eat and drink. You may eat and drink when I am finished'? ⁹ Is he grateful to that servant because he did what was commanded? ¹⁰ So should it be with you. When you have done all you have been commanded, say, 'We are unprofitable servants; we have done what we were obliged to do.' "

NT: Luke 12:35–38; 22:27

7 Jesus continues to speak to his disciples (see 17:1), asking them, **Who among you would say to your servant**: the word translated as **servant** is literally "slave" throughout this passage. Jesus is asking his disciples

---

BACKGROUND: SERVANT, SLAVE Both servants and slaves did the bidding of others and may even have done identical work, but with a major difference: servants were hired, slaves were owned. A servant was free to decide whom to work for and could quit; a slave had no choice but to work for his or her owner. At the time of Jesus, one became a slave by being born to a woman slave, by being taken as a prisoner of war, by incurring a debt one could not pay off, by voluntarily becoming a slave, or by being kidnapped. Slaves made up around a fifth of the population in the Roman Empire. There are important differences between slavery in the first-century Roman Empire and slavery in the Americas in the seventeenth to nineteenth centuries, and further differences between slavery in Palestine and slavery in other parts of the Roman Empire. In the world of Jesus, slavery was not based on race: the slaves referred to in Jesus' parables are usually Jews owned by other Jews. Many owners treated their slaves badly, but slaves could own property (including other slaves!) and hold important positions; a few slaves were better educated than their owners. Some slaves served as managers, doctors, and bankers, although most were farm workers or domestic servants. A few freely chose slavery because it offered them guaranteed employment, preferring it over working as day laborers. Most slaves, however, wanted to be free. Slaves could be freed after a certain period of service; a slave of a Roman citizen was generally given citizenship upon being freed. There are different Greek words for servant and slave, but in the Gospels the New American Bible usually translates the Greek word for slave as "servant" (e.g., Luke 2:29; 12:37; 14:17; 15:22; 19:13; 20:10; 22:50), apparently to avoid confusing the ancient practice of slavery with slavery in the American experience.

---

to put themselves in the sandals of someone who owns a slave and to imagine what they would **say** to their slave **who has just come in from plowing or tending sheep in the field.** The slave worked on his owner's farm and is coming into the house at the end of the day. Jesus asks whether any master would say to his slave, **Come here immediately and take your place at table**—sit down and eat your dinner right away. The disciples can only answer, "No, that is not what a slave is told in such a situation." Even if the disciples do not own slaves, they know how slaves are treated.

8   **Would he not rather say to him, "Prepare something for me to eat. Put on your apron and wait on me while I eat and drink. You may eat and drink when I am finished"?** Jesus again asks a question, this time one that would be answered, "Yes, of course." The owner has only one slave, who does both farm work and housework. When the slave is done in the fields, then it is time for him to prepare his master's evening meal and serve it. A full day's work is expected of a slave. When his master is done eating, then the slave's duties are done for the moment and he may eat.

9   **Is he grateful to that servant**—does the slave deserve special thanks—**because he did what was commanded?** Such a question would be answered, "No, the slave is due no gratitude for carrying out his duties and doing what he was **commanded.**" If a friend does one a favor, she or he deserves gratitude. But the work a slave performs is not a favor; in the thinking of the time, it is what the master is entitled to because he owns the slave.

10 **So should it be with you. When you have done all you have been commanded, say, "We are unprofitable servants."** An owner has a right to his slave's doing **all** that he or she has been **commanded.** The word translated **unprofitable** is best understood as having the sense of no profit or benefit to the master beyond what is due him. The case is the same for the disciples in relation to God. When they **have done all** they **have been commanded** by God, they have done no more than given God his due. **We have done what we were obliged to do:** disciples

should view their obedience and service to God as what they are **obliged to do** and not as an extra that merits a special reward (see 1 Cor 9:16). To do what is expected of them does not put God in debt to them, any more than a slave carrying out his master's orders makes the master beholden to him.

For reflection: To what extent do I consider myself to belong to God? Do I think that my service of God entitles me to any special consideration?

We may find it distasteful to think of ourselves as slaves of God, but the New Testament exhibits no such distaste. Mary literally called herself "the slave of the Lord" (1:38). Paul called himself a slave of Christ (Rom 1:1; Gal 1:10; Phil 1:1) and characterized Christians as slaves of God (Rom 6:22; see also Eph 6:6; Col 3:24; 4:12; 2 Tim 2:24; Titus 1:1; James 1:1; 1 Pet 2:16; 2 Pet 1:1; Jude 1:1).

For reflection: What do I find helpful in considering myself God's slave? What do I find abhorrent in being a slave of God?

Even though we owe total service to the God who created us and holds us in being, Jesus presents another side of the picture. He portrays himself as someone who goes against all custom and waits on his slaves (12:35–38). He will tell his disciples, "I am among you as the one who serves" (22:27). God has the right to demand everything of us, but out of love God came among us in Jesus to serve us.

A Grateful Samaritan's Faith

¹¹ As he continued his journey to Jerusalem, he traveled through Samaria and Galilee. ¹² As he was entering a village, ten lepers met [him]. They stood at a distance from him ¹³ and raised their voice, saying, "Jesus, Master! Have pity on us!" ¹⁴ And when he saw them, he said, "Go show yourselves to the priests." As they were going they were cleansed. ¹⁵ And one of them, realizing he had been healed, returned, glorifying God in a loud voice; ¹⁶ and he fell at the feet of Jesus and thanked him. He was a Samaritan. ¹⁷ Jesus said in reply, "Ten were cleansed, were they not? Where are the other nine? ¹⁸ Has none but this foreigner returned to give

thanks to God?" ¹⁹ **Then he said to him, "Stand up and go; your faith has saved you."**

> OT: Lev 13–14; Num 5:1–4
> NT: Luke 5:12–14

11 **As he continued his journey to Jerusalem**: Jesus is traveling to Jerusalem (9:51–53; 10:38; 13:22; 14:25), where, he knows, he will be put to death (9:22, 44; 13:33). **He traveled through Samaria and Galilee**; another translation would be, "he was passing between Samaria and Galilee." It may seem that Jesus has made little progress: near the beginning of his journey he came near a Samaritan village (9:51–53), and he is still in the vicinity of **Samaria** and **Galilee**. Luke does not provide the information needed to reconstruct the route Jesus took to Jerusalem nor to calculate how long the trip took. One conjecture: the Jezreel Valley (see Joshua 17:16; Judges 6:33; Hosea 1:5) formed the border between **Samaria** to its south and **Galilee** to its north. Running through the valley was an east-west trade route that connected with a north-south trade route in the Jordan River valley. Those traveling from Galilee to Jerusalem would often go south to the Jezreel Valley, east to the Jordan, and then south to Jericho on their way to Jerusalem. This could be the route that Jesus is taking (see 19:1).

> Jerusalem: See page 516
> Samaria, Samaritans: See page 277
> Galilee: See page 114

12 **As he was entering a village, ten lepers met [him]. They stood at a distance from him**: those with skin diseases classified as leprosy had to keep apart from others (Lev 13:46; Num 5:1–4). As Jesus is about to go into a village, **ten lepers** see him from **a distance**. While those with leprosy could not enter towns, they often lived close to towns so that they could receive charity.

13 They **raised their voice,** shouting to be heard at a distance, **saying, "Jesus, Master! Have pity on us!"** They recognize **Jesus**, for reports about him have spread throughout the region (4:14; 7:17), including an account of him cleansing a man with leprosy (5:12–15). They call him **Master**, a title for a person with authority. They plead, **Have pity on us!**

Those afflicted with leprosy usually had to depend on the generosity of others for their survival, for their exclusion from society made it difficult for them to earn a living. The **pity** or mercy that they would normally ask from others would be alms, but they are pleading for more from Jesus as **Master**. He has the authority to cleanse people with leprosy from their affliction (5:12–15; 7:22), and that is the **pity** they ask Jesus to show them.

For reflection: Where am I most in need of Jesus' mercy?

14 **And when he saw them**—when he heard their shouts and looked at them and **saw** that they had leprosy—**he said, "Go show yourselves to the priests."** When a skin condition considered leprosy went away, a **priest** was to make an examination and certify that the person no longer had the disease (Lev 14:1–3). This was the first step toward the person being restored to society. On a previous occasion, Jesus told a man with leprosy, "Be made clean" and "the leprosy left him immediately" (5:13). But Jesus does not utter a healing command now, nor are the men with leprosy healed immediately. Rather, Jesus tells them, **Go show yourselves to the priests,** sending them off unhealed. He asks them to act as if they had been cleansed of their leprosy, even though they could see that they were still diseased. Perhaps they were disappointed that he did not heal them as they had requested, but they nevertheless do what he tells them. **As they were going** on their way to priests, **they were**

BACKGROUND: LEPROSY In the Old and New Testaments, the Hebrew and Greek words translated "leprosy" refer to a variety of skin conditions and infections. In the New Testament period, one of these conditions may have been what is called leprosy today (Hansen's disease). Some of these skin conditions went away in time; some did not. A skin condition that resulted in a certain kind of abnormal appearance made the afflicted person ritually impure, or unclean. Old Testament regulations specified that priests were to determine whether a skin condition was "leprosy"; if it was, the person with the skin disease was excluded from the community as unclean (Lev 13). Priests likewise judged whether a person's leprosy had gone away, in which case the person underwent purification rituals before rejoining the community (Lev 14). These procedures indicate that what was at stake was ritual purity. Exclusion of the afflicted person from the community prevented the spread of ritual uncleanness; there was little understanding of the nature of diseases or of how they were spread.

cleansed. They are healed, but only in the course of their acting with obedience and faith, doing what Jesus told them.

Priests and Levites: See page 302

For reflection: What lesson might there be in healing taking place only when the men with leprosy do what Jesus asks of them? How are they models of faith for me?

15 **And one of them, realizing**—literally, seeing—**he had been healed, returned, glorifying God in a loud voice.** He can see that his leprosy is gone, and he perceives that **he had been healed** by God: what he sees with his eyes gives rise to spiritual insight and faith (verse 19). In gratitude he glorifies **God in a loud voice**, praising God publicly for healing him. Glorifying God is the proper response when God does great things (see 2:20; 5:25–26; 7:16; 13:13). The biblical model for gratitude to God is not a private feeling of thankfulness but public praise, honoring and glorifying God by proclaiming to others what he has done (see Psalm 9:2; 30:2; 35:18, 28; 52:11; 105:2; 106:2; 107:32; 111:1; 145:4; 150:2).

For reflection: How do I glorify God? What has God done for me that deserves being proclaimed to others?

The man not only glorified God, but he **returned** to Jesus. His certification by a priest could be delayed for a few hours (it would lead to an eight-day purification process—Lev 14:4–32). What could not be delayed was expressing his gratitude to Jesus: if he did not reach Jesus before he left the village (verse 12), it might be some time before he found him again.

16 He returned **and he fell at the feet of Jesus**—literally, fell on his face at the feet of Jesus, a posture of reverence and homage. Previously he could only shout at Jesus from a distance because of his leprosy (verses 12-13), but now that he has been freed of leprosy he can come to Jesus and throw himself at his feet. He **thanked him**, recognizing that Jesus was God's agent in his healing. His thanksgiving to Jesus likely took the same form as his glorifying of God (verse 15): a public acknowledgment of what Jesus had done for him, offered as testimony and praise. We can

note that this is the only time in the Gospels that anyone thanks Jesus for anything.

Luke notes that **he was a Samaritan**. The band of ten people with leprosy living on the border between Samaria and Galilee (verses 11–12) included a **Samaritan**, whom Jews would consider an outcast because of his religion and ethnic identity. God's grace, however, knows no boundaries (see also 7:9).

17 **Jesus said in reply** to the man's expression of profuse gratitude, **"Ten were cleansed, were they not?"** In verse 19 Jesus addresses the man cleansed of his leprosy, so Jesus is presumably speaking now to his disciples. He asks them three questions. **Ten were cleansed, were they not?** Yes, ten were cleansed. **Where are the other nine?** Not here; they are likely on their way to priests.

18 **Has none but this foreigner returned to give thanks to God?** The words translated **give thanks** are literally "give glory" and mean to glorify (see verse 15). Jesus refers to the Samaritan as **this foreigner**, this non-Jew. Jesus seemingly indicates that the other nine who were healed of leprosy were Jews. **None** of them **returned** to Jesus **to give thanks to God** and acknowledge that God healed them through him. Only **this foreigner**, this Samaritan, of whom Jews did not expect much, came back to Jesus.

> For reflection: When did someone of whom I did not expect much prove to be a better follower of Jesus than I?

19 **Then he said to him, "Stand up and go; your faith has saved you."** All ten who had leprosy showed some **faith** in Jesus by setting off at his word to see priests before their leprosy was visibly healed (verse 14). But by returning to Jesus, the Samaritan demonstrated **faith** in Jesus as the one through whom God healed. He has been **saved**—rescued in a more profound sense than simply being physically cleansed of leprosy. Jesus said **your faith has saved you** to a woman whose sins were forgiven (7:50) and to a woman healed of hemorrhaging (8:48); for these women and for this man, their **faith** that Jesus is God's agent brings them

salvation. They have been released from evil so that they may embrace Jesus' message and enter into the kingdom of God.

For reflection: How have I experienced the saving power of faith in Jesus?

The Presence of the Kingdom of God
²⁰ **Asked by the Pharisees when the kingdom of God would come, he said in reply, "The coming of the kingdom of God cannot be observed, ²¹ and no one will announce, 'Look, here it is,' or, 'There it is.' For behold, the kingdom of God is among you."**
NT: Luke 7:22; 10:9, 11; 11:20; 12:54–56

20 **Asked by the Pharisees when the kingdom of God would come**: most **Pharisees** shared the expectation of many Jews that God would act to set things right for his people and usher in a golden age. Jesus refined such expectations. The keynote of his preaching, and the message he had his disciples preach, was that God was establishing his **kingdom** or reign (4:43; 8:1, 10; 9:2, 11, 60; 10:9, 11). Jesus taught his followers to pray to their Father, "your kingdom come" (11:2). Some Pharisees wanted to know **when** the kingdom of God **would come** and **asked** Jesus to tell them. **He said in reply, "The coming of the kingdom of God cannot be observed."** The significance of Jesus' answer lies in the word translated as **observed**. The word was used for observing symptoms to diagnose a medical condition and for scientific observation of data. Jesus is asked when God's kingdom will come, and he answers that the symptoms or signs of its coming **cannot be observed**. The time of its coming cannot be calculated because there will be no observable data that will indicate that its coming is imminent.

Pharisees: See page 143
Kingdom of God: See page 381

21 **And no one will announce, "Look, here it is," or, "There it is."** Just as the time of the coming of God's kingdom cannot be determined, neither can it be localized in a specific place. The implication would seem to be that God will establish his reign over the entire world and not just over a particular nation or people.

461

While there will be no signs that will announce that the ultimate establishment of God's reign is imminent, there are signs that indicate that God's reign is being inaugurated through the ministry of Jesus. **For behold, the kingdom of God is among you.** The sense of **For behold** is, open your eyes and see. Jesus invited John's disciples to "tell John what you have seen and heard: the blind regain their sight, the lame walk, lepers are cleansed, the deaf hear, the dead are raised, the poor have the good news proclaimed to them" (7:22). Jesus said, "If it is by the finger of God that [I] drive out demons, then the kingdom of God has come upon you" (11:20). Jesus asked, "Why do you not know how to interpret the present time?" (12:56)—interpret what is presently happening. Jesus tells the Pharisees to perceive that **the kingdom of God is among you**, made present in the person and ministry of Jesus and in the lives of those who have responded to him. The Pharisees shouldn't be preoccupied with when the kingdom of God will be established in its fullness (verse 20); they should perceive what God is doing here and now through Jesus and, like the grateful Samaritan, respond to him with faith (17:19).

For reflection: How have I experienced the presence of the kingdom of God in my life? What are the signs of Jesus at work today?

ORIENTATION: *After telling Pharisees that there will be no signs announcing the ultimate coming of the kingdom of God (17:21–22), Jesus speaks to his disciples about its ultimate coming (17:22–37). His words play on different meanings of "day" and "days" and are sometimes cryptic.*

The Day of the Son of Man
²² **Then he said to his disciples, "The days will come when you will long to see one of the days of the Son of Man, but you will not see it. ²³ There will be those who will say to you, 'Look, there he is,' [or] 'Look, here he is.' Do not go off, do not run in pursuit. ²⁴ For just as lightning flashes and lights up the sky from one side to the other, so will the Son of Man be [in his day]. ²⁵ But first he must suffer greatly and be rejected by this generation. ²⁶ As it was in the days of Noah, so it will be in the days of the Son of**

Man; ²⁷ they were eating and drinking, marrying and giving in marriage up to the day that Noah entered the ark, and the flood came and destroyed them all. ²⁸ Similarly, as it was in the days of Lot: they were eating, drinking, buying, selling, planting, building; ²⁹ on the day when Lot left Sodom, fire and brimstone rained from the sky to destroy them all. ³⁰ So it will be on the day the Son of Man is revealed. ³¹ On that day, a person who is on the housetop and whose belongings are in the house must not go down to get them, and likewise a person in the field must not return to what was left behind. ³² Remember the wife of Lot. ³³ Whoever seeks to preserve his life will lose it, but whoever loses it will save it. ³⁴ I tell you, on that night there will be two people in one bed; one will be taken, the other left. ³⁵ And there will be two women grinding meal together; one will be taken, the other left." [³⁶] ³⁷ They said to him in reply, "Where, Lord?" He said to them, "Where the body is, there also the vultures will gather."

Gospel parallels: Matt 10:39; 24:17–18, 23, 26–28, 37, 41;
Mark 8:35; 13:15–16, 21; John 12:25
OT: Gen 6–8; 13:12–13; 19:1–29
NT: Luke 9:22–26, 62; 12:35–48; 17:20–21; 21:5–36; 24:26

22 **Then he said to his disciples, "The days will come when you will long to see one of the days of the Son of Man."** Jesus refers to himself as **the Son of Man**. He tells his disciples that **the days will come when** they will **long** for something, apparently referring to the **days** after his ascension into heaven (24:51). By **the days of the Son of Man** that they will long for, Jesus might mean the time of his public ministry: after his ascension (24:51), his disciples will long to have him bodily present with them as he was during his life on earth. However, since he has just spoken about the coming of the kingdom of God (17:20–21), **the days of the Son of Man** more likely refers here to the period after he comes in glory to establish God's reign in its fullness (see 9:26; 12:40). His disciples will long **to see one of the days of the Son of Man**, to have even a single day's experience of God's complete reign. They will be persecuted as they proclaim the Gospel (Acts 5:40–41; 12:1–5). Paul will maintain that "It is necessary for us to undergo many hardships to enter the kingdom of God" (Acts 14:22). In the midst of these hardships they will **long**

for Jesus to return to deliver them from their suffering and bring them into the kingdom. Jesus tells them **but you will not see it**: they will not experience his return as quickly as they would like.

Disciple: See page 149
Son of Man: See page 147

23 **There will be those who will say to you, "Look, there he is," [or] "Look, here he is."** False reports will circulate during the period after Jesus' ascension, claiming that he has returned and is in this or that place. The disciples will be vulnerable to being misled by these reports because they will long intensely for his return. Jesus advises them to give no credence to any claims about his having come; he tells them **do not go off** to wherever he is reported to be, **do not run in pursuit,** looking for him.

24 The disciples can dismiss all reports of his return because when he comes, reports will be unnecessary. **For just as lightning flashes and lights up the sky from one side to the other, so will the Son of Man be [in his day].** Not all manuscripts of Luke's Gospel have the words **in his day**, which is why the New American Bible encloses them in brackets. The day of the Son of Man is the moment of his coming again (see verse 30). It will be like a great **lightning** flash that **lights up the sky** from one horizon to the other; his coming will be sudden and universal and observable by all. As a comparison, the false reports of his coming will be like a claim, "There is a lamp burning in the next room," while his actual coming will be like lightning illuminating the entire earth. There will be no mistaking his coming, and no need for one person to tell another about it. Nor, as Jesus told the Pharisees, will there be any advance warning signs (17:20); it will simply happen.

25 Although Jesus is addressing the subject of what will happen in the future, he wants his disciples to keep it in the perspective of more immediate events. He tells them, **but first he must suffer greatly and be rejected by this generation. By this generation** Jesus refers to those who do not accept him as an agent of God (see 7:31–34; 11:29). He has already spoken of or alluded to his suffering and death (9:22, 44; 12:50; 13:33). He **must** suffer as God's will for him; he cannot come "in his glory

and in the glory of the Father and of the holy angels" (9:26) without first enduring suffering and death (see 24:26). His disciples must bear in mind that suffering is his path to glory, and theirs as well (see verse 33).

26 Because there will be no signs announcing that his coming is imminent (17:20), many will be going about life as usual and will not be prepared when he comes. Jesus uses two comparisons to illustrate this. **As it was in the days of Noah, so it will be in the days of the Son of Man.** In this verse, **the days of the Son of Man** refer to the time preceding his coming. People will behave then as they behaved **in the days of Noah**. The story of **Noah** and the flood is told in chapters 6 through 8 of Genesis.

27 God instructed Noah to build an ark to escape the coming flood (Gen 6:14–22). While Noah was building the ark, the people of his time **were eating and drinking, marrying and giving in marriage**. The word translated **giving in marriage** literally means "being given in marriage"; men married, and woman were given in marriage by their fathers. God judged the people of Noah's time to be wicked, and he regretted that he had created them (Gen 6:5–6), but their sinfulness is not at issue here. **Eating and drinking, marrying and giving in marriage** are simply the normal activities of life. Although God's judgment was pending against them, they went on with life as usual **up to the day that Noah entered the ark**. Then **the flood came and destroyed them all**. They never saw it coming.

28 A second comparison: **Similarly, as it was in the days of Lot**: Abraham's nephew **Lot** settled in the Jordan Plain southeast of the Dead Sea, "pitching his tents near Sodom" (Gen 13:12) and apparently eventually moving into the town (see Gen 19:1–3). Genesis notes that "the inhabitants of Sodom were very wicked in the sins they committed against the LORD" (Gen 13:13). While Lot lived with them, the people of Sodom **were eating, drinking, buying, selling, planting, building**. They were going about the normal activities of life; there is no implication that these activities were why God judged them to be wicked.

29 **On the day when Lot left Sodom**: the story is told in chapter 19 of Genesis. **Lot** was warned by angels to flee from **Sodom** with his family

(Gen 19:12–22). Once he was a safe distance away, **fire and brimstone rained from the sky to destroy them all**—all the people of Sodom (Gen 19:23–25).

30 Jesus draws the lesson of the two comparisons: **so it will be on the day the Son of Man is revealed**. The **day** when the Son of Man **is revealed** refers to the time when he will come in glory (9:26). He will be **revealed**: he will be made manifest to everyone, and his identity will be made clear (see also 1 Cor 1:7; 2 Thess 1:7; 1 Pet 1:7, 13; 4:13). People will be going about the normal activities of life, oblivious to the cataclysmic event that is about to occur, since there will be no signs to warn them that he is about to come (17:20).

> *For reflection: Do I go about life as usual, as if Jesus will certainly not come during my lifetime?*

31 Jesus is implicitly warning his disciples against living life as usual. How then should they live, in light of his coming unexpectedly? He tells them, **on that day, a person who is on the housetop and whose belongings are in the house must not go down to get them.** Most houses had a flat roof, accessible by an outside stairway, that was used for drying crops (Joshua 2:6), for sleeping on hot nights (1 Sam 9:25–26), and as a place where one could have some privacy (Acts 10:9). Jesus advises that **on that day**, a person on a **housetop** should not go down into the house to gather up **belongings**. The significance of Jesus' advice hinges on the meaning of **that day**. It is unlikely that it is the day of Jesus' coming (verse 30), for his lightning-fast coming (verse 24) will leave no time to gather possessions even if one wanted to. If by **that day** Jesus had in mind the day when Jerusalem will be besieged (see 21:20), then he would be advising a quick escape from the city (see 21:21), without any delay to collect possessions. But Jesus does not seem to have the siege of Jerusalem in mind here. Rather, by **that day** he seems to mean the period before his coming, comparable to the period before the flood and to the period before Sodom was destroyed (verses 26–29). He uses the example of someone leaving **belongings** behind in order to flee swiftly to save his or her life as a comparison for the urgency of being prepared for his coming, for being unencumbered by possessions. Jesus warned his

disciples that they must not let themselves be governed by money (16:13) and told them, "Everyone of you who does not renounce all his possessions cannot be my disciple" (14:33). The prospect of his coming in glory makes it all the more urgent for his followers not to be weighed down by belongings. He has spoken about the need to be vigilant while awaiting his return (12:35–48) and now makes detachment from possessions part of that vigilance.

For reflection: If I lost all my possessions in a disaster like a tornado or hurricane but was physically unharmed, how grateful would I be that I was still alive?

And likewise a person in the field must not return to what was left behind. Again, Jesus' advice could be taken literally if an enemy army was advancing: when you see war horses on the horizon, flee right away. Don't go back to your house to gather up belongings; don't have the slightest regard for **what was left behind**. In this context, however, Jesus is using the example of fleeing from danger as a comparison for his disciples' not returning to what they **left behind** in order to follow him. When he called his first disciples, "They left everything and followed him" (5:11). He warned that "no one who sets a hand to the plow and looks to what was left behind is fit for the kingdom of God" (9:62). Not having second thoughts about what one has left behind to follow Jesus is all the more important in light of the prospect of his coming.

32 Jesus reinforces his point by telling his disciples, **Remember**—pay heed to the example of—**the wife of Lot**. When Lot and his family were about to flee Sodom, angels warned them, "Don't look back or stop anywhere on the Plain. Get off to the hills at once" (Gen 19:17). Despite this warning, "Lot's wife looked back" on what she had left behind, "and she was turned into a pillar of salt" (Gen 19:26). She serves as an image for the importance of not looking "to what was left behind" (9:62).

For reflection: Have I given up anything for Jesus that I now regret parting with? Do I have any second thoughts about the course my life has taken as a disciple of Jesus?

33 Jesus generalizes his instructions about not hanging on to possessions or looking back on what one has given up, echoing what he earlier told his disciples (9:24): **Whoever seeks to preserve his life will lose it, but whoever loses it will save it**. The word translated as **life** could also be translated as "self." Whoever tries to **preserve** his or her earthly life, or self, trying to hang on to it as a possession, will **lose** what he or she is trying to preserve. Jesus has told parables that provide examples of death and God's judgment depriving people of that which they treasured (12:20; 16:22–25). On the other hand, **whoever loses** his or her life, his or her self, **will save it**. The word translated **will save** literally means "keep alive": it is by forsaking oneself for the sake of Jesus that one keeps oneself alive—eternally alive. Jesus previously told his disciples that they will save their lives by losing their lives (9:24) after telling them that "the Son of Man must suffer greatly and be rejected by the elders, the chief priests, and the scribes, and be killed and on the third day be raised" (9:22). He repeats the pattern here, first telling them that the Son of Man must suffer greatly and be rejected (verse 25) before telling them that by losing their lives they will save their lives. Disciples must follow in the footsteps of Jesus to enter into the kingdom of God, forsaking all as he forsook all.

> *For reflection: What does Jesus' warning, "Whoever seeks to preserve his life will lose it," mean for me? What does Jesus' promise, "Whoever loses it will save it," mean for me?*

34 **I tell you, on that night there will be two people in one bed; one will be taken, the other left.** By **that night** Jesus means the time of his coming, which he also refers to as "the day the Son of Man is revealed" (verse 30). He may come at day or at night; the setting here is at **night** because there are **two people in one bed**—presumably a married couple. When Jesus comes in glory, **one** of them **will be taken** into the kingdom of God (see 16:22) and **the other left** outside (see 13:25). Jesus' words presume that God judges one of them worthy to enter the kingdom and the other not, but Jesus does not go into the reasons for God's judgments. His point is that his coming will entail a division between those who are ready to be taken into the heavenly kingdom and those who are excluded. The division will occur suddenly and unexpectedly (see verses

24, 26–30); the couple went to bed that night expecting to get up in the morning.

35 Jesus provides a second illustration to make the same point: **And there will be two women grinding meal together; one will be taken, the other left**. The type of millstones used in homes indicate that we should envision the **two women** kneeling, facing each other with a large flat stone between them, pushing a second smaller stone back and forth, **grinding** grain between the two stones. **One** of the women **will be taken** into the kingdom of God when Jesus comes, and **the other** woman **left** outside. Again, Jesus does not provide the reasons for their respective fates but simply indicates that his coming will mean a great and permanent divide between humans (see 16:26). There is also the note of unexpectedness: the women would not be bothering to grind grain into flour if they realized that the end would come before they had time to bake bread.

Jesus' two examples warn his disciples against complacency and assure them that they will be judged by God and assigned an eternal fate.

For reflection: What particular message do Jesus' examples of one being taken and one left have for me?

[36] (Some manuscripts of Luke's Gospel include at this point the verse "There will be two men in the field; one will be taken, the other left behind." These words are not found in the most reliable manuscripts and were probably added by a scribe who adapted them from Matthew 24:40. The New American Bible omits this verse.)

37 **They said to him in reply, "Where, Lord?"** The disciples seem puzzled by what Jesus has told them, for their question is odd. Are they asking **where** will the one person in bed and the one woman grinding grain be taken? That would indicate that they missed the point he was trying to make by using these examples. Are they asking **where** Jesus will appear when he comes—even though Jesus has indicated that his coming will be universally observable and not limited to a specific place (verses 23–24)? Perhaps it is the latter, for Jesus seems to speak of his coming in his reply to them. **He said to them, "Where the body is, there also**

the vultures will gather." These are among Jesus' most enigmatic words anywhere in the Gospels. Their likely meaning is that his coming will be as evident as a **body** marked by hovering **vultures**. When the disciples saw vultures circling in the sky, they knew that there was a dead or dying human or animal below. The coming of Jesus will be just as obvious, and there will be no need to wonder **where** he is. We might find lightning flashing across the sky (verse 24) to be a more palatable image for his coming than vultures gathered at a corpse. Either image, however, conveys that his coming will be clearly evident.

Lord: See page 137

CHAPTER 18

ORIENTATION: *Jesus continues to speak to his disciples about his coming in the future to establish God's reign in its fullness (17:22–37). They are to be faithful in prayer as they await his return (18:1–8).*

A Parable about Persistence in Prayer

¹ **Then he told them a parable about the necessity for them to pray always without becoming weary. He said, ² "There was a judge in a certain town who neither feared God nor respected any human being. ³ And a widow in that town used to come to him and say, 'Render a just decision for me against my adversary.' ⁴ For a long time the judge was unwilling, but eventually he thought, 'While it is true that I neither fear God nor respect any human being, ⁵ because this widow keeps bothering me I shall deliver a just decision for her lest she finally come and strike me.' " ⁶ The Lord said, "Pay attention to what the dishonest judge says. ⁷ Will not God then secure the rights of his chosen ones who call out to him day and night? Will he be slow to answer them? ⁸ I tell you, he will see to it that justice is done for them speedily. But when the Son of Man comes, will he find faith on earth?"**

OT: Sirach 35:14–19
NT: Luke 11:1–13; 17:22–37

1   **Then he told them**—his disciples (see 17:22)—**a parable about the necessity for them to pray always without becoming weary.** The sense of **pray always** is to continue to pray, not to pray continuously. Jesus is not asking his disciples to spend all their waking hours in prayer but telling them that it is necessary for them to persevere in prayer. They must do so **without becoming weary**, literally, without losing heart. If God seems slow to answer their prayers, they may be tempted to lose hope and abandon prayer. Jesus' words **pray always without becoming weary** apply to all prayer. But since he is speaking about his coming to bring God's reign to fulfillment (verse 8; 17:22–37), it is particularly the prayer, "your kingdom come" (11:2), that his disciples must **pray always without becoming weary**. During the time after his ascension they will "long to

471

see one of the days of the Son of Man" but they "will not see it" (17:22). They must nevertheless persevere in praying for his coming without losing heart. To illustrate perseverance in prayer he tells them a **parable**.

Parables: See page 217

For reflection: How faithfully do I pray? What do I pray for? How do I react when God does not answer my prayers when I think he should?

2 He said, **"There was a judge in a certain town"**: a local **judge** could decide lawsuits. This particular judge **neither feared God nor respected any human being**. Fear of God is reverence and respect for God (see 1:50; 12:5), required of all (Lev 19:14; Deut 4:10; 6:13; 14:23) as the basis for just dealings (Lev 25:17, 36, 43). Since it was the duty of judges to render just decisions (Lev 19:15; Deut 1:16-17; 16:18–20), it was all the more important for them to have a proper fear of God (see 2 Chron 19:5–9). This judge, however, had no fear of God. Nor did he **respect any human being**: he did not care about others or what they thought of him. He had neither divine nor human motives for judging justly—exactly the wrong kind of person to be a judge!

3 **And a widow in that town**: in the society and economy of the time, a **widow** without a man to support her and protect her rights was often poor and powerless. Sirach proclaimed that God "is not deaf to the wail of the orphan, / nor to the widow when she pours out her complaint; / Do not the tears that stream down her cheek / cry out against him that causes them to fall?" (Sirach 35:14–15). The implication is that orphans and widows often have grievances because they are oppressed. A **widow in that town used to come to** the judge **and say, "Render a just decision for me against my adversary."** The connotation of **used to come** is that she came repeatedly to him. She apparently has a lawsuit against an **adversary**, likely seeking some kind of financial settlement that is due her. She seeks a **just decision**, which would be in her favor, but the judge does not do his duty and render a verdict (is he waiting for a bribe?). Hence she keeps coming back to him, demanding justice; she does not grow weary of asking.

4 **For a long time the judge was unwilling** to render a verdict in her favor **but eventually he thought, "While it is true that I neither fear God nor respect any human being"**: he acknowledges that he has no concern for God or for people or interest in justice being done. He does not seem bothered by his deplorable condition and does not give the least indication that he would like to change.

5 But, he tells himself, **because this widow keeps bothering me I shall deliver a just decision for her lest she finally come and strike me**. The word translated **strike** specifically means to strike under the eye, to give a black eye. It was used metaphorically for beating someone down or wearing someone out, and that seems to be the sense here. The judge is probably not afraid that the widow will physically harm him, but she **keeps bothering** him, and she will eventually wear him out if he does not **deliver a just decision for her**. Although he does not fear God or respect others, he does value his own peace of mind. The widow will keep coming back until she gets what she wants, so he will grant her the **just decision** she desires in order to put an end to her pestering.

6 **The Lord said, "Pay attention to what the dishonest judge says."** Luke refers to Jesus as **the Lord**. He directs his disciples to **pay attention to** and reflect on **what the dishonest judge says**. Jesus does not hold up the **judge** as a person to be imitated; he is **dishonest**—the word could also be translated unjust. But there is a lesson to be learned from his reasoning in giving the widow what she wants. He is worn down by her continual pleas for justice even though he has no interest in justice being done; he gives in to her because of her persistence.

Lord: See page 137

7 Jesus asks, **Will not God then secure the rights of his chosen ones who call out to him day and night?** The words translated **secure the rights** mean to do justice and are an echo of the widow's quest for justice from an unjust judge. Disciples are to pray that God will establish justice, overcoming evil, setting things right. The Old Testament refers to God's people and those who serve him as the **chosen** (see Deut 4:37; 7:6–7; 1 Chron 16:13; Sirach 47:22; Isaiah 42:1; 43:20; 45:4; 65:9; 15, 22); in the New Testament the **chosen** are Jesus' first and subsequent disciples (see

Rom 8:33; Eph 1:11; Col 3:12; 1 Thess 1:4; 2 Tim 2:10; Titus 1:1; 1 Pet 1:1; 2:9; Rev 17:14). Calling out to God **day and night** means imploring him perseveringly (see 2:37). If an amoral judge who respects no one will grant justice to a widow because of her persistence, how much more will a just **God** grant justice to his **chosen ones** who persistently ask him? Jesus used a similar logic in teaching about prayer when he told his disciples, "If you then, who are wicked, know how to give good gifts to your children, how much more will the Father in heaven give the holy Spirit to those who ask him?" (11:13). **Will he be slow to answer them?** The question demands the answer, "Of course not!" They are his **chosen ones**.

> *For reflection: Do I consider myself among God's chosen ones? What does this imply about God's attitude toward me?*

8   Jesus assures his disciples, **I tell you, he will see to it that justice is done for them speedily**. Since Jesus is speaking to his disciples about "the necessity for them to pray always without becoming weary" (verse 1), **speedily** does not necessarily mean "immediately." If God immediately answered every prayer, there would be no need for Jesus to exhort his disciples to persevere in prayer. If the prayer in question is the disciples' petition, "your kingdom come" (11:2), it is likewise clear that **speedily** is not "immediately." Luke is writing his Gospel a half-century after Jesus' ascension, and Jesus has not come yet to usher in God's kingdom. Perhaps there is a paradox in the disciples expecting that God will act **speedily** even as they must continue to pray without growing weary. God may not act immediately, but Jesus' disciples must nevertheless pray with the confidence that God will not be slow to answer their prayers and set things right (verse 7). They must have the lively expectation that what they pray for is just around the corner.

> *For reflection: What has been my experience of God answering my prayers? How do I understand Jesus' promise that God responds speedily?*

Jesus asks, **But when the Son of Man comes, will he find faith on earth?** He has spoken of his coming as **the Son of Man**, saying that it will be like a lightning flash that lights up the sky from one horizon to the other (17:24, 30). When he comes, Jesus will set things right once and for all. In the present context, **faith** means remaining faithful, vigilant for his coming (see 12:35–48), perseveringly praying, "your kingdom come." If his coming is delayed, will his followers lose heart and hope (see 2 Pet 3:3–4)? By asking **will he find faith on earth**, Jesus is not asking for a yes or no answer but exhorting his followers to persevere to the end despite any delay, remaining faithful to prayer, filled with hope and expectation.

Son of Man: See page 147

For reflection: In the Creed, we profess, "He will come again in glory to judge the living and the dead." How firmly do I believe what I profess?

A Parable about Two Prayers

⁹ He then addressed this parable to those who were convinced of their own righteousness and despised everyone else. ¹⁰ "Two people went up to the temple area to pray; one was a Pharisee and the other was a tax collector. ¹¹ The Pharisee took up his position and spoke this prayer to himself, 'O God, I thank you that I am not like the rest of humanity—greedy, dishonest, adulterous—or even like this tax collector. ¹² I fast twice a week, and I pay tithes on my whole income.' ¹³ But the tax collector stood off at a distance and would not even raise his eyes to heaven but beat his breast and prayed, 'O God, be merciful to me a sinner.' ¹⁴ I tell you, the latter went home justified, not the former; for everyone who exalts himself will be humbled, and the one who humbles himself will be exalted."

OT: Ezra 9:6; Psalm 51
NT: Matt 23:12; Luke 5:33; 11:42; 14:11

9 **He then addressed this parable to those who were convinced of their own righteousness.** The words translated **were convinced of their own righteousness** might also be translated "trusted in themselves that they were righteous" or "were confident in themselves because they were righteous." Jesus addresses those who are sure that their conduct is acceptable to God. Along with their self-assurance, they **despised**

everyone else: they scorned others as lacking their righteousness. Jesus addresses a **parable** to all who think that they are righteous and disdain others, whether these self-assured individuals be his disciples (17:22) or in the crowd traveling with him (14:25)—or readers of Luke's Gospel.

Parables: See page 217

> *For reflection: How well do I think I measure up to what God expects of me? How do I look upon those who do not appear to measure up as well as I think I do?*

10 **Two people went up to the temple area to pray.** Communal prayers were offered twice daily at the Temple (see 1:10; Acts 3:1), but Jews also came at other times **to pray**. In Jesus' parable, **two people** go to the Temple for private prayer. **One was a Pharisee and the other was a tax collector.** Pharisees tried to observe God's laws carefully; they were widely respected, even by those who did not adopt their practices. Tax collectors, on the other hand, were widely despised as corrupt agents of a foreign power. For his parable, Jesus chooses two individuals who are at the opposite ends of the religious spectrum, a respectable **Pharisee** and a disreputable **tax collector**. Jesus could just as well have chosen two other diverse types of individuals—say, a priest and a prostitute—and shaped his parable around them.

Temple: See page 519
Pharisees: See page 143
Tax collectors: See page 94

11 **The Pharisee took up his position**—literally, "the Pharisee stood"; prayers were often offered while standing (see 1 Sam 1:26; 1 Kings 8:22–23; Neh 9:4; Psalm 134:1; Matt 6:5). He **spoke this prayer to himself**. The words translated **to himself** are ambiguous. It is unlikely that they mean that he prayed silently, for prayers were customarily said in a low murmur (see 1 Sam 1:13). Perhaps a better translation for **to himself** would be "with reference to himself," for his prayer is all about himself with "I" occurring repeatedly. He begins his prayer, **O God, I thank you.** This is a good opening for a prayer; a number of psalms begin by thanking or praising God (for example, Psalm 30; 92; 118; 136; 138). These psalms go on to state the reason why God is to be thanked and

praised, and the Pharisee does this as well: he thanks God **that I am not like the rest of humanity**. He thinks he is different from other people, for he views others as being **greedy, dishonest,** and **adulterous.** The word translated **greedy** can refer to robbers and swindlers. The Pharisee views others in a bad light, attributing serious sins to them. He can see the tax collector, and he thanks God that he is not **even like this tax collector**. In the Greek of Luke's Gospel, **this** has a disdainful ring: this one, this contemptible person. The Pharisee considers tax collectors to be sinners who should be shunned (see 5:30; 7:34; 15:1–2). He thanks God that he is not like others, especially like this tax collector.

So far the Pharisee's prayer has been about what he isn't: he says he isn't like other people, whom he views as despicable sinners.

12 Having expressed his superiority, he lists his achievements. He says, **I fast twice a week**. The law of Moses required fasting on only one day a year, the Day of Atonement (Lev 16:29), but some Jews voluntarily abstained from food and drink on other days as an act of piety (see 5:33). He fasts **twice a week**: the *Didache*, a Christian book of instruction written shortly after the time of Jesus, mentions Jews fasting on Mondays and Thursdays. He says, **I pay tithes on my whole income**, literally, "on everything I receive." The law of Moses required farmers to give **tithes**— ten percent—of their harvests for the support of Levites and priests (Num 18:21–32; Deut 14:22), but some Jews went beyond the requirements of the law and gave a tithe of everything they grew or received—"tithes of mint and of rue and of every garden herb," in Jesus' earlier characterization of Pharisees' tithing (11:42). This Pharisee is proud of his religious achievements, of his fasting and tithing more than was required. He is satisfied with himself and thanks God for who he is; he does not ask God for anything.

Fasting: See page 153

For reflection: Do my good deeds and acts of piety give me a sense of satisfaction? Why do I do them?

13 The Temple courtyards covered more than thirty-five acres, with the Temple itself on an elevated area near the middle. **The tax collector stood off at a distance** in an outer courtyard. He came no closer **and**

would not even raise his eyes to heaven, as Jews often did while praying (9:16; see also Psalm 123:1; Mark 7:34; John 11:41; 17:1). His attitude is like that of Ezra when he prayed, "My God, I am too ashamed and confounded to raise my face to you, O my God, for our wicked deeds are heaped up above our heads and our guilt reaches up to heaven" (Ezra 9:6). He **beat his breast** over his heart, a gesture expressing sorrow (see 23:48) and, here, contrition. He **prayed, "O God, be merciful to me a sinner."** He looks upon himself as **a sinner**. The word translated **be merciful** has connotations of atonement and reconciliation (the word is translated as "expiate" at Heb 2:17); the tax collector prays that God will remove his sinfulness. His prayer echoes Psalm 51's pleas for God's mercy and restoration. He has no achievements to parade before God; he does not even claim that he will change his life. He simply admits that he is a sinner and relies on God's mercy.

> Have mercy on me, God, in your goodness;
>> in your abundant compassion blot out my offense.
> Wash away all my guilt;
>> from my sin cleanse me.
>
> Psalm 51:3–4

14 Jesus solemnly proclaims, **I tell you, the latter went home justified**, found acceptable by God. Jesus knows how God responds to those who, like the tax collector, make no pretense about themselves and throw themselves on his mercy: God is merciful to them. The tax collector went home justified by God, but **not the former**: the Pharisee asked nothing from God and received nothing from him. He had an acute eye for the sins of others but was blind to his own, and did not ask for God's mercy.

Jesus generalizes from the two figures in his parable, invoking words he has uttered previously (14:11): **for everyone who exalts himself will be humbled** by God, **and the one who humbles himself will be exalted** by God. The Pharisee in his prayer exalted himself, thinking himself to be better than others, but God does not look favorably on those who in their pride look unfavorably upon everyone else. The tax collector humbled himself, standing off at a distance, not daring to raise his eyes to heaven, beating his breast and asking for mercy. He left the Temple area justified, **exalted** by God.

Jesus addressed his parable "to those who were convinced of their own righteousness and despised everyone else" (verse 9) as a warning against self-satisfied complacency and disdain for others. The tax collector provides an example for them to imitate in his humility and in his prayer, "O God, be merciful to me a sinner."

For reflection: What do I see of myself in the Pharisee? In the tax collector? What is the chief lesson of Jesus' parable for me?

ORIENTATION: *Jesus uses teaching opportunities to address the conditions for entering the kingdom of God (18:15–34).*

Receiving the Kingdom Like a Child

¹⁵ **People were bringing even infants to him that he might touch them, and when the disciples saw this, they rebuked them.** ¹⁶ **Jesus, however, called the children to himself and said, "Let the children come to me and do not prevent them; for the kingdom of God belongs to such as these.** ¹⁷ **Amen, I say to you, whoever does not accept the kingdom of God like a child will not enter it."**

Gospel parallels: Matt 19:13–15; Mark 10:13–16

NT: Matt 18:3; Luke 9:46–48; 10:21; 12:22–34; 18:13–14

15 **People were bringing even infants to him that he might touch them**, perhaps to heal them (see 5:13; 6:19) or to impart a blessing (see Gen 48:14–16). **And when the disciples saw this, they rebuked them** and tried to stop them. Did they think that Jesus was too important to waste his time on babies? Had they forgotten that Jesus "took a child and placed it by his side and said to them, 'Whoever receives this child in my name receives me' " (9:47–48)? At the very least they could have asked Jesus, "Are these infants bothering you?" and found out what he wanted them to do. This is not the only time that the disciples act on the basis of their own impulses and preferences without first seeking Jesus' desires (see 9:49–50).

Disciple: See page 149

For reflection: To what extent are my actions guided by my own preferences, and to what extent are they guided by Jesus' way for me?

16 **Jesus, however, called the children to himself**, welcoming them. To make his desires clear, Jesus expresses them both positively—**let the children come to me**—and negatively—**and do not prevent them**. He welcomes children for a profound reason: **the kingdom of God belongs to such as these**. Those who heard these words were probably startled. It is unlikely that their expectations of what **the kingdom of God** would be like included any prominent place or role for children. Children—especially infants—had no status or influence. Yet Jesus proclaims that the kingdom of God is made up of children and those who are like children. His mission is to inaugurate the reign of God (4:43; 11:20; 17:21); it is natural for him to welcome children, because **the kingdom of God belongs to** them.

Kingdom of God: See page 381

17 Jesus solemnly makes another startling pronouncement: **Amen, I say to you, whoever does not accept the kingdom of God like a child will not enter it**. The word translated **accept** can also be translated "receive." What does it mean to accept or receive the kingdom of God **like a child**? Young children do not earn their keep but receive what they need from their parents. Receiving the kingdom of God **like a child** means receiving it as a gift, not earning it as an achievement. Jesus taught his disciples to trust their Father to provide for them (12:22–34), telling them, "Do not be afraid any longer, little flock, for your Father is pleased to give you the kingdom" (12:32). Trust comes naturally for children, who depend on their mothers and fathers to provide for them; accepting **the kingdom of God like a child** means entrusting oneself into the hands of the Father. The childlike—those who receive like a child—put up no barriers to receiving what God gives. Jesus praised his Father, saying "for although you have hidden these things from the wise and the learned you have revealed them to the childlike" (10:21). The tax collector in Jesus' parable made no claims about his own achievements but simply prayed for God's mercy—the proper stance for receiving from God (18:13–14).

For reflection: How do I understand accepting God's kingdom like a child? What are its implications for my relationship with God?

Whoever does not accept the kingdom of God like a child **will not enter it**. Those who do not depend on God rather than on their own achievements will not enter the kingdom. Yet Jesus elsewhere taught that one must "strive to enter through the narrow door" of the kingdom, "for many, I tell you, will attempt to enter but will not be strong enough" (13:24). Jesus said that "the kingdom of God is proclaimed, and everyone who enters does so with violence" (16:16). How does one strive hard, even violently, to enter the kingdom even while accepting it like a child? How does one exert one's utmost efforts while at the same time being completely dependent on God? This seems to be a paradox that must be lived out, rather than thought out and solved.

For reflection: How do I balance my striving to do God's will with accepting that eternal life is God's gift to me?

Wealth and Eternal Life

¹⁸ An official asked him this question, "Good teacher, what must I do to inherit eternal life?" ¹⁹ Jesus answered him, "Why do you call me good? No one is good but God alone. ²⁰ You know the commandments, 'You shall not commit adultery; you shall not kill; you shall not steal; you shall not bear false witness; honor your father and your mother.' " ²¹ And he replied, "All of these I have observed from my youth." ²² When Jesus heard this he said to him, "There is still one thing left for you: sell all that you have and distribute it to the poor, and you will have a treasure in heaven. Then come, follow me." ²³ But when he heard this he became quite sad, for he was very rich.

²⁴ Jesus looked at him [now sad] and said, "How hard it is for those who have wealth to enter the kingdom of God! ²⁵ For it is easier for a camel to pass through the eye of a needle than for a rich person to enter the kingdom of God." ²⁶ Those who heard this said, "Then who can be saved?" ²⁷ And he said, "What is impossible for human beings is possible for God."

Gospel parallels: Matt 19:16–26; Mark 10:17–27

OT: Exod 20:12–16; Deut 5:16–20

NT: Luke 9:23–26; 10:25–28; 12:33; 14:33; 16:8–13; 18:16–17

18 **An official asked him this question**: the **official** might have been a synagogue leader (8:41) or a judge (the word for **official** is translated as "magistrate" at 12:58) or in some other position of authority. He addresses Jesus as **good teacher** and asks him, **What must I do to inherit eternal life?** Calling Jesus a **good teacher** is respectful; there is no indication that his question is insincere or that he is out to trap Jesus. He asks about entering into **eternal life**, everlasting life after death (see 2 Macc 7; Dan 12:2). He recognizes that eternal life cannot be earned; it is something that one must **inherit** or receive as a gift from God. Perhaps he heard Jesus say that "whoever does not accept the kingdom of God like a child will not enter it" (18:17) and perceived that this meant accepting eternal life in the kingdom as a gift. He wants to know what he must **do** to be eligible to **inherit eternal life**. Even if an inheritance is a free gift, there can be conditions attached to receiving it.

Life after death: See page 298

19 **Jesus answered him, "Why do you call me good? No one is good but God alone."** Jesus surprisingly rebuffs the assertion that he is **good**. Perhaps the point that Jesus wishes to make is that **God alone** is supremely good; Jesus' goodness comes from God. Jesus wants to deflect attention from himself as a teacher to the one who is the source of his teaching, as is clear from what he says next to the official.

20 He tells him, **You know the commandments**. If you wish to inherit eternal life from God, then do what you **know** God commands you to do. Jesus reminds him of some of the **commandments** that God gave his people when he established a covenant with them at Mount Sinai: **you shall not commit adultery; you shall not kill; you shall not steal; you shall not bear false witness; honor your father and your mother** (Exod 20:12–16; Deut 5:16–20). Jesus does not recount the commandments in the same order in which they are found in Exodus and Deuteronomy, but there does not appear to be any significance in the order in which he gives them. Jesus reminds the official of the commandments that deal with how people treat each other; he does not recount the commandments that deal with their relationship with God (Exod 20:2–11; Deut 5:6–15). It should be obvious that if one wishes to

482

receive eternal life from God, then one must be faithful to and worship God. It may be less apparent that how one treats other people determines whether God will grant one eternal life, and Jesus may want the official to focus on this aspect of his conduct.

Another person had asked Jesus the same question: "Teacher, what must I do to inherit eternal life?" (10:25). Jesus directed his attention to what was written in the law: "You shall love the Lord, your God, with all your heart, with all your being, with all your strength, and with all your mind, and your neighbor as yourself" (10:26–27). Both times Jesus teaches that one must keep God's commandments to inherit eternal life.

For reflection: How eligible am I for inheriting eternal life, if obeying God's commandments is the prerequisite?

21 **And he replied, "All of these I have observed from my youth."** He is now an adult if he is an official (verse 18). He claims that he has obeyed **all** of God's commandments since he was a **youth**, since his young teenage years. There is no reason to believe that he is deceived about his conduct or lying; obeying God's commandments is not an impossible ideal. Luke described Zechariah and Elizabeth as "righteous in the eyes of God, observing all the commandments and ordinances of the Lord blamelessly" (1:6), and Paul will write that "in righteousness based on the law I was blameless" (Phil 3:6). The official is among those who obey God's commandments, and he had been doing so since he was a youth. He is an upright person.

22 **When Jesus heard this he said to him, "There is still one thing left for you."** The word translated **left** means "lacking" or "missing": although the official obeys God's commandments, there is still **one thing** more for him to do if he wishes to inherit eternal life. Jesus tells him, **sell all that you have**. The word **all** should be read as if it is underlined for emphasis; Jesus tells him to sell everything, as much as he possesses. He is to take the proceeds **and distribute it to the poor**, the abjectly poor. Jesus has a special concern for the very poor (4:18; 6:20; 7:22) and has taught that the proper use of money is to help the poor (11:41; 12:33; 14:13; 16:9). If the official gives away all he has as alms, Jesus promises

him, **you will have a treasure in heaven**. Jesus earlier said much the same thing to his disciples: "Sell your belongings and give alms. Provide money bags for yourselves that do not wear out, an inexhaustible treasure in heaven" (12:33). Jesus concludes, **then come, follow me**. Jesus explicitly or implicitly issued the call **follow me** to others, and they left behind their jobs and possessions to become his disciples (see 5:10–11, 27–28; 9:59–62). Now Jesus makes the same invitation to this upright official. He asks no more of him than he asked of others: "Everyone of you who does not renounce all his possessions cannot be my disciple" (14:33).

Alms: See page 332

Disciple: See page 149

After telling the official that he was lacking "one thing" (verse 22) Jesus seems to instruct him to do several things: sell all he has and give to the poor and follow him. However, these are aspects of one fundamental response to God—of totally entrusting oneself to God through generosity to others and allegiance to Jesus. Jesus has made it clear that following him requires absolute commitment: "If anyone wishes to come after me, he must deny himself and take up his cross daily and follow me. For whoever wishes to save his life will lose it, but whoever loses his life for my sake will save it" (9:23–24). He has made it clear that his disciples must trust in God rather than in their possessions (9:2–3; 10:3–4; 12:22–34; 16:13). Hence Jesus invites the official to sell his possessions and give to the poor and follow him. Then he will receive the eternal life he wants to inherit, an everlasting treasure in heaven.

For reflection: What are the implications for me of Jesus telling the official to give all he has to the poor in order to follow him? How complete is my allegiance to Jesus and dependence on God?

23 **But when he heard this he became quite sad, for he was very rich.** The official counts the cost of becoming Jesus' disciple, and for him it is very high, **for he was very rich**. He must leave behind far more than a fishing boat or a tax collector's booth (5:11, 27–28); he must cast aside a fortune, along with the security and comforts it affords him. **He became quite sad** at the prospect of giving up his wealth, and he cannot bring

himself to do it—at this time anyway. In Luke's account, he does not go away but remains with Jesus. Luke leaves it open whether he will eventually do what Jesus asks of him. The official can thereby represent all those who have heard Jesus' invitation but have not yet been able to bring themselves to respond to him wholeheartedly. There is hope for the official, and for us.

For reflection: What has Jesus asked me to do that I have not yet done? What holds me back?

24 **Jesus looked at him [now sad]**: the New American Bible puts the words **now sad** in brackets because they are not found in all ancient manuscripts of Luke's Gospel. The words would refer to the rich official, who became sad when he learned the cost of discipleship for him (verse 23). Jesus **looked at him** and continues to address him, although what he says is directed as well to all others who are present. He said, **How hard it is for those who have wealth to enter the kingdom of God!** The word translated **wealth** does not necessarily mean great wealth; it simply means money or property. One cannot serve God and mammon (16:13), and **how hard it is** to put God ahead of mammon! The official's failure to respond to Jesus demonstrates how difficult it can be to part with one's possessions for the sake of Jesus and the poor, and therefore **how hard it is for those who have wealth to enter the kingdom** and inherit eternal life. As addressed to the rich official, Jesus' words are an acknowledgment that what he asks of him is indeed difficult and **hard.** As an observation meant for the others present, Jesus' words warn that possessions can be an obstacle to the wholehearted dependence on God that is necessary if one is to receive the kingdom like a child (18:17). Jesus has repeatedly taught about the dangers of wealth (6:24; 8:14; 12:15–21; 16:13, 19–31).

Kingdom of God: See page 381

For reflection: How hard do I find it to give what I have to those in need, trusting in God's care for me? What limits do I put on my charity?

25 As he is fond of doing (see 6:41–42), Jesus uses an outlandish image to drive his point home: **For it is easier for a camel to pass through the eye of a needle than for a rich person to enter the kingdom of God**. A **camel** was the largest animal in the region, and **the eye of a needle** was the smallest opening that Jesus' listeners would have been familiar with. Jesus proclaims that **it is easier** for the largest animal to pass through the smallest opening **than for a rich person to enter the kingdom of God**. Here Jesus speaks not simply of wealth but of riches, significant wealth. If we were to embellish his imagery we might say, the greater the wealth, the larger the camel: the more one has, the more difficult it is **to enter the kingdom of God**. For those bloated by riches, the narrow door of the kingdom (13:24) is like the eye of a needle.

26 **Those who heard this said, "Then who can be saved?"** They might be perplexed because they share a view, based on Scripture (Deut 28:1–14; Job 1:9–10; 42:10; Sirach 11:21–22), that riches are a sign of God's favor. If those whom God favors have great difficulty entering the kingdom, **then who can be saved?** Who can inherit eternal life? What hope is there for ordinary people if it easier for a camel to pass through the eye of a needle than for God's favorites to enter his kingdom?

27 **And he said, "What is impossible for human beings is possible for God."** When Mary wondered how she could conceive a child since she had no relations with a man (1:34), the angel Gabriel told her, "Nothing will be impossible for God" (1:37). What humans cannot achieve, God can. God can change the rich official's heart so that he is willing to give his fortune to the poor and cast his lot with Jesus. God can touch the hearts of every woman and man, moving them to have more faith and be more compassionate, drawing them beyond themselves and to himself. God can grant eternal life to those who cannot attain it through their efforts—which is everyone. Eternal life is not our present life unendingly prolonged in a better setting but transformed life, a new mode of personal existence with God. It is impossible for any human to effect this transformation into a new mode of existence, but **what is impossible for human beings is possible for God**.

For reflection: What are my ultimate hopes for myself? How great is my faith that God can do the impossible for me?

The Path to Eternal Life

28 Then Peter said, "We have given up our possessions and followed you." 29 He said to them, "Amen, I say to you, there is no one who has given up house or wife or brothers or parents or children for the sake of the kingdom of God 30 who will not receive [back] an overabundant return in this present age and eternal life in the age to come."

31 Then he took the Twelve aside and said to them, "Behold, we are going up to Jerusalem and everything written by the prophets about the Son of Man will be fulfilled. 32 He will be handed over to the Gentiles and he will be mocked and insulted and spat upon; 33 and after they have scourged him they will kill him, but on the third day he will rise." 34 But they understood nothing of this; the

---

BACKGROUND: THE AGE TO COME There was no expectation of meaningful life after death in early Old Testament times; if God was to reward good and punish evil it had to be in this life. Most of the prophecies of the Old Testament share this perspective: God will rescue or punish his people through the events of history. Late in the Old Testament era a new perspective developed that is expressed in a first-century Jewish writing: "The Most High has made not one age but two" (4 Ezra 7:50—a book not in the Bible). According to this perspective, God would bring an end to the present age and inaugurate a new age. The age to come was conceived of differently in different writings; there was general agreement that God would bring human history with all its evils to an end and reward good and punish evil at a judgment. This was often associated with God fully establishing his reign over his people and all peoples, but there were different expectations for how this would happen. Jesus spoke of the present age and the age to come (Mark 10:30; see also Luke 20:34–35) and proclaimed that the kingdom of God was at hand (Mark 1:15), which meant that the present age was drawing to an end (Matt 13:39–40, 49; 24:3; 28:20). Paul speaks of Christians as living in the present age (Rom 8:18; 12:2) and yet having been rescued from it (2 Cor 5:17; Gal 1:4): Jesus began establishing the reign of God, but we still await its fullness. *Related topics: Judgment (page 327), Kingdom of God (page 381), Life after death (page 298), Nonbiblical writings (page 342).*

word remained hidden from them and they failed to comprehend what he said.

Gospel parallels: Matt 19:27–29; 20:17–19; Mark 10:28–34

OT: Isaiah 50:6; 52:13—53:12; Dan 7:13

NT: Luke 5:11, 28; 9:22, 44–45; 14:26–27; 18:18–27; 24:25–27, 45–46

28 The disciples were present when Jesus told the official to sell all he had, distribute it to the poor, and then come and follow him (18:15, 22). The official held back, saddened by the prospect of giving up his riches (18:23). **Then Peter said, "We have given up our possessions and followed you":** Peter states that he and the other disciples have done what the official was invited to do (see 5:11, 28). Perhaps Peter is implicitly asking Jesus to reassure them that they will receive the eternal life the official was seeking (18:18), despite its being hard to enter the kingdom of God (18:24–25). Will God do the impossible (18:27) for them?

29 **He said to them, "Amen, I say to you, there is no one who has given up house or wife or brothers or parents or children for the sake of the kingdom of God":** here **house** may have the sense of household, those who live together. Jesus speaks about those who have **given up** their families for the sake of serving and entering God's **kingdom**. Giving up **wife** or husband and **children** can include remaining single for the sake of the kingdom. Jesus has made it clear that his disciples' first allegiance must be to him rather than to their families (9:59–62; 14:26). He realizes that some families will be torn apart because some members become his disciples (12:51–53). Now he acknowledges those who have given up their families **for the sake of the kingdom of God.**

Kingdom of God: See page 381

For reflection: What relationships have I forsaken for the sake of God? What relationships might be holding me back from serving him?

30 Jesus promises that there is no one who has given up family relationships for the sake of the kingdom of God **who will not receive [back] an overabundant return in this present age.** Jesus does not specify what the **overabundant return** will be. However, he has spoken of a family gathered around him, made up of "those who hear the word of God and

act on it"; his disciples are brothers and sisters to him and to each other (8:21). In Acts, Luke will recount that "the community of believers was of one heart and mind, and no one claimed that any of his possessions was his own, but they had everything in common" (Acts 4:32; see also Acts 2:42–47). Those who leave behind their families to follow Jesus receive a loving welcome into a new family **in this present age**.

> *For reflection: What overabundant return have I received because of what I have given up for Jesus? What is my experience of life in his new family?*

Jesus also promises that those who have given up their families for the sake of the kingdom of God will receive **eternal life in the age to come**. Although this is the first time in Luke's Gospel that Jesus refers explicitly to **the age to come**, he has taught about what will happen in the next life. Men and women will rise from death to face God's judgment (10:14; 11:31–32); some will be welcomed into the eternal banquet of the kingdom of heaven, and some will be excluded (13:28–29; 16:22–26). Jesus has addressed the conditions for entering the banquet of the kingdom by speaking of what it is necessary to do to receive the kingdom of God (18:17), to be saved (13:23–24; 18:26–27), to be welcomed into eternal dwellings (16:9), to receive eternal life (10:25–28; 18:18–22). He now promises **eternal life in the age to come** to those who have given up their families to be his disciples.

> *For reflection: How firm are my hopes for eternal life in the age to come? What must I do to receive eternal life?*

The rich official is presumably still present (see 18:24) as Jesus assures his disciples that there will be an overabundant return and eternal life for those who give up their possessions and family to follow him. Did Jesus' assurance give him the resolve to divest himself of his riches in order to inherit the eternal life he sought (18:18)? Luke continues to leave it open whether he will respond, thereby holding out hope for all who find it hard to do what Jesus asks of them.

31 The rich official lacks one thing (18:22), and there may be something that the disciples lack as well, for **then he took the Twelve aside** to speak with

them privately. He reminds them, **Behold, we are going up to Jerusalem** (see 9:51–53; 13:22; 17:11). They are now approaching Jericho (18:35), seventeen miles from Jerusalem. Jesus tells his disciples that in Jerusalem **everything written by the prophets about the Son of Man will be fulfilled**. Although God addresses Ezekiel as "son of man" (Ezek 2:1, 3, 6, 8, etc.), there are no passages in the **prophets** that are explicitly **about the Son of Man** save for the book of Daniel's reference to "one like a son of man" coming on the clouds of heaven (Dan 7:13). It is best, therefore, to understand Jesus to be referring to himself as **the Son of Man**, and saying that **everything written by the prophets about** him—whether or not they used the term "Son of Man"—**will be fulfilled**. The word **fulfilled** can carry the connotation of fulfilled by God; God's purposes will be accomplished.

Jerusalem: See page 516

Son of Man: See page 147

32 Jesus tells his disciples what the prophets have foretold will happen to him in Jerusalem. **He will be handed over to the Gentiles**: here **Gentiles** means the Roman authorities. **And he will be mocked and insulted and spat upon**, to disgrace and humiliate him.

33 **And after they have scourged him they will kill him.** If Jesus is handed over to Romans who will have him **scourged** before they **kill him**, then the implication is that Jesus will be crucified. Romans crucified rebels and violent criminals, first scourging them to weaken them and increase their suffering. **But on the third day he will rise.** Death, even a horrible death, is not the final word; God's purpose for Jesus will be fulfilled in his rising.

It is difficult to know which prophecies Jesus had in mind when he said that "everything written by the prophets" will be fulfilled (verse 31) by his being mocked, scourged, and killed and by his rising on the third day. Some passages in Isaiah about a suffering servant of God find fulfillment in Jesus (see Isaiah 50:6; 52:13—53:12), but prophets provide no detailed blueprint for Jesus' dying and rising. Perhaps what Jesus intends to convey is that his suffering, dying, and rising fulfill God's purpose, a purpose expressed in the Scriptures (see also 24:25–27, 45–46).

Jesus has repeatedly alluded to his death (5:35; 12:50; 13:33; 17:25), speaking most directly about it as he was about to begin his journey to

Jerusalem (9:22, 44, 51). Now, as his journey to Jerusalem nears its conclusion, he again tells his disciples what lies ahead for him. He assured them of "an overabundant return in this present age and eternal life in the age to come" (verse 30), but they should have no illusions about the cost of eternal life: they must follow the way of Jesus. After previously speaking of his suffering and dying, he told them, "If anyone wishes to come after me, he must deny himself and take up his cross daily and follow me" (9:23; see also 14:27). By reminding them that he will die and rise in fulfillment of God's purpose, he implicitly conveys that in God's plan their own path to eternal life may require giving up more than possessions and family; it may require giving up their lives.

34 But they understood nothing of this; the word remained hidden from them and they failed to comprehend what he said. Luke emphasizes their incomprehension by stating it three times. They have no idea what Jesus is talking about, despite his having spoken previously about his dying and rising. They still do not grasp that the path into the kingdom is the way of the cross (see 9:44–45). They do not understand that this is in fulfillment of Scripture and God's will; they still lack an understanding of God's way for Jesus, and for them.

> *For reflection: How well do I grasp that the way of Jesus is the way of the cross? How well do I embrace the cross in my life?*

A Blind Beggar Is Saved by His Faith in Jesus

³⁵ Now as he approached Jericho a blind man was sitting by the roadside begging, ³⁶ and hearing a crowd going by, he inquired what was happening. ³⁷ They told him, "Jesus of Nazareth is passing by." ³⁸ He shouted, "Jesus, Son of David, have pity on me!" ³⁹ The people walking in front rebuked him, telling him to be silent, but he kept calling out all the more, "Son of David, have pity on me!" ⁴⁰ Then Jesus stopped and ordered that he be brought to him; and when he came near, Jesus asked him, ⁴¹ "What do you want me to do for you?" He replied, "Lord, please let me see." ⁴² Jesus told him, "Have sight; your faith has saved you." ⁴³ He imme-

diately received his sight and followed him, giving glory to God.
When they saw this, all the people gave praise to God.

Gospel parallels: Matt 20:29–34; Mark 10:46–52
NT: Luke 4:18–19; 7:22, 50; 8:48; 17:19

35 **Now as he approached Jericho**: Jesus is nearing the end of his journey
to Jerusalem. A popular route from Galilee to Jerusalem ran through the
Jordan River valley, avoiding Samaria and the hostility Jewish travelers
might encounter there (see 9:51–53). At **Jericho** travelers turned west
onto the road to Jerusalem (see 10:30). **A blind man was sitting by the
roadside begging.** Those who were **blind** were often reduced to **begging** to survive. **Sitting by the roadside** near an entrance to Jericho
was a choice site for begging. Since the feast of Passover was drawing
near (22:1), crowds of pilgrims on their way to Jerusalem would be passing
through Jericho, and they might be generous in giving alms—a Jewish
pious deed (Tobit 4:7–11, 16; 12:8–9; Sirach 3:29; 7:10).

Jericho: See page 496

36 **And hearing a crowd going by, he inquired what was happening.**
The **crowd** is probably made up of those traveling with Jesus (see 14:25)
as well as his disciples, for it is a large enough crowd that its noise attracts
the beggar's attention. He asked **what was happening**—why are so
many people on the road?

37 **They told him, "Jesus of Nazareth is passing by."** Jesus is identified as being from **Nazareth**, which is how he is popularly known (see
24:19). But he is not simply a man named Jesus who happens to be from
Nazareth; he is the well-known **Jesus of Nazareth**, whose reputation for
healing and expelling demons has spread throughout the land (4:14, 37;
5:17; 6:17–19; 7:17).

Nazareth: See page 19

38 **He shouted, "Jesus, Son of David, have pity on me!"** Luke's readers know that **Jesus** is a descendant of **David** through Joseph (1:27, 32,
69; 2:4) and in that sense can be called **Son of David**. But this is the
only time in Luke's Gospel that anyone calls him **Son of David**, and we

must wonder why the beggar addresses him in this way. **Son of David** is not a title for the Messiah in the Old Testament. The Old Testament does, however, refer to Solomon as the "son of David" (2 Chron 1:1; 13:6; 30:26; 35:3; Prov 1:1), and Jewish tradition at the time of Jesus ascribed to Solomon the power to exorcise demons and heal. The blind beggar had likely heard that Jesus healed the infirm and restored sight to the blind (see 7:22). Some scholars suggest that the beggar was calling upon Jesus as a latter-day Solomon with healing powers when he called out to him as **Jesus, Son of David** and implored him, **have pity on me!** The **pity** or mercy beggars normally asked for was alms (see Acts 3:1–3), but this blind man wishes for considerably more from Jesus.

39 **The people walking in front rebuked him, telling him to be silent.** It is not clear whether **the people walking in front** are Jesus' disciples or others in the crowd accompanying him. In any case, they **rebuked** the beggar, **telling him to be silent.** Jesus' disciples **rebuked** those bringing infants to him (18:15), and there seems to be a similar attempt here to shield Jesus from someone considered a bothersome nobody. **But he kept calling out all the more, "Son of David, have pity on me!"** His persistence shows that he is asking for more than alms: anyone might give

---

BACKGROUND: SON OF DAVID Broadly speaking, any descendant of David could be called a son of David (as Joseph is—Matt 1:20). The Messiah was commonly expected to be a descendant of David (Matt 22:42; Mark 12:35; Luke 20:41; John 7:42) and therefore could be called the Son of David. While the Old Testament provides ample basis for such expectation, no Old Testament passage uses the title "Son of David" as a title for the Messiah. The Messiah is, however, called the Son of David in one of the *Psalms of Solomon,* a nonbiblical writing from around 50 B.C. It is striking that during Jesus' public ministry, others call him the Son of David only in conjunction with his healings (Matt 9:27; 12:23; 15:22; 20:30–31; Mark 10:47–48; Luke 18:38–39; Matt 21:9 may not be an exception: see Matt 21:14–15). There is evidence that popular Jewish tradition looked upon Solomon, a son of David, as an exorcist and a healer, and some scholars suggest that Jesus was hailed as the Son of David during his ministry because he, too, exorcised and healed. Matthew proclaims Jesus to be the Son of David who is the Messiah (Matt 1:1, 16–17). Luke's Gospel makes it explicit that Jesus is the descendant of David through whom God's promise of an everlasting reign for the house of David will be fulfilled (2 Sam 7:12–16; Psalm 89:3–5, 29–38; Luke 1:32–33). *Related topics: Nonbiblical writings (page 342), Psalms of Solomon (page 259).*

him alms, but he wishes something specifically from the **Son of David**. He **kept calling out**, repeatedly imploring Jesus, **have pity on me!** Like the persistent widow (18:1–5), he has little to lose: what can those trying to silence him do to a man who is blind and forced into a life of begging? He has much to gain if the **Son of David** takes pity on him and heals him.

For reflection: How persistently do I implore Jesus for his healing mercy? What do I have to gain by turning to him? What do I have to lose by turning to him?

40 **Then Jesus stopped**, pausing in his journey to Jerusalem, where he will be killed and rise in fulfillment of prophecy (18:31–33). Jesus is eager for his baptism of suffering to be accomplished (12:49–50), but he takes time for a man whom no one else considers of any significance. His mission is to bring good news to the destitute and sight to the blind (4:18–19). He **ordered that he be brought to him**—led to him, since he is blind. **And when he came near, Jesus asked him,**

41 **What do you want me to do for you?** Jesus can see that he is blind and destitute and in need of many things, but he leaves it to the man to ask for what he wants. He allows a man whose freedom has been restricted by his blindness to chose freely, and to exercise however much faith he may have. **He replied, "Lord, please let me see."** The man calls Jesus **Lord,** recognizing Jesus as a man with authority. He believes that Jesus has the power to give him sight, and he asks for that: **let me see**.

Lord: See page 137

For reflection: What do I most want Jesus to do for me?

42 **Jesus told him, "Have sight."** Jesus can heal with a word (see 7:7–8), and he speaks a healing word to the man, commanding, **have sight**. He tells him, **your faith has saved you.** The beggar demonstrated **faith** by persistently calling out to Jesus despite the crowd's opposition, believing that Jesus could heal him. The word translated **saved** can mean "healed," but the man is receiving more than a physical healing from Jesus because

of his **faith**. Like those whom Jesus previously told, **your faith has saved you** (7:50; 8:48; 17:19), the man has been rescued from infirmity and evil. His life has been transformed by the one who came to establish God's reign on earth; by his **faith** in Jesus he is entering into God's reign. Who can be **saved** (18:26)? Those who have faith in Jesus.

43 **He immediately received his sight,** as Jesus commanded, **and followed him**—implied, followed him as a disciple (see 5:27–28; 9:23, 57–62; 18:28). The rich official could not bring himself to give up his wealth in order to respond to Jesus' call, "Follow me" (18:22–23), but the formerly blind beggar has no possessions to hold him back. Those who have nothing need leave nothing behind to follow Jesus. The beggar whose sight Jesus restored is an example of those whom Jesus praises in his beatitude, "Blessed are you who are poor, / for the kingdom of God is yours" (6:20). He followed Jesus, **giving glory to God**: he recognizes that God worked through Jesus to give him sight. Praising and glorifying God by recounting what he has done is the proper response to make to God (see 1:64; 2:20; 5:25–26; 7:16; 13:13; 17:15, 18). **When they saw this, all the people gave praise to God**, joining the man in glorifying God for what he is doing through Jesus.

For reflection: What are all the ways in which the blind beggar sets an example for me to imitate?

CHAPTER 19

A Just and Generous Tax Collector

¹ He came to Jericho and intended to pass through the town. ² Now a man there named Zacchaeus, who was a chief tax collector and also a wealthy man, ³ was seeking to see who Jesus was; but he could not see him because of the crowd, for he was short in stature. ⁴ So he ran ahead and climbed a sycamore tree in order to see Jesus, who was about to pass that way. ⁵ When he reached the place, Jesus looked up and said to him, "Zacchaeus, come down quickly, for today I must stay at your house." ⁶ And he came down quickly and received him with joy. ⁷ When they all saw this, they began to grumble, saying, "He has gone to stay at the house of a sinner." ⁸ But Zacchaeus stood there and said to the Lord, "Behold, half of my possessions, Lord, I shall give to the poor, and if I have extorted anything from anyone I shall repay it four times over." ⁹ And Jesus said to him, "Today salvation has come to this house because this man too is a descendant of Abraham. ¹⁰ For the Son of Man has come to seek and to save what was lost."

OT: Ezek 34:11, 16
NT: Luke 5:27–32; 7:34; 15:1–2, 4, 8; 18:22–26

1 **Jesus came to Jericho and intended to pass through the town.** Jesus is traveling to Jerusalem (9:51–53; 13:22, 33; 17:11; 18:31) by way of

---

BACKGROUND: JERICHO can lay claim to being both the lowest and the oldest city on earth. Jericho lies in the Jordan Valley, ten miles from where the Jordan River empties into the Dead Sea. The city is about 850 feet below sea level (for comparison, Death Valley in the United States is about 280 feet below sea level). Jericho was built at the site of a powerful spring that flows to this day. In ancient Jericho, archaeologists have discovered a thirty-foot-high tower and city walls dating from around 8,000 B.C.—almost seven thousand years before Joshua came along. At the time of Jesus, the tower and the wall had long been buried in a pile of rubble. Jericho lay along one of the most commonly used routes for travel between Galilee and Jerusalem. The road from Jericho to Jerusalem went by a palace that Herod the Great had built to enjoy Jericho's warm winter weather; Jerusalem, only seventeen miles away but twenty-five hundred feet above sea level, is cold and damp in the winter.

496

Jericho, following a route commonly taken by Jews going from Galilee to Jerusalem.

2 **Now a man** lived **there named Zacchaeus** (a Jewish name—see 2 Macc 10:19), **who was a chief tax collector and also a wealthy man.** Jericho lay near the eastern border of Judea on a trade route; the primary source of **tax** revenue was likely customs imposed on transported goods. As a **chief tax collector**, Zacchaeus may have been in charge of all the taxes or customs collected at Jericho. It would then be no surprise that he is **a wealthy man**: those who contracted with Roman authorities to be responsible for tax collection in a region could become wealthy. Because of his position and wealth, Zacchaeus is well known in Jericho (see verse 7).

Tax collectors: See page 94

Jesus said that "it is easier for a camel to pass through the eye of a needle than for a rich person to enter the kingdom of God" (18:25). Readers of Luke's Gospel must wonder whether wealthy Zacchaeus can be saved (18:26).

3 Zacchaeus **was seeking to see who Jesus was**: he has apparently heard about Jesus but never met him. **But he could not see him because of the crowd, for he was short in stature.** He is not tall enough to see over the **crowd** around Jesus, and they are not about to clear a way for him (see verse 7). Examination of first-century burial remains in Galilee indicate that the average adult Jewish man was five feet five inches; Zacchaeus was probably less than five feet tall.

4 **So he ran ahead and climbed a sycamore tree in order to see Jesus, who was about to pass that way.** Zacchaeus is more than idly curious about Jesus, for **in order to see Jesus** he does things that would invite ridicule for a public official. He **ran** to get ahead of the crowd: men of substance never ran; they walked with slow dignity (see Sirach 19:26). A chief tax collector sprinting past the crowd would have raised some eyebrows. He **climbed a sycamore tree**, an undignified act even less befitting a wealthy adult. The sight of Zacchaeus with his (expensive?)

cloak gathered up, climbing a tree, would have brought hoots of derision. But Zacchaeus seems oblivious to what people might think of him; he wants **to see Jesus**. He does not act like he wants to meet Jesus; climbing a tree is hardly the way to have a face-to-face encounter with someone passing by. Zacchaeus seems to be very attracted to Jesus but at the same time reluctant to approach him personally.

> *For reflection: Do I have any ambivalence about drawing too close to Jesus? What holds me back?*

5 **When he reached the place** where Zacchaeus was sitting in the tree, **Jesus looked up and said to him, "Zacchaeus, come down quickly."** Jesus knows who **Zacchaeus** is and calls him by name. Perhaps Jesus exhibits more than human knowledge (see 5:22; 6:8; 7:39–40; 11:17), or perhaps he had asked someone in the crowd, "Who is that man up in the tree?" Jesus cannot fail to notice that Zacchaeus has cast aside his dignity to catch a glimpse of him, and Jesus responds to those who disregard themselves for his sake (see 7:37–38, 44–50). He tells Zacchaeus to **come down quickly, for today I must stay at your house**. The connotation of **stay** is remain for a while. Jesus **must** accept hospitality from Zacchaeus and eat with him: it is part of his mission from God. Jesus was passing through Jericho on his way to Jerusalem, not intending to stop there (verse 1). But upon seeing Zacchaeus in the tree, he changed his plans. He is on his way to Jerusalem to suffer, die, and rise in fulfillment of God's will for him (9:22), but **today** he also has an opportunity to do God's will and he **must** take advantage of it. He tells Zacchaeus to come down **quickly** to receive him as a guest. Jesus responds to Zacchaeus' interest in him by taking the initiative to enter into Zacchaeus' life.

Hospitality: See page 314

> *For reflection: When have I disregarded myself or sacrificed my dignity in order to draw closer to Jesus? How has he responded to me?*

6 **And he came down quickly and received him with joy.** Zacchaeus complies **quickly** and with **joy**. Although he apparently was hesitant to approach Jesus, he is very happy to have an opportunity to meet him.

He **received him** into his home, just as had Martha (in 10:38; the word translated there as "welcomed" is translated here as **received**).

7   **When they all saw this, they began to grumble, saying, "He has gone to stay at the house of a sinner."** The word translated here as **to stay** literally means to unharness pack animals, and hence to lodge for the night. Zacchaeus is considered to be a **sinner**, undoubtedly because he is a tax collector. Jesus is regularly criticized for associating with "tax collectors and sinners" (5:27–30; 7:34; 15:1–2) by those who think that befriending sinners puts a stamp of approval on their conduct. When Jesus goes to the house of Zacchaeus to **stay** with him, **all** who **saw** him do so **began to grumble**. We can best take **all** to refer to the crowd (verse 3); his disciples, who included at least one former tax collector (5:27–28), were probably not upset by Jesus' conduct, especially after having heard him explain why he welcomes sinners (5:31–32; 15:2–32). Zacchaeus' undignified actions (verse 4) probably caused the crowd to murmur, but Jesus' associating with him leads them to **grumble**.

8   **But Zacchaeus stood there and said to the Lord:** Zacchaeus reacts to the grumbling. He tells Jesus, **Behold, half of my possessions, Lord, I shall give to the poor.** He respectfully addresses Jesus as **Lord**, acknowledging his authority. Giving **half** of one's **possessions** to the **poor** as alms is extremely generous. It is to love one's neighbor as one loves oneself (10:27) by giving to those in need as much as one keeps for oneself. Zacchaeus continues, **and if I have extorted anything from anyone I shall repay it four times over.** The tax system lent itself to extortion (see 3:12–14); as a chief tax collector, Zacchaeus probably received his cut of whatever his subordinates extorted. The law of Moses required restitution of ill-gotten goods plus one-fifth their value (Lev 5:21–24; Num 5:7), save for stolen livestock, where two- or four- or fivefold restitution was required (Exod 21:37; 22:3, 8). By repaying **four times over** whatever he gained from extortion, Zacchaeus applies the more exacting standard for restitution to himself. John the Baptist demanded, "Produce good fruits as evidence of your repentance" (3:8); Zacchaeus' giving half of his considerable wealth to the poor and his

making fourfold restitution is evidence of a life transformed by Jesus' visit to his house.

Lord: See page 137
Alms: See page 332

There is, however, another way to understand Zacchaeus' words. Although the New American Bible translates his statements in the future tense (**I shall give . . . I shall repay**), in the Greek of Luke's Gospel they are in the present tense and can be interpreted as Zacchaeus' telling Jesus what he is already doing: "I give half my possessions to the poor; I repay four times over whatever I receive from extortion." Scholars are divided over whether Zacchaeus speaks of what he will do or of what he is already doing; both interpretations are grammatically possible. If Zacchaeus responds to the grumbling by telling Jesus what he already does, then his response has the sense, "Even though I am a tax collector, I am not the sinner others suppose; I am generous in helping the poor, and I am more than fair in my dealings." Jesus does not need to feel embarrassed to stay in his house.

For reflection: How well do I measure up to the standard set by Zacchaeus for generosity? For restitution?

9 **And Jesus said to him, "Today salvation has come to this house."** The word **salvation** broadly means any rescue from danger and distress or from death (see 1:69, 71) but can have the more specific meaning of deliverance by God from eternal death. When Simeon saw the infant Jesus, he exclaimed to God, "My eyes have seen your salvation" (2:30): Jesus is God's agent on a rescue mission. Jesus tells Zacchaeus, **Today salvation has come to this house**: Jesus, God's agent of **salvation**, has come into Zacchaeus' **house**. Whether Jesus' visit resulted in Zacchaeus becoming generous and just, or whether Zacchaeus was already generous and just, Jesus is assuring him that he is on the path to **salvation**. Jesus' next words seem to be addressed to the grumbling crowd as a vindication of Zacchaeus: **because this man too is a descendant of Abraham**, a member of God's people. Jesus defends Zacchaeus as a generous and fair man, who has as much right to the **salvation** that God offers through Jesus as any other **descendant of Abraham**.

10 **For the Son of Man has come to seek and to save what was lost.**
Jesus echoes a prophecy of Ezekiel, in which God promises to tend his
sheep: "The lost I will seek out, the strayed I will bring back, the injured
I will bind up, the sick I will heal" (Ezek 34:16). Like the shepherd searching for his lost sheep and the woman searching for her lost coin (15:4,
8), Jesus is on a mission **to seek** the **lost**. He has **come** to **save** them,
to bring them salvation (verse 9). If Jesus' visit resulted in a change in
Zacchaeus' behavior, then Jesus has sought out and saved a person who
had been lost. If Zacchaeus was already generous and fair but despised
as a sinner, then Jesus' public vindication of Zacchaeus has saved him
from exclusion from God's people. Who can be saved (18:26)? Those who
receive Jesus with joy (verse 6) and embrace his message with wholehearted generosity.

Son of Man: See page 147

*For reflection: How did Jesus seek me out and find me? What has he saved
me from?*

Jesus clearly approves of Zacchaeus's giving half his possessions
to the poor and making fourfold restitution. Yet Jesus demanded that
another rich official give all that he possessed to the poor (18:22). Jesus
does not set an absolute standard of giving for everyone, but he demands
that all his followers put him ahead of their possessions and that all be
generous in helping those in need. Some leave everything to follow him
(5:11, 28; 18:28). Yet Jesus was happy to have Mary Magdalene, Joanna,
and Susanna provide for him out of their resources (8:2–3), apparently
not asking them to completely divest themselves of their resources. He
accepted hospitality in the home of Martha and Mary (10:38–42) and
apparently did not demand that they sell their home to follow him. Each
disciple must hear the specific call of Jesus, and respond to it.

*For reflection: What is Jesus asking me to do with my money and
possessions?*

Doing One's Duty until the Kingdom Comes

¹¹ While they were listening to him speak, he proceeded to tell a parable because he was near Jerusalem and they thought that the kingdom of God would appear there immediately. ¹² So he said, "A nobleman went off to a distant country to obtain the kingship for himself and then to return. ¹³ He called ten of his servants and gave them ten gold coins and told them, 'Engage in trade with these until I return.' ¹⁴ His fellow citizens, however, despised him and sent a delegation after him to announce, 'We do not want this man to be our king.' ¹⁵ But when he returned after obtaining the kingship, he had the servants called, to whom he had given the money, to learn what they had gained by trading. ¹⁶ The first came forward and said, 'Sir, your gold coin has earned ten additional ones.' ¹⁷ He replied, 'Well done, good servant! You have been faithful in this very small matter; take charge of ten cities.' ¹⁸ Then the second came and reported, 'Your gold coin, sir, has earned five more.' ¹⁹ And to this servant too he said, 'You, take charge of five cities.' ²⁰ Then the other servant came and said, 'Sir, here is your gold coin; I kept it stored away in a handkerchief, ²¹ for I was afraid of you, because you are a demanding person; you take up what you did not lay down and you harvest what you did not plant.' ²² He said to him, 'With your own words I shall condemn you, you wicked servant. You knew I was a demanding person, taking up what I did not lay down and harvesting what I did not plant; ²³ why did you not put my money in a bank? Then on my return I would have collected it with interest.' ²⁴ And to those standing by he said, 'Take the gold coin from him and give it to the servant who has ten.' ²⁵ But they said to him, 'Sir, he has ten gold coins.' ²⁶ 'I tell you, to everyone who has, more will be given, but from the one who has not, even what he has will be taken away. ²⁷ Now as for those enemies of mine who did not want me as their king, bring them here and slay them before me.' "

Gospel parallels: Matt 25:14–30
NT: Luke 8:18; 12:35–48; 16:10; 19:1–10

11 **While they were listening to him speak**: Jesus is in Jericho, speaking to Zacchaeus in the presence of a crowd (19:1–10). While everyone was listening **he proceeded to tell a parable because he was near Jerusalem and they thought that the kingdom of God would appear there immediately**. Jesus is **near Jerusalem**, which is seventeen miles from Jericho; his journey is nearing its end. Jesus has proclaimed the good news of the **kingdom of God** and sent his disciples to announce it (4:43; 8:1; 9:2, 11, 60; 10:9, 11; 16:16); he has spoken of God's kingdom as a present reality, inaugurated by his ministry (11:20; 17:21). Some in the crowd, perhaps including some of his disciples, **thought that the kingdom of God would appear** in its fullness **immediately** and that it would be established in **Jerusalem**, the capital established by David. Their expectations for the **kingdom** likely included the overthrow of Roman rule; Jesus' disciples will ask him after his resurrection, "Lord, are you at this time going to restore the kingdom to Israel?" (Acts 1:6). Jesus addresses expectations that the kingdom of God will be established **immediately** by telling a **parable**. It is a complex parable that makes several points.

Parables: See page 217

Jerusalem: See page 516

Kingdom of God: See page 381

Jewish expectations at the time of Jesus: See page 69

12 **So he said, "A nobleman went off to a distant country to obtain the kingship for himself and then to return."** A **nobleman** is someone who is part of the ruling class. Jesus' audience would have immediately thought of several Jewish rulers who **went off** to Rome to obtain the title of king for themselves. Rome had ruled Palestine since 63 B.C. and appointed kings who governed under its authority. Herod the Great traveled to Rome and was given the title of king in 40 B.C. In his will, he divided his kingdom among three of his sons, but they needed Roman approval to assume office after he died. In Jesus' parable, the nobleman's journey to and from a **distant** country, along with the lobbying it will take for him to be made a king, will take some time.

13 Before the nobleman left, **he called ten of his servants and gave them ten gold coins**. The word translated **servants** here and throughout the parable literally means "slaves." The **gold coins** in question were each

worth about one hundred days' wages for an ordinary laborer. The parable goes on to make it clear that the slaves received one coin each. This was not a trivial amount, but neither was it a fortune. The nobleman **told them, "Engage in trade with these until I return."** He entrusts money to ten of his slaves so that they can conduct business while he is gone; his intent is that they earn him a profit. Slaves sometimes served as stewards or financial managers for their masters.

Servant, slave: See page 454

If Jesus' disciples are perceptive, they might suspect that Jesus' parable will be similar to some of his previous parables. Jesus spoke of slaves being vigilant for their master's return from a wedding feast (12:35–38) to convey the message, "You also must be prepared, for at an hour you do not expect, the Son of Man will come" (12:40). Jesus spoke of a steward given duties to perform in his master's absence and the master on his return rewarding or punishing the steward according to how well he carried out his duties (12:42–48). Now Jesus is addressing expectations that the kingdom of God will come immediately (verse 11) by telling a parable about a nobleman traveling abroad and giving his slaves financial responsibilities in his absence. Jesus is indicating that the kingdom will not come immediately, and that his disciples will have duties to carry out while they await his coming to establish God's reign in its fullness.

For reflection: What responsibilities and duties has Jesus given me?

14 **His fellow citizens, however, despised him and sent a delegation after him to announce, "We do not want this man to be our king."** Those listening to Jesus' parable would have thought of Archelaus, a son of Herod the Great to whom Herod bequeathed half of his kingdom. After Herod died in 4 B.C., Archelaus went to Rome to be confirmed as king. A delegation of fifty Jews and Samaritans followed him and pleaded with Emperor Augustus not to make Archelaus king over them. Augustus compromised by confirming him as a ruler but denying him the title of king until he proved himself worthy of it. Archelaus ruled so incompe-

tently and aroused so many protests that Rome removed him in A.D. 6 and appointed a Roman governor to rule his territory.

15 **But when he returned after obtaining the kingship**: in Jesus' parable, the nobleman receives the kingdom or rule he was seeking. He **returned** from the distant country and **had the servants called, to whom he had given the money, to learn what they had gained by trading**. He wishes an accounting of how well they used the money entrusted to them.

16 **The first came forward and said, "Sir, your gold coin has earned ten additional ones."** The first slave to report was amazingly successful in his business dealings and had **earned** a tenfold profit for his master the king. Such extraordinary returns are not achieved overnight; his master must have been away for some time.

17 **He replied, "Well done, good servant!"** He commends him and praises his success. He tells him, **You have been faithful in this very small matter**. One hundred days' wages are a **very small matter** for someone who has just obtained kingship, but the slave has proven himself to be **faithful**—reliable—by his successful business dealings with what was entrusted to him. In light of that, his master tells him to **take charge of ten cities**. The king shares his rule with his slave, giving him authority over ten cities in his realm, presumably to manage them and collect taxes and receive a share of the proceeds. Being given charge of **ten cities** is an extremely generous reward compared with the value of the ten coins the slave had earned for his master, a reward out of all proportion to what the slave had accomplished. Jesus earlier taught that "the person who is trustworthy in very small matters is also trustworthy in great ones" (16:10), and the same logic is at work in this parable.

18 **Then the second came and reported, "Your gold coin, sir, has earned five more."** His business dealings have also been very successful, even though not as successful as those of the first slave.

19 **And to this servant too he said, "You, take charge of five cities."** His master does not praise him as he did the slave who earned a tenfold return, but he nonetheless rewards his success by putting him in charge of five cities—still a very generous reward compared with what the slave had accomplished for him.

> *For reflection: What kind of return have I given Jesus for the gifts and responsibilities he has entrusted to me? How has he rewarded me?*

20 While ten slaves were entrusted with money (verse 13), Jesus' parable only follows up on three of them. After two have given their reports, **then the other servant came and said, "Sir, here is your gold coin; I kept it stored away in a handkerchief."** The word translated **handkerchief** is literally "sweat cloth," used for wiping perspiration from the neck and face. Although the slave was told to engage in business with the gold coin (verse 13), he did not do so. Instead he kept the coin wrapped up in a rag to hide it and keep it safe.

21 He explains to his master why he hid the coin instead of trading with it: **for I was afraid of you, because you are a demanding person.** He views his master as a **demanding person,** someone who is harsh and exacting, and he is **afraid** of him. He tells him, **you take up what you did not lay down,** a proverbial expression that can cover various kinds of misappropriation. He tells him, **you harvest what you did not plant**: you reap what is not yours, what others have sown. It is unclear how accurate is the slave's assessment of his master; the master has just rewarded two of his slaves quite lavishly for successfully carrying out their duties. What is clear is that the third slave views his master as stern, grasping, and unscrupulous, and is **afraid** of him. Immobilized by fear, he did nothing with the money entrusted to him.

> *For reflection: How do I view God: as stern and demanding, or as generous in his rewards?*

22 **He said to him, "With your own words I shall condemn you, you wicked servant."** He calls the slave **wicked** because he was disobedient and did not engage in business as he was ordered to do. He will judge

and **condemn** the slave with his **own words**, on the basis of what the slave said about him. He tells him, **You knew**—or thought you knew—**I was a demanding person, taking up what I did not lay down and harvesting what I did not plant**. The slave thought that his master demanded a profit from his dealings, making it any way that he could.

23 The master tells the slave, if that is how you view me, if you know that I demand a profit, then **why did you not put my money in a bank?** The words translated **in a bank** are literally, "on a table," referring to a moneylender's table; moneylenders served as the banks of the time. (Money lenders were likely Gentiles, for the law of Moses did not allow Jews to charge interest on loans to other Jews—Exod 22:24; Lev 25:36–37; Deut 23:20–21.) **Then on my return I would have collected it with interest.** A moneylender would have paid **interest**, and while the master would not have received the five- or tenfold return that the other slaves had earned him, he would have gotten some return nonetheless. The third slave did not make even a minimal effort to put the money entrusted to him to any fruitful use.

24 **And to those standing by he said, "Take the gold coin from him and give it to the servant who has ten."** Those who are **standing by** are presumably the king's attendants. If the first slave still **has ten** coins, then it would appear that the king is letting him retain them, perhaps so that he can use them to do future business on the king's behalf. The king has the unproductive slave's coin transferred to the slave who earned the tenfold return. While the first two slaves were lavishly rewarded, the master says nothing about punishing the unproductive slave; he simply relieves him of what he had entrusted to him. This might be evidence that he is not as stern as the third slave views him.

25 **But they said to him, "Sir, he has ten gold coins."** The attendants' observation is a little puzzling. The first slave not only has **ten gold coins** but he is now in charge of ten cities (verse 17), a position that should earn him far more than the ten coins are worth. Perhaps the point of the attendants' remark should simply be taken to be, why bother to give another coin to someone who already has so much?

26 The king responds by telling his attendants, **I tell you, to everyone who has, more will be given, but from the one who has not, even what he has will be taken away**. The general sense of his words is, the rich get richer and the poor get poorer. The king does not give a specific justification for why he gives his favored slave the coin (kings do not need to justify their actions to underlings) but simply invokes a proverb about the fortunes of the haves and the have-nots. He says in effect, what I have done is nothing out of the ordinary. A wealthy person gets wealthier; a poor person loses even the little she or he has.

These words could also be understood as spoken by Jesus, as an aside that interrupts the parable, for he said something very similar on another occasion (8:18). Jesus would then be applying the parable to his disciples as a promise and as a warning. He promises that if they make good use of what they have been given—such as knowledge of the mysteries of the kingdom of God (8:10; 10:21), the charge to proclaim the kingdom of God to others (9:2; 10:9), and power to cast out demons and heal the sick (9:1; 10:9, 17)—then they will be given even greater gifts and responsibilities. But if they do not make use of what they have been entrusted with, if they hide away the good news of the kingdom of God in a sweat cloth, as it were, then it will be taken from them and turned over to more reliable servants.

For reflection: What promise do I find in these words? What warning do I find in them?

27 The king continues, **Now as for those enemies of mine who did not want me as their king, bring them here and slay them before me**. The newly appointed **king** acts decisively toward his **enemies** (verse 14), executing them as traitors or rebels. His act seems brutish to us, but in the ancient world, those on the losing side of wars and power struggles were usually treated brutally (see 1 Sam 15:32–33). There was unrest in Jerusalem after Herod died; Archelaus dispatched soldiers to restore order, and they killed three thousand Jews gathered in the Temple at Passover time. While Archelaus was in Rome, more disturbances broke out, and Roman soldiers crucified two thousand rebels. Those who did

not want Archelaus to be their king were permanently excluded from his kingdom!

The king in Jesus' parable (much less Archelaus!) should not be taken simply and completely as an image for Jesus. Jesus employs unsavory characters in his parables, for example, the dishonest steward (16:1–8) and the dishonest judge (18:1–8), without endorsing all that they are or do. Nevertheless, the conclusion of the parable does convey a sobering warning: those who do not want Jesus to reign over them will not be part of the reign he will establish.

The kingdom of God (verse 11) will not be established when Jesus reaches Jerusalem. Rather, Jesus is on his way to the "exodus that he was going to accomplish in Jerusalem" (9:31), his "being taken up" (9:51) to God through suffering and death. He will not return immediately to establish God's reign in its fullness. When he does come, he will reward his servants according to how well they carried out the duties he assigned them. Those who are faithful and reliable in carrying out what has been entrusted to them will be rewarded extremely generously: the eternal banquet of the kingdom (13:29) is a recompense out of all proportion to what anyone may accomplish in this life. Those who reject Jesus and God's reign will be excluded from it.

For reflection: What is the single most important lesson of Jesus' parable for me?

ORIENTATION: *After addressing expectations that God's kingdom would come upon his arrival in Jerusalem (19:11–27), Jesus acts out a prophecy to dispel any notions that he will establish God's kingdom by force.*

Jesus' Royal Ride

²⁸ After he had said this, he proceeded on his journey up to Jerusalem. ²⁹ As he drew near to Bethphage and Bethany at the place called the Mount of Olives, he sent two of his disciples. ³⁰ He said, "Go into the village opposite you, and as you enter it you will find a colt tethered on which no one has ever sat. Untie it and bring it here. ³¹ And if anyone should ask you, 'Why are

you untying it?' you will answer, 'The Master has need of it.'"
³² So those who had been sent went off and found everything just as
he had told them. ³³ And as they were untying the colt, its owners
said to them, "Why are you untying this colt?" ³⁴ They answered,
"The Master has need of it." ³⁵ So they brought it to Jesus, threw
their cloaks over the colt, and helped Jesus to mount. ³⁶ As he rode
along, the people were spreading their cloaks on the road; ³⁷ and
now as he was approaching the slope of the Mount of Olives, the
whole multitude of his disciples began to praise God aloud with joy
for all the mighty deeds they had seen. ³⁸ They proclaimed:
"Blessed is the king who comes / in the name of the Lord.
Peace in heaven
    and glory in the highest."
³⁹ Some of the Pharisees in the crowd said to him, "Teacher,
rebuke your disciples." ⁴⁰ He said in reply, "I tell you, if they keep
silent, the stones will cry out!"

Gospel parallels: Matt 21:1–11; Mark 11:1–10; John 12:12–16
OT: Psalm 118:26; Zech 9:9–10
NT: Luke 2:13–14; 19:11–27

28 **After he had said this**, after he had told a parable "because he was near
Jerusalem and they thought that the kingdom of God would appear there
immediately" (19:11), **he proceeded on his journey up to Jerusalem.**
The word **proceeded** has the connotation of going in front; Jesus went
ahead of his disciples, leading them. They have been in Jericho (19:1)
and are now traveling **up to Jerusalem**, a 3,500-foot ascent through

---

BACKGROUND: BETHANY was a village on a southeastern slope of the Mount of
Olives, about two miles from Jerusalem (John 11:18). During major feasts Jerusalem
was crowded with pilgrims and accommodations were scarce; hence Jesus spent his
nights in Bethany when he came to Jerusalem for Passover (Matt 21:17; Mark 11:11–12;
see Luke 21:37). The Gospels do not make it clear whether Jesus stayed with friends
in Bethany or simply camped out. The Gospel of John presents Mary, Martha, and
Lazarus as residents of Bethany (John 11:1). Luke seems to situate Mary and Martha
in a village near Galilee (Luke 10:38–42); Matthew and Mark do not mention the two
sisters or Lazarus. Matthew and Mark describe Jesus eating at the home of Simon the
leper in Bethany (Matt 26:6–13; Mark 14:3–9); John describes a similar meal in Bethany
with Martha, Mary, and Lazarus (John 12:1–8).

the Judean wilderness. Jesus is on the last leg of his journey to Jerusalem (9:51–53; 13:22, 33; 17:11; 18:31), where he will be "taken up" to God (9:51) through suffering, dying, and being raised (9:22).

Jerusalem: See page 516

29 As he drew near to Bethphage and Bethany at the place called the Mount of Olives: the **Mount of Olives** is a ridge of hills immediately east of Jerusalem, separated from the city by the Kidron Valley. **Bethphage** and **Bethany** were villages on the Mount of Olives. **Bethany** was about two miles east of Jerusalem and is today the site of the Palestinian village of al-Azariyeh; the exact location of **Bethphage** is unknown. As Jesus **drew near** these villages, **he sent two of his disciples** ahead of him with a mission.

Disciple: See page 149

30 He said, "Go into the village opposite you": Luke's Gospel does not clarify whether the **village opposite** the disciples is Bethany or Bethphage. Jesus tells his disciples that **as you enter it you will find a colt**—a young donkey—**tethered on which no one has ever sat**. There is no indication in Luke's Gospel that Jesus has made any advance arrangements for the colt; rather, Jesus seems to have more than human knowledge of what his disciples will find in the village, including that **no one has ever sat** on the **colt** that they will find **tethered** there. Other than demonstrating Jesus' knowledge of the colt, the fact that it has never been ridden does not play any role in what happens, nor is there any obvious Old Testament significance in a donkey that has never been ridden. Jesus tells his two disciples, **Untie it and bring it here**.

31 And if anyone should ask you, "Why are you untying it?" you will answer, "The Master has need of it." The word translated as **Master** can also be translated as "Lord." Jesus refers to himself as **Master** or Lord and uses his **need** for the colt as the justification to be given for his disciples' borrowing it.

Lord: See page 137

511

32 **So those who had been sent went off and found everything just as he had told them.** The Greek verb for **had been sent** is related to the noun that gives us the word "apostle" (6:13); apostles are those who are sent by Jesus on a mission—here the mundane mission of bringing a donkey to Jesus. His foreknowledge of what the two disciples would find in the village proves correct; **everything** is **just as he had told them.**

For reflection: What has Jesus sent me to do? How have things worked out when I have accepted his word and followed his instructions?

33 **And as they were untying the colt, its owners said to them, "Why are you untying this colt?"** The fact that the **owners** of the colt question Jesus' disciples makes it unlikely that Jesus had made advance arrangements with them to borrow their colt. Their question, however, is one more indication that Jesus had foreseen what would happen, for he prepared his disciples to answer the owners' question (verse 31).

34 **They answered** as Jesus instructed them to answer, **"The Master has need of it."** This satisfies the owners of the colt, and they allow the disciples to take it. Perhaps they had heard of Jesus and knew that he was the **Master** or Lord on whose behalf the disciples were borrowing the colt.

35 **So they brought it to Jesus** and **threw their cloaks**, their outer garments, **over the colt** as a makeshift saddle **and helped Jesus to mount.** He will ride a colt on the final mile or two of his journey to Jerusalem.

Clothing: See page 175

At this point we must ponder why Jesus made such rather elaborate arrangements to ride rather than walk into Jerusalem. This is the only time in Luke's Gospel that he rides a beast; his entire ministry—which has involved constant travel—has been carried out on foot. His motive is thus hardly one of practicality or convenience. Furthermore, pilgrims normally walked rather than rode into Jerusalem to celebrate feasts. He is violating rather than conforming to usual practice. It would appear then that Jesus sees some symbolic significance in his riding a colt into Jerusalem.

The best candidate for helping us understand the significance of Jesus' act is a prophecy of Zechariah in which a king enters Jerusalem on a colt as a sign that he comes to bring peace (Zech 9:9–10). Kings did ride mules or donkeys (1 Kings 1:32–44), but not into war; in wars, kings rode on horses or in chariots (1 Kings 22:34–35). Zechariah prophesied that a king would come to Jerusalem, humbly riding a colt, to establish a dominion of peace. Jesus has just addressed expectations that he would establish the kingdom of God upon his arrival in Jerusalem (19:11–27); these expectations usually included overthrow of Roman rule (see Acts 1:6). By acting out Zechariah's prophecy, Jesus wants to convey that although he is entering Jerusalem as a king (verse 38), he is not going to establish God's reign by force of arms.

> Rejoice heartily, O daughter Zion,
>> shout for joy, O daughter Jerusalem!
> See, your king shall come to you;
>> a just savior is he,
> Meek, and riding on an ass,
>> on a colt, the foal of an ass.
> He shall banish the chariot from Ephraim,
>> and the horse from Jerusalem;
> The warrior's bow shall be banished,
>> and he shall proclaim peace to the nations.
>
> Zech 9:9–10

36 As he rode along, the people were spreading their cloaks on the road. The extent to which those traveling with Jesus understood the full significance of his riding a colt is unclear. They do, however, view Jesus as a kingly figure (see verse 38) and give him a royal welcome. We might think that **spreading their cloaks on the road** is akin to giving him a red-carpet treatment, but there is a deeper meaning to what they did. Their act signifies personal submission to Jesus as king, with **cloaks**, or clothing, representing those who wear them. When Jehu was made king of Israel around 840 B.C., "At once each took his garment, spread it under Jehu on the bare steps, blew the trumpet, and cried out, 'Jehu is king!'" (2 Kings 9:13). Spreading their **cloaks** on the road for Jesus to ride upon

513

seems to have a similar significance: they are symbolically accepting Jesus as their king.

For reflection: How do I express or symbolize my submission to Jesus?

37 **and now as he was approaching the slope of the Mount of Olives**: the word translated **slope** means descent. When coming from Jericho, travelers climb up the eastern side of the **Mount of Olives**, reach its summit, and then begin the descent to Jerusalem. It is at this point that travelers catch their first sight of Jerusalem and especially of the Temple, which lay at the foot of the Mount of Olives across the Kidron Valley. The sight inevitably brings a surge of joy to pilgrims, weary from a journey on foot that has as its final leg an uphill climb through the arid and dangerous (10:30) Judean wilderness. As they caught sight of Jerusalem, **the whole multitude of his disciples began to praise God aloud**. Jesus is accompanied by **the whole multitude of his disciples** (see 6:17). They **began to praise God aloud**—loudly—**with joy for all the mighty deeds they had seen**. Those who have followed Jesus have been with him on many occasions when he performed **mighty deeds**, healing the sick, expelling demons, raising the dead (see 4:40–41; 6:17–19; 7:21–22). They **praise God** for what he has accomplished through Jesus. They are filled with **joy**, treating Jesus' arrival within sight of Jerusalem as a culminating moment in his mission. It is, but not in the way in which they understand it (see 18:31–34). They are in a triumphant mood, but Jesus must endure suffering and death in order to enter into his glory (24:26).

38 Their shouts reveal their perception of Jesus' arrival in Jerusalem. **They proclaimed: / "Blessed is the king who comes / in the name of the Lord."** The disciples adapt words from Psalm 118, a psalm traditionally used to welcome the king into the Temple and to greet pilgrims entering Jerusalem. Verse 26 of this psalm contains a beatitude and a blessing. It proclaims the blessedness or good fortune of those who come to the Temple on pilgrimage on account of God: "Blessed is he / who comes in the name of the LORD." This is followed by a blessing pronounced upon the pilgrims by priests in the Temple: "We bless you from the LORD's house." The disciples apply the first part of the verse to Jesus, but modify it so that it proclaims his blessedness as **the king** who comes in

the name of the Lord. **Comes in the name of the Lord** has the sense, comes on behalf of God. The disciples perceive Jesus as a **king** who is empowered by God to establish his reign. They were probably among those who expected God's kingdom to be established when Jesus reached Jerusalem (19:11), and they apparently associated Jesus' riding of a colt with Zechariah's prophecy about a king coming to Jerusalem on a colt (Zech 9:9). Now, catching sight of Jerusalem they loudly praise God for what he is doing through Jesus (verse 37) and proclaim the blessedness of Jesus as **the king who comes in the name of the Lord**.

Beatitudes: See page 169

> Blessed is he
> who comes in the name of the LORD.
> We bless you from the LORD's house.
>
> Psalm 118:26

The disciples add words not found in Psalm 118: **Peace in heaven and glory in the highest**. The words **in the highest** mean in the highest heaven. The sense of the disciples' exclamation seems to be, God reigns in peace and glory in heaven. Perhaps there is the implication that his reign of peace and glory will be established on earth by Jesus the king who comes in God's name. This exclamation of a "multitude of his disciples" (verse 37) is similar to that of the "multitude of the heavenly host" who proclaimed at Jesus' birth, "Glory to God in the highest / and on earth peace to those on whom his favor rests" (2:13–14).

39 **Some of the Pharisees in the crowd said to him, "Teacher, rebuke your disciples."** They address Jesus not as a king but as a **teacher**, which is how Pharisees and scholars of the law have addressed him in the past (7:40; 10:25; 11:45). **Some of the Pharisees** want him to **rebuke** his disciples and prevent them from hailing him as a king. The motive of these particular Pharisees for asking Jesus to silence his disciples is unclear. They may be among those who are critical of Jesus (5:21, 30; 6:2, 7; 11:53) and who reject the idea that he is God's agent (11:15–16), much less a king who comes on behalf of God. Or they may be among those Pharisees who are concerned for Jesus' safety (13:31). It was very dangerous for anyone whom Rome had not appointed to be hailed as a king,

especially in Jerusalem at Passover time (22:1). Rome did not take rivals to its rule lightly; extra troops were moved to Jerusalem at Passover to put down any unrest and rebellion. As it will turn out, the charge posted on the cross as the reason for executing Jesus will read, "This is the King of the Jews" (23:38). Some Pharisees may fear that Jesus is putting his life at risk by allowing his disciples to hail him as a king.

Pharisees: See page 143

40 **He said in reply, "I tell you, if they keep silent, the stones will cry out!"** Jesus is indeed the coming one foretold by John the Baptist (3:16; 7:18–20), he who comes in the name of the Lord to establish his reign. He will not do it in the manner his disciples may be expecting, and he may not be the kind of king they have in mind when they hail him as king. Nevertheless, he is approaching the culmination of his mission, an event so significant in God's plan that not only his disciples but even inanimate **stones** should **cry out** in acknowledgment of what is happening. If God can raise up children to Abraham from stones (3:8), God can raise up cries of praise from stones. However, Jesus is not speaking so much about what stones can do as about what his disciples should do: they must praise God for what he is accomplishing through Jesus.

BACKGROUND: JERUSALEM lies on rocky hills about twenty-five hundred feet above sea level; hence the Bible speaks of "going up" to Jerusalem and "going down" from Jerusalem. In Old Testament times, Jerusalem's importance was political and religious rather than geographic or economic. It did not lie on any trade routes, nor is the region a lush agricultural area: the eastern outskirts of Jerusalem border on the Judean wilderness. However, David had chosen Jerusalem to be his capital, and Solomon had built the first Israelite Temple in Jerusalem. Jerusalem remained the religious center of the Jews even after Israelite political independence was lost. Jerusalem's population at the time of Jesus is estimated to have been around forty thousand. Well over one hundred thousand more people would crowd into the city during pilgrimage feasts (Passover, Weeks, Booths). The Temple was the mainstay of Jerusalem's economy, by one estimate accounting for 20 percent of the city's income. The massive revamping of the Temple complex that Herod the Great began in 20 B.C. continued almost until the time of the Jewish revolt in A.D. 66—a major public-works project. Offerings brought to the Temple and the sale of animals for sacrifice brought income to Jerusalem and to those who controlled the Temple. Jerusalem was a company town, and that company was the Temple. *Related topic: Temple (page 519).*

For reflection: Have I kept too silent about what God has accomplished through Jesus? How often in the course of a day do I praise him?

Jesus Mourns for Jerusalem

⁴¹ As he drew near, he saw the city and wept over it, ⁴² saying, "If this day you only knew what makes for peace—but now it is hidden from your eyes. ⁴³ For the days are coming upon you when your enemies will raise a palisade against you; they will encircle you and hem you in on all sides. ⁴⁴ They will smash you to the ground and your children within you, and they will not leave one stone upon another within you because you did not recognize the time of your visitation."

OT: Isaiah 29:3; Jer 6:6; Ezek 4:2
NT: Luke 12:54–56; 13:34–35; 19:35–38; 23:27–31

41 Jesus is riding a colt down the Mount of Olives into Jerusalem (19:35–37). Those accompanying him are filled with exuberance as they catch sight of the city (19:37–38), but Jesus reacts very differently: **As he drew near, he saw the city and wept over it.** As Jesus rode down the western side of the Mount of Olives, he had a panoramic view of Jerusalem lying below. Most prominent would have been the Temple and its surrounding courtyards and colonnades—magnificent structures on Jerusalem's eastern side. Jesus **wept over** what he **saw** (one of the two times in the Gospels that Jesus weeps, his weeping at the tomb of Lazarus being the other—John 11:35). Some pilgrims may have wept for joy when they caught sight of Jerusalem, but Jesus' tears are of profound sorrow. He not only **saw** Jerusalem as it was but foresaw the ruins it would become (verse 44). Just as Jeremiah wept over the fate he foresaw for Jerusalem (Jer 8:18–21; 14:17), so too does Jesus. He is well aware that he will suffer and be put to death in Jerusalem (18:31–33), but he weeps not for himself but for the people of Jerusalem (see also 23:27–31).

For reflection: What does Jesus' weeping not for himself but for others tell me about him?

42 Jesus wept over Jerusalem, **saying, "If this day you only knew what makes for peace."** The biblical concept of **peace** is broader than an absence of strife and includes notions of harmony, well-being, wholeness. God sent Jesus to bring the peace of heaven (19:38) to earth (2:14), to "guide our feet into the path of peace" (1:79). Jesus told those he healed and made whole, "go in peace" (7:50; 8:48). His exclamation to Jerusalem implies that it faces dire consequences because it does not know **what makes for peace**—it does not realize what it should do for its well-being. It does not know it **this day**, the day of his arrival in Jerusalem. **But now it is hidden from your eyes**: the people of Jerusalem, in particular its leaders (9:22; 19:47; 20:1–2, 19; 22:2, 52, 66; 23:10; 24:20), do not perceive the significance of Jesus and are missing the opportunity he presents for receiving God's peace and avoiding disaster. This tragedy moves Jesus to tears.

43 Jesus prophesies to Jerusalem, **For the days are coming upon you when your enemies will raise a palisade against you; they will encircle you and hem you in on all sides**. Jesus describes what sometimes happens when armies lay siege to a city: they **encircle** it **on all sides**, erecting a **palisade** or wall to prevent food from being brought into the city and to cut off all avenues of escape. Then the besieging army can wait until famine sets in (2 Kings 6:24–29), weakening its defenders, before storming the walls. That was how Jerusalem was besieged and conquered by the Babylonians (2 Kings 25:1–4), and it will be how Rome will capture Jerusalem in A.D. 70 (the first-century Jewish historian Josephus will describe in graphic detail the starvation caused by the Roman siege). While Jesus' words echo prophecies of past sieges of Jerusalem (Isaiah 29:3; Jer 6:6; Ezek 4:2), they also foretell what Rome will do in putting down the Jewish revolt of A.D. 66–70.

44 Conquering armies often destroyed cities after capturing them, in order to preclude a later revolt (see 2 Kings 25:9–10). Jesus prophesies that this will be the fate of Jerusalem, declaring that **they will smash you to the ground and your children**—your inhabitants—**within you, and they will not leave one stone upon another within you**. The imagery Jesus uses—smash to the ground, not leave one stone on another—could be used to portray the utter destruction of any city. Jesus is not neces-

sarily providing a detailed description of what Roman troops will do to Jerusalem, but he knows that the city will be destroyed. In A.D. 70 the Temple was destroyed, the walls of Jerusalem were torn down, and buildings and houses were burned or leveled.

Jesus tells Jerusalem it will be destroyed **because you did not rec-ognize the time of your visitation**. Jesus earlier asked a crowd, "Why do you not know how to interpret the present time?" (12:56). Jerusalem **did not recognize** what was a decisive moment for it, its **visitation**. The word **visitation** means "coming to rescue"; here it refers to God's coming to rescue his people (1:68, 78; 7:16) in Jesus. Jesus yearns to gather the people of Jerusalem together as a hen gathers her brood under her wings to shelter and protect them, but they are unwilling (13:34). If Jerusalem were to embrace him and follow his teachings to "love your enemies" and "to the person who strikes you on one cheek, offer the other one as well"

BACKGROUND: TEMPLE In the ancient Near East, a temple was thought of as the "house" or "palace" of God. Solomon, who ruled from about 970 to 931 B.C., built the first Israelite Temple in Jerusalem. From the time of King Josiah, who ruled from about 640 to 609 B.C., this Jerusalem Temple was the only site where Jews could offer animal sacrifices. Solomon's Temple was destroyed by the Babylonians in 586 B.C. A second Temple was built after the Exile and dedicated in 515 B.C. Herod the Great rebuilt and refurbished this second Temple, enlarging the surrounding courtyard to more than thirty-five acres. Around the perimeter of the courtyard, Herod erected magnificent colonnaded halls similar to structures found elsewhere in the Greek and Roman world. The Temple itself was not a huge building; the precedent established by Solomon's Temple limited its interior floor plan to about 30 by 90 feet (see 1 Kings 6:2). Herod added auxiliary rooms and a grand entrance, substantially increased the height of the façade of the structure, and plated its exterior with gold. Worshipers gathered outside the Temple rather than within it. An altar for offering burnt sac-rifices stood in a courtyard reserved for priests that was in front of—east of—the Temple. East of the Court of Priests was a small Court of Israel, which ritually clean Jewish men could enter, and to its east was a Court of the Women for ritually clean Jews of any age or sex. The remaining, and by far the largest, portion of the Temple area was a Court of the Gentiles, available to both Jews and non-Jews. The open spaces and colonnaded halls in the Court of the Gentiles provided places for meet-ings, instruction, the selling of animals for sacrifice, and the changing of coins for Temple taxes and offerings. The Temple also served as a national religious treasury and depository for savings (see 2 Macc 3:5–12). Rome destroyed the Temple in A.D. 70 while putting down a Jewish revolt. It was never rebuilt.

(6:27, 29), it would not join in the ill-advised revolt against Rome and it would be spared destruction. But it is missing its opportunity; it does not recognize the moment of God's visitation in Jesus and what makes for its peace. Jesus weeps over Jerusalem's tragic fate and needless suffering.

For reflection: What have been the decisive moments in my life? How have I recognized and seized the opportunities God has provided for me?

ORIENTATION: *Jesus completes his journey to Jerusalem by entering the Temple courtyards. There he disrupts commercial activities before beginning to teach.*

Jesus Teaches in His Father's House

⁴⁵ Then Jesus entered the temple area and proceeded to drive out those who were selling things, ⁴⁶ saying to them, "It is written, 'My house shall be a house of prayer, but you have made it a den of thieves.' " ⁴⁷ And every day he was teaching in the temple area. The chief priests, the scribes, and the leaders of the people, meanwhile, were seeking to put him to death, ⁴⁸ but they could find no way to accomplish their purpose because all the people were hanging on his words.

Gospel parallels: Matt 21:12–13; Mark 11:15–18; John 2:14–17

OT: Isaiah 56:7; Jer 7:11

NT: Luke 2:49; 19:41–44; 21:37–38

45 **Then,** after coming down the Mount of Olives (19:36–44), **Jesus entered the temple area**. The **temple** lay on the east side of Jerusalem, across from the Mount of Olives. Visiting the Temple might seem like a natural and convenient first stop for any pilgrim arriving in Jerusalem, but Jesus is not coming to Jerusalem as a simple pilgrim. He comes "in the name of the Lord" (19:38), on behalf of God; he comes to reveal "what makes for peace" (19:42). He wept for Jerusalem because it does not recognize the time of its visitation and will be destroyed (19:41, 44). All this must have been fresh on his mind as he **entered the temple area**, and was perhaps part of his motive for going there. He **proceeded to drive out those who were selling things**. The sales would have been

of unblemished animals, required for sacrificial offerings at the Temple (Lev 1:3). Such commerce took place in the Court of the Gentiles, the outermost courtyard surrounding the Temple itself. Jesus' act was more likely a symbolic disruption rather than a complete elimination of all selling in the Temple area. The Temple courtyards extended over an area of roughly thirty American football fields, and it would have been difficult for Jesus to have single-handedly expelled every merchant. Had Jesus created a large disturbance, Temple guards (22:4, 52) or Roman soldiers from the adjacent Antonia fortress (see Acts 21:30–34) would have quickly stepped in to restore order. We can best understand his driving out of merchants as a prophetic act, just as Old Testament prophets used symbolic acts to convey God's message (Isaiah 20:1–6; Jer 13:1–11; 19:1–13; Ezek 4—5). Jesus goes on to use Scripture to explain and justify his act.

46 He said to the merchants he was expelling, **It is written, "My house shall be a house of prayer, but you have made it a den of thieves."** Jesus invokes what is **written** in Scripture, borrowing words from prophecies. Isaiah prophesied that the Temple would be a house of prayer for all who turned to God, foreigners as well as Israelites (Isaiah 56:6–8). Jesus selects words from Isaiah's prophecy to highlight that the Temple is to be a place of **prayer**. Jeremiah excoriated those who committed grave sins and then used the Temple as a refuge, making it a **den** or hangout **of thieves** (Jer 7:9–11). They believed that they were safe in the Temple because God would protect his house, but Jeremiah reminded them that God had allowed his shrine at Shiloh to be destroyed (Jer 7:12–15). Jesus uses the words **den of thieves** from Jeremiah's prophecy to characterize what the Temple has become.

> My house shall be called
> a house of prayer for all peoples.
>
> Isaiah 56:7

> Has this house which bears my name become in your eyes
> a den of thieves?
>
> Jer 7:11

Scholars have proposed various explanations for the significance of Jesus' action and words. Luke's emphasis in recounting the scene seems to be on the contrast between what the Temple should have been, **a house of prayer**, and what it had become, a commercial center. The sellers were not necessarily cheating their customers, but the priests who controlled the commerce became wealthy from it and lived in luxury—a condition Jesus considered woeful (6:24; 12:16–21; 16:19–31). Those in charge had become, as it were, **thieves** who enriched themselves from Temple worship, using the Temple as their **den**. Jesus symbolically protests their commercialization of his Father's house (2:49), which should be a place of prayer rather than profit. Their putting mammon ahead of God (16:13) was one reason why they were unable to recognize the time of their visitation (19:44): they could not see what made for peace (19:42) because their eyes were on their own status and wealth rather than on what God was doing through Jesus.

For reflection: How have I used my service of God for my own advantage? How has my self-interest blinded me to what God is doing?

47 Having symbolically cleared away the clutter of commercial activity, Jesus puts the Temple courtyard to a proper use: **And every day he was teaching in the temple area**. Jesus began his ministry in Galilee by teaching in synagogues (4:14–15), and he begins his ministry in Jerusalem by teaching **every day** in the Temple courtyard. Luke will recount some of the things Jesus taught there (20—21). **The chief priests, the scribes, and the leaders of the people, meanwhile, were seeking to put him to death.** The high priest and **chief priests** ran the Temple, which was the source of their wealth. They would naturally be upset that Jesus disrupted activities in an area under their authority. **Scribes**, or teachers of the law, including some from Jerusalem, have been critical of Jesus in the past (5:17–21, 30; 6:7, 11; 11:53–54; 15:2) and may resent his popularity with the people (verse 48). The **leaders of the people**, also referred to as elders (20:1; 22:52, 66), are lay aristocrats from influential families. The Sanhedrin—the Jewish ruling council in Jerusalem—was made up of chief priests, scribes, and elders (22:66; see Mark 15:1). The Jewish

leadership of Jerusalem is **seeking to put him to death**—literally, to destroy him. Jesus told his disciples that he "must suffer greatly and be rejected by the elders, the chief priests, and the scribes, and be killed" (9:22), and now they are looking for a way to make it happen.

High priest, chief priests: See page 605

Scribes: See page 146

Elders: See page 189

48 **but they could find no way to accomplish their purpose because all the people were hanging on his words.** Jesus finds a receptive audience for his teaching; **all the people** are eager to listen to him. Luke will later note that "all the people would get up early each morning to listen to him in the temple area" (21:38). When Jesus spoke of Jerusalem being unwilling to have him gather her children to himself (13:34), he was primarily referring to the leaders of Jerusalem, not to the ordinary people. At the same time, Luke does not say that Jesus made a large number of new disciples: the people of Jerusalem are attracted to him and listen to his teachings but without necessarily becoming his disciples. Nevertheless, Jesus has become "a sign that will be contradicted" (2:34) and a source of division (12:51): some reject him and seek to destroy him, while others are receptive to him. Jesus' popularity with ordinary people restrains those who wish him put to death.

For reflection: Do I hang on Jesus' every word? How willing am I to live by his words?

CHAPTER 20

Jesus' Authority Is Questioned

¹ One day as he was teaching the people in the temple area and proclaiming the good news, the chief priests and scribes, together with the elders, approached him ² and said to him, "Tell us, by what authority are you doing these things? Or who is the one who gave you this authority?" ³ He said to them in reply, "I shall ask you a question. Tell me, ⁴ was John's baptism of heavenly or of human origin?" ⁵ They discussed this among themselves, and said, "If we say, 'Of heavenly origin,' he will say, 'Why did you not believe him?' ⁶ But if we say, 'Of human origin,' then all the people will stone us, for they are convinced that John was a prophet." ⁷ So they answered that they did not know from where it came. ⁸ Then Jesus said to them, "Neither shall I tell you by what authority I do these things."

Gospel parallels: Matt 21:23–27; Mark 11:27–33
NT: Luke 3:2–3, 15–17; 7:24–30; 19:45–48

1   **One day as he was teaching the people in the temple area**: since his arrival in Jerusalem (19:45), Jesus has been **teaching the people** every day **in the temple area** (19:47). He is **proclaiming the good news** of the kingdom of God, announcing that God is establishing his reign on earth and inviting women and men to enter into it. Proclaiming the good news of the kingdom is Jesus' mission from God; he told his disciples, "I must proclaim the good news of the kingdom of God, because for this purpose I have been sent" (4:43). He has carried out his mission (7:22; 8:1; 16:16) and sent his disciples out with the same good news (9:2; 10:9). Now Jesus is bringing the good news of the kingdom to the **people** of Jerusalem. While he was teaching and proclaiming the good news, **the chief priests and scribes, together with the elders, approached him**. These leaders were upset when Jesus disrupted commerce in the Temple courtyard (19:45–47), and they are not happy that he is teaching in the Temple precincts and attracting crowds that are eager to hear him (19:48; 21:38). They **approached** Jesus, interrupting him **as he was teaching**.

Temple: See page 519
Gospel, good news: See page 59
High priest, chief priests: See page 605
Scribes: See page 146
Elders: See page 189

2　They **said to him, "Tell us, by what authority are you doing these things?"** By **these things** they mean his teaching every day in a Temple courtyard (verse 1; 19:47) after interfering with the sale of sacrificial animals (19:45–46). They demand to know **what authority** he has to teach or to disrupt activities in the Temple area. He has not studied under a religious scholar, yet he teaches as if his words are authoritative. In the synagogue of Capernaum those who heard him "were astonished at his teaching, because he spoke with authority" (4:32). The chief priests, scribes, and elders demand a justification for his actions: **tell us** the nature of your authority. They also demand that Jesus tell them, **Who is the one who gave you this authority?** The high priest and chief priests are in charge of the Temple; along with scribes and elders of the Sanhedrin (22:66) they have authority over religious matters. They most certainly have not authorized Jesus to teach, nor have they delegated him any authority over what goes on at the Temple. **Who** then **gave you this authority?** What right have you to come to the Temple and do what you are doing?

3　**He said to them in reply, "I shall ask you a question."** Responding to a question with a question was a common debating tactic of the time, in order to solicit information or an opinion from the questioner that could be used in answering his or her question. Jesus says, **Tell me,**

4　**was John's baptism of heavenly or of human origin?** By **John's baptism** Jesus implicitly refers to John's entire mission and message, which had baptism as its central component (3:2–14). **Of heavenly or of human origin** is literally, "from heaven or from humans"; from heaven means from God. Jesus is asked who gave him authority, and he responds by asking who gave John the Baptist his authority. There were only two possible sources for John's authority. If he did not receive it from God, then it was **of human origin** and he had no mandate from God to baptize.

Baptism: See page 88

5 **They discussed this among themselves.** Their deliberations, however, are not about the source of John's authority but about the consequences for themselves of the answers they might give in response to Jesus' question. They are not interested in the truth but in preserving their own status. In their deliberations they **said, "If we say, 'Of heavenly origin,' he will say, 'Why did you not believe him?' "** It is evident that they did not accept John's baptism or **believe** his message, and they know that Jesus is aware of this. Luke earlier noted that "the Pharisees and scholars of the law, who were not baptized by him, rejected the plan of God for themselves" (7:30), and those who are now questioning Jesus likewise rejected John and God's plan for them.

6 **"But if we say, 'Of human origin,' then all the people will stone us, for they are convinced that John was a prophet."** After John's birth, his father Zechariah prophesied, "And you, child, will be called prophet of the Most High" (1:76), and Zechariah's words were borne out. "The word of God came to John" (3:2), as it had come to previous prophets (Isaiah 38:4; Jer 1:2, 4, 11, 13; Ezek 1:3; 3:17), and crowds went into the desert to hear his message and be baptized (3:7). Jesus characterized John as a prophet "and more than a prophet" (7:26). Those questioning Jesus realize that if they dismiss John's authority as being merely **of human origin** and not the authority of a **prophet** sent by God, **then all the people will stone us**. They fear the kind of mob violence stemming from offended religious beliefs that will result in the stoning of Stephen (Acts 7:54–60).

> *For reflection: When have I allowed concern for my reputation or well-being to override what is true and right?*

7 **So they answered that they did not know from where it came.** They plead ignorance in order to dodge Jesus' question. They did not try to determine where John's authority came from, although their not believing in him (verse 5) indicates that they did not accept that his authority

was from God. Because there will be problems for them no matter which way they answer Jesus' question, they evade answering. Their failure to answer nevertheless indicts them: as religious leaders of God's people, they are expected to discern the authenticity of anyone who claims to be sent by God, and they are supposed to provide guidance for the people in light of their discernment. Their feigned ignorance about someone as significant as John the Baptist amounts to dereliction of duty.

8 **Then Jesus said to them, "Neither shall I tell you by what authority I do these things."** Since they refused to answer his question, he refuses to answer theirs. Yet his question to them is in itself an implicit answer to their question, since Jesus recognizes that John's authority came from God (7:26–28). If those questioning Jesus would acknowledge that John's authority comes from God, then Jesus could respond that his authority does as well. Furthermore, he can appeal to John to back up his claim. John proclaimed that "I am baptizing you with water, but one mightier than I is coming" (3:16), and he recognized, although with some perplexity, that Jesus was the one who was coming after him (7:18–19). Jesus considered John to be his forerunner and a fulfillment of the Scripture, "Behold, I am sending my messenger ahead of you, / he will prepare your way before you" (7:27; Mal 3:1). If John's authority is accepted, then his testimony to Jesus as the mightier one with greater authority should also be accepted, and this would answer the religious authorities' question. But those who reject John also reject Jesus, and do not recognize the time of their visitation (19:44).

For reflection: Do I accept Jesus' authority over me? What difference does it make in how I lead my life?

The Parable of the Tenant Farmers
9 **Then he proceeded to tell the people this parable. "[A] man planted a vineyard, leased it to tenant farmers, and then went on a journey for a long time. 10 At harvest time he sent a servant to the tenant farmers to receive some of the produce of the vineyard. But they beat the servant and sent him away empty-handed. 11 So he proceeded to send another servant, but him also they beat**

and insulted and sent away empty-handed. ¹² Then he proceeded to send a third, but this one too they wounded and threw out. ¹³ The owner of the vineyard said, 'What shall I do? I shall send my beloved son; maybe they will respect him.' ¹⁴ But when the tenant farmers saw him they said to one another, 'This is the heir. Let us kill him that the inheritance may become ours.' ¹⁵ So they threw him out of the vineyard and killed him. What will the owner of the vineyard do to them? ¹⁶ He will come and put those tenant farmers to death and turn over the vineyard to others." When the people heard this, they exclaimed, "Let it not be so!" ¹⁷ But he looked at them and asked, "What then does this scripture passage mean:

'The stone which the builders rejected
    has become the cornerstone'?

¹⁸ "Everyone who falls on that stone will be dashed to pieces; and it will crush anyone on whom it falls." ¹⁹ The scribes and chief priests sought to lay their hands on him at that very hour, but they feared the people, for they knew that he had addressed this parable to them.

Gospel parallels: Matt 21:33–46; Mark 12:1–12
OT: Psalm 118:22; Isaiah 5:1–7
NT: Luke 3:22; 20:1–8

9   Jesus is "teaching the people in the temple area and proclaiming the good news" (20:1; see also 19:47). Some chief priests, scribes, and elders interrupted him, challenging his authority (20:1–8). In light of their challenge, **then he proceeded to tell the people this parable**. He addresses his words to **the people**, but those who challenged him over-hear the parable (see verse 19). Jesus begins his parable by saying, **[A] man planted a vineyard**. Any of his listeners who were familiar with the book of Isaiah would likely have suspected that the **vineyard** represents God's people, as it does in a memorable prophecy of Isaiah: "The vineyard of the LORD of hosts is the house of Israel" (Isaiah 5:7). In Jesus' parable, the vineyard owner **leased it to tenant farmers**. Leasing vineyards or crop land to **tenant farmers** was a common practice; tenants would give the owner an agreed-upon share of the harvest, retaining the rest for themselves. If the vineyard represents God's people, then the tenants presumably represent the leaders into whose care God has entrusted

his people. **Then** the owner **went on a journey for a long time**. The word translated **went on a journey** simply means "went away"; he is away **for a long time**.

Parables: See page 217

The vineyard of the LORD of hosts is the house of Israel,
and the men of Judah are his cherished plant.

Isaiah 5:7

10 **At harvest time he sent a servant to the tenant farmers to receive some of the produce of the vineyard.** The word translated **servant** literally means "slave" here and throughout the parable. The vineyard owner is due **some of the produce of the vineyard** from each harvest as part of the contractual arrangement he made with the **tenant farmers** in leasing the vineyard to them. **At harvest time** he sends one of his slaves as his agent to collect what is due him, **but they beat the servant and sent him away empty-handed**. Some tenants tried to short-change owners if they thought they could get away with it, but these tenants behave brutishly and lawlessly.

Servant, slave: See page 454

11 **So he proceeded to send another servant**: the owner wants the share of the harvest that is due him and makes another attempt to collect it. The second slave he sends as his emissary is treated no better than the first: **but him also they beat and insulted and sent away empty-handed**. The tenants not only refuse to give the owner his portion of the harvest, but treat his slaves shamefully and brutally.

12 Despite the tenant's behavior, the owner persists in trying to obtain what is due him. **Then he proceeded to send a third, but this one too they wounded and threw out.** Do the tenants think that if they mistreat and turn away all the slaves the owner sends, the owner will eventually give up trying to collect his share and they will have the entire harvest for themselves?

Those in Jesus' audience who grasped that the vineyard represents God's people may have made another association by now. The Old Testament refers to prophets as servants or slaves of God (1 Kings

14:18; 2 Kings 9:7; Ezra 9:11; Isaiah 20:3; Jer 7:25; Baruch 2:20; Ezek 38:17; Dan 9:6; Amos 3:7; Zech 1:6). The slaves sent by the owner in the parable represent prophets that God sent to his people; the "long time" of verse 9 represents the centuries during which God sent them. Prophets frequently experienced rejection and even violence when they brought messages from God that his people did not want to hear (11:47; 13:34; 1 Kings 19:10; 22:26–28; 2 Chron 16:10; 36:15–16; Neh 9:26; Jer 2:30; 7:25–26; 38:4–6), just as the owner's slaves were ill-treated by the tenants.

13 **The owner of the vineyard said**: The word translated **owner** is in some contexts translated "lord"; those listening to the parable who realize that the vineyard represents God's people understand that the **owner** represents the Lord God. The owner deliberates and asks himself, **What shall I do?** It would be pointless to send any more of his slaves to collect his share of the harvest; they would receive the same treatment as the first slaves he sent. The owner decides to send someone who would have more authority than his slaves: **I shall send my beloved son**. The word translated **beloved** can have the connotation of "only." The owner cannot dictate how the tenants will respond to his **beloved son**, but he will **send** him in the hope that he will be treated with the deference due him as his son: **maybe they will respect him**.

Lord: See page 137

Luke's readers have no difficulty perceiving that the **beloved son** in the parable represents Jesus. While Jesus was praying after being baptized by John, "A voice came from heaven, 'You are my beloved Son; with you I am well pleased' " (3:22). Until the time of John, God sent prophets to his people (16:16), whom they mistreated (11:47). Then God sent Jesus (4:18, 43), his beloved and only son.

For reflection: What does it reveal to me about God, that he "so loved the world that he gave his only Son" (John 3:16)?

14 The owner's son does as his father asks of him and goes to the vineyard. **But when the tenant farmers saw him they said to one another, "This is the heir."** The tenants seem to interpret the son's arrival as an indica-

tion that his father has died and that, as his only son, he has come to take possession of the vineyard as his **heir.** They resolve, **Let us kill him that the inheritance may become ours.** While our knowledge of first-century legal practices is limited, it seems that if a property became ownerless, such as by its owner dying without leaving an heir, then tenants occupying the property had first claim to it. That seems to be behind the tenants' deciding to kill the son so that **the inheritance may become ours.**

15 **So they threw him out of the vineyard and killed him.** They follow through on their evil resolve. Jesus' own death will follow the same pattern: he will be led out of the city to be crucified (23:26, 33; see also Heb 13:12). Jesus asks the people to whom he is addressing the parable (verse 9), **What will the owner of the vineyard do to them?**

16 Jesus answers his own question: **He will come and put those tenant farmers to death.** The owner will follow the law of Moses, which calls for strict retributive justice: "eye for eye, tooth for tooth! . . . whoever slays a man shall be put to death" (Lev 24:20, 21; see also Exod 21:23–24; Deut 19:21). The outcome will be the same whether the owner turns the murderous tenants over to the authorities or takes the law into his own hands. Then having seen that justice is done, he will **turn over the vineyard to others.** The vineyard still requires workers to tend it and harvest its crops; **others** will be brought in to replace the original tenants.

When the people heard this, they exclaimed, "Let it not be so!" They seem to understand that Jesus' parable is about the leaders of God's people, those to whom God has entrusted his vineyard. Their dismayed **Let it not be so!** can apply to much of the parable as well as to its outcome: let it not be so that our leaders do not give God what is due him; let it not be so that our leaders reject prophets and kill God's ultimate envoy; let it not be so that their behavior results in their destruction and replacement.

For reflection: Is there anything in my life that might cause others to utter in dismay, "Let it not be so!"?

17 **But he looked at them:** the word used here for **looked** has the connotation of an intense gaze. Jesus sees their dismay and addresses it. He

asked, **"What then does this scripture passage mean?"** Jesus directs their attention to **scripture** as a revelation of God's will. The sense of his question is, "You say, 'Let it not be so!' But doesn't **this scripture passage** make the same point as my parable?" Jesus quotes words from Psalm 118: **The stone which the builders rejected / has become the cornerstone**. The **cornerstone** of a building is a foundation block linking two walls at a corner; the positioning of the cornerstone determines the placement of the building and the alignment of its walls. A **stone which the builders rejected** and cast aside as unfit ends up being the most important stone in the building, an utter reversal of its fortunes. That the stone is **rejected** links this Scripture passage with Jesus' parable: the owner's son is rejected and killed by tenants, the stone is rejected by builders. The tenants and the builders represent the leaders of God's people. The Scripture passage does not end with the stone's rejection but goes on to speak of its exaltation. In conjunction with the parable it is an implicit extension of it, conveying the message that the death of the son will be a prelude to his exaltation.

> The stone the builders rejected
> has become the cornerstone.
>
> Psalm 118:22

Luke's readers know that Jesus "must suffer greatly and be rejected by the elders, the chief priests, and the scribes, and be killed and on the third day be raised" (9:22); this is God's will for him. He will be rejected but will become the cornerstone of a new edifice. The leaders who reject him will be replaced; Jesus is establishing new leadership for God's people. In Acts, Luke will portray the Twelve as the core leaders of the early Church (Acts 1:13–26; 2:14; 6:2). In response to those who say, "Let it not be so!" Jesus cites Psalm 118 to proclaim, "This is the way that it will be."

18 When Jesus was an infant, Simeon prophesied that "this child is destined for the rise and fall of many in Israel" (2:34), and Jesus addresses the situation of those who fall. Continuing to use the image of a stone and borrowing from Scripture, he proclaims, **Everyone who falls on that stone will be dashed to pieces.** Isaiah spoke of "an obstacle and a stum-

bling stone" that would cause many to stumble and fall (Isaiah 8:14–15). Jesus proclaimed, "Blessed is the one who takes no offense in me" (7:23); by implication, woe to the one who takes offense, who is tripped up because of me. It will be like falling from a height and being smashed on a rock. **And it will crush anyone on whom it falls**: here Jesus uses the opposite image, that of a boulder falling upon and crushing someone. A faintly similar image is used in the book of Daniel (Dan 2:34, 44–45). Being dashed to pieces or crushed by a huge stone are harsh images, but Jesus invokes them because there is a harsh fate in store for Jerusalem unless it changes course (13:34–35; 19:41–44). Jesus is warning the people who are listening to disassociate themselves from the leaders who reject him. He is inviting them to accept him and the way that makes for peace, because now is the time of Jerusalem's visitation (19:42, 44).

For reflection: In what area of my life am I in the greatest danger of stumbling and falling?

19 **The scribes and chief priests sought to lay their hands on him at that very hour, but they feared the people, for they knew that he had addressed this parable to them.** Some **scribes and chief priests** heard Jesus' parable and realized that it was about **them**. They grasp that Jesus has compared them to tenants who refuse a vineyard owner his due, who brutalize his slaves, who kill his beloved son, who will be destroyed and replaced. They want to **lay their hands on him**—seize him violently and arrest him. After Jesus disrupted commerce in the Temple courtyards, they "were seeking to put him to death, but they could find no way to accomplish their purpose because all the people were hanging on his words" (19:47–48). Now Jesus' parable infuriates them even more, and they wish to seize him **at that very hour**, but are again held back by his popularity, for **they feared the people**. They could have taken Jesus' parable as a warning and changed their course, but instead they became more intent on destroying him.

For reflection: How do I react to criticism and warnings that I should change my behavior? When have I become even more set in my ways?

Who Is Due What?
²⁰ They watched him closely and sent agents pretending to be righteous who were to trap him in speech, in order to hand him over to the authority and power of the governor. ²¹ They posed this question to him, "Teacher, we know that what you say and teach is correct, and you show no partiality, but teach the way of God in accordance with the truth. ²² Is it lawful for us to pay tribute to Caesar or not?" ²³ Recognizing their craftiness he said to them, ²⁴ "Show me a denarius; whose image and name does it bear?" They replied, "Caesar's." ²⁵ So he said to them, "Then repay to Caesar what belongs to Caesar and to God what belongs to God." ²⁶ They were unable to trap him by something he might say before the people, and so amazed were they at his reply that they fell silent.

Gospel parallels: Matt 22:15–22; Mark 12:13–17
NT: Luke 2:1–3; 3:1; 19:47–48; 20:19; 23:2; Acts 5:37

20 **They watched him closely**: the chief priests, scribes, and elders who were seeking to destroy Jesus (19:47) and wanted to seize him (20:19) **watched him closely**, scrutinizing his behavior and monitoring his words with malicious intent (see 6:7; 14:1). They are reluctant to confront Jesus in person because he has publicly shamed them by telling a parable that compared them to murderous tenants (20:9–18). Instead they **sent agents pretending to be righteous**. The word translated **agents** has the connotation of spies. **Righteous** in this context means sincere: the spies are **pretending** to be sincere in their approach to Jesus, but their mission and intent is **to trap him in speech in order to hand him over to the authority and power of the governor**. The Roman **governor** at the time was Pontius Pilate (3:1), who had **authority** over Judea and the **power** to put people to death. The agents were to **trap** Jesus into saying something that could be used as a charge against him and would justify their handing him over to Pilate.

Pontius Pilate: See page 617

21 **They posed this question to him**, addressing him as **Teacher**. Their question has to do with the law of Moses, and they ask it of Jesus as a **teacher** who can be expected to interpret how the law is to be observed. Before asking their question they use flattery to lull Jesus into giving an

answer that will get him into trouble. They tell him **we know that what you say and teach is correct**: Jesus is **correct** in his teachings, faithful to the law of Moses. **You show no partiality** to people—Jesus is not swayed by anyone's status or office, even that of the Roman authorities—**but teach the way of God in accordance with the truth**. The **way of God** is the way of life prescribed by God for his people. Jesus teaches the kind of life God requires **in accordance with the truth**: what Jesus teaches is an authentic expression of God's will. Those flattering Jesus are setting him up to give a strict interpretation of the law of Moses without regard for how his answer will be taken by the Roman authorities.

Ironically, everything said in guileful flattery about Jesus is true. Jesus does not tailor his message in order to tell his listeners what they want to hear; Jesus truly teaches what is **the way of God** for them.

For reflection: What have I learned from Jesus' teachings in the Gospel of Luke about the way of God for me?

22 The agents pose a loaded question: **Is it lawful for us to pay tribute to Caesar or not?** Julius Caesar was the Roman emperor from 49 to 44 B.C.; emperors who immediately succeeded him assumed the name **Caesar**. The **tribute** was an annual head tax imposed on every adult male when Judea came under direct Roman rule in A.D. 6. The census taken at that time (2:1–3) was done to enroll men in the tax roster. While the tax itself was small, about a day's wages, it was one more tax in an already oppressive tax system. More important, paying this tax was a sign of submission to Roman rule. When the tax was first imposed, a man known as Judas the Galilean led a revolt against it (see Acts 5:37). The first-century Jewish historian Josephus wrote that Judas the Galilean called Jews "cowards for consenting to pay tribute to the Romans and tolerating mortal masters, after they had God for their Lord." Rome put down the tax revolt, but repugnance at the tax remained.

Roman Empire: See page 52

Jesus is asked whether it is **lawful** for Jews to pay this head tax to the Roman emperor, meaning whether it is permitted by the law of Moses. If he declares that paying the tax is unlawful, then he can be denounced to Pontius Pilate as a troublemaker stirring up another tax revolt; Pilate brutally quashed threats to Roman sovereignty (see 13:1). If Jesus declares the tax lawful, then he will not only uphold a resented tax but acquiesce to Roman rule and dash popular hopes for Jewish independence and rule by God. His popularity with the people will be diminished—the popularity that prevents the chief priests, scribes, and elders from taking action against him (19:47–48; 20:19). Their agents have tried to put Jesus in a lose-lose situation.

23 Jesus is not taken in by their appearance of sincerity and their flattery. **Recognizing their craftiness** and trap **he said to them,**

24 **Show me a denarius.** A **denarius** was a widely circulated silver Roman coin equivalent to a day's wages for an ordinary worker (the plural of **denarius** is translated as "days' wages" at 7:41 and as "silver coins" at 10:35). The annual Roman head tax was one **denarius.** Jesus asks to see the coin used to pay the tax; presumably he is not carrying such a coin himself. He asks, **whose image and name does it bear?** Like modern coins, ancient coins bore some sort of image and inscription. Those trying to trip Jesus up over Roman taxes have no trouble producing a denarius and telling Jesus whose image and name is on it; they carry and use such coins. **They replied, "Caesar's."** Tiberias Caesar was the current emperor (3:1), and a denarius minted during his reign bore an image of his head and the inscription, "Tiberias Caesar Augustus, Son of the Divine Augustus." A second inscription called him the "Supreme Pontiff," meaning that he was the highest priest mediating between the people and the gods.

25 **So he said to them, "Then repay to Caesar what belongs to Caesar and to God what belongs to God."** The word translated **repay** can mean either give or give back; the New American Bible here interprets it to mean give back. **What belongs to Caesar** is more literally, "the things of Caesar." Jesus says that because a denarius bears the emperor's image and name, therefore it should be returned to him. Coins in some sense belonged to the one who minted them; the emperor's image and inscription on a coin were like a property seal, similar to the imprint of a signet ring on a blob of wax. Paying the required tax is simply giving the emperor what is his. In a broader sense, Roman minting and control of the currency made trade and business possible. Without coins of

dependable value, commerce would be reduced to bartering. Those who participate in the economic system of the Roman Empire and profit from it can be expected to share the cost of running it. Roman taxes are the price for using Roman coins.

For reflection: Do I resent paying taxes, or do I accept that they are payment for the services and benefits that I and others receive?

Jesus does not let matters rest there; he adds quite emphatically, **and** repay **to God what belongs to God**—more literally, repay to God "the things of God." What are the things of God? What belongs to God? "The earth is the LORD's and all it holds, / the world and those who live there. / For God founded it on the seas, / established it over the rivers" (Psalm 24:1-2). Everything God created is his; God's claim on his creation is total. Paul will invoke words of a Greek writer: "In him we live and move and have our being" (Acts 17:28). All that we have is his, loaned to us out of love. And just as a coin bears the image of the emperor who minted it, so women and men bear the image of the one who created them: "God created man in his image; / in the divine image he created him; / male and female he created them" (Gen 1:27). Humans are God's unique possession, bearing his image. An emperor or government may have a claim to our taxes (see Rom 13:1-7), but God has an unlimited claim on all we have and all we are.

For reflection: What have I given to God? Where did I get it? What am I holding back from him?

26 **They were unable to trap him by something he might say before the people**: Jesus has said nothing seditious against Roman authority, nor has he said anything **before the people** that would turn them against him. The people can hardly object to his reminding them of their obligations to God, with the clear implication that their obligations to God far outweigh whatever obligations they have to civil authority. Jesus has escaped the **trap** set for him and done so skillfully; **so amazed were they at his reply that** the agents questioning him **fell silent**. They cannot think of anything else to say to Jesus to trap him in his speech; they have failed in their mission (verse 20).

537

Resurrected Life

²⁷ Some Sadducees, those who deny that there is a resurrection, came forward and put this question to him, ²⁸ saying, "Teacher, Moses wrote for us, 'If someone's brother dies leaving a wife but no child, his brother must take the wife and raise up descendants for his brother.' ²⁹ Now there were seven brothers; the first married a woman but died childless. ³⁰ Then the second ³¹ and the third married her, and likewise all the seven died childless. ³² Finally the woman also died. ³³ Now at the resurrection whose wife will that woman be? For all seven had been married to her." ³⁴ Jesus said to them, "The children of this age marry and remarry; ³⁵ but those who are deemed worthy to attain to the coming age and to the resurrection of the dead neither marry nor are given in marriage. ³⁶ They can no longer die, for they are like angels; and they are the children of God because they are the ones who will rise. ³⁷ That the dead will rise even Moses made known in the passage about the bush, when he called 'Lord' the God of Abraham, the God of Isaac, and the God of Jacob; ³⁸ and he is not God of the dead, but of the living, for to him all are alive." ³⁹ Some of the scribes said in reply, "Teacher, you have answered well." ⁴⁰ And they no longer dared to ask him anything.

Gospel parallels: Matt 22:23–33; Mark 12:18–27
OT: Gen 38:6–11; Exod 3:1–15; Deut 25:5–6
NT: Acts 23:6–8; 1 John 3:2

27 Jesus is in a courtyard of the Temple, teaching and responding to challenges (19:47; 20:1–26). **Some Sadducees, those who deny that there**

BACKGROUND: SADDUCEES These Jews were an aristocratic group or party centered in Jerusalem and largely made up of high-priestly families and members of the upper class. They were an elite and hence a rather small group within Jewish society. Sadducees were religiously conservative, upholding their own interpretation of the law of Moses and rejecting traditions developed by Pharisees. The Sadducees also rejected beliefs in a resurrection of the dead and relatively new beliefs about angels that had arisen in the second century B.C. (see Acts 23:8). Sadducees cooperated with Roman rule in order to maintain their privileged status. Sadducees as an identifiable group did not survive the Roman destruction of Jerusalem in A.D. 70.

---

is a resurrection, came forward and put this question to him. This is the first appearance of **Sadducees** in the Gospel of Luke. They were a small, elite group living chiefly in Jerusalem, unlikely to be encountered by Jesus in Galilee. **Sadducees** were religiously conservative, holding to what they found written in Scripture, particularly in the law of Moses, and rejecting recent developments, such as belief that there would be a **resurrection** of the dead (see Acts 23:8). Some books written in the previous two centuries spoke of the dead being raised (2 Macc 7; Dan 12:2), but Sadducees did not accept such books as Scripture. Some Sadducees have heard about Jesus and apparently know that he teaches that women and men will be raised from the dead to be judged by God (10:14; 11:31–32; 14:14). They challenge him with a **question** designed to show the folly of believing that there will be a resurrection.

Resurrection: See page 401

28 They address Jesus as **Teacher,** someone responsible for knowing the law of Moses. They tell him, **Moses wrote for us, "If someone's brother dies leaving a wife but no child, his brother must take the wife and raise up descendants for his brother."** They cite a law (Deut 25:5–6) that made provision for carrying on the name and preserving the inheritance of a man who died without a male child: his brother should take his widow as his wife and beget an heir for him (see also Gen 38:6–11). It is doubtful whether this was a common practice at the time of Jesus, but the law was on the books, and as a **teacher** Jesus could be questioned about it.

> When brothers live together and one of them dies without a son, the widow of the deceased shall not marry anyone outside the family; but her husband's brother shall go to her and perform the duty of a brother-in-law by marrying her. The firstborn son she bears shall continue the line of the deceased brother, that his name may not be blotted out from Israel.
>
> Deut 25:5–6

29 The Sadducees propose a test case. **Now there were seven brothers; the first married a woman but died childless.** Following the law

meant that one of his six brothers would take the widow as his wife, in order to beget a son who would carry on the dead brother's name and be his heir.

30 **Then the second**: the Sadducees tell their story very tersely, implying that the woman's **second** husband also died without their marriage producing a son.

31 **And the third married her**, and also died childless, **and likewise all the seven** married her and **died childless**. The Sadducees' story is highly improbable, but they are putting it forward as a "What if?" situation in order to pose a question to Jesus.

32 Their story concludes, **Finally the woman also died**.

33 They ask their question: **Now at the resurrection**—they mean, if there is a resurrection—**whose wife will that woman be? For all seven had been married to her**. Their question presumes that while a man may

---

BACKGROUND: MARRIAGE PRACTICES The love of wife and husband for each other could be just as heartfelt in ancient as in modern times and sexual attraction just as passionate (see the Song of Songs). Yet the understanding and practice of marriage in the Old Testament has its differences from marriage in the modern Western world. The primary purpose of marriage was to beget children, specifically sons who could continue the father's family name and inherit the father's family lands. Hence shame befell a barren wife, however much her husband might love her (1 Sam 1:1–8). If a husband died without leaving a son, his brother was to marry his widow and beget an heir for him (Deut 25:5–6). A man could have more than one wife (Deut 21:15–17), but a wife could not have more than one husband, for that would create family heritage tangles. Inheritance passed to sons, with a double share to the oldest (Deut 21:17). Only by exception could daughters inherit (Num 27:8), and then with restrictions to keep the inheritance within the father's clan (Num 36:6–9). Marriages were arrangements between families as well as between husband and wife. Particularly when those getting married were young, as early as puberty for a girl and a few years older for a boy, their fathers arranged their betrothal, sometimes drawing up a contract (see Tobit 7:13). A betrothed woman might continue to live with her family for a period of time (Matt 1:18). There was no wedding ceremony as such but a party or feast to celebrate a wife moving into the home of her husband (Matt 22:2–10; 25:1–13; Mark 2:19; John 2:1–10).

---

have more than one wife (Solomon was credited with seven hundred—1 Kings 11:3), a wife may not have more than one husband. Inheritances passed from fathers to sons; a wife having several husbands would raise paternity and inheritance issues. Their question also assumes that resurrected life will be basically a continuation of this life in a different setting. Hence what is impossible in this life—a woman having more than one husband at the same time—will be impossible in the next life. If the woman in the Sadducees' example had seven husbands in this life but only one can be her husband after **the resurrection**, then **whose wife** will she be? In the Sadducees' scenario, each of the **seven** men who **had been married to her** has an equal claim to her. The point the Sadducees wish to make with their story and question is that there cannot be a resurrection, because if there were, then impossible situations like this would arise.

34 Jesus takes their concern seriously and addresses it in two ways. First he explains why situations like the one they propose will not occur. **Jesus said to them, "The children of this age marry and remarry."** The word translated **age** can also mean "world"; **the children of this age** refers to people living in this world. There is, however, an important nuance of meaning. **The children of this age** is literally "the sons of this age," with "sons of" being a biblical idiom for sharing the characteristics of or participating in something (the words translated "a peaceful person" at 10:6 are literally "a son of peace"). **The children of this age** not only live in this world but share the character of this world. Flesh and blood, they are born, live, and pass away, as everything in this world passes away. They **marry and remarry**: the word translated **remarry** is more properly translated "are given in marriage"; a closely related word with the same meaning is used in the next verse. Men marry their wives, and women are given in marriage by their fathers to their husbands (see 17:27). Since every man and woman will eventually die, marriage and the begetting of new generations of children is necessary to continue the human race.

35 **But those who are deemed worthy to attain to the coming age and to the resurrection of the dead**: Jesus refers to "this age" (verse 34) being replaced by **the coming age** or the age to come. God will

bring human history to an end, vanquishing evil, and ushering in a new era in which he reigns in fullness over all. Women and men **who are deemed worthy** by God **to attain** it will enter into God's reign in **the coming age** through **the resurrection of the dead**. Jesus previously referred to this as "the resurrection of the righteous" (14:14). All will rise to face God's judgment (11:31–32); "some shall live forever, / others shall be an everlasting horror and disgrace" (Dan 12:2). Jesus focuses on those **deemed worthy** by God to receive everlasting life in the coming age. He does not go into what they must do to be **deemed worthy**, but he has previously answered those who asked him, "What must I do to inherit eternal life?" (10:25–28; 18:18–22), he has urged his listeners to "strive to enter through the narrow door" leading into the heavenly banquet (13:24–29), and he has promised that those who give up everything for him will receive "eternal life in the age to come" (18:28–30). Those who **attain** eternal life **neither marry nor are given in marriage**. Strictly speaking, Jesus says only that no new marriages will take place in the age to come: men will not **marry**, nor will women be **given in marriage**. However, what Jesus goes on to say indicates that human relationships such as marriage, like humans themselves, will be transformed in the age to come.

The age to come: See page 487

For reflection: What am I doing so that I will be deemed worthy of eternal life? What do I need to receive from God so that I will be made worthy?

36 Those who attain eternal life in the age to come will not marry or be given in marriage because **they can no longer die, for they are like angels**. Being **like angels** does not mean being disembodied spirits; at the time of Jesus, **angels** were often thought of as human in form but with heavenly rather than earthly bodies (24:4; Acts 1:10; see also 2 Macc 3:26; Dan 8:15–16). Those who are raised to eternal life are **like angels** in that angels do not die and neither do those who have been raised: they **can no longer die**. Hence they do not marry (verse 35): marriage and the begetting of children are necessary to continue the human race as older generations die off, but this is no longer necessary when men and women can no longer die. But what about the loving personal relationship between a husband and wife, which can continue long after

their childbearing years are over? It is difficult to imagine that God will separate those whom he has joined together (see Mark 10:6–9), but it is also beyond our imagining how married couples will experience their relationship in the age to come.

Angels: See page 11

And they are the children of God because they are the ones who will rise—literally, "they are sons of God, being sons of the resurrection." The expression "sons of God" has a variety of meanings in the Old Testament. The key to understanding its significance here lies in why Jesus says that those who are raised are the sons or children of God: it is **because** they are sons of the resurrection. As in verse 34, "sons of" means to share the characteristics of or to participate in. Because of their participating in or experiencing resurrection, those who are raised participate in and take on characteristics of God. Resurrection transforms the flesh and blood "children of this age" (verse 34); they become **like angels**, they become **children of God**. The first letter of John speaks of the same transformation: "What we shall be has not yet been revealed. We do know that when it is revealed we shall be like him, for we shall see him as he is" (1 John 3:2).

Son of God: See page 25

For reflection: How often do I think about what I will be in eternity? To the extent I can, what do I imagine my life will be like when I am with God?

The constraints of this life do not apply in the next life because resurrected life is transformed life and not a mere continuation of present life. The Sadducees based their test case on a mistaken assumption; the kind of problem they envision will not arise at the resurrection. Jesus is not content, however, simply to demonstrate that their reasoning is faulty. He goes on to show that a book they accept as Scripture contains an implicit affirmation of the resurrection.

37 **That the dead will rise even Moses made known**: the word translated **will rise** literally means "are raised," implying are raised by God. That God will raise the dead **even Moses made known in the pas-**

543

sage about the bush when he called "Lord" the God of Abraham,
the God of Isaac, and the God of Jacob. Jesus refers to a text in the
book of Exodus as something that **Moses made known**, following the
tradition that Moses was the author of the first five books of the Bible.
Since chapter divisions and verse numbers had yet to be introduced into
Scripture, Jesus cannot tell the Sadducees to recall what is written in
Exodus 3:1–15. Instead he refers to this section of Scripture as **the passage about the bush**, which recounts how God spoke to Moses out of
a burning bush. God told Moses to say to the Israelites, "The LORD, the
God of your fathers, the God of Abraham, the God of Isaac, the God
of Jacob, has sent me to you" (Exod 3:15). In the Old Testament, the
expression, "the God of" someone is not simply a way of identifying who
someone worships. It expresses a personal relationship between God and
a person, with God acting as the person's protector and benefactor. For
the Lord God to be the God of Abraham, Isaac, and Jacob means that
he is in a personal, caring relationship with them. Moses, as the traditional author of Exodus, did not say that the Lord God was formerly the
God of Abraham, Isaac, and Jacob; Moses speaks as if God is presently
the God of Abraham, Isaac, and Jacob. God's relationship with them
continues, even though they died centuries earlier. And if that relationship continues, then Abraham, Isaac, and Jacob must nevertheless still
be alive.

God's name: See page 546

> God spoke further to Moses: "Thus shall you say to the
> Israelites: The LORD, the God of your fathers, the God of
> Abraham, the God of Isaac, the God of Jacob, has sent me
> to you."
>
> Exod 3:15

*For reflection: What is my personal relationship with God? How have I
experienced God's care for me?*

38 Jesus proclaims that God **is not God of the dead, but of the living**.
Only the **living** can be in a relationship with God, enjoying his care and
protection. Death cannot rupture God's relationship with his people, **for
to him all are alive**. Jesus does not explain their mode of existence; he

simply states that **all are alive**—implicitly, alive in God, maintained in existence despite having died. Jesus earlier spoke of "Abraham, Isaac, and Jacob and all the prophets" being in the heavenly banquet in the kingdom of God (13:28–29), and he told a parable in which a poor man named Lazarus died and was carried by angels "to the bosom of Abraham" (16:22), an image for reclining next to Abraham at the heavenly banquet. Abraham, Isaac, and Jacob are alive and with God.

If in the first part of his response to the Sadducees (verses 34–36), Jesus taught that resurrected life is not the same as this life; in the second part of his response Jesus affirms that it is real life nonetheless: in God **all are alive**. Death cannot separate us from the love of God (see Rom 8:38–39); the relationship we begin with God in this life continues and reaches its fulfillment in the next. Because God's love is undying, so are those whom he loves.

For reflection: What are the implications for me that in God I am forever alive?

39 **Some of the scribes said in reply, "Teacher, you have answered well."** The **scribes** encountered so far in the Gospel of Luke have generally been associated with the Pharisees (see 5:21, 30; 6:7; 11:53; 15:2), and that seems to be the case here. Pharisees believed in the resurrection of the dead while Sadducees did not, and this was a point of contention between them (see Acts 23:6–10). Some **scribes** who overheard Jesus' response to the Sadducees address Jesus as a religious **teacher** and tell him, **you have answered** the Sadducees **well**. As scribes who were also Pharisees, they would agree with Jesus' teaching about resurrection and be happy that he had refuted the Sadducees.

Scribes: See page 146
Pharisees: See page 143

40 **And they no longer dared to ask him anything.** Here **they** seems to refer not just to Sadducees but to everyone who was trying to trip up Jesus or "trap him in speech" (20:20). Jesus so skillfully met all challenges that no one **dared** to challenge him again, lest he publicly show them up. The next time Jesus is asked hostile questions, he will be under arrest (22:66–71).

Who Is the Son of David?
⁴¹ Then he said to them, "How do they claim that the Messiah is the Son of David? ⁴² For David himself in the Book of Psalms says:
'The Lord said to my lord,
"Sit at my right hand
⁴³   till I make your enemies your footstool."'
⁴⁴ "Now if David calls him 'lord,' how can he be his son?"
    Gospel parallels: Matt 22:41–46; Mark 12:35–37
    OT: Psalm 110:1
    NT: Luke 1:26–35; 2:11, 26; 3:22–31; 9:20

41 **Then he said to them:** Jesus is "teaching the people in the temple area and proclaiming the good news" (20:1). He has been challenged and questioned by various people (20:1–2, 20–22, 27–33), and he now poses a question of his own. He asks the crowd, **How do they claim that the Messiah is the Son of David?** By **they** Jesus might mean people in general, but some scribes are present (20:39) and Jesus might be specifically referring to them. Belief that God would send a **Messiah** to rescue his people had developed in the two centuries before Jesus, based on Scripture texts that promised that the dynasty of David would rule over God's people (2 Sam 7:8–16; Psalm 89:3–5; see also Isaiah 9:5–6; 11:1–10; Jer 23:5–6; Ezek 34:22–24; 37:24–25; Micah 5:1–3). As "scholars of the law" (11:52), scribes would be familiar with these Scripture passages. Even though there were different views of what the Messiah would do, scribes

BACKGROUND: GOD'S NAME The English word "God" is the generic term for the Supreme Being. In addition to the equivalent generic Hebrew term for God, the Old Testament also uses the personal name for God, which in Hebrew is written with letters that correspond to the English letters YHWH. Biblical Hebrew was written largely without vowels, and thus it is impossible to be certain how this name was pronounced; it may have been pronounced "Yahweh." The Old Testament presents God revealing his name, *YHWH*, to Moses at the burning bush (Exod 3:15). Out of reverence, Jews in the time of Jesus, as still today, avoided saying the name of God; when they read Scripture aloud and came to the name *YHWH*, they substituted a Hebrew word for "Lord." When the Hebrew Scriptures were translated into Greek, the Greek word for Lord was used to translate *YHWH*. The Old Testament of the New American Bible uses the word "Lᴏʀᴅ" (printed with large and small capitals), and on rare occasions "Gᴏᴅ," to stand for the Hebrew *YHWH*.

would generally agree that he would be **the Son of David**—a descendant of David. Yet, Jesus asks, why do they make this claim? How is it that they think that the Messiah will be descended from David?

Scribes: See page 146
Messiah, Christ: See page 257
Son of David: See page 493

42 Some in Jesus' audience probably want to protest, "Well of course he will be a descendant of David—that's what Scripture says!" But before they can respond to his question, Jesus invokes Scripture to raise a difficulty: **For David himself in the Book of Psalms says: "The Lord said to my lord, / 'Sit at my right hand.' "** In the **Book of Psalms**, seventy-three psalms are attributed to David; Psalm 110 is one of them (this is indicated in the heading which the New American Bible includes as part of verse 1). Jesus accepts the traditional attribution of Psalm 110 to David, which means that **David himself** is the one saying, **The Lord said to my lord**. The first **Lord** mentioned is the Lord God. In verses 1, 2, and 4, Psalm 110 uses the Hebrew word *YHWH*, the personal name for God. Out of reverence, Jews did not speak God's name but pronounced a Hebrew word for "Lord" when they came to *YHWH* in Scripture. Jesus interprets the second **lord** mentioned in Psalm 110 to be the Messiah. Thus David is saying, **The Lord** God **said to my lord** the Messiah, **"Sit at my right hand."** God invites the Messiah to sit at his **right hand**, the place of honor and power.

Lord: See page 137

For reflection: What does it mean for me that Jesus is my Lord?

> *A psalm of David.*
> *The LORD says to you, my lord:*
> *"Take your throne at my right hand,*
> *while I make your enemies your footstool."*
>
> Psalm 110:1

43 Jesus quotes the remainder of the psalm verse: **till I make your enemies your footstool**. The Messiah is to sit at the right hand of God until God brings the **enemies** of the Messiah into abject submission to him, symbolized by their lying prostrate as his **footstool**.

44 Jesus points out the difficulty of claiming that the Messiah is the Son of David in light of what David says in Psalm 110: **Now if David calls him "lord," how can he be his son?** While a son might address his father as **lord** (which can also be translated as a respectful "sir"—13:8; 14:22; 19:16, 18, 20, 25), a father would never address his son as **lord.** A **lord** is someone with authority; fathers are superior to their sons and have authority over them, not the other way around. But in Psalm 110 **David calls** the Messiah **"lord,"** so **how can** the Messiah **be his son?** As David's **lord,** the Messiah is someone who is superior to David. In what sense then is the Messiah **his son?**

Luke does not recount anyone being able to offer an explanation of **how** the Messiah is both a descendant of David and yet superior to him. In its immediate context in Luke's Gospel, Jesus' question provides another example of why "they no longer dared to ask him anything" (20:40): his critics recognize that his perceptive knowledge of Scripture means that they will be shamed in any debate with him.

Readers of Luke's Gospel have been given the information they need to answer Jesus' question. They know that Jesus is the Messiah (2:11, 26; 9:20). Because Jesus' legal father, Joseph, is "of the house and family of David" (2:4), so is Jesus; Luke traced Jesus' genealogy through Joseph (3:23) back to David (3:31). The angel Gabriel told Mary, "Behold, you will conceive in your womb and bear a son, and you shall name him Jesus. He will be great and will be called Son of the Most High, and the Lord God will give him the throne of David his father" (1:31–32). Jesus is not only a descendant of David who will be given his throne; he is also the "Son of the Most High." Through the power of the Holy Spirit, the Messiah born into the house of David is "the Son of God" (1:35), and therefore David must acknowledge him as his **lord.**

For reflection: Jesus is Son of David and Son of God. How well am I able to accept both his full humanity and his full divinity?

Beware of Exalting Oneself and Victimizing Others
⁴⁵ **Then, within the hearing of all the people, he said to [his] disciples,** ⁴⁶ **"Be on guard against the scribes, who like to go around in long robes and love greetings in marketplaces, seats of honor in**

synagogues, and places of honor at banquets. ⁴⁷ They devour the houses of widows and, as a pretext, recite lengthy prayers. They will receive a very severe condemnation."

Gospel parallels: Matt 23:6–7; Mark 12:38–40

NT: Luke 11:37–54; 14:7–14

45 **Then, within the hearing of all the people:** Jesus is "teaching the people in the temple area and proclaiming the good news" (20:1). **He said to [his] disciples,** who are present but have not been heard from since his entry into Jerusalem (19:37–40). While Jesus addresses his words specifically to his **disciples,** he does so **within the hearing of all the people** because he wants them to hear what he has to say as well. Some scribes may be present in the crowd (20:39).

Disciple: See page 149

46 Jesus tells his disciples, **Be on guard against the scribes**. The role of the **scribes** to whom Jesus refers was to help people understand God's laws and put them into practice (they are also called "scholars of the law" by Luke—14:3). Jesus has criticized them for hindering rather than helping people to follow God's way (11:46). The sense of **be on guard against** them is not only, be wary of them, but also, do not follow their example. Jesus characterizes the scribes he is speaking about as those **who like to go around in long robes**. Most robes or outer garments were long; Jesus is referring to something distinctive about these **long robes** that would draw the notice of others. These scribes **like to go around** in distinctive garb, strutting around in them so as to be seen. Clothing proclaimed social status (7:25; 15:22; 16:19); these scribes made sure others were aware of their claim to elevated status. They **love greetings in marketplaces**—not just friendly hellos but elaborate respects paid to them because they are scribes. **Marketplaces** were commercial and social centers where people crossed paths; these scribes **love** to be publicly honored. They love **seats of honor in synagogues**: they love to sit in prominent places where they will be noticed when people gather to hear Scripture read and to pray. Similarly, they love **places of honor at banquets**, at the head table next to the host, reserved for those of high status. Jesus previously criticized Pharisees for loving such honors (11:43–44) and advised taking the lowest place at banquets (14:7–11).

Now he warns his disciples not to imitate scribes who want to be the center of attention and exalt themselves before others.

Scribes: See page 146

Synagogue: See page 115

Banquets: See page 386

For reflection: What do I do to be the center of attention? To gain public recognition? Do I make sure that I get credit for my accomplishments?

47 **They devour the houses of widows.** In the society of the time, **widows** without sons to support them and safeguard their rights were often poor and powerless. Jesus does not specify how scribes **devour the houses of widows**, but the context suggests that they in some way use their status as scribes to take advantage of vulnerable women. Jesus has taught that the poor and vulnerable are to be assisted (11:41; 12:33; 14:12–14; 18:22; 19:8–9); he certainly does not want his disciples to follow the example of those who prey on the helpless. Not only do they take advantage of widows; **as a pretext**, they **recite lengthy prayers**. The word translated **as a pretext** may have the sense, "for appearance's sake." **Lengthy prayers** has the connotation of ostentatious prayer, recited publicly. The scribes Jesus criticizes put on a show of religiosity, perhaps to induce widows to trust them and make it easier for them to gain control of their property. Their pride, hypocrisy, and use of their status to defraud others will not go unpunished: **They will receive a very severe condemnation** by God.

Jesus points out faults of some scribes not only to bring them to repentance, if they are present in the crowd, but especially to warn his disciples (verse 45) not to succumb to the same pitfalls. It is an occupational hazard for anyone in a religious position or ministry to use his or her status for his or her own benefit. Jesus wants his disciples to shun all self-aggrandizement; they are not to pursue prestige or take advantage of others to benefit themselves.

For reflection: When have I used my status and gifts for my own benefit? How might I more selflessly serve others?

CHAPTER 21

ORIENTATION: *Jesus is teaching in a Temple courtyard (19:47; 20:1). His last words were addressed to his disciples within the hearing of a larger audience (20:45), and this continues to be the setting.*

A Poor Widow's Contribution

¹ **When he looked up he saw some wealthy people putting their offerings into the treasury ² and he noticed a poor widow putting in two small coins. ³ He said, "I tell you truly, this poor widow put in more than all the rest; ⁴ for those others have all made offerings from their surplus wealth, but she, from her poverty, has offered her whole livelihood."**

Gospel parallels: Mark 12:41–44

NT: Luke 20:45–47; 21:5–6

1   **When he looked up**: teachers normally sat while teaching. Jesus **looked up and he saw some wealthy people putting their offerings into the treasury**. There were receptacles in a Temple courtyard for voluntary **offerings** for the upkeep and adornment of the Temple; Luke refers to these receptacles as the Temple's **treasury**. Some offerings were being made by **wealthy people**; the Greek text of Luke's Gospel puts emphasis on the word **wealthy**.

2   Jesus also **noticed a poor widow putting in two small coins**. The Greek word used here for **coins** referred to the smallest and least valuable coin in circulation in Palestine at the time. The **widow** who donates them is **poor**, and her donation would not seem to amount to much compared with what those who are wealthy give.

3   **He said** to those around him, **I tell you truly, this poor widow put in more than all the rest**. The **widow** is again characterized as **poor**, this time with the word used for those who are destitute. Jesus solemnly proclaims—**I tell you truly**—that the poor widow **put in more than all the rest**: her two tiny coins were **more** than everyone else gave, including the wealthy (verse 1). This is a startling pronouncement. Whoever

was in charge of tallying up the donations to the Temple that day would probably have calculated the relative value of her offering quite differently.

4 Jesus explains his startling pronouncement: **for those others have all made offerings from their surplus wealth**. The word translated **surplus wealth** has the connotation of excess abundance, of being far more than enough. The chief tax collector Zacchaeus was a wealthy man (19:2), and he remained wealthy even after he gave half of his possessions to the poor (19:8): Zacchaeus donated from his surplus wealth, as did **all** those, other than the widow, who **made offerings** to the Temple that day. Jesus contrasts the poor widow's offering with those of the wealthy: **But she, from her poverty, has offered her whole livelihood**. The word translated **poverty** means deficiency, lack: while **others** donated from their surplus, she donated from her insufficiency. She **offered her whole livelihood**: the word for **livelihood** literally means "life," and by extension the means of sustaining life. She could have kept one of her two coins for herself and still matched Zacchaeus' standard for generosity, but she put in all the means that she had to live on. As Jesus evaluates her offering, she "put in more than all the rest" (verse 3) because she gave her whole life while they gave from their leftovers. The true measure of generosity is not what one gives but what one retains for oneself.

> *For reflection: To what extent does God get just my leftovers? Or am I putting all my possessions and my entire life in his hands?*

If the poor widow's offering is considered in itself, she can serve as a model for disciples of Jesus. She is among those who are blessed and fortunate because they are poor and, consequently, are heirs to the kingdom of heaven (6:20). Disciples of Jesus are to trust their Father in heaven to care for them (12:22–34), as she has put her survival in the hands of God. They are to be detached from money and possessions (14:33), as she is detached; they are to be generous (12:33; 18:22), as she is.

> *For reflection: What does the poor widow's example mean for me?*

If the poor widow's offering is considered in its context in Luke's Gospel, there may be another level of significance. Jesus has just criticized scribes who "devour the houses of widows and, as a pretext, recite lengthy prayers" (20:47). Might he have been referring to scribes who exhorted even those who were very poor to donate generously to the Temple, backing up their exhortations with a pretense of piety? Jesus will go on to react to the Temple's being "adorned with costly stones and votive offerings," saying that "the days will come when there will not be left a stone upon another stone" (21:5–6). It is unlikely that Jesus looked favorably upon the poor being exploited and their means devoured to adorn an already extravagant building whose days were numbered. While Jesus may praise the poor widow's great generosity and trust in God, he may also lament her exploitation by religious leaders.

Jesus Foretells the Destruction of the Temple
⁵ While some people were speaking about how the temple was adorned with costly stones and votive offerings, he said, ⁶ "All that you see here—the days will come when there will not be left a stone upon another stone that will not be thrown down."
> Gospel parallels: Matt 24:1–2; Mark 13:1–2
> NT: Luke 13:34–35; 19:42–44

5   **While some people were speaking**: those **speaking** may be Jesus' disciples or some in the crowd gathered in a Temple courtyard to listen to his teachings (see 20:45; 21:38). They are impressed by **how the temple was adorned with costly stones and votive offerings**. In 20 B.C., Herod the Great began a massive reconstruction project, beautifying the Temple and doubling the size of its courtyards. Herod sheathed the Temple exterior with white marble and gold plating. According to the first-century Jewish historian Josephus, the columns in the colonnades surrounding the Temple complex were thirty-seven feet high, each cut from a single block of white marble—**costly stones** indeed! Wealthy individuals made donations of **votive offerings**; Josephus mentions a man named Alexander who donated gold and silver plating for the tall

door that was the entrance to the Court of the Women. Herod intended his expanded and refurbished Temple complex to be the most magnificent temple in the Roman world, and by all accounts he succeeded. The first-century Roman historian Tacitus wrote that the Temple was "immensely opulent." For Jews, not only was the Temple the place of God's special presence where sacrificial offerings could be made; it was also the most impressive building they would ever see. No wonder those around Jesus remark on **how the temple was adorned with costly stones and votive offerings**.

Jesus is not impressed by such ostentation and knows what will become of it. **He said,**

6 **All that you see here**—the Temple itself, the colonnaded halls, everything—**the days will come when there will not be left a stone upon another stone that will not be thrown down**. Jesus prophesies the total destruction of the Temple. **The days will come:** there will be a time when there is nothing left but rubble. Jesus earlier foretold of Jerusalem, "Your house will be abandoned" (13:35); it is clear now that destruction and abandonment will befall even the house of God. Jesus lamented the fate of Jerusalem because "you did not recognize the time of your visitation"; it will be besieged and conquered, and "they will not leave one stone upon another within you" (19:41–44). In putting down a Jewish revolt, Roman armies will besiege and conquer Jerusalem and destroy the Temple in A.D. 70.

Jesus' foretelling of the Temple's destruction is a shocking pronouncement. There had been a Temple, a house of God, in Jerusalem since the time of Solomon a millennium earlier, interrupted only by the seventy years it lay in ruins after the Babylonian conquest of 586 B.C. The destruction of the Temple would mean the end of Jewish religious life centered on sacrificial worship of God at the Temple. It would be a world coming to an end.

For reflection: If I had been one of Jesus' disciples present that day, how would I have reacted to Jesus' pronouncement?

ORIENTATION: *When Jesus is asked when the Temple will be destroyed (21:7), he responds by speaking of this and of other events that will happen in the future (21:8–36). His followers will be persecuted; Jerusalem will be destroyed; he will come in glory. He begins by warning his disciples not to be misled.*

Do Not Be Deceived or Led Astray or Terrified!

⁷ Then they asked him, "Teacher, when will this happen? And what sign will there be when all these things are about to happen?" ⁸ He answered, "See that you not be deceived, for many will come in my name, saying, 'I am he,' and 'The time has come.' Do not follow them! ⁹ When you hear of wars and insurrections, do not be terrified; for such things must happen first, but it will not immediately be the end." ¹⁰ Then he said to them, "Nation will rise against nation, and kingdom against kingdom. ¹¹ There will be powerful earthquakes, famines, and plagues from place to place; and awesome sights and mighty signs will come from the sky."

Gospel parallels: Matt 24:3–8; Mark 13:3–8

OT: Isaiah 19:2

BACKGROUND: REVELATIONS OF THE END A number of books written in the centuries around the time of Jesus employed a distinctive type of writing, called apocalyptic, to convey a vision of God triumphing over evil. Two of these books are Daniel, in the Old Testament, and Revelation, in the New Testament; there were similar writings that were not accepted as inspired Scripture. The book of Revelation's Greek title is *Apokalypsis,* a word that means "an uncovering" or "a revelation." This Greek word is the source of the name for writings of this sort, which unveil what is hidden, characteristically employing symbols and imagery to do so. This type of writing grew out of Old Testament prophecies that described a future quite different from the present (Isaiah 24–27; 34–35; 56–66; Ezek 38–39; Joel 3–4; Zech 9–14; Mal 3). Apocalyptic writings often contain an account of a revelation given to a human being by an angel, telling what is going to happen in the future by means of symbolic accounts of events on earth and in heaven. This type of writing flowered in difficult times, when evil seemed to be winning out and the only hope was for God's intervention. Different books described different futures, but they commonly spoke of God judging and destroying the wicked, transforming this world, and beginning a new age. Those who remained faithful to God would be rewarded in an afterlife. *Related topics: The age to come (page 487), Jewish expectations at the time of Jesus (page 69), Nonbiblical writings (page 342).*

NT: Luke 21:5–6

7 **Then they asked him**: Jesus has been speaking to his disciples in the hearing of a crowd (20:45), making it unclear whether **they** are disciples or others. He foretold the destruction of the Temple (21:5–6) and is asked, **Teacher, when will this happen?** Until now, Jesus has not been addressed as **Teacher** by his disciples in the Gospel of Luke, but perhaps they do so here, wanting to be taught by him about what lies ahead (some of his response will clearly be directed to them—21:12–19). **When will this happen**: when will the days come when there will not be left one stone of the Temple upon another? **And what sign will there be when all these things are about to happen?** What warning **sign** will announce that the destruction of the Temple and the events that accompany it **are about to happen?**

8 **He answered, "See that you not be deceived."** Jesus does not immediately address the question of when the Temple will be destroyed. Instead he warns those listening against being **deceived** and misled by events that are going to occur. He tells them that they must be on their guard because **many will come in my name**—will come using his name and claiming that they speak for him. Jesus has in mind the period between his "being taken up" (9:51) and his coming in glory (9:26; 12:40; 17:24–30; 18:8). Some will say **I am he,** apparently claiming to be Jesus returned. They will say, **the time has come**—the end is at hand. Jesus tells his disciples and those listening, **Do not follow them!** Do not be taken in by their claims; do not go along with them.

For reflection: How do I discern whether people are truly speaking for Jesus today when they claim to do so?

9 **When you hear of wars and insurrections**: Jesus knows that there will be **wars** and **insurrections**. One of the **insurrections** that many of his disciples will certainly **hear of** will be the Jewish revolt against Roman rule that will begin in A.D. 66. Jesus tells them, **do not be terrified** by reports of wars and uprisings, **for such things must happen first, but it will not immediately be the end**. By **the end** Jesus means the end of the present age and the beginning of the age to come (see 18:30;

20:35). There were various speculations at the time of Jesus, fed by writings that presented revelations or scenarios of the end, about how God would bring the present age to an end. Some thought that the end of this age would be marked by great upheavals and wars. Jesus warns that wars and insurrections are not to be taken as signs that **the end** is at hand. They **must happen first**: here **must** conveys the point that God is ultimately in charge of human history and even evils like wars cannot derail his plans. (The book of Revelation uses "must" in the same way when it presents itself as a revelation of "what must happen soon"—Rev 1:1.) Consequently, Jesus' disciples should **not be terrified** by wars and revolts, as dreadful as they might be; his disciples are in the hands of God. Nor should they interpret wars and insurrections as indications that "the time has come" (verse 8): **it will not immediately be the end**.

The age to come: See page 487

10 **Then he said to them**, expanding on what he has just said, **Nation will rise against nation, and kingdom against kingdom**. The word **nation** means a people; one people will fight against another people. **Kingdom against kingdom** echoes a prophecy of Isaiah that speaks of escalating violence: "Brother will war against brother, / Neighbor against neighbor, / city against city, kingdom against kingdom" (Isaiah 19:2). The interval between Jesus' being taken up and his coming in glory will be marred by violence and wars, just as all human history is marred by violence and wars.

11 **There will be powerful earthquakes, famines, and plagues from place to place.** Along with human disasters such as wars, there will be natural disasters. **Earthquakes, famines,** and **plagues** have occurred in various places since the dawn of history and will continue to occur until the end of the age. (In Acts, Luke will write of a famine and an earthquake occurring—Acts 11:28; 16:26.) There will be **awesome sights and mighty signs will come from the sky**. The **awesome sights** may be eclipses of the sun or of the moon, or they may be meteorites, which were then thought to be stars falling from the sky. The word translated **sky** can also be translated "heaven"; since these **awesome sights** took place in God's heavenly domain, they were taken to be cosmic **signs** that God was doing, or about to do, something. Jesus speaks of them, however, as

557

things that may occur without being signs that the end is at hand. His disciples are to take care that they are not deceived (verse 8), either by those claiming that the end is at hand or by wars or natural disasters or sights in the sky. All these things will occur, "But it will not immediately be the end" (verse 9).

Cosmic signs: See page 565

Jesus was asked when the Temple will be destroyed and what warning sign will there be, and he will address the destruction of Jerusalem (21:20–24). But he prefaces what he will say with some "do nots" for his disciples: do not be deceived, do not be led astray, do not be terrified. No matter what happens, even in the midst of wars and tumult, keep calm and stay the course of discipleship.

For reflection: To what extent am I able to read or watch the news with a calm confidence that God is ultimately in charge? That he will bring me safely to himself?

The Coming Persecution

12 "Before all this happens, however, they will seize and persecute you, they will hand you over to the synagogues and to prisons, and they will have you led before kings and governors because of my name. 13 It will lead to your giving testimony. 14 Remember, you are not to prepare your defense beforehand, 15 for I myself shall give you a wisdom in speaking that all your adversaries will be powerless to resist or refute. 16 You will even be handed over by parents, brothers, relatives, and friends, and they will put some of you to death. 17 You will be hated by all because of my name, 18 but not a hair on your head will be destroyed. 19 By your perseverance you will secure your lives."

Gospel parallels: Matt 10:17–22; 24:9–13; Mark 13:9–13
NT: Luke 6:22–23; 12:11–12, 51–53; 21:5–11; John 16:2

12 Jesus has just said that wars and natural disasters are not signs that the end of the age is at hand (21:8–11). **Before all this happens, however**—even before there are wars and disasters—**they will seize and**

persecute you. It will become clear that he is speaking to his disciples and that they will be seized and persecuted precisely because they are his disciples (see also 6:22–23). Jesus warns them that **they will hand you over to the synagogues and to prisons, and they will have you led before kings and governors**. Jesus' disciples will face persecution both by religious authorities (those in charge of **synagogues**) and by civil authorities (**kings** and **governors**). Luke will recount instances in Acts of followers of Jesus being seized and interrogated or persecuted by religious authorities (Acts 4:1–21; 5:17–41; 7:58—8:3) and by Jewish kings and Roman governors (12:1–4; 23:33—26:32). Jesus tells his disciples that they will be persecuted **because of my name**—because of their identification with him, their allegiance to him, their service of him. There are about thirty references to the **name** of Jesus in Acts. Peter and John are taken into custody for proclaiming Jesus and are ordered "not to speak or teach at all in the name of Jesus" (Acts 4:18). They persist in their preaching and are arrested a second time, flogged, and are ordered again "to stop speaking in the name of Jesus" (5:40). They go away "rejoicing that they had been found worthy to suffer dishonor for the sake of the name" (5:41). When the risen Jesus sends Ananias to the blinded Saul, he tells him "this man is a chosen instrument of mine to carry my name before Gentiles, kings, and Israelites, and I will show him what he will have to suffer for my name" (Acts 9:15–16). Before undergoing his own suffering and death, Jesus warns his disciples that they may have to suffer **because of my name**.

Synagogue: See page 115

For reflection: What have I suffered because of the name of Jesus—because I am a Christian, because I proclaim him and his message?

13 Jesus tells his disciples to regard their being arrested as an opportunity to take advantage of: **It will lead to your giving testimony**—testimony to him before religious and civil authorities. In Acts, Luke will provide numerous examples of the testimony given by Jesus' followers. As the climax of his speech on Pentecost, Peter will proclaim, "Let the whole house of Israel know for certain that God has made him both Lord and Messiah, this Jesus whom you crucified" (Acts 2:36; see also Acts 2:22–35; 3:12–26; 4:8–12, 33; 5:30–32; 10:34–43; 13:23–41).

14 **Remember, you are not to prepare your defense beforehand**: Luke's sentence in Greek contains a "therefore," and the words translated **remember** are literally, "put in your hearts." Jesus' disciples will be hauled before authorities and have opportunities to bear witness to him; therefore, they are to take to heart his injunction, **you are not to prepare your defense beforehand**. The word translated **prepare** specifically means to practice what one will say, rehearsing a memorized speech. Normally those hauled into court would prepare their **defense** in advance, but Jesus' disciples are not to do so.

15 Jesus tells his disciples that they are not to prepare their defense beforehand, **for I myself shall give you a wisdom in speaking**. Luke's Greek puts an emphasis on **I myself**. The disciples are not to rely on their own ideas and words but are to rely on Jesus to give them **a wisdom in speaking** at the moment when it is needed. He previously told his disciples, "When they take you before synagogues and before rulers and authorities, do not worry about how or what your defense will be or about what you are to say. For the holy Spirit will teach you at that moment what you should say" (12:11–12). Jesus can speak of either himself or the Holy Spirit as the one providing his followers with what they are to say, because the divine assistance they receive can be attributed equally to the Holy Spirit or to the risen Jesus (see Rom 8:10–11). The help they receive will be so effective **that all** their **adversaries will be powerless to resist or refute** what they say. Luke recounts in Acts how religious leaders were "amazed" by the boldness of Peter and John in their testimony, whom they took to be "uneducated, ordinary men"; the leaders "could say nothing in reply" (Acts 4:13–14). On another occasion, opponents "debated with Stephen, but they could not withstand the wisdom and the spirit with which he spoke" (Acts 6:9–10).

> *For reflection: When have I been aware of being given the right words to bear witness to Jesus?*

16 Being given irrefutable wisdom in testifying will not mean that followers of Jesus will be immune to rejection and suffering. Jesus tells his disciples, **You will even be handed over by parents, brothers, relatives, and friends**. In context, **handed over** means handed over to the authorities

who are persecuting followers of Jesus (verse 12). One is normally safe with family and friends, but those closest to Jesus' disciples will betray them. Jesus asked his followers to give their allegiance to him rather than to their families (9:59–62; 14:26; 18:29), realizing that this could result in painful divisions (12:51–53). When persecutions come, those **parents, brothers, relatives, and friends** who are alienated from Jesus' disciples may turn them over to persecutors, perhaps to escape persecution themselves. **And they will put some of you to death**: some of Jesus' followers will die in persecutions. In Acts, Luke recounts the execution of Stephen (Acts 7:54–60) and of James the brother of John (Acts 12:1–2).

17 **You will be hated by all because of my name.** Again, **because of my name** means because of being identified with Jesus and serving him (see verse 12). **All** is best understood to mean people in general rather than every single person. Those who became followers of Jesus were generally scorned in the Roman world because they followed their own way of life and did not worship the Roman gods. In Acts, Luke will recount Paul reaching Rome toward the end of his life and being told that Christians are a "sect" that is "denounced everywhere" (Acts 28:22). The first-century Roman historian Tacitus portrayed Christians as easy targets for Emperor Nero's persecution in the mid-60s because they were so widely despised.

18 Despite the persecution and even martyrdom that his followers will face, Jesus promises them that **not a hair on your head will be destroyed**, invoking a proverbial assurance of safety (see 12:7; 1 Sam 14:45; 2 Sam 14:11; 1 Kings 1:52; Acts 27:34). While some of Jesus' followers will experience extraordinary deliverance from persecution and danger (Acts 12:3–11; 16:19–34; 28:3–6), some will be put to death (verse 16). Jesus' assurance is therefore best understood as a promise of eternal life. He told his disciples, "Do not be afraid of those who kill the body but after that can do no more" (12:4); persecutors cannot deprive them of eternal life. His followers will be brought safely through the storms of this life into everlasting life and need not fear even death itself.

For reflection: What do Jesus' words of assurance mean to me personally?

19 **By your perseverance you will secure your lives.** Jesus has spoken before about the need for **perseverance**—steadfast endurance. In his explanation of the parable of the seed, the seed that fell on rich soil "are the ones who, when they have heard the word, embrace it with a generous and good heart, and bear fruit through perseverance" (8:15; see also 18:1–8). In its context here, **perseverance** means remaining steadfast despite persecution. The word translated **secure** literally means to gain or acquire; Jesus is promising that those who persevere will receive eternal life in the "resurrection of the righteous" (14:14). Jesus taught, "Whoever wishes to save his life will lose it, but whoever loses his life for my sake will save it" (9:24). His disciples may lose their lives because they bear witness to him during a persecution (verses 12–16), but they will thereby save their lives eternally (see 12:8).

For reflection: What do Jesus' words ask of me? What do Jesus' words promise me?

The Destruction of Jerusalem
²⁰ **"When you see Jerusalem surrounded by armies, know that its desolation is at hand. ²¹ Then those in Judea must flee to the mountains. Let those within the city escape from it, and let those in the countryside not enter the city, ²² for these days are the time of punishment when all the scriptures are fulfilled. ²³ Woe to pregnant women and nursing mothers in those days, for a terrible calamity will come upon the earth and a wrathful judgment upon this people. ²⁴ They will fall by the edge of the sword and be taken as captives to all the Gentiles; and Jerusalem will be trampled underfoot by the Gentiles until the times of the Gentiles are fulfilled."**

Gospel parallels: Matt 24:15–22; Mark 13:14–20
OT: Deut 28:64; Sirach 28:18; Hosea 9:7
NT: Luke 13:34–35; 19:41–44; 21:5–7; 23:27–31

20 After Jesus foretold the destruction of the Temple, he was asked when it would happen and what sign would announce it (21:5–7). He did not immediately address these questions, but instead he warned against being misled by purported signs that the end was at hand (21:8–11) and

he told his disciples that they would be persecuted (21:12–19). Now Jesus addresses the destruction of Jerusalem, which will include the destruction of the Temple: **When you see Jerusalem surrounded by armies, know that its desolation is at hand.** During wars, **armies** besieged walled cities by surrounding them, cutting off food supplies. Jesus previously warned Jerusalem that "the days are coming upon you when your enemies will raise a palisade against you; they will encircle you and hem you in on all sides" (19:43). When the people of Jerusalem see the city **surrounded by armies**, they should realize that the **desolation** or devastation of the city **is at hand.** Jesus does not say when this will happen, but an army laying siege to the city will be a sign that it is about to be destroyed. Romans will lay siege to Jerusalem in A.D. 70 in order to put down a Jewish revolt against Roman rule—one of the "wars and insurrections" Jesus alluded to earlier (21:9–10).

Jerusalem: See page 516

21 **Then those in Judea must flee to the mountains.** When an enemy army arrives, it is time for civilians to get out of the way. **Judea** was the region surrounding Jerusalem. **Mountains** or hills provided hiding places where people could escape conflict (1 Sam 26:1; 1 Macc 2:28; 2 Macc 5:27). **Let those within the city escape from it, and let those in the countryside not enter the city.** Normally, a walled city like Jerusalem provided safety for its inhabitants and was a place where those living outside the city could take refuge, but the opposite will be true when Jerusalem is besieged. **Those** living **within the city** should **escape from it** while they have the chance, and **those** living **in the countryside** should **not enter** it, lest they perish. Several ancient sources speak of Christians who lived in Jerusalem at the time of the Jewish revolt fleeing the city to take refuge in Pella, a city east of the Jordan River.

Judea: See page 40

22 Jesus explains that **these days are the time of punishment when all the scriptures are fulfilled.** By **these days** Jesus means the period when Jerusalem is besieged and destroyed, and he characterizes this period as the time when **all the scriptures are fulfilled.** Jesus apparently has in mind Scripture passages that speak of God punishing the defiance and disobedience of his people by destroying their cities and sending them

563

into exile (see Lev 26:27–33; Deut 28:15, 49–57, 63–68; 1 Kings 9:6–9; Jer 6:1–8; 7:30–34; 17:27; 19:10–15; 22:5; Micah 3:9–12). While these **scriptures** were fulfilled by the Babylonian destruction of Jerusalem in 586 B.C., Jesus applies them to the coming Roman devastation of the city. Just as the earlier destruction of Jerusalem was a **punishment** for or consequence of not walking in the way of God, so will be its coming destruction. Jerusalem has not recognized the time of its visitation (19:44) and is following a path to insurrection and war rather than to peace (19:42). Jesus borrows the expression **time of punishment**—literally, "days of punishment"—from the prophet Hosea (Hosea 9:7) and he will go on to echo several other **scriptures** as signals that what will befall Jerusalem is not simply an accident of history but a fulfillment of God's will as discerned in Scripture.

23 Jesus wept over Jerusalem (19:41), and he is still filled with compassion for its people (see also 13:34–35; 23:27–31). He exclaims, **Woe to pregnant women and nursing mothers in those days**. Invading armies usually treated those they conquered quite cruelly, and **pregnant women** and **nursing mothers** were among the most vulnerable (see 1 Macc 1:60–61; Amos 1:13). They will be in a woeful and unfortunate situation in the **days** when Jerusalem is besieged, **for a terrible calamity will come upon the earth**. The word translated **earth** can also mean land or territory (it is translated as "land" in the sense of territory at Acts 7:3–4), and that is its meaning here. **A terrible calamity** will come upon Judea and other Jewish areas, **and a wrathful judgment upon this people**— the Jewish people. The Greek word translated **wrathful judgment** is elsewhere translated as "wrath" (3:7) and refers to God's wrath against sin and sinners (see Rom 1:18; 2:5–8). Jesus sees the horrible destruction and great suffering that will take place during the Jewish revolt to be a consequence of not following God's ways.

Woes: See page 171

For reflection: What were the consequences for me when I did not follow God's ways? Am I doing anything now that deserves God's wrath?

24 **They will fall by the edge of the sword and be taken as captives to all the Gentiles**: when the terrible calamity comes upon Jerusalem,

some within the city will be killed and others taken away as prisoners of war. Josephus reports that a great many died when Jerusalem fell to the Roman army, and that some Jews were taken to Rome to be paraded as a conquered people while others were exiled to Egypt. In his description of what will happen—**fall by the edge of the sword** and **be taken as captives**—Jesus echoes Scripture passages (Deut 28:64; Sirach 28:18; see also Isaiah 3:25; 13:15; Jer 20:4; 21:7) to indicate that what will happen is in fulfillment of the Scriptures (verse 21). **Jerusalem will be trampled underfoot by the Gentiles**: Jesus invokes the image of a victorious army swarming through a conquered city, trampling it (see 1 Macc 3:51; 4:60; Isaiah 63:18). His final words—**until the times of the Gentiles are fulfilled**—are cryptic. Some scholars believe that they refer to the period during which the Gospel is preached to Gentiles, an interpretation suggested by chapter 11 of Paul's letter to the Romans: "A hardening has come upon Israel in part, until the full number of the Gentiles comes in" (Rom 11:25). Jesus' words, in any case, indicate that the end of the age (see 21:9) will not follow immediately upon the destruction of Jerusalem; **the times of the Gentiles** must first be **fulfilled**. Jesus does not say how

---

BACKGROUND: COSMIC SIGNS Ancient conceptions of the universe led people to believe that events observed in the heavens carried significance for the unfolding of God's plans on earth. The universe was sometimes thought to consist of the earth under the dome of the sky (Gen 1:6–9), with sun, moon, and stars set in this dome (Gen 1:14–18), and God's dwelling was imagined to be in or above the sky (Gen 28:12; Deut 26:15; 1 Kings 8:30; 2 Macc 3:39—the Hebrew and Greek words for sky also mean "heaven"), although the heavens could not contain him (1 Kings 8:27). Stars looked small—small enough to fall from the sky as meteorites. Eclipses of the sun were known to occur. Eclipses of the moon can give it a deep red or copper hue, due to the refraction of its light by the earth's atmosphere; Joel spoke of the sun being "turned to darkness, / and the moon to blood" (Joel 3:4). Since these events happened in God's heavenly domain, they were taken as signs of God's action. Furthermore, when the prophets announced that God was going to act, as on a "day of the Lord," they sometimes used cosmic upheavals as symbolic images for God's acting (Isaiah 13:9–10; Joel 2:10–11; 3:3–4). At the time of Jesus, cosmic imagery was used to indicate that God was acting in some very significant way, but did not mean that the physical universe was coming to an end. *Related topic: The day of the Lord (page 91).*

long these **times** will last but goes on to speak of what will happen when they come to an end (21:25–28).

The Coming of the Son of Man

²⁵ **"There will be signs in the sun, the moon, and the stars, and on earth nations will be in dismay, perplexed by the roaring of the sea and the waves. ²⁶ People will die of fright in anticipation of what is coming upon the world, for the powers of the heavens will be shaken. ²⁷ And then they will see the Son of Man coming in a cloud with power and great glory. ²⁸ But when these signs begin to happen, stand erect and raise your heads because your redemption is at hand."**

Gospel parallels: Matt 24:29–31; Mark 13:24–27
OT: Dan 7:13–14; Haggai 2:6, 21
NT: Luke 9:26, 34–35; 12:40; 17:22–37; 18:8; Acts 1:9–11

25 After "the times of the Gentiles are fulfilled" (21:24), **there will be signs in the sun, the moon, and the stars**. Jesus does not describe the nature of these **signs,** but his listeners would have been familiar with prophecies that spoke of the sun being darkened, the moon turning red, and other unusual heavenly phenomena (Isaiah 13:10; 24:23; Ezek 32:7–8; Joel 2:10; 3:4; 4:15). Since heaven was God's domain, extraordinary occurrences in the heavens were taken as **signs** of God's activity, indicating that something momentous was at hand. There will be terrifying signs on earth as well as in the heavens: **and on earth nations will be in dismay, perplexed by the roaring of the sea and the waves**. Merchants and travelers feared storms at sea, whose chaotic ferocity could be tamed only by God (Psalm 65:8; 89:10; 107:23–32). When the heavenly and earthly signs appear, **nations**—the peoples of the earth—**will be in dismay, perplexed** by what is happening. The heavenly phenomena are signs that God is acting—but what is he doing?

The day of the Lord: See page 91

26 **People will die of fright in anticipation of what is coming upon the world**: the word translated **die** literally means "stop breathing": the cosmic chaos will take one's breath away. Isaiah speaks of similar **fright**

on the day of the Lord: "all hands fall helpless . . . / every man's heart melts in terror. / Pangs and sorrows take hold of them" (Isaiah 13:7–8). Jesus previously spoke of what was in store for Jerusalem (21:20–24); now he is talking about **what is coming upon the** entire inhabited **world**. People will be terrified, **for the powers of the heavens will be shaken**—shaken by God, producing the signs Jesus alluded to (verse 25). Jesus echoes a prophecy of Haggai in which God proclaims, "I will shake the heavens and the earth" (Haggai 2:6, 21). Clearly, something momentous is unfolding.

27 **And then they will see the Son of Man coming in a cloud with power and great glory**: in the wake of the cosmic signs all the people of the earth will see Jesus coming in great glory. Jesus echoes a passage in the book of Daniel in which Daniel sees "One like a son of man coming, / on the clouds of heaven" who is given everlasting dominion by God over all nations (Dan 7:13–14). Jesus has previously referred to himself as the Son of Man coming in glory (9:26) and has told his disciples his coming would be at a time they did not expect (12:40; see also 17:22–37; 18:8). By echoing the book of Daniel, Jesus indicates that he will come endowed with the **power** of God to have dominion over all people. He will come **in a cloud**: at his ascension, Jesus will be lifted up in a cloud and his disciples will be told that he will "return in the same way as you have seen him going into heaven" (Acts 1:9–11). Yet there may be a deeper significance to the **cloud**. A cloud manifested yet concealed God's presence and glory on Mount Sinai (Exod 19:9; 24:15–18), in the Temple (1 Kings 8:10–12), and at Jesus' transfiguration (9:34–35). Jesus will come "in his glory and in the glory of the Father" (9:26); he will come **in a cloud** that manifests yet conceals the glory of God imparted to Jesus.

Son of Man: See page 147

> As the visions during the night continued, I saw
> One like a son of man coming,
> on the clouds of heaven;
> When he reached the Ancient One
> and was presented before him,
> He received dominion, glory, and kingship;

> *nations and peoples of every language serve him.*
> *His dominion is an everlasting dominion*
> *that shall not be taken away,*
> *his kingship shall not be destroyed.*
>
> Dan 7:13–14

For reflection: What does it tell me about Jesus that he will come with power and great glory? In light of this, what should be my relationship with him now?

28 Jesus tells his disciples, **But when these signs begin to happen,** the cosmic signs that precede his coming (verses 25–26), **stand erect and raise your heads because your redemption is at hand**. To **stand erect** and to **raise your heads** is to assume a posture of vigor and confidence (see Judges 8:28; Job 10:15; Psalm 83:3), the opposite of cowering in fear. While others may "die in fright in anticipation of what is coming upon the world" (verse 26), Jesus' disciples should be filled with joyful anticipation. Jesus' coming will mean that their **redemption is at hand**. Here **redemption** is equivalent to salvation, being delivered from affliction and persecution (see 21:12–19) and receiving fullness of life. Before Jesus' birth, Zechariah prophesied about him, saying that God "has raised up a horn for our salvation" (1:69); after Jesus was born, Simeon saw him and proclaimed, "My eyes have seen your salvation" (2:30). The salvation they anticipated will be consummated when Jesus comes again. His followers should be eager for his coming, confident that he brings them **redemption** and eternal life.

For reflection: What are my expectations about Jesus' coming? What changes should I make in the way I live, so that if he were to come today, I could stand tall and confident to greet him?

The Coming of God's Kingdom
²⁹ **He taught them a lesson. "Consider the fig tree and all the other trees. ³⁰ When their buds burst open, you see for yourselves and know that summer is now near; ³¹ in the same way, when you see these things happening, know that the kingdom of God is near.**

³² **Amen, I say to you, this generation will not pass away until all these things have taken place.** ³³ **Heaven and earth will pass away, but my words will not pass away."**

Gospel parallels: Matt 24:32–35; Mark 13:28–31
NT: Luke 21:5–28, 36

29 **He taught them a lesson**—literally, told them a parable. Jesus asks his disciples to **consider the fig tree and all the other trees**. The **fig tree** loses its leaves during the winter, as do many **other trees**.

Parables: See page 217

30 **When their buds burst open**, as they do in the spring, **you see for yourselves** that fresh foliage is appearing **and know that summer is now near**. The appearance of new leaves on trees is a signal that summer is just around the corner.

31 Jesus draws the lesson of the parable or comparison he is making: **in the same way, when you see these things happening, know that the kingdom of God is near**. By **these things**, Jesus means the cosmic signs that announce his coming (21:25–26). Jesus inaugurated the **kingdom** or reign **of God** through his preaching and conquest of evil (4:43; 8:1, 10; 9:11; 11:20; 16:16; 17:21), but God's reign will only be established in its fullness and all evil vanquished at the dawning of the age to come (13:28–29; 14:15; 18:30; 20:35; 22:30). The signs that announce Jesus' coming (21:25–26) thus also indicate that **the kingdom of God is near**: Jesus will complete his mission of establishing God's reign when he comes in glory (21:27). When his disciples pray, "Your kingdom come" (11:2), they are asking as well for the coming of Jesus.

Kingdom of God: See page 381

For reflection: What do I have in mind when I pray, "Your kingdom come"?

32 **Amen, I say to you, this generation will not pass away until all these things have taken place.** If **this generation** means Jesus' generation, and if **all these things** refers to the signs that announce his coming (21:25–26), then Jesus is saying that he will come before his

569

contemporaries die off. However, it is unlikely that this is what Luke understood Jesus to be saying, for Luke wrote his Gospel a half-century after the time of Jesus, and Jesus' generation had pretty well passed away without Jesus coming. It is therefore best to understand **all these things** to refer to wars and insurrections, to persecutions, and to Jerusalem being destroyed (21:5–24), events that did occur within the lifetime of some who were alive at the time of Jesus. In favor of this interpretation is what Jesus will go on to say: he will tell his disciples to "pray that you have the strength to escape the tribulations that are imminent" (21:36), literally, "to escape *all these things* that are about to happen" (emphasis added). Disciples of Jesus can pray to escape from wars and persecution, but they have no need to be delivered from what will happen when Jesus comes (see 21:28).

33 Jesus concludes his teaching with a solemn assurance: **Heaven and earth will pass away, but my words will not pass away**. Here **heaven and earth** represent the entire universe, which will eventually **pass away.** Jesus taught that "it is easier for heaven and earth to pass away than for the smallest part of a letter of the law to become invalid" (16:17): God's word stands firm forever (Psalm 119:89, 160; Isaiah 40:8; Baruch 4:1). So too, Jesus' **words will not pass away,** for his word is the word of God (5:1). Jesus' **words** can refer to what he is teaching about what lies ahead (21:5–36), but it can also refer to all that he taught in the course of his ministry. Jesus assures his listeners that his words are authoritative and enduring, and should be taken to heart.

> For reflection: What does it tell me about Jesus that his words will outlast the universe? What are the implications for me of Jesus' words remaining forever?

Be Prepared for Jesus
34 **"Beware that your hearts do not become drowsy from carousing and drunkenness and the anxieties of daily life, and that day catch you by surprise 35 like a trap. For that day will assault everyone who lives on the face of the earth. 36 Be vigilant at all times and**

pray that you have the strength to escape the tribulations that are imminent and to stand before the Son of Man."

OT: Eccl 9:12

NT: Luke 8:14; 12:35–48; 17:26–30; 21:9–23

34 **Beware that your hearts do not become drowsy:** to **beware** is to be on guard (17:3), to be vigilant lest something happen. Jesus' disciples are to take care that their **hearts do not become drowsy.** In the biblical view, the **heart** is the seat of feeling, thinking, and willing. Those who are **drowsy are** oblivious to what is going on. This can result **from carousing and drunkenness.** While excess drinking is always wrong, Jesus' message is more pointed: his followers are not to be dulled by dissipation and drunkenness lest they be unprepared for his coming in glory (21:27). Jesus warned his disciples to be vigilant, "for at an hour you do not expect, the Son of Man will come" (12:35–40); he illustrated his warning with a parable about a servant who uses an apparent delay in his master's return "to eat and drink and get drunk" (12:45). Followers of Jesus must remain sober and alert. They must also beware lest they be distracted by **the anxieties of daily life.** In Jesus' interpretation of the parable of the seeds, some who accept the word of God "are choked by the anxieties and riches and pleasures of life" (8:14). Jesus assured his disciples that they did not need to be anxious about their needs, for their Father cares for them (12:22–31). He warns them not to be dulled by drunkenness or anxieties lest **that day catch you by surprise,** literally, come upon you suddenly. By **that day** Jesus means the day of his coming. He previously spoke of people going about life as usual on "the day the Son of Man is revealed" (17:26–30), oblivious to what was about to happen.

For reflection: What distracts me from wholehearted devotion to Jesus?

35 That day will come **like a trap** that ensnares those who do not expect it. Ecclesiastes uses the images of "fish taken in the fatal net, or birds trapped in the snare" as a comparison for something suddenly befalling a person (Eccl 9:12); Jesus uses similar imagery to convey the point that his coming will catch people by surprise. **For that day will assault**—literally, come upon—**everyone who lives on the face of the earth.** The **face of the earth** is a biblical idiom for the whole world (Exod 32:12;

Deut 7:6; Isaiah 23:17; Jer 25:26). Jesus' coming in glory will have world-wide consequences, affecting **everyone**. Jesus does not spell out what the consequences of his coming will be. However, he has spoken of God's final judgment (10:14; 11:31–32), and he has said that when he comes in glory he will be ashamed of those who have been ashamed of him (9:26; see also 12:8–9). It is therefore implicit that what will happen at his coming will determine the eternal destiny of every woman and man on earth, along with those who rise from the dead to face judgment (11:31–32; see also Acts 10:42; 17:31).

36 Jesus urges his disciples to be ever prepared for his coming: **Be vigilant at all times**. Since they do not know when he will come (12:40), they must be constantly **vigilant** and alert lest his arrival surprise them like a trap snapping shut (verses 34–35). He tells them to **pray that you have the strength to escape the tribulations that are imminent**. The words translated **the tribulations** are literally, "all these things," an expression Jesus used earlier (21:32), most likely to refer to wars, insurrections, and persecutions (21:9–24). They are about to happen and are even **imminent**. Jesus tells his disciples to **pray that you have the strength to escape** these upheavals, avoiding them or coming through them safely (see 21:21). They are also to pray that they are able **to stand before the Son of Man**. Everyone will stand before God and **the Son of Man** to face judgment, but here **stand** has the connotation of standing tall and unafraid. Jesus told his disciples to "stand erect and raise your heads" at his coming "because your redemption is at hand" (21:28). They are to pray that they will be able to stand before him unafraid because they will be receiving redemption and eternal life.

Son of Man: See page 147

For reflection: Am I ready to stand before Jesus? What do I need to pray for and do to get ready?

Jesus Continues to Teach in the Temple
37 During the day, Jesus was teaching in the temple area, but at night he would leave and stay at the place called the Mount of

Olives. **³⁸ And all the people would get up early each morning to listen to him in the temple area.**

NT: Matt 21:17; Mark 11:11, 19; Luke 19:47-48; 20:1; 22:1, 39; John 8:1-2

37 **During the day, Jesus was teaching in the temple area**: Jesus continues to spend his days teaching in a Temple courtyard (19:47; 20:1). Luke has devoted two chapters to Jesus' teachings and to controversies that arose there (Luke 20—21). **But at night he would leave and stay at the place called the Mount of Olives.** Luke will shortly note that "the feast of Unleavened Bread, called the Passover, was drawing near" (22:1). Pilgrims came by the tens of thousands to Jerusalem to celebrate Passover, tripling the population of the city. Not all of them could be accommodated within the city, so pilgrims sought hospitality in nearby villages or camped out in open areas. Jesus and his disciples spend their nights on **the Mount of Olives**, a ridge of hills immediately east of Jerusalem. Luke does not specify where on the Mount of Olives Jesus stayed, leaving it open whether he found hospitality in a village such as Bethany or Bethpage (see 19:29) or camped out, perhaps at Gethsemane (see 22:39-40).

Temple: See page 519

38 **And all the people would get up early each morning to listen to him in the temple area.** Although Jesus has met opposition from various religious leaders (19:47; 20:1-2, 19-22, 27-33), he continues to be very popular with **all the people**. They are eager **to listen to him**, getting **up early each morning** to come to the Temple to hear him. At the beginning of his days of teaching at the Temple, "all the people were hanging on his words" (19:48), and they continue to do so.

For reflection: What example is set for me by the people who arose early to listen to Jesus? How might I spend more time listening to him?

CHAPTER 22

The Conspiracy Against Jesus

¹ Now the feast of Unleavened Bread, called the Passover, was drawing near, ² and the chief priests and the scribes were seeking a way to put him to death, for they were afraid of the people. ³ Then Satan entered into Judas, the one surnamed Iscariot, who was counted among the Twelve, ⁴ and he went to the chief priests and temple guards to discuss a plan for handing him over to them. ⁵ They were pleased and agreed to pay him money. ⁶ He accepted their offer and sought a favorable opportunity to hand him over to them in the absence of a crowd.

Gospel parallels: Matt 26:1–5, 14–16; Mark 14:1–2, 10–11
NT: Luke 4:13; 6:12–16; 19:47–48; 20:19; John 11:47–53; 13:2, 27

1 Since arriving in Jerusalem, Jesus has been teaching every day in a Temple courtyard, attracting crowds (19:47–48; 21:38). **Now the feast of Unleavened Bread, called the Passover, was drawing near**. The feasts of **Unleavened Bread** and of **Passover** were celebrated together. **Passover** was celebrated by a meal eaten with unleavened bread after sundown on the fourteenth day of the spring month of Nisan; no leavened bread was eaten during the following seven days, which made up **the feast of Unleavened Bread**.

The feasts of Passover and Unleavened Bread: See page 577

2 As Passover was approaching, **the chief priests and the scribes were seeking a way to put him to death**, literally, "how to do away with him." This has been their intent ever since Jesus disrupted commercial activities in the Temple courtyard, "but they could find no way to accomplish their purpose because all the people were hanging on his words" (19:45–48). They want to get rid of Jesus and scheme how they might do so, but are at an impasse, **for they were afraid of the people** (see also 20:19). The crowds who get up early in the morning to listen to Jesus' teaching (21:38) would riot if anyone tried to harm him.

High priest, chief priests: See page 605
Scribes: See page 146

3   The impasse is broken in a startling way: **Then Satan entered into
Judas, the one surnamed Iscariot, who was counted among the
Twelve**. Before Jesus began his public ministry, **Satan** tried to deflect
him from his mission, tempting him for forty days in the wilderness
(4:1–13). Jesus did not succumb to his enticements, and "when the devil
had finished every temptation, he departed from him for a time" (4:13;
the words translated "for a time" have the connotation of until the
opportune time). Now Satan is provided with an opportunity by **Judas**,
who is one of **the Twelve** chosen by Jesus to be apostles (6:13–16). Jesus
made his choice of **the Twelve** after spending a night in prayer (6:12), so
we must presume that Judas was once a true disciple, worthy of his call
by Jesus. Judas must have given Satan some kind of opening, but Luke
does not tell us what it was. Somehow, though, a disciple whom Jesus had
chosen for a special role "became a traitor" (6:16), giving his allegiance to
Jesus' enemies rather than to Jesus.

Satan: See page 108

*For reflection: What warning am I given by Judas' defection? Where in my
life am I providing an opening for evil?*

4   Judas knows that Jesus has aroused the opposition of religious leaders;
their confrontations have been in public (20:1–26, 45–46). He also seems
to be aware that they want to do away with Jesus but are held back by fear
of what the crowds would do if they tried. **He went to the chief priests
and temple guards**: the word translated **temple guards** means those in
charge of the Temple's security. As Gentiles, Roman soldiers would not
have been able to enter into the inner courtyards of the Temple, so a
Jewish police force was necessary. Judas takes the initiative to go to those
in charge of the Temple **to discuss a plan for handing him over to
them**, literally, "to discuss how he might hand him over to them." What
unfolds later indicates that Judas offers to lead them to Jesus at a time
and place when Jesus can be arrested quietly, without a crowd around to
protect him (in Acts, Peter will say that Judas was "the guide for those
who arrested Jesus"—Acts 1:16).

5   **They were pleased**, literally, "rejoiced." Those who want to get rid of
Jesus are overjoyed that someone who is in Jesus' inner circle and knows

his movements now offers to help them arrest him. They **agreed to pay him money**: Judas apparently demanded payment for his help. In modern idiom, Judas sold Jesus out. We may speculate that Judas wanted something to live on once he no longer traveled with Jesus and was supported as one of the Twelve (see 8:1–3). In any case, Judas chooses mammon over God (see 16:13) and Jesus' enemies over Jesus—manifestations of Satan's influence over him (verse 3).

6 **He accepted their offer**, consenting to what they offered to pay him. Luke does not say how much he was paid but in Acts he will recount that Judas used the money to buy "a parcel of land"—presumably income-producing farmland—but did not live long enough to benefit from it (Acts 1:18). Then he **sought a favorable opportunity to hand him over to them in the absence of a crowd**. Judas does not know when the **favorable opportunity** will arise, but he keeps his eyes open for a situation in which Jesus can be quietly arrested.

What happens in the wake of Judas' betrayal must be understood from multiple perspectives. A trusted friend turns against Jesus and bears responsibility for his death: a wrenching, sinful tragedy (22:21–22). The battle between Jesus and Satan reaches a climax in an hour of darkness: a cosmic struggle between good and evil (22:53). Jesus must be handed over, suffer, and die in fulfillment of Scripture: the working out of God's providential plan (9:22; 12:50; 17:25; 18:31–33; 22:37; 24:26–27, 44–47).

For reflection: How do I understand and balance the different perspectives on Jesus' death?

ORIENTATION: *Events move swiftly once Passover arrives. The remainder of Luke's Gospel covers four days during which Jesus has a final meal with his followers; is arrested, tried, and crucified; rises from the dead and is taken up to heaven.*

Surreptitious Preparations for Passover
⁷ **When the day of the Feast of Unleavened Bread arrived, the day for sacrificing the Passover lamb, ⁸ he sent out Peter and John, instructing them, "Go and make preparations for us to eat the**

Passover." ⁹ They asked him, "Where do you want us to make the preparations?" ¹⁰ And he answered them, "When you go into the city, a man will meet you carrying a jar of water. Follow him into the house that he enters ¹¹ and say to the master of the house, 'The teacher says to you, "Where is the guest room where I may eat the Passover with my disciples?"' ¹² He will show you a large upper room that is furnished. Make the preparations there." ¹³ Then they went off and found everything exactly as he had told them, and there they prepared the Passover.

Gospel parallels: Matt 26:17–19; Mark 14:12–16
OT: Exod 12:1–28; Lev 23:4–8, 15; Deut 16:1–8
NT: Luke 19:28–35; 22:1–6, 21–22

7 **When the day of the Feast of Unleavened Bread arrived, the day for sacrificing the Passover lamb**: for each home, a **lamb** was sacrificed at the Temple during the afternoon (Exod 12:6; Deut 16:5–6), in preparation for the Passover meal that would be eaten after sundown

---

BACKGROUND: THE FEASTS OF PASSOVER AND UNLEAVENED BREAD These originated as different feasts but were celebrated in conjunction with each other. Passover was celebrated by a meal that included lamb; it commemorated God's freeing the Israelites from captivity in Egypt (Exod 12). Some scholars believe than an ancient precursor of Passover was the sacrifice of a young lamb as an offering for the safety of the flock, made by shepherds in the spring before moving the flock to new pastures. The feast of Unleavened Bread (Exod 23:15; 34:18; Lev 23:6) was an agricultural festival celebrating the beginning of the grain harvest. In Palestine during biblical times, grain crops grew only during the winter rainy season, with barley being the first grain to ripen in the spring. To celebrate the barley harvest, bread made from only newly harvested grain was eaten for seven days. This bread was unleavened because leaven was kept in the form of starter dough, and no starter dough from previously harvested grain could be used during this feast (Exod 12:18–20). The Passover meal was eaten with unleavened bread after sundown on the fourteenth day of the spring month of Nisan—a night of a full moon in the lunar calendar followed by Jews. The seven-day celebration of the feast of Unleavened Bread began at the same time. The feasts of Passover and Unleavened Bread incorporated traditions of nomadic shepherds and settled farmers but gave them greater meaning as part of a celebration of liberation from Egypt (see Exod 13:3–10; 34:18; Deut 16:1–8). After sacrificial worship was restricted to the Temple in Jerusalem by King Josiah (ruled 640–609 B.C.), Passover was celebrated in Jerusalem, since the sacrificing of lambs had to be done at the Temple.

(Exod 12:8). In the Jewish way of reckoning, days ran from sundown to sundown rather than from midnight to midnight, with the seven-day **Feast of Unleavened Bread** beginning at the same sundown (Exod 12:18; 23:15) that the **Passover** meal was eaten. However, in popular usage the preceding day was also spoken of as **the day of the Feast of Unleavened Bread**, since that was when all leavened bread and leaven were removed from the house in preparation for the feast. The preparations for the feasts of Passover and Unleavened Bread thus took place together. This **day** of preparation has **arrived** for Jesus and his disciples.

8 Jesus **sent out Peter and John, instructing them, "Go and make preparations for us to eat the Passover."** Jesus favors sending out disciples on mission in pairs (10:1); he sent two disciples to prepare for his entry into Jerusalem (19:29–35). Now he sends **Peter** and **John** to make **preparations** for the **Passover** meal. Jesus had singled out **Peter** and **John,** along with James, to witness his raising the daughter of Jairus to life (8:51–56) and his transfiguration (9:28–36). **Peter** and **John** will also be linked together and play prominent roles in the early Church (Acts 3:1—4:31; 8:14–17). Now, apparently in light of their prominence among the Twelve, Jesus sends them on a mission that includes some rather menial tasks. Making **preparations** for a Passover meal included buying, sacrificing, and roasting a lamb; baking or obtaining unleavened bread; buying wine and other provisions necessary for the meal (Exod 12:8); and preparing the place where the meal would be eaten. A Passover meal, like any rather formal meal for a significant number of people, was a lot of work. Jesus asks two of the leaders among the Twelve to do this work, perhaps to serve as a demonstration of what he will teach his disciples during the course of the meal: "Let the greatest among you be as the youngest, and the leader as the servant" (22:26). Jesus asks them to make preparations **for us to eat the Passover**: Jesus eagerly desires to share the Passover meal with his disciples before he suffers and dies (22:15–16).

For reflection: What is the lesson for me in Jesus asking Peter and John to prepare the Passover meal?

9 **They asked him, "Where do you want us to make the preparations?"** Since final **preparations** were made where the Passover meal

was eaten, the sense of their question is, Where will you eat the Passover meal with us? Jesus and presumably his disciples have been staying on the Mount of Olives at night (21:37), since there were not sufficient accommodations within Jerusalem to house all the pilgrims who came for Passover. However, the law of Moses was interpreted to require that the Passover meal be eaten within the city (see Deut 16:7). Residents of Jerusalem made their extra rooms available to pilgrims for the Passover meal. Peter and John ask Jesus **where** there is a room for them.

10 Jesus does not tell them the location of the room. Instead **he answered them, "When you go into the city, a man will meet you carrying a jar of water."** Jesus knows what will happen when Peter and John enter the **city** of Jerusalem. It is not clear from Luke's account whether Jesus made arrangements in advance or he has more than human knowledge of what will happen (as he apparently had when he earlier sent two disciples on a mission—19:29–35). A **man will meet** Peter and John inside the city, and they will be able to identify him because he will be **carrying a jar of water**. Normally it was women who transported water in jars for their families; it would have been unusual for a man to do so. Jesus does not ask Peter and John to say anything to the man but simply to **follow him into the house that he enters**.

11 There they are to **say to the master of the house, "The teacher says to you, 'Where is the guest room where I may eat the Passover with my disciples?'"** The man with the water jug will not be the **master** or owner **of the house** but will lead Peter and John to him. It is unclear whether the house owner is a disciple of Jesus. He will understand that Jesus is the **teacher** that Peter and John are referring to, but many people think of Jesus as a teacher (7:40; 8:49; 9:38; 10:25; 12:13; 18:18; 19:39; 20:21, 28, 39; 21:7). Peter and John are to ask about a **guest room** in his house: the Greek word translated **guest room** means a place where people might stay (the word is translated as "inn" at 2:7). Jesus wants to make use of the room to **eat the Passover** meal **with** his **disciples**.

Disciple: See page 149

12 **He will show you a large upper room that is furnished.** An **upper room**—that is, an "upstairs room"—may be a second-story room, or an

additional room built on the flat roof of a house, accessible by an outside stairway. It is a **large** room, able to accommodate a sizable number of people (if it is the same upper room where Jesus' disciples stayed after his ascension, then it can hold one hundred twenty people—Acts 1:13, 15). **Furnished** has the connotation of furnished with cushions or couches used for reclining at a formal meal. The owner of the house has furnished the room for a Passover meal, likely with the intent of making it available to pilgrims. Peter and John are to **make the preparations there** for the Passover meal.

13 **Then they went off and found everything exactly as he had told them**: they do what Jesus asks them to do, and everything happens **exactly** as Jesus had said it would, just as it did when Jesus had sent two disciples to prepare for his entry into Jerusalem (19:32). Even as Jesus' life is in danger (22:1–6), he remains in charge of events as they unfold. **There they prepared the Passover** meal for Jesus to eat with his disciples that evening.

Jesus sends Peter and John in a surreptitious manner to the place where they can prepare the Passover meal. They are not told the location of the room or the names of the water carrier or the homeowner. Jesus wants to keep the location where he will eat the Passover meal a secret, even to anyone who overhears his instructions. He knows that religious leaders in Jerusalem want to do away with him (19:47; 22:2), and he knows that they will succeed (9:22, 44; 18:31–33). He also knows that Judas will hand him over to be put to death (22:21–22), but he does not want this to happen until he has eaten the Passover meal with his disciples (22:15). If Judas had been able to inform Jesus' enemies of the place where Jesus will eat the Passover meal or lead them there, they would have been able to arrest Jesus when the crowds who keep him safe (19:47–48; 22:2) are dispersed and preoccupied by their own Passover meals. Hence Jesus keeps Judas in the dark about where they will celebrate Passover. Peter and John may not have grasped why Jesus was instructing them as he was, but everything worked out when they followed his instructions.

For reflection: When have I known what Jesus wanted me to do, but without completely understanding why he was asking it of me? What was the outcome when I did as he asked?

Jesus Gives His Body and Blood

¹⁴ When the hour came, he took his place at table with the apostles. ¹⁵ He said to them, "I have eagerly desired to eat this Passover with you before I suffer, ¹⁶ for, I tell you, I shall not eat it [again] until there is fulfillment in the kingdom of God." ¹⁷ Then he took a cup, gave thanks, and said, "Take this and share it among yourselves; ¹⁸ for I tell you [that] from this time on I shall not drink of the fruit of the vine until the kingdom of God comes." ¹⁹ Then he took the bread, said the blessing, broke it, and gave it to them, saying, "This is my body, which will be given for you; do this in memory of me." ²⁰ And likewise the cup after they had eaten, saying, "This cup is the new covenant in my blood, which will be shed for you."

Gospel parallels: Matt 26:20, 26–29; Mark 14:17, 22–25
OT: Exod 12:1–14, 24–27; 24:3–8; Jer 31:31–34
NT: John 6:51–58; 1 Cor 10:16–17; 11:23–27; 15:1–3; Heb 10:10–18

14 Peter and John prepared the Passover meal as Jesus had instructed them (22:7–13), and **when the hour came** for the meal to be eaten **he took his place at table with the apostles**. The word translated as **he took his place at table** literally means, "he reclined." The Passover meal may originally have been eaten while standing (see Exod 12:11), but Jews had adopted the Greek custom of reclining on one's side at banquets. Reclining at the Passover banquet was interpreted as a sign of liberation from slavery in Egypt, since slaves did not banquet. Jesus reclined **with the apostles,** the Twelve whom he chose to be his ambassadors and messengers (6:13–16). Artistic depictions of Jesus' last supper with his disciples portray him seated at a table surrounded by twelve men. We might wonder, however, where the rest of the "whole multitude of his disciples" who accompanied him into Jerusalem (19:37), women as well as men (23:49, 55; 24:10, 22), ate the Passover meal. The "large upper room" (22:12) in which Jesus and the apostles ate would likely have accommodated more than thirteen people (far more if it is the same upper room as in Acts 1:13, 15). Some of what Jesus will go on to say appears to be directed to a larger group of the disciples than the Twelve reclining alongside him (see 22:35).

Apostle: See page 164
Banquets: See page 386

When the hour came may have a deeper level of significance than simply that it was time to begin eating the Passover meal. The **hour** or time has come for the will and plan of God (7:30; 10:21; 22:42) to be fulfilled (18:31; 22:37; 24:44) by the exodus Jesus is going to accomplish in Jerusalem (9:31), his being taken up to God (9:51) through suffering and death (9:22; 17:25; 24:26).

15 **He said to them, "I have eagerly desired to eat this Passover with you before I suffer."** The word **suffer** conveys not only enduring physical pain but suffering death (see 24:46; Acts 1:3; 17:3). Jesus knew that his death was imminent (22:21–22); he **eagerly desired** to have a last meal with his closest friends and followers before he died. While he has shared meals with them since the beginning of his ministry (4:38–39), it is especially appropriate for him to share the **Passover** meal, which celebrates Israel's exodus from Egypt, before he accomplishes his own exodus to his Father (9:31). Each exodus marks a new stage in God's liberation of his people.

The feasts of Passover and Unleavened Bread: See page 577

For reflection: What does it tell me about Jesus' relationship with his disciples that he eagerly desired to eat with them before he suffered? What does it imply about his relationship with me?

16 Jesus explains why he eagerly desired to eat this Passover meal with his apostles: **for, I tell you, I shall not eat it [again] until there is fulfillment in the kingdom of God**. The Greek word translated **there is fulfillment** is literally, "it is fulfilled" and implies, it is fulfilled by God. Jesus will not eat the Passover meal again until what it celebrates is fulfilled by God in his **kingdom**. Passover celebrates God's liberation of the Israelites from slavery in Egypt; the full establishment of the reign of God will liberate men and women from slavery to sin and bondage to suffering and death. Jesus' mission was to establish God's reign through his preaching and healing (11:20); he was sent by God "to proclaim liberty to captives / . . . to let the oppressed go free" (4:18). His mission will culminate when the kingdom of God is established in its fullness at his coming in glory (21:27, 31). His coming will usher in the age to come and the banquet of the kingdom of God (13:29; 14:15); the Passover meal is an

anticipation of this heavenly banquet. Jesus will not again eat a Passover meal on earth, but he will be the host and servant (12:37; 22:27) of the banquet in the age to come.

Kingdom of God: See page 381

17 **Then he took a cup** of wine. There is no mention in the Old Testament of wine being drunk during the Passover meal, but wine accompanied any banquet. Later Jewish practice calls for four cups of wine to be drunk at the Passover meal, but we do not know how many cups were customary at the time of Jesus. Luke recounts Jesus' action over two cups of wine. Jesus took the first of them and **gave thanks** to God for it, as would the host at any formal Jewish meal. A traditional Jewish thanksgiving or blessing for wine is, "Blessed are you, O Lord our God, king of the universe, creator of the fruit of the vine" ("fruit of the vine" is an expression for wine). He said to those sharing the meal with him, **Take this** cup **and share it among yourselves**: drinking from a common cup expresses fellowship.

18 Jesus adds, **for I tell you [that] from this time on I shall not drink of the fruit of the vine until the kingdom of God comes.** The sense of Jesus' words is the same as his statement that he will not eat the Passover meal again until it is fulfilled in the kingdom of God: he will not again drink wine until **the kingdom of God comes** in its fullness. Jesus is not making a vow of abstinence but rather indicating that this very night he will begin his exodus to God; he will be unable to continue the fellowship meals he has shared with his followers in the past. However, his fellowship with them will continue and become more intimate through a new meal that he now institutes.

19 **Then he took the bread**: bread accompanied every meal, unleavened bread at Passover. He **said the blessing**—literally, "gave thanks." The Greek word Luke uses for "gave thanks" gives us the word "Eucharist." Jesus gives thanks to God for the bread, as the host at any Jewish meal would do. A traditional Jewish thanksgiving or blessing over the bread is, "Blessed are you, O Lord our God, king of the universe, who bring forth bread from the earth." He **broke it and gave it to them** to eat: one loaf of bread, broken into pieces and shared among those at a meal, expressed

fellowship, as did the shared cup of wine. Jesus gave the bread to his disciples **saying, "This is my body, which will be given for you."** During the Passover meal, the host explains the significance of its various elements (see Exod 12:26–27). A traditional explanation of the bread eaten during the Passover meal is, "This is the bread of affliction which our ancestors ate in the land of Egypt" (see also Deut 16:3). It was to be expected that Jesus would say something about the significance of the bread he was distributing to his followers; what he said was unexpected: **this is my body**. In the Hebrew way of thinking, one's **body** or flesh was one's whole person as a physical being (see Rom 12:1; Phil 1:20). Jesus gives his disciples bread to eat as his **body**, his person, his self.

These words of Jesus must be pondered, for they are a great mystery. What does it mean for bread to be the body of Jesus? What is the significance of eating bread that is the body of Jesus? What bonds of fellowship are created between those who share the bread that is the body of Jesus?

For reflection: What do Jesus' words, "This is my body," mean for me?

Jesus tells them that the bread is his body **which will be given for you**. Jesus repeatedly warned his followers that he would suffer and die (9:22, 44; 13:33; 18:31–33) and has just referred to his suffering (verse 15): his body **will be given** in death. His death will be a death **for you,** a death on behalf of his followers, for their sake. He does not immediately explain what his death will accomplish for them but instructs them, **do this in memory of me**. The form of the word **do** signifies repeated action: keep doing this. **In memory of me** has a fuller meaning than simply recalling what Jesus did. Passover is a memorial of the exodus (Exod 12:14), celebrated as if each person sharing the meal experienced the effects of liberation from Egypt: "The LORD brought *us* out of Egypt" (Deut 6:21, emphasis added). So too, when followers of Jesus share bread that is his body **in memory** of him, each one benefits from his body being given for them. The death of Jesus on their behalf is re-presented, made present, for those who celebrate it **in memory** of him.

For reflection: What does it mean to me that Jesus gave his body for me? What do I experience when I join with others in celebrating it in memory of him?

20 **And likewise the cup after they had eaten**: Jesus had earlier taken a cup of wine, thanked God for it, and given it to his disciples to share, and he does **likewise** with another cup of wine **after they had eaten** the Passover meal. He said to them, **This cup is the new covenant in my blood, which will be shed for you.** By speaking of **this cup** Jesus implicitly refers to the wine it holds and identifies the wine with his **blood**, just as he said that the bread he gave them is his body. In Hebrew thought, **blood** is the life of a human or an animal (Lev 17:11, 14; Deut 12:23). For Jesus to give his blood to his disciples is to share his life with them. A **covenant** is an agreement or pact that establishes a binding relationship between two parties. God entered into a covenant with his people at Mount Sinai; what we refer to as the Ten Commandments are the terms of this covenant (Exod 20:1–17; Deut 5:6–21). This covenant was sealed in blood: bulls were sacrificed, with one portion of their blood poured on an altar as an offering to God and the other portion sprinkled on the people (Exod 24:6, 8). Jesus tells his followers that the covenant or bond he now establishes between God and his people is a **covenant in my blood**—by means of my blood— **which will be shed for you.** Jesus will **shed** his **blood**, pouring out his life as a sacrificial offering for the sake of his followers (see Eph 5:2; Heb 7:27; 9:14; 10:10–14).

COMMENT: THE EUCHARIST Luke's first readers would have known about Jesus' final meal with his followers even before they read Luke's Gospel. Proclaiming what Jesus did and said on the night before he died was part of the gospel message, as Paul makes clear (1 Cor 11:23–26). The Church from its earliest days celebrated "the breaking of the bread" (Acts 2:42), that is, "the Lord's supper" (1 Cor 11:20). Luke's audience would have understood his account of what Jesus did during the Last Supper in light of their own celebration of the Eucharist. The same is true for us today. Our understanding of the Eucharist rests not only on what we read in Luke but also on what we read in the other Gospels and writings of the New Testament. We are also the heirs of two millennia of theological reflection on the meaning of the Eucharist. St. Thomas Aquinas in the thirteenth century employed concepts from the Greek philosopher Aristotle in characterizing bread and wine becoming the body and blood of Christ as "transubstantiation"—a change of their underlying reality. The Roman Catholic Church embraces this term, even as it acknowledges that bread and wine becoming the body and blood of Christ surpasses our understanding.

> *Then he took the blood and sprinkled it on the people,*
> *saying, "This is the blood of the covenant which the LORD*
> *has made with you".*
>
> Exod 24:8

For reflection: What does it mean for me that the cup of wine is the blood
of Jesus shed for me?

Jesus tells his disciples that the cup of wine that he is giving them is a **new** covenant in his blood. God spoke through Jeremiah to promise that he would make a "new covenant" with his people in which he would "forgive their evildoing and remember their sin no more" (Jer 31:31, 34). Jesus establishes a new relationship between God and his people in which their sins are forgiven because of Jesus' death for them (see 24:46–47; Heb 10:12–18). From the earliest days of the Church the core of the gospel message is that "Christ died for our sins" (1 Cor 15:1–3; see also Gal 1:4; 1 Pet 3:18). Through sharing in bread that is his body and wine that is his blood, his followers are joined to God under the new covenant established by Jesus' pouring out his life for them, and they obtain forgiveness of their sins. This mystery of faith deserves our lifetime's reflection.

> *The days are coming, says the LORD, when I will make*
> *a new covenant with the house of Israel and the house of*
> *Judah. . . . I will forgive their evildoing and remember*
> *their sin no more.*
>
> Jer 31:31, 34

Jesus Foretells His Betrayal
²¹ "And yet behold, the hand of the one who is to betray me is with me on the table; ²² for the Son of Man indeed goes as it has been determined; but woe to that man by whom he is betrayed." ²³ And they began to debate among themselves who among them would do such a deed.

Gospel parallels: Matt 26:21–25; Mark 14:18–21; John 13:21–30

NT: Luke 22:3–6, 14–20; Acts 2:23

21 **And yet behold, the hand of the one who is to betray me is with me on the table.** Jesus has just given his disciples bread and wine as his body and blood and told them that he would be giving his life for their sake (22:19–20), **and yet**, despite his complete gift of himself to and for them, **one** of them who is at **the table** with him will **betray** him. The word translated **betray** can also be translated "hand over" (see 9:44; 18:32). Jesus knows that Judas is looking for an opportunity to hand him over to the chief priests (22:3–6), which is why Jesus kept the location of their Passover meal a secret (22:7–13). Yet even though Judas will betray him, Jesus did not exclude him from the meal or refuse to give him his body and blood! Nor does Jesus name Judas as his betrayer. Had he done so, the other disciples would have restrained Judas and prevented him from carrying through on his betrayal. Only Judas knows that Jesus is talking about him. Jesus seems to be giving Judas a chance to change his mind, even though Jesus realizes that he will not. Judas will **betray** him, handing him over to death; yet in an ironic twist, Jesus' death will bring forgiveness of sins (see 22:20; 24:46–47), even making forgiveness possible for those responsible for his death (see 23:34).

> *For reflection: What significance do I find in Jesus' including Judas at the last supper and giving him bread and wine as his body and blood? What significance do I find in Judas' nonetheless betraying Jesus? What are the lessons for me?*

22 **for the Son of Man indeed goes as it has been determined**—implied, determined by God. Jesus, **the Son of Man,** "must" suffer and die (9:22; 12:50; 13:33; 17:25) in order to carry out his mission from God and enter into glory (24:26). In Acts, Peter will proclaim that Jesus was "delivered up by the set plan and foreknowledge of God" (Acts 2:23; the word translated as "set" is translated as **determined** in Luke's Gospel). Jesus is following God's path for him, **but woe to that man by whom he is betrayed.** The working out of God's plans incorporates freely made human decisions; divine sovereignty eliminates neither free will nor the responsibility of men and women for their actions. Judas is in a woeful

condition because he has **betrayed** Jesus, having offered to hand him over to those who will put him to death (22:2–6). Jesus' **woe** is a warning for Judas: he will be held accountable by God if he continues down the path of betrayal.

Son of Man: See page 147

Woes: See page 171

For reflection: Do I hold myself accountable for my actions? Where am I trying to evade responsibility for what I have made of myself?

23 **And they began to debate among themselves who among them would do such a deed.** Jesus' words catch his disciples by surprise and they ask themselves, **who among** us **would do such a deed?** Their discussion apparently produces only puzzlement, for Luke gives no indication that they settle on anyone as the likely culprit. Their **debate** seems to be over which of them is the worst disciple, and from that they will turn to debating which of them is the greatest (22:24).

True Greatness Is Humble Service

²⁴ **Then an argument broke out among them about which of them should be regarded as the greatest. ²⁵ He said to them, "The kings of the Gentiles lord it over them and those in authority over them are addressed as 'Benefactors'; ²⁶ but among you it shall not be so. Rather, let the greatest among you be as the youngest, and the leader as the servant. ²⁷ For who is greater: the one seated at table or the one who serves? Is it not the one seated at table? I am among you as the one who serves. ²⁸ It is you who have stood by me in my trials; ²⁹ and I confer a kingdom on you, just as my Father has conferred one on me, ³⁰ that you may eat and drink at my table in my kingdom; and you will sit on thrones judging the twelve tribes of Israel."**

Gospel parallels: Matt 19:28; 20:25–28; Mark 10:42–45
NT: Luke 9:46–48; 10:22; 12:32, 37; 22:14–23; John 13:1–17

24 **Then**, after the disciples debated which of them might betray Jesus (22:21–23), **an argument broke out among them about which of them should be regarded as the greatest**. This is not the first time

they have squabbled over which of them is **the greatest** (see 9:46), but their present **argument** could not have occurred at a more inappropriate time. Jesus has made it clear that this is his last meal with them before he suffers and dies for their sake; he has given them bread that is his body and wine that is his blood (22:14–20). Followers of Jesus should never argue over which of them should be honored as the most important or greatest (9:47–48), but for the disciples to do so immediately after Jesus' solemn words and actions reveals that they still do not grasp what Jesus has told them about his coming suffering and death (18:31–34) and its implications for them (9:22–25).

> *For reflection: How do my self-concerns and preoccupations reveal that I do not fully grasp the implications of what Jesus has done for me?*

25 **He said to them, "The kings of the Gentiles lord it over them"**: in the ancient world those who were **kings** had virtually absolute authority over their subjects and could **lord it over them**, exercising their authority as they saw fit. **And those in authority over them are addressed as "Benefactors"**: their subjects honor those **in authority** as their **benefactors**, as those who do good for them. Those who were a position to be patrons and do favors for others expected to be honored for it. Having power over others and being praised by them was an appealing prospect in the ancient world, as it is in our time.

Patrons: See page 216

> *For reflection: How do I behave when I am in charge of others? Do I enjoy being praised?*

26 Acquiring power and prestige may be the driving force for many people, but Jesus tells his disciples that **among you it shall not be so**. The way of Jesus is quite different: **Rather, let the greatest among you be as the youngest**. In the culture of the time, the young had no status or power and were assigned menial tasks. Some of Jesus' disciples will be in positions of leadership, but even those with the **greatest** authority and office should behave as if they were **the youngest** and least important members of the family of Jesus. **The leader** in any group of disciples must be **as the servant**: a **servant** carries out the wishes of others, caring for their

needs. Jesus turns the way the world operates on its head: instead of lording it over others and seeking praise, disciples of Jesus must behave as if they are socially insignificant and at the disposal of others. That is what it means to be **the greatest** among the followers of Jesus. His disciples were misguided in their dispute over which of them was the greatest (verse 24), for they were following the world's understanding of greatness rather than that of Jesus. They should have remembered his words: "The one who is least among all of you is the one who is the greatest" (9:48).

Servant, slave: See page 454

For reflection: In at least one area of my life, what does it mean in practical terms for me to be as the youngest and servant of all?

27 Jesus explains why greatness lies in humble service. He begins with a rhetorical question: **For who is greater: the one seated at table or the one who serves?** In the normal way of understanding roles, someone **seated at table**—literally, "reclining," as at a banquet—is in a position superior to the waiter who **serves** the meal. Jesus used the superiority of the one being served over the one serving as the basis of a parable (17:7–10). Jesus answers his rhetorical question with a second rhetorical question: **Is it not the one seated at table** who is greater? His disciples would have to answer, "Of course." Against this backdrop of normal status relationships Jesus makes a startling pronouncement: *But* **I am among you as the one who serves** (the word *but* is in the Greek text of Luke's Gospel). Jesus' disciples should have no difficulty recognizing that he is **greater** than they are: he raises the dead, heals the sick, expels demons, calms storms, and speaks for God. Although Jesus is unquestionably **greater** than his disciples, he is in their midst **as the one who serves**. He has dedicated his life to service of God and service of others. He has gone "about doing good and healing all those oppressed by the devil" (Acts 10:38) and now will give his body and shed his blood for the sake of others (22:19–20). There can be no greater act of service than to give up one's life. Jesus asks his followers to be servants (verse 26) in imitation of him (see also 12:37). His words take on added solemnity because they are in effect his farewell discourse to his disciples, his last instruction to them before he dies.

For reflection: What does it mean for me that Jesus came into our midst to serve? What does his example ask of me in my daily life?

28 **It is you who have stood by me in my trials:** Jesus acknowledges that his disciples have been faithful to him and remained with him in his **trials**, the hardships and tribulations Jesus has endured in carrying out his mission. Jesus has had no assured lodgings or meals (9:58); he has been besieged by crowds who press upon him with their needs (4:42; 5:1, 15, 19; 6:17–19; 7:11; 8:4, 19, 40, 45; 9:11, 37; 12:1; 14:25; 18:36; 19:3). Being constantly available to others in need is draining. Jesus has faced rejection and opposition, even to the point of some seeking his death (4:28–29; 6:11; 11:53–54; 13:31; 19:47; 20:19–21; 22:2). Through all this his disciples have **stood by** him, sharing in his hardships and trials, and Jesus acknowledges their faithfulness.

For reflection: What does it mean in my life to stand by Jesus? To remain faithful to him even through hardships and trials?

29 Jesus tells his disciples that, in response to their faithfulness, **I confer a kingdom on you, just as my Father has conferred one on me**. For Jesus to **confer a kingdom** on his disciples can have several senses. It can mean that Jesus is bringing them into the reign of God. Jesus told them, "Your Father is pleased to give you the kingdom" (12:32), meaning pleased to make them part of his reign. The word translated **kingdom** can also have the sense of kingship or rule, and to confer a kingdom can mean to convey a share of that rule. The **Father** has **conferred** his kingship or rule on Jesus: "all things have been handed over" to him by his Father (10:22). Jesus now confers kingship on his disciples, sharing his authority with them.

30 Jesus tells his disciples that he confers the kingdom on them so **that you may eat and drink at my table in my kingdom**. Jesus brings them into the reign of God so that they may take part in the banquet of the kingdom (13:29; 14:15; 22:15–18)—a banquet that will be foreshadowed when they break bread in memory of him (22:19–20; 24:30–35; Acts 2:42, 46; 20:7, 11). Jesus shared his authority with his disciples (verse 29) and now tells them, **you will sit on thrones judging the twelve tribes of**

Israel. To **sit on thrones** signifies having authority. **Judging** does not narrowly mean passing judgment but leading and ruling, the sense it has in some Old Testament passages. Ten of the twelve **tribes** of Israel disappeared in exile (2 Kings 17:21–23); prophets expressed hopes for their restoration (Isaiah 11:11–13; Jer 3:18; Ezek 37:15–22). Jesus uses **the twelve tribes of Israel** as an expression for the reconstituted people of God, the new Israel made up of his followers. The role Jesus assigns his disciples will begin with his ascension; Luke will recount in the first half of Acts how the apostles led the early Church. They stood by Jesus during his trials; they will continue his work after his return to his Father.

Jesus Foretells Peter's Denials and Repentance
31 "Simon, Simon, behold Satan has demanded to sift all of you like wheat, 32 but I have prayed that your own faith may not fail; and once you have turned back, you must strengthen your brothers." 33 He said to him, "Lord, I am prepared to go to prison and to die with you." 34 But he replied, "I tell you, Peter, before the cock crows this day, you will deny three times that you know me."

Gospel parallels: Matt 26:31–35; Mark 14:27–31; John 13:36–38
OT: Job 1—2
NT: Luke 22:28–30, 54–62; John 21:15–19

31 Jesus acknowledged that his disciples have stood by him in his trials, and he promised them that they would dine with him in his kingdom (22:28–30). But past faithfulness and future reward do not mean that there will not be some rough sailing. Satan, in mounting an assault on Jesus (see 4:13), found a weak link in Judas (22:3), and Satan would like to subvert other disciples as well. Jesus addresses this, directing his words to Peter: **Simon, Simon, behold Satan has demanded to sift all of you like wheat**. Jesus calls Peter **Simon**, his name before Jesus gave him the name Peter (4:38; 6:14). He calls out his name twice—**Simon, Simon**—to emphasize the seriousness of what he is saying to him. **Satan has demanded to sift all of you like wheat**: Satan has demanded that God allow him to tempt and test Jesus' disciples. **Sift all of you like wheat** has the connotation of shaking the disciples, seeing if he can get some of them to fall away, like wheat that falls through a sieve. Jesus tells Peter

that Satan wants to assault **all of you**—all the disciples. All followers of Jesus of all time will be tested.

Satan: See page 108

32 Jesus says, **but I have prayed that your own faith may not fail**, speaking specifically to Peter. Satan wants to shake the faith of Jesus' disciples, but Jesus interceded and **prayed** for Peter. **Faith** here means faithfulness, fidelity, loyalty to Jesus. Jesus prayed that Peter's faith **may not fail**: the word **fail** has the sense of completely give out. Jesus' intercession for Peter will be answered. While Peter's faithfulness will be tested and he will deny knowing Jesus (verse 34), Peter will not completely fall away; he will weep bitterly over his denials (22:62). Jesus tells Peter that **once you have turned back, you must strengthen your brothers**. In the Old Testament, the Hebrew word used for "repent" means to turn back or return (see Hosea 14:2). The New Testament also uses the notion of turning for repentance: the risen Jesus tells Paul that he is sending him to the Gentiles so that "they may turn from darkness to light and from the power of Satan to God, so that they may obtain forgiveness of sins" (Acts 26:18). Repentance and forgiveness are always possible, no matter how far one has fallen away. Jesus tells Peter that once he has repented and turned back, **you must strengthen your brothers**. Peter's **brothers** are not only his fellow disciples but the men and women who will join the Church (see Acts 6:3; 9:30; 11:1, 29; 15:1, 3, 32). To **strengthen** them means to strengthen their faith, encouraging them in their fidelity to Jesus (see Acts 14:22; 15:32; 18:23). Jesus calls Peter to serve him despite his sins (5:8) and weakness. Someone whose own strength has failed should have special compassion for others in their frailty.

Repentance: See page 92

For reflection: What am I able to do to strengthen my brothers and sisters in the faith?

33 Peter will not acknowledge that he will fail Jesus and need to repent. **He said to him, "Lord, I am prepared to go to prison and to die with you."** Peter has apparently grasped that Jesus may be arrested and be put to death, but he is confident that he will be faithful to Jesus no matter what happens. He tells Jesus that he is **prepared** for what lies ahead; he

will remain loyal to Jesus as his **Lord** even if it means being imprisoned and dying with him. As it will turn out, Peter will be arrested and jailed several times (Acts 4:3; 5:18; 12:3); ancient tradition recounts his crucifixion in Rome during Emperor Nero's persecution of Christians in the 60s A.D. But these lie down the road, after Peter has fallen and turned back to Jesus.

Lord: See page 137

34 **But he replied, "I tell you, Peter, before the cock crows this day, you will deny three times that you know me."** By **this day** Jesus refers to the day which began at sundown, when they reclined at the Passover meal (22:14). A **cock** or rooster might begin crowing anytime in the early morning hours. Since Jesus is speaking with his disciples after the meal (the second cup marked its end—22:20), a cock crow can be expected in a few hours. The force of Jesus' words to Peter is, You think you are prepared to go to prison and die with me? Very shortly **you will deny three times that you know me**. For Peter to refuse to acknowledge that he is even acquainted with Jesus is a far cry from remaining loyal to him at the cost of his life.

Luke does not record any response by Peter to Jesus' stark prediction. Had Peter accepted that Jesus was right, it would have tempered his overconfidence in himself. But Peter apparently thinks that he gauges his loyalty and fortitude better than does Jesus.

For reflection: What do I think I am prepared to do or undergo for Jesus? What has my experience taught me about the frailty of my resolutions?

Preparation for the Coming Crisis
³⁵ **He said to them, "When I sent you forth without a money bag or a sack or sandals, were you in need of anything?" "No, nothing," they replied.** ³⁶ **He said to them, "But now one who has a money bag should take it, and likewise a sack, and one who does not have a sword should sell his cloak and buy one.** ³⁷ **For I tell you that this scripture must be fulfilled in me, namely, 'He was counted among the wicked'; and indeed what is written about me is coming to**

fulfillment." ³⁸ Then they said, "Lord, look, there are two swords here." But he replied, "It is enough!"

OT: Isaiah 53:12

NT: Luke 10:1–12; 22:31–34, 49–53

35 He said to them, "When I sent you forth without a money bag or a sack or sandals, were you in need of anything?" Jesus **sent** seventy or seventy-two disciples out to cure the sick and proclaim the kingdom of God (10:1–12), instructing them to "carry no money bag, no sack, no sandals" (10:4). Jesus earlier sent out the Twelve with similar instructions (9:1–5) but without forbidding sandals (9:3). Jesus' reference to **sandals** now may indicate that he is speaking to a larger group of disciples than the Twelve. Jesus sent them on mission without the provisions travelers normally carry—coins in a **money bag** so that they could buy food, a **sack** to carry food and other items, **sandals** to make walking easier. They were to rely on God to provide for them through the hospitality of people along the way. Jesus asks them, **were you in need of anything** when you traveled as I instructed you? **"No, nothing," they replied.** They survived quite well because others fed and sheltered them (see 10:5–8).

Hospitality: See page 314

36 He said to them, "But now one who has a money bag should take it." The words translated **but now** are emphatic: the disciples must deal with a new situation. **One who has a money bag should take it, and likewise a sack**: they can no longer count on the hospitality of others but must be more self-reliant. **And one who does not have a sword should sell his cloak and buy one.** The Greek word here for **sword** referred to a small sword, such as a traveler might carry for protection against robbers (see 10:30). A **cloak** was an outer garment, often used at night as a blanket (see Exod 22:25–26). Selling one's **cloak** to buy a **sword** meant placing one's safety ahead of one's comfort and being prepared for conflict.

Clothing: See page 175

Jesus' disciples should have realized that his words were not meant as instructions to be followed literally but were a figurative way of telling them that they were entering a new situation where they needed to be prepared to face rejection and hostility (see Acts 8:1–3; 12:1–5), as well as sifting by Satan (22:31). Would the Jesus who required renouncing possessions (14:33) now tell them that they needed money bags and sacks? Would the Jesus who told them to accept slaps (6:29) have them carry swords? Jesus is talking about what their attitude should be, not giving them a shopping list.

37 Jesus explains why his followers will find themselves in a new situation of rejection and hostility: **For I tell you that this scripture must be fulfilled in me, namely, "He was counted among the wicked."** The **scripture** Jesus quotes is from a passage in Isaiah that speaks of a servant of God who suffers for the sake of others (Isaiah 52:13—53:12). The servant **was counted among the wicked**—was treated like a criminal. Jesus proclaims that these words **must be fulfilled in me:** he will be treated as a criminal (see 22:52) in fulfillment of this Scripture. The word **must** indicates that it is a divine necessity, part of God's plan for Jesus (see 2:49; 4:43; 9:22; 12:50; 17:25; 24:7). Jesus adds, **and indeed what is written about me is coming to fulfillment**. Jesus began his ministry by reading aloud a passage from Isaiah and proclaiming, "Today this scripture passage is fulfilled in your hearing" (4:17–21; Isaiah 61:1–2). After his resurrection he will remind his disciples that he told them that "everything written about me in the law of Moses and in the prophets and psalms must be fulfilled" (24:44). Jesus' being treated as a criminal is a **fulfillment** of what is **written about** him in Scripture. And if Jesus is treated as a criminal, his disciples can expect to fare no better; they must be prepared to face hardship.

> Therefore I will give him his portion among the great,
> and he shall divide the spoils with the mighty,
> Because he surrendered himself to death,
> was counted among the transgressors.
> Isaiah 53:12

For reflection: What does it tell me about Jesus' attitude toward me that he is concerned for the well-being of his disciples even as his suffering and death is imminent?

38 The disciples take Jesus' instructions literally, missing the point. **Then they said, "Lord, look, there are two swords here."** They apparently carried two swords with them from Galilee—a normal precaution for normal travelers, but strange for those who have put their lives in the hands of Jesus. **But he replied, "It is enough!"** Enough of such foolishness! Jesus seems exasperated by his disciples' incomprehension. He does not try to explain further (that might be futile: see 18:31–34) but leaves the upper room (22:39) to embrace what "must be fulfilled" (verse 37).

Lord: See page 137

Jesus' Agony in Prayer

³⁹ Then going out he went, as was his custom, to the Mount of Olives, and the disciples followed him. ⁴⁰ When he arrived at the place he said to them, "Pray that you may not undergo the test." ⁴¹ After withdrawing about a stone's throw from them and kneeling, he prayed, ⁴² saying, "Father, if you are willing, take this cup away from me; still, not my will but yours be done." [⁴³ And to strengthen him an angel from heaven appeared to him. ⁴⁴ He was in such agony and he prayed so fervently that his sweat became like drops of blood falling on the ground.] ⁴⁵ When he rose from prayer and returned to his disciples, he found them sleeping from grief. ⁴⁶ He said to them, "Why are you sleeping? Get up and pray that you may not undergo the test."

Gospel parallels: Matt 26:36–46; Mark 14:32–42; John 18:1
NT: Luke 11:4; 21:37; 22:31–38

39 **Then going out** from the room in Jerusalem where he had eaten the Passover meal after sunset with his disciples (22:11–20) **he went, as was his custom, to the Mount of Olives**. The **Mount of Olives** is a ridge of hills immediately east of Jerusalem. Luke has noted that after Jesus came to Jerusalem, he spent the days "teaching in the temple area, but at night he would leave and stay at the place called the Mount of Olives" (21:37). Now, **as was his custom**, Jesus returns **to the Mount of Olives**, apparently to the place (verse 40) where he had been staying at night. **And the disciples followed him**: while this might simply indicate that

they had been staying at the same place on the Mount of Olives, their following him also has symbolic significance. Disciples of Jesus must follow him and remain with him wherever he leads them.

Disciple: See page 149

For reflection: Am I willing to follow Jesus no matter where he leads me? What conditions do I put on my willingness to follow?

40 **When he arrived at the place he said to them, "Pray that you may not undergo the test."** The Greek word translated **test** can also be translated as temptation (as at 4:13) or trial (as at 8:13 and 22:28). Jesus is concerned about a **test** that his disciples will face, a trial that will tempt them to fall away. He warned them to be prepared for his being taken as a criminal; Peter's faith will fail when Jesus is arrested (22:34–38). Satan wants to sift them, shaking their loyalty to Jesus (22:31). In light of the impending crisis, Jesus urges them to **pray that you may not undergo the test**. They are to ask God to spare them testing that is beyond their strength; they are to pray that they will not succumb to temptation and fall away from Jesus. He taught them to make a similar petition to God when he told them to pray, "Do not subject us to the final test" (11:4).

For reflection: What do I mean when I pray the words of the Lord's Prayer, "Lead us not into temptation"?

41 **After withdrawing about a stone's throw from them and kneeling, he prayed.** Jesus goes off a little bit from his disciples, out of earshot but not out of sight. He **prayed** just as he had prayed throughout his life, particularly at critical moments (3:21; 5:16; 6:12; 9:18, 28–29; 11:1); he **prayed** as he urged his disciples to pray in anticipation of the impending crisis for him and for them. Jesus prays while **kneeling**. Jews normally stood while praying (see 18:11, 13); **kneeling** was done for special prayers (see Acts 9:40; 20:36; 21:5), as a posture of submission to God.

42 Jesus prayed **saying, "Father, if you are willing, take this cup away from me."** Jesus addresses God as his **Father**: he is the Son of God (1:32, 35; 3:22; 9:35; 10:21–22). Jesus has spoken of and called upon God

as his **Father** from his first words in Luke's Gospel (2:49) until this very night (22:29). Jesus begins his prayer to his **Father** by saying, **if you are willing:** he has been sent to carry out his Father's will (see 4:18, 43; 9:48; 10:16) and he remains submitted to his will. Yet he asks that if his Father is willing, **take this cup away from me**. A **cup** is used in the Old Testament as a metaphor for one's fate or destiny (Psalm 16:5), oftentimes unpleasant (Psalm 11:6; 75:9; Isaiah 51:17, 22; Ezek 23:31–34). By a **cup** Jesus refers to the suffering and death that he knows awaits him (22:15), and he asks his Father to spare him, to **take this cup** of suffering **away** if his Father is **willing** to do so.

It is a surprising request. Until this moment, Jesus has calmly spoken of and accepted the fact that he must suffer and die (9:22, 44; 13:33; 17:25; 22:15–20, 22) in fulfillment of God's will as made known in Scripture (18:31–33; 22:37); he has even been eager for it to be accomplished (12:50). Yet now that the moment is at hand he looks for a way out—a way that would be in accord with his Father's will, to be sure, but nevertheless a way different from his present destiny. In his prayer, Jesus offers no explanation for why he asks his Father to take the cup of suffering and death from him, so we are left to speculate. Jesus surely shared the aversion to pain and death that every human experiences; perhaps the enormity of what will happen to him hits home now that the hour for it is at hand. In any case, Jesus prays, **take this cup away from me**, but continues, **still, not my will but yours be done.** Jesus' prayer to his Father begins and ends with his submission to his Father's will, even as he asks his Father to change what he wills.

For reflection: What do I learn from Jesus' prayer? When have I found it hardest to say to my heavenly Father, "Not my will but yours be done"?

43 (Verses 43 and 44 are missing from some ancient manuscripts of Luke's Gospel, which the New American Bible indicates by enclosing them in brackets.) **[And to strengthen him an angel from heaven appeared to him.** God sent angels as his messengers to Zechariah (1:11–20), to Mary (1:26–38), and to shepherds (2:8–14), but angels can also carry out other tasks (16:22). In response to Jesus' prayer, God sends **an angel from heaven** whose mission is to **strengthen him**—strengthen Jesus to pray more intensely to embrace his Father's will for him.

Angels: See page 11

44 He was in such agony and he prayed so fervently that his sweat became like drops of blood falling on the ground.] The key for understanding what Jesus was experiencing lies in what Luke meant when he wrote that Jesus was in **agony**. For modern readers, **agony** means extreme pain. **Agony** is a near transliteration of the Greek word that Luke uses, *agonia*, but *agonia* meant something different from extreme pain for Luke's first readers. It was a word associated with athletics and was used to describe an athlete's struggle for victory; a closely related word is translated as "strive" at 13:24, as "struggle" at 1 Tim 4:10, and as "compete" at 1 Tim 6:12. Luke's readers would have understood Luke to mean that Jesus was in an intense struggle as he prayed. He **prayed so fervently that his sweat became like drops of blood falling on the ground**. Jesus did not sweat blood but, like an athlete in vigorous competition, perspired so profusely that his **sweat** fell from him like **drops of blood**. Luke uses athletic language and imagery to convey the intensity with which Jesus, strengthened by an angel, prayerfully strived to align himself with his Father's will. It was not easy for him to tell his Father, "not my will but yours be done"; it was spiritually comparable to a superb athlete exerting every bit of his or her strength and energy in a grueling race. Luke does not immediately tell his readers the outcome of Jesus' struggle, but Jesus' words and behavior in the following hours demonstrate that he was victorious in aligning himself with his Father's will.

For reflection: What insight into Jesus am I given by Luke's portrayal of him struggling fervently in prayer?

45 When he rose from prayer and returned to his disciples, he found them sleeping from grief. After his victory in prayer Jesus goes back to his **disciples**. He had told them to "pray that you may not undergo the test" (verse 40), but he finds them not at prayer but **sleeping from grief**. It is not evident why they are filled with **grief**. Perhaps Jesus' words about his coming suffering and death had finally sunk in, and they were grieving for him and for their loss. Whatever the cause of their grieving, for Luke's first readers **grief** had a connotation of weakness. Those whose lives were well-ordered did not let themselves become overwhelmed by emotions such as grief. Luke's readers would have seen a contrast not only between Jesus praying and his disciples sleeping, but also between Jesus struggling vigorously and his disciples letting themselves be overcome by emotion. These contrasts reinforce the importance of praying lest one succumb to temptation and weakness.

For reflection: What example does Jesus at prayer set for me?

46 **He said to them, "Why are you sleeping? Get up and pray that you may not undergo the test."** An armed crowd is on its way to arrest Jesus (22:47–53); it is no time for Jesus' disciples to be **sleeping.** Jesus tells them to **get up,** and he repeats his previous instruction to them: **pray that you may not undergo the test.** Even at this last minute, they are to pray that they not succumb to the crisis that is at hand.

The Hour of Darkness

⁴⁷ While he was still speaking, a crowd approached and in front was one of the Twelve, a man named Judas. He went up to Jesus to kiss him. ⁴⁸ Jesus said to him, "Judas, are you betraying the Son of Man with a kiss?" ⁴⁹ His disciples realized what was about to happen, and they asked, "Lord, shall we strike with a sword?" ⁵⁰ And one of them struck the high priest's servant and cut off his right ear. ⁵¹ But Jesus said in reply, "Stop, no more of this!" Then he touched the servant's ear and healed him. ⁵² And Jesus said to the chief priests and temple guards and elders who had come for him, "Have you come out as against a robber, with swords and clubs? ⁵³ Day after day I was with you in the temple area, and you did not seize me; but this is your hour, the time for the power of darkness."

Gospel parallels: Matt 26:47–56; Mark 14:43–52; John 18:2–11
NT: Luke 6:27–29, 35; 22:1–6, 21–23, 39–46

47 **While he was still speaking,** telling his disciples to "pray that you may not undergo the test" (22:46), the test begins. **A crowd approached**

and in front, leading it as its guide, **was one of the Twelve, a man named Judas**. He took part in the Passover meal with Jesus and the other disciples (22:21) but at some point slipped away. He had earlier agreed to hand Jesus over to the chief priests and Temple guards in return for money, and he had been looking for a "favorable opportunity to hand him over to them in the absence of a crowd" (22:3–6). Now it is night, and there are no friendly crowds around Jesus. Judas, knowing the place where Jesus spends his nights on the Mount of Olives (21:37; 22:39–40), leads an arresting party there. **He went up to Jesus to kiss him**. A **kiss** on the head or hand was a customary greeting (see 7:45), an expression of affection and friendship; a disciple might kiss his teacher as a sign of respect. It would be natural for Judas, **one of the Twelve** specially chosen by Jesus (6:12–16), to kiss him; he was one of Jesus' closest associates.

48 Jesus, however, knows why Judas has come, leading others to him (see 22:21). **Jesus said to him, "Judas, are you betraying the Son of Man with a kiss?"** The primary meaning of the Greek word translated **betraying** is to give over or hand over. Even though there is a full moon at Passover, Jesus might not be quickly identified in the dark; a **kiss** from Judas would single him out. It would be a vilely hypocritical act: the Greek word for **kiss** is derived from the word for "love," but Judas' intention is to hand Jesus over to those who would put him to death (22:2–6). It is not clear from Luke's account whether Judas actually kissed Jesus or was forestalled by Jesus' question. In any case, by going up to Jesus, Judas identifies him for those who came to seize him.

Son of Man: See page 147

49 **His disciples realized what was about to happen and they asked, "Lord, shall we strike with a sword?"** Jesus' disciples realize that the crowd has come to seize Jesus, and their instinctive reaction is to protect him. They have two swords at their disposal (22:38) and ask Jesus, **Lord, shall we strike with a sword?** They fail to grasp that when Jesus spoke of procuring a sword (22:36), he was speaking figuratively to make the point that they needed to be prepared for adversity, not asking them to literally arm themselves. Jesus has made it clear that violence is not to be met with violence (6:29).

50 Without waiting for Jesus' permission **one of them struck the high priest's servant and cut off his right ear.** The **high priest's servant,** literally, slave, may have been acting as his personal representative. If he was in front of the crowd that came to seize Jesus, he would make a handy target for the disciple's sword. Along with being misguided, the blow was inept: having an ear cut off is painful and disfiguring but not disabling. As soon as the test begins (22:40, 46), Jesus' disciples demonstrate that they are unable to respond to it as Jesus would have them respond.

High priest, chief priests: See page 605

Servant, slave: See page 454

For reflection: When have I charged ahead on a course of action without considering what Jesus would have me do?

51 **But Jesus said in reply, "Stop, no more of this!"** Jesus puts an end to the amateur sword-play. He is resolved to do his Father's will (22:42), which means that he must suffer and be put to death (9:22; 12:50; 13:33; 17:25; 22:22, 37). However well-intentioned, his disciples' attempt to prevent his arrest thwarts his Father's will, and does so with a violence that Jesus condemns. **Then he touched the servant's ear and healed him.** Jesus demonstrates what it means to "love your enemies and do good to them" (6:35). Taking the initiative, he **healed** a man who had come to seize him for those who wanted to put him to death (22:2). Jesus healed many women and men in the course of his ministry; he is willing to heal and do good even to those who treat him as their enemy. This healing foreshadows the healing and forgiveness that will be granted through his death and resurrection (see 23:34; Acts 2:36–38; 5:30–31; 10:39–43).

For reflection: What does Jesus' healing of the high priest's servant reveal to me about Jesus? What hope does it give me that he is willing to heal me where I am wounded?

52 **And Jesus said to the chief priests and temple guards and elders who had come for him:** Luke identifies the crowd who came to Jesus (verse 47) as made up of **chief priests,** that is, high ranking priests, often from high priests' families, **temple guards,** who were in charge of the Temple's security, and **elders,** influential lay leaders. **Chief priests**

and **elders** sat on the Sanhedrin (22:66), the Jewish ruling council; the opposition to Jesus comes from the highest circles. He asks them, **Have you come out as against a robber, with swords and clubs?** The word **robber** has the connotation of a violent criminal. Those coming to seize Jesus treat him as if he is a man of violence, someone who has to be subdued **with swords and clubs**. It is a charade: Jesus has provided no basis for being considered a violent criminal, but it serves the purpose of those arresting him to treat him as if he is a threat to the social order (see 23:2).

Elders: See page 189

53 Jesus reminds those who have come to arrest him, **Day after day I was with you in the temple area, and you did not seize me**, literally, "did not stretch out your hands against me." After his arrival in Jerusalem, Jesus taught daily in a courtyard of the Temple (19:47; 20:1; 21:37), in plain view in daylight. It would have been a simple matter for the Temple guards to arrest him in the **temple area**, but it would have attracted a good deal of notice, for crowds gathered to hear Jesus when he taught (21:38). The fact that his adversaries seize Jesus at night, away from the crowds (20:19; 22:2), is an indication that what they are doing will not stand up to public scrutiny. Jesus tells them, **but this is your hour, the time for the power of darkness.** The word **darkness** has multiple associations. It refers to Jesus' surreptitious arrest under cover of **darkness**. It alludes to the spiritual and moral **darkness** of those who want to do away with him. Its ultimate association is with Satan: Paul will describe his mission as helping people "turn from darkness to light and from the power of Satan to God" (Acts 26:18). Now is the **hour** that Satan has been waiting for (4:13) to assault Jesus and his followers (22:3, 31). For the moment, **the power of darkness** will prevail, but only so that the plan of God will come to fulfillment (22:22).

Temple: See page 519

For reflection: What am I doing that will not stand up to scrutiny? How has God worked even through my failings to bring his plan for me to fulfillment?

Peter Denies Knowing Jesus

⁵⁴ After arresting him they led him away and took him into the house of the high priest; Peter was following at a distance. ⁵⁵ They lit a fire in the middle of the courtyard and sat around it, and Peter sat down with them. ⁵⁶ When a maid saw him seated in the light, she looked intently at him and said, "This man too was with him." ⁵⁷ But he denied it saying, "Woman, I do not know him." ⁵⁸ A short while later someone else saw him and said, "You too are one of them"; but Peter answered, "My friend, I am not." ⁵⁹ About an hour later, still another insisted, "Assuredly, this man too was with him, for he also is a Galilean." ⁶⁰ But Peter said, "My friend, I do not know what you are talking about." Just as he was saying this, the cock crowed, ⁶¹ and the Lord turned and looked at Peter; and Peter remembered the word of the Lord, how he had said to him, "Before the cock crows today, you will deny me three times." ⁶² He went out and began to weep bitterly. ⁶³ The men who held Jesus in custody were ridiculing and beating him. ⁶⁴ They blindfolded him and questioned him, saying, "Prophesy! Who is it that struck

---

BACKGROUND: HIGH PRIEST, CHIEF PRIESTS The office of high priest is traced back to Aaron in the Old Testament. Over the course of time, high priesthood became restricted to descendants of Zadok, the high priest at the time of Solomon. This succession was broken by Syrian and Maccabean rulers in the second century B.C., when the office of high priest was made into a political appointment. The Essenes considered these latter high priests illegitimate, since they were not descendants of Zadok. The high priest had religious functions, and he alone could enter the Holy of Holies of the Temple, once a year, on the Day of Atonement. The importance of the high priest extended beyond religious matters. The high priest had authority over the Temple and its income, which was the mainstay of the economy in Jerusalem. Because the high priest was the highest-ranking Jewish authority, he served as an intermediary between Rome and the Jewish people. Rome expected the high priest to help keep the nation in line and to ensure payment of tribute, or taxes, to Rome, and the high priest remained in office at the pleasure of Rome. The Gospels refer to "chief priests," a group that would have included the current high priest, former high priests, other high-ranking priests and members of high-priestly families. The chief priests were a wealthy aristocracy within the priesthood; ordinary priests carried out their assigned duties in the Temple but had little say over how it was run.

---

you?" ⁶⁵ **And they reviled him in saying many other things against him.**

> Gospel parallels: Matt 26:57–58, 67–75; Mark 14:53–54, 65–72;
> John 18:12–18, 25–27
> NT: Luke 12:8–9; 18:32; 22:31–34, 39–40, 46–53

54 Judas led an armed crowd that included Temple guards to the place where Jesus spent his nights on the Mount of Olives (21:37; 22:39–40, 47–53). **After arresting him they led him away and took him into the house of the high priest.** Jesus was arrested but not his disciples, despite one of them having struck the high priest's servant with a sword (22:49–50). Apparently the authorities did not think that his disciples posed a serious threat. The current **high priest** was Caiaphas (see 3:2). High priests came from aristocratic priestly families and derived considerable income from Temple offerings and activities. Archaeologists have found the remains of several mansions in Jerusalem that apparently belonged to members of high-priestly families. These mansions incorporated Greek and Roman architectural features and had interior courtyards. What follows indicates that Jesus is being held by guards in a courtyard of the **house of the high priest** until daybreak, when the Sanhedrin will convene to interrogate him (22:55, 61, 66). **Peter was following at a distance.** Peter said that he was willing to go with Jesus to prison and death (22:33) and continues **following** him as his disciple, going into the courtyard of the high priest's house. He wants to be near Jesus and see what happens to him. He follows, however, **at a distance**, as if he is leery of being too closely identified with Jesus, his claim to be willing to die with him notwithstanding.

> Houses: See page 186

For reflection: What do I see of myself in Peter's following of Jesus at a distance?

55 **They lit a fire in the middle of the courtyard and sat around it, and Peter sat down with them.** Luke's account leaves it vague who **they** are who **lit a fire**, but they could be members of the group that arrested Jesus and the maids and servants attached to the high priest's house (see verse 56). It is now the early morning hours, which can be chilly at Passover time in Jerusalem. **Peter** joins those sitting **around** a **fire in the middle of the courtyard** to keep warm. Perhaps he thinks he can blend in with the crowd.

56 **When a maid saw him seated in the light, she looked intently at him.** The word translated **maid** can refer to a female slave or servant girl. She first **saw** Peter indistinctly in the flickering **light** of the fire and then **looked intently at him**, examining and trying to identify him. Where had she seen him before? She remembered **and said, "This man too was with him."** She doesn't know Peter's name and refers to him as **this man;** she is sure that he **was with him**—with Jesus. We might imagine her gesturing first toward Peter, and then toward Jesus, who is being held by guards in the courtyard. Luke does not tell his readers when and where the maid saw Peter **with** Jesus. It could have been when Jesus was teaching in a Temple courtyard (19:47—21:38), or she may have been in the crowd that Judas led to Jesus on the Mount of Olives (22:47). She has in any case seen them together and comments on it to those around her. Her words are not so much an accusation as an observation: there are no arrest warrants out for disciples of Jesus or bounties offered for their capture.

57 **But he denied it**—literally, "but he denied"—**saying, "Woman, I do not know him."** Peter does not deny the maid's assertion as much as he denies Jesus. Applied to a person, **denied** has the sense of repudiate or disown (see 12:9). He addresses the maid as **woman**, a more formal way of speaking than would normally be used for a slave or servant girl. Peter claims, **I do not know him**: I am not acquainted with the man you are talking about. This is an outrageous lie coming from Peter, who is not only one of Jesus' intimate followers (see 8:51; 9:28) but the one who professed that Jesus is "the Messiah of God" (9:20). His denial begins to fulfill Jesus' warning that Satan wants to sift the disciples like wheat (22:31) and his prediction to Peter that "before the cock crows this day, you will deny three times that you know me" (22:34).

Luke does not tell his readers what was going through Peter's mind. We can speculate that Peter feared that admitting his relationship with Jesus would place him in jeopardy. Despite his promise to remain with Jesus no matter the cost (22:33), Peter crumbles the first time he is tested:

he cannot admit even to a maid, a person of lowly and unthreatening status, that he was with Jesus.

For reflection: How has my fidelity to Jesus been tested? When have I done what I was firmly determined not to do?

58 **A short while later someone else saw him and said, "You too are one of them."** This person, a man, addresses Peter directly and tells him that he is **one of them**—one of Jesus' disciples. Perhaps he was part of the crowd that seized Jesus on the Mount of Olives and saw Peter with the other disciples. Like the maid's comment (verse 56), his words are more an observation than an accusation. **But Peter answered, "My friend, I am not."** The word translated **my friend** might also be translated as "man" or "sir." Peter says, **I am not** one of Jesus' disciples, even though Jesus designated him as one of the specially chosen Twelve (6:13–14). Peter is not on the periphery of Jesus' disciples but among the core of his followers.

For reflection: When have I denied or downplayed my association with followers of Jesus or with the Church? What led me to do so?

59 **About an hour later**: about an **hour** goes by without anyone else commenting on Peter's association with Jesus. Luke continues to remain silent about what is going through Peter's mind, but an hour is ample time for Peter to reflect on the enormity of what he has done. Did he remember Jesus' teaching about the importance of acknowledging him before others (12:8–9)? Did Peter berate himself for having denied that he knew Jesus and was his disciple? Did Peter steel himself to acknowledge Jesus should the occasion to do so arise again? The only thing that is clear is that Peter remained in the courtyard of the high priest's house with Jesus, even though at a distance from him. After about an hour, **still another insisted, "Assuredly, this man too was with him."** There is no doubt in this man's mind that Peter was **with** Jesus; he **insisted** on it very **assuredly**, as if he had seen them together. He can be sure it is not a case of mistaken identity because Peter **also is a Galilean** like Jesus (see 23:6–7) and his other disciples (see Acts 1:11; 2:7). He can tell that Peter is a Galilean because of his accent (see Matt 26:73) or possibly from his

style of clothing. For a Galilean stranger to show up in the middle of the night in the courtyard of the high priest's house as the Galilean Jesus is being held there cannot be dismissed as a mere coincidence: **this man too was with him**.

Galilee: See page 114

60 **But Peter said, "My friend, I do not know what you are talking about."** Peter professes to be puzzled by what the man is saying. Given yet another opportunity to declare his association with Jesus, Peter takes refuge in evasion. Earlier that night he had not remained awake to pray that he not undergo the test (22:40, 45–46), and now he repeatedly fails the test. Satan has sifted Peter like wheat (22:31); Peter's fidelity to Jesus has been tried and found wanting in an hour of darkness (22:53). **Just as he was saying this, the cock crowed**, as Jesus had said it would (22:34).

61 **And the Lord turned and looked at Peter.** Jesus has apparently been within Peter's sight while Peter was denying that he knew him. Now Jesus **turned** to Peter and **looked** at him. The word translated **looked** has the connotation of Jesus fixing his gaze upon Peter, looking squarely at him. Luke does not describe the expression on Jesus' face, but from Peter's reaction we can imagine that it is a look of compassion and love, tinged with sadness. Peter has fallen, as Jesus knew he would (22:34). But Jesus has also prayed that Peter's faith would not completely fail and that when he had turned back he would strengthen the other disciples (22:32). Jesus **turned** to Peter so that Peter would turn back to him; Jesus **looked** at Peter to assure him of his understanding and love. **And Peter remembered the word of the Lord, how he had said to him, "Before the cock crows today, you will deny me three times."** Had Peter totally forgotten these words of Jesus and only now remembered them? Or had he rejected these words when Jesus uttered them but now their truth hits home? Luke hints that Jesus' words to Peter now have an impact on him as if they were a word of God spoken to him, for he characterizes Jesus' words as **the word of the Lord**. Luke's first readers would have found the expression, "the word of the Lord," meaning the word of God, many times in the Greek translation of the Old Testament, particularly in the prophets. Jesus' gaze and words touch Peter to his core.

Lord: See page 137

For reflection: What do I imagine to be the expression on Jesus' face as he gazes at me? What are the most personal and significant words he has spoken to me?

62 **He went out and began to weep bitterly.** Peter cries in heartfelt remorse for having denied Jesus. He is the weak and sinful person he has always been (5:8), but he realizes that Jesus nonetheless loves him and has a mission for him (5:10). He likely remembers that Jesus told him, "Once you have turned back, you must strengthen your brothers" (22:32), and resolves to do just that. The risen Jesus will appear to Peter (24:34); we may speculate that he did so to accept Peter's repentance and bring about reconciliation. The Peter that Luke's readers will meet in Acts will be fearless in the face of opposition, unfazed by imprisonment, and bold in proclaiming Jesus despite attempts to silence him (Acts 4:1–31; 5:17–42).

For reflection: What do I see of Peter in myself? What has been my most heartfelt repentance?

63 **The men who held Jesus in custody were ridiculing and beating him.** Jesus is being held **in custody** until daybreak, when the Sanhedrin will convene (22:66). Those holding Jesus amuse themselves by abusing him; they apparently enjoy inflicting shame and pain on those within their power. Jesus foretold that it would happen, telling his disciples that "he will be mocked and insulted and spat upon" (18:32).

64 **They blindfolded him and questioned him, saying, "Prophesy! Who is it that struck you?"** Those guarding Jesus **blindfolded** him so that they could play a rough game of guess-who-hit-you, an ancient variation on blindman's buff. They tauntingly demand that Jesus **prophesy**, apparently aware that Jesus is widely regarded as a prophet (7:16; 9:7–8, 18–19; 24:19). If he cannot name his assailant, well then, he is no prophet. Ironically, Jesus has demonstrated his prophetic insight by foretelling their abuse (18:32) and Peter's denials (22:34).

65 **And they reviled him in saying many other things against him.** Luke might seem to be repeating himself, for he has already said that Jesus' guards were ridiculing him (verse 63). But Luke's choice of words

suggests a deeper meaning: he literally writes that "blaspheming, they were saying many other things against him." The Greek word for blaspheme means to revile and defame, but it takes on weightier significance when God is the one who is reviled and defamed. By choosing this word to express how Jesus is **reviled**, Luke implies that the ridicule and abuse heaped on Jesus is equivalent to reviling God. The one who endures the mockery and blows of his captors is no mere prophet but God's beloved Son (3:22; 9:35). As his Son, he embraces his Father's will (22:42), submitting himself to the abuse and suffering he knew would be inflicted on him (9:22; 18:32).

For reflection: What insight into Jesus am I given by his acceptance of mockery and pain?

Jesus before the Sanhedrin
⁶⁶ When day came the council of elders of the people met, both chief priests and scribes, and they brought him before their Sanhedrin. ⁶⁷ They said, "If you are the Messiah, tell us," but he replied to them, "If I tell you, you will not believe, ⁶⁸ and if I question, you will not respond. ⁶⁹ But from this time on the Son of Man will be seated at the right hand of the power of God." ⁷⁰ They all

BACKGROUND: SANHEDRIN At the time of Jesus, it was common for cities to have some form of city council, with what we think of as legislative, judicial, and executive responsibilities. In Jerusalem this council was called the Sanhedrin, from the Greek for "sitting together." Its members were drawn from the aristocracy of high-priestly families and wealthy or influential citizens, called elders, and included some religious scholars, called scribes: see Mark 15:1. The high priest presided over the council's deliberations. Since A.D. 6, Judea and Jerusalem had been under direct Roman rule, exercised through governors such as Pontius Pilate. Rome normally allowed subject peoples to manage their own affairs, as long as public order was maintained and taxes were paid. The Sanhedrin was the chief Jewish ruling body in Jerusalem under Roman authority. It dealt primarily with religious matters, but since religion pervaded all of Jewish life, authority in religious matters covered a wide range of concerns. The Sanhedrin's religious authority extended beyond Jerusalem, because of its makeup and the importance of the Jerusalem Temple in Jewish life. *Related topics: Elders (page 189), High priest, chief priests (page 605), Scribes (page 146).*

asked, "Are you then the Son of God?" He replied to them, "You say that I am." ⁷¹ Then they said, "What further need have we for testimony? We have heard it from his own mouth."

Gospel parallels: Matt 26:59–66; Mark 14:55–64
OT: Psalm 110:1; Jer 38:15
NT: Luke 3:22; 9:20–22, 35; 19:47; 20:19–20; 22:2, 53–54; John 10:24–26

66 **When day came:** Jesus was arrested in darkness and held overnight at the house of the high priest (22:53–54). After daybreak, **the council of elders of the people met, both chief priests and scribes, and they brought him before their Sanhedrin.** The **Sanhedrin** was the Jewish ruling body in Jerusalem, made up of **chief priests** including the high priest, **scribes** who were scholars of the law of Moses, and **elders**—influential lay leaders. Luke characterizes the whole **Sanhedrin** as **the council of elders of the people**, since all who served on it were leaders of the people (see Acts 22:5). The **Sanhedrin** was the most authoritative Jewish council, but subject to Roman rule. When day came, **they brought** Jesus to stand before the Sanhedrin, perhaps inside the house of the high priest, or perhaps in the Sanhedrin's regular meeting chamber. Their intent is plain: "The chief priests, the scribes, and the leaders of the people . . . were seeking to put him to death (19:47; see also 22:2). They previously wanted to seize him "but they feared the people," so they sent agents "to trap him in speech, in order to hand him over to the authority and power of the governor" (20:19–20). Now he is in their hands away from the crowds; now they can try to trap him into saying something that will justify their handing him over to the Roman governor to be executed. Jesus is well aware of their intent and accepts the outcome as his Father's will for him (9:22; 18:31–33; 22:42).

Elders: See page 189
High priest, chief priests: See page 605
Scribes: See page 146

67 **They said, "If you are the Messiah, tell us."** The Sanhedrin interrogates Jesus and begins their questioning with a blockbuster. While there were different expectations of what **the Messiah** would do when he came, the most common view was that he would liberate the Jewish people from Roman rule. One of the *Psalms of Solomon*, a first-century

B.C. Jewish nonbiblical writing, asked God to strengthen the Messiah "to shatter unrighteous rulers, to cleanse Jerusalem from gentiles"—references to the Romans. Even after his resurrection, Jesus' disciples expected that he might "restore the kingdom to Israel" (Acts 1:6), meaning restore its sovereignty as a nation. If Jesus admits that he is **the Messiah**, then he can be handed over to the Roman governor and accused of being a revolutionary intent on winning independence for Jews from Rome. Rome did not take challenges to its rule lightly; it crucified rebels in order to eliminate them and to graphically warn others of what awaited those who stirred up rebellion. The Sanhedrin asks the question that will make all other questioning superfluous if Jesus answers yes: **If you are the Messiah, tell us**.

Messiah, Christ: See page 257
Psalms of Solomon: See page 259

But he replied to them, "If I tell you, you will not believe." Assuredly, Jesus *is* the Messiah (2:11, 26; 4:41; 9:20). Gabriel told Mary that she would bear a son and that "the Lord God will give him the throne of David his father, and he will rule over the house of Jacob forever, and of his kingdom there will be no end" (1:32–33). But the kingdom that Jesus establishes is not like earthly kingdoms, and he does not establish it by conquering nations. When Peter told Jesus that his disciples thought he was the Messiah of God, Jesus rebuked them and forbade them to tell this to anyone, saying, "The Son of Man must suffer greatly and be rejected by the elders, the chief priests, and the scribes, and be killed and on the third day be raised" (9:20–22). Jesus is not the kind of Messiah people are expecting. He will fulfill his mission as the Messiah by suffering and dying, not by leading a revolt against Rome. Jewish leaders ask Jesus to tell them if he is the Messiah, and he responds, **If I tell you, you will not believe**. If I tell you the kind of Messiah I am, you will not believe me; you will not accept me as the Messiah sent by God. Jesus knows how firmly they are set against him; they seek his death, not the truth about him. Were they to accept him as a Messiah who was not out to end Roman rule, then they would undercut the case they wish to make to the Roman governor against him. Jesus knows it is useless to **tell** them who he is.

68 Jesus continues, **and if I question, you will not respond**. Discussion is also useless. Jesus previously used a **question** to engage with chief priests, scribes, and elders, but without getting an answer from them (20:1–8; see also 20:39–44). It is no different now; they **will not respond**, because they have already made up their minds to put him to death. Jesus' words to the Sanhedrin faintly echo Jeremiah's response to King Zedekiah when the king questioned him: "If I tell you anything, you will have me killed, will you not? If I counsel you, you will not listen to me!" (Jer 38:15).

69 Jesus accepts the fact that the Sanhedrin will hand him over to the Roman governor, who will have him put to death, but he knows that his suffering and dying are a prelude to his being raised by God (9:22; 18:32–33). He speaks of his exaltation after he is raised: **But from this time on the Son of Man will be seated at the right hand of the power of God.** Jesus refers to himself as **the Son of Man**, as he has often done (5:24; 6:5; 7:34; 9:22; 11:30; 12:10; etc.). He proclaims that from now on, he will **be seated at the right hand of the power of God**. The seat at one's **right hand** was a place of honor and authority. In Psalm 110, God tells an Israelite king, "Sit at my right hand" (Psalm 110:1); Jesus interpreted these words as addressed to the Messiah (20:41–44). To be seated at the right hand **of the power of God** means being seated at the right hand of God and sharing the power of God. The present hour is "the time for the power of darkness" (22:53), but the darkness will be vanquished by the power of God. He will vindicate Jesus by raising him from the dead and exalting him at his right hand (see Acts 2:32–36; 5:31; 7:55–56). Jesus faces suffering and death confident that it is the path to his exaltation.

Son of Man: See page 147

For reflection: Do I view death more as an end or as a beginning? How confident am I that God will raise me to be with him?

70 **They all asked, "Are you then the Son of God?"** Just as Luke's readers know that he is the Messiah (2:11, 26; 4:41; 9:20), so they also know that he is **the Son of God,** conceived through the Holy Spirit (1:35) and proclaimed by God to be his beloved Son (3:22; 9:35). But those question-

ing Jesus were not present when Gabriel appeared to Mary or when God spoke to Jesus after his baptism and during his transfiguration; they do not realize the profound and unique sense in which Jesus is **the Son of God**. Rather, when they speak of **the Son of God,** the expression carries only the general Old Testament meaning of someone with a special relationship to God, such as an Israelite king (2 Sam 7:14; Psalm 2:7) or a righteous person (Wisd 2:18). Jesus proclaimed that he will be seated at the right hand of the power of God (verse 69); their asking him, **Are you then the Son of God**, has the sense, Do you claim to have an exalted relationship with God such that he would seat you at his right hand?

Son of God: See page 25

For reflection: What does it mean for me that Jesus of Nazareth is the Son of God?

He replied to them, "You say that I am." Jesus response is equivocal. He does not deny that he is the Son of God but tells them, **you** are the ones who are saying that I am the Son of God. He does not accept their understanding of what it means that he is the Son of God, for their understanding is inadequate, but neither can he deny that he is the Son of God. It would be fruitless for him to proclaim to them his unique relationship with his Father (10:22), for they would not accept it. Discussion continues to be pointless (verses 67–68) when the minds of those questioning him were made up before the hearing began.

71 **Then they said, "What further need have we for testimony? We have heard it from his own mouth."** They construe his "You say that I am" as a claim to be the Son of God, and they take this to be tantamount to claiming to be the Messiah (see 23:2). They say that they have **heard it from his own mouth**: they have heard something sufficient for their purposes, enabling them to hand him over to the Roman governor (see 20:20). They have no **further need** of **testimony** because they consider Jesus' words about himself to be incriminating testimony. Luke's next verse recounts their bringing Jesus before Pilate, the Roman governor (23:1).

CHAPTER 23

Jesus before Pilate

¹ **Then the whole assembly of them arose and brought him before Pilate. ² They brought charges against him, saying, "We found this man misleading our people; he opposes the payment of taxes to Caesar and maintains that he is the Messiah, a king." ³ Pilate asked him, "Are you the king of the Jews?" He said to him in reply, "You say so." ⁴ Pilate then addressed the chief priests and the crowds, "I find this man not guilty." ⁵ But they were adamant and said, "He is inciting the people with his teaching throughout all Judea, from Galilee where he began even to here."**

⁶ On hearing this Pilate asked if the man was a Galilean; ⁷ and upon learning that he was under Herod's jurisdiction, he sent him to Herod who was in Jerusalem at that time.

Gospel parallels: Matt 27:1–2, 11–14; Mark 15:1–5; John 18:28–38
NT: Luke 18:32; 20:19–26; 22:66–71; 23:14

1 After the chief priests, scribes, and elders questioned Jesus and decided they had testimony to use against him (22:66–71), **then the whole assembly of them arose and brought him before Pilate**. ontius **Pilate** was the Roman governor of Judea (3:1); he had the authority to impose the death penalty. His headquarters were in Caesarea on the Mediterranean coast, but he came with troops under his command to Jerusalem to keep order during major religious feasts such as Passover. When in Jerusalem, Pilate likely stayed in a grand palace-fortress built by Herod the Great near the main western gate of the city; it had a court-yard that could be used for legal proceedings. Roman trials customarily began at daybreak. Jesus foretold that he would be "handed over to the Gentiles" (18:32); those bringing Jesus to Pilate fulfill his prediction.

Roman Empire: See page 52

2 **They brought charges against him, saying, "We found this man misleading our people."** They accuse Jesus of being a rabble-rouser who is leading the Jewish people astray. Religious leaders had their differences with Jesus throughout his ministry, but Pilate has no interest in Jewish

616

religious disputes. For the charge that Jesus was **misleading our people** to have any weight with Pilate, Jesus' accusers have to show how Jesus' words or actions are a threat to Roman rule. They make two accusations of this sort: **he opposes the payment of taxes to Caesar and maintains that he is the Messiah, a king**. Their allegations match up with two of Pilate's most important duties as governor: he is responsible for the collection of taxes and for maintaining Roman rule. Those accusing Jesus charge that **he opposes the payment of taxes to Caesar**—to the Roman emperor, who had assumed the name **Caesar** (3:1). Previously when the chief priests sent agents to trap Jesus in speech "in order to hand him over to the authority and power of the governor," their agents asked him, "Is it lawful for us to pay tribute to Caesar or not?" (20:19–22). Jesus replied, "Repay to Caesar what belongs to Caesar and to God what belongs to God" (20:25): an emperor may have a legitimate claim to taxes, but God has an unlimited claim on all we have and are. It is a tendentious misinterpretation of Jesus' words to charge that he **opposes the**

BACKGROUND: PONTIUS PILATE Pilate was the Roman governor of Judea and the adjacent regions of Samaria and Idumea from about A.D. 26 to 36. His official title was prefect, or military commander, but he also carried out the duties of procurator, or civil administrator, keeping order and collecting taxes. Pilate was a member of the lower Roman nobility that Rome drew on for governors of unimportant but sometimes troublesome provinces like Judea. Pilate lived in Caesarea, on the Mediterranean coast, using a seaside palace built by Herod the Great as his headquarters, or praetorium. Paul was later held captive here (Acts 23:35). Pilate commanded about twenty-five hundred to three thousand soldiers, most of whom were stationed in Caesarea but some of whom manned the Antonia Fortress, adjacent to the Temple in Jerusalem. During Jewish pilgrimage feasts, when Jerusalem was crowded with pilgrims, Pilate and his Caesarea troops went to Jerusalem to keep order. Pilate could be quite heedless of Jewish sensitivities, and he aroused anger by bringing images of the Roman emperor into Jerusalem and by taking money from the Temple treasury to pay for an aqueduct. The Gospels portray Pilate as weak and indecisive. Philo, a first-century Jewish writer living in Egypt, might have been exaggerating when he characterized Pilate as arrogant, corrupt, cruel, and given to executing people without trial. Pilate seems to have been a man who made ill-considered decisions but backed down under pressure. He was removed as governor after his troops killed some Samaritans. The fact that Pilate kept Caiaphas as high priest during his whole term as governor indicates that the two men established a working relationship.

---

payment of taxes to Caesar. It is also an ironic charge to make against someone who was so friendly with tax collectors (5:27–30; 7:34; 15:1–2; 19:1–10; see also 18:10–14)!

Roman Empire: See page 52

Those accusing Jesus also charge that he **maintains that he is the Messiah, a king**. Earlier that morning they demanded of Jesus, "If you are the Messiah, tell us," and he responded, "If I tell you, you will not believe" (22:67). Jesus did not deny that he is the **Messiah**, but neither did he claim to be the Messiah. Jesus' accusers distort his equivocal response and tell Pilate that Jesus **maintains that he is the Messiah**. Because Pilate might not be familiar with the Jewish concept of a Messiah, the accusers interpret **Messiah** to mean **a king**. Pilate would certainly understand the implications of someone claiming to be **a king**: it would be a declaration that one is a rival to Caesar and would be an incitement for people to revolt against Roman rule (see 23:14). Some people did hail Jesus as a **king** when he entered Jerusalem (19:38), perhaps expecting that he had come to town to replace Roman rule with the kingdom of God (19:11)—an expectation Jesus discouraged by telling a parable (19:12–27) and by riding peaceably into Jerusalem on a donkey (19:35–36). Nevertheless, Jesus is charged with claiming to be **the Messiah, a king**—a charge Pilate cannot dismiss lightly.

Messiah, Christ: See page 257

3 Pilate ignores Jesus' supposed opposition to paying Roman taxes and addresses the weightier charge: **Pilate asked him, "Are you the king of the Jews?"** Pilate gives Jesus an opportunity to defend himself. **He said to him in reply, "You say so."** The sense of his response is, The word "king" is yours, not mine. Jesus cannot deny that he is the Messiah, but he is not the kind of rebel king that Pilate has in mind. Jesus responds to Pilate as he did to the Sanhedrin when asked whether he was the Son of God (22:70): he cannot deny his identity, but neither can he agree with how others misperceive him.

For reflection: How accurate are my perceptions of Jesus? To what extent have I made him fit into my ways of thinking instead of forming my thinking by what is revealed about him in Scripture and the teaching of the Church?

4 **Pilate then addressed the chief priests and the crowds, "I find this man not guilty."** The **crowds** present at Jesus' hearing before Pilate are best identified with the crowd that seized him on the Mount of Olives (22:47) rather than with the crowds who listened to him teaching in the Temple (see 19:47–48; 21:38; 22:2, 6). Those accusing Jesus would want their supporters with them at Pilate's hearing; it is doubtful that word of Jesus' nighttime arrest has already reached the ordinary people of Jerusalem. Pilate **addressed the chief priests** and those who were with them, telling them, **I find this man not guilty.** Luke has recounted only a brief exchange between Pilate and Jesus (verse 3), but it was apparently enough to convince Pilate that the accusations made against Jesus were not compelling. We can speculate that Pilate had dealt with enough dangerous criminals through the years to know that the man standing calmly in front of him is not a violent fanatic. Pilate could be very brutal in dealing with perceived threats to Roman rule (see 13:1), but he does not consider Jesus such a threat. He pronounces him **not guilty.**

High priest, chief priests: See page 605

5 **But they were adamant and said, "He is inciting the people with his teaching."** They repeat their charge (verse 2) that Jesus is **inciting the people,** implying that he is inciting them against Rome. They say that he is doing so by **his teaching** but provide no instances of Jesus saying anything treasonous. They claim that he is not just a local problem but has been spreading his teachings **throughout all Judea,** using **Judea** to refer to the whole of Palestine (see 4:44; 6:17; 7:17). Jesus has taught **from Galilee where he began** (4:14–15) **even to here,** to Jerusalem (19:47). Their **adamant** insistence that Jesus is a dangerous troublemaker puts Pilate in a bind. On the one hand, he does not think that Jesus is guilty of what he is being charged with. On the other hand, sheer force goes only so far in governing a subject people; Pilate depends on the Jewish aristocracy to be his partners in maintaining peaceful Roman rule. If he expects them to cooperate with him, then he has to take their interests into account, and they are set on doing away with Jesus.

Judea: See page 40
Galilee: See page 114

619

6 **On hearing this Pilate asked if the man was a Galilean.** Pilate's ears seem to perk up when he hears them mention Galilee, for it might provide him with a way out of his bind. Pilate is not responsible for governing Galilee. **If the man** standing accused before him is **a Galilean**, then Rome's agent for governing Galilee can deal with him instead of Pilate.

7 **and upon learning that he was under Herod's jurisdiction, he sent him to Herod who was in Jerusalem at that time.** Galilee, where Jesus grew up and carried out much of his ministry, was under the **jurisdiction** of **Herod** Antipas (3:1). His capital was the city of Tiberias on the Sea of Galilee, but Herod Antipas **was in Jerusalem at that time**. He may have come for Passover and stayed in a family palace near the Temple. Since Jesus as a Galilean could be considered **under Herod's jurisdiction**, Pilate **sent him to Herod**, apparently hoping to be rid of the matter. Pilate has no love for Herod Antipas (23:12); let Herod Antipas worry about placating the chief priests.

Herod Antipas: See page 99

Jesus before Herod
8 Herod was very glad to see Jesus; he had been wanting to see him for a long time, for he had heard about him and had been hoping to see him perform some sign. 9 He questioned him at length, but he gave him no answer. 10 The chief priests and scribes, meanwhile, stood by accusing him harshly. 11 [Even] Herod and his soldiers treated him contemptuously and mocked him, and after clothing him in resplendent garb, he sent him back to Pilate. 12 Herod and Pilate became friends that very day, even though they had been enemies formerly.

OT: Isaiah 53:7
NT: Luke 3:19–20; 9:7–9; 13:31–33; 18:32; 23:1–7; Acts 8:32–35

8 Pilate sent Jesus to **Herod** Antipas (23:6–7), who **was very glad to see Jesus; he had been wanting to see him for a long time, for he had heard about him**. Earlier, Herod had "heard about all that was happening" (9:7)—heard about Jesus and his disciples traveling throughout Galilee, proclaiming the kingdom of God and healing the sick (7:22; 8:1;

9:6). Herod had been "greatly perplexed" by speculations about Jesus and "he kept trying to see him" (9:7–9). Now he is **very glad to see Jesus** at last. Herod **had been hoping to see him perform some sign**: he had heard of the works Jesus performed and wanted him to put on a show for his entertainment. Herod Antipas seems ambivalent toward Jesus. At one time he wanted to kill Jesus (13:31); at other times he seems merely curious about Jesus and hopes to be entertained by him.

Herod Antipas: See page 99

9 **He questioned him at length.** Luke does not recount what Herod Antipas asked Jesus but notes that it was a lengthy interrogation. No matter what Herod asked, Jesus **gave him no answer.** Jesus stands silently before him, not working signs to amuse him, not satisfying his curiosity. Jesus neither respects nor fears Herod. When some Pharisees urged Jesus to leave Galilee because Herod wanted to kill him, Jesus told them to tell "that fox" that he would continue to carry out his mission (13:31–33). So too now: Jesus is determined to carry out God's will for him, and he will not try to evade death by appeasing those in authority. The early Church understood Jesus' silence before his interrogators to be a fulfillment of Isaiah's prophecy about a servant of God who remains silent before his oppressors (Acts 8:32–35; Isaiah 53:7).

> Though harshly treated, he submitted
> and did not open mouth;
> Like a lamb led to slaughter
> or a sheep silent before shearers,
> he did not open his mouth.
>
> Isaiah 53:7

10 **The chief priests and scribes, meanwhile, stood by accusing him harshly.** They accompanied Jesus to Herod in order to make a case against him, and they try to do so, **accusing him harshly**, vehemently. They likely repeated their charge that Jesus incited the people of Galilee by his teaching (23:5); they may have tried to persuade Herod that Jesus was a threat to him. Herod had imprisoned and beheaded John the Baptist after John censured him for his illicit marriage "and because of all

the evil deeds Herod had committed" (3:19–20; 9:9). Would Herod now do likewise with Jesus?

High priest, chief priests: See page 605

Scribes: See page 146

11 Jesus will not answer Herod's questions, and Herod becomes hostile toward this uncooperative man standing before him. **[Even] Herod and his soldiers treated him contemptuously and mocked him.** Jesus foretold that he would be "mocked and insulted and spat upon" (18:32); his words continue to be fulfilled (see also 22:63–65). **And after clothing him in resplendent garb, he sent him back to Pilate.** The significance of **clothing** Jesus **in resplendent**, literally, bright **garb** is not entirely clear. Some biblical scholars understand it as one of the ways in which Jesus is treated **contemptuously**: he is wrapped in regal garb to mock him for his alleged pretensions. Other scholars connect the **resplendent garb** with his being sent **back to Pilate**: Jesus is clothed in a bright white garment to signify to Pilate that Herod finds him innocent. In favor of the latter interpretation is Pilate's declaration that Herod did not find Jesus guilty of the charges made against him (23:14–15). In either case the outcome is clear: Herod treats Jesus **contemptuously** but takes no further action against him. He does not think that Jesus is such a threat to him that he should get rid of him as he did John the Baptist; instead he **sent him back to Pilate** for Pilate to do with him as he would.

Pontius Pilate: See page 617

12 **Herod and Pilate became friends that very day, even though they had been enemies formerly.** Luke does not explain why **Herod** and **Pilate** had been **enemies**. Herod may have been angered by Pilate's killing of some of his Galilean subjects who had come to the Temple in Jerusalem (13:1), or perhaps the two were simply neighboring rulers who did not naturally get along. But because of their handling of Jesus, they **became friends that very day**. They may have interpreted their shuttling of Jesus back and forth between them as signs of professional courtesy to each other, breaking the ice of their enmity. In Acts, the col-

lusion of **Herod** and **Pilate** against Jesus will be seen as a fulfillment of Psalm 2 (Acts 4:24–28; Psalm 2:1–2).

Jesus Back before Pilate

¹³ **Pilate then summoned the chief priests, the rulers, and the people** ¹⁴ **and said to them, "You brought this man to me and accused him of inciting the people to revolt. I have conducted my investigation in your presence and have not found this man guilty of the charges you have brought against him,** ¹⁵ **nor did Herod, for he sent him back to us. So no capital crime has been committed by him.** ¹⁶ **Therefore I shall have him flogged and then release him." [**¹⁷**]**

¹⁸ **But all together they shouted out, "Away with this man! Release Barabbas to us."** ¹⁹ **(Now Barabbas had been imprisoned for a rebellion that had taken place in the city and for murder.)**

Gospel parallels: Matt 27:15–21; Mark 15:6–11; John 18:39–40
NT: Luke 23:1–12

13 Jesus' hearing before Pilate (23:1–6) had been recessed while Jesus was being examined by Herod Antipas (23:7–11). After Herod had sent Jesus back to Pilate (23:11), **Pilate then summoned the chief priests, the rulers, and the people,** reconvening the hearing. The word translated as **rulers** means officials who have some kind of authority (it is translated as "official" at 8:41; 18:18) and refers to the elders and scribes who, along with **chief priests,** served on the Sanhedrin and brought Jesus before Pilate (22:66; 23:1). The **people** would include the crowds who accompanied them to the hearing (23:4), presumably their supporters rather than the people of Jerusalem in general. The ordinary people of Jerusalem have been very favorable toward Jesus (19:48; 20:19; 21:38; 22:2), and Luke has recounted nothing that would turn them against him. Some of them will lament his execution (23:27, 48).

Pontius Pilate: See page 617
High priest, chief priests: See page 605

14 Pilate **said to them, "You brought this man to me and accused him of inciting the people to revolt,"** which was the force of the charges they made against Jesus (23:2, 5). Pilate would ruthlessly suppress uprisings against Roman rule; if Jesus was a rebel, he would be executed. However, Pilate declares, **I have conducted my investigation in your presence and have not found this man guilty of the charges you have brought against him.** Pilate's **investigation,** which Jesus' accusers witnessed, determined that Jesus is not guilty of the **charges** made against him: he is not an insurrectionist. This is the second time that Pilate pronounces Jesus not guilty (see 23:4); that should be the end of the matter. As governor, Pilate has the authority to pronounce judgment in cases such as this.

15 Knowing that Jesus' accusers are adamant in their quest for Jesus to be convicted (23:5), Pilate adds another reason for judging Jesus innocent: **nor did Herod** find him guilty, **for he sent him back to us.** Even if clothing Jesus in resplendent garb (23:11) was not a signal that Herod Antipas found him innocent, the very fact that **he sent him back** to Pilate is an indication that Herod found Jesus not guilty. Herod would have dealt decisively with Jesus, as he had with John the Baptist (3:19–20; 9:9), if he thought he was a threat to his rule. Pilate concludes, **So no capital crime has been committed by him.** Jesus has done nothing that deserves the death penalty.

Herod Antipas: See page 99

16 Pilate knows that finding Jesus not guilty of a capital crime will be hard for his accusers to accept, and so he proposes a compromise: **Therefore I shall have him flogged and then release him.** The word translated **flogged** literally means to educate or discipline—teach a lesson, we would say—and was used for light whippings. As a concession, Pilate will have Jesus **flogged,** treating him as a petty criminal, to assuage his accusers. Then he will **release him.** If Jesus is not guilty of the charges made against him, then he does not deserve a whipping. But Pilate is less interested in justice being served than in coming up with a solution that will appease Jesus' accusers and resolve the situation.

[17] (Some manuscripts of Luke's Gospel include at this point the verse "He was obliged to release one prisoner for them at the festival." These words are not found in the most reliable manuscripts and were probably added by a scribe who adapted them from Matt 27:15 or Mark 15:6. The New American Bible omits this verse.)

18 **But all together they shouted out, "Away with this man! Release Barabbas to us."** They are not satisfied with Jesus' being flogged; they shout, **Away with this man**—do away with him! Jesus' accusers construe his release (verse 16) to be a pardon Pilate is granting him despite his guilt, rather than the consequence of his being not guilty (verses 14–15). And if Pilate is going to pardon a criminal, then let it be someone other than Jesus: they cry out, **Release Barabbas to us**.

19 This is the first mention of Barabbas in Luke's Gospel, so Luke in an aside to his readers explains who Barabbas is: **(Now Barabbas had been imprisoned for a rebellion that had taken place in the city and for murder.)** Jesus was charged with "inciting the people to revolt" (verse 14), and Barabbas is guilty of this and more: he took part in a **rebellion** in Jerusalem and committed **murder**. For this he has been **imprisoned**, held in jail until his case could be heard and he could be executed.

Those who brought Jesus to Pilate continue to be adamant (22:5) in their desire that Pilate do away with Jesus, even to the point of clamoring for the release of a violent insurrectionist in place of Jesus. Pilate is still in a bind, caught between his desire to release an innocent Jesus and his accusers' determination that Jesus be eliminated. What will Pilate do?

Pilate Delivers a Verdict
[20] Again Pilate addressed them, still wishing to release Jesus, [21] but they continued their shouting, "Crucify him! Crucify him!" [22] Pilate addressed them a third time, "What evil has this man done? I found him guilty of no capital crime. Therefore I shall have him flogged and then release him." [23] With loud shouts, however, they persisted in calling for his crucifixion, and their voices

prevailed. ²⁴ The verdict of Pilate was that their demand should be granted. ²⁵ So he released the man who had been imprisoned for rebellion and murder, for whom they asked, and he handed Jesus over to them to deal with as they wished.

Gospel parallels: Matt 27:22–26; Mark 15:12–15; John 19:16
NT: Luke 23:1–5, 13–19

20 **Again Pilate addressed them**, those who are determined that Jesus be done away with (23:18). He was **still wishing to release Jesus**: he has declared Jesus not guilty (23:4, 14) and proposed that he be flogged and released (23:16).

Pontius Pilate: See page 617

21 **But they continued their shouting, "Crucify him! Crucify him!"** The chief priests and their allies shouted, "Away with this man!" (23:18) and **they continued their shouting**, now clamoring, **Crucify him! Crucify him!** Crucifixion was a gruesome method of execution that

---

BACKGROUND: CRUCIFIXION was an exceedingly cruel form of execution used by a number of ancient peoples. Rome adopted crucifixion as its way of executing slaves, rebels, and lower-class, violent criminals. The Romans crucified many both before and after Jesus, including thousands when Rome put down the Jewish revolt of A.D. 66–70. Crucifixions were done in a variety of ways using different styles of crosses. Common Roman practice was first to scourge the one to be crucified, to increase suffering. Then the condemned was forced to carry a crossbeam to the place of execution, where an upright beam would already be in place. Roman crucifixions were done at public sites, such as along a busy road, in order to make them a public display. The one to be crucified was stripped of his clothing, and his arms were tied or nailed to the crossbeam. The crossbeam was then lifted up and fixed to the upright beam at a notch cut either in its top or in its side. Sometimes the person's feet were nailed or tied to the upright beam. Romans often posted a sign indicating the crime for which the person was being crucified. Despite their suffering, those who were crucified could survive for several days, tormented by pain, thirst, insects, and the shame of dying naked before others. Death usually resulted from shock or suffocation when chest muscles gave out. A body was sometimes left on the cross until it disintegrated, eaten by rats and vultures. Crucifixion was designed to be as painful and degrading a death as possible. Rome used crucifixion not merely as a punishment but also as a warning of what would happen to those who challenged Roman authority.

Rome used for rebels and those considered the dregs of society. Chief priests and other leaders have accused Jesus of "inciting the people to revolt" (23:14); they now demand that he be crucified as an insurrectionist. There was no more agonizing and degrading form of death that they could have asked be inflicted on Jesus. Crucifixion would not only dispose of him but would publicly discredit him.

22 **Pilate addressed them a third time, "What evil has this man done?"** His response has the sense, Why crucify him? What evil has this man done that justifies crucifixion? Pilate proclaims, **I found him guilty of no capital crime**—guilty of no crime deserving the death penalty— a judgment he has previously stated (23:15). This is the **third time** that Pilate has declared Jesus not guilty (23:4, 14), once also invoking Herod's similar conclusion (23:15). There does not seem to be the least doubt in Pilate's mind that the charges made against Jesus are unsubstantiated. He

---

COMMENT: WHO WAS RESPONSIBLE FOR JESUS' DEATH Along with the four Gospels, two other ancient writings help determine responsibility for Jesus' death. The Roman historian Tacitus (who lived from about A.D. 56 to 118) wrote that Christ "had been put to death by the procurator Pontius Pilate during the reign of Tiberius" (*Annals*, 15.44). The notice posted on the cross charged Jesus with being "The King of the Jews" (Matt 27:37; Mark 15:26; Luke 23:38; John 19:19)—an insurrectionist. Jesus was executed in the manner that Rome used to get rid of insurrectionists: crucifixion. At the time of Jesus, only Romans, not Jews, could crucify. Jesus died at Passover, when Jerusalem was filled with pilgrims. A city seething with religious and nationalistic fervor could generate sparks of revolt, and Pilate apparently treated Jesus as such a spark, crucifying him. The Jewish historian Josephus (who lived from about A.D. 37 to 100) wrote that Pilate, "upon hearing him accused by the men of the highest standing among us," condemned Jesus to be crucified (*Jewish Antiquities*, 18.3.3). Pilate acted at the urging of the high priest and his associates. They controlled the Temple, which was the source of their power and income. Jesus disrupted commerce in the Temple precincts, upsetting those in charge (Mark 11:15-18). More ominously, Jesus spoke about the Temple being destroyed (Mark 13:1-2). Religious disagreements certainly led some people to oppose Jesus. But those who were personally responsible for his death were a Roman governor bent on maintaining order and religious leaders whose status depended on the Temple. The Second Vatican Council stated, "Even though the Jewish authorities and those who followed their lead pressed for the death of Christ (cf. John 19:6), neither all Jews indiscriminately, nor Jews today, can be charged with crimes committed during his passion" (*Nostra Aetate*, 4).

decides to impose his compromise solution (see 23:15–16): **Therefore**, since he is not guilty of a capital crime, **I shall have him flogged and then release him**. The word translated **flogged** again means disciplined, taught a lesson (23:16).

For reflection: At this point, what do I think of Pilate's handling of Jesus' case?

23 **With loud shouts, however, they persisted in calling for his crucifixion.** They are not willing to settle for Jesus being flogged; they do not want him to be released. They will accept nothing less than his **crucifixion**. They make their demand to Pilate as loudly as they can, a frenzy of shouting.

And their voices prevailed: Pilate gives in. Luke does not explain Pilate's rationale for agreeing to crucify a man he has repeatedly declared innocent of any crime justifying the death penalty. We can speculate that Pilate judged it the most expedient course of action for him. He had nothing to gain by setting Jesus free; rather, it was to his advantage to placate Jewish leaders whose cooperation made Roman rule easier. Furthermore, the crowd of people clamoring for Jesus' death is getting unruly, and the last thing that Pilate would want to do is to foment unrest during Passover, when Jerusalem is crowded with pilgrims celebrating Israel's liberation from Egypt. Pilate came to town to preserve order, not to stir things up.

For reflection: When have I stood my ground on a matter of principle, even though doing so was to my disadvantage? When have I capitulated in a situation in which I should have stood firm?

24 **The verdict of Pilate was that their demand should be granted.** Pilate sentences Jesus to crucifixion, acceding to their **demand** (verses 21, 23). He had the authority to acquit Jesus, but expediency won out over justice.

25 **So he released the man who had been imprisoned for rebellion and murder** (23:19), **for whom they asked** (23:18). Barabbas, guilty of capital crimes, goes free, while Jesus, though repeatedly proclaimed innocent (23:4, 14–15, 22), is sentenced to death. The freeing of Barabbas, despite

his **rebellion** and **murder**, serves as an image for Jesus freeing men and women from their sins, however heinous, through his death.

For reflection: How am I as Barabbas in relation to Jesus?

And he handed Jesus over to them to deal with as they wished—literally, "He handed over Jesus to their will." While the New American Bible translation may make it sound as if Pilate turns Jesus over to the chief priests and their allies to execute, it is clear that soldiers under Pilate's command carried out Jesus' crucifixion. Roman authority reserved for itself the right to crucify (see John 18:31). Roman soldiers could impress people to carry burdens, which the soldiers here will do when they force Simon to carry Jesus' crossbeam (23:26). Roman soldiers received the clothing of those they executed (23:34). There will be an inscription of the charge against Jesus posted on the cross, which was a common Roman practice (24:38). A centurion—an officer in the Roman army—will be present at the crucifixion (23:47). That Pilate handed Jesus over to the will of those who sought his death means that he had Jesus crucified as they demanded. Whatever the complicity of others in Jesus' death, Pilate was the governor who ordered him crucified as a supposed insurrectionist (23:38), and soldiers under his command carried it out.

On the Way of the Cross
26 As they led him away they took hold of a certain Simon, a Cyrenian, who was coming in from the country; and after laying the cross on him, they made him carry it behind Jesus. 27 A large crowd of people followed Jesus, including many women who mourned and lamented him. 28 Jesus turned to them and said, "Daughters of Jerusalem, do not weep for me; weep instead for yourselves and for your children, 29 for indeed, the days are coming when people will say, 'Blessed are the barren, the wombs that never bore and the breasts that never nursed.' 30 At that time people will say to the mountains, 'Fall upon us!' and to the hills, 'Cover us!' 31 for if these things are done when the wood is green what will happen when it is dry?" 32 Now two others, both criminals, were led away with him to be executed.

Gospel parallels: Matt 27:31–32; Mark 15:20–21; John 19:17
OT: Prov 11:31; Hosea 10:8
NT: Luke 13:34–35; 19:41–44; 21:5–6, 20–24; 22:37; 23:23–25

26 Pilate condemned Jesus to crucifixion (23:23–25). **They led him away to the place where he would be crucified** (23:33), outside the city. Along the way, **they took hold of a certain Simon, a Cyrenian, who was coming in from the country**. Being a **Cyrenian** meant that **Simon** was born in Cyrene, a city near the northern coast of Africa that had a sizable Jewish population (Jews from Cyrene are mentioned at Acts 6:9; 11:20; 13:1); the site of Cyrene is in present-day Libya. Simon may have come to Jerusalem for Passover and spent his nights in the countryside because Jerusalem was crowded, or he may have moved from Cyrene to somewhere near Jerusalem. There is no indication that Simon had any previous involvement with Jesus; he is simply someone who was coming into Jerusalem as Jesus was being led out. The soldiers in charge of Jesus' crucifixion **took hold** of Simon **and after laying the cross on him, they made him carry it behind Jesus**. Normally, those being crucified were made to carry a crossbeam on their shoulders to the place of crucifixion, where upright beams were already in place. Jesus is apparently unable to carry a crossbeam, so Simon is conscripted to carry one for him. In countries ruled by Rome, its soldiers had the authority to press people into service as temporary burden-bearers (see Matt 5:41). Luke does not indicate why Jesus could not carry the crossbeam himself. However, Luke's first readers were familiar with how Romans carried out crucifixions and knew that those being crucified were first scourged to weaken them and increase their agony. Luke's readers would presume that Jesus was scourged so severely that he was unable to carry a crossbeam.

Crucifixion: See page 626

Jesus said that "if anyone wishes to come after me," he must "take up his cross daily and follow me" (9:23), later repeating this requirement (14:27). Simon, carrying a cross **behind** Jesus, provides a vivid image for what Jesus' disciples must do.

For reflection: What crosses have been laid upon me without my volunteering to carry them? What crosses have I taken up because of Jesus?

27 **A large crowd of people followed Jesus, including many women who mourned and lamented him.** The **large crowd** is best identified with those sympathetic to Jesus, those who hung on his words in the Temple courtyard (19:48; 21:38), and who will mourn his death (23:48). **Many women** in the crowd already **mourned and lamented** for Jesus in anticipation of his suffering and death. The word translated **mourned** means to beat one's breast as an expression of sorrow (see 18:13). Those who **followed Jesus** to the place of his execution were familiar with crucifixions and knew the horror of what awaited him there, and they were profoundly moved.

> *For reflection: What emotions do I experience when I read a Gospel account of Jesus' crucifixion or meditate on his death?*

28 **Jesus turned to them and said, "Daughters of Jerusalem, do not weep for me."** The idiom **daughters of Jerusalem** means the women of Jerusalem. Jesus tells the women mourning for him, **do not weep for me; weep instead for yourselves and for your children**. The sense of Jesus' words is, Do not weep so much for me as for yourselves and your children (see 10:20 for another use of the do-not-do-this-but-do-that idiom). Crucifixion is horrible, but what is in store for these women and their children is also horrible. Jesus wept over Jerusalem because it would be encircled by a siege (19:41–43), inflicting starvation and terrible suffering on its people. He foretold of the city, "They will smash you to the ground and your children within you" (19:44); now he tells the women who are mourning for him to mourn instead for what will befall them and their **children**—the next generation. In the course of putting down a Jewish revolt, Roman armies will lay siege to Jerusalem in A.D. 70, bringing horrible suffering upon those within the city. Although Jesus is on his way to suffer crucifixion, his concern is for the people of Jerusalem (see 13:34) and the agonies they will endure.

Jerusalem: See page 516

> *For reflection: What insight into Jesus am I given by his words to those who were mourning for him?*

29 **for indeed, the days are coming when people will say, "Blessed are the barren, the wombs that never bore and the breasts that never nursed."** Jesus invokes a beatitude that overturns the usual notion of a woman's blessedness. For Jews, children were a blessing from God (see 11:27) and being **barren** was a tragic disgrace (see 1:7, 24–25; Gen 16:1–5; 1 Sam 1:1–11). But **the days are coming** when the reverse will be true, when those who are **barren** will be **blessed** and fortunate. Regarding the time when Jerusalem will be surrounded by armies (21:20), Jesus earlier proclaimed: "Woe to pregnant women and nursing mothers in those days" (21:23). The siege will take a terrible toll on them, and it will be better to be barren than to have borne children who will suffer so horribly during the siege.

Beatitudes: See page 169

30 The suffering during the siege of Jerusalem will be so great that its citizens will long to be put out of their misery. **At that time people will say to the mountains, "Fall upon us!" and to the hills, "Cover us!"** Jesus invokes words of the prophet Hosea in which, in the face of an invasion, people cry out for swift release from life, preferring to be instantly killed by an avalanche than to endure prolonged suffering. The first-century Jewish historian Josephus will vividly describe the starvation and ensuing horrors caused by the Roman siege of Jerusalem, making death a welcome prospect. The women of Jerusalem should indeed weep for what will befall their children.

> Then they shall cry out to the mountains, "Cover us!"
> and to the hills, "Fall upon us!"

Hosea 10:8

31 Jesus concludes with a comparison: **for if these things are done when the wood is green what will happen when it is dry?** Everyone knows that **dry** wood burns more easily than moist, **green** wood. Jesus seems to be comparing himself to the green wood, with **these things** being his suffering and death. If Jesus, though innocent (see 23:4, 14–15, 22), receives such horrible treatment, then **what will happen** to those who are not innocent, to those who are, as it were, dry kindling that can easily burst

into flame? Jesus may be poetically alluding to a proverb that says that if God passes judgment even on the just, then how much more will he do so upon the wicked (Prov 11:31, also alluded to at 1 Pet 4:17–18). If the innocent Jesus suffers, then what is in store for the people of Jerusalem?

> If the just are recompensed on the earth,
>   how much more the wicked and the sinner!
>   Prov 11:31

Jesus' words to the women of Jerusalm are a lamentation for what will happen to them and to their children. They are also an implicit call for Jerusalem to change course in order to avoid what will otherwise befall it. It is not too late for the leaders of Jerusalem to follow the path that makes for peace (see 19:42).

For reflection: What does Jesus' lamentation mean for me? What dry kindling do I have in my life that could go up in flames?

32 **Now two others, both criminals, were led away with him to be executed.** Jesus is not the only one **to be executed** that day. The two **criminals** likely had been charged with capital crimes and held in jail until Pilate was in town to hear their cases; having found them guilty, he ordered that they be crucified along with Jesus.

ORIENTATION: *Luke omits the details of Jesus' crucifixion and does not describe his sufferings. Instead he emphasizes the mockery Jesus endured and the saving mercy Jesus extended. Some of the mockery is ironically a true proclamation of who Jesus is and what he does.*

The Savior Is Crucified

33 **When they came to the place called the Skull, they crucified him and the criminals there, one on his right, the other on his left.** 34 **[Then Jesus said, "Father, forgive them, they know not what they do."] They divided his garments by casting lots.** 35 **The people**

stood by and watched; the rulers, meanwhile, sneered at him and said, "He saved others, let him save himself if he is the chosen one, the Messiah of God." ³⁶ Even the soldiers jeered at him. As they approached to offer him wine ³⁷ they called out, "If you are King of the Jews, save yourself." ³⁸ Above him there was an inscription that read, "This is the King of the Jews." ³⁹ Now one of the criminals hanging there reviled Jesus, saying, "Are you not the Messiah? Save yourself and us." ⁴⁰ The other, however, rebuking him, said in reply, "Have you no fear of God, for you are subject to the same condemnation? ⁴¹ And indeed, we have been condemned justly, for the sentence we received corresponds to our crimes, but this man has done nothing criminal." ⁴² Then he said, "Jesus, remember me when you come into your kingdom." ⁴³ He replied to him, "Amen, I say to you, today you will be with me in Paradise."

Gospel parallels: Matt 27:33–44, 48; Mark 15:22–32, 36; John 19:17–24, 29
OT: Psalm 22:8, 19; 69:22
NT: Luke 2:11; 4:1–13; 6:27–28; 9:20, 35; 22:37; 23:3

33 **When they came to the place called the Skull**: in Aramaic, the **place** was known as Golgotha (Matt 27:33; Mark 15:22; John 19:17), but Luke translates the name as **Skull** for his readers. It was a rounded knoll of rock just outside the walls of Jerusalem; those being crucified atop it were in plain view of those entering or leaving the city. Rome used crucifixion as a public warning of what was in store for those who ran afoul of its authority. There **they crucified him**. Luke does not describe the procedures they followed; his first readers were sufficiently familiar with what cruci-

---

BACKGROUND: GOLGOTHA During the Old Testament era, the limestone hillside west of Jerusalem was quarried for building blocks. Seams of high quality limestone were dug out; poor stone was left unquarried. Eventually the good stone played out, and the quarry was abandoned. At the time of Jesus, the old quarry lay just outside the western wall of Jerusalem, near a city gate. A hump of unquarried rock jutted up perhaps twenty to thirty feet from the quarry floor. Romans used this mound of rock as a place to crucify criminals, since it made a public display of their deaths. The site was called Golgotha, from the Aramaic word for skull, likely because the unquarried hump of rock was shaped like the top of a skull. The Latin word for skull gives us the name "Calvary." Today the site of Golgotha is within the Church of the Holy Sepulchre in Jerusalem. *Related topic: Tomb of Jesus (page 651).*

fixion involved. The arms of those being crucified were affixed to a beam of wood, and the beam was hoisted up into a slot on an upright beam, perhaps seven feet tall, already in place. Death came slowly, with great pain, but Luke is silent about the physical suffering Jesus endured. Luke notes that they also crucified **the criminals there, one on his right, the other on his left**. Jesus foretold that in fulfillment of Scripture he would be "counted among the wicked" (22:37; Isaiah 53:12); he will depart from this life in the close company of two **criminals**.

Crucifixion: See page 626

Even if Luke seems to pass rather quickly over Jesus' crucifixion, we should not. We who believe that he is the Son of God, conceived through the Holy Spirit and sent to establish the reign of God, must be brought up short by God's plan for him taking him to the cross. How could his mission culminate in the agony of crucifixion? God proclaimed through Isaiah,

> My thoughts are not your thoughts,
>> nor are your ways my ways, says the LORD.
> As high as the heavens are above the earth,
>> so high are my ways above your ways
>> and my thoughts above your thoughts
>>>> (Isaiah 55:8–9)

Nowhere is this more true than in the way the Son of God died.

For reflection: What meaning do I find in the crucifixion of Jesus? What mystery do I find in it?

34 The following sentence is missing from some ancient manuscripts of Luke's Gospel, which the New American Bible indicates by enclosing it in brackets. It is nonetheless part of inspired Scripture. **[Then Jesus said, "Father, forgive them, they know not what they do."]** Jesus' first words from the cross are a prayer. He addresses God as **Father,** as is his practice in prayer (10:21; 11:1–2; 22:42). Even though his Father's will for him means enduring the agony of the cross, he does not renounce his relationship with his **Father**. He prays for those who are responsible for

635

his death as well as for those who are carrying it out, asking his Father to **forgive them** for what they are doing to him; implicitly he has forgiven them himself. Psalm 51 uses images of washing away sins, almost as if they had never been committed, to convey what it means for God to **forgive** (Psalm 51:3–4, 9, 11). Jesus taught, "Love your enemies, . . . pray for those who mistreat you" (6:27, 28), and he provides the ultimate example of what his teaching means. He makes an excuse for those responsible for his suffering and death: **they know not what they do**. Jesus pleads ignorance on their behalf, as a defense attorney might plead to a judge on behalf of a guilty client. Jesus' significance in God's plans was hidden from their eyes (19:41–44); he invokes their ignorance as a mitigating factor (see 12:48).

> For reflection: "He is always able to save those who approach God through him, since he lives forever to make intercession for them" (Heb 7:25; see also Rom 8:34). What confidence in Jesus' intercession for me does his prayer from the cross give me? What does his example ask of me?

They divided his garments by casting lots. Those being crucified were stripped of their clothes to shame them, inflicting the ignominy of dying naked in public (see Heb 12:2). Soldiers apparently had the right to the clothing and minor possessions of those they crucified. They **divided his garments** among themselves **by casting lots**. Luke invokes words from Psalm 22 to describe their action, conveying that what is happening is a fulfillment of Scripture (Psalm 22:19).

> They divide my garments among them;
> for my clothing they cast lots.
>
> Psalm 22:19

35 **The people stood by and watched.** A large crowd of people had followed Jesus as he was led out of Jerusalem to be crucified, including "many women who mourned and lamented him" (23:27). Now they **stood by and watched,** silently witnessing his crucifixion (see 23:48). **The rulers, meanwhile, sneered at him**: by **rulers** Luke refers to the Jewish leaders who accused Jesus before Pilate (23:13–14). They **sneered at him,** mocking him by saying, **"He saved others, let him save himself**

if he is the chosen one, the Messiah of God." The word **save** means rescue from danger or disease or death. Jesus **saved** those he healed (7:3, 50; 8:36, 48; 17:19; 18:42) and brought back to life (8:50). Those mocking Jesus refer to **the Messiah of God** as **the chosen one**. Psalm 89 speaks of David as God's chosen and anointed (Psalm 89:21); the **Messiah**, literally, anointed one, would be a descendant of David (20:41) and, like him, could be called God's **chosen one**. Jesus did not deny that he was the Messiah (22:67–68). Now he is taunted, If you are the Messiah, if you could rescue others, then rescue yourself from crucifixion. They have no more expectation that he can save himself than they have faith that he is the Messiah.

Messiah, Christ: See page 257

Luke's choice of words in writing that the leaders **sneered** at Jesus suggests that Luke sees their sneering to be a fulfillment of other verses from Psalm 22, which in its Greek translation uses the same rare word for sneer or mock (Psalm 22:8). The leader's mockery faintly echoes the mockery in this Psalm (Psalm 22:9).

> *All who see me mock me;*
> *they curl their lips and jeer;*
> *they shake their heads at me:*
> *"You relied on the LORD—let him deliver you;*
> *if he loves you, let him rescue you."*

Psalm 22:8–9

There is unwitting truth in the mockery heaped on Jesus. Luke's readers know that Jesus *is* **the Messiah of God**, as Peter professed (9:20), and *is* God's **chosen**, as God himself testified (9:35). Jesus has **saved others**, and he will fulfill his mission of bringing salvation (1:69, 71; 2:30; 19:9) precisely by not saving himself. He will give his body and shed his blood on the cross in order to establish a new covenant between God and humans (22:19–20), bringing forgiveness of sins (see 24:46–47; Jer 31:31, 34). That is the mission of "a savior . . . who is Messiah and Lord" (2:11), a "savior to grant Israel repentance and forgiveness of sins" (Acts 5:31).

For reflection: What do the words said in mockery of Jesus teach me about him? What does it mean to me that Jesus is my savior?

36 **Even the soldiers** who crucified him **jeered at him,** joining in the sneering. **As they approached to offer him wine:** the word translated **wine** refers to a sour wine or vinegar that soldiers drank as a cheap thirst quencher. Their words as they offer Jesus the wine (verse 37) make it clear that they are offering it to him in mockery. Luke again likely has a Psalm verse in mind that is being fulfilled by what happens to Jesus: "For my thirst they gave me vinegar" (Psalm 69:22).

> *They put gall in my food;*
> *for my thirst they gave me vinegar.*
>
> Psalm 69:22

37 **they called out, "If you are King of the Jews, save yourself."** Pilate asked Jesus if he was the **King of the Jews** (23:3), and this title will be posted on the cross as the charge justifying his crucifixion (verse 38). The soldiers incorporate the charge in their mockery, offering him cheap rough wine as fit for the kind of king he is. They taunt him, **If you are King of the Jews, save yourself**, echoing the Jewish leaders' mockery (verse 35). To them he appears to be one more miserable Jewish wretch being crucified—hardly a king!

38 **Above him there was an inscription that read, "This is the King of the Jews."** Romans sometimes hung a written charge around the neck of a person being led off to be crucified, giving the reason he was being put to death and serving as a warning to others not to commit the same crime. In the case of Jesus they posted **an inscription** of the charge **above him** on the upright beam of the cross. Jesus was crucified as an insurrectionist **King of the Jews**. Even if Pilate was not convinced that Jesus was guilty of any capital crime (23:4, 14–15, 22), he had ordered Jesus' crucifixion and needed a charge against him that justified it. The **inscription** not only labeled Jesus as an insurrectionist but also mocked him: **This**—literally "this one," which has a contemptuous tone—**is the King of the Jews**.

39 Now one of the criminals hanging there reviled, literally, blasphemed, **Jesus, saying, "Are you not the Messiah? Save yourself and us."** A criminal joins in the mockery, echoing the refrain **save yourself** (see verses 35, 37). He says, save **us** as well if you are really **the Messiah.** He does not have any expectation that the three of them being crucified will be rescued from their fate, much less faith that Jesus is the Messiah.

On the eve of his public ministry, Jesus was tempted three times by the devil to compromise his identity and abandon his mission (4:1–13). The devil's refrain was, "If you are the Son of God" (4:3, 9). Now at the culmination of his ministry there is again a threefold call to compromise who he is and forsake his mission (verses 35, 37, 39): If you are the Messiah, a king, save yourself. But to save others he will not save himself; from beginning to end Jesus is faithful to who he is and to his mission from his Father.

40 The other criminal, **however, rebuking** the first criminal, **said in reply** to him, **"Have you no fear of God, for you are subject to the same condemnation?"** The word translated **condemnation** can mean either sentence or judgment, and the criminal's question can have both senses. He points out to the criminal mocking Jesus that he has received the same sentence as Jesus, death by crucifixion. He asks him, **have you no fear of God,** whom you will shortly face, **for you are subject to the same** judgment by God that every human faces. **Fear of God** means awe of God and respect for who he is and what he can do (see 12:5).

For reflection: Do I have a proper fear of God? What is my attitude toward facing God's judgment?

41 And indeed, we have been condemned justly, for the sentence we received corresponds to our crimes. Both criminals had committed **crimes** that justified death by crucifixion. They were getting what they deserved, **but this man has done nothing criminal.** It is obvious to the second criminal that Jesus, unlike them, **has done nothing** that deserves the death penalty.

42 Then he said, "Jesus, remember me when you come into your kingdom." He addresses Jesus simply by name, as **Jesus,** not using titles such as Lord, Master, or Teacher; he appeals to Jesus as one person to another. He asks Jesus to **remember me**, be graciously mindful of me and act on my behalf (see Judges 16:28; 1 Sam 1:11, 19; Psalm 106:4; 115:12). He asks Jesus to do so **when you come into your kingdom**. Luke does not explain exactly what he has in mind when he speaks of Jesus coming into his **kingdom**. It is clear to him that Jesus has done nothing deserving execution (verse 41) but is nevertheless being crucified as the "King of the Jews" (verse 38). He seems to make an intuitive leap of faith that Jesus is indeed a king and that his death will mean the beginning of his kingly rule. Readers of Luke's Gospel know that his intuition is correct: Jesus is accomplishing his exodus (9:31), his being taken up (9:51) to his Father; Jesus' **kingdom** (1:33; 22:29–30) is the reign of God, which he will bring to fulfillment when he comes in glory (21:27, 31).

Kingdom of God: See page 381

43 **He replied to him, "Amen, I say to you, today you will be with me in Paradise."** Jesus solemnly assures him of the truth of what he is telling him: **Amen, I say to you**. The criminal asked Jesus to remember him when he comes into his kingdom; Jesus will do so **today**. He tells him, this very day **you will be with me in Paradise**. Where Jesus is going, the criminal will also go, being **with** Jesus and sharing in his destiny. Jesus calls where he is going **Paradise**, a word that means "garden" and has associations with the garden of Eden (Gen 2:8). **Paradise** is an

---

BACKGROUND: PARADISE The word "paradise" in Hebrew and Greek is taken from a Persian word that originally meant an enclosure and came to mean a park or garden. In the Greek translation of the Old Testament, the "garden in Eden" is literally the "paradise in Eden" (Gen 2:8); similarly, in Isaiah "the garden of the LORD" is literally "the paradise of the LORD" (Isaiah 51:3). In some Jewish nonbiblical writings, Eden became an image for an idyllic life with God after death—a life in paradise. In one of these writings, the *Psalms of Solomon,* those who love God and obey his commandments will inherit a life of happiness in "the Lord's paradise," while sinners are consigned to Hades. The word "paradise" is used once in the Gospels (Luke 23:43), once by Paul (2 Cor 12:4), and once in Revelation, where it is translated as "garden" by the New American Bible: "To the victor I will give the right to eat from the tree of life that is in the garden of God" (Rev 2:7). There was no single coherent view of the afterlife at the time of Jesus; paradise was one image for what we think of as heaven. *Related topics: Nonbiblical writings (page 342), Psalms of Solomon (page 259).*

---

image for a life of happiness that the righteous will enjoy after death. **Today** the criminal will die and **be with** Jesus in a place of bliss.

This unnamed criminal becomes the only saint personally canonized by Jesus. What did he do, that Jesus should assure him of his eternal salvation? His criminal past certainly did not merit it. His repentance simply consisted of acknowledging his crimes and accepting that the punishment he was receiving was justified. He did not call upon Jesus as his Lord and Savior. He did, however, refrain from mocking Jesus and he rebuked another criminal who did. He professed Jesus' innocence and acknowledged that he did not deserve crucifixion. He had faith that Jesus' death would lead to his coming into his kingdom, and he asked Jesus to be mindful of him when he did. In response, Jesus solemnly spoke the only words that will ultimately matter for every woman and man: **today you will be with me in Paradise**. Jesus looks for grounds to grant salvation rather than for a reason to condemn (see John 3:17), and this criminal provided him with sufficient grounds. Jesus indeed saves (verse 35): he pleads for forgiveness for those crucifying him (verse 34); he grants eternal life to a dying man who asks to be remembered.

For reflection: How does the exchange between Jesus and this criminal give me hope?

Jesus Goes to His Father

⁴⁴ It was now about noon and darkness came over the whole land until three in the afternoon ⁴⁵ because of an eclipse of the sun. Then the veil of the temple was torn down the middle. ⁴⁶ Jesus cried out in a loud voice, "Father, into your hands I commend my spirit"; and when he had said this he breathed his last. ⁴⁷ The centurion who witnessed what had happened glorified God and said, "This man was innocent beyond doubt." ⁴⁸ When all the people who had gathered for this spectacle saw what had happened, they returned home beating their breasts; ⁴⁹ but all his acquaintances stood at a distance, including the women who had followed him from Galilee and saw these events.

Gospel parallels: Matt 27:45–56; Mark 15:33–41; John 19:25–30
OT: Psalm 31:6

NT: Luke 8:1–3; 9:31, 51; 22:53; 23:27, 35, 43

44 Jesus has been crucified between two criminals (23:33). **It was now about noon and darkness came over the whole land until three in the afternoon.** The word translated **land** can also mean "earth." It is unclear whether Luke wants to convey that **darkness** came over the whole land of Palestine or over the whole earth. The significance of the darkness is likewise not entirely clear. Some biblical scholars associate it with the darkness of the "day of the Lord," when God would come in judgment: "On that day, says the Lord GOD, / I will make the sun set at midday / and cover the earth with darkness in broad daylight" (Amos 8:9; see also Isaiah 13:9–10; Joel 2:1–2, 10; 3:4; Zeph 1:14–15). However, there is otherwise no indication in Luke's Gospel that he understands the death of Jesus to be a fulfillment of prophecies about the "day of the Lord." Rather, Luke's readers might most naturally associate the **darkness** enveloping Jesus on the cross with his pronouncement that his arrest marked "the time for the power of darkness" (22:53). **Darkness** is a stark image for the forces of evil that brought Jesus to the cross.

The day of the Lord: See page 91

45 The darkness came over the land or earth **because of an eclipse of the sun.** While **eclipse** is a near transliteration of the Greek word Luke uses, it can also be misleading for modern readers. We understand that an **eclipse of the sun** is caused by the moon passing between the sun and the earth. This is impossible at full moon, and Jesus is being crucified at Passover, which is celebrated at a full moon. The word translated **eclipse** has "fail" or "give out" as its basic meaning (it is translated as "fails" at 16:9 and as "fail" at 22:32). Luke simply writes that darkness covered the land or earth because the sun failed; he does not offer an explanation of how its light failed. **Then the veil of the temple was torn down the middle.** The **veil of the temple** likely refers to the curtain covering the doorway to the innermost room of the Temple, the Holy of Holies (Exod 26:31–33; 40:21; Lev 24:3). The Holy of Holies was the place of God's special presence; it could be entered only by the high priest once a year, on the Day of Atonement (Lev 16:1–19). **Was torn** implies, was torn by God. The rending of the veil can have multiple symbolic meanings. It might foreshadow the destruction of the Temple (see 13:35; 21:5–6). It

might signify that access to God is being opened to everyone (see Heb 10:19–20). However, coming as it does in Luke's Gospel before the death of Jesus, it is best understood as God's response to Jesus on the cross. Just as heaven opened for God to speak to Jesus on the eve of his ministry (3:21–22), so at the culmination of his ministry God opens the veil shielding his presence in the Temple to signify that he is present to his Son despite the surrounding **darkness**. Jesus is accomplishing his exodus (9:31), his being taken up (9:51) to his Father, bringing a criminal along with him to Paradise (23:43); God opens the door to welcome them, so to speak.

Temple: See page 519

For reflection: What significance for me do I find in the veil of the Temple being torn open?

46 Jesus cried out in a loud voice: he still has sufficient strength to cry out in a **loud voice**. He cries, **"Father, into your hands I commend my spirit."** Jesus continues to call upon God as his **Father** during his crucifixion (see 23:34). He prays words from Psalm 31, a psalm that expresses confidence in God in a time of misery and distress. Its words take on special meaning when prayed by a person near death. **Into your hands I commend my spirit**: the word for **commend** could also be translated as "entrust." **Spirit** can have the sense of self, and it can also mean "breath": and **when he had said this he breathed his last**. At death, "the life breath returns to God who gave it" (Eccl 12:7; see also Psalm 104:29). Jesus breathes out his final breath to God, entrusting himself into the **hands** of his **Father**, serenely confident in his Father's care for him. Death holds no terror for him; he knows that his dying means his being taken up to God (9:51) and entering into his glory (24:26). He confidently foretold that "from this time on the Son of Man will be seated at the right hand of the power of God" (22:69).

> *Into your hands I commend my spirit;*
> *you will redeem me, LORD, faithful God.*
>
> Psalm 31:6

For reflection: How can Jesus' attitude in the face of death help me grow in my understanding of death? Reflect on Psalm 31:6 as Jesus' prayer, and as your prayer.

47 **The centurion who witnessed what had happened**: the rank of **centurion** meant he commanded one hundred soldiers. He was under Pilate's authority and was in charge of the soldiers carrying out the crucifixions that day. The centurion **witnessed what had happened** at least from the time Jesus was led out of the city (23:26) until his death. He heard Jesus' prayers from the cross, asking forgiveness for his executioners and entrusting himself into the hands of God (23:34, 46); he observed his demeanor as he died. His soldiers have been jeering at Jesus (23:36), but his reaction to Jesus is quite different. He **glorified God and said, "This man was innocent beyond doubt."** Pilate, Herod, and a criminal have declared Jesus to be **innocent** (23:4, 14–15, 22, 41); now a Gentile **centurion** does so as well. Jesus' serenity as he dies, despite the pain and mockery he is enduring, manifests that he is not a criminal and that his crucifixion is a miscarriage of justice. The centurion has the fairness and honesty to admit that he has seen to the execution of a man who **was innocent beyond doubt**. The word translated **innocent** also means "just" or "righteous" (see Acts 3:14; 7:52; 22:14); the centurion recognizes that Jesus is not simply an unfortunate victim but an upright man. Luke writes that by his words he **glorified God**. Throughout Luke's Gospel, people have glorified God in response to God's saving power being exercised through Jesus (5:25–26; 7:16; 13:13; 17:15; 18:43). God is exercising his saving power now, establishing a new covenant in the blood of Jesus (22:20). A Gentile becomes the first person to glorify God for it, even if he does not understand the full significance of Jesus' death.

48 **When all the people who had gathered for this spectacle**: a "large crowd" had followed Jesus to the place of crucifixion, "including many women who mourned and lamented him" (23:27). Once at the place, they "stood by and watched" (23:35). After they **saw what had happened** and witnessed the death of Jesus, **they returned home beating their breasts**, a gesture of anguished sorrow (see 18:13). Although some joined with the religious leaders in seeking Jesus' death (23:13), **the people** of Jerusalem in general have been very favorable toward Jesus since his

arrival in town (19:48; 20:19; 21:38; 22:2), and they are traumatized by his execution.

49 Most of the crowd of onlookers dispersed after Jesus' death, **but all his acquaintances stood at a distance**, lingering at the scene. **All his acquaintances** presumably includes Jesus' disciples. Among them are **the women who had followed him from Galilee**. Many women had accompanied Jesus as he journeyed from village to village in Galilee (8:1–3) and had **followed him from Galilee** to Jerusalem. Jesus' acquaintances **stood at a distance** during his crucifixion, perhaps afraid to come nearer or perhaps kept away by soldiers exercising crowd control. They nevertheless **saw these events**, saw what had taken place that day, and could bear witness to what had happened (see Acts 1:21–22; 5:29–32; 10:39; 13:26–31).

Galilee: See page 114

For reflection: What would have been going through my mind and heart if I had been among those who watched from a distance as Jesus died on a cross? What is in my heart now as I meditate on his death?

Joseph Buries the Body of Jesus
⁵⁰ Now there was a virtuous and righteous man named Joseph who, though he was a member of the council, ⁵¹ had not consented to their plan of action. He came from the Jewish town of Arimathea and was awaiting the kingdom of God. ⁵² He went to Pilate and asked for the body of Jesus. ⁵³ After he had taken the body down, he wrapped it in a linen cloth and laid him in a rock-hewn tomb in which no one had yet been buried. ⁵⁴ It was the day of preparation, and the sabbath was about to begin. ⁵⁵ The women who had come from Galilee with him followed behind, and when they had seen the tomb and the way in which his body was laid in it, ⁵⁶ they returned and prepared spices and perfumed oils. Then they rested on the sabbath according to the commandment.

Gospel parallels: Matt 27:57–61; Mark 15:42–47; John 19:38–42
OT: Deut 21:22–23
NT: Luke 8:1–3; 23:49

50 **Now there was a virtuous and righteous man named Joseph**. At the beginning of his Gospel, before Jesus' birth, Luke introduced his readers to Zechariah and Elizabeth who were "righteous in the eyes of God" (1:5–6). Now, after Jesus' death on the cross (23:46), Luke introduces another **virtuous and righteous** person, a man **named Joseph**. He is **a member of the council**, that is, of the Sanhedrin, the chief Jewish ruling body in Jerusalem (22:66). **Joseph** is among the elite of Jerusalem, one of its leaders. Members of the Sanhedrin brought Jesus before Pilate, charging that he was inciting the people to revolt (23:1–2, 13-14) and demanding that he be crucified (23:18–23). Joseph, however, had not gone along with them, for **though he was a member of the council,**

Sanhedrin: See page 611

51 he **had not consented to their plan of action.** The words translated **their plan of action** signify both the decision to do away with Jesus (see 19:47; 22:2) and the actions they took to carry it out. Joseph **had not consented** to their decision and was not involved in bringing Jesus before Pilate. Luke provides additional background about Joseph: **He came from the Jewish town of Arimathea.** Calling Arimathea a **Jewish** town has the connotation that it lies in Judea (the Greek word

---

BACKGROUND: BURIAL PRACTICES Jewish burials took place as soon as possible after death. The corpse was washed and anointed with ointments and perfumes and wrapped in cloth. Ordinary Jews were buried in simple graves dug in the ground; wealthy Jerusalem Jews were buried in cave-like tombs carved into the limestone hillsides surrounding the city. These tombs usually contained several chambers and served entire families for several generations. Burials were usually a two-step process. First, the corpse lay on a shelf in the tomb for about a year. Then, after the flesh had decayed away, the bones were collected and placed in a pit containing the bones of the person's ancestors. Or, in Jerusalem at the time of Jesus, bones were often placed instead in an ossuary, a lidded box carved from limestone; typically such boxes were about twenty-four by eighteen by twelve inches. The box was then set in a recess in the tomb complex. Sometimes the bones of several members of a family were placed in the same box. In 1990, archaeologists excavating a tomb on the southern edge of Jerusalem found a bone box with an Aramaic form of the name "Caiaphas" inscribed on it. Inside were bones identified as those of a man about sixty, an adult woman, a teenage boy, a young child, and two infants. Archaeologists believe that the bones of the man are those of the Caiaphas who was high priest from A.D. 18 to 36. *Related topic: Tomb of Jesus (page 651).*

for "Jewish" comes from the Greek word for "Judea"), but the location of **Arimathea** is otherwise uncertain today. That Joseph **came from** Arimathea indicates that he was born there; as a member of the Sanhedrin, he likely was now residing in Jerusalem (see also verse 53).

Joseph **was awaiting the kingdom of God**. When Jesus was brought to the Temple after his birth, he was met by Simeon, a "righteous and devout" man was "awaiting the consolation of Israel" (2:25), and by the prophetess Anna, who was "awaiting the redemption of Jerusalem" (2:36–38). Joseph similarly was **awaiting the kingdom of God**—looking forward in hope to God consoling and redeeming his people by establishing his reign. While **the kingdom of God** was the keynote of Jesus' preaching and teaching (4:43; 8:1; 9:11; 13:18–21; 16:16; 17:20–21; 18:16–17, 24–25), Joseph's awaiting the kingdom does not necessarily mean that he is a disciple of Jesus. The references in the Old Testament to God reigning as king (Psalm 84:4; 89:19; 93:1; 95:3; 96:10; 97:1; 98:6; 99:1; Isaiah 52:7) would have been sufficient for some Jews to have formulated their hopes in terms of God definitively establishing his reign. Joseph of Arimathea is a virtuous and righteous man who awaited God's reign and did not go along with the plot to do away with Jesus.

Kingdom of God: See page 381

52 After Jesus' death on the cross (had Joseph been among the onlookers?), **he went to Pilate and asked for the body of Jesus**. Romans often left crucified bodies on crosses to be eaten by scavenging animals and birds, so that the gruesome sight would serve as a crime deterrent. When those who were crucified were buried, it was usually in a common grave with other criminals. Joseph **asked for the body of Jesus** so that he could bury it. The law of Moses forbade leaving the corpse of an executed criminal hanging on a tree overnight (Deut 21:22–23), and this law was interpreted to cover crucifixion. It was an act of charity to provide burial for those who would otherwise go unburied (see Tobit 1:16–18). As a virtuous and righteous man (verse 50), Joseph might want to bury the body of Jesus before nightfall in order to uphold the law and perform a charitable deed. But Joseph's behavior must surely also be understood in light of his being a member of the Sanhedrin that bore responsibility for Jesus' death. By providing a proper burial for Jesus, Joseph disassociates himself from the action of the Sanhedrin and tries to alleviate, as best he can, the harm they have done. Joseph cannot undo Jesus' suffering and death, but he can treat his body with respect. Since **Pilate** is in charge of the soldiers stationed at the cross of Jesus, Joseph asks him to order that Jesus' body be turned over to him. Pilate grants his request, perhaps recognizing that he is a respected leader, perhaps simply to bring the whole affair of Jesus' death to a quiet conclusion.

Pontius Pilate: See page 617

53 **After he had taken the body down, he wrapped it in a linen cloth.** Bodies were normally washed, anointed with spices and perfumes, and **wrapped** in burial shrouds. **Linen cloth** was somewhat expensive; Joseph is giving the body of Jesus an honorable burial. The approach of sundown, marking the beginning of the Sabbath (verse 54), apparently forces Joseph to bury the body of Jesus rather quickly, temporarily foregoing the customary anointing with spices and perfumes. Joseph **laid him in a rock-hewn tomb in which no one had yet been buried.** The tomb would belong to Joseph and be intended for several generations of burials; having a family tomb at Jerusalem is another indication that Joseph lives in Jerusalem. Owning a tomb **hewn** in limestone rock indicates that Joseph had some wealth; only the upper class could afford to have such tombs dug for them. **No one had yet been buried** in the tomb: it was apparently quite new.

Tomb of Jesus: See page 651

For reflection: Despite risking criticism from other members of the Sanhedrin, Joseph nevertheless did what he could for Jesus. What am I able to do for Jesus?

54 **It was the day of preparation, and the sabbath was about to begin.** The day before **the sabbath** was a **day of preparation** for the Sabbath. Work that could not be done on the Sabbath, such as cooking meals, was done in advance so that there would be no occasion to break the Sabbath rest. The body of Jesus was buried late in the day, as the sun was setting **and the sabbath was about to begin.**

55 **The women who had come from Galilee with him followed behind.** They had followed Jesus in **Galilee** (8:1–3), and had come **with**

him to Jerusalem. They had stood off at a distance watching as he was crucified and died (23:49). They had lingered near the place of his crucifixion until Joseph came for his body, and then they **followed behind** him as he brought the body of Jesus to the tomb. They **followed** until **they had seen the tomb and the way in which his body was laid in it**. They observe that Jesus' body did not receive the customary anointing with spices and perfumes before it was **laid** on a broad rock shelf in the tomb. The fact that they only watched and did not take part in the burial of Jesus may indicate that Joseph was not a disciple of Jesus. Were he a fellow disciple, it would have been natural for them to step forward and help with the burial.

Galilee: See page 114

56 After seeing where and how Jesus' body was buried, **they returned and prepared spices and perfumed oils**. They apparently have sufficient time to do so before the Sabbath begins. Their intent is to return to the tomb as soon as they can and anoint Jesus' body with the **prepared spices and perfumed oils**, completing what was customary for proper burial. From the first time we meet these women (8:2–3) until the end, we see them providing for Jesus. **Then they rested on the sabbath according to the commandment** that forbade work on the Sabbath (Exod 20:10; Deut 5:14). Like Zechariah and Elizabeth, who observed "all the commandments and ordinances of the Lord blamelessly" (1:6), and like Mary and Joseph, who did what the law required for a mother and her newborn child (2:22–24), so those who are involved in the burial of Jesus are "virtuous and righteous" (verse 50), observing the Mosaic law faithfully. In birth and death Jesus is in the company of devout Jews.

For reflection: What can I learn from the example of these women?

CHAPTER 24

ORIENTATION: *Save in his final verse (24:53), Luke recounts events that take place during the course of a single day (24:1–52). Jesus' disciples come to realize that he has been raised from the dead and that all that has happened is in fulfillment of God's will made known through the Scriptures.*

The Empty Tomb

¹ But at daybreak on the first day of the week they took the spices they had prepared and went to the tomb. ² They found the stone rolled away from the tomb; ³ but when they entered, they did not find the body of the Lord Jesus. ⁴ While they were puzzling over this, behold, two men in dazzling garments appeared to them. ⁵ They were terrified and bowed their faces to the ground. They said to them, "Why do you seek the living one among the dead? ⁶ He is not here, but he has been raised. Remember what he said to you while he was still in Galilee, ⁷ that the Son of Man must be handed over to sinners and be crucified, and rise on the third day." ⁸ And they remembered his words. ⁹ Then they returned from the tomb and announced all these things to the eleven and to all the others. ¹⁰ The women were Mary Magdalene, Joanna, and Mary the mother of James; the others who accompanied them also told this to the apostles, ¹¹ but their story seemed like nonsense and they did not believe them. ¹² But Peter got up and ran to the tomb, bent down, and saw the burial cloths alone; then he went home amazed at what had happened.

Gospel parallels: Matt 28:1–8; Mark 16:1–8; John 20:1–10
NT: Luke 8:1–3; 9:22, 44–45; 17:25; 18:31–34; 23:49–56

1   Although a chapter break was later introduced here into Luke's Gospel, the present verse is a continuation of the previous verse: "Then they rested on the sabbath according to the commandment" (23:56), **but at daybreak on the first day of the week they took the spices they had prepared and went to the tomb.** Sabbath being the seventh day of the week (Exod 20:10), the following day is **the first day of the**

week—Sunday on our calendar. Some women had followed Jesus from Galilee to Jerusalem and witnessed his crucifixion (23:49). They trailed behind Joseph of Arimathea after he took down the body of Jesus from the cross and laid it in a tomb (23:53–55). They observed that Jesus' body did not receive an anointing as was customary for burials, so they prepared spices and perfumes before the Sabbath began (23:56), intending to anoint the body of Jesus at their first opportunity. The Sabbath ended at sunset, but it was impractical to go to the tomb and anoint the body of Jesus in darkness. Then **at daybreak**, at first light, **on the first day of the week** they take **the spices they had prepared** and go to the **tomb** of Jesus.

We should note that the women fully expected to find the body of Jesus in the tomb. Although he had told his disciples that he would be raised from the dead on the third day (9:22; 18:33), "they understood nothing of this; the word remained hidden from them and they failed to comprehend what he said" (18:34). While they expected that there would be a resurrection of the dead at the end of this age (see 11:31–32; 20:34–35), they apparently could not conceive that God could raise Jesus to resurrected life before this age ended.

BACKGROUND: TOMB OF JESUS At the time of Jesus, an abandoned limestone quarry lay just outside the western wall of Jerusalem. Here Golgotha rose as a hump of unquarried rock. Tombs were dug in the old quarry, just as tombs were dug into virtually all the hills surrounding biblical Jerusalem. The tomb in which Jesus' corpse was buried, located less than two hundred feet from Golgotha, was cut into the side of the quarry. This tomb had at least two chambers: a small antechamber at its entrance and a second chamber with a shelf cut into its wall where a corpse could be laid. There were likely other chambers for other corpses or for their bones after the flesh had decayed away. After Jesus' body was taken down from the cross, it was placed on the shelf in the second chamber. In the fourth century, the Roman emperor Constantine ordered a church to be built at the site of Golgotha and the tomb of Jesus. Workers cut away the hillside surrounding the tomb of Jesus in order to isolate it as a freestanding chapel. This chapel was largely destroyed in the eleventh century and has been rebuilt several times since. Today Golgotha and the tomb of Jesus are within the Church of the Holy Sepulchre in Jerusalem. *Related topics: Burial practices (page 646), Golgotha (page 634).*

For reflection: When have I heard the words of Jesus without comprehending their meaning? How did I later come to grasp them?

2   **They found the stone rolled away from the tomb.** Cave-like tombs from the time of Jesus have been found in the hills around Jerusalem. They have small entrances, perhaps a yard square, that can be blocked with a **stone** disc rolled across them to keep out scavenging animals. The stone can be rolled back to provide access to the tomb for additional burials. After Joseph of Arimathea laid the body of Jesus in the tomb (23:53), he would have blocked its entrance with a stone. When the women arrive at dawn at the **tomb,** they find **the stone rolled away**. They had seen Joseph rolling the stone into place and were probably perplexed to find it now rolled back. Had someone gotten to the tomb ahead of them?

3   **but when they entered** the tomb, **they did not find the body of the Lord Jesus**. Luke sometime refers to Jesus as **the Lord** (7:13; 10:1; 11:39), reflecting Christian practice. The women came to the tomb with spices (verse 1) to anoint the body of Jesus, and even more perplexing than finding the stone rolled back is not finding his body. They saw Joseph of Arimathea lay Jesus' body in the tomb (22:55), but it is no longer there. What happened to it?

Lord: See page 137

4   **While they were puzzling over this**, quite bewildered (had someone taken Jesus' body? who would do such a thing?), **behold, two men in dazzling garments appeared to them**. Those who appear in **dazzling garments** are heavenly figures (9:29–31; Acts 10:30); the **two men** are angels (see 24:23). In Scripture, angels characteristically manifest themselves under the appearance of men (2 Macc 3:26; Dan 8:15; Acts 1:10; 10:30).

Angels: See page 11

5   **They were terrified**: the women who were puzzled that Jesus' body was no longer in the tomb are now **terrified** by angels in dazzling array suddenly appearing to them. They **bowed their faces to the ground** in fear and awe. Their visit to the tomb has turned out unexpectedly

indeed! **They said to them, "Why do you seek the living one among the dead?"** The angels reproach the women for expecting to find **among the dead** someone who is **living**. The angels' words proclaim that Jesus is alive, despite having been crucified a couple of days earlier. The women must wonder, "How can this be?" even though they are being assured by angels that Jesus is **living**.

6 The angels continue, **He is not here, but he has been raised.** The women can see for themselves that **he is not here**. Far more significant is the reason the angels give for Jesus not being in the tomb: **he has been raised**—implied, raised by God from the dead. The angels' words explaining why Jesus is not here will be echoed by the early Church as the core of the gospel: "God raised him from the dead" (Acts 3:15; see Acts 2:24, 32; 4:10; 5:30; 10:40; 13:30, 34, 37; Rom 4:24–25; 6:4, 9; 7:4; 8:11, 34; 10:9; 1 Cor 6:14; 15:1–20; etc.).

> For reflection: When I talk to others about Jesus, what importance do I place on his having been raised?

The women should not be surprised that the tomb is empty for, the angels tell them, **Remember what he said to you while he was still in Galilee,**

Galilee: See page 114

7 **that the Son of Man must be handed over to sinners and be crucified, and rise on the third day.** The women were among his followers in Galilee (8:1–3; 23:49), where he had spoken about his being put to death and being raised from the dead **on the third day** (9:22; 18:33). They should be able to remember Jesus saying that these things **must** happen (9:22; 17:25), even if at the time they did not understand what he was talking about (9:45; 18:34). The angels characterize those responsible for Jesus' death as **sinners**, and they specify that he was put to death by being **crucified**. Rising **on the third day** can take the day of his death as the first day, the next day, the Sabbath, as the second day, and the following day, the first day of the week, as the third day. Luke does not describe the actual resurrection of Jesus; he only recounts the

653

women going to the tomb and finding it empty because Jesus was already risen.

Son of Man: See page 147
Crucifixion: See page 626

> *For reflection: None of the four Gospels describes the actual resurrection of Jesus. Why do I think that they are silent about something so important?*

8 **And they remembered his words.** It would appear from what subsequently happens (verses 9–12, 22–23) that they not only **remembered** but began to grasp and believe Jesus' **words**. They can see that Jesus is not in the tomb, and they accept that "he has been raised" (verse 6) as he said he would be.

9 **Then they returned from the tomb and announced all these things to the eleven and to all the others.** The women who had witnessed his death and burial (23:49, 55) are the first witness to his resurrection. Although the angels did not instruct them to tell others that Jesus has been raised, it was such marvelous news that it had to be **announced** to others. **They returned from the tomb** to where the **eleven** (the Twelve—6:13—minus Judas) and **all the others** who were his disciples were gathered. Luke does not specify the location or how many were together there, but in Acts he will speak of a hundred twenty being gathered in an "upper room where they were staying" (Acts 1:13, 15) and this might be the setting here as well. The women **announced all these things**: they reported that they found the stone rolled back and the tomb empty, that angels appeared to them and told them that Jesus had been raised from the dead, that the angels reminded them that Jesus had told them that he must die and be raised.

> *For reflection: Is the gospel message such good news for me that I tell it to others? Is anything holding me back?*

10 **The women** who announced all these things **were Mary Magdalene, Joanna, and Mary the mother of James**. Two of the women who had traveled with Jesus in Galilee and used their resources to provide for him were **Mary Magdalene** and **Joanna**, the wife of Herod's stew-

ard Chuza (8:1–3). Many other women did the same (8:3), one of them likely being **Mary the mother of James**; later they followed Jesus to Jerusalem (23:49). Since Mary and James were very common names, this **Mary** and **James** cannot be identified with certainty with anyone else in the Gospels named Mary or James. **The others**—other women—**who accompanied them** to the tomb of Jesus **also told this to the apostles**, the eleven who remained of the Twelve (6:13). The other women also report to the apostles all the things that had happened that morning (verse 9), including the angels' announcement that Jesus has been raised (verse 6).

Apostle: See page 164

11 **but their story seemed like nonsense and they did not believe them.** The word translated **nonsense** was used as a medical term for the delirious ravings of someone with a high fever. The apostles may have been able to accept that the body of Jesus was no longer in the tomb and perhaps even believe that angels appeared to the women. But the apostles **did not believe** the women when they told them that Jesus had been raised; that struck them as delirious **nonsense**. Scholars point out that in the world of Jesus, the testimony of women was often dismissed out of hand as unreliable. However, in this situation it seems to have been the message rather than messengers that the apostles found unbelievable. They had not understood Jesus when he told them that he would be raised (18:34); now they do not believe the women's announcement that it has happened.

For reflection: How do I react when others dismiss my convictions as nonsense?

12 One thing was verifiable, however: the condition of the tomb. Was it empty, as the women said? **Peter got up and ran to the tomb**, urgently wanting to find out for himself. There he **bent down** to peer in through the low entranceway, **and saw the burial cloths alone:** he saw only the cloths that the body of Jesus had been wrapped in (23:53). At least that part of the women's story is true: Jesus is no longer in the tomb. **Then he went home amazed at what had happened.** The word translated **amazed** means wondering: Peter is mystified about **what had hap-**

pened. Why would anyone remove the body of Jesus but leave the burial cloths behind? Peter cannot understand why the tomb is empty, but he does not believe it is because Jesus has been raised.

For reflection: What lesson might there be for me in the first disciples' reactions to news of Jesus' resurrection?

On the Way to Emmaus

¹³ Now that very day two of them were going to a village seven miles from Jerusalem called Emmaus, ¹⁴ and they were conversing about all the things that had occurred. ¹⁵ And it happened that while they were conversing and debating, Jesus himself drew near and walked with them, ¹⁶ but their eyes were prevented from recognizing him. ¹⁷ He asked them, "What are you discussing as you walk along?" They stopped, looking downcast. ¹⁸ One of them, named Cleopas, said to him in reply, "Are you the only visitor to Jerusalem who does not know of the things that have taken place there in these days?" ¹⁹ And he replied to them, "What sort of things?" They said to him, "The things that happened to Jesus the Nazarene, who was a prophet mighty in deed and word before God and all the people, ²⁰ how our chief priests and rulers both handed him over to a sentence of death and crucified him. ²¹ But we were hoping that he would be the one to redeem Israel; and besides all this, it is now the third day since this took place. ²² Some women from our group, however, have astounded us: they were at the tomb early in the morning ²³ and did not find his body; they came back and reported that they had indeed seen a vision of angels who announced that he was alive. ²⁴ Then some of those with us went to the tomb and found things just as the women had described, but him they did not see." ²⁵ And he said to them, "Oh, how foolish you are! How slow of heart to believe all that the prophets spoke! ²⁶ Was it not necessary that the Messiah should suffer these things and enter into his glory?" ²⁷ Then beginning with Moses and all the prophets, he interpreted to them what referred to him in all the scriptures. ²⁸ As they approached the village to which they were going, he gave the impression that he was going on farther. ²⁹ But they urged him,

"Stay with us, for it is nearly evening and the day is almost over." So he went in to stay with them. ³⁰ And it happened that, while he was with them at table, he took bread, said the blessing, broke it, and gave it to them. ³¹ With that their eyes were opened and they recognized him, but he vanished from their sight. ³² Then they said to each other, "Were not our hearts burning [within us] while he spoke to us on the way and opened the scriptures to us?" ³³ So they set out at once and returned to Jerusalem where they found gathered together the eleven and those with them ³⁴ who were saying, "The Lord has truly been raised and has appeared to Simon!" ³⁵ Then the two recounted what had taken place on the way and how he was made known to them in the breaking of the bread.

Gospel parallels: Mark 16:12–13

NT: Luke 9:16, 22; 17:25; 18:31–34; 22:19, 37; 24:1–12; 1 Cor 15:1–5

13 **Now that very day**: it is still the first day of the week (24:1). Women who had gone to the tomb of Jesus reported that his body was not there

---

BACKGROUND: EMMAUS Three different sites have been venerated as Emmaus. During the fourth to seventh centuries, Christians identified Emmaus with the Emmaus mentioned in 1 Maccabees (1 Macc 3:40, 57; 4:3; 9:50) even though it was about nineteen miles west of Jerusalem rather than the seven miles (literally, sixty *stadia*) specified by Luke (Luke 24:13; some copyists revised Luke's Gospel to read one hundred sixty *stadia*, which is roughly nineteen miles). This Emmaus, near today's Latrun, was abandoned after a plague in A.D. 639. After the crusaders conquered Jerusalem in 1099, they settled on a site for Emmaus about nine miles west of Jerusalem. This site, at today's Abu Ghosh, was venerated as Emmaus during the crusader era but later fell out of use. Christians visiting the Holy Land thereafter settled on a third site for Emmaus, called Qubeiba today, seven miles northwest of Jerusalem. The Emmaus mentioned by Luke was very likely at a fourth site. At the time of Jesus there was village named Emmaus three and a half miles west of Jerusalem; Romans changed its name to Colonia later in the first century. The Palestinian village of Qaluniya marked the site until 1948; today it is Motza, a suburb of Jerusalem. When Luke wrote that Emmaus was seven miles from Jerusalem he was apparently referring to a round trip. The chronology of events in chapter 24 of Luke's Gospel works best if Emmaus was only three and a half miles from Jerusalem. The two disciples could have eaten an afternoon meal with Jesus (24:29–31) and returned to Jerusalem to meet with the other disciples (24:33–35), with there still being time for the risen Jesus to appear to them (24:36–49) and lead them to Bethany (24:50–52).

---

and that angels had told them that he had been raised, "but their story seemed like nonsense" to the eleven and the other disciples, who did not believe them (24:1–11). Now **two of them**, two of these other disciples (24:9), **were going to a village seven miles from Jerusalem called Emmaus**. Possibly they are disciples of Jesus who live in the **village** of **Emmaus**, just as Martha and Mary have a house in a village (10:38–42). Or they may have come with Jesus from Galilee to Jerusalem (see 19:37) and generally spent their nights in Emmaus because lodgings in Jerusalem were crowded at Passover. Whether they have permanent or temporary lodgings in Emmaus is not significant; what is important is that they are disciples of Jesus who were in Jerusalem when he was crucified and who do not believe that he has been raised from the dead.

Jerusalem: See page 516

14 **and they were conversing about all the things that had occurred.** It will become clear that **the things that had occurred** include Jesus' being crucified despite his being a mighty prophet (verses 19–20). His death dashed their hopes that he would redeem Israel, and not even the disappearance of his body and a report that he has been raised have restored their hopes (verses 21–24). As the two disciples walked along the road to Emmaus, they were **conversing** about all these things, rehashing events and trying to make sense of them. They had dedicated their lives to Jesus as his disciples; what would become of them now that he was dead?

> *For reflection: How would my life change were I to become convinced that Jesus was not raised from the dead?*

15 **And it happened that while they were conversing and debating** about the things that had occurred, **Jesus himself drew near and walked with them**. Luke emphasizes that it is Jesus **himself** walking with the two disciples. He had **walked with** his disciples throughout his ministry (7:11; 8:1–3; 9:10); chapters 9 to 19 of Luke's Gospel recount his journey with them to Jerusalem. The risen Jesus continues to walk alongside his disciples as they journey through life.

16 **but their eyes were prevented from recognizing him.** They take him to be a stranger who happens to be traveling along the same road from Jerusalem. Jesus' appearance must be such that he can be mistaken for an ordinary man. **Their eyes were prevented from recognizing him:** Luke does not say what **prevented** them from **recognizing** Jesus, but Jesus' subsequent words to them suggest that their failure to understand and believe what Scripture says about him (verse 25) is one obstacle to recognizing him. Because they do not grasp the message of Scripture, they are not expecting to ever see Jesus again, and their expectations shape their perceptions.

For reflection: How am I most aware of the presence of Jesus? What allows me to recognize his presence to me?

17 **He asked them, "What are you discussing as you walk along?"** It was obvious that they were having an animated discussion. When Jesus asked them what they are talking about, **they stopped** in their tracks, **looking downcast.** What they were **discussing** made them despondent.

18 **One of them, named Cleopas, said to him in reply:** Luke provides a name for one of the two disciples. This is the only time the name **Cleopas** occurs in Scripture (Clopas is a different name—John 19:25). Luke leaves the second disciple unnamed and does not indicate whether the second disciple is a woman or a man, making it easier for his readers to identify with this disciple. Cleopas asks the stranger who came up alongside them, **Are you the only visitor to Jerusalem who does not know of the things that have taken place there in these days?** His question presumes that what happened recently in Jerusalem is so momentous that it would be unthinkable for anyone to be talking about anything else. (As a modern comparison: the day after 9/11, no American needed to ask others what they were talking about.) If the stranger is coming from **Jerusalem**, surely he should know about **the things that have taken place there** in the last few days. How could anyone be unaware of them? There is irony here: Cleopas thinks Jesus must be obtuse if he does not know what has been going on in Jerusalem, but Jesus is the only one who fully comprehends **the things that have taken place.**

19 **And he replied to them, "What sort of things?"** For the moment, Jesus will let Cleopas and the other disciple do the talking. Jesus is willing to listen to his disciples, even if he understands things better than they do. **They said to him, "The things that happened to Jesus the Nazarene."** They identify **Jesus** as **the Nazarene**, the Jesus from Nazareth (see 18:37), to distinguish him from other Jewish men having the rather common name of Jesus. They say he was **a prophet.** Jesus was commonly thought of as a **prophet** (7:39; 9:7–8, 18–19), indeed a great prophet (7:16), **mighty in deed and word before God and all the people.** Jesus' words had authority (4:32, 36), and he undeniably performed mighty deeds (7:22). **Before God and all the people** means not only in their sight but with their acknowledgment and approval. Jesus was God's agent, freeing men and women from evil and teaching them God's ways. Cleopas and the other disciple had been discussing **the things that happened to Jesus,**

Nazareth: See page 19

20 **how our chief priests and rulers both handed him over to a sentence of death and crucified him**—handed him over to the Romans to be sentenced to death and crucified. This was a profoundly shocking and baffling turn of events. How could **chief priests** and other Jewish leaders seek the death of a mighty prophet sent by God? How could a man who did so much good to so many people end up being **crucified**? Cleopas and the other disciple would have been among "all his acquaintances" who "stood at a distance" and watched Jesus die on a cross (23:49), a sight that filled them with anguish. Now they were discussing how it could have happened and what it meant. They were perplexed and distraught.

High priest, chief priests: See page 605
Crucifixion: See page 626

For reflection: What do I find perplexing about Jesus' death?

21 Jesus had been put to death, **but we were hoping that he would be the one to redeem Israel**. The word **redeem** means to liberate or ransom, as when a slave is freed or a captive is ransomed. To **redeem Israel** can broadly mean to free God's people from bondage

and affliction; the hopes of these two disciples likely included God's people being freed from Roman rule (see Acts 1:6). Yet instead of Jesus prevailing over the Romans, he was crucified by them. Instead of God's reign being established, as Jesus proclaimed it would be, Rome continues to rule. The hopes of the two disciples died with Jesus on the cross and were buried with him in the tomb. It is no wonder that they are downcast (verse 17): they staked their lives on Jesus, and now he and his message are dead.

For reflection: Have I so thoroughly staked my life on Jesus that I would be utterly lost without him?

Besides all this, it is now the third day since this took place. The two disciples do not seem to remember that Jesus said he would be raised on **the third day** (9:22; 18:33) or, if they remember, they do not grasp and believe what he said (see 18:34). Had they expected Jesus to be raised on **the third day**, they surely would have remained in Jerusalem, waiting in eager anticipation. But instead they left Jerusalem. Jesus died shortly before the beginning of the Sabbath, and they waited until the Sabbath was over to go to Emmaus because it was farther away than it was permitted to walk on the sabbath (Exod 16:29 and Num 35:5 were interpreted to limit travel on the Sabbath to two thousand cubits or about one thousand yards; see Acts 1:12). The sense of their remarking that **it is now the third day since this took place** seems to be, even though it is the third day since Jesus was crucified, nothing has happened since to undo their devastation at his death. They watched Jesus die, and they passed the Sabbath in Jerusalem with a profound sense of loss and emptiness. Nothing has filled their emptiness.

22 True, some things did happen. **Some women from our group, however, have astounded us: they were at the tomb early in the morning.** The two disciples on the road to Emmaus were with the other disciples of Jesus earlier that day when **some women** who had gone to the **tomb** of Jesus came and reported what had happened (24:1–10). The two disciples were **astounded** by what the women said.

Tomb of Jesus: See page 651

23 After the women **did not find his body** in the tomb, **they came back and reported that they had indeed seen a vision of angels who announced that he was alive**. Although the disciples were astounded by what they said, they dismissed it as "nonsense and did not believe them" (24:11); they do not believe that Jesus is **alive**.

24 **Then some of those with us went to the tomb and found things just as the women had described, but him they did not see.** Luke recounted Peter going to the tomb and being amazed that the body of Jesus was no longer in it (24:12). The empty tomb is not in itself sufficient grounds for faith; it is a testimony to the absence of Jesus rather than a sign of his presence. **Him they did not see**: apart from the women, none of the disciples are prepared to accept that he is alive unless they **see** him. Consequently, after hearing the reports of the women and of those who went to the tomb, Cleopas and his companion left Jerusalem downcast. They think that Jesus is dead and their discipleship is over. Again there is irony: the two disciples do not **see** Jesus even though he is at their side and they are talking with him about him!

For reflection: What might be the lesson for me in the two disciples' not realizing that Jesus is at their side?

25 **And he said to them, "Oh, how foolish you are!"** Jesus rebukes his two disciples for being **foolish** and obtuse. He is disappointed with them because they are **slow of heart to believe all that the prophets spoke!** They may be familiar with the **prophets**, but they have not taken their words to **heart**. In the biblical view, the **heart** is the seat of thinking, willing, and feeling. To be **slow of heart** is to resist understanding and be reluctant to accept—here, understand and accept God's revelation made known through the prophets, and through all of Scripture (verse 27). Because the disciples do not understand and **believe** what is written in Scripture, they are unable to discern God's will in "the things that have taken place" in Jerusalem (verse 18) and do not accept the women's report that Jesus has been raised and is alive.

For reflection: How eager of heart am I to embrace what I read in Scripture? How has Scripture enabled me to make sense out of my life?

26 Jesus tells the two disciples, **Was it not necessary that the Messiah should suffer these things and enter into his glory?** If they had understood and accepted "all that the prophets spoke" (verse 25), they would have realized that it was **necessary** for **the Messiah** to **suffer these things**. By **necessary** Jesus means necessary in God's plan, something that must happen. Throughout his life, Jesus carried out his Father's will, explaining that it was what he *must* do (2:49; 4:43; 13:33; 19:5). When Peter proclaimed him to be **the Messiah** (9:20), Jesus told his disciples that he "must suffer greatly and be rejected by the elders, the chief priests, and the scribes, and be killed and on the third day be raised" (9:22; see also 12:50; 17:25; 24:6–7). All **these things** had to happen for God's will to be carried out (see 22:42) and for Jesus to **enter into his glory**. His suffering and death were the "exodus" he accomplished in Jerusalem (9:31), his "being taken up" (9:51) to his Father and **glory**. Jesus spoke of his coming "in his glory and in the glory of the Father and of the holy angels" (9:26), "coming in a cloud with power and great glory" (21:27), to bring the reign of God to fulfillment (21:31). What the two disciples took to be a tragic failure was just the opposite: his crucifixion fulfilled God's plan and was Jesus' entering **into his glory**.

Messiah, Christ: See page 257

For reflection: Jesus' death was his entry into glory. What hope does this give me in the face of death?

27 **Then beginning with Moses and all the prophets, he interpreted to them what referred to him in all the scriptures,** explaining how his suffering and death fulfilled Scripture. Jesus begins his interpretation with **Moses and all the prophets,** "the law and the prophets" (16:16), but extends it to include **all the scriptures,** the entire Old Testament.

Luke does not tell his readers which passages in Scripture Jesus interpreted, but a number of Scripture passages have been quoted or alluded to in the course of his Gospel, especially in connection with the suffering and death of Jesus. Jesus began his ministry by reading a passage from Isaiah and proclaiming, "Today this scripture passage is fulfilled in your hearing" (4:17–21; Isaiah 61:1–2). He referred to himself as a stone rejected by the builders that becomes the cornerstone (20:17; Psalm 118:22). He invoked words from Psalm 110 to teach that the Messiah is greater than David (20:41–44; Psalm 110:1). He told his disciples, "this scripture must be fulfilled in me, namely, 'He was counted among the wicked'; and indeed what is written about me is coming to fulfillment" (22:37; Isaiah 53:12). After his arrest, he remained silent before Herod Antipas, just as, in Isaiah, a servant of God does not open his mouth to those treating him harshly (23:9; Isaiah 53:7). This prophecy of Isaiah speaks of a servant of God whose sufferings atone for the sins of others (Isaiah 52:13—53:12). Luke uses words from Psalm 22 to describe Jesus' executioners dividing his clothing by casting lots (23:34; Psalm 22:19), and he invokes this Psalm again in recounting how Jesus was mocked while on the cross (23:35; Psalm 22:8–9). Jesus is offered sour wine, just as the psalmist is in Psalm 69 (23:36; Psalm 69:22). Jesus prays words from Psalm 31 as he dies (23:46; Psalm 31:6). Jesus could have cited these passages as well as others as he interpreted what referred to him in **all** the Scriptures. He could have drawn attention to themes and patterns in the Scriptures and shown how his death and resurrection fit a biblical pattern. For example, prophets sent by God were rejected and even killed (see 6:22–23; 11:47–51; 13:34; 20:9–17), and it was no different with God's envoy and prophet Jesus (see 4:24; 7:16; 13:32–33).

Jesus **interpreted** the Scriptures: Scripture requires interpretation. Jesus explained how the Scriptures applied to him and how he fulfilled them. No single Scripture passage explicitly speaks of the Messiah having to suffer in order to enter into glory (verse 26; Isaiah 52:13—53:12 does not identify the servant of God with the Messiah). Jesus is able to draw connections, however, between different passages. Individual Scripture passages are like stones in a mosaic portraying him. No single stone contains his entire image; it is all the stones joined together in the mosaic that forms the image of Jesus—if Jesus is the pattern by which the stones are arranged. Jesus can be understood in light of Scripture when Scripture is understood in light of Jesus.

For reflection: How well am I able to find foreshadowings of Jesus when I read the Old Testament? What are the clearest foreshadowings that I am aware of?

Just as Jesus explained his suffering, dying, and rising in light of the Scriptures, so will the early Church: "They reached Thessalonica, where there was a synagogue of the Jews. Following his usual custom, Paul joined them, and for three sabbaths he entered into discussions with them from the scriptures, expounding and demonstrating that the Messiah had to suffer and rise from the dead, and that 'This is the Messiah, Jesus, whom I proclaim to you' " (Acts 17:1–3; see also Acts 26:22–23; 28:23; 1 Cor 15:1–4).

28 **As they approached the village to which they were going, he gave the impression that he was going on farther.** As they are about to enter Emmaus, Jesus acted as though he would continue on along the road.

29 **But they urged him, "Stay with us, for it is nearly evening and the day is almost over."** The word translated **urged** means strongly urged, almost compelled. **Stay with us**: the two disciples offer Jesus hospitality in their dwelling, food and lodging for the night. Prevailing on travelers to accept hospitality is a deeply rooted biblical tradition (see Gen 18:1–8; 19:1–3; Acts 16:15). As a reason for Jesus to accept their hospitality they say, perhaps with some exaggeration, that **it is nearly evening and the day is almost over**. Since people generally rose with the sun, the main part of the work **day** was regarded as **almost over** by early afternoon. It might now only be mid to late afternoon but the two disciples use the approach of **evening** as an excuse for Jesus to **stay with** them. They are listening to his explanation of Scripture with rapt attention (see verse 32), and they want to continue listening to him as long as they can. They relish the prospect of his staying overnight in their house. Whoever he is (see verse 16), he certainly has great insight into Scripture, even if he seemed oblivious to the events that have taken place recently in Jerusalem (verse 18). **So he went in to stay with them.** Jesus accepted meals and hospitality throughout his ministry (4:38–39; 5:29; 7:36; 10:38–40; 11:37; 14:1; 19:5; 22:8–13) and depended on others for his lodgings (9:58). The risen Jesus continues to accept the invitations of those who ask him to **stay with** them.

Hospitality: See page 314

For reflection: "Behold, I stand at the door and knock. If anyone hears my voice and opens the door, [then] I will enter his house and dine with him, and he with me" (Rev 3:20). How have I invited Jesus to be with me? How have I experienced his response?

30 There is some evidence that, save for special occasions, Jewish custom at the time of Jesus was to eat two meals a day: a simple breakfast between ten and eleven in the morning, and the main meal in late afternoon. The two disciples share their afternoon main meal with Jesus. **And it happened that, while he was with them at table, he took bread, said the blessing, broke it, and gave it to them.** Even though they are in the house or lodgings of Cleopas and the other disciple, Jesus acts as the host at the meal, saying the **blessing** over the **bread**. Perhaps the two disciples deferred to him in light of his amazing grasp of Scripture: he was obviously someone who had meditated deeply on God's revelation and ways. Jesus does what the host at any Jewish meal would do, taking bread, offering a blessing to thank God for the bread, breaking the round loaf of bread into portions, and distributing the portions to those sharing the meal. Jesus has done this many times over the course of his adult life. When he fed a crowd of more than five thousand, he took five loaves of bread and two fish, "and looking up to heaven, he said the blessing over them, broke them, and gave them to the disciples to set before the crowd" (9:16). At his last supper with his disciples, "he took the bread, said the blessing, broke it, and gave it to them, saying, 'This is my body, which will be given for you; do this in memory of me'" (22:19). The two disciples may have been present at these occasions and in any case would have been present at other meals when Jesus blessed and broke the bread.

31 **With that their eyes were opened and they recognized him.** If their failure to grasp the message of Scripture had been an obstacle to their recognizing that the risen Jesus was with them (see verses 16, 25), that obstacle has been removed by Jesus (verse 27). Yet it was not until he blessed and broke bread that **they recognized him** to be Jesus. It was not simply that they had seen him doing this before and the sight of it triggered memory and recognition. Luke writes that **their eyes were opened**, implying, opened by God. Discerning the presence of the risen Jesus requires divinely implanted eyes of faith. **But he vanished from their sight.** Luke does not write that Jesus went away but that he literally became invisible from them. Jesus has entered into his glory (verse

26) and is no longer subject to the limitations of space and time. He can manifest his presence, as he did to the two disciples, but he is always present, even if his presence is not perceived.

32 **Then they said to each other, "Were not our hearts burning [within us] while he spoke to us on the way and opened the scriptures to us?"** In retrospect they recognize even more clearly the impact Jesus had on them as he **spoke to** them **on the way** to Emmaus and **opened the scriptures** to them. They realize that their **hearts** were **burning** with intense emotion as Jesus explained Scripture to them and it took on meaning for them.

> *For reflection: What have been my most heartfelt moments while reading Scripture? Which passages came alive for me? When have I had a sense that Jesus was speaking to me through the words of Scripture?*

33 **So they set out at once and returned to Jerusalem.** They left Jerusalem feeling downcast because their hopes had been dashed by the crucifixion of Jesus (verses 17, 21); they return filled with exuberant joy. Jesus is alive, and his crucifixion was not the tragic failure that they had thought. **They found gathered together the eleven and those with them**, whom the two disciples had been with earlier that day (24:9, 13). There was no need for Jesus to tell the two disciples to announce to the rest of his disciples that he was alive; it was not something they could keep to themselves. Like the women who had been at the tomb early that day, they had to tell others the good news (24:9–10).

34 Before they can report what had happened they are preempted by the rest of Jesus' followers, who also have good news that they cannot keep to themselves. They **were saying,** undoubtedly quite excitedly, **The Lord has truly been raised and has appeared to Simon!** Luke does not recount the appearance of the risen Jesus to **Simon** Peter (Paul mentions an appearance of Jesus to Peter, referring to him as Cephas, the Aramaic counterpart to Peter—1 Cor 15:5). The appearance had to take place after Peter went to the tomb, found it empty, and reported this to the other disciples (24:12, 24). Previously the disciples had no faith that Jesus was alive because "him they did not see" (verse 24). Now they believe that he **has truly been raised**, because he **has appeared to Simon**. They refer to Jesus as **the Lord**: they have often addressed Jesus as **Lord** (5:8; 9:54; 10:17, 40; 11:1; 12:41; 17:37; 22:33, 38, 49), but now they are beginning to grasp that Jesus is **the Lord**, sharing the lordship of God (see John 20:28; Phil 2:11).

Lord: See page 137

35 **Then the two recounted what had taken place on the way**, how a stranger walked with them and explained Scripture to them, how their hearts were on fire as they listened to him and Scripture took on meaning for them. They recounted **how he was made known to them in the breaking of the bread** and then disappeared from their sight.

In Acts, Luke refers to the Eucharist as **the breaking of the bread** (Acts 2:42; see also 2:46; 20:7, 11). Luke described what happened during the meal in Emmaus in a manner that evokes the Eucharist (compare verse 30 with 22:19), and he reinforces the link by referring to it as **the breaking of the bread**. He wants his readers to realize that Jesus is present in the Church's celebration of the Eucharist, **the breaking of the bread**.

The experience of the two disciples during the meal is the culmination of their transformation from disciples who were downcast over the death of Jesus to disciples who have a heartfelt realization that he is alive. Their transformation occurred in stages: first, Jesus *opened* the Scriptures to them (verse 32), explaining their meaning, showing how his death fulfilled God's will as made known through Scripture (verses 26–27). Then their eyes were *opened* to his presence (verse 31) through the breaking of the bread (verse 35). These two elements—breaking open the Scriptures, breaking the bread—will be at the heart of the worship of the Church when it gathers every first day of the week (24:1, 13; Acts 20:7) to fulfill Jesus' command, "Do this in memory of me" (22:19). Luke wants the eyes and hearts and minds of his readers opened to the presence of the risen Jesus; he wants his readers to recognize Jesus through the Scriptures and in the breaking of the bread. He wants his readers to be transformed into joyful witnesses bearing the good news that Jesus is alive.

For reflection: What are the most important lessons for me in what happened to the two disciples?

Jesus Appears to His Disciples

³⁶ While they were still speaking about this, he stood in their midst and said to them, "Peace be with you." ³⁷ But they were startled and terrified and thought that they were seeing a ghost. ³⁸ Then he said to them, "Why are you troubled? And why do questions arise in your hearts? ³⁹ Look at my hands and my feet, that it is I myself. Touch me and see, because a ghost does not have flesh and bones as you can see I have." ⁴⁰ And as he said this, he showed them his hands and his feet. ⁴¹ While they were still incredulous for joy and were amazed, he asked them, "Have you anything here to eat?" ⁴² They gave him a piece of baked fish; ⁴³ he took it and ate it in front of them.

⁴⁴ He said to them, "These are my words that I spoke to you while I was still with you, that everything written about me in the law of Moses and in the prophets and psalms must be fulfilled." ⁴⁵ Then he opened their minds to understand the scriptures. ⁴⁶ And he said to them, "Thus it is written that the Messiah would suffer and rise from the dead on the third day ⁴⁷ and that repentance, for the forgiveness of sins, would be preached in his name to all the nations, beginning from Jerusalem. ⁴⁸ You are witnesses of these things. ⁴⁹ And [behold] I am sending the promise of my Father upon you; but stay in the city until you are clothed with power from on high."

Gospel parallels: Mark 16:15; John 20:19–20

NT: Matt 28:18–20; Luke 4:14–21; 12:11–12; 24:33–35; Acts 1:4–8; 10:34–43

36 **While they were still speaking about this**: the eleven and the other disciples (24:9, 33) are talking about how Jesus appeared to Simon Peter and made himself known to two disciples in Emmaus (24:34–35). Peter and the two disciples are recounting their firsthand experiences of Jesus. As they are **speaking about this, he stood in their midst**. Jesus appears abruptly and unexpectedly, suddenly standing **in their midst** and interrupting their discussion. Having entered into his glory (24:26), Jesus can manifest himself anywhere at any time. He **said to them, "Peace be with you."** Wishing others **peace** was a traditional greeting (1 Sam 25:6); Jesus instructed his disciples to say, "Peace to this household," when entering a house (10:5). Jesus is not mouthing a polite pleasantry when he

wishes his disciples **peace**. He came to guide God's people "into the path of peace" (1:79), the way that makes for harmony, wholeness, total well-being (see also 19:42). Ultimately, the peace that Jesus brings is salvation (see 2:11, 14; 7:50; 8:48; Acts 10:36–38).

For reflection: When have I experienced Jesus giving me peace?

37 **But they were startled and terrified**: their reaction is anything but peaceful! They were rattled and in a **terrified** panic because they **thought that they were seeing a ghost**, a disembodied spirit, a ghostly apparition (see 1 Sam 28:8–19). Even though Jesus appeared to Simon Peter and made himself known to the two disciples in Emmaus, they along with the other disciples do not recognize that it is Jesus who is standing before them. Even though they believe that "the Lord has truly been raised" (24:34), they take him for a **ghost** and are **terrified**. This puzzling turn of events is an indication that there is a profound mystery in the transformation effected by resurrection. Had Jesus simply been brought back to life, his disciples would have had no more trouble recognizing him than the widow had recognizing her son or Jairus his daughter when Jesus brought them back to life (7:11–15; 8:51–56). In being raised from the dead, Jesus has not returned to his former mode of existence but has been transformed in a manner that makes it difficult for his disciples to recognize him.

For reflection: What are my expectations of being transformed through death and resurrection?

38 **Then he said to them, "Why are you troubled?"** Jesus' question implies that they should not be **troubled**, "startled and terrified" (verse 37), by seeing him. **And why do questions arise in your hearts?** In this context, the word translated as **questions** could also be translated as "doubts." Jesus asks them why they doubt whether it is truly he, raised from the dead, who is standing in their midst. He implies that they should not be troubled or have doubts. In light of the message of the angel to the women at the tomb, and in light of Jesus' explanation of Scripture to the two disciples on the road to Emmaus, all his disciples

should understand that he had to suffer, die, and be raised (24:6–7, 26) in fulfillment of God's plan found in Scripture (24:27). They should have been prepared to recognize him even in his transformed state and welcome him with joy. Instead, they doubt that it is really he.

39 Jesus tells them, **Look at my hands and my feet,** and see **that it is I myself.** Presumably Jesus' crucifixion left marks on his **hands** and his **feet,** and these remain in the risen body of Jesus. (Luke's readers may have heard that Jesus was nailed to the cross, a not uncommon Roman practice; see also John 20:25–27.) The disciples had seen Jesus be crucified (23:33, 49); the marks of crucifixion should be evidence that it is he himself standing in their midst. Because they take him for a ghost (verse 37), Jesus tells them, **Touch me and see** that I am not a ghost, **because a ghost does not have flesh and bones as you can see I have.** The disciples are able to **touch** the risen Jesus and feel his **flesh** and **bones,** and **see** for themselves that he is not a **ghost.**

40 **And as he said this, he showed them his hands and his feet,** allowing them to examine him closely.

41 **While they were still incredulous for joy and were amazed:** they do not know what to think or how to respond. They are **amazed,** wondering what is happening—the same reaction Peter had when he found the tomb of Jesus empty (24:12). They are filled with **joy** at the sight of Jesus. But they are also **incredulous,** not believing what they are seeing. Jesus standing before them—that's too good to be true! Jesus knows they are befuddled and need help accepting that it is he. **He asked them, "Have you anything here to eat?"**

42 **They gave him a piece of baked fish,** perhaps a leftover from their late afternoon meal.

43 **he took it and ate it in front of them** to demonstrate that he was not a ghost or apparition. After Jesus raised the daughter of Jairus to life, "he then directed that she should be given something to eat" (8:53–55): her eating would be proof that she really was alive.

Luke does not describe what the risen Jesus looks like, and he does not try to reconcile the various things he tells his readers about Jesus' bodily state after being raised from the dead. The risen Jesus is not a ghost or disembodied spirit: he has flesh and bones than can be touched, he can eat food, he bears marks of crucifixion. But the risen Jesus can become present (verse 36) and vanish (24:31) suddenly; his appearance is such that even those who are his disciples and knew him well before his death have difficulty recognizing him. The risen Jesus is a transformed Jesus with a bodily existence that is not subject to the limitations of earthly existence.

For reflection: What does Luke's account tell me about the risen Jesus? What questions does it leave in my mind?

44 Jesus does not attempt to provide his disciples with further proofs of his bodily presence. He seems to diagnose their fundamental problem as continuing incomprehension of God's plan for him, for this is what he addresses. **He said to them, "These are my words that I spoke to you while I was still with you,"** meaning before his death and being raised. Jesus is still with them, but not in the manner in which he was previously with them. He reminds them that he told them **that everything written about me in the law of Moses and in the prophets and psalms must be fulfilled**. Jesus reflects a traditional threefold division of Scripture when he refers to the **law** of Moses, the **prophets**, and the **psalms**, perhaps meaning the psalms and the other scriptural writings. While he was with them before his death, Jesus spoke of Scripture being **fulfilled** in him (4:17–21; 18:31; 22:37) and applied the **psalms** to himself (13:35—Psalm 118:26; 20:17—Psalm 118:22; 20:41–44—Psalm 110:1; 22:69—Psalm 110:1). In recounting Jesus' passion, Luke drew from or invoked Psalms 22, 31, and 69.

45 **Then he opened their minds to understand the scriptures**, just as he had done for the two disciples on the road to Emmaus: "Beginning with Moses and all the prophets, he interpreted to them what referred to him in all the scriptures" (24:27).

*For reflection: Where am I in need of my mind being opened to the meaning
of Scripture? What are the most significant passages that puzzle me?*

**46 And he said to them, "Thus it is written that the Messiah would
suffer and rise from the dead on the third day."** Jesus opens the
minds of his disciples to understand that his suffering, death, and rising are a fulfillment of what **is written** in Scripture. He told the two
disciples on the way to Emmaus, "Was it not necessary that the Messiah
should suffer these things and enter into his glory?" (24:26). It was necessary that he suffer, because it was God's will for him as made known
through Scripture.

Messiah, Christ: See page 257

In the course of this first day of the week (24:1), an angel reminded
the women at the tomb that Jesus had told them that "the Son of Man
must be handed over to sinners and be crucified, and rise on the third
day" (24:7)—"must" because it is God's will (see 9:22; 12:50; 13:33; 17:25;
22:42). Then Jesus opened the minds of two disciples to understand that
he had to suffer and die to enter into glory, in fulfillment of Scripture
(24:26–27). Now he opens the minds of all his disciples to understand
how his death and rising are in fulfillment of Scripture. Luke had to be
selective in what he included in his Gospel to keep it to a manageable
length (even so, it is the longest of the Gospels). If he recounts something multiple times, as he is doing in this chapter, it is to emphasize its
importance. Luke wants his readers to understand that Jesus' crucifixion
was not a tragic failure but the fulfillment of God's plan made known
through Scripture. The reactions of Jesus' disciples demonstrate that it
was not easy for them to comprehend and accept this. Luke knows that
it may be difficult as well for his readers to really comprehend and fully
accept it. Hence he drive homes the point: Jesus' crucifixion and being
raised fulfilled Scripture and God's will.

*For reflection: How fully do I comprehend why Jesus died on a cross?
What still puzzles me? How completely do I accept that this was God's
will?*

47 "Thus it is written that the Messiah would suffer and rise from the dead on the third day" (verse 46) **and that repentance, for the forgiveness of sins, would be preached in his name to all the nations, beginning from Jerusalem**. Jesus proclaims that just as it is written in Scripture that the Messiah would suffer and rise from the dead, so it is also written in Scripture that **repentance** leading to the **forgiveness of sins** would be **preached** to **all the nations**, peoples, of the world. Calling men and women to repentance was part of Jesus' mission; he had "not come to call the righteous to repentance but sinners" (5:32). He spoke of the joy in heaven over even one sinner repenting (15:7, 10). Jesus carried out his ministry almost entirely among Jews, but God's plan as found in Scripture calls for the people of all nations to be invited to repentance so that their sins may be forgiven.

Repentance: See page 92
Jerusalem: See page 516

For reflection: Where am I in need of repentance and forgiveness?

Jesus does not say which Scriptures indicate that this is God's plan, but a number of passages touch on one or more of its elements. A call to **repentance**, to turn to God and away from sin, is heard throughout the Old Testament, particularly in the prophets: "Return, O Israel, to the LORD, your God" (Hosea 14:2). Repentance leads to **forgiveness of sins** (see 2 Sam 12:13; Psalm 32:1–5; 130:4). In some cases, sacrificial offerings were to be made at the Temple to atone for sins (Lev 5; 19:20–22). Isaiah spoke of a servant of God who would give his life as an offering, taking away the sins of many (Isaiah 53:5–6, 8, 10, 12). Jeremiah prophesied that God would establish a new covenant with his people, forgiving their sins (Jer 31:31, 34). There are foreshadowings in the Old Testament of God's mercy and forgiveness being extended **to all the nations**. In Isaiah, God says to his servant, "I will make you a light to the nations / that my salvation may reach to the ends of the earth" (Isaiah 49:6). Isaiah speaks of the peoples of the earth streaming to **Jerusalem** as the dwelling place of God (Isaiah 56:6–8; 60:11–14), and the word of God going forth from Jerusalem (Isaiah 2:2–3).

Whichever Scripture passages Jesus may have invoked, he opened the minds of his disciples (verse 45) so that they could understood that, in fulfillment of Scripture, **repentance, for the forgiveness of sins, would be preached in his name to all the nations, beginning from Jerusalem**. There is a link in God's plan between Jesus' suffering and rising (verse 46) and repentance for the forgiveness of sins being preached to all nations. At his last supper with his disciples, Jesus took a cup of wine and said, "This cup is the new covenant in my blood, which will be shed for you" (22:20). By his death, Jesus established the new covenant prophesied by Jeremiah, bringing forgiveness of sins (Jer 31:31, 34). Paul will proclaim, "Christ died for our sins in accordance with the scriptures" (1 Cor 15:3; see Isaiah 53:5–12; Rom 4:25; 5:6–8; 1 Pet 2:22–24; 3:18). Because of Jesus' crucifixion and rising, forgiveness of sins is available to all.

For reflection: What forgiveness have I received because of the death and rising of Jesus?

48 **You are witnesses of these things.** In God's plan, Jesus was to suffer, die, and rise, creating a new covenant between God and his people, bringing them forgiveness. Now his disciples are to be **witnesses of these things** to all the nations, proclaiming the death and rising of Jesus, inviting women and men into the new covenant, calling them to repentance and offering them forgiveness. They are to do so "in his name" (verse 47), meaning as his representatives (see Exod 5:23; Deut 10:8).

These few words—**You are witnesses of these things**—summarize the content of Luke's second volume, the Acts of the Apostles. Jesus will tell his disciples, "You will be my witnesses in Jerusalem, throughout Judea and Samaria, and to the ends of the earth" (Acts 1:8). Peter will conclude the first sermon in Acts by inviting his audience to "repent and be baptized, every one of you, in the name of Jesus Christ for the forgiveness of your sins" (Acts 2:38). Peter will proclaim that "God has thus brought to fulfillment what he had announced beforehand through the mouth of all the prophets, that his Messiah would suffer. Repent, therefore, and be converted, that your sins may be wiped away" (Acts 3:18–19). Peter will say that Jesus "commissioned us to preach to the people and testify . . . To him all the prophets bear witness, that everyone who believes in him will receive forgiveness of sins through his name" (Acts 10:42, 43). Paul will also proclaim that Jesus fulfilled what is written in Scripture (13:29;

17:2–3; 26:22–23), bringing forgiveness of sins (Acts 13:38); Paul will bring this message to the Gentiles (Acts 13:47; 20:21; 26:17–18; 28:28).

For reflection: What witness am I able to give about Jesus and about what God accomplished through him? How often do I act as his witness?

49 And [behold] I am sending the promise of my Father upon you; but stay in the city until you are clothed with power from on high. At the beginning of Acts, Luke will again recount Jesus' final instructions to his disciples, making it clear that **the promise of my Father** is the Holy Spirit: "He enjoined them not to depart from Jerusalem, but to wait for 'the promise of the Father about which you have heard me speak; for John baptized with water, but in a few days you will be baptized with the holy Spirit' " (Acts 1:4–5). The **Father** promised through the prophets that his Spirit would be poured out upon his people and upon all mankind (Isaiah 32:15; 44:3; Ezek 39:29; Joel 3:1–5). Jesus tells his disciples **I am sending** the Holy Spirit upon you: Jesus will baptize them with the holy Spirit and fire (3:16), immersing them in the Spirit. The Holy Spirit will descend as tongues of fire on Pentecost, fulfilling the Father's promise (Acts 2:1–21; Joel 3:1–5 is quoted by Peter to explain what happened).

Jesus, conceived through the power of the Holy Spirit (1:35), filled with and led by the Spirit (4:1), carried out his mission in the power of the Spirit (4:14; 5:17; 6:19). Now his disciples are to be his witnesses (verse 48) **clothed with power from on high**, from heaven. To be **clothed** with something is a biblical image for being enveloped with a quality or capacity (see 2 Chron 6:41; Job 8:22; Psalm 104:1; 132:9; Prov 31:25). The disciples are to be equipped with the **power** of the Holy Spirit, the power Jesus exercised in his ministry, so that they can carry out their ministry. Jesus tells them to **stay in the city until** they receive the power of the Spirit: they cannot carry out their mission as witnesses simply by their own abilities and talents. Jesus told his disciples not to worry about what they would say when they had to testify before authorities, "for the holy Spirit will teach you at that moment what you should say" (12:11–12). On another occasion he made a similar promise: "I myself shall give you a wisdom in speaking" (21:14–15). The Spirit who empowered Jesus will inspire them, so that their words will be his words; the Spirit will clothe them with the power they need to be Jesus' witnesses to all the nations of the earth. If the witness of Jesus' disciples is the contents of Acts, the power of the Holy Spirit is its dynamism.

The Spirit: See page 100

For reflection: What is my God-given mission in life? How has the Holy Spirit empowered me to carry out my mission?

Jesus Is Taken Up to Heaven

⁵⁰ Then he led them [out] as far as Bethany, raised his hands, and blessed them. ⁵¹ As he blessed them he parted from them and was taken up to heaven. ⁵² They did him homage and then returned to Jerusalem with great joy, ⁵³ and they were continually in the temple praising God.

Gospel parallels: Mark 16:19

OT: Num 6:24–26

NT: Luke 9:31, 51; 24:44–49; Acts 1:1–12

50 **Then he led them [out] as far as Bethany.** Jesus **led** the eleven and the other disciples (24:9, 33) out of Jerusalem, providing a final image for discipleship: Jesus leads, his disciples follow him. He led them **as far as Bethany**: Bethany lay on an eastern slope of the Mount of Olives. Jesus began his entry into Jerusalem, riding on a colt, from the vicinity of Bethany (19:28–35), and he will make his final departure from the same area. He **raised his hands, and blessed them**. To bless someone is to ask for God's favor upon them. The premier blessing in the Old Testament is, "The LORD bless you and keep you! / The LORD let his face shine upon you, and be gracious to you! / The LORD look upon you kindly and give you peace!" (Num 6:24–26). Priests **raised** their **hands**, extending them over those they **blessed** (Lev 9:22; Sirach 50:20); Jesus' blessing of his disciples is also akin to the blessings made by Jacob (Gen 49:25–26) and Moses (Deut 33) before they died. It is Jesus' farewell blessing as he is taken up to heaven, his final prayer on earth for them (see 22:32).

Bethany: See page 510

> *For reflection: Jesus' final act on earth was asking God's blessings upon his disciples. What does this reveal to me about Jesus?*

51 **As he blessed them he parted from them**: he leaves in the act of praying for God's blessings upon them. He parted from them **and was taken up to heaven**. During Jesus' transfiguration, Moses and Elijah "appeared in glory and spoke of his exodus that he was going to accomplish in Jerusalem" (9:31). His "exodus" is his "being taken up" (9:51) to his Father through crucifixion (23:46) and resurrection. Jesus has entered into his glory (24:26; see also 9:26; 21:27; 23:43); his being **taken up** to heaven marks the conclusion of his bodily appearances to his disciples. Before his death, he said that from this time on he "will be seated at the right hand of the power of God" (22:69); from there he will clothe his disciples with "power from on high" (24:49). Peter will explain the outpouring of the Holy Spirit on Pentecost by saying, "God raised this Jesus; of this we are all witnesses. Exalted at the right hand of God, he received the promise of the holy Spirit from the Father and poured it forth, as you [both] see and hear" (Acts 2:32–33). Paul will speak of Jesus at the right hand of God interceding for his followers (Rom 8:34), continuing his departing prayer for God's blessings upon them.

Jesus was taken up to **heaven**: the word translated **heaven** also means "sky," which was figuratively thought of as the dwelling place of God (3:21–22; Job 22:14; Psalm 11:4). Luke's first readers probably could visualize Jesus being taken up to heaven much as they could Elijah being taken up bodily to heaven (2 Kings 2:11). Our modern understanding of the universe may make this more difficult for us to imagine. Since God created space and time, God transcends space and time, and heaven—being with God—is itself beyond our imagining. Those who would like to suggest a more sophisticated account than Luke's of how Jesus was taken up to God will quickly discover the limits of our space- and time-bound human imaginations.

52 **They did him homage**: the word translated **did . . . homage** means to prostrate oneself before another, as the centurion Cornelius will do before Peter (Acts 10:25). Prostrating oneself before God is an act of worship, and the word for **homage** became an expression for worship (it is translated as "worship" at 4:8; Acts 8:27; 24:11). That is its sense here:

the disciples prostrated themselves before Jesus as an act of worship—the first time they do so in Luke's Gospel. They finally grasp that Jesus has risen and entered into his glory; they finally begin to comprehend what it means that he is the Lord (24:34) and deserves their worship. **Then** they **returned to Jerusalem with great joy**, obeying Jesus' instruction to "stay in the city until you are clothed with power from on high" (24:49). When Jesus appeared in their midst, they were "incredulous for joy" (24:41), but now their doubts are gone and they are filled with **great joy**. They realize that Jesus' crucifixion did not mark an end but a beginning. In joyful anticipation they await being clothed with the power of the Spirit (24:49).

Jerusalem: See page 516

53 **and they were continually in the temple praising God.** Jesus' disciples continue to worship in the **temple** (see also Acts 2:46; 3:1). Luke's Gospel ends as it began, with devout Jews coming to the Temple (1:8–9; 2:22–38, 41–50). Jesus' disciples were continually **praising God**, glorifying him for what he accomplished in Jesus (see 5:26; 7:16; 13:13; 17:15; 18:43). Now that Jesus has opened their eyes to understand the significance of his crucifixion and resurrection (24:25–32, 44–47), they have much to thank and praise God for.

Temple: See page 519

For reflection: How continually or intermittently do I praise God for what he has done for me in Jesus?

Luke began his Gospel by telling his readers that his aim was to "compile a narrative of the events that have been fulfilled among us" (1:1). At the end of his Gospel his readers are able to understand what he means by "fulfilled," for the risen Jesus in his last words to his followers proclaimed that his death and rising into glory fulfilled God's plan as found in Scripture (24:26–27, 44–46). In his second volume, the Acts of the Apostles, Luke will recount how the early Church continued to fulfill God's plan by preaching repentance in Jesus' name to all the nations (24:47; Acts 1:8). Luke compiled his narrative so that his readers "may realize the certainty of the teachings you have received" (1:4), the certainty of the gospel message. Now it is up to his readers to embrace that message and allow themselves to be swept up in God's grand plan in Jesus for their salvation.

For reflection: What are the most important insights that I am taking away from my reading of Luke's Gospel? What have I heard as God's word spoken particularly to me?

THE WRITING AND INTERPRETATION OF THE GOSPEL OF LUKE

The Writing of the Gospels

Each of the four Gospels is a product of a three-stage process.[1]

The *first stage* is what Jesus did and taught while on earth.[2] He called disciples who saw his works and heard his teachings and could serve as his witnesses after his resurrection and ascension. In his teachings, "Jesus accommodated himself to the mentality of his listeners,"[3] speaking as a Palestinian Jew of the first third of the first century to other Palestinian Jews.

In the *second stage* the apostles and other witnesses handed on to their hearers what Jesus had said and done but "with that fuller understanding which they, instructed by the glorious events of Christ and enlightened by the Spirit of truth, now enjoyed."[4] The apostles in their preaching took into account the circumstances of their audiences and interpreted Jesus' words and deeds according to the needs of their listeners. They used modes of speaking that were suited to their purposes and to the mentality of their listeners.[5]

In the *third stage* the authors of the four Gospels "selected certain of the many elements which had been handed on, either orally or already in written form," and incorporated them in their Gospels, sometimes synthesizing these elements or explaining them in light of the situation of those for whom they wrote, "but always in such a fashion that they have told us the honest truth about Jesus."[6]

> *From what they had received, the sacred writers above all selected the things which were suited to the various situations of the faithful and to the purposes which they had in mind, and adapted their narration of them to the same situations and purpose. Since the meaning of a statement also depends on the sequence, the evangelists, in passing on the words and deeds of our savior, explained these now in one context, now in another, depending on (their) usefulness to the readers. . . . For the truth of a story is not at all affected by the fact that the evangelists relate the words and deeds of the Lord in a different order, and express his sayings not literally but differently, while preserving their sense.[7]*

That the written Gospels are the result of a three-stage process has implications:

- The Gospel authors present incidents and teachings from Jesus' public ministry in an order suited to their purposes in writing, which is not necessarily the order in which they historically occurred. Accounts from the four Gospels cannot be synthesized to produce an actual timeline of events from Jesus' baptism by John to the Last Supper. Each Gospel narration must be read for the meaning that events have in the order in which they are recounted.

- In expressing the teachings of Jesus, the Gospels do not necessarily transmit the exact words Jesus used. Jesus taught in Aramaic; the Gospels were written in Greek. Just as Jesus accommodated his teachings to his listeners, so those who passed on his teachings also formulated them in light of the needs of their audiences while preserving the sense of Jesus' words.

- Because the Gospel authors were writing for different audiences and had different purposes in writing, each of the four Gospels has its distinctive traits and emphases. The four Gospels cannot be combined or harmonized into a single document that preserves the unique riches of each. Rather, each Gospel must be read as an inspired presentation of the life and teachings of Jesus and relished for its particular perspective.

That the Gospels came to be written by a three-stage process does not mean that they are not reliable witnesses to Jesus. The Second Vatican Council stated that "Holy Mother Church has firmly and with absolute constancy maintained and continues to maintain, that the four Gospels, whose historicity she unhesitatingly affirms, faithfully hand on what Jesus, the Son of God, while he lived among men, really did and taught for their eternal salvation, until the day when he was taken up."[8]

Luke

Neither Luke nor any of the Gospel authors signed his name to his Gospel. However, the oldest surviving copy of the Gospel of Luke, dating from around A.D. 200, adds at its end, "According to Luke." This Luke is traditionally identified with the Luke whom Paul mentions as one of his coworkers in his letter to Philemon (Phlm 24) and with "Luke the beloved physician" mentioned in Colossians (Col 4:14; see also 2 Tim 4:11). A late second-century writing describes Luke as a Syrian from Antioch who was a companion of Paul and wrote his Gospel in Greece and died there.

The opening verses of the Gospel of Luke present its author as a careful researcher who examined what had been handed down orally and in written form about Jesus and drew on these sources to compile his own well-ordered narrative about Jesus (Luke 1:1–4). The author had a good command of the Greek language and was well acquainted with the Old Testament Scriptures in their Greek translation. The same author also wrote Acts (compare Luke 1:1–4 with Acts 1:1–2). Portions of Acts that recount some of Paul's journeys are written as eyewitness accounts, indicating that the author sometimes traveled with Paul: "When he had seen the vision, we sought passage to Macedonia at once, concluding that God had called us to proclaim the good news to them" (Acts 16:10).

Putting the bits of evidence together indicates that Luke was a Gentile, a Syrian who grew up in Antioch, a Greek-speaking city. Perhaps he converted to Judaism or became a "God-fearer," a Gentile who worshiped Israel's God and attended synagogue but did not fully convert to Judaism (see Acts 13:16, 26). He became a follower of Christ. As a member of the Church in Antioch he was familiar with events that happened there recounted in Acts (Acts 11:19–30; 13:1–3; 14:26—15:2; 15:30–35). Sometime before A.D. 50 he left Antioch, joined Paul at Troas, on the western coast of present-day Turkey, and sailed with him to Philippi in northern Greece (Acts 16:10–17). He may have remained in Philippi, for he next joins up with Paul in Philippi in 58 and travels with him to Jerusalem (Acts 20:5–15; 21:1–18) and then to Rome around 61 (Acts 27:1—28:16). Most scholars believe that the Gospel of Luke was written sometime around A.D. 85, possibly in Greece, for churches predominantly made up of Gentile converts.

Interpreting the Gospel of Luke

Biblical scholars have developed various methods for analyzing the Gospels; some of these methods address the process by which the Gospels came to be written. Some methods try to reconstruct the first stage of Gospel tradition—what Jesus did and said. Other methods address how the gospel message was handed on during the second stage of tradition, examining the modes of speech or literary forms employed. Still other methods examine how a Gospel author edited the written and oral traditions he incorporated in his Gospel or analyze the narrative techniques he employed in telling the good news of Jesus Christ.

Each of these methods can contribute to our understanding of the Gospels, but each of them also has its limitations.[9] Reconstructions of what Jesus did and said are inevitably shaped by the methods employed in making the reconstruction as well as by the data provided by the Gospels. While the modes of speaking that might have been used during the oral transmission of the gospel can be studied, it is each Gospel as a written document that is inspired Scripture, not reconstructed earlier versions of individual stories and teachings.

If we know or can reconstruct the sources a Gospel writer used in writing his Gospel, then the way he edited his sources can be an indication of the message he wanted to convey in his Gospel. Most scholars hold that the author of the Gospel of Luke drew on the Gospel of Mark; material from the Gospel of Mark makes up about a third of the content of Luke. Where there is material common to Luke and Mark, the way Luke edited Mark provides clues to Luke's interests and emphases. I made use of such clues in writing my exposition of Luke's Gospel, even though I do not make explicit comparisons of the two Gospels in my exposition.

Luke drew not only on the Gospel of Mark but also on various written and oral traditions in circulation in the early Church. Matthew in writing his Gospel also used Mark and other sources. The material that is not found in Mark but that is found in both Luke and Matthew appears to be drawn from a common source; such material makes up over a fifth of Luke's Gospel. However, studying how Luke and Matthew made use of this common source is difficult because we can reconstruct this source only on the basis of what is found in Luke and Matthew. Up to forty percent of the material in the

Gospel of Luke is from sources unique to Luke, and it is virtually impossible to determine how he may have edited these sources.

The exposition of the Gospel according to Luke contained in this book focuses on the Gospel of Luke as it is found in the Bible—on the final product, not on the pieces that Luke might have assembled in producing the final product.

The Second Vatican Council spoke of the inspired meaning of Scripture in terms of the meaning expressed by the authors of the biblical books: "Since, therefore, all that the inspired authors, or sacred writers, affirm should be regarded as affirmed by the Holy Spirit, we must acknowledge that the books of Scripture, firmly, faithfully and without error, teach that truth which God, for the sake of our salvation, wished to see confided to the sacred Scriptures."[10] The council also spoke of "the meaning which the sacred writers really had in mind, that meaning which God had thought well to manifest through the medium of their words."[11] The council linked the meaning an inspired author "intended to express" with what he "did in fact express" by his words.[12] The focus of this exposition of the Gospel of Luke is on what Luke expressed by his words, since they convey the inspired meaning of his Gospel. Fr. Raymond E. Brown suggested that one writing a commentary on the Gospel of John "should limit commentary to what most likely was meant by the first-century author and most likely understood by the first-century audience."[13] I have tried to heed his advice in writing about the Gospel of Luke.

Understanding the meaning expressed by Luke's words involves an interaction between his words and the reader. By analogy, music is not simply notes on a piece of paper but exists in performance and listening. Meaning comes alive in this encounter between the text and the reader. Each reader brings his or her perspective, knowledge, experiences, questions, and interests to a text, and these influence what a reader takes away from a text. This does not mean that a biblical text is a blank slate on which we can write whatever meaning we like; it does mean that there is a richness of meaning in Scripture that no single reading or reader can fully capture.

In reading the Gospel of Luke all of us bring our knowledge and experience of Jesus to the text: none of us is hearing about Jesus for the very first time. Our understanding of Jesus is shaped by many factors: by what we have read in the rest of the New Testament about him, by centuries of theological reflection on him, by Church pronouncements on him, and by our own experiences of him in private prayer, public worship, and the Christian community. Even if we wanted to, we would not be able to set all this aside in reading the Gospel of Luke. As we read Luke's words about Jesus, we understand them in light of our previous understanding of Jesus, even as Luke's words enrich, challenge, and modify our understanding of Jesus and his message.

My exposition of the Gospel of Luke represents my understanding of this Gospel. If my life experiences and education had been different, if I were part of a different culture or Church body, I would have been alert to facets of meaning in Luke that escape my notice. I hope that my reading of Luke will aid others in arriving at their own reading of Luke, and in encountering the Jesus he proclaims.

Endnotes

1. The Second Vatican Council in its decree on revelation summarizes the three stages that culminated in the written Gospels (Second Vatican Council, *Dogmatic Constitution on Divine Revelation [Dei Verbum]* [1965], 19; hereafter abbreviated as *Revelation*. The decree cites the Pontifical Biblical Commission's *Instruction on the Historical Truth of the Gospels* (1964; hereafter abbreviated as *Truth*), which described "the three stages of tradition by which the teaching and the life of Jesus have come down to us" (*Truth*, 6).
2. *Revelation*, 19.
3. *Truth*, 7.
4. *Revelation*, 19.
5. *Truth*, 8.
6. *Revelation*, 19.
7. *Truth*, 9.
8. *Revelation*, 19.
9. See Pontifical Biblical Commission, *The Interpretation of the Bible in the Church* (Rome: Libreria Editrice Vaticana, 1993), chap. 1.
10. *Revelation*, 11.
11. Ibid., 12.
12. Ibid.
13. Raymond E. Brown, SS, *An Introduction to the Gospel of John*. Edited, updated, introduced, and concluded by Francis J. Moloney, SDB (New York: Doubleday, 2003), 111.

SELECTED BIBLIOGRAPHY

Commentaries on the Gospel of Luke

Bock, Darrell L. *Luke*. 2 vols. The Baker Exegetical Commentary on the New Testament. Grand Rapids, Michigan: Baker Academic, 1994–1996.
Bovon, Francois. *Luke 1*. Hermenia. Minneapolis: Fortress Press, 2002.
Caird, G.B. *Saint Luke*. The Pelican New Testament Commentaries. Baltimore: Penguin Books, 1963.
Evans, C.F. *Saint Luke*. TPI New Testament Commentaries. Philadelphia: Trinity Press International, 1990.
Fitzmyer, Joseph A., SJ. *The Gospel According to Luke*. 2 vols. The Anchor Bible. Vol. 28–28a. New York: Doubleday, 1979–1985.
Green, Joel B. *The Gospel of Luke*. The New International Commentary on the New Testament. Grand Rapids, Michigan: Eerdmans, 1997.
Johnson, Luke Timothy. *The Gospel of Luke*. Sacra Pagina Series. Vol. 3. Collegeville, Minnesota: Liturgical Press, 1991.
Marshall, I. Howard. *The Gospel of Luke*. The New International Greek Testament Commentary. Grand Rapids, Michigan: Eerdmans, 1978.
Nolland, John. *Luke*. 3 vols. Word Biblical Commentary. Vol. 35A–C. Dallas: Word Books, 1989–1993.
Talbert, Charles H. *Reading Luke: A Literary and Theological Commentary on the Third Gospel*. New York: Crossroad, 1988.

Studies and Resources

The Ante-Nicean Fathers, vol. 1, *The Apostolic Fathers, Justin Martyr, Irenaeus*. Grand Rapids, Michigan: Eerdmans, 1987.
———. vol. 4, *Tertullian, Minucius Felix, Origen*. Grand Rapids, Michigan: Eerdmans, nd.
Bailey, Kenneth E. *Poet & Peasant, and Through Peasant Eyes*. Grand Rapids, Michigan: Eerdmans, 1983.
Binz, Stephen J. *The Passion and Resurrection Narratives of Jesus: A Commentary*. Collegeville, Minnesota: Liturgical Press, 1989.

Brown, Raymond E., SS. *The Birth of the Messiah*, 2nd ed. New York: Doubleday, 1993.

————. *The Death of the Messiah: From Gethsemane to the Grave: A Commentary on the Passion Narratives in the Four Gospels*. 2 vols. The Anchor Bible Reference Library. New York: Doubleday, 1994.

————. *An Introduction to the New Testament*. The Anchor Bible Reference Library. New York: Doubleday, 1997.

————. *An Introduction to New Testament Christology*. New York: Paulist Press, 1994.

————. *An Introduction to the Gospel of John*. Edited, updated, introduced, and concluded by Francis J. Moloney, SDB. New York: Doubleday, 2003.

————. *A Risen Christ at Eastertime*. Collegeville, Minnesota: Liturgical Press, 1990.

Brown, Raymond E., SS, Karl P. Donfried, Joseph A. Fitzmyer, SJ, and John Reumann, eds. *Mary in the New Testament*. Philadelphia: Fortress Press, 1978.

Brown, Raymond E., SS, Karl P. Donfried, and John Reumann, eds. *Peter in the New Testament*. Minneapolis: Augsburg, 1973

Cassidy, Richard J. *Jesus, Politics, and Society: A Study of Luke's Gospel*. Maryknoll, New York: Orbis, 1978.

Cassidy, Richard J. and Philip J Sharper, eds. *Political Issues in Luke-Acts*. Maryknoll, New York: Orbis, 1983.

Catechism of the Catholic Church, 2nd ed. Washington, DC: United States Catholic Conference, 1997.

Chancey, Mark A. *The Myth of a Gentile Galilee*. Society for New Testament Studies Monograph Series 118. Cambridge: Cambridge University Press, 2002.

Charlesworth, James H., ed. *The Old Testament Pseudepigrapha*. 2 vols. Garden City, New York: Doubleday, 1983–1985.

Charlesworth, James H., and Petr Pokorny, eds. *Jesus Research: An International Perspective*. Grand Rapids, Michigan: Eerdmans, 2009.

Collins, John J. *The Apocalyptic Imagination: An Introduction to the Jewish Matrix of Christianity*. New York: Crossroad, 1987.

Davies, W.D. *The Sermon on the Mount*. London: Cambridge University Press, 1966.

Donahue, John R., SJ. *The Gospel in Parable*. Minneapolis: Fortress Press, 1990.

Dunn, James D.G. *Jesus Remembered.* Christianity in the Making. Vol. 1. Grand Rapids, Michigan: Eerdmans, 2003.

Durkin, Daniel, OSB, ed. *Sin, Salvation, and the Spirit.* Collegeville, Minnesota: Liturgical Press, 1979.

Early Christian Writings: The Apostolic Fathers. Maxwell Staniforth, trans. New York: Penguin, 1968.

Evans, Craig A., and Stanley E. Porter, eds. *Dictionary of New Testament Background.* Downers Grove, Illinois: InterVarsity Press, 2000.

Fitzmyer, Joseph A., SJ. *The Biblical Commission's Document "The Interpretation of the Bible in the Church": Text and Commentary.* Rome: Pontificio Istituto Biblico, 1995.

———. *A Christological Catechism: New Testament Answers.* New York: Paulist Press, 1991.

———. *Luke the Theologian: Aspects of His Teaching.* New York: Paulist, 1989.

———. *Responses to 101 Questions on the Dead Sea Scrolls.* New York: Paulist Press, 1992.

———. *The One Who Is to Come.* Grand Rapids, Michigan: Eerdmans, 2007.

———. *To Advance the Gospel: New Testament Studies.* Grand Rapids, Michigan: Eerdmans, 1998.

Flannery, Austin P., OP, ed. *Documents of Vatican II.* New York: Pillar Books, 1975.

Fredriksen, Paula. *Jesus of Nazareth, King of the Jews: A Jewish Life and the Emergence of Christianity.* New York: Vintage Books, 2000.

Freedman, David Noel, ed. *The Anchor Bible Dictionary.* 6 vols. New York: Doubleday, 1992.

Freyne, Séan. *Galilee, from Alexander the Great to Hadrian, 323 BCE to 135 CE: A Study of Second Temple Judaism.* Wilmington, Delaware: Michael Glazier, 1980.

———. *Galilee, Jesus, and the Gospels: Literary Approaches and Historical Investigations.* Philadelphia: Fortress Press, 1988.

———. *The World of the New Testament.* Wilmington, Delaware: Michael Glazier, 1980.

García Martínez, Florentino, ed. *The Dead Sea Scrolls Translated: The Qumran Texts in English.* Translated by Wilfred G.E. Watson. 2nd ed. Grand Rapids, Michigan: Eerdmans, 1996.

Green, Joel B. *The Theology of the Gospel of Luke*. Cambridge: Cambridge University Press, 1995.

Green, Joel B., and Scot McKnight, eds. *Dictionary of Jesus and the Gospels*. Downers Grove, Illinois: InterVarsity Press, 1992.

Hamm, Dennis, SJ. *The Beatitudes in Context*. Wilmington, Delaware: Michael Glazier, 1990.

Harrington, Daniel J., SJ. *Jesus: A Historical Portrait*. Cincinnati: St. Anthony Messenger Press, 2007.

Hendrickx, Herman. *The Passion Narratives of the Synoptic Gospels*. London: Geoffrey Chapman, 1984.

———. *The Resurrection Narratives of the Synoptic Gospels*. London: Geoffrey Chapman, 1984.

Hengel, Martin. *Crucifixion in the Ancient World and the Folly of the Message of the Cross*. Philadelphia: Fortress Press, 1977.

Horsley, Richard A. *Bandits, Prophets, and Messiahs: Popular Movements in the Time of Jesus*. With John S. Hanson. San Francisco: Harper & Row, 1988.

Hultgren, Arland J. *The Parables of Jesus: A Commentary*. Grand Rapids, Michigan: Eerdmans, 2000.

Jonge, Marinus de. *God's Final Envoy: Early Christology and Jesus' Own View of His Mission*. Grand Rapids, Michigan: Eerdmans, 1998.

Karris, Robert J. *Luke: Artist and Theologian. Luke's Passion Account as Literature*. New York: Paulist, 1985.

Kodell, Jerome, OSB. *The Eucharist in the New Testament*. Wilmington, Delaware: Michael Glazier, 1988.

Kurz, William S., SJ. *Reading Luke-Acts: Dynamics of Biblical Narrative*. Louisville: Westminster John Knox Press, 1993.

Lambrecht, Jan. *The Sermon on the Mount*. Wilmington, Delaware: Michael Glazier, 1985.

Leaney, A.R.C. *The Jewish and Christian World 200 BC to AD 200*. Cambridge: Cambridge University Press, 1984.

Léon-Dufour, Xavier, SJ. *Sharing the Eucharistic Bread: The Witness of the New Testament*. Translated by Matthew J. O'Connell. New York: Paulist Press, 1987.

Moloney, Francis J., SDB. *Women First Among the Faithful*. Notre Dame, Indiana: Ave Maria Press, 1986.

Matera, Frank J. *Passion Narratives and Gospel Theologies: Interpreting the Synoptics Through Their Passion Stories*. New York: Paulist, 1986

Mackowski, Richard M., SJ. *Cities of Jesus*. Rome: Pontifical Oriental Institute, 1997.

McNamara, Martin, MSC. *Intertestamental Literature*. Wilmington, Delaware: Michael Glazier, 1983.

———. *Palestinian Judaism and the New Testament*. Wilmington, Delaware: Michael Glazier, 1983.

Meier, John P. *A Marginal Jew: Rethinking the Historical Jesus*. 4 vols. New York: Doubleday, 1991–2009

Montague, George T., SM. *The Holy Spirit: Growth of a Biblical Tradition*. New York: Paulist, 1876.

Murphy-O'Connor, Jerome, OP. *The Holy Land: From Earliest Times to 1700*. 4th ed. Oxford Archaeological Guides. Oxford: Oxford University Press, 1998.

Neyrey, Jerome, SJ. *The Passion According to Luke*. New York: Paulist, 1985.

Nickle, Keith F. *Preaching the Gospel of Luke*. Louisville: Westminster John Knox Press, 2000.

O'Toole, Robert F., SJ. *The Unity of Luke's Theology: An Analysis of Luke-Acts*. Wilmington, Delaware: Michael Glazier, 1984.

Pontifical Biblical Commission. *Instruction on the Historical Truth of the Gospels*. 1964. Translation and commentary in Fitzmyer, *A Christological Catechism*.

———. *The Interpretation of the Bible in the Church*. Rome: Libreria Editrice Vaticana, 1993.

Powell, Mark Allan. *What Are They Saying About Luke*. Mahwah, New Jersey: Paulist Press, 1989.

Reed, Jonathan L. *Archaeology and the Galilean Jesus: A Reexamination of the Evidence*. Harrisburg, Pennsylvania: Trinity Press, 2000.

———. *The HarperCollins Visual Guide to the New Testament: What Archaeology Reveals about the First Christians*. New York: HarperCollins, 2007.

Rousseau, John J., and Rami Arav. *Jesus and His World: An Archaeological and Cultural Dictionary*. Minneapolis: Fortress Press, 1995.

Saldarini, Anthony J. *Pharisees, Scribes and Sadducees in Palestinian Society: A Sociological Approach*. Wilmington, Delaware: Michael Glazier, 1988.

Sawicki, Marianne *Crossing Galilee*. Harrisburg, Pennsylvania: Trinity Press International, 2000.

Senior, Donald, CP. *The Passion of Jesus in the Gospel of Luke*. Wilmington, Delaware: Michael Glazier, 1989.

Stanley, David M., SJ. *Jesus in Gethsemane*. New York: Paulist Press, 1980.

Sweetland, Dennis M. *Our Journey with Jesus: Discipleship according to Luke-Acts*. Collegeville, Minnesota: Liturgical Press, 1990.

Tanner, Norman P., SJ, ed. *Decrees of the Ecumenical Councils*. 2 vols. Washington, DC: Georgetown University Press, 1990.

VanderKam, James C. *The Dead Sea Scrolls Today*. Grand Rapids, Michigan: Eerdmans, 1994.

Wilkinson, John. *Jerusalem as Jesus Knew It: Archaeology as Evidence*. London: Thames and Hudson, 1978.

The Works of Flavius Josephus. 4 vols. William Whiston, trans. Grand Rapids, Michigan: Baker Book House, 1974.

INDEX OF BACKGROUND MATERIAL
AND COMMENTS

Comments

Palestine
at the time of Jesus

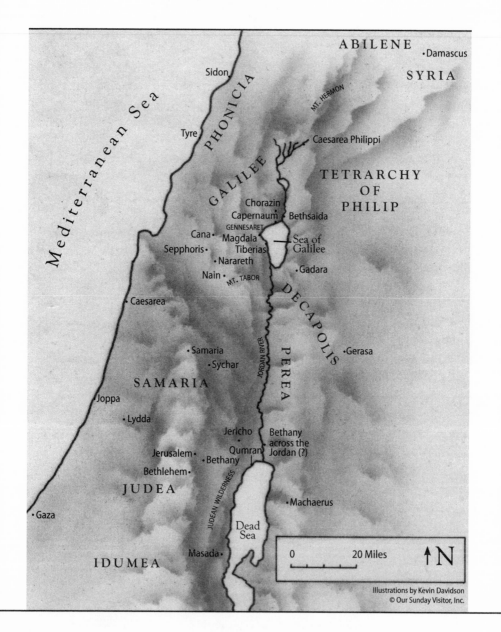

ABILENE

• Damascus

SYRIA

Sidon

PHONICIA

MT. HERMON

Mediterranean Sea

Tyre

GALILEE

Caesarea Philippi

TETRARCHY
OF
PHILIP

Chorazin

Capernaum • Bethsaida

GENNESARET

Cana •

Magdala

Sepphoris •

Tiberias

Sea of
Galilee

• Narareth

Nain • MT. TABOR

• Gadara

• Caesarea

DECAPOLIS

• Samaria

JORDAN RIVER

PEREA

• Sychar

• Gerasa

SAMARIA

Joppa

• Lydda

Jericho

•

Bethany
across the
Jordan (?)

Jerusalem •

Qumran

• Bethany

Bethlehem •

JUDEA

JUDEAN WILDERNESS

• Machaerus

• Gaza

Dead
Sea

IDUMEA

Masada •

0   20 Miles

↑ N

Illustrations by Kevin Davidson
© Our Sunday Visitor, Inc.

Jerusalem

at the time of Jesus

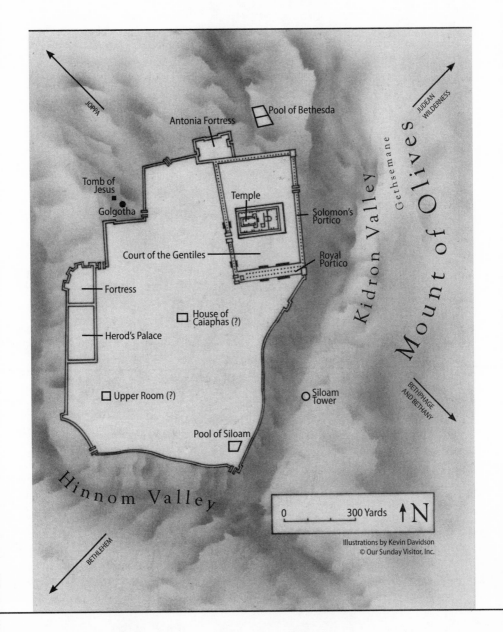

Illustrations by Kevin Davidson
© Our Sunday Visitor, Inc.